SUSPECT DOCUMENTS

Suspect Documents

THEIR SCIENTIFIC EXAMINATION

BY
WILSON R. HARRISON, M.Sc., Ph.D.
Director, Home Office Forensic Science Laboratory,
Llanishen, Cardiff

CHICAGO
NELSON-HALL PUBLISHERS

Published in the United States of America in 1981 by Nelson-Hall Inc., 111 N. Canal St., Chicago, IL 60606

Library of Congress Cataloging in Publication Data

Harrison, Wilson R
Suspect documents, their scientific examination.

Reprint of the 1958 ed. published by Praeger, New York.
Bibliography: p.
Includes index.
1. Forgery. 2. Legal documents. 3. Writing --Identification. I. Title.
[HV8074.H32 1981] 363.2'565 80-22803
ISBN 0-88229-759-7

CONTENTS

PREFACE

THIS book is based largely on the practical experience I have acquired during the past twenty-four years in dealing with nearly 7,000 cases, ranging from murder to the sending of anonymous letters, most of which were submitted by the police and various Government Departments to the Home Office Forensic Science Laboratory, Cardiff, of which I am and have been the Director since January, 1938.

Having been trained as a physical chemist, I believe that what cannot be demonstrated is not evidence; in criminal cases, in particular, there should never be any appeal to conclusions based on flair or on the "eye of the expert." Consequently, I have endeavoured to treat the subject as a branch of physical science with a broad basis of demonstrable fact for every opinion I have expressed.

The objects of the book are to give an up-to-date account of the materials which make up a document, to describe the analysis to which the examiner subjects the document referred to him and by so doing to inform and guide the many police officers and members of the legal profession who have to deal with documents suspected to be false, or whose authorship they wish to determine.

Within this framework, I have given particular attention to three matters which my official position has given me special opportunities to investigate: firstly, disguised handwriting; secondly, forgeries of the signatures of near-illiterate persons—a class of crime which the advent of the Welfare State has considerably increased; thirdly, complaints of the receipt of anonymous letters. For those who are not entirely familiar with scientific terms a brief glossary has been provided at the end of the text.

I have to thank the Home Office for permission to write this book and the Stationery Office for allowing me to publish those photographs to which Crown copyright attaches. My thanks are also due to the Commissioner of Police for the Metropolis and to the many Chief Constables who have given me permission to publish photographs of documents they have submitted to the Laboratory. In this connection special mention must be made of the West Riding Constabulary who so kindly procured for me some thousands of specimens of both normal and disguised hands on which the chapter on Disguise has largely been based.

I wish to express my gratitude to the many others who have assisted me. These include the Cardiff Public Library who supplied for publication specimens of old-fashioned British handwriting, those who have permitted me to publish specimens of their handwriting and the various commercial undertakings who have supplied information on typewriters, ball-point pens, inks, dyestuffs, etc.

A special word of thanks is due to my colleagues at the Laboratory. They have provided sketches, given advice and friendly criticism of the original draft as well as a measure of clerical assistance. To the staff of the Chemistry Department

I am indebted for the spectrographic analysis of the various inks and the provision of the X-ray powder diffraction photographs of paper ash and associated material. In particular the photographic staff have achieved much in producing acceptable copies of photographs where the original documents were no longer available. This accounts for the fact that not all of the reproductions of handwriting and typescript have reached the same standard of perfection.

Many of the photographs refer to criminal cases where the wrongdoer has paid his debt to society. I feel that nothing should be done to reopen old wounds so I have taken care, whenever possible, to eliminate from both the reproductions and the text, any clues as to either the persons or the cases concerned. Such information, I feel, can well be dispensed with, for it would do little to enhance the value of the photographs for the purposes they are intended to serve.

Dr. H. S. Holden, Adviser on Forensic Science to the Home Office, painstakingly read through the original manuscript and I am deeply indebted to him for many suggestions for its improvement as well as for supplying and allowing me to publish a specimen of his most outstanding handwriting shown in Figure 10–5.

Above all, I must thank my wife, who not only constructively criticised the original drafts and effected the removal of many obscure passages but who drew several of the sketches and assisted in the arduous work of proof-reading and index compiling.

In conclusion it must be emphasised that any opinions and views expressed are those of the author and are not intended in any way to represent the official views of the Home Office.

WILSON R. HARRISON.

LLANISHEN,
CARDIFF.
August 6, 1958.

1

INTRODUCTION

It is well known that documents are not always what they are represented to be. The crime of forgery is probably quite as ancient as writing and on a number of occasions history has been changed by documents subsequently proved to be forgeries.

When one considers the importance of the issues which often hang on the authenticity of a document—the disposal of vast estates or of large sums of money where the signature on a will or agreement is questioned; the good name of anyone accused of forgery, blackmail or libel [1]; the liberty and possibly the life of a man accused of murder and implicated by forged documents—one would think that today, after so many centuries of reliance upon documents, there would have been established reliable methods for testing the authenticity of any suspect document. It might well be thought that trustworthy experts, skilled in such arts, would be easily available: experts regarded as competent to assist those members of the legal profession whose task it is to advise clients and argue cases when documents are in dispute. One would have considered it as taken for granted that recognised experts in the by no means modern art of examining suspect documents would be so experienced and reliable that their conclusions would be accepted in the courts with the same confidence as those of experts in the other fields of physical science, such as chemistry, physics and geology.

No one who has had any practical experience in legal matters is under any such misapprehension. In spite of the thousands of important documents which must pass through his hands, the average lawyer, confronted with a case whose outcome may hang upon the authenticity of a document, usually does not know whom to consult or what reliance he can place on the results of an investigation.

Most lawyers are aware that there exist certain individuals often loosely referred to as " handwriting experts " or " graphologists " to whom they may refer their problems, but unless he has been unusually fortunate in the past, the more experienced a lawyer is, the less likely is he to place much reliance upon the opinions of the majority of these gentlemen. In the past, not only in this, but in other countries as well, " handwriting experts " and " graphologists " in general have enjoyed a very low status in the courts. The general and usually well-justified feeling has been that their findings are largely intuitive and that consequently there are often as many opinions as there are experts in the case. The contrary opinions expressed by the experts on the two sides often cancel each other out with the result that the case has to be settled on other, and, it is to be hoped, more reliable grounds.

[1] According to the *Criminal Statistics,* during 1956 in England and Wales the following offences were known to the police, blackmail 119, falsifying accounts 874, forgery and uttering 4,001, libel 60.

A number of factors make for the understandable reluctance of the courts to place much reliance upon the opinions of many of the " handwriting experts " who appear to testify in them. In professions such as law and medicine, there are powerful governing bodies who see that the standards of those practising are maintained by a system of prescribed study and qualifying examinations. This means that anyone consulting a doctor or lawyer is guaranteed a certain minimum standard of professional experience and attainments.

Similarly if anyone is engaged to testify as an expert witness in such sciences as chemistry, physics or medicine he will have to be a most exceptional man to be accepted as an expert unless he possesses one or more degrees granted by a university, or the diploma of fellowship of a learned society or institute of accepted standing, such as the Royal Institute of Chemistry in the case of analytical chemists, or the Fellowship of the Royal College of Surgeons when expert evidence in surgical matters is to be given.

The demand for specialists in the examination of documents is so small that comparatively few qualified men are ever likely to be wholly engaged in this work. No university college of any standing either in Great Britain or America offers a course of study leading to a degree [2] and if such a course were contemplated it would be a difficult matter to provide either teachers or anything like full employment for any substantial number of students when qualified.

Apart from the occasional examples of sheer incompetence there are several good reasons for the low status formerly enjoyed by the document examiners in the courts.

The first and undoubtedly the most important reason is that, even today when full advantage can be taken of elaborate and often very expensive apparatus embodying the most recent developments in microscopy, photography and micro-chemical analysis, the complete physical examination of a suspect document is by no means a simple matter. In spite of considerable advances in technique, a number of problems such as that of the relative ages of ink writings of documents still await complete solution and others such as the absolute age of an ink or pencil writing show no signs as yet of yielding to attack.

A price has to be paid for every advance in technique. Such is the complexity of modern analytical methods that the complete examination of documents, even as far as our still imperfect knowledge allows, demands from the examiner not only a broad basic education in the physical sciences such as chemistry and physics, but a number of other skills which have to be acquired by subsequent study and

[2] In England and Wales the only regular instruction on document examination is that given by the author, by means of lectures, demonstrations and practical work which form part of the syllabus of the Home Office Detective Training Courses held at Hendon, Wakefield, Mill Meece (No. 4 Police District Training Centre) and Stanley Grange (Lancashire County Constabulary Training Centre).

These lectures are specifically designed for the benefit of detective officers in order to make them familiar with the work of the Questioned Document Department of the Home Office Forensic Science Laboratory at Cardiff, where the majority of the investigations involved in the examination of documents submitted by the Police Forces in England and Wales are carried out by the author and his staff.

A certain amount of more specialised training for government experts of other countries has also been carried out at this laboratory, but this is very limited because the laboratory is primarily staffed and equipped for actual work on documents rather than for training expert witnesses on this subject.

experiment. In view of this, the wonder is not that the document examiners of a former age were often unreliable, but that, armed solely with their crude magnifying glasses and primitive photographic apparatus, they accomplished so much.

The second reason is that it is only now being realised that the exposure of a forgery, the establishment of the authorship of an anonymous manuscript or of the source of a typewritten document is a co-operative process which must pass through certain well-defined stages and involves persons with three quite different functions. Each of the three must be aware of both the needs and the capabilities of the others, and to some extent, at least, be acquainted with what they have to do and how they set about it.

In the first place we have the legal adviser, who is generally the first to be consulted if civil proceedings are being contemplated, or the investigating officer, who takes charge of the preliminary investigation when obvious breaches of the criminal law, such as blackmail or criminal libel, are concerned. The ordinary duty of either is to establish the facts surrounding the first appearance of the suspect documents and to investigate both the " stories " and the standing of the witnesses in the case. This must be accomplished by the preliminary examination of the documents, upon which will usually rest the decision as to whether or not an expert is to be consulted. If it is decided that an expert is to be consulted it is necessary to gather the data which will almost certainly be needed when he is brought into the investigation.

The legal adviser or investigating officer must be in a position to anticipate the needs of the expert in the way of comparative material such as specimens of handwriting or typescript, not only to save time once an expert examination has been decided on, but also and mainly because the earlier such material is sought the better is the chance of obtaining satisfactory specimens. Witnesses to forged documents, like most other suspects, are invariably more willing to co-operate by talking freely and giving specimens of their handwriting early in the investigation than later when their confidence in their immunity from discovery has begun to ebb and doubts are creeping in. (Other good reasons may necessitate a speedy investigation. When questioned typewriting is involved, the specimens should be taken from suspect machines before use and abuse has so altered the characteristics of the machines that specimens taken at a later date. are practically useless for comparison.)

Once the decision to seek expert advice has been taken there must follow the closest co-operation between the investigator and the expert. The expert, being remote from the matter, has only the material supplied to him by those who have carried out the preliminary investigation to guide him during his examination of the documents. No expert can express a stronger opinion than is justified by the nature of the standard of comparative material with which he has been supplied. Long experience has shown that the limiting factors in over 90 per cent. of such cases is the nature of the standards. Poor standards result in inconclusive opinions and many of the mistakes made by the " handwriting experts " in the past have been due to their attempting to do too much with inadequate material in the way of standards. The provision of adequate standards of comparison is by far the most important phase of the preliminary investigation, and experience has shown that it is the investigator with the most comprehensive knowledge of the ways of the expert who is most likely to provide the most suitable standards.

This question will be treated very fully in a later chapter, for one of the most gratifying results of the lectures on document examination given at the Home Office Detective Training Courses to detective officers of both this and other countries is the steady improvement in the nature of the standard material furnished in cases submitted by those officers who have attended the courses. This matter is so important and so little that is reliable has been written on it, that a whole chapter in this book has been devoted to it.

When the expert has completed his examination he must render his report in a form suitable to the third person involved. This is the advocate whose duty it is to present the facts uncovered by the expert, together with any opinion he—the expert—feels justified in expressing, in such a manner that a jury will appreciate the issues involved.

This demands from the expert a report which is quite different in form from that in which he would report his findings to a learned society. The report should enable the advocate to appreciate not only the strong points but the weak ones also, because those are the ones which are likely to be stressed both by expert testimony called by the other side and in cross-examination. It is only the advocate who is fully instructed and has made himself familiar with the outline of the methods used in examining a document who will be in the best position to counter the effects of cross-examination when he re-examines his own expert, and also to cross-examine in the most effective way the expert called to testify on the opposite side.

In this way the court is assisted in arriving at a just decision on facts which have been adequately presented instead of having to make a blind decision, as it may have to where uninstructed advocates content themselves with destructive attacks upon the ability of expert witnesses in general and on those called by the other side in particular.

In no single volume can the whole subject of document examination be treated in such detail that it will provide complete instruction in the art. The primary reason for writing this book is to assist the investigating officer or legal adviser to perform his part whenever he becomes concerned in a case involving suspect documents or anonymous documents. To this end, an outline is given of all the important methods of laboratory examination of documents, particular attention being paid to their limitations. Added to this, the preliminary examination to which any suspect document should be subjected has been treated in some detail. The all-important preliminary phase of any case involving questioned documents has also been given a fairly exhaustive treatment.

It is also hoped that those with some experience in the examination of documents will find some interest in the account of methods used in the physical examination of documents and of the principles upon which handwriting and typescript is identified in the specially equipped and staffed British Government laboratory.

The advocate may possibly learn something which will enable him to extract the greatest measure of assistance from his document experts when presenting his case, and also find some suggestions to help him in his attack on testimony he knows to be either mistaken or not over-scrupulous.

A certain amount of duplication may be observed, but this is the price which has to be paid for the elimination of excessive cross-reference and for making each chapter a coherent whole.

Finally, if the readers of this book conclude that the competent specialists who have given serious study to the problems involved in the examination of suspect documents are entitled to the same respect as that accorded to experts in other branches of knowledge, then the purpose of the book will have been fulfilled.

Bibliography

Hilton, Ordway, "Education and Qualification of Examiners of Questioned Documents," *Journal of Forensic Sciences,* 1 (3), July, 1956.

Osborn, A. S., "A New Profession," *Journal of the American Judicative Soc.*, Vol. 24, No. 1, June, 1940.

At the end of Chapter 15 a list of books dealing generally with the subject of Document Examination is given and mention is made of some of the journals and other publications in which articles on this work are occasionally published.

2

MATERIALS FROM WHICH DOCUMENTS ARE MADE

THE work of the document examiner is not concerned wholly with the comparison of handwriting or typescript. Among other things, he is frequently called upon to decipher or restore erased or faded handwriting or typescript. He may also be required to estimate the age of a document or determine the relative times of writing of different entries.

To appreciate his work in these and other directions, it is necessary to know something of the history as well as the properties of the materials, paper, ink, adhesives, etc., which together make up a document. The following notes are by no means exhaustive, because on the subject of paper-making alone there exists a very substantial bibliography. All that has been attempted is to select for mention those matters which affect the work of the document examiner. At the end of the chapter a brief bibliography is given for the benefit of those for whose purposes the treatment given here is inadequate.

PAPER

The majority of documents are written, typed or printed on paper. It is said that paper was invented by the Chinese more than two thousand years ago, but knowledge of its manufacture was slow to spread into Europe. The exact date when paper was first made in Europe is not known; it was certainly being made in France in the twelfth century and knowledge of the paper-making process had spread to England by A.D. 1600. Incidentally, it is no coincidence that the invention and manufacture in quantity of the iron-tannin ink are contemporary with the spread of paper-making in Europe. Both are complementary, for the production of writing paper in quantity called for the invention of an improved type of pen and ink for use with this new material.

The earliest European papers were made from fibres derived from the mechanical disintegration of linen and cotton rags in the presence of water. At first, paper was made by hand. Improvements in the art accumulated slowly, the great step forward being taken at the end of the eighteenth century when a paper-making machine which produced a continuous web of paper was invented.

As the demand for paper soon outstripped the supply of linen and cotton rags, strenuous efforts were made in the early part of the last century to prepare cellulose fibres suitable for paper-making from more abundant sources.

Straw was considered a source of cellulose which was well worth exploitation, and by the middle of the nineteenth century straw was being used along with rag pulp for the manufacture of cheap wrapping paper. Shortly afterwards, about 1861, esparto fibre was introduced, but its use has been largely confined to the preparation of paper for book production as it is light and bulky and takes printing ink very satisfactorily.

During the first half of the last century experiments were also being carried out to determine whether wood could be used as a source of paper-making fibres. By the seventies, these efforts were entirely successful and very shortly afterwards wood pulp processes were being worked on a very large scale.

The first wood pulps were made by the action of calcium sulphite on wood chips to prepare what is now known as chemical wood pulp. Eventually it was discovered that an even cheaper paper could be made largely from wood which had simply been finely ground without any chemical treatment except bleaching to improve its colour. This is known as " mechanical " wood pulp or sometimes more simply as " groundwood."

In its essence, paper-making is an extremely simple process. A dilute suspension of cellulose fibres is shaken whilst being drained of its excess water through a wire sieve. The shaking causes the fibres to interlace to form a web or mat of fibres resting on the sieve, from which it is removed to be pressed and dried to form a sheet of paper.

A sheet of paper consisting of cellulose fibres alone would closely resemble blotting paper and be of little use for writing with ink, for the ink would spread laterally causing the line to " feather " and the writing to become illegible.

Paper is made suitable for ink writing by a double treatment. The pores between the cellulose fibres are partially filled with what is known as a " loading " material and the surface is improved by one of a number of treatments. The simplest is sizing by dipping the sheet into a tub containing a dilute solution of gelatine which is allowed to dry on the paper. Other cheaper but less satisfactory treatments involve the precipitation of rosin on the surface of the paper with alum followed by hot rolling and glazing. Instead of rosin, a variety of substances may be used including starch, wax, rubber, latex, casein and synthetic resins.

The choice of fibre as well as the treatment it receives during the beating process has a great influence on the nature of the paper. The best papers contain a high proportion of rag pulp whilst the cheapest, used almost exclusively for newsprint, consist largely of groundwood, which should be absent from any paper which is expected to maintain its quality substantially unchanged over a period of years. If the beating process is arranged to effect a rapid cutting of the fibres into short lengths, the resultant paper, if left unfilled and unsized, absorbs water so readily that its main use is for blotting paper. On the other hand, if the same fibres are beaten for a very long time so that they are fibrillated and rendered highly water absorbent, the resultant paper resembles parchment in its texture.

When the sheet of paper comes from the paper-making machine, it may be subjected to further treatment so as to modify its properties. It may be impregnated with wax to render it waterproof, partially nitrated by treatment with nitric acid to give it wet-strength, parchmentised by the action of sulphuric acid, or coated with casein and a mineral filler to endow it with a superfine surface on which high quality illustrations may be printed.

Paper-makers, in the endeavour to improve their products, have not been unaware of the progress made in other industries. Twenty years ago, no commercial additions of plastics to give wet-strength to paper were being made, but at the present time papers containing melamine or urea resins for this purpose are being made at a rate of over a million tons annually.

Polyethylene coated paper is used for waterproofing, and plasticised synthetic resins are used in pressure-sensitive tapes. Special plastic coatings are applied to improve printability and to form the laminations of identification cards as well as to give scuff-resistance to documents.

Improvements in the sizing of paper have been made by the use of chemicals which react with the hydroxyl groups of the cellulose molecule to form agglomerates which bind the fibres together. This sizing material being part of the cellulose molecule cannot be removed by anything short of the most drastic chemical treatment.

Papers have been made on the laboratory scale from the synthetic fabric fibres orlon, terylene and nylon. A commercial run of nylon paper has been made in North America, and experimental quantities of synthetic fibre paper have been produced in the United Kingdom for use as a filter medium. It has proved by no means a simple matter to make paper of synthetic fibres, for fibre-to-fibre bonding cannot be achieved by beating and felting as with cellulose fibres. The problem of bonding has been solved in two ways. The first relies upon the fact that aqueous solutions of certain salts in high concentrations are solvents or swelling agents for polymer fibres. Consequently, when a dilute solution is allowed to evaporate from a web of synthetic fibres, it concentrates at the points of contact and dissolves some of the polymer. Complete evaporation precipitates the polymer and bonds the fibres. The second method is carried out by evaporating a solution or dispersion of a binding agent which is deposited at the points of contact of the fibres and completing the binding by heat and pressure.

The papers made from synthetic fibres have high bursting and tearing strength as well as high folding endurance, but it is very unlikely that paper made from anything other than cellulose will ever be in extensive use as a writing material; the use of papers made from synthetic fibres is likely to be restricted to those purposes where their unique strength and peculiar properties justify their greatly increased cost over that of cellulose paper.

When burned, pure cellulose fibre leaves but little ash so that the sometimes voluminous ash left after paper is burned is derived almost exclusively from the filler and any pigments which may have been added to modify the colour of the paper.

The best writing paper is that made from linen and cotton rags, containing little loading and which has been sized by immersion in gelatine size. This type of paper is expensive but is both strong and durable, taking ink well; it is the paper of choice for important documents which are expected to have the maximum useful life.

Most good quality writing paper in common use consists largely of chemical wood pulp with a small admixture of rag pulp to improve its properties. On the other hand, the cheapest writing papers often contain groundwood along with the chemical wood pulp. To improve their appearance they are sometimes heavily loaded with mineral matter which does nothing to improve the other qualities of the paper.

The filler with which paper is loaded usually consists of mineral matter which may be either natural or synthetic. The best known of the loading materials is kaolin or china clay, but others, based upon calcium sulphate or, for special purposes, barium sulphate, are extensively used.

A sheet of paper is the end product of long preparation from a multitude of materials, many of which may have some influence on its behaviour when it is subjected to scientific examination by a document examiner.

Writing Paper Pads

Whilst the greater part of writing paper is supplied as loose sheets, a fair amount of the cheaper varieties is sold in the form of writing pads. This is fortunate for the document examiner, because writing impressions are transmitted through the paper to appear on the lower sheets. These impressions may sometimes be deciphered, to the undoing of the writers of anonymous letters.

In the past, the sheets making up a pad of writing paper were fastened together by a layer of glue applied to the edge of the pad. When a sheet was torn off, the traces of glue adhering to one edge afforded unmistakable evidence that it once had formed part of a pad. When the glueing had not been done with care, a sheet would tear in an irregular fashion so that it was sometimes possible to match sheets with each other or with the pad from which they had been torn.

Nowadays it is often the practice to substitute a soft strip of unvulcanised rubber for the glue. When a sheet is torn from such a pad, it comes away clean with the rubber strip remaining intact. It is invariably difficult, and sometimes impossible, to prove that such sheets once formed part of a pad, and there is no possibility of linking sheets with each other or with the pad from which they were detached, since there are no torn edges.

Carbon Paper

In essentials, carbon paper is a good quality tissue paper which has been heavily coated with a waxy layer which holds sufficient colouring matter to give a clearly defined transferred impression in use.

Whilst carbon papers have been in use for many years, research is still being vigorously prosecuted in order to improve their quality. This is shown by the number of new patents taken out every year in practically every industrialised country.

The basis of the pigmented layer is a mixture of hard waxes of various origin. Natural waxes such as carnauba and beeswax have been in use for the better qualities for many years, but these are being replaced to some extent by synthetic wax-like materials.

Black carbon papers generally contain finely divided carbon which is absent from the coloured papers which owe their colour to the presence of coloured pigment, lakes or dyestuffs.

Impressions containing carbon are reasonably permanent but some of the others are by no means satisfactory. Some, especially those which depend solely on dyestuffs for their colour, fade rapidly; this is very unfortunate as no satisfactory method of restoration is known.

For many years, efforts have been made to dispense with the use of carbon paper for the preparation of copies. One development which seems satisfactory for use with continuous stationery was placed upon the American market in 1954 before being introduced in England in July, 1955. This is the N.C.R. paper (No Carbon Required). No separate carbon paper is used to make copies of either typewritten or handwritten matter but the appropriate surfaces of the various sheets are coated with layers of colourless chemicals which, when brought into close contact, react to form a temporary blue copy on the required sheet. The temporary blue copy gradually turns into a more permanent green.

No details are available as to the identity of the coating materials, but experiments have shown that the temporary blue colour is probably caused by the reaction of liberated iodine with starch. The final green colour of the copy is probably formed by the action of the iodine, which is a mild oxidising agent, on a dyestuff leuco-base which is also present in the coating. The liberation of the iodine can be effected by one of a number of chemical reactions. The source of the iodine may be an iodide mixed with an oxidising agent which is energised by contact with an acid held bound on the surface of the opposing sheet. The initial blue colour due to the iodine may easily be discharged by the action of heat, alkaline solutions or a number of organic solvents but the final green colour cannot easily be erased. Vigorous chemical treatment is needed to remove the green colouring matter from the paper. There is a slight odour associated with one of the chemical components of the coating which is likely to continue throughout the life of the paper, but it is stated that the chemicals present are unlikely to decrease the useful life of the paper.

Under normal conditions of storage, the green copy is stated to have adequate legibility after four years, which is the greatest limit of age which can at present be given because of the very recent development of the process.

Many an ingenious swindle has been worked by means of concealed carbon paper and the introduction of this new material, which can be used to give copies without the use of a separate sheet of carbon paper, will undoubtedly stimulate certain minds with criminal instincts. If a suspicious document is encountered which has been drawn up in a bright green, the possibility of its having been produced by trickery should be borne in mind so that the appropriate investigations may be made into its authenticity.

Safety Paper

Safety paper is the term applied to paper which has been treated in such a way as to minimise the chances of a successful forgery by erasure, whether mechanical or chemical, being carried out on any document of which it forms the basis.

The simplest and the most common safety paper bears a printed design which varies from a set of fine parallel lines to one of elaborate patterns which cover the surface of the paper wherever any writing has to be done.

This overprinting is lightly carried out in a pale unobtrusive colour using fugitive dyes which are affected by the application of any chemicals sufficiently active to bleach ink. If an erasure by rubbing is attempted, then the pattern is removed along with the writing.

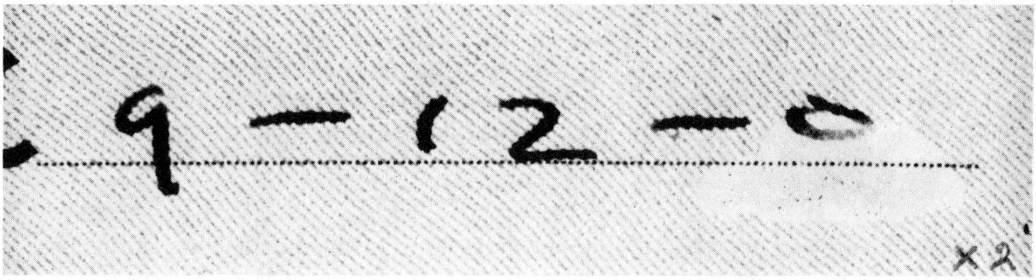

Fig. 2–1. The safety printing has been damaged by the action of the ink eradicator.

Whilst this simple device may deter the crude forger, the skilled operator will re-draw by hand those portions of the pattern which have been erased, and incidentally take advantage of the presence of the pattern to hide the erasure.

Any document which is protected in this way should be scrutinised with great care because even if a microscopic examination of the pattern shows that it is still intact, this does not necessarily mean that no erasure has been effected.

The author has examined motor-vehicle registration books which had been protected against erasure by this system of overprinting and failed to find any visible trace of damage to the overprinting which should have been sensitive to the action of pure water, even more so powerful chemical bleaches. However, photography by infra red revealed that a whole mass of entries had been bleached out. The printers who prepared the registration books were obviously incompetent, for the overprinting had been carried out with one of the most stable and bleach-resisting printing inks available, thus completely defeating the object of the operation.

A whole series of devices has been patented with the object of protecting documents against alteration by chemical erasure of the ink. The most highly developed material hitherto devised is the paper to which the application of either oxidising

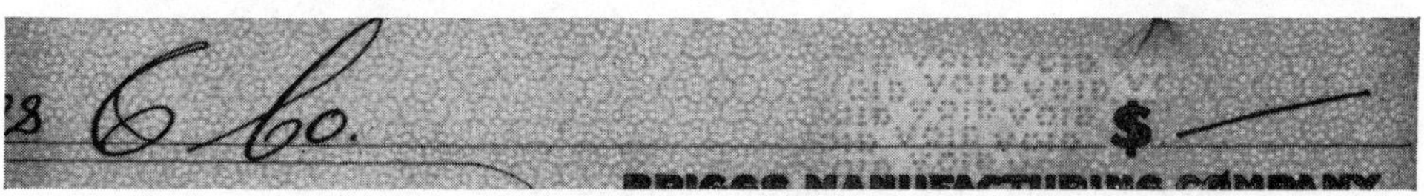

Fig. 2–2. The action of the ink eradicator has (1) removed the pattern, and (2) caused the word " void " to appear. (By courtesy of the Todd Co., Rochester N.Y.)

or reducing agents, either of which may be used for bleaching out ink, causes a reaction with the chemicals with which the paper has previously been impregnated to reveal a repetition of the word " void " wherever the chemicals have been applied.

This word is black in colour and cannot be erased without serious destruction of the surface of the paper.[1]

The development of safety paper reaches its highest peak in the production of identity cards, where there is the possibility of their being altered or imitated by organisations which might be expected to have the resources of a government behind them.

These cards are protected by a number of devices the details of which are rightly kept secret, but the general practice is to seal the card and any accompanying photograph inside a casing of synthetic resin which is itself engraved to reveal tampering as well as coded with markings which are not apparent to the naked eye.

Cheque-Writing Machines

A device which is intended to prevent either erasure or alteration of entries on cheques is the cheque-writer. This machine may be regarded as a very simple form of typewriter which drives ink-covered type faces into the very paper of the cheque. To produce this " shredding " action as it is termed, the faces of the type are scored with parallel cuts. The sharp edges so formed cut into the paper and carry with them the colouring matter of the ink. So thorough is the penetration of the paper that the colour can usually be seen quite clearly on the opposite side.

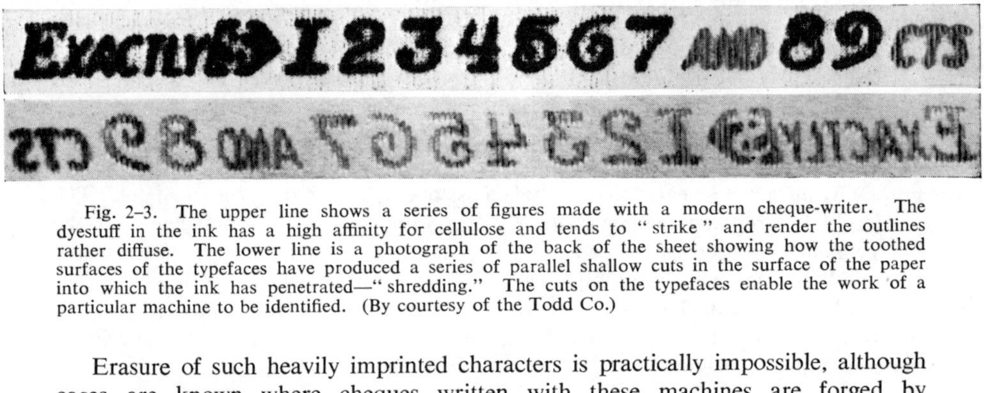

Fig. 2–3. The upper line shows a series of figures made with a modern cheque-writer. The dyestuff in the ink has a high affinity for cellulose and tends to " strike " and render the outlines rather diffuse. The lower line is a photograph of the back of the sheet showing how the toothed surfaces of the typefaces have produced a series of parallel shallow cuts in the surface of the paper into which the ink has penetrated—" shredding." The cuts on the typefaces enable the work of a particular machine to be identified. (By courtesy of the Todd Co.)

Erasure of such heavily imprinted characters is practically impossible, although cases are known where cheques written with these machines are forged by increasing the amount for which they have been drawn, a procedure commonly known as " raising."

Ink

Although some authorities consider that the earliest ink was a form of vegetable varnish, there is no doubt that the oldest type of ink whose use became widespread is that invented by the Chinese some thousands of years ago. The Chinese are given no credit for its invention in the name by which it is commonly known—Indian Ink. This ink is still in extended use in the East and, in a modified form, by artists all over the world.

[1] The Todd Co. Inc., Rochester, New York.

Indian Ink

Indian Ink is simple in composition, consisting of amorphous carbon in the form of lamp-black made into a cake with hide glue. The best lamp-black is considered to be that made by burning oily matter such as tung oil in a restricted supply of air and condensing the smoke on a cool surface. The ink is marketed in the form of sticks or cakes and has to be prepared for use by grinding the solid with water to form a suspension of the carbon in a dilute glue medium.

The colour of the ink, which can vary from dark brown to blue-black, is governed by the quality of the lamp-black, which again depends largely upon the materials from which the lamp-black is made. The darker tints are the more highly esteemed; this is why it is the practice to modify the original brown colour of some batches of ink by the judicious addition of blue pigment such as Prussian Blue.

Liquid preparations in which the carbon is kept in suspension were introduced at a later date. These are more convenient but not so highly esteemed by the more critical, who prefer to grind their own ink from the solid cake.

This turbid carbon ink is admirably adapted for use with the reed pen. When it is applied to paper or parchment, the water soaks in or evaporates so that the finished writing consists of a layer of amorphous carbon held bound to the surface of the document by a film of dried glue. If correctly prepared, Indian ink is practically neutral in reaction so that it neither corrodes the writing instrument, if this be metal, nor causes any deterioration of the paper or parchment.

As carbon is extremely stable, being unaffected by the action of light, air, moisture, acid fumes or microbiological attack, Indian ink can be counted on to last and retain its full colour as long as the material on which it has been written remains intact.

Carbon ink cannot be removed from a document by the action of chemical bleaches, to which it is extremely resistant, but as it rests largely on the surface of the paper or parchment it is possible to remove the greater part of the ink by scrubbing with a suitable detergent solution.

Modern carbon ink supplied in liquid form utilises carbon-black rather than soot as the source of the amorphous carbon whilst the hide glue is replaced by a solution of shellac in borax. Manufacture is facilitated by the use of a wetting agent which assists the mixing of the shellac solution with the carbon-black. Carbon inks of this class are usually kept slightly alkaline by the addition of ammonia, but care is needed in the formulation because too much alkali makes the ink liable to spread on the paper. If these ammoniacal inks are acidified the carbon coagulates, which is why they are immiscible with iron-tannin inks, which are almost invariably acid in reaction.

Sometimes forgers attempt to darken a freshly made ink writing by mixing Indian ink with ordinary ink in an effort to make the writing look as if it had been written some time previously. The attempt is usually unsuccessful because the muddy liquid produced in this way leaves unmistakable traces on the paper.

In its present form carbon ink, whether liquid or prepared from the solid cake, is unsuitable for use with a pen, especially with a fountain pen, although research devoted to the problem may result in the production of an ink similar in some respects to the new emulsion paints. If there could be formulated an ink consisting of colloidal carbon bound with one of the newer plastics such as polystyrene or polyvinyl acetate, the mixture being brought into suspension in water with an emulsifying agent, it would be of inestimable value for the preparation of documents intended to last a very long time. The final state of such an ink would be finely divided carbon bonded to the paper by a tough resin film. There would be no prospect of the writing being attacked by corrosive atmospheres, light, moisture or moulds. The neutral reaction of the ink, to say nothing of the absence of iron, would ensure the longest possible life to the paper.

Printing Ink

Modern printing inks have progressed far from the time when they were made by grinding carbon in the form of vegetable char with a varnish made of natural gums and drying oils. Nowadays a bewildering variety of materials is employed to produce special printing inks to meet the exacting demands of the trade. These materials include the latest synthetic resins as well as the older oils which have been modified by chemical treatment. Every year a host of new patents appear, so that finality can scarcely be said to have been reached. Nevertheless, it can be taken that most printing inks contain carbon in some form and all are resistant to fading and bleaching. It is sometimes possible to remove printing ink from a document by scrubbing with an aqueous solution of a suitable detergent. The rubbing breaks up the surface of the ink, and the detergent facilitates the suspension and eventual removal of the carbon and other ingredients by the water.

Cancelling Inks

Cancelling inks often contain carbon and this fact should be borne in mind when it is required to decipher faint cancellation marks on postage stamps and wrappers. Carbon is opaque to infra-red radiation and consequently photography of the mark with an infra-red sensitive plate can be relied upon considerably to improve the legibility of any markings effected with a carbon-containing cancelling ink.

Erasure of cancelling ink on valuable stamps is usually effected by attack on the medium which binds the carbon to the surface of the stamp, and it is to be regretted that many cancelling inks are manufactured with media which offer poor resistance to attack, so that the resistant carbon can simply be swabbed off. This treatment, colloquially known as " washing the stamps," can usually be detected by infra-red photography which will reveal the traces of carbon which almost invariably remain on the stamp.

Iron-Tannin Inks

As far back as the eighth century, or, as some authorities believe, at a much earlier date, it was discovered that when soluble salts of iron were mixed with extracts from the vegetable materials such as tan-bark and nut-galls, which were already in use for tanning hides, a mobile liquid was obtained which rapidly darkened on exposure to the air. This dark liquid was found to be far more suitable for use with the contemporary newly invented type of pen, the quill, than the carbon ink of antiquity.

In spite of its many advantages over carbon ink, the writing fluid made in this way was found to have a number of serious faults. When freshly prepared, it was practically colourless so that it had to be allowed to mature in open vats until its colour attained sufficient depth to allow it to be used as ink. Unfortunately, it was found that as the colour developed on storage, a large proportion of the iron-tannin compounds which gave body to the ink was precipitated to form a thick mud which clogged the pens.

Many additions to the ink were tried until it was discovered that gum arabic would act as a protective colloid and hinder, even if it did not prevent, the formation of the unwanted precipitate.

Iron-tannin ink protected by the addition of gum arabic remained the standard writing fluid for centuries as chemical science was not sufficiently advanced to allow of any substantial improvements being made in its composition. It was gradually realised that the best tanning materials for hides were not necessarily the most satisfactory for the preparation of ink of good colour. As ink made from tannin derived from nut-galls proved to be by far the most satisfactory in this respect, nut-galls were used to such an extent that iron-tannin ink is sometimes known as iron-nutgalls ink.

It was not until the middle of the last century that any considerable advance was made in the preparation of this ink. The iron salts, the chloride and the sulphate in use for ink making are slightly acid in solution so that the resulting inks are also slightly acid. The important discovery was, that if the acidity of the ink were deliberately increased by the addition of mineral acid, oxidation of the ink in storage was so reduced that the iron salts remained in solution even in the absence of gum arabic, which was henceforth omitted from the iron-tannin ink-making formulae.

Unfortunately the acidified liquid resulted in an ink which was practically colourless. The colour developed but slowly after writing, a period of some months having to elapse before the ink line reached anything like its full depth of colour.

To overcome this serious defect, Stephens in 1836 added to the ink of his manufacture a small proportion of indigo. Incidentally, this use of indigo as a temporary colouring matter for ink had been mooted in Germany over seventy years before Stephens carried the suggestion into effect.

The indigo imparted a bright blue initial colour to the writing, and this was slowly masked by the violet-black tint of the iron-gallotannate complexes produced by the action of the oxygen of the air upon the other constituents of the ink. It is from this colour change from blue to black that this improved ink was named " Blue-black," a term which is still in use today to designate iron-tannin inks which use a blue dyestuff to give a temporary colour to the writing, although indigo is no longer regarded as the best dyestuff for this purpose.

Today a fair number of suitable dyestuffs are available to the ink manufacturer, but the one which is in greatest use is known as " Soluble Blue."

Whilst it is possible to make ink-like products by mixing, in almost any proportions, iron salts and tannin, which itself may be drawn from one of a number of sources, inks prepared haphazardly are unlikely to be of satisfactory quality. For centuries after the discovery of iron-tannin ink, no systematic work was done on the methods of preparation so as to ensure the production of ink of good colour and long life. Between 1870–80 this work was carried out in Germany at the request of the Prussian Government, and so well was it done that the recommendations of the investigators Schuttig and Neumann form the basis of the official specifications to which iron-tannin inks are made to this day.[2]

Though by no means perfect, iron-tannin ink is still the most popular ink where good colour and permanence are required. Unlike carbon ink, which remains largely on the surface of the paper, the iron-tannin ink soaks into the paper, so that the insoluble iron compounds formed when the ink ages are firmly held as an integral part of the paper surface. Mature writing with this ink is difficult to erase and resists the action of water so that it does not become smudged should the document be wetted.

The period over which an ink writing retains its colour depends upon its quality and the conditions of storage. All iron-tannin inks can be expected to fade eventually but the residual oxide of iron will last as long as the paper, and its presence ensures that writing with the most faded ink may be deciphered, albeit with some difficulty, should the occasion arise.

Iron-tannin ink has the added advantage that it is relatively cheap and easy to make from materials which are available in good supply. When properly made this ink does not deteriorate appreciably, even on long storage.

The greatest defect of iron-tannin ink is that it contains acid. It is this acid which corrodes pen nibs and, what is far worse, accelerates the deterioration of the paper to which it is applied.

Record Ink

This is the term applied to inks of high quality which are assured of long life under reasonable conditions of storage of the documents. Following the recommendations of Schuttig and Neumann it is laid down in most government specifications that a record ink should contain between 0·5 to 0·6 per cent. of iron with the minimum concentration of acid which is consistent with the good performance of the ink.

Any iron-tannin ink is necessarily slow-drying, but as it is essential to maintain the concentration of iron in the ink, the temptation to use blotting paper should be resisted. Blotting paper is the enemy of ink, and there is no point in ensuring that an ink contains a high proportion of iron compounds if the greater part of these are to be removed by the action of the blotting paper before they have had the opportunity of soaking into the paper, where they will form the insoluble black iron-gallotannate which gives the mature ink line its body.

The availability of a good long-lasting ink for the preparation of important documents is considered so important that in 1932 the League of Nations published a report dealing with the permanence of papers, which included recommendations as to the qualities of a permanent ink.[3]

Among the recommendations it was stated that a satisfactory ink should be

[2] O. Schluttig and G. S. Neumann, *Die Eisengallustinten* (The Iron-Gall Inks), (v. Zahn and Jaensch, Dresden, Germany, 1890).

[3] *Report by League of Nations on the Permanence of Papers* (1932 Ottawa Meeting of the National Research Council).

thin and easy-flowing, remaining substantially unaltered in an unstoppered bottle but quick-drying with no suggestion of stickiness. The ink should contain sufficient iron and tannin so that when dry it will blacken and resist the fading action of light and smudging by water yet not be so acid as to attack steel.

Some of these requirements are contradictory, as an ink which contains the recommended concentration of iron and tannin will necessarily contain sufficient acid to corrode a steel pen.

Fountain Pen Inks

The inks described as " fountain pen inks " can be divided into two classes. The first class, which is usually called " Blue-black Permanent," is nothing more than a record ink which contains about half the normal concentration of iron compounds but an increased proportion of dyestuff.

Incidentally, there is no reason whatsoever why record ink itself should not be used in the conventional fountain pen, for which it is quite as satisfactory as any specially labelled fountain pen ink.

The other class of ink, which is sometimes termed " non-staining," contains no iron salts, being little more than a dilute aqueous solution of one or more synthetic dyestuffs. Unlike iron-tannin inks, these dyestuff inks are usually neutral in reaction and are consequently non-corrosive to steel pen nibs.

The colour of these inks does not change appreciably on exposure to air, nor does the dye become insoluble in water after it has been applied to the paper. This means that writing done with these inks is apt to smear should the paper be wetted.

By a careful selection of the dyestuffs, it is possible to prepare what are termed " Washable Inks." This term does not mean what at first sight might be assumed—that writing done with these inks would resist the action of water, as is the case with washable distemper. On the contrary, it means that stains on fabrics caused by these inks can easily be washed out without any risk of leaving behind a stain of iron mould.

Coloured Inks

Synthetic dyestuffs form the basis of practically all coloured inks whether intended for use in fountain pens or not. There is no black dyestuff commercially available which has sufficient tinctorial power to make a satisfactory black ink by itself in the concentrations usually employed, so that black inks generally contain a dark blue dyestuff as their main constituent with its colour modified by the addition of red and yellow dyestuffs.

Unfortunately, the very best of the dyestuffs available for ink-making are by no means fast to light, so that writing done with these inks slowly fades under even the best conditions of storage. Whilst they are quite satisfactory for everyday use, dyestuff inks cannot be recommended for important documents.

Some blue dyestuff inks utilise a copper compound as the blue colouring matter. As these inks contain a compound of a metal which forms a coloured oxide, the writing can be expected to be permanent.

It is perhaps unfortunate that the use of copper compounds in ink is apt to bring other problems in its train. Traces of this metal catalyse the perishing of a variety of materials, among them being rubber and the rubberlike compounds used in the manufacture of fountain pens. This deleterious action of copper compounds can, however, be inhibited by the addition of suitable antoxidants to the ink, but every addition to an ink is likely to bring its own peculiar difficulties with it, to say nothing of the additional trouble and expense incurred.[4]

The document examiner has at his disposal a variety of methods whereby faded iron-tannin inks can be deciphered or if necessary restored in colour, but where a faded dyestuff ink which contains no metal is concerned, it is only rarely that anything can be done to decipher the faded writing and nothing to restore its colour.

In recent years, it has become the practice to add to inks small concentrations of wetting agents. Although these are sometimes given quaint names by the manufacturers, they are very similar to the active ingredients found in domestic detergents. These additions effect some improvement in the flow of the ink in a fountain pen and may to some extent facilitate the absorption of the ink into the paper and so accelerate the drying of the writing.

Copying Ink

Copying ink is substantially a concentrated record ink to which has been added chemicals such as glycerine or dextrin. The additions retard the oxidation of the ink, which remains on the document to be copied in a soluble state, so that a partial transfer of the colouring matter may be effected some hours after writing.

Logwood Ink

This is but one of a number of different types of ink formerly in extensive use but rarely encountered today, when about 80 per cent. of writing ink is dyestuff ink, the remainder being iron-tannin ink.

Logwood ink was one of the most satisfactory of these older inks, being simply made by mixing chromium salts with an aqueous extract of logwood chips. Many of the older books on document examination give details of the preparation and properties of these obsolete inks together with tests for distinguishing between them. There is no advantage to be gained by repeating this useless information here, for if it is required reference may be made to one of the books mentioned in the bibliography at the end of this chapter.

Quick-Drying Inks

Although a satisfactory general purpose quick-drying ink has been sought for many years, progress has been very slow, and until recently quick-drying inks have not proved at all satisfactory.

The replacement in whole or in part of the slow-drying water by a more volatile vehicle such as alcohol or acetone was an obvious move, but inks made in this way have had but a limited success. One of their disadvantages was that the ink dried quickly, not only on the paper but also in those places where it was required to remain liquid—in the bottle and at the pen point.

In more recent years, a different line of approach has been tried. Instead of

[4] G. H. Sayler. U.S. Patent 2,528,390. 1950.

accelerating the evaporation of the ink, modifications in its composition have been made to encourage its more rapid absorption into the paper. The first efforts in this direction involved the addition of non-volatile organic solvents to the ink. Being non-volatile, their presence did not increase the rate at which they dried up in the bottle or fountain pen, so that these inks did not share the disadvantages of those containing alcohol or acetone. Nevertheless, experience showed that inks made in this way were not only expensive but were too slow-drying to be of any practical value.[5]

The next discovery was that the addition of a wetting agent to ordinary ink would facilitate its penetration into the paper, but this line of approach was barred because if sufficient wetting agent were added to ensure rapid absorption of the ink, this was accompanied by an undesirable degree of lateral spreading over the surface, resulting in the broadening and sometimes the feathering of the ink line.

The problem was eventually solved by the adoption of a radically different line of approach. It has been known for many years that solutions of alkali not only penetrate well into cellulosic materials such as paper, but also increase the affinity of the fibres for substantive dyestuffs such as those used in ink. This suggested that an alkaline ink should not only be quick-drying by absorption, but when dry, resistant to moisture.

As early as 1912, suggestions were made that an alkaline ink containing potassium carbonate might prove quick-drying through absorption, as well as moisture-resistant when dry, but inks containing this alkali were found to be too slowly absorbed to be considered quick-drying because the carbonate solution in the concentrations allowable was insufficiently alkaline.[6]

Work on alkaline inks continued, and in 1927 a patent was taken out to cover an ink containing caustic soda, which proved to be sufficiently alkaline to be quick-drying by absorption.[7]

This was a considerable step forward, but it was soon found that the high alkalinity which was necessary to ensure quick-drying of the ink brought other troubles in its train. The most serious proved to be the flooding of fountain pens, the inability to use any really suitable ink-forming iron salts in the presence of alkali and the lack of dyestuffs suitable for use in strongly alkaline solutions. This latter fact is surprising, for many thousands of synthetic dyestuffs have been prepared and it might well be thought that among them would be some which were suitable for use in an alkaline ink. It must be remembered that dyestuffs are produced commercially primarily for dyeing textiles, which is usually done from solutions which are acid, neutral or mildly alkaline, so that until recently little effort had been made to produce dyestuffs suitable for use in ink and at the same time stable to light and to oxidation when in the presence of strong alkali.

Research in this direction has been prosecuted vigorously and, to date, well over a thousand new dyestuffs have been specially synthesised and tested in an effort to find the mere half-dozen or so required to furnish a suitable range of colours for alkaline inks.[8]

[5] G. B. Ottley. U.S. Patent 1,897,071. 1933.
[6] Margival, *Les Encres* (Gautier-Villars, Paris, 1912).
[7] Schladebach and Hahle. U.S. Patent 1,645,117. 1927.
[8] W. B. Reynolds. U.S. Patent 2,489,463. 1949.

The flooding of fountain pens when used with alkaline inks was also investigated. It was discovered that the surface tension of an alkaline ink did not differ appreciably from that of ordinary inks which had proved quite suitable for use in fountain pens, so that too low a surface tension was not the reason why alkaline inks flooded. Eventually it was found that the main cause of the flooding was that the alkaline solution had a zero contact angle with the metal of the pen nib. This encouraged the flow of the ink across the nib and resulted in the excess rate of flow which led to flooding of the pen.

By analogy with the method used to concentrate ores by the process known as "froth flotation," where the crude ore is treated with chemicals which allow unwanted dirt to be wetted and the desired particles of ore to remain dry on subsequent treatment with water, it was discovered that the addition of small quantities of similar agents to the ink would control its tendency to flood. A recent patent discloses the use of amyl xanthate for this purpose.[9]

This was not the end of the difficulties encountered in the attempt to develop an alkaline ink. If an ink containing caustic soda is kept in a stoppered bottle, it will remain practically unaltered, but this is not the case when it is exposed to air, when it will speedily absorb carbon dioxide. This will not only reduce its alkalinity, but it will tend to clog the slit of the nib with an incrustation of sodium carbonate crystals.

At first sight, the problem of preventing the absorption of carbon dioxide might appear to be insuperable, but recent theoretical work on the properties of thin films, such as soap bubbles, has indicated how an alkaline ink can be protected from deterioration from this cause. Success was achieved by the addition to the ink of a carefully chosen wetting agent which concentrates in the surface of the film of ink on the pen nib to block off the carbon dioxide in the air from the alkali in the ink, which consequently remains substantially unaltered for long periods.[10]

The rapid absorption of an alkaline ink into the paper is accompanied by a certain amount of undesired lateral spreading. This problem has also been attacked and it has been discovered that if a colloidal material such as corn starch or a colloidal clay such as Bentonite is added to the ink, the tendency towards lateral spreading and feathering of the ink line is reduced to negligible proportions.

When the foregoing researches had been completed, the problem of rendering an alkaline ink permanent was very simply solved. For this purpose iron salts are not suitable, but vanadium in the form of ammonium metavanadate may be added to the blue-black inks and copper in the form of a modified copper phthalocyanine compound to the blue and green inks of this class.[11]

There is no doubt that the introduction of these modern alkaline inks is an important new departure. As they contain compounds of metals which form coloured oxides they are likely to be as permanent as the best record inks containing iron. Their alkaline reaction (pH approximately 11·6) is probably too slight to do any harm to the cellulose or other constituents of the paper, and as they are acid-free

[9] C. S. Miner and G. H. Sayler. U.S. Patent 1,932,248. 1933.

[10] W. B. Reynolds, "The Development of Quick-drying Writing Inks," *Chem. and Eng. News*, April, 1946.

[11] British Patent 619,972. 1946.

they are unlikely to accelerate the deterioration of the paper with age, which is the most serious fault of acid iron-tannate inks.

On being applied to paper, they are speedily absorbed so that there is little temptation to remove the greater part of the ink with blotting paper. The dyestuff present is rapidly and thoroughly fixed on to the surface of the cellulose fibres so that these inks are very resistant to the action of water.

Although the problems associated with the production of a quick-drying alkaline ink have been solved, these inks as at present formulated are unlikely to supersede the conventional inks for most ordinary purposes. Not only are they necessarily more expensive but their use is restricted to a special range of fountain pens, as the alkali present will attack the hard metal points of the conventional gold nib as well as the nitrocellulose from which the majority of fountain pens are constructed.

Special nib alloys have been devised for use with alkaline inks and the pens themselves have to be made from an alkali-resistant plastic such as polymethacrylate.

Modern inks are far more complicated mixtures than the simple fluids from which they have been derived; mention has been made of the parts played by alkali, colloidal materials, antoxidants, flotation agents, metal complexes and specially developed dyestuffs. The story is by no means complete, for a survey of contemporary patent literature reveals that this list has already been extended by the addition of humectants, such as the glycols, etc., in an endeavour to develop yet more satisfactory writing fluids.[12]

Hectograph Inks

A hectograph consists of a layer of either a gelatine-glycerol mixture or of a special clay. The document to be copied is heavily written with a special ink which consists of a suitable dyestuff mixed with glucose, glycerol or a glycol, whose function is to assist the transfer of the ink. When the document is placed face down upon the gelatine or clay surface, some of the dye is absorbed by it. When the document is replaced by a sheet of absorbent paper, some of the dyestuff migrates from the gelatine to the paper to form a copy of the original.

To ensure the production of a reasonable number of copies before the hectograph surface becomes depleted of colouring matter a dyestuff, such as crystal violet, with a high tinctorial power must be employed.[13]

All the suitable dyestuffs are fugitive, so that copies made in this way are unlikely to have a long life especially if they are exposed to sunlight. There is no known procedure by means of which faded hectograph copies may be restored or deciphered; it is a matter of some difficulty to make a satisfactory photograph of a faded hectograph copy even if the best choice is made of the filters which are available.

Stamp-Pad Inks

These inks are very similar to hectograph inks except that they are heavily loaded with humectants, such as glycerol or glycol, which prevent the pad from

[12] R. S. Casey, "Writing Ink," *Encyclopaedia of Chemical Technology* (Polytechnic Institute of Brooklyn, New York, 1952).

[13] Inks Circular C.426, United States Department of Commerce, National Bureau of Standards, 1940.

drying up. Some of the quick-drying stamp-pad inks contain solvents such as acetone, methyl alcohol or ethyl acetate, instead of the more common aqueous solutions.[13]

Typewriter Ribbon Inks

Typewriter ribbons are made of silk, cotton or rayon cloth, which has been impregnated with an ink that has been the subject of a great deal of research still being vigorously prosecuted so as to improve the final product. An ink which is commonly employed consists of a slow-drying oil such as castor oil mixed with olein and an oil-soluble dyestuff. The choice of dyestuffs is limited and the light-resisting properties of the dyestuffs in common use leave a great deal to be desired. Where a greater degree of permanency is required, a " record " ribbon must be employed. This is loaded with carbon black and a blue pigment whose function is to improve the rather brown tone of the carbon. Some of the carbon black-blue pigment mixture is transferred to the document from the ribbon and this gives a fair measure of permanency to the typescript. Blue record ribbon inks make use of Prussian Blue alone as the colouring matter. Colour lakes may be used as the source of the colour instead of the pure dyestuff; these are finely ground into the vehicle with which the ribbon is impregnated.

Copying ribbons usually contain a water-soluble dye in a glycerol or similar base. Some copying ribbons contain carbon as well as the water-soluble dyestuff, so that they produce a black original impression derived from the carbon, and a blue copy due to the dye which alone is capable of easy transfer during the copying process.

A typewriter ribbon made of woven cloth will necessarily give typescript impressions with uneven outlines. Certain makes of typewriter have an alternative arrangement whereby a strip of carbon paper which is fed once through the machine is used instead of a woven ribbon. This device permits the production of clear-cut impressions which are in no way inferior to letterpress printed characters.

Ball-Point Pen Ink

The success of the ball-point pen has been bound up with the provision of suitable inks. The problems presented in the formulation of an ink which answers most of the requirements are formidable and research continues apace to discover both better colouring matter and vehicles than those in use at the present time.

The ball-point pen works on a very simple principle—a tiny rotating ball picks up a supply of ink by contact with that contained in a reservoir and then transfers it to the paper. The gap between the ball and its housing is very narrow—something less than a thousandth of a centimetre—so that this rules out the use of inks containing suspended colouring matter. With the exception of colloidal carbon, which was tried for a short time but eventually abandoned by many manufacturers, the colouring matter in a ball-point pen ink must be in solution.

Apart from any other considerations, the physical properties of the ink are all-important. Whilst the ink must never seep through the gap when the pen is not in use, its passage through that same gap must be regular and continuous when the ball is rotated while writing. The writing trace must be even but not excessive. No excess globules of ink can be allowed to collect around the gap or smudging of the writing will result. To this end, the viscosity of the ink must be carefully adjusted between fairly fine limits. In addition, there must be sufficient adhesion between the ball and the ink to enable the ball to do its work of transferring the ink from the reservoir to the paper, but the adhesion of the ink to the ball must not be so great that it cannot easily be stripped from it by contact with the paper. Not only the viscosity and the adhesive powers, but the surface tension of the ink must lie within narrow limits if the pen is to work satisfactorily. Finally, the vehicle in which the colouring matter is dissolved must have a low vapour pressure so that it does not evaporate in storage and so solidify in the reservoir or form crusts on the ball.

The chemical properties required by a suitable ink are no less difficult to achieve. In the first place, the ink and all its major constituents must be non-hygroscopic and there must be no chance of the ink altering through oxidation or polymerisation on storage. Secondly, the ink must be non-corrosive to the materials of which the pen is made; and finally, the dyestuffs which are chosen must be of an acceptable colour and of high tinctorial power, because of the small amount of ink which is transferred, as well as being reasonably resistant to fading by light. This is a very uncommon combination of characters for a range of dyestuffs to possess. In addition, any dyes which are used should adhere firmly to the paper surface and not be transferable. This latter consideration is not to obviate the possibility of forgery by transfer, the danger of which has been greatly overrated, but dyes which fail in this respect give writing which easily smudges.

In view of the foregoing, it is not surprising that a great deal of research has been necessary to bring the inks to their present stage of development. When the ball-point pen was first introduced towards the end of the war, the inks used were oily in nature and " dried " on the paper by virtue of the extremely small amount transferred. The trace of oily ink was almost completely absorbed into the surface of the paper so that no true drying by loss of solvent or oxidation took place.

The oily base consisted of olein with or without an admixture of castor or similar oil. Colophony was usually added to increase the viscosity of the ink.[14] A feature of all ball-point pen inks is the high proportion of dyestuff present—averaging no less than about 15 per cent. of the whole.

The dyestuffs utilised were all oil-soluble, which restricted the choice very severely, and the early inks were unsatisfactory in many respects. Many of the dyestuffs available were fugitive and the only one which gave a good bright blue—Victoria Blue—was found to " strike " very badly on certain papers. Striking is the term given to the continued spreading of the colour over the surface of and into the paper so that the line of writing tends to lose its character and degenerate into a broad structureless streak of colour.

A.

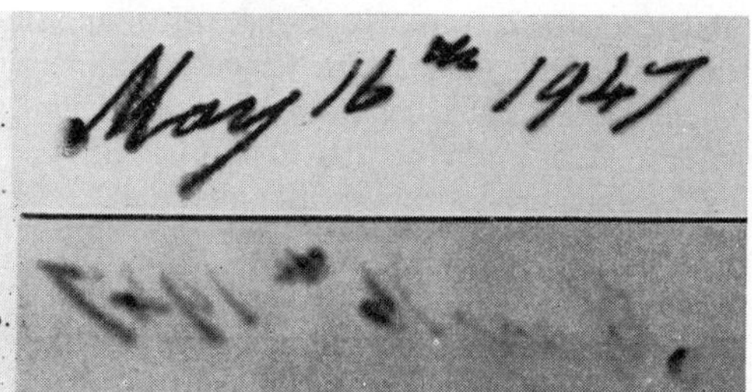

B.

Fig. 2–4. *Striking of ball-point pen ink*
" A " shows how the dye has diffused laterally. " B " is a photograph of the back of the sheet showing how the dye has diffused through the sheet.

[14] British Patents 621,847; 629,226; 629,283; 652,359.

The possibility of a ball-point writing such as a signature being fraudulently transferred from one document to another is considered to be a serious risk, but the author knows no case of this having been attempted with a view to committing forgery.

Some of the cheaper pens still use inks based on olein as these inks are quite satisfactory for most purposes, although not nearly so effective as an improved class of ink which was introduced in 1952.

These improved inks are based on polyethylene glycols of suitable viscosity. In these polar solvents a different and much superior range of dyestuffs can be dissolved to overcome many of the disadvantages of the oily inks. The dyestuffs, which are similar to those used in "steam setting" printing inks, adhere very firmly to the cellulose fibres so that the writing can neither be smudged or transferred.

Attempts have been made to design a ball-point pen which can use ordinary ink. One such pen has been marketed in which the ball consists of a tiny sphere of sapphire working in a housing of platinum.

Liquid Lead Pencil Ink

The "liquid lead" pencil is in all respects an ordinary ball-point pen with a fluid containing finely divided carbon substituted for the usual dyestuff-containing ink.

In use, the ball deposits an irregular smear of finely divided carbon on the surface of the paper and, as there is no reaction between the inert carbon and the cellulose fibres, it is possible to erase the line by vigorous rubbing with a soft eraser. From this description it would appear that this liquid lead pencil has little to recommend it over a propelling pencil fitted with a very soft lead.

When the line made by one of these liquid lead pencils is examined with a microscope and compared with one of similar depth of colour made by a soft lead pencil, it will be found that the line made by the ball-point contains much less black material than the other and it is a matter of some surprise that so dark a line is made by such a meagre deposit. Whilst the greater part of this deposit may be seen heaped in discrete patches among the paper fibres, there will also be observed a continuous grey background to the line which is absent from the pencil mark. This grey background is formed of a multitude of tiny particles precipitated from the liquid ink. These are far more numerous and very much smaller than those which can be detached from the lead of an ordinary pencil by its passage over the paper. It is probable that it is this extreme degree of subdivision which produces such a dark mark from so little material.

Pencils

The glazed surface of writing paper is sufficiently hard to abrade any soft material which is rubbed across it. If a rod of soft metal such as silver or lead alloy is used, the abraded metal being optically dense, though minute in quantity, forms a visible mark. Soft metals are no longer used as marking materials but they are mentioned here because the document examiner might very well come across marks on documents made by soft metal which are very difficult to distinguish visually from marks made by hard pencils.

It was early discovered that natural graphite sawn into strips supported between pieces of wood was much superior to metal as a marking material, and it is from this crude device that the modern pencil has been developed.

The " lead " of a modern pencil consists of an intimate mixture of graphite and clay, which is extruded whilst moist, dried, baked, and finally boiled in tallow before being glued into its wooden sheath. Other substances such as carbon black for artists' pencils or dyestuffs such as methyl violet to make copying or so-called indelible pencils are sometimes added to the graphite and clay mix.

When the pencil point is drawn over the surface of the paper, fragments of the " lead " are dislodged to form the line. The graphite particles become piled up against those paper fibres which lie at right angles to the direction of motion whilst longitudinal striae are formed by the abrasive action of the clay which is present. The greater the proportion of graphite in the lead, the darker is the line which is made with a fixed pressure.

Indelible or copying pencils leave fragments of the dyestuff intermingled with the graphite and clay which forms the line. These particles of dyestuff " strike " into the paper and are partially adsorbed on to the surface of the cellulose fibres. This is why they resist abrasion and so to some extent justify the use of the term " indelible." If a heavy line made with one of these pencils is pressed into intimate contact with a damp sheet of paper, some of the dye is transferred to make a copy, hence the term " copying lead."

Whilst pencil writing may be almost wholly erased by abrasion, it is immune to the action of ink eradicators. Pencil writing will not fade, and if carefully preserved, it may be expected to last as long as the paper on which it is written. It is, however, apt to smudge, so that pencil entries in diaries carried in the coat pocket may become practically illegible through the rubbing caused by the relative motion of the pages.

Pencil writing or drawings may be preserved from deterioration from this cause by being coated with a protective varnish which binds the loose fragments which make up the line. Shellac dissolved in methylated spirit is favoured by artists for this purpose but it is probable that a solution of polyvinyl acetate in alcohol or acetone would prove even more satisfactory when it is desired to preserve an important document written in pencil.

Crayons

Coloured pencils are more correctly described as crayons, whether in the form of a cored rod or as a stick of coloured material which may or may not be surrounded by a paper jacket. The active ingredient is almost invariably a mixture of waxes coloured by the addition of oil-soluble dyestuffs, or more likely, pigments or colouring matters produced by depositing a dye on a white mineral base known as lakes.

The exact composition of the waxy base varies, but most wax crayons contain the cheap paraffin wax modified by the addition of more expensive waxes such as carnauba. The mark made by a wax crayon on paper is hard to distinguish from that made by carbon paper because both are produced by colouring matter bound in a waxy base.

Coloured Chalks

These, though popular with artists, are infrequently encountered by the document examiner. These chalks rarely contain what the chemist knows as chalk but are composed of a selected grade of calcium sulphate coloured by the addition of pigments or lakes. Writing or drawings made with these " pastels," as they are sometimes termed, rub off the paper very easily. They can be treated with a protective varnish similar to that used for pencil, albeit with some loss of quality.

Adhesives

It was once thought that only substances of a gelatinous nature could serve as adhesives for paper, hence the almost universal use of glue derived from both animal and fish sources, together with pastes based on starch or modified starches such as dextrin, and solutions of natural products such as gum arabic. The fact that frozen water, which is not of a gummy nature, made an excellent adhesive for paper and paper products was overlooked. It is now realised that good adhesion can be attained by the use of any liquid which will wet both surfaces to be joined and subsequently become transformed to a solid either by drying or chemical action.[15]

Research and experiment have added to the above rather restricted list adhesives based on sodium silicate solution, albumen, casein, rubber latex, resins and the esters and ethers of cellulose.

Those adhesives which are based on animal and vegetable products, especially glue and albumen, are subject to microbiological attack which causes their adhesive quality to be impaired. As this is so, it is necessary to add small quantities of preservatives to adhesives of this nature. The substances chosen for this purpose are many and varied and include zinc salts, formaldehyde, fluorides and derivatives of phenol.

Post-war development has resulted in the production of a range of emulsions based on polyvinyl acetate which are excellent adhesives. They are stable aqueous dispersions of water-soluble material which range from thin milky liquids to stiff pastes.

The way in which these emulsions act as adhesives is quite different from that of the older adhesives which become solid by loss of solvent. The emulsion adhesives consist of two balanced phases which remain intact on storage. Contact with porous paper upsets this balance so that stability is lost and the solid matter present coalesces on the surfaces to be joined to form a solid bond. These adhesives possess a high resistance to humidity, to acids and alkalis, to oils, whether vegetable or mineral, as well as to many common solvents. They are subject neither to microbiological attack nor insect or rodent infestation.

Unvulcanised rubber which has been applied to the paper in the form of latex is now used as an adhesive for envelopes. These are sealed by merely pressing the treated surfaces together, and unlike gum or glue these adhesives cannot be broken down by steaming. If force is used to open the envelope, resealing becomes a

[15] McBain and Lee. Proc. Roy. Soc. A 1927, 113, 606.

difficult task. If solvent is used to soften the rubber or rubber substitute, it will spread into the surrounding paper and leave traces which show that the adhesive strip has been tampered with.

Bibliography

Any public library should be able to supply a list of the older standard books on the manufacture of paper and ink, so these are not included here. More recent publications include:

Norris, F. H., *Paper and Papermaking* (Oxford University Press, 1952).

Labarre, E. J., *Dictionary and Encyclopaedia of Paper and Papermaking* (2nd ed., Oxford, 1952).

Hunter, D., *Paper Making. History and Technique of an Ancient Craft* (2nd ed., London Pleiades Books, 1947).

Stephenson, J. N., *Pulp and Paper Manufacture* (four volumes) (McGraw-Hill, New York, 1950).

Clapperton, R. H., *Modern Papermaking* (Blackwell, 1952).

Gilmour, F. C. (Ed.), *Paper, Its Making, Merchanting and Usage* (Nat. Assoc. of Paper Merchants, London, with Longmans Green, 1955).

Gaskell, P., "Notes on 18th Century British Paper," *The Library,* Fifth Series, Vol. XII, March, 1957.

Directory of Paper Makers (Marchant Singer and Co., High Holborn, London).

Phillips Paper Trade Directory of the World (S. C. Phillips and Co., London).

The Stationers Guide (Trade Periodicals, Ltd., London).

Grant, J., *Books and Documents* (Grafton and Co., London, 1937).

Mitchell, C. A. *Inks, Their Composition and Manufacture* (4th ed., C. Griffin & Co., London, 1937).

Wolfe, H. F., *The Manufacture of Printing and Lithographic Ink* (MacNair-Dorland Co., New York, 1933).

Waters, C. E., "Inks" Circular, C426 (U.S. Department of Commerce, 1940).

Lucas, A., "The Inks of Ancient and Modern Egypt," *The Analyst* 47, 1922.

Zimmerman, E. W., "Coloured Waterproof Drawing Inks," *Ind. Eng. Chem.* 25, 1033, 1933.

Waters, C. E., "Quick-drying Stamp-pad Inks," *Journ. Research Nat. Bur. Standards* 20, 543–547, 1938.

Mally, Rudolf, "The Ball Point Pen," *Kriminalistik,* 10 (2) 55–60, February, 1956.

Lindsly, G. H., and Casey, R. S., "Behaviour of the Ballpoint pens and Inks as Seen by a Principal Manufacturer," *Amer. Bar. Assocn. Journal,* Vol. 34, May, 1948.

Souder, W., "Composition, Properties and Behaviour of Ballpoint Pens and Inks," *Journ. Crim. Law and Crim. and Police Science,* Vol. 45, March–April, 1945.

"Making Ball-Point Pens," *Machinery,* January 25, February 1, 1951.

"Ball Point Pens," *Science Illustrated,* August, 1946.

Mitchell, C. A., "Blacklead Pencils and their Pigments in Writing," *Journ. Soc. Chem. Ind.* 38, 1919. "Graphites and other Pencil Pigments," *The Analyst* 47, 1922.

Locard, J., *L'analyse des traits de crayon en criminalistique* (Desvigne et Cie, Lyon, 1936).

Simons, Francis L., *Safety Papers,* "Safety Papers—A Review of Theory and Practice," TAPPI, 34 (10), 113–122, October, 1951.

Mosher, R. H. (Ed.), *Speciality Papers* (Remsen Press, Brooklyn, N.Y., 1950).

Dulac, R., *Industrial Cold Adhesives,* Eng. ed., J. L. Rosebaum (C. Griffin & Co., Ltd., London, 1937).

Reports of the Adhesive Research Committee, 1922, 1926, 1932, Her Majesty's Stationery Office.

3

THE PRELIMINARY EXAMINATION

INTRODUCTION

THE majority of forgeries are crude, and it is surprising what obvious fakes are accepted as genuine when their falsity should be apparent to anyone giving them more than the most cursory scrutiny.

There are in existence business agreements bearing obvious erasures or traces of pencil associated with important signatures; wills, allegedly signed by the aged on their death-beds, bearing bold well-written signatures characteristic of writers in full possession of their faculties; documents with vital clauses curiously compressed in marked contrast with the remainder of the writing, to say nothing of torn and dilapidated papers with all their significant portions miraculously preserved intact. Whenever a crude forgery has been exposed, astonishment is expressed that such a poor thing should have been advanced as genuine and, what is more surprising, accepted by so many at its face value.

There is no doubt that forgeries owe their immunity from immediate detection to the fact that by far the greater part of the documents handled by the business man, and even by the lawyer, is genuine—it is only the rarity which is forged. If this were not so, and every important document had to be subjected to an expensive and time-consuming scrutiny by an expert before being accepted as genuine, business would be soon brought to a standstill.

Fortunately, there is a happy mean between the blind acceptance of a document as genuine and its submission to a document examiner to ensure that all is in order. This is to make an examination of any suspect document on the lines laid down below. For this examination little apparatus and no specialised scientific knowledge are required, but when carried out thoroughly, the scheme to be outlined for the preliminary examination of a suspect document can be counted on to expose the majority of forgeries which might otherwise be accepted as genuine: the scheme will also indicate the authors of a fair proportion of anonymous letters if they are examined according to the principles laid down.

Equipment

No elaborate optical equipment need be acquired; a microscope in the hands of the inexperienced is more likely to be a hindrance than an aid. A simple magnifying glass will suffice. Apart from this magnifying glass and possibly a metal rule, all that is required is a comfortable chair, a table of convenient height placed in a good light, ample patience, and last but not least, a healthy scepticism which refuses to take things at their face value. As an example of the latter, it is a good rule to regard as suspect every document, such as a will or agreement, which has some romantic story attached to its discovery. Whilst the stories associated with the romantic discoveries of documents may vary in detail, it is safest to regard them all as unreliable, however circumstantial they may be, and to concentrate the attention on the documents themselves in an endeavour to discover factual evidence on which they can safely be judged.

The emphasis which must be placed on the various tests to be described must be governed by the nature of the document under examination. For example, an observation which might be of vital importance when a forgery is suspected may prove of little moment when the problem is the entirely different one of deducing the probable source of an anonymous communication.

Background Details

The full story surrounding the appearance of any document on the scene should be ascertained and *written down in the fullest detail.* This is important for two reasons.

In the first place, by writing down the full story, the examiner will render his mind alert to the significance of any discovery he may make during his examination of the documents which is inconsistent with the story. Anachronisms and incongruities which constitute the most damning evidence of the spurious nature of a document can only be recognised as such by an examiner who is fully aware of what the document he is examining is supposed to represent.

Secondly, once the story has been put on record, no modification can, with impunity, subsequently be introduced in an endeavour to reconcile it with the later discovery of inconvenient facts.

Description of Documents

As each of the tests is applied, a comprehensive note should be made. As explained elsewhere, no document can be regarded as something which has the permanence of an inscription on stone, for every time a document is exposed to light and handled, some deterioration takes place, however carefully it may be dealt with. Apart from this normal fair wear and tear, it may very well happen that an important document may later fall into the hands of an inexperienced or unskilful document examiner who will cause ink writings or typescript to fade through overlong exposures to powerful light sources, or even deface it to a considerable extent by daubing with chemicals in abortive attempts to conduct a chemical analysis of the ink.

If the notes made during the examination are properly kept, they will constitute a comprehensive description of the document as first received. Indeed the notes may be the only means whereby track may be kept of any changes which may subsequently take place.

One example which comes to mind concerns a document which, when first received and examined at the author's laboratory, exhibited well-defined impressions in the paper which indicated that the signature it bore was a traced forgery. When the same document was produced at the trial at Assizes a few months later, not a trace of the impressions could be detected. Impressions do tend naturally to disappear with the passage of time, but not so completely in such a short period. Inquiries established that the document had been left for examination with a "handwriting expert" called for the defence and that it was during this period that the impressions disappeared. Fortunately a very full record of the original appearance of the document was available together with a photograph of some of the impressions which had so completely disappeared by the time of the trial. Note: It is possible to remove impressions from paper by pressing with a hot iron!

The Appearance of the Document

Folds and Creases

Most documents are produced in a folded condition. When a folded document is received it should be examined back and front for any impressions it may bear before being unfolded. The impressions which are especially sought are those caused by the cancelling stamp if the document has passed through the post. Sometimes, when a document has been re-addressed, two cancellation marks may be visible. If both are on the same side of the folded document, well and good, but if one is on one side and the other on the other, it will indicate that the contents of the envelope had been removed from the envelope and replaced in a different way before the envelope was put back into the post.

It is important to note which portions of a folded document are on the outside. When preparing false documents which are supposed to have had a chequered career, few forgers are so stupid as to leave them in their pristine freshness. The paper is made to appear old and worn by being rubbed on the floor or sometimes by being soaked in tea or coffee. A mistake is made if this maltreatment is effected before the document is folded, for a genuine document, which is really old, will be found to have its outer surfaces, with the possible exception of the edges, soiled, stained and discoloured to a much greater extent than those on the inside which have received some measure of protection. This distinction is rarely found with documents which have been artificially aged. Here the inside surfaces are often indistinguishable by their condition from those on the outside.

If anything significant is observed as the result of this examination, a sketch should be made showing how the folds ran when the document was first opened by the examiner and care should be taken to keep the document in its original folds.

New folds should never be introduced. Folded documents are sometimes described as having been found in specified envelopes when an actual trial will show that it is impossible to insert the document into the envelope if the original folds are adhered to. Sometimes it is possible partially to insert the document so that a portion protrudes. If such is the case, there should be some trace of a line of demarkation, because that part of the document which protrudes should have been affected either by light or dust.

When the document has been unfolded, the hand lens should be used to scrutinise each fold, with particular attention being paid to the places where ink writing crosses a fold. In the laboratory examination of a document, a powerful stereoscopic microscope is invariably used for this purpose, but even a hand lens may reveal sufficient to put the examiner on his guard against accepting a false document as genuine.

The reason for this is that a well-creased fold is apt to break up the surface of the paper along the line of the fold. If an ink line is made across a fold, the ink often tends to spread into the impaired surface on each side of the line where it crosses the fold. If, on the other hand, the ink line had dried before the paper is folded, there can be no subsequent spreading. As this is so, any spreading will indicate that the ink line was made *after* the paper was folded; but it must not lightly be assumed that if there is no spreading, the ink line was necessarily made before the fold. (See Figure 3–1.) No hasty conclusions should be drawn if no ink can be seen to run into a fold, for experiments have been made which show that it is possible to draw a pen quickly across a well-defined fold without producing any apparent spreading of the ink line at the intersection. This point is dealt with in more detail in Chapter 7.

A scrutiny of the intersection of the ink line and any folds in the paper will often yield evidence which is in conflict with the story which has been related of the preparation of the document, especially so where wills are concerned. The signature of one or possibly both witnesses can sometimes be shown to have been written subsequent to the folding of the document and that of the testator before these particular folds were made. This may be a finding which is at complete variance with the detailed story of the attestation of the will.

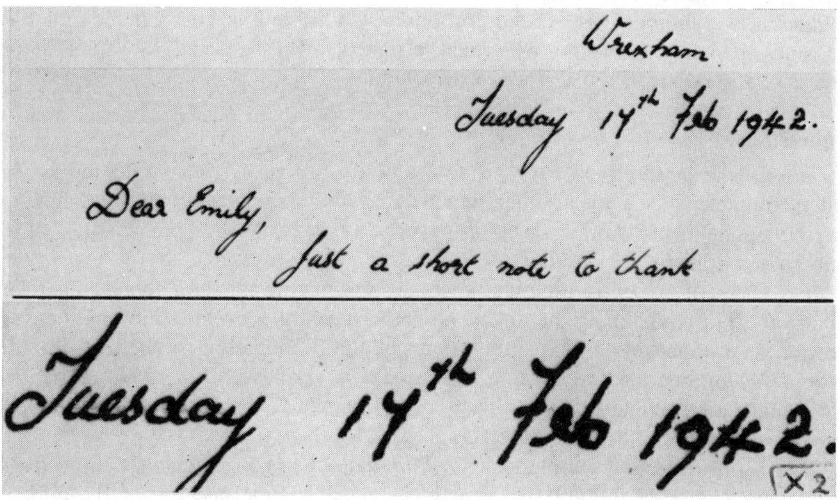

Fig. 3–1. There is no spreading of the ink of the heavily written "Tuesday" into the crease in the paper. On the other hand, there is well-defined spreading of the ink line of the date "17th Feb 1942." This indicates that "Tuesday" was written before, and "17th Feb 1942" after the folding of the paper.

Odour

Paper will readily absorb the volatile components which give rise to the odour characteristic of tobacco, cosmetics and certain fungi. As this is so, the odour associated with a document, especially one which has been stored in the same place for an appreciable time, may well provide a clue as to where it had been kept, or possibly more important, where it had *not* been, prior to its production. Whilst the evidential value of the odour may be small, this test should never be omitted.

Certain cosmetics have a well-defined scent, and as the great majority of anonymous letters are written by women and often kept in their hand-bags before posting, the possibility of obtaining a clue to the writer in this way should be borne in mind.

Again, if a long-lost will is alleged to have been found within the covers of an ancient Bible, a favourite place for the discovery of wills, it might be remembered that many old books possess a distinctive odour caused by the action of moulds and bacteria on the adhesives used in their bindings. Any document stored for some years in such a hiding-place should have a pronounced musty odour associated with it. If this does not prove to be the case, justifiable doubt may be felt as to whether the document had indeed rested for any length of time in the place where it is alleged to have been discovered.

If the odour associated with the document is elusive, it may be intensified by enclosing the document in a clean and consequently odourless metal box fitted with a tight lid which is then placed for a short time near a fire or over a radiator. After the box and its contents have warmed up, the lid is removed and the air inside the box immediately tested for odour. This test is best carried out by a non-smoker or by someone who has refrained from smoking for some hours, otherwise any odour of tobacco may escape notice.

Impressions

The tensile strength of paper is low and its recovery from stretching is slow and incomplete. This means that paper takes impressions very well and much of the immediate history of a sheet of paper may be gleaned from a study of the impressions it bears.

If a sheet of paper is illuminated in the ordinary way, with the incident light falling at approximately right angles to its surface, the irregularities in the sheet are not very noticeable. It is only when oblique illumination, or better still, what is termed illumination "at grazing incidence," is employed that those impressions which make a fair angle with the direction of illumination are thrown into prominence as dark shadows on a bright surface.

It is by no means a simple task to illuminate at grazing incidence more than a few square inches of the surface of a document at a time because of the difficulty of making a sheet of paper lie perfectly flat. This is why it is generally impossible to photograph the whole of any document of reasonable size so as to reproduce in permanent form all those details which can easily be seen by the exploration of the surface of the document a square inch or so at a time.

To obtain illumination at grazing incidence, the source of light, which is preferably in the form of a flat beam, should be adjusted so that the light travels nearly, but not quite, parallel with the surface of the document. The effect then obtained resembles that at dusk, when the beams of the setting sun graze the surface of the earth in the neighbourhood of the observer. The shadows thrown by the smallest obstacles are so apparent that they reveal details which otherwise would have gone unnoticed in any other form of lighting.

It must be emphasised that the shadow formations observed when a document is illuminated at grazing incidence are by no means replicas of the impressions which give rise to them. It must be borne in mind that a shadow is produced only when the direction of the light subtends an angle with the depression or elevation which is on the surface being examined. Any depression or elevation which lies parallel with the direction of light will throw little, if any, obvious shadow.

This point is very well illustrated if a depression in the surface of a sheet of paper which is made up of four similar grooves to form a hollow square is illuminated at grazing incidence.

See Figure 3–2 in which the left-hand diagram A represents the appearance the hollow square would present when illuminated from above. All four grooves would be equally ill-defined and, if shallow, may escape notice. When the light is moved so that it passes over the surface of the paper at grazing incidence from right to left, the shadow pattern produced will throw two of the four grooves into prominence as shown in the centre diagram B. These will be the grooves which are at right angles to the direction of the incident light. It will be noted that these two similar vertical grooves are not represented by equal shadow patterns because of the interference of the two horizontal grooves which themselves are not outlined by the light.

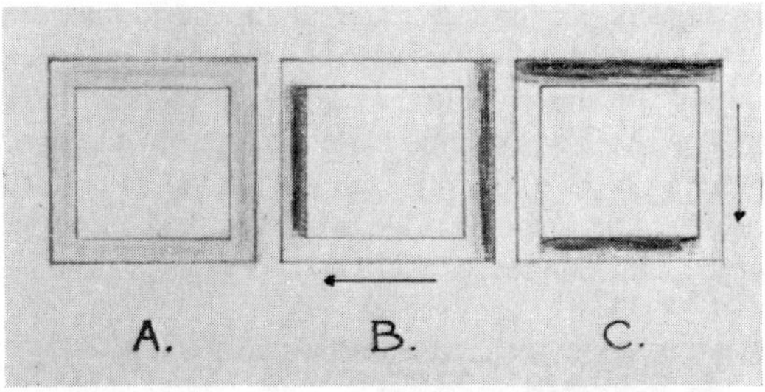

Fig. 3–2. This diagram illustrates the shadow pattern arising from the oblique illumination of a depression which takes the form of a hollow square. The arrows indicate the direction of the light. It is only when the centre and right-hand shadow patterns are combined in the brain that any resemblance to a hollow square is apparent.

When the light is moved around, the shadow pattern will change to that shown in the right-hand diagram C. This shadow pattern is similar to the centre diagram except that its orientation has been changed.

This simple illustration shows why it is necessary to have a moving light before any shadow pattern can be interpreted. When a moving light is employed, the brain is able to memorise the various patterns as they appear and so effect a synthesis, something which cannot be accomplished anything like so well from a photograph, or even from a series of photographs taken with the incident light at different angles.

To examine a document for the presence of significant impressions, the operator should seat himself in a comfortable chair before a fairly high table in a room which is dimly lit rather than entirely dark. The document is placed on a stiff sheet of cardboard and its surface is explored a little at a time, by lowering on to it an electric light bulb of low wattage contained in an opaque dome-shaped shade with a smooth edge. The shade is adjusted until its edge nearly touches the surface of the paper. A lamp of low wattage is essential because any glare reflected from the surface of the paper will entirely defeat the experiment.

If the shade is held in this position, either in the hand, or more conveniently in a fitting of the "Anglepoise" type, a small area of the document just outside the edge of the opaque shade will be intensely illuminated with light at the most favourable angle for the discovery of impressions.

To read any impressions which might be discovered, the light should be moved so that the impression being studied is lit from a diversity of angles. The light should be kept moving rather than placed in a number of set positions.

The warning should be given that the interpretation of shadow patterns is not nearly as easy as might appear to those whose acquaintance with the method is theoretical rather than practical. Although patience and perseverance are essential, such work should never be carried on for long periods without a rest. As the eyes and brain tire, the shadow patterns seem to form a muddled mass capable of the most diverse interpretations.

Laborious though this test may be, it should never be neglected, for relatively few fraudulent or anonymous documents are totally devoid of impressions which are worth deciphering. Special attention should be paid to the neighbourhood of the ink line of every important signature even when it is known to be genuine, for it may prove to have been used as the model for a traced forgery. A signature which has been treated in this way generally retains unmistakable evidence of the passage of the tracing point along its outline. (See Figure 3–3.)

This will take the form of a shallow groove which follows very closely the outline of the signature. The groove is often far more apparent when the back of the sheet is examined, for what from the front may appear to be but a shallow groove, more or less obscured by the ink of the signature, will show up on the back as an obvious ridge which stands out boldly when the surface is illuminated at grazing incidence.

Fig. 3–3. This shows a genuine signature which has been used as the basis of a traced forgery. The indentation, caused when the signature was traced over with a stylus, is rendered more apparent by the oblique lighting of the document.

If the signature has been written with a ball-point pen, care should be taken not to jump to hasty conclusions. When these instruments are not working in a satisfactory fashion, there is a temptation to apply excess pressure in the effort to make a continuous line. This extreme pressure will produce a groove along the line of the signature which is sometimes accompanied by an extra fragmentary line where surplus ink is being wiped off the housing of the ball. The groove may well be mistaken for the impression of a tracing point.

Once the signature has been dealt with, the examination for impressions should be extended to the remainder of the surface of the document. Surprising though it may seem, many a will and agreement has been found to bear impressions made when the forger was practising the forgery on scraps of paper placed on the document itself. The importance of such a discovery may be considerable, for it may prove difficult for a forger to provide any convincing last-minute explanation for their presence.

Cancellation Stamps

The pressure employed in the application of Post Office cancellation marks, especially when a hand stamp is used, sometimes results in corresponding impressions appearing on the contents of the envelopes and sometimes on the back of the envelope itself.

If any importance attaches to the date, it is as well to check with any impressions found on the contents of the envelope or on the back of the envelope, because the author has had experience of an investigation wherein a number of very carefully altered date stamps were exposed as forgeries by their not agreeing with impressions which had been overlooked by the forger; these unnoticed impressions enabled the true date of posting to be determined.

It may happen, on the other hand, that the absence of any impression will constitute valuable evidence of attempted fraud. A swindle constantly being tried on bookmakers who cater for the postal backer is to pass an empty envelope through the post to the home of the backer, whose address is lightly pencilled on the envelope or written on a slip of paper wrapped around it, and then to insert a winning bet in the already post-marked envelope before delivering it by hand to the bookmaker's premises.

Most bookmakers in a fair way of business, and incidentally all football-pool proprietors, take precautions with respect to the receipt of their mail which can be relied upon to defeat this device, but it is constantly being tried on the small bookmakers, and occasionally succeeds until a phenomenal run of luck excites suspicion.

In the majority of these cases the envelope is passed through the post empty, and occasionally an impression of the cancellation mark may be seen on the inside surface of the back of the envelope. If the sheet of paper bearing the winning bet has been preserved in its original folds, it may be shown that it must have intercepted the impression of the date stamp had it been inside the envelope when the stamp was cancelled. In practically every case, it will be found that the sheet of paper bearing the bet is innocent of any such impression, a finding which is sufficient to prove that it must have been inserted *after* the envelope had passed through the post.

Writing Paper

Impressions are often found on writing paper. These are to be expected if the paper forms part of a writing pad but they may also be present on sheets which are not sold in pads. In this latter case they occur because, although loose, the sheets concerned were superimposed when the writing was being done. Impressions on writing paper are more common now than hitherto, which is perhaps the only good thing that the introduction of the ball-point pen has done for the document examiner. With these writing implements, considerable pressure is usually applied so that bold impressions are made on any sheets which may be below that being written on.

The only difficulty in the investigation, and it is one which is very real, is that impressions from several sheets of writing may be found superimposed, especially when the sheet was derived from a writing pad. This is because the impressions from writing with a ball-point pen often travel far into the pad.

Fig. 3–4. Impressions found on a writing pad at the home of a suspect after a " smash and grab " raid. They read—

" Dear A
Did a job last night for C
which came unstuck If things
go haywire be a sport & collect my
gear & look after it for me will you?
the van got damaged a bit but this "

etc.

A ballpoint pen was used for writing the original letter which was never recovered. The impressions were so distinct that they enabled the authorship of the handwriting to be proved—evidence which was of material assistance in procuring a conviction.

Where anonymous letters are concerned, the most useful impressions are those which give the address of the writer at the top right-hand corner of the sheet. These are discovered far more frequently than might be supposed, but in all cases the examiner should be on the alert for the " planted " impression. This warning is given in the light of the author's experience, for during the routine examination of one of a group of anonymous letters, excellent impressions of an address were found. Not only were these impressions both clear-cut and complete but they occurred where there was no handwriting which might cause their presence to pass unnoticed or cause difficulty in their decipherment.

Suspicion was aroused when no other impressions whatsoever could be found and added weight was given to the theory that they had been " planted " when it became evident that the writer of the anonymous material used far too gentle a pen-pressure to occasion such deep and well-defined impressions in the natural way of writing.

As was anticipated, inquiries at the address showed that none of the occupants had had anything to do with the offence; the additions were deliberately made to mislead the investigation and to cause annoyance to innocent parties.

Typescript

To preserve the surface of the rubber roller, it is customary to use a backing sheet when typing; professional typists generally use a special sheet for this purpose but more often than not, another sheet of typing paper is substituted for a proper backing sheet. Unless the typist has a very light touch or the paper is both thick and strong, impressions of much of the typescript will appear on the backing sheet. These impressions are by no means obvious when the backing sheet itself is typed on and so escape notice unless carefully looked for.

In view of this, every suspect typewritten document should be examined for the presence of these impressions; it is surprising how many typewritten documents examined at the author's laboratory have yielded valuable evidence of their place of origin in this way. In this connection, the modern practice of typing names under illegible signatures has much to recommend it. See Chapter 8 for a further discussion on impressions caused by typescript.

You are the talk of the neighbourhood and if you dont
soon get out of the district your house will be burned
down. Your family is rotten like you and your husband
is a disgrace to decent neighbours.

Fig. 3–5. An example of an anonymous typewritten letter bearing impressions of matter typed when the paper was used as a backing sheet.

Police officers attending the lectures on the examination of documents given by the author at the Home Office Detective Training Courses are advised, when searching premises, to remove for laboratory examination any apparently blank sheets of paper they may find if typewriters are in use as well as any pads of writing paper. The pad illustrated in Figure 3–4 was discovered in such a search. On many an occasion the value of this advice has been proved by the evidence discovered following the examination of sheets of apparently blank paper with light at grazing incidence.

The moving light is by far the most efficient as well as the safest method for discovery and interpretation of impressions. Many a valuable document has been defaced and ruined for further investigation by the stupid practice of dusting the surface with a black powder such as graphite or the graphite mixture used for developing finger prints. This dusting is carried out in the pious hope that the powder will obligingly collect in the depressions, which will then be rendered decipherable by direct lighting. What actually happens is that the relatively rough surface of the paper retains the powder so securely that the whole surface becomes black and stays so in spite of the efforts made to persuade the powder to migrate to any impressions in the surface.

If an eraser is used in an attempt to remove the graphite, the final state of the document is made worse as the black powder is rubbed into the surface of the paper to form a series of streaks which defy all attempts at removal.

Examination by Transmitted Light

This may be accomplished by holding the document before a strong light. The light which passes through the paper gives some indication of its colour and also reveals those places where the translucency of the sheet has been changed through tampering, such as scraping, rubbing or oiling.

Where a document comprises more than a single sheet of paper, all the sheets should be examined in this way, for a change in tint may be the first indication that the substitution of one or more sheets has taken place.

It is often a simple matter to find a substitute sheet which apparently matches the remainder of the document, but it is infinitely more difficult to find a substitute sheet which will also appear the same by transmitted light, because here thickness and fibre make-up have also to be matched.

Wiremarks and Watermarks

The variations in transparency known as " wiremarks " and " watermarks " are well known as identifying features of a sheet of paper. The term " wiremark " is given to the fine markings which are often seen to cover the surface of the paper

Fig. 3–6. Transmitted light photograph of (left) laid paper, and (right) wove paper. The " K " portion of the watermark is a code letter, indicating the year of manufacture of the paper.

when examined by transmitted light; if these wiremarks are parallel, the paper is referred to as " laid " paper, whereas if they take the form of a mesh or are not discernible, the paper is known as " wove " paper.

Both wire and watermarks are introduced into the paper at a very early stage in its manufacture. The paper pulp flows on to a travelling endless wire belt which, while the water is draining away through its meshes, retains and felts the cellulose fibres through its vibratory motion. The moist web of fibres then passes under the " dandy roll " which is covered with the wire which produces the wiremarks. It is the dandy roll which also carries raised letters or designs which press into the moist web to compress and thin out the fibres as they pass beneath it to form the watermark.

Wiremarks become of importance when a document has become torn and has then apparently been repaired. To tear a document and then to substitute another piece is a simple alternative to making extensive erasures and alterations.

If on a torn document the genuine piece has been restored, the wiremarks will be seen to continue smoothly over the join. If a different piece of paper has been substituted, then there is a good chance of some discontinuity being apparent.

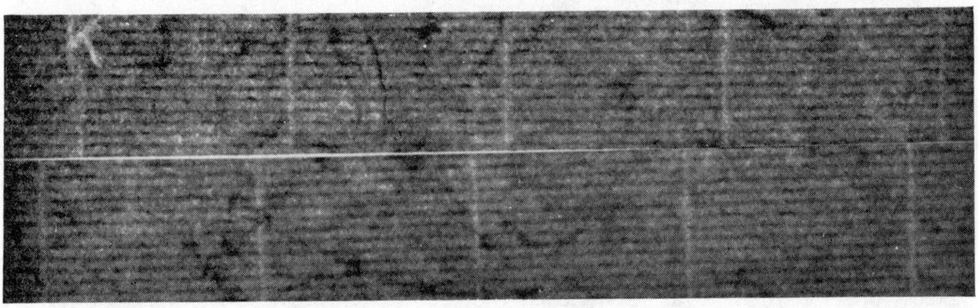

Fig. 3–7. The two pieces of paper, joined by cellulose tape, were not originally derived from the same sheet because the wire marks, brought into prominence by transmitted light, do not coincide.

The use of the watermark as an identifying feature of paper is dealt with in some detail in Chapter 7.

Erasures

Patches which exhibit a greater degree of transparency to transmitted light than the remainder of the document are either the sites of erasures or places where oil or grease has been applied to the paper. When an erasure has been effected, not only is the paper reduced in thickness by the removal of some of its substances, but the rubbing with a hard smooth object which is generally resorted to in an effort to smooth the roughened surface often produces an increased translucency

Fig. 3–8. This photograph, by transmitted light, shows that two erasures have been effected. In the photograph the contrasts have been increased by control of exposure and development to enhance the effect of increased translucency.

in the paper. The further examination of the suspected site of an erasure is dealt with in some detail below.

Very occasionally, patches which are more opaque to transmitted light may be seen. There are a number of reasons for the presence of an opaque patch. Sometimes such a place is the site of an erasure where a more elaborate treatment has been used to restore the damaged surface of the paper than the mere smoothing of the roughened surface by rubbing with a hard object. Such a more thorough repair is often necessary because, with certain papers, it is difficult to produce a satisfactory ink writing on the site of an erasure because of the spreading of the ink to produce what is known as a " feathered " ink line. A feathered ink line would immediately betray the fact that the paper had been tampered with.

Fig. 3–9. The feathered edges of the ink lines which make up the " 5 " and the vertical stroke of the " 2 " which are written on the site of an erasure, may be contrasted with the smooth edges of the other ink lines which are written where the paper surface is unabraded.

The feathering can be avoided by first painting the defective surface with a dilute aqueous solution of gum or starch. When this has dried, a rub with a hot domestic iron will seal the surface to such an extent that ink may be used on it once more. The excess opacity which invariably betrays the site of such repair is due to an excessive amount of reglazing material having been applied.

An opaque patch may have an innocent explanation, for the absorption by the paper of anything other than oily or greasy matter will cause increased opacity, but every opaque patch should be regarded with suspicion until an explanation for its presence is forthcoming.

The Surface

Whenever possible, the examination should be conducted in strong daylight; artificial light, however powerful, is much less satisfactory. This is because the faint yellow tinge, which is often all that betrays the presence of a carefully effected chemical erasure, can only be seen in contrast with the remainder of the paper in a light which is rich in the shorter wavelengths—the extreme blue and violet of the spectrum. The tungsten filament lamp has such a preponderance of yellow and red light that the faint yellow tinge of a chemical erasure may pass unnoticed if this illuminant is relied on. A good " daylight " fluorescent lamp is superior to the metal filament lamp but even this is inferior to daylight.

Both sides of the paper should be examined, and when making a note of the colour—few papers are dead white—the sheet should be twisted so that a portion of the back and the front can be examined at the same time. Some papers are tinted differently on back and front and a fair proportion have a different finish on the two surfaces. Discolorations should be noted as they may yield evidence as to the origin of the document, even if they are not the site of chemical erasures, for anonymous letters have been traced to their source through stains on the paper.

The surface of the paper should be examined with care as it is practically impossible to " work " on a document without affecting the tint or the sheen of the surface. If a document is wetted, the surface will present a curious wavy appearance when it dries; if there is abrasion of any sort, there will follow a disturbance of the surface sheen which sometimes is sufficient to modify the tint of the paper. The appearance of the surface waviness on the flap of an envelope may be the only indication that the envelope has been steamed to render the adhesive ineffective prior to opening.

Blots and Smears

A blot may occur on a document through carelessness, but the experienced document examiner regards every blot on a suspect document with suspicion. He tends to regard a blot as a device for obscuring something a forger wishes to hide rather than a manifestation of the careless use of a pen. Whilst smears and smudges usually result from the smearing of the writing on the document itself, occasionally they may arise from contact with other writings. In these cases, they may prove of great evidential value especially when they occur in note books or books of counterfoils which might have had pages removed or substituted.

Any dense blots, especially in cases where the ink bottle appears to have been emptied on to the document and no attempt made to remove any of the ink by blotting, should be regarded as almost certain evidence of an attempt to cover up the site of an erasure. This suspicion may be regarded as confirmed should a close examination of the surface of the paper in the centre of the blot reveal a roughening which is absent elsewhere. In an attempt to effect a complete elimination of an unwanted entry on a document, it is not unknown for the forger to erase the entry by vigorous rubbing and then to allow a fair quantity of ink to dry naturally over the surface of the erasure. The treatment of such a dense blot in an endeavour to decipher what has been erased should be conducted only in a document laboratory.

Whatever process has been used for making a traced forgery—see Chapter 11 for details—the forger runs the risk of leaving smears on the document wherever it has been in contact with the carbon paper or graphite-covered sheet used for making the guide line. As this is the case, any smudges on a document, especially if they are coloured, should arouse suspicion that a traced forgery might be present as well.

When anonymous letters are being examined, the edges of flaps of envelopes and stamps, or indeed any part of the document carrying an adhesive, should be examined for traces of lipstick. If these are discovered, they will suggest that a woman is concerned. Some idea of her colouring, whether dark or fair, may be obtained from the colour of the lipstick but little more is likely to be learned even from a chemical analysis of the stain.

If a smear resulting from contact with another document bearing wet ink is noticed, a mirror should be used for the examination. This will correctly re-orientate the smeared impression and greatly assist its interpretation. If a number of small indecipherable smears are seen, a tracing of their outline and position should be made by placing a sheet of tracing paper on the document and marking the outlines with a soft pencil *gently* applied to the tracing paper so that *no impression passes through on to the document.* The alternative device of placing the document over a sheet of carbon paper and outlining the smears with sufficient pressure to transfer a clear impression on to a sheet of paper beneath the carbon paper should never be employed, because the document would thereby be defaced by the addition of a set of new impressions.

The tracing paper can be used as a template to be applied over any other pages of writing which may be encountered and which show signs of having been smudged. If there is complete agreement, there can be little doubt that the sheet giving rise to the original smudges has been found. When applying the tracing paper as a template, care should be taken to apply it so that it is correctly orientated. The outlines on the tracing paper form a mirror-image of the original writing so the tracing paper should be turned over before it is applied. If any difficulty is experienced in understanding how the tracing paper has to be applied, an experiment should be performed with some writing which is deliberately smudged and a tracing made of the transferred marks. Trial and error will soon indicate how the tracing paper should be orientated before being applied to the original writing.

Erased Typescript

Whilst it is possible to erase typescript with an abrasive-loaded rubber, inconspicuous smears are often left on the paper. If these are noticed, a search should be made for the indentations associated with punctuation marks for these cannot be erased without removing a considerable amount of the paper as well. The presence of these indentations not only constitutes good evidence that typescript has been erased, but offers a means whereby it may be possible to link a carbon copy with the erased material. This method is described in some detail in Chapter 8.

Dimensions

It may sometimes prove advantageous for a note to be made of the dimensions and shape of a document which is the subject of examination. If the edges of the document are straight but the sheet does not appear to be rectangular, the four edges and a diagonal should be measured to form a complete record of its outline.

It is a common practice to commit forgery by the careful trimming of what is otherwise a genuine document. It is far simpler and much surer to trim off unwanted entries rather than to attempt to erase them and to risk having the erasure detected and possibly restored. That is why any document which consists of a sheet or sheets of paper of unconventional size should be regarded with suspicion until a satisfactory explanation for the unusual shape is forthcoming. Trimming is often resorted to in an attempt to alter the apparent date of a document. Dates usually appear near one of the edges, so that they can often be trimmed off without removing an undue amount of the paper. If a new date is then inserted, the most careful search will fail to reveal either alteration or erasure.

On occasion, evidence that the document has been trimmed may be obtained by the microscopical examination of the edges for this may reveal that one edge is more freshly cut than the others and possibly that a different type of cutting tool was used.[1]

It is not unheard of for a portion of a document to be trimmed off after it has left the possession of the examiner and in this case, in the absence of a photograph, a note of the original dimensions may prove to be the only conclusive evidence of what has taken place.

If the edge of a suspect document is seen to be irregular, an accurate record of its outline should be preserved, as it may prove possible to match this irregular edge with that of another document which subsequently comes to hand. Evidence such as this has on occasion proved to be of value when anonymous letters are being investigated, for these are often written on scraps of paper torn from sheets which later become available to the investigators.

The record of an irregular edge should never be made by carelessly tracing round it with a pencil, a procedure which is calculated to destroy the finer details of the outline. If possible, an accurate photograph should be prepared; but this can be replaced or even supplemented with a replica of the edge made, by placing the document on a sheet of bromide paper with a heavy sheet of glass placed on top so as to force the document into intimate contact with the sensitive surface. This is carried out in a dark room so that the bromide paper can be given a controlled exposure to light. If the exposure has been sufficient, a permanent record of the outline in silhouette is obtained after processing the bromide paper. Unfortunately, even if great care is taken not to stretch the paper whilst it is being processed, the final print will not be a perfect replica of the original outline. The problem of dimensional stability of photographs is considered in Chapter 6.

When small cardboard documents such as railway tickets are the subject of examination, it may be advisable to make a determination of the thickness of the card so that it can be compared with that of an admittedly genuine specimen. This may seem a counsel of perfection, but on one occasion, when the author received a railway ticket for examination for a suspected altered date, no erasure or tampering with the clear-cut date could be seen. The ticket was, however, found to be slightly thicker than a genuine specimen and this gave a clue to what had happened. The original ticket bearing an unwanted date had been split through the cardboard and the back of a much cheaper ticket with the required date had been pasted on to the front half of the original ticket. As most cardboard is composite, such a fraud may very well escape detection if the join is carefully made, but unless the forger is very careful, the final composite ticket is unlikely to be of the same thickness as the original, and it is this which should lead to the detection of the fraud.

Perforations

Paper rarely tears evenly along the perforations. The slight irregularities in tearing may prove of value should it be required to prove that a sheet was torn from a particular counterfoil.

Whilst many books of receipts are numbered this is not always the case, and

[1] Chavigny, P., "Identification of Scissors by Traces left on Paper," *Journal of Criminal Law and Criminology*, 36, 1936. Purtell, D. J., "The Identification of Paper-cutting Knives and Paper Cutters," *Journal of Criminal Law and Criminology*, Vol. 44, July–August, 1953.

even when numbered books are concerned it will often be found that the number is missing from the cheque or receipt being examined. In these circumstances the matching of the perforations may often be all that can be done to establish correspondence.

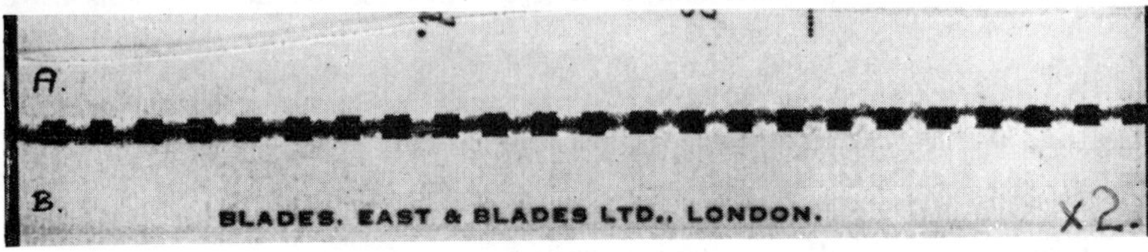

Fig. 3–10. An enlarged photograph (X2) provides the best evidence of matching through the uneven tearing of perforations.

Perforations, wherever they occur, should always be scrutinised for the presence of traces of adhesives. More than one swindle has been carried out by having a substitute form held tightly against a counterfoil so that an official stamp which is essential to the fraudulent scheme can be obtained at the hand of an unsuspecting person. The substitute form is usually held in place by the application of a thin line of adhesive along the perforations and it is the traces of this adhesive which can be used to expose the *modus operandi* of the fraud.

Some variation of this trick is usually employed when stolen crossed cheques are cashed by being put through an official banking account in such a manner as to deceive the auditors. The bank clerk sees the correct official stamp on the fraudulent paying-in slip, yet the auditors are presented with a counterfoil which bears little relation to what was presented to the bank clerk. This description of a method whereby crossed cheques were stolen and cashed, and yet paid into the account of the authority to which they had been made payable, has deliberately been left obscure as it is inadvisable to publish the working details of this ingenious swindle which was eventually uncovered by the finding of traces of adhesive on the counterfoil perforations. (See Figure 3–23.)

Fig. 3–11. The unsymmetrical perforations of the stamps with respect to the engraving may prove of significance when questions of possible contiguity are raised.

Adhesive Stamps

If a sheet of stamps is examined it will sometimes be discovered that, although the stamps themselves are printed symmetrically on the sheet, the perforations are by no means accurately spaced with respect to the printed outline of each stamp. With some rows, the perforations will be seen almost to impinge on the coloured portion to leave a more than ample margin on the stamps of the adjacent row. This lack of symmetry may sometimes be used to test whether two or more stamps were or were not contiguous on the sheet, a test which has, on occasion, proved important when the statement of a witness is being tested for accuracy.

Sometimes it is possible to show that stamps were once contiguous on the sheet by matching the perforations as already described. This rather difficult task may be simplified if the stamps are torn in such an irregular fashion that a recognisable fragment from one remains attached to another. The proof that stamps on receipts supposed to have emanated from different firms were at one time contiguous has proved of vital importance when the authenticity of insurance claims was tested.

Fig. 3–12. The perforations in the lower right-hand corner can be seen to be covered with adhesive. This indicates that the stamp has been re-affixed with fresh adhesive.

When stamps have been removed from one document and reaffixed to another by the use of extra adhesive, examination of the perforations with a good lens will almost invariably show the presence of excess adhesive on the upper surface of the perforated edges as it is almost impossible to refix a stamp without the fresh adhesive spreading to these areas.

Holes and Tears

It is wise, in the first instance, to regard all holes and torn places on a suspect document, even if there appears good reason for their presence, *e.g.,* a hole for fastening the sheets together, as deliberately made to cover up a forgery. Any perforation in an unusual place or one which is abnormally large has probably been made to eliminate unwanted data which, if allowed to remain, would betray the fraud.

Important documents are often drawn up on stamped paper. Most British Government stamped paper bears two figures inside a small circle to indicate the year the sheet was officially stamped. This circle is generally sited near the top left-hand corner of the sheet and it is remarkable how often in a suspect document the whole of this tiny circle will be found to have been neatly removed by the punch which made the hole for filing the document. Figure 3–13 shows how this occurred in connection with a document which bore a suspect signature of a man who died in 1932. Unfortunately for the forger the punch left sufficient of the final figure for it to be positively identified as "4." This evidence was overlooked and the document submitted for comparison of the signature thereon with others known to be by the alleged signatory. Whilst the signature on the document could have been shown to have been forged—see Figure 11–15, in Chapter 11—the evidence from the hole was sufficient in itself to brand the document as a forgery.

It is equally remarkable how often in documents, such as receipts, there occur tears which have the effect of removing the serial number. It is good policy to regard as fraudulent every receipt which has had its serial number torn off. It sometimes happens that great care has apparently been taken to reaffix the torn-off portion, bearing the printed number or other identifying data, with stamp edging or cellulose tape. Whilst such a repair might pass muster on casual

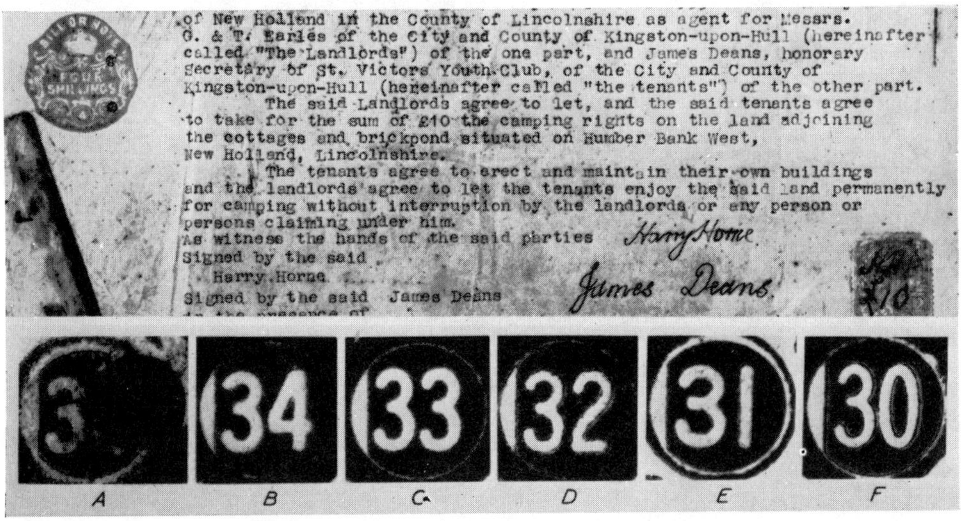

of New Holland in the County of Lincolnshire as agent for Messrs.
G. & T. Earles of the City and County of Kingston-upon-Hull (hereinafter called "The Landlords") of the one part, and James Deans, honorary Secretary of St. Victors Youth Club, of the City and County of Kingston-upon-Hull (hereinafter called "the tenants") of the other part.
The said Landlords agree to let, and the said tenants agree to take for the sum of £10 the camping rights on the land adjoining the cottages and brickpond situated on Humber Bank West, New Holland, Lincolnshire.
The tenants agree to erect and maintain their own buildings and the landlords agree to let the tenants enjoy the said land permanently for camping without interruption by the landlords or any person or persons claiming under him.
As witness the hands of the said parties Harry Horne
Signed by the said
Harry Horne
Signed by the said James Deans James Deans

Fig. 3–13. The upper photograph shows a portion of an agreement wherein two perforations occur in the official stamp at the top left-hand corner. The signatory died in 1933. In the lower photograph " A " is an enlarged photograph of one of the perforations showing two tiny remnants from the second of the two figures which represents the year of stamping. Whilst this figure could very well have been " 4 " as shown in " B " it could not have been " 3," " 2," " 1 " or " 0 " as shown in " C," " D," " E " and " F " because perforations made in these figures could not have yielded the two tiny remnants shown in " A." This proved quite conclusively that the signature was a forgery. An enlarged photograph of the signature is shown in Chapter 11, figure 11–15, wherein traces of fraudulent retouching can be seen.

examination, the sceptical will study the restored portion with the greatest care wondering the while whether the restored piece ever formed part of the original document. The wiremarks already referred to are sometimes of vital importance when such a question is raised, as by their aid it is sometimes possible to show that the restored fragment is foreign to the rest of the document.

Tears in documents are not always the result of genuine wear. It is quite a simple operation to get rid of an inconvenient date which cannot be trimmed off by making two parallel folds which narrowly contain the date and then tearing the document along the folds. The narrow strip bearing the unwanted date is removed and the two remaining portions carefully joined with a thin strip of adhesive. Such a join will often pass unnoticed. Some forgers join the two portions with stamp edging or cellulose tape whilst others just place the two portions back into the envelope. This latter is perhaps the safest course for few will take the trouble to place the parts together and then examine them for continuity of wiremarks or for other evidence which will show that a strip has been removed.

A document vital to a case is sometimes produced in a torn and tattered condition to give colour to the story of the vicissitudes through which it is supposed to have passed. If examination shows that nothing of real importance has been lost or rendered illegible and that the damage has been done only to those parts of the document which are not very significant, the document should be regarded with suspicion. If this happy state of affairs proves to be the case with not one but with a whole group of documents, then it can safely be concluded that they are forgeries because the odds against this happening are too great for it to be fortuitous. In the literature there are many examples of forgeries being exposed after suspicion has been aroused in this way. One of the best known is that quoted by A. C. Mitchell, in which a series of forged letters, alleged to have been written by Burns, Scott, Thackeray and other celebrities, contained worm holes; but in every instance the worms had been careful to avoid damaging the writing! The more reasonable explanation, that the forger had avoided the worm holes, was subsequently proved to be true.

Most forgers of ancient documents are well aware of the importance of using genuinely old paper, the most convenient source of which is the fly leaves of old books. As one book can yield but a limited amount of material, leaves from a number of books must be collected when fabricating a document of any size and imperfect sheets may have to be pressed into service. With this in mind, any reputedly ancient document made up of a number of different papers must be regarded with suspicion. At the same time, the examiner will be on his guard for the appearance of variable spacing of the writing or of cramped and unnatural phraseology on a damaged document, which often indicate that the writer has used material which was already in a damaged state and has taken care to avoid writing anything of importance on the damaged or fragile portions of the sheet.

Holes Made by Fastenings

The tiny perforations made by wire stapling machines may easily be overlooked; often they can only be seen by holding the document up to a strong light. These holes occur in pairs and should more than one pair be present because more than one staple was used, it may be possible, from the relative position of the holes, to discover which of a number of separate documents had at one time been stapled together.

This is the basis on which the author has investigated thefts of pay-packets. It is the custom in many organisations to staple the bank notes to the pay-packet envelope which bears the name or number of the employee. As more than a single staple is almost invariably used for this purpose, it has been found possible to link bank notes found in the possession of a suspect with the stolen pay-packet which, as it bears the name of the loser, is thrown away at the earliest opportunity but may be found on thorough search of the vicinity. If two wire staples have been used, then the pay-packet and the notes it once contained will all have groups of four holes which are perfectly matched. The odds against these coinciding with the holes in other pay-packets or in other notes are exceedingly great. In the illustration Figure 3–14, three wire staples were used in which case the degree of certainty is even greater.

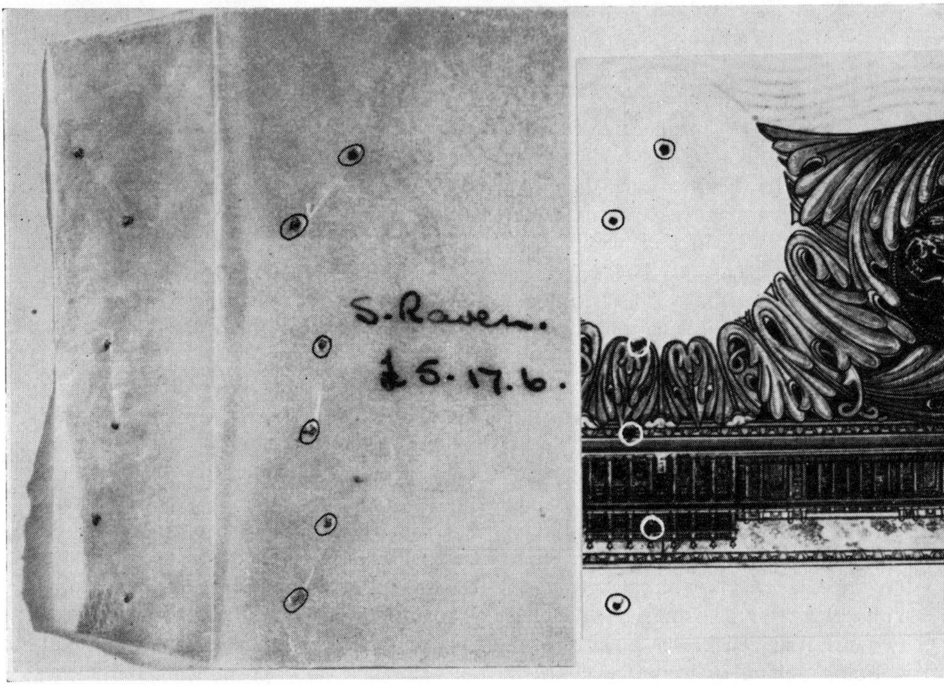

Fig. 3–14. Pin-holes in the Treasury Notes, indicated with circles, match the staple holes in the transparent envelope (one set indicated with circles). This proves that the Notes, shown on the right, had been fastened into the envelope, shown on the left.

The Content of the Document

When the physical examination of the document has been comp'eted, attention can be paid to what has been printed, written or typed thereon.

Secret Writing

If there is any reason to suspect the presence of secret writing, the attention should first be directed to the spacing of the visible handwriting or typescript present, generally referred to as the " overt text." It is comparatively common practice to space widely the overt text so as to accommodate the secret writing—the " covert text." If this is not done, there is the risk of the pen used for the secret writing crossing some of the overt text and producing a defect in the line which might lead to discovery of the secret writing. Apart from this, it is far simpler to decipher the covert text when it rests clear of any overwriting.

Many simple secret inks are revealed on warming the document. A simple test for such an ink may be made by holding the document over an inverted electric light bulb until that portion of the document immediately over the bulb becomes hot to the touch. If this reveals some of the secret writing, the document can be moved over the bulb until it has become sufficiently heated to reveal the whole of the covert text.

If this fails to reveal any secret writing, nothing further should be done to the document as the detection of secret writing is a matter for laboratory treatment; amateur efforts are almost certain to cause damage. The laboratory treatment of a document for the detection of secret writing is dealt with in some detail in Chapter 5.

Extraneous Markings

An examination should be made for the presence of ink and other marks which are not part of the writing. In some instances, these will be the ends of words from writing which had run off the edges of other sheets of paper on to the document being examined. When writing on slightly over-lapping sheets of paper, it is not always easy to distinguish the edge of the top sheet being written on, so that it is by no means unusual for the writing to stray from this to the sheet underneath. The significance of these overlappings may be great, for they may enable it to be demonstrated that two sheets of paper were once in very intimate contact.

Documents may also be linked by the partial transfer of writing from one, which has been carelessly handled whilst the ink is wet, on to another which has come into contact with it. This transferred writing is best examined with a mirror for it is hard to recognise traces of words and letters when they appear as mirror-images of their conventional forms.

If blots and smears are found on one of the pages of a notebook, the writing which gave rise to the smears should be sought on the opposite page. If this blotted and smeared writing cannot be found, a search should be made through the rest of the book on the off-chance that some rearrangement or removal of pages had been effected. The blots and smears may constitute the main evidence that pages have been removed from notebooks or from books of counterfoils.

Even the edges of sheets of paper and of envelopes should not be exempt from an examination for blots, smears and other markings such as impressions. This is especially important if the sheet once formed part of a writing pad. These writing pads, as well as tightly packed bundles of envelopes, sometimes become soiled or smeared on their edges, and these markings may enable a sheet of paper or an envelope to be linked with a particular pad or packet of envelopes and, on occasion, to show approximately where in the pad or packet it originally appeared.

When the markings on the edges of packets or pads are in the form of impressions, these would be represented as shallow notches in the sides of the individual sheets. These shallow notches might well escape the notice of anyone who did not appreciate their significance. (See Figure 3–15.)

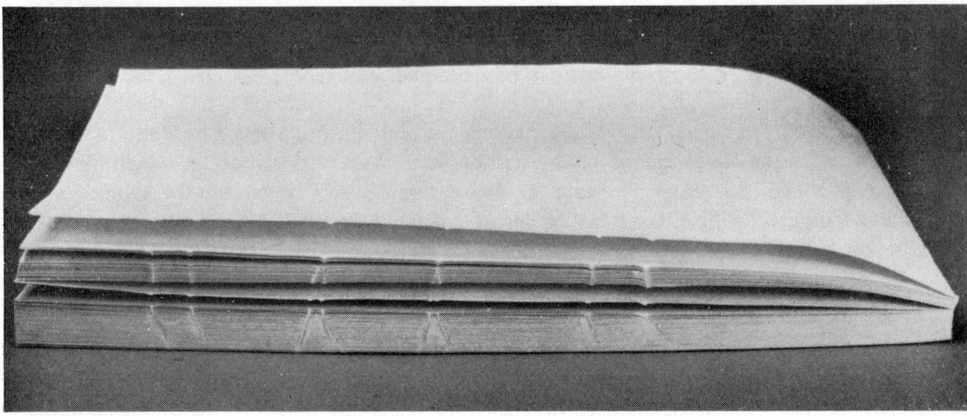

Fig. 3–15. The scratches on the side of the pad (specially emphasised, so as to show up in the photograph) are represented by nicks in the edges of the individual sheets. The position of the nicks would roughly indicate the position of the sheet in the pad.

Typescript

The first and simplest test is to examine the colour of the typescript, for a forger, wishing to make a fraudulent addition to a typewritten document, is likely to find some difficulty in matching some of the coloured ribbons now in use. Even with a similar ribbon, there may be obvious differences between the original and the added typescript because of the differential fading which has taken place.

If no colour changes are apparent, the typescript should be examined to discover whether the ribbon was in the same state throughout. If additions are made on the same machine after a fair amount of work has been done with the same ribbon, or better still if the ribbon has been changed, some difference will probably be apparent. Care should be taken not to jump to hasty conclusions for the ribbon feeds through the machine and it may differ in condition from place to place. If changes in depth of impression occur in the middle of a word or in a phrase, it may safely be concluded that the change has no significance. On the other hand, if a sudden change occurs at the beginning of a significant passage, and particularly if the ribbon is seen to revert to its original state at the end of the passage, the change may well be indicative of a fraudulent addition.

Any postscript should be examined with especial care, for this forms the most convenient site for a fraudulent addition. There is usually a fair amount of space between the postscript and the remainder of the typescript so that slight errors in alignment caused by the reinsertion of the sheet into the machine are rarely obvious on casual inspection.

Whilst the fact that a document has been reinserted in a machine for additions to be typed thereon will be betrayed by the failure of the added materials to appear in perfect alignment with that already on the sheet, it should be remembered that a practised typist may be so skilled in reinserting paper into the machine that a laboratory examination will be called for before it is certain that any significant degree of misalignment exists.

A rough test of alignment may be carried out with the metal scale previously referred to. Horizontal misalignment is tested for by placing the scale under each line in turn, but unless the typist has been very careless when reinserting the paper, this test is unlikely to reveal anything which is not already obvious. The test for vertical misalignment is far more likely to reveal errors. Few typists are aware that typescript is aligned quite as accurately in a vertical direction as it is horizontally so that they fail to take the necessary precautions to ensure good vertical alignment when reinserting the paper in the machine.

To carry out this test, the scale should be applied at right angles to the line of type so that it falls along the centres of a selected letter such as i, e, o, which happens to occur in the same vertical column in several of the lines. Any misalignment is immediately apparent.

The design of letters such as t, r, g, a and w, and of any figures in a suspected addition should be compared with that of the remainder of the typescript, for these are the characters in which the greatest variation is found among the different makes of machine. This simple test is all too rarely carried out, with the result that many important typewritten documents with obviously fraudulent additions are allowed to pass unchallenged.

If the regular cleaning of the typefaces is neglected, certain of the characters such as e, a, o, d, 6, 8, will become clogged with debris from the ribbon to reproduce faulty impressions with "filled" ovals. The presence or absence of such imperfect reproductions will sometimes constitute another simple test for the presence of additions.

Whenever typescript is being examined, a note should be kept of any obvious imperfections in the characters or of gross examples of misalignment, for it may happen that the typescript on documents subsequently examined will be found to exhibit similar imperfections.

Such observations prove important when doubtful claims for compensation following fires and burglaries are being investigated. Forged receipts are often produced to support inflated claims, and it may prove that receipts which presumably should have little or nothing in common can be shown to have been typed on the same machine.

Erased Typescript

On paper of good quality, it is possible to erase typescript so completely that all trace of the coloured ink is removed. If the paper has a matt surface, it may be difficult to prove that an erasure has been effected except for the fact that it is virtually impossible completely to erase the small pits in the paper left behind by punctuation marks.

Whenever it is suspected that typescript has been erased, these tiny depressions should be looked for. The manner in which these remnants of punctuation marks can be utilised to trace a carbon copy of the erased typescript is dealt with in some detail in Chapter 8.

Ink Lines

Whilst the complete examination of the ink line on a document is a laboratory matter, important observations may be made during the preliminary examination.

The colour of the ink lines should be studied in daylight, special attention being paid to any entries which appear either lighter or darker than the remainder. These differences, where not caused by blotting, may indicate either the use of different inks or that the writing was done at different times.

The earlier these observations of the colour of the ink lines are made the better, because when the differences are due to the writings having been made at different times, they tend to become less apparent with lapse of time and finally disappear altogether if similar ink has been used.

Examination of the ink line will probably show whether blotting-paper has been used and also whether it has been used at constant intervals throughout the writing, a fixed habit of some persons. Any departure from consistency in this respect should be noted, for when additions are fraudulently made, the ink is often allowed to dry without being blotted so that the line will tend to dry darker and so appear to be older than it really is. If blotting-paper has been used at regular intervals throughout the remainder of the writing, the fact that it has not been used on a suspect entry may prove to be a discovery of some evidential value.

If " feather-edging " of the ink line is noticed, the area where it occurs should be investigated for the presence of an erasure which has so disturbed the surface layer of the paper that the ink has tended to spread. See Figure 3–9 for an illustration of a feather-edged ink line.

Signatures

It often happens that the signature on a questioned document is all that is examined critically in spite of the valuable evidence which is so frequently available from other parts of the document. Even when the examination is restricted to the signature, it is often conducted in the most perfunctory manner, attention being paid only to the design of the letters. As the crudest traced forgery can be counted on to reproduce the letter design most faithfully, it is obvious that any examination of a suspect signature must be more searching than this.

The position of the signature on the document should first be considered. Many a fraudulent document is prepared from a sheet of paper which already bears a genuine signature. As it is rare to find a genuine signature conveniently placed at the bottom of an otherwise blank sheet, the forger has to make do with less favourable material. His efforts will often result in the production of a forged document which bears the signature in an unconventional place because it has had to be constructed around a pre-existing signature. As this is so, the most sceptical eye should be directed towards any document which exhibits several lines of cramped writing or typescript above a signature which has a considerable area of blank paper below it.

The great majority of signatures are written in a fairly straight line even though this line may slope upwards, or more rarely downwards, with respect to the remainder of the writing. Any signature which has been written so that it changes direction should be regarded with suspicion. (See Figure 3–16.)

The only reasonable explanation for such an abrupt change in direction is the sudden realisation by the writer that if the signature is continued along the same line on which it started it will be certain to run into some other writing on the document. This will indicate that the signature must have been written after the writing it has avoided.

In the case illustrated in Figure 3–16, the writing which was avoided was the signature of the first witness whereas the " story " was that the testator signed first.

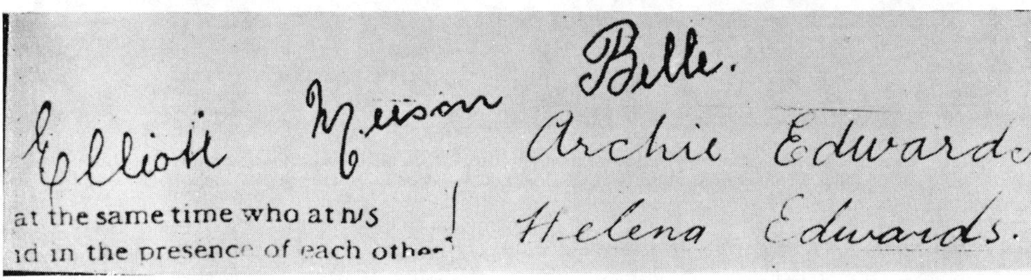

Fig. 3–16. The sudden change in the alignment of this signature in the middle of the word " Elliott " suggests that the signature of the " witness " " Archie Edwards " was already on the Will. This was inconsistent with the story that the Will was " witnessed " after it had been signed.

Any suspect signature should be examined with a lens for the presence of a guide line which might indicate that it is a tracing. Doubling of the line in whole or in part, whilst a very suspicious feature of any questioned signature, does not invariably indicate that the signature is a forgery. The matter is dealt with in some detail in Chapter 11 which should be consulted if a double line is found in any suspect signature.

It may be stated here that there are two innocent explanations for the presence of a double line in a suspect signature. The first is that a defective ball-point pen has been used, a matter which can easily be checked, and the second that the signature has been used as a model by a forger.

Sometimes a genuine signature is overwritten as part of a scheme of forgery. Many forgeries are prepared by adding to or altering a genuine document. If, when completed, the additions appear to be foreign to the remainder of the entries, the forger will ink-in all the genuine entries including the signature, in the hope that the difference in appearance will be submerged by the overwriting. (See Figures 3–17 and 11–23.)

Any partial overwriting or retouching of a signature should be regarded with extreme suspicion. The significance of the presence of retouching in a suspect signature is dealt with in some detail in the chapter on forged signatures.

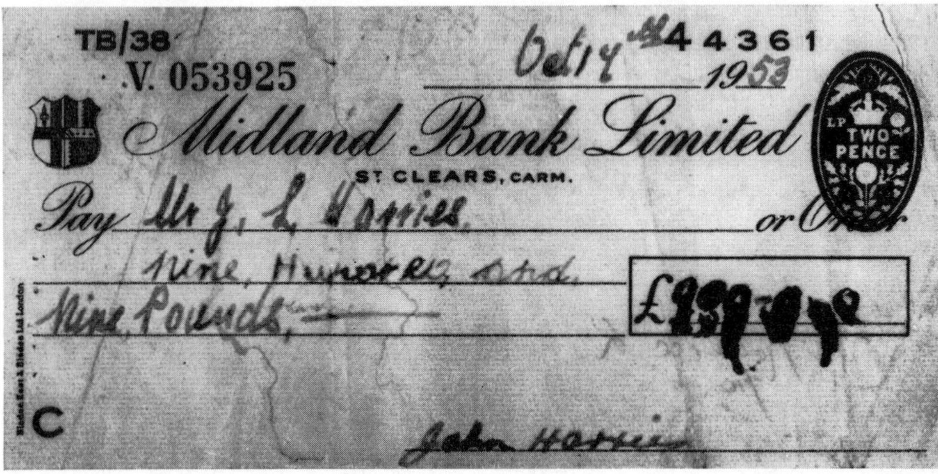

Fig. 3–17. This shows a cheque, originally drawn for £9, altered to £909, overwritten to hide the alterations, and finally wetted and smudged to hide the overwriting.

Signatures Obtained by Trickery

Genuine signatures may be acquired for forged documents by trickery. Many tricks have been devised to this end; the simplest is when the victim is induced to sign some simple document of little significance, such as a receipt for some trivial thing, in the course of which a copy of his signature is simultaneously made to appear on an underlying sheet which forms the basis of the forgery. Carbon paper is the usual medium of transference so that the trick demands a certain amount of stage-management on the part of the trickster who has to run the risk that the victim may become suspicious and discover the carbon paper.

The introduction of the N.C.R. paper, described in Chapter 2, will undoubtedly simplify the task of the trickster for this special paper bears no outward sign of its peculiar properties and no carbon paper or anything resembling carbon paper has to be used. If the victim can be induced to sign on one sheet of this special paper which has been placed in full view over another white sheet which also gives no hint of its unique properties, then a signature which might well be taken for one written with a ball-point pen or stylo will be formed on the lower sheet.

The initial blue colour of this forgery will soon turn to a bright green, in which condition the writing can neither be easily erased nor affected by most chemical reagents. The impression will be clear cut and not smudged or faded as though it had been made with ordinary carbon paper.

Any questioned signature made with carbon paper or which is a bright green should be regarded with suspicion, and the document on which it appears should be deemed fraudulent unless there is some satisfactory explanation for the failure to use ink.

Stamps

The examination of the perforated edges of stamps for evidence of refixing, etc., has already been touched on and the significance of the watermark and the printed design as evidence of dating is considered in some detail in Chapter 7.

Where a signature crosses the stamp the colour of the ink on the stamp should be compared with that which overlaps and appears on the paper. The edges of the stamp where the ink line crosses from the paper should also be examined with a lens. This is because a stamp with a genuine signature may be removed from a document to be refixed on a forgery. As few signatures are so small that the whole can be accommodated on a stamp, there is almost certain to be an overlapping portion which has to be supplied by the forger after the signature-bearing stamp has been stuck down. When this has to be done, it is difficult to make a convincing matching of the ink and the lining up of the two extremities of the signature on the stamp with the added portions on the paper is by no means as simple as it might sound. The ink is liable to collect at the edge of the stamp, and if the stamp has not been stuck down very securely right to its edge, some of the added ink line will run under the stamp. (See Figure 11–23 in Chapter 11.)

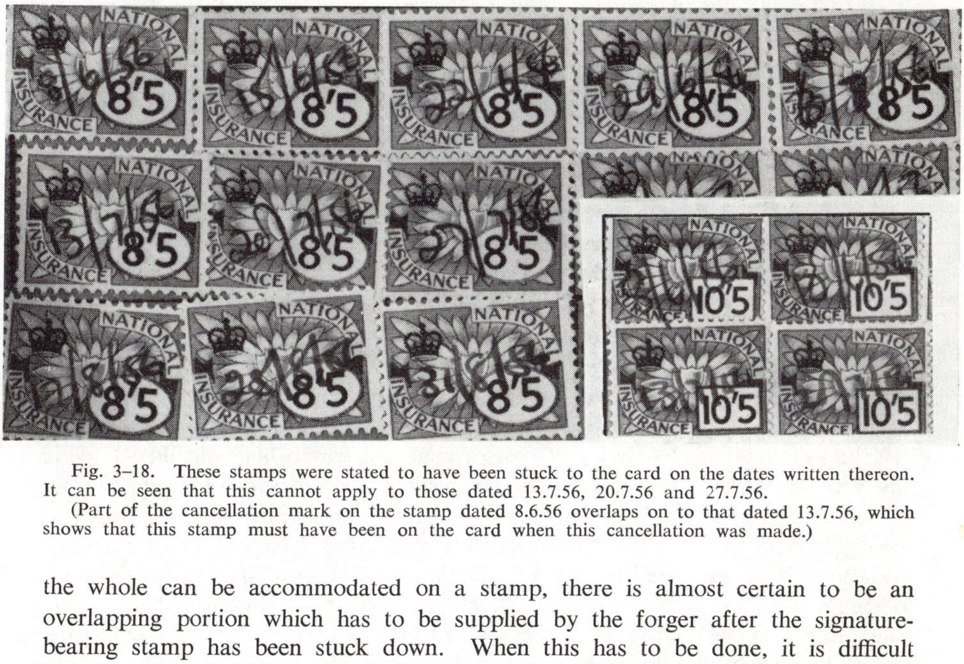

Fig. 3–18. These stamps were stated to have been stuck to the card on the dates written thereon. It can be seen that this cannot apply to those dated 13.7.56, 20.7.56 and 27.7.56.
(Part of the cancellation mark on the stamp dated 8.6.56 overlaps on to that dated 13.7.56, which shows that this stamp must have been on the card when this cancellation was made.)

Receipts

The preliminary examination of a receipt should be devoted to the detection of anachronisms such as the use of a ball-point pen or post-war stamps on receipts bearing dates prior to 1939. At the same time, any printed matter should be scrutinised for evidence that the receipt was printed at a time subsequent to the date it bears. Addresses and telephone numbers are the most obvious sources of this type of information but even subtle differences in the design of the block used for the printed heading may indicate a later date of printing.

Many forged receipts are based upon genuine receipts which have been " raised " either by the addition of whole items or, more frequently, by the addition of extra strokes to either the shillings or pounds column which will have the effect of greatly increasing the sum represented by the receipt.

The addition of single strokes for this purpose may appear to be a simple and detection-proof task, but it is surprising how often even the most carefully made additions stand out from the remainder of the entries once attention has been focused upon them.

If different inks have been used to make the additions, their detection is usually a matter for the laboratory, but the effect of examining the suspect receipt under different conditions of lighting should be tried. What might appear to be a perfect match by daylight is sometimes no match at all when the receipt is viewed by the light of a fluorescent lamp.

Any receipt which has been torn from a book should be examined for the presence of impressions which would indicate what was written on the receipt which preceded it in the book. This information has often allowed a receipt which has lost its printed number to be " placed " in a book of counterfoils. An impression of the date of the preceding receipt may be discovered and this may provide some indication of the probable maximum age of the receipt.

Ballot Papers

Ballot papers are sometimes the subject of examination when a fraudulent election of the officers of a society is suspected.

The examination of a series of crosses might appear to hold out little hope of any success, but on one occasion about twenty ballot papers were submitted to the author. Little could be learned from the design of the various crosses as the secretary of the society, who was eventually shown to have fraudulently marked the whole batch, had used a variety of markings. The examination was extended to the impressions borne by the ballot papers when it was discovered that every ballot paper had a number of impressions of crosses upon it. With a little care, it was found possible to arrange the ballot papers one above the other in the order in which they had been marked as a *group,* and not singly, which would have been the case if they had been sent out to the individual electors. The only person who could have marked the papers in a group in this fashion was the secretary responsible for issuing the papers.

This case is quoted to show how careful observation followed by common-sense interpretation of the evidence will thus sometimes throw an unexpected light on what, at first sight, appears to be a problem to which there is no apparent solution.

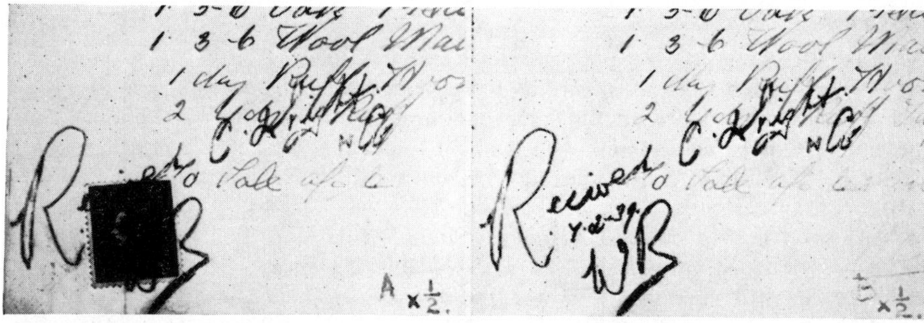

Fig. 3–19. " A " is a reduced photograph of a portion of a disputed receipted account. " B " shows the same account photographed from a filter to render the endorsement more legible. It will be seen that the " & Co " portion of the endorsement has been written below the name " Light." This hinted that this endorsement had been traced from a genuine receipt in which the endorsement came so near the edge that there was no room for writing the " & Co." as a continuation of the name of the firm. Search through the counterfoils in the possession of the firm brought to light a duplicate, part of which is shown in " A " of figure 3–20.

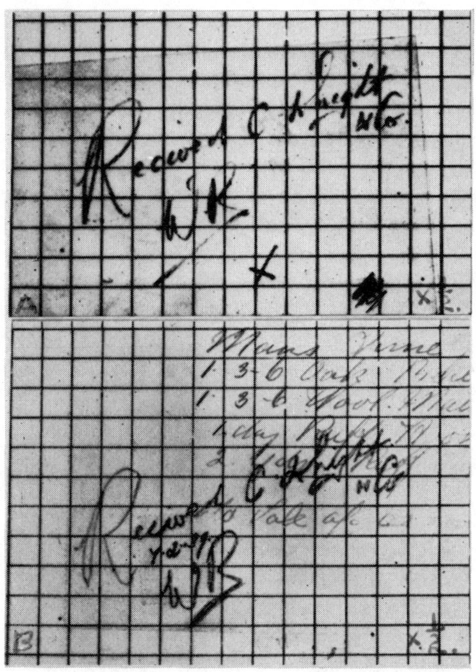

Fig. 3–20. The upper photograph " A " shows the counterfoil referred to in figure 3–19, photographed under a transparent scale of squares whilst " B " is a portion of the disputed receipt treated in the same way. Comparison of the two photographs will show that with the exception of the date the disputed endorsement on " B " is a perfect replica of that on the counterfoil " A." This proved that the disputed endorsement must have been traced from the account of which " A " is the counterfoil. Further investigation showed that the suspect had gained possession of this account and a conviction followed.

Envelopes

It is interesting to watch an envelope being opened. Many people pull out the obvious contents before discarding the envelope, which is never looked at again unless it has to be searched for some unnoticed enclosure which is mentioned in the letter. Others, and anyone who is about to examine the letter critically should be among this number, extract the contents and then thoroughly search the envelope to the bottom before putting it on one side.

An experienced document examiner opening an envelope will follow a definite procedure designed to preserve all the available evidence. Before opening the envelope, he will scrutinise it at the bottom and at the edges for traces of its having been opened and resealed. He will then note the exact place on the envelope where the post office cancellation mark, if any, appears.

Before taking the contents right out of the envelope, he will check whether impressions of the cancellation marks appear in the expected places on the contents or whether they are to be found in some other place, which will indicate that the envelope has been opened and the contents replaced in a different manner after the envelope has been postmarked. This test should always be applied to the contents of envelopes which have been redirected from their first place of receipt.

If the cancellation mark on the envelope has been applied by hand and is very heavy, and yet no trace of any impression can be found anywhere on the contents, the possibility that the envelope was empty when it was postmarked or that the original contents have been removed must be considered. Empty envelopes are often postmarked in an effort, usually unsuccessful, to obtain money from bookmakers who cater for the postal backer. Sometimes the date stamp impression may be found on the inside surface of the envelope if the envelope was empty or its contents small. In these cases, the impression should be compared with the postmark to see whether this has been altered after receipt.

Envelopes of thick opaque paper enclosing what appears to be bundles of uninteresting documents should be investigated with especial care during a search through papers. One of the best and simplest ways of concealing a document which must be readily available when required, is to fix it at the bottom of such an envelope with a spot of adhesive and then to fill the envelope with some harmless document. The casual searcher will pull the decoy document wholly or partially out of the envelope and never think of looking inside for something which will not fall out on shaking.

Another good reason for the thorough searching of an envelope is that it may contain debris which will afford some clue to the history of the envelope or its contents. This is especially important when anonymous letters are the subject of the examination.

Whenever there is suspicion that an envelope has been opened and surreptitiously resealed it is curious how often the investigation is confined to a close inspection of the flap of the envelope. No criminal who knows his business ever opens an envelope by tampering with the upper flap. If the envelope is of foolscap size, it is simplest to slit open the bottom fold and after the abstraction of the contents, to trim off the double strip at the bottom of the envelope and then cut the flap which remains to a suitable outline before sticking it down to complete the envelope once more. The total time for this operation is about two minutes and the chance of detection is almost nil, for few are likely to measure the envelope and discover that it is now a fraction of an inch shorter than formerly.

With the smaller envelope, where the bottom flap extends up to the centre of the back, this reconstruction of the bottom flap cannot be accomplished. The procedure with such an envelope is to shave off about a twentieth of an inch from the bottom. This will open the envelope without harming the contents, but the problem of resealing remains. This is accomplished by running a thin line of good quality adhesive along the inside of the cut edges. When these are pressed together and the adhesive has dried, little trace of the operation remains and the repair will escape notice unless a special search is made for it by someone who knows of the method. The crude operator will tear or steam open the flap of an envelope and hope to conceal traces of his handiwork by a liberal use of adhesive to reseal the flap. Steaming will result in the paper surface which has been so treated becoming wavy when dry instead of smooth and flat, and the use of extra adhesive can be detected by examining the edges of the flap where it will be seen as a shiny streak which is absent when an envelope is sealed by means of its original gum. If the date on the cancellation mark is in question, which is the case when envelopes which contain winning bets for surprisingly large sums of money are being examined, it should be remembered that there are two ways in which a suitable date stamping can fraudulently be obtained. The first is to send through the post an empty envelope addressed to the swindler bearing the address very lightly written in pencil, which can be subsequently erased. The second, which avoids the risk of the erased pencil writing being deciphered, is to fix a band of paper around the middle of the envelope with the address written thereon. The stamp, however, is stuck on to the envelope, which consequently receives the required date stamping. When the envelope is received, the band of paper bearing the address is removed

Fig. 3–21. *Forged First-Day Cover*
The simple circular form of date stamp is that used in a cancelling machine, so that if the three impressions were genuine they should have appeared in a straight line. The cover was date-stamped by hand, using a forged machine stamp.

and the address of the bookmaker written on the envelope. The only way in which such a band can be held in place is by a spot or two of adhesive or the use of adhesive tape. A knowledge of the ways in which this trick can be carried out will indicate what evidence is likely to be discovered.

Sometimes names and addresses which have been partially erased are found on envelopes which enclose anonymous letters. It is only in the rarest cases that these names and addresses have anything to do with the sender; generally the envelopes have been picked up and re-used to save expense, although on occasion the names and addresses have been deliberately written and then partially erased in an effort to implicate an innocent party.

Finally, the edges of the flap of an envelope should always be examined for traces of lipstick which would indicate that it was sealed by a woman who uses that type of lipstick. In the case of an anonymous letter, too much must not be hoped for from the discovery of lipstick on the envelope, because more than four-fifths of anonymous letters are sent by women, many of whom use lipstick.

Notebooks

Entries in notebooks or in diaries are sometimes produced to support inflated claims for expenses, loss of earnings, etc. Sometimes, not only are the entries made much later than the dates they bear, but whole pages may be removed to get rid of unwanted material which might expose the fraud. Removal of pages may immediately be suspected if the binding appears too loose and wide for the book.

With printed books, the pages are always in batches (called signatures) made by folding a large sheet. Thus an octavo sheet may be folded eight times to give a signature of sixteen pages, a 12mo sheet folded twelve times to give twenty-four pages, and so on. Many notebooks are made in the same way, so that by determining the number of sheets in a signature it is possible to determine whether any pages have been torn out of any notebook constructed in this way.

Occasionally single pages are torn out and the corresponding loose pages are left in the book. On occasion, new pages are substituted unobtrusively by careful work on the sewing threads which hold the book together. If pages from a similar book are available, it is not always easy to detect a carefully made substitution. If this is suspected, the safest procedure is to examine any impressions of writing and other markings which have passed through the pages flanking the page which is thought to have been substituted. A substituted page will be devoid of these impressions.

On occasion, blots and smears may be used to show that two pages which originally faced each other are no longer in that position, and even the edges of the notebook should be scrutinised as scratches which cause slight notches in the edges of sheets may serve to distinguish the genuine from the inserted pages.

Where diaries are concerned, the usual question is whether certain entries, which are relied on to prove some matter, are genuinely of the date alleged, or have been inserted at a more recent time. This is a question which cannot always be answered in a satisfactory fashion and which has been treated more fully in Chapter 7, but suffice it to say that questioned entries which are genuine rarely seem to stand out from other contemporary writings about which there is no dispute. If the questioned entries have all been written at the same time, instead of over a period as they purport to have been, they will often appear to have something in common with each other which excites sufficient suspicion to justify further examination by a document examiner. Longstanding pencil entries in a diary which is carried in the pocket tend to become smudged and to lose their precision of outline owing to the relative motion of the pages. This is an effect which is very difficult for the forger to imitate even if he realises that the new entries appear too fresh. (See Figure 7–4.)

Forged account books are often written up specially for an investigation. In these the entries are usually supposed to have been written up at short intervals over a long period of time. The forger rarely makes the mistake of using the same pen and ink throughout, but does something which is almost as revealing. The invariable habit is to get together about three different pens with different widths of nib and to use these with three different inks. By ringing the changes with the pens and inks, it is hoped that the entries will appear sufficiently diverse to pass muster. The trick usually fails because the entries are written in approximately equal groups before a change of pen or ink is made. When an account book written up in this manner is compared with a genuine specimen, the differences become obvious.

Unlike notebooks, many account books are ornamented with an embossed device or are given a class name by the stationer who markets them. On more than one occasion, account books have been proved to have been fraudulent because inquiry with the stationer has shown that the particular design of account book in question had not been marketed until some time after the date of the earlier entries. If the account books purport to go back before 1945, the presence of writing with a ball-point pen will be evidence of an anachronism which is sufficient to condemn them as forgeries.

Blotting-paper

Although the idea of examining blotting-paper by means of a mirror is very old, it should never be neglected because the eye can much more easily pick out significant fragments of letters and words when these are presented in their correct orientation.

Every piece of blotting-paper which comes to hand in any search through documents should be examined for the presence of markings which can never legitimately appear on blotting-paper. Probably the most important and revealing of these is a post office cancellation mark or date stamp. If these are found, it means that a swindle involving the Post Office Savings Bank, or a bookmaker, or possibly those who deal in "first day covers" is being perpetrated. (See Figure 3–21.)

Occasionally a piece of blotting-paper may be discovered which has been used for blotting whole columns of what appears to be the same signature. This will prove to be an important find, because, before attempting to write a simulated forgery, which, unlike a traced forgery, has no guiding line, a forger will often practise writing the signature on a piece of scrap paper until he feels that he has acquired sufficient facility to make a convincing specimen on the document itself.

On occasion, it is not what is *on* a piece of blotting-paper which may be significant. For example, if a document bears three or more lines of writing all of which have been blotted, and one of these lines is not represented on a piece of blotting-paper in spite of all the others being present in the correct spacing, this, in the absence of any other reasonable explanation, will suggest that the line which is missing from the blotting-paper was not written at the same time as the others.

When fraudulent account books are being hastily prepared, with different pens and inks so as to deceive the investigator, blotting-paper may be found with traces of entries supposedly written in different inks on different occasions, all correctly orientated in such a way that the only conclusion which can be drawn is that all the entries must have been blotted at the same time. If the same piece of blotting-paper is used on different occasions, it would be a very difficult matter, even if by some chance anyone wished to do so, to ensure that the traces on the blotting-paper are sited in the same relative position as the different entries in the account book. It is consequently impossible to conceive of this happening by pure chance.

Bibliography

"Artificially Aged Documents," *The Analyst,* 50, 1925.

Fig. 3–22. " A " is a portion of an address on an anonymous letter. " B " is a reversed photograph of a piece of blotting paper found in the house of a suspect. Owing to the thickening of the ink line on the blotting paper and the failure of some of the ends of strokes on the envelope to be reproduced, the writing on the blotting paper appears to be smaller than that on the envelope. When, however, a transparency of " B " was superimposed on " A " an exact register was observed.

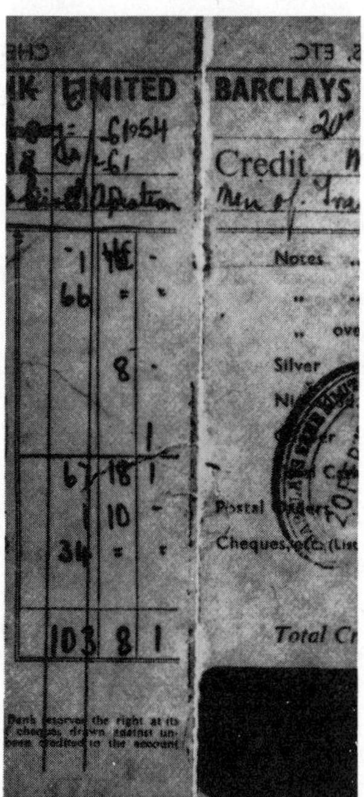

Fig. 3–23. This illustrates how a forged paying-in slip was temporarily attached to a counterfoil so as to deceive the bank clerk. The vertical dark strips indicate the thin line of adhesive which was used. The detection of this adhesive on the edges of some of the counterfoils was the first clue to the method whereby stolen crossed cheques were paid into an official banking account so that the thief could receive cash.

4

THE EQUIPMENT OF A DOCUMENT LABORATORY

Introduction

The author is often asked for information concerning the equipment which is needed in a laboratory dealing with the various phases of document examination, and this is the reason why the subject is being considered here.

Document examination is not unique in that the equipment needed is governed almost entirely by the scope and character of the examinations which have to be carried out. As already pointed out in the chapter on the preliminary examination of documents, a great deal may be learned from the examination of a suspect document with little more equipment than a table situated in a good light, a wooden scale and a pocket magnifier. At the other end of the scale, where a laboratory, such as the one directed by the author, has to be equipped to carry out every conceivable test on a document, such as the analysis of a few milligrammes of paper ash by the aid of the spectrograph, or the X-ray diffraction powder-camera, or the microanalysis of a trace of ink by methods based on chromatography or electrophoresis, a formidable amount of highly specialised apparatus will be needed. Some items of equipment will cost hundreds or even thousands of pounds and need specialist attention to keep them properly maintained and utilised to the limit of their capacity.

In the description which follows, any very complicated apparatus which is only used for very highly specialised examinations will be given but the briefest reference, for the details of such examinations are better sought in other publications; on the other hand, the comparatively simple apparatus which will suffice for the greater part of what might be termed the everyday examinations will be treated in considerably more detail. No attempt will be made to describe conventional laboratory apparatus and equipment, except where it has been adapted to the special requirements of the document examiner.

Bench Space

One of the most essential facilities for document examination is one of the simplest to provide—ample bench space over which a considerable number of documents can be spread within easy sight and reach of the examiner. There are a number of reasons why bench space should never be restricted.

If all the documents concerned in an investigation can be spread out before the examiner, there will be little time lost in seeking any particular document. Not only this, but the extent to which they are handled will be reduced to a minimum, which is most desirable. Every time a document has to be drawn from, or inserted into, an envelope, some deterioration takes place; every time it is folded or unfolded, there is a reduced expectation of life for the paper in the vicinity of the folds. These considerations are important for all documents, but vital when old fragile documents are the subject of the examination.

The final and perhaps the most compelling reason for having sufficient bench space to accommodate a large number of documents is that, on occasion, the attention will be drawn to some relationship between certain of the documents which otherwise might be overlooked.

For example, several out of a large group of signatures may be noticed to bear a very close resemblance to one another, an observation which might lead to the discovery that all were traced from the same original signature. Such a resemblance might escape notice if a large number of signatures were viewed in succession instead of simultaneously.

Again, the spreading out of documents in chronological order will often serve to focus attention on any which might fail to fit into the general pattern, and it is among these that forgeries are more likely to be found.

Storage of Documents

A cool, dry, well-ventilated storage place should be provided for the documents submitted to the laboratory for examination. Any risk of accidental damage, fire and theft should be minimised by the employment of all the conventional safety measures.

In the laboratory directed by the author, documents under examination are kept in cellophane or polythene bags in steel boxes, which are stored over-night in a well-ventilated strong room free from chemical fumes and sufficiently warm to remain dry whatever the outside conditions may be.

General Lighting of Laboratory

Any critical examination of a suspect document should be carried out in a good white light, for many significant stains such as those caused by chemical eradicators

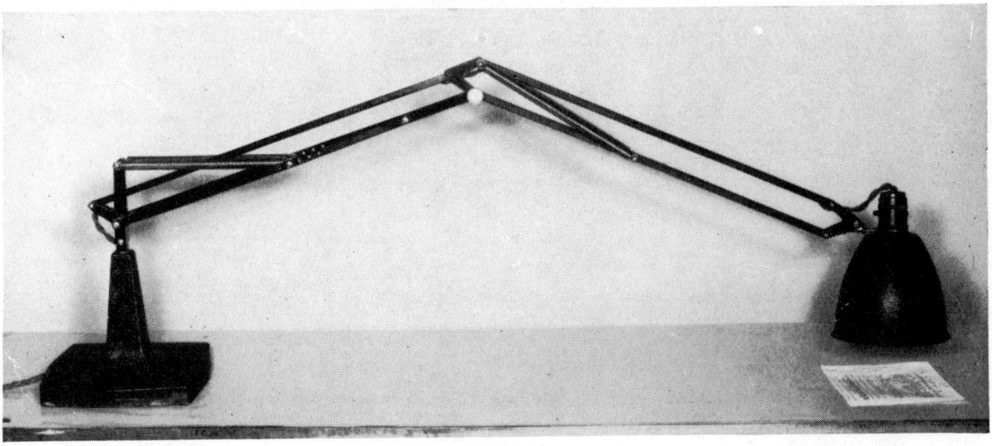

Fig. 4–1. The Anglepoise lamp suitable for the examination of documents for the presence of impressions.

are pale yellow and are extremely difficult to distinguish if the incident light is lacking in the shorter wavelengths. North daylight is by far the most satisfactory illuminant for general document examination but, except in the most favoured parts of the world, natural lighting can be relied on for neither quality nor intensity. As this is so, it is good practice to examine all documents by artificial light. This has the great merit of constancy, although it must be confessed that some workers feel that they cannot do their best work in rooms lit solely by artificial light. The room lighting should be with discharge-lamps of the "daylight" type rather than the somewhat warmer tints which are more popular for domestic use. These lamps should be supplemented with a desk lamp of the "Anglepoise" type fitted with a blue tinted "daylight" bulb. For special lighting apparatus, see *post,* p. 82.

Chemical Examinations

Whenever possible, all chemical examinations should be carried out in a properly equipped chemical laboratory, particularly those where noxious vapours are evolved. Failing this, a certain amount of improvisation will permit the majority of the chemical tests applied to documents to be carried out with little loss of efficiency at the price of some inconvenience.

Fig. 4–2. Simple apparatus for the controlled heating of material on microscope slides.

When a teak-topped bench with gas laid on is not available, a table covered with well waxed linoleum of good quality and a simple form of spirit lamp will make a good substitute.

Liquid reagents should be kept in small bottles fitted with stoppers which allow a single drop of reagent to be delivered at a time. There should also be a supply of fine glass capillary tubes fitted with rubber teats, for the transference of liquids on to and from ink lines and stains on documents.

As practically all of the chemical reactions will have to be carried out on microscope slides, some simple arrangement for heating these will have to be devised. The simplest is made from a 16g. brass strip, about two inches wide and fifteen inches long, bent into an "S" shape with all three horizontal portions flattened to carry the slides.

As only the bottom end of the strip is heated, there will be a temperature gradient along it so that the heating rate can be controlled by moving the slide along the strip. Figure 4–2 shows the strip supported on a stand with microscope slides placed at different positions. The heating apparatus shown is a Bunsen burner although a more convenient arrangement would be to stand the strip on an electric hot plate.

Special Heating Equipment

For the development of fingerprints on paper by the ninhydrin technique, the heating of the document after spraying is best accomplished in a thermostatically controlled electrically heated oven. This is an expensive piece of apparatus which might not always be available, in which case a substitute will have to be improvised.

A full-size biscuit tin should have a hole pierced in one side near the bottom so that a lampholder can be fitted in such a way that a 100-watt electric light bulb will project into the tin to act as a source of heat. The document to be heated rests on a tray near the top of the box. A hole is pierced in the lid to take a cork through which a thermometer passes so that its bulb is just above the document as it rests on its tray.

With this improvised electric oven, it will be necessary to watch the thermometer so that the temperature can be controlled by switching the light on and off. If the lamp gives too little heat to enable the required temperature of 80°C. to be reached, the sides of the biscuit tin should be lagged with felt rather than the power of the lamp increased, for this might result in the document being scorched by the radiant energy which will heat the document rather than the air in the tin.

For the local heating of a document, it is hard to improve on the small infra-red lamp. These lamps, which are run directly from the mains, are silvered on the back so as to concentrate the radiation into a broad beam. When mounted on a stand of the "Anglepoise" type, complete control of the heating may be exercised by altering the distance between lamp and document.

Fume Cupboards

Certain operations on documents should never be carried out in the open laboratory because of the poisonous nature of the gases involved. These include the fuming of documents with iodine vapour or thiocyanic acid gas and the spraying with an acetone solution of ninhydrin. For these operations, there is no substitute for an efficient fume cupboard such as that which forms part of the equipment of any chemical laboratory; if this is not available, the operations will have to be carried out in the open air.

Humid Chamber

This is the apparatus in which a document may be subjected to a hot humid atmosphere for an indefinite period. Its uses are described in detail in the chapter which deals with the laboratory examination of documents.

A completely satisfactory humid chamber may be fashioned from a large rectangular glass storage battery cell. If the edge is in good condition, it may be closed with a sheet of glass, but unless a fairly tight fit can be guaranteed, the closure should be made with a sheet of polythene or polyvinyl chloride held in position with a rubber band. If a glass jar of suitable dimensions cannot be obtained, it will be possible to make an excellent, though expensive, substitute out of stout sheets of "perspex," cemented together with the special adhesive supplied by the makers.

The source of the water vapour is a pool of water in the bottom of the cell and the heating is simply accomplished by directing the radiation from an electric lamp of suitable wattage up through the transparent base of the cell. The water acts as an efficient absorber of the longer wavelengths and saturates the air space above it with water vapour.

The document is supported on a stainless steel wire gauze placed well clear of the water. To protect the document from drops of condensed moisture falling on it, it can be loosely wrapped in polythene film or, better still, placed inside an inverted glass beaker supported on the wire gauze. The most favourable temperature for the humid chamber is about 50°C., which is rather warm to the touch. It should be possible to maintain this temperature with a 100-watt bulb unless the chamber is very large indeed.

Chromatography

In its essentials, the apparatus needed for chromatographic analysis, whether along a strip or over the surface of a circular filter paper, is simple in the extreme. All that is required is a vessel both to support and enclose the filter paper so as to prevent evaporation from its surface and to accommodate the container for the running fluid. Whilst commercial apparatus, which is simple to use and reasonable in price, is available from a number of firms of laboratory suppliers, quite satisfactory substitutes may be improvised for use on the rare occasions where chromatographic analysis has to be attempted.

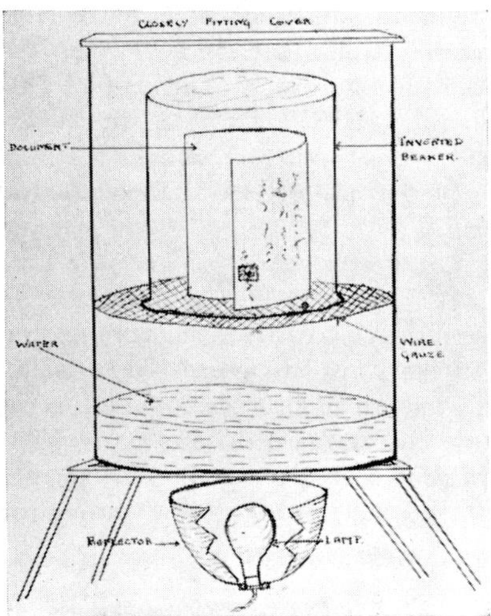

Fig. 4–3. A diagram showing the construction of an improvised humid chamber.

For chromatography along a strip of paper, a container about fifteen inches high and not less than four across will prove satisfactory; whilst a rectangular cross-section is the more convenient, most commercial glass containers will be found to be circular. The top of the container is ground flat so as to make an airtight fit with the plate which acts as a closure. Near the top of the container there will have to be a horizontal glass or metal rod over which the filter paper strip can hang, as well as a support for the trough which contains the running fluid.

For horizontal paper chromatography, the apparatus is even simpler. If a conventional desiccator of the correct size is not available, the edges of two pie-dishes about four inches in diameter should be ground by rubbing on a sheet of glass which is liberally smeared with a mixture of carborundum powder and machine oil until they make a good fit when placed face to face. To use this apparatus, the filter paper, which is of a diameter slightly greater than the pie-dishes, has a hole cut in its centre so that it is a tight fit on a standard Soxhlet thimble about an inch in diameter. The materials to be analysed are spotted on a circle surrounding the thimble before the filter paper is placed in one pie-dish so that the thimble rests on the bottom. The running-fluid is poured into the thimble and the second pie-dish is inverted on the first so as to enclose the filter paper in a vapour-filled space. The running fluid diffuses up the walls of the thimble on to the filter paper.

In a comparatively short time, the running-fluid streams to the edge of the filter paper carrying with it some of the constituents of the materials being analysed. Special filter papers cut with five equally spaced slits to minimise lateral diffusion (the Kamerau modification) are commercially available for use with this type of apparatus.

Electrophoretic Separations

Commercial apparatus should be purchased if more than occasional work on electrophoresis is contemplated. Whilst excellent results may be achieved on improvised apparatus, the high voltages employed in these separations may be a source of danger to anyone not well acquainted with the running of electrical equipment.

For the electrophoretic separation of inks, all that is required is a horizontal support for a strip of filter paper, about a foot in length, each end of which dips into a trough of electrolyte, and a source of high voltage which can be regulated. The simplest support is a strip of glass, and the vessels for holding the buffer solution which forms the electrolyte can be those made of polythene for the domestic preparation of ice cubes. Each vessel into which the end of the filter paper strip dips should be put into electrical communication with another similar vessel full of the same electrolyte, through the medium of a short strip of filter paper which dips into both vessels.

The platinum wires which form the electrodes dip into these outer vessels. The source of high voltage—of the order of some hundreds of volts—may be a group of high tension batteries such as those made for radio sets, but if mains are available it is better to construct a suitable rectifying and smoothing unit. The mains should be isolated by using a double wound transformer, the cost of which may be reduced by employing a voltage doubling circuit as good regulation is not called for.

Selenium rectifiers are quite suitable and smoothing should be done in the conventional way with a choke and electrolytic condensers. The output is controlled by means of a variable high resistance and the output voltage measured with a voltmeter wired permanently in circuit so that the smoothing condensers are automatically discharged on switching off. As a smoothed output of about 50 m.a. at 350 volts should be sufficient for most purposes, all the necessary parts may be purchased at comparatively reasonable prices at electrical disposal stores.

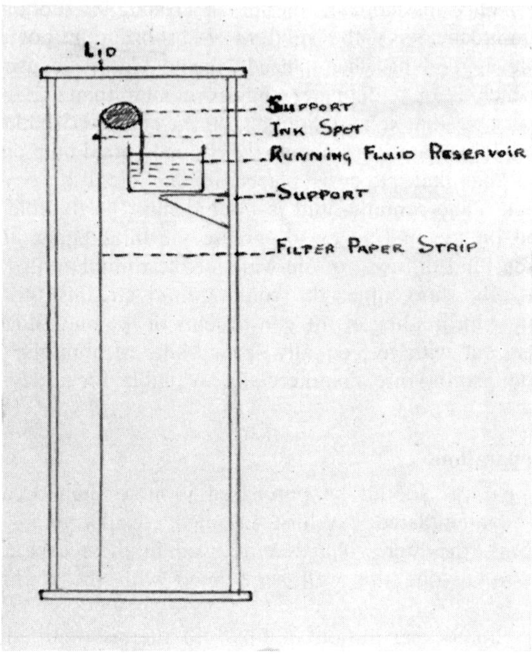

Fig. 4–4a. Sketch of apparatus used for vertical chromatography.

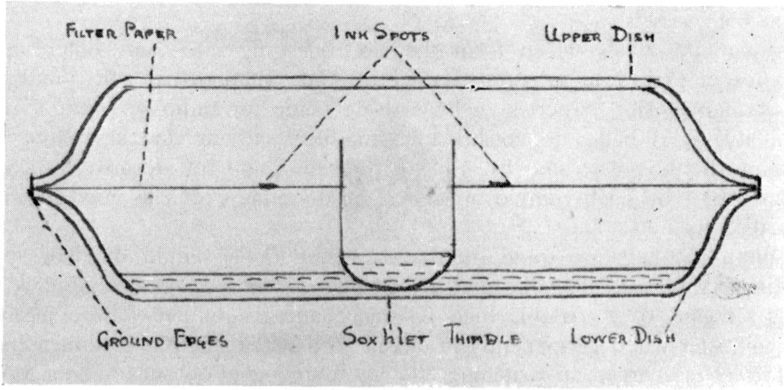

Fig. 4–4b. Sketch of apparatus used for horizontal chromatography.

No circuit diagrams or further details of the electrical arrangements will be given, as anyone who cannot assemble a mains unit from the outline provided should, in the interests of safety, purchase a commercial unit.

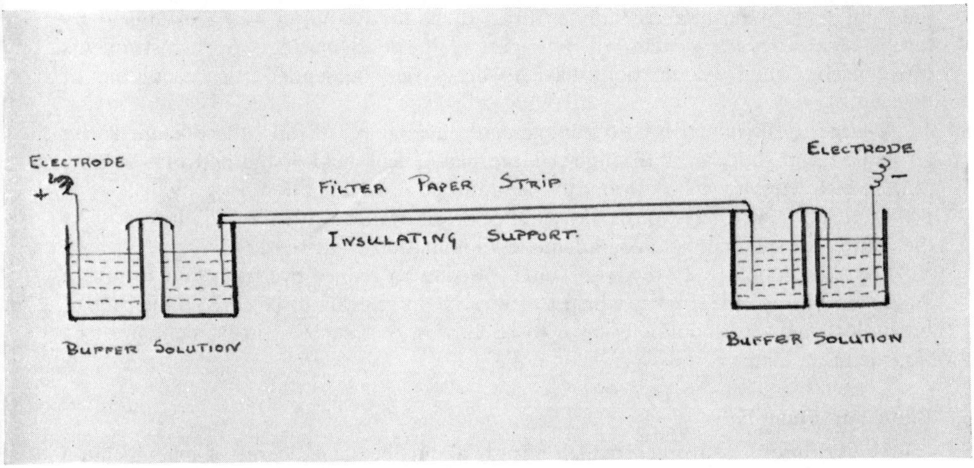

Fig. 4–5. Diagrammatic representation of the apparatus used in the electrophoretic separation of the constituents of ink.

For the details of the operation of apparatus for electrophoretic separation, the choice of a buffer solution for the electrolyte, the control of the applied voltage and the levelling of the electrolyte in the four containers, etc., the references at the end of the chapter should be consulted.

OPTICAL EQUIPMENT

Whilst a great deal of the apparatus in a document laboratory may be improvised, there should be no improvisation or cheese-paring where optical equipment such as magnifiers, microscopes and camera lenses are concerned, for good work cannot be carried out with inferior optical apparatus in unsteady and flimsy mountings.

Hand Magnifiers

For many document examinations, a linear magnification of about four times is all that is required, and for this a hand magnifier will be most appropriate. Because of its very restricted field of view, the small pocket magnifier favoured by the botanist is much less satisfactory than the engraver's glass. A glass by a good maker will be corrected for both colour and the most obvious aberrations and, having a diameter of nearly two inches, will afford a reasonably wide field of view. The linear magnification given by these instruments is in general about three to four times, which is just what is required for work with documents.

Illuminated Magnifier

This instrument comes in a number of forms. One, used extensively by the Forces for map-reading, consists of a hand magnifier of the reading-glass type with an illuminating system built into the handle. A dry battery supplies the power, and the light from a flash-lamp bulb is directed on to the object being examined by means of a reflecting system which is part of the lens housing. Such instruments prove useful when examinations have to be carried out under poor conditions of lighting.

A larger desk model is also commercially available. In this, the document can be viewed with both eyes through a large plastic lens held at the end of a folding arm, which enables its position to be adjusted. Illumination is provided by a powerful lamp which is housed in a reflector associated with the lens holder. As the lamps are mains-operated, adequate illumination is assured.

The use of both eyes tends in some measure to reduce eyestrain and to give a magnified view of the object, which to some extent appears to be three dimensional, but unless many examinations have to be carried out, such an instrument must be regarded as a luxury.

Binocular Magnifiers

Another useful instrument which affords about the same degree of magnification as the engraver's glass, but which has the double advantage of giving binocular magnification and leaving the hands free for any manipulation, is the binocular magnifier which is fixed to the forehead with a headband. The distance between the eyes and the twin lens is adjustable and the whole lens system can be turned up out of line of vision when necessary. The only disadvantage in the use of such an instrument is that as focusing has to be done by moving the position of the head relative to the document, definition is lost whenever the head has to be moved. This is apt to cause a certain degree of eyestrain. For fine manipulations when the head can be kept in a steady position, the binocular magnifier is unsurpassed.

Microscopes

Stereoscopic microscopes

A good stereoscopic microscope is essential for serious work on documents, and a really satisfactory instrument should be chosen. This type of microscope is unique in that it gives a stereoscopic or three dimensional image which is both erect and correctly orientated, which is vital for many types of investigation. It is true that such a microscope fails to give the high degree of enlargement which can be attained with a monocular instrument, but it is only on the rarest occasion that any difficulty is experienced through insufficient enlargement of the image. Great enlargement brings with it a correspondingly small field of view and a reduction in the stereoscopic effect.

A modern instrument by a good maker should be chosen because in recent years the stereoscopic microscope has been improved out of recognition, but before any final choice is made a number of instruments should be tested under working conditions. This is important because at least one well-known maker markets an instrument which, though very expensive, is practically useless for document examination. In this design, the twin optical systems are so inclined that an excessive degree of distortion is found at the higher magnifications. If a square object is examined, it appears anything but square, exhibiting a marked amount of what photographers speak of as " pincushion " distortion.

The maker's excuse that all stereoscopic microscopes suffer from this defect is not acceptable, because in many cheaper instruments this form of distortion is so slight that it is imperceptible at any magnification. When a series of parallel lines is examined with this instrument it will present the appearance shown in Figure 4–6, where the lines at the extremities appear anything but parallel.

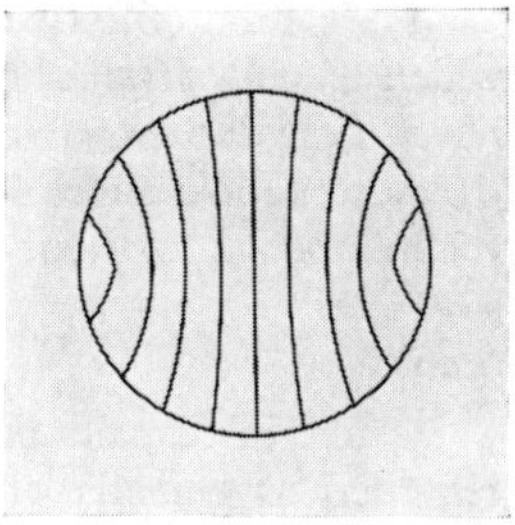

Fig. 4–6. Illustrating the pin cushion type of distortion produced when a series of parallel lines is viewed with an unsatisfactory stereoscopic microscope.

Before purchasing the microscope, a simple test should be carried out. A fine line should be drawn on a sheet of paper and observed at the highest power of the instrument. When the microscope has been focused, the paper should be moved so that the line is advanced across the field of view in a direction at right angles to its length. With an unsatisfactory instrument, the line will appear straight only when it is in the centre of the field; at the extremities, it will appear obviously bowed. Whatever other virtues may be claimed by the makers, a microscope exhibiting this fault is useless for document examination. Stereoscopic microscopes require careful adjustment, otherwise serious eyestrain will follow their use for any extended period. Before taking delivery of an instrument, a period of about thirty minutes of serious work should be undertaken with it. If, at the end of this period, there is any sense of strain, the instrument is either faulty in design, out of adjustment, or both.

In the laboratory directed by the author there are four stereoscopic microscopes. One is unusable for any length of time by anyone, the second is usable by some of the workers but not all; the third, a much cheaper instrument than the second, can be used without eyestrain by all, whilst the fourth, a good instrument in its day, gives an image which is too dim to be acceptable to anybody accustomed to more modern apparatus.

Eyepieces and Objectives

These should be chosen to suit the work which is expected of the instrument, bearing in mind that it is preferable to vary the magnification by altering the objectives rather than the eyepieces. As this is so, one pair of eyepieces should suffice. Wide-angle eyepieces giving a magnification of about seven times will be the best choice. An additional single eyepiece of the same type with a permanently fitted scale or graticule is a useful accessory. These scales and graticules may be purchased in a variety of forms, but the most useful has proved to be one in which a large square has been subdivided into a hundred small squares. This, when used with the appropriate pair of objectives, will cover an area of about a fifth of an inch square on any document under examination. This area will cover most typewritten and many handwritten characters.

Before accepting any eyepiece fitted with a scale or graticule, it should be tested, for it is not unknown for the graticule to be misplaced in the eyepiece so that both document and graticule cannot be brought into focus in the same plane. The graticule may appear to be floating in the air well above the character on the document it is desired to measure, and, when this happens, severe eyestrain will follow on any attempt to use it.

The paired objectives should be chosen so that they give a range of magnification which extends from about eight to thirty times when used with the eyepieces which have been chosen. No greater degree of magnification should be sought, for as the stereoscopic effect disappears at high magnification, there is little advantage over the monocular instrument at twice the cost for the optics.

Stands

Whilst three pairs of objectives and a single pair of wide-angle eyepieces may be regarded as essential, there will be no need to purchase an elaborate microscope stand fitted with mirrors and substage condensers, for the simplest form of stand should prove quite satisfactory. It is rarely necessary to make a stereoscopic examination of a document by transmitted light, but should occasion arise, the document should be placed on a sheet of glass which is strongly illuminated from below, and the microscopic examination then carried out in the normal way. Such a simple arrangement is unlikely to afford the intense illumination which can be achieved with a mirror and substage condenser, but it will suffice for most purposes.

When it is necessary to examine a document without the microscope having to rest on it, the microscope body can be removed from its stand and fixed to the end of a long metal arm which extends over the document from a heavy base which ensures stability. Such extension arms are marketed by most manufacturers of microscopes.

Illuminating Equipment

Many stereoscopic microscopes can be purchased with built-in illuminating systems, and one of these is in use at the author's laboratory. Experience with this instrument has shown that any advantage is more apparent than real. A separate source of light such as a lamp of the " Anglepoise " type is far more convenient for normal work on documents. As stereoscopic microscopes have long working distances, the lamp may be moved in the hand to give the required intensity and direction of illumination. This convenient and speedy alteration of lighting is needed when impressions and similar faint markings are being examined.

The Compound Microscope

For all investigations which necessitate a high degree of magnification, the monocular compound microscope must be used. An expensive instrument with optics capable of working at the extreme limits of magnification is not necessary, for a simple design of microscope equipped with a single eyepiece and three objectives ranging from one inch to a sixth should be sufficient to cover all normal requirements.

Oil-immersion objectives are rarely needed for document examination, and if an extra objective is purchased, it should be a two-inch rather than one of a higher power. Such an objective will be found very useful for bridging the gap between the short-focus camera lens and the one-inch microscope objective when photomicrographs of low magnification are required.

There is little point in buying expensive apochromatic objectives for achromats of good quality should prove satisfactory. Cheap and consequently inferior objectives should be avoided, as there is little difference in price between the cheapest and the best except where the highest powers are concerned. As but a single eyepiece is needed, this should be of the highest quality wide-angle type; there is no reason why one of the eyepieces from the stereoscopic microscope should not be used where funds are restricted. Few accessories, apart from a mechanical stage and a simple form of substage condenser, are needed. A built-in vertical illumination system is a luxury for document examination, as a conventional form of microscope lamp should suffice for most purposes.

Some provision should be made for the taking of photomicrographs; if a special camera designed for use with the microscope is not available, quite satisfactory results may be obtained with improvised equipment, and details are given in the chapter on Photography of Documents on methods for making suitable photographs with such makeshift apparatus.

Comparison Microscopes

It is sometimes necessary to bring two objects into the same field of view so that they may be compared under the same degree of magnification. This is done with a "comparison microscope," although some makers apply special names to the instruments they sell for this purpose.

In essentials, a comparison microscope comprises two separate objectives and ancillary equipment arranged side by side with an eyepiece so designed that the images from both objectives can be seen in the same field of view. Comparison microscopes are necessarily expensive, with the result that there are on the market special "comparator" heads which enable two similar compound microscopes to be used together in such a way that they become equivalent to a comparison microscope. The two microscopes are set

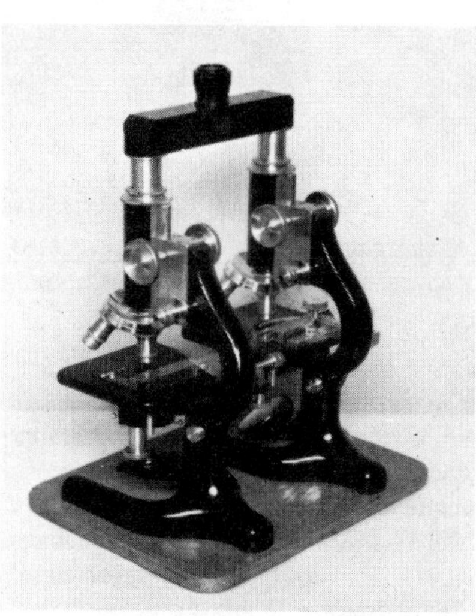

Fig. 4–7. Two Compound Microscopes fitted with Comparison eye pieces.

up side by side and the eyepieces are removed, to be replaced by the comparison head with its single eyepiece in which the two separate images can be seen together.

The Measurement of Colour

In the laboratory directed by the author, the comparison microscope has been modified so that it can be used for the measurement of the colour of ink lines. The tubes, to the bottom of which the eyepieces are screwed, have been slotted to allow slides holding a series of standard Lovibond glasses to be slid into position behind the objectives.

Fig. 4–8. Comparison Microscope fitted with racks carrying the Lovibond tinted glasses.

When a colour measurement is to be made, the ink line is focused under one of the objectives whilst a " standard white " — a block of magnesium carbonate — is placed under the other. The slides holding the graded slips of coloured glass are adjusted until the colour of the block, as seen through the tinted glass, matches that of the ink line being measured. The comparison is facilitated by both being visible side by side in the same field of view.

A wide range of standard Lovibond coloured glasses is available and details of the glasses which are most suitable for any particular problem in colour measurement should be sought from the makers, who are in the best position to give advice.

Measuring Apparatus

Measurement plays an important part in document examination, and many ingenious scales have been devised to facilitate the work. Whilst these devices have their uses, experience has shown that practically every measurement of importance can be made with one or other of a small number of standard instruments, most of which were not available to the document examiners of a former generation.

Metal Scales

A metal scale about a foot or fifteen inches in length will suffice for general measurements on handwriting or typescript. This scale is best made of stainless steel and should be graduated in both inches and centimetres. At one end of the scale, the subdivisions should extend to thirty-seconds of an inch with half-millimetres on the metric scale. With such a scale, rough measurements may be made directly on the document, but for more accurate work the distances should be spanned with needle-pointed dividers, which should then be transferred to the scale for measurement. This metal scale will also serve as a straight edge when typescript is tested for the alignment errors which arise when a document has been reinserted in the machine.

Even when dividers are used, measurements may have an error which can amount to a quarter of a millimetre, irrespective of the skill of the operator. For certain investigations this uncertainty will rule out the use of the scale and necessitate the employment of some form of measuring machine. These machines take many forms, but in the document laboratory some type of travelling microscope will be found most useful.

The Measuring Microscope

A measuring microscope consists of a low-power microscope mounted in such a way that the distance the microscope, or alternatively the document under examination, moves between observations, can be accurately assessed.

Any measuring microscope which is worth acquiring is certain to be very expensive, so that care should be exercised in the choice of this essential piece of apparatus. The cheaper forms of measuring microscope are restricted to movement along a straight line; such an instrument is practically useless for general measurements on documents, for which an instrument which can be moved to make measurements along two directions at right angles is essential. Ample capacity is also needed, and the observing microscope should be able to range over the width of a sheet of foolscap in one direction, and also have a movement of about five or six inches at right angles to the first direction.

Suitable machines fall into one of two classes. In the first class, the observing microscope is moved along well-fitting slides by the rotation of accurately threaded rods which not only move the microscope but which also indicate the amount of movement by the extent to which they have been turned. The construction of the threaded rods and of nuts which remain free of backlash and maintain their accuracy over long periods of service is by no means easy to accomplish. Measuring microscopes based on this principle are generally limited in capacity and very expensive and difficult to maintain in their initially accurate state as wear develops.

In the second class of instrument, the threaded rods which are used to adjust the position of the observing microscope, are not employed for measurement as well. This function is performed by a scale which is fixed to the guides along which the body of the observing microscope moves. The scale is generally read by means of a subsidiary microscope which will often carry an eyepiece micrometer to effect a further subdivision of the scale so as to increase the accuracy with which it can be read.

Whilst the movement of the observing microscope along its guides enables measurements to be made in one direction, measurements at right angles to this are made by observing the movement of the carriage carrying the document. Gross movements of both observing microscope and carriage are made by hand, after which a fine adjustment actuated by screwed rods is brought into play.

With this type of instrument, wear has little effect on the heavy guides on which both observing microscope and carriage move, and all measurements are made with reference to scales which undergo no wear at all. The scales are generally made of an alloy which has a negligible change in dimensions with change of temperature, and as eyepiece micrometers can be used with the subsidiary microscopes with which they are read, the graduations need not be excessively fine.

Although either type of measuring instrument can measure directly only those distances which lie along the direction of motion of either observing microscope or carriage, distances in other directions can be calculated by applying the principle of Archimedes to the measurements made in two directions at right angles.

The measuring machine used by the author is illustrated in Figure 4–9 below: it is of the second type, which employs scales for the measurements. That portion of the document being examined with the observing microscope is illuminated by built-in lamps and each of the subsidiary microscopes has its own source of illumination. The document is held on the carriage between two heavy sheets of plate glass which can be turned through a small angle to assist in the adjustment of the document, so that any required distance to be measured can be made to coincide with the direction of motion of the observing microscope. Provision is also made for examinations and measurements to be carried out by transmitted light.

The scales are graduated in half-millimetres, and the rotating drums on the eyepiece micrometers on the subsidiary microscopes are graduated into fifty well-spaced intervals. There is no difficulty in estimating to the nearest fifth of a division on the drums, so that measurements can be made to an accuracy of less than a hundredth of a millimetre. This is more than is required for any measurement made on paper which lacks any great degree of dimensional stability.

Measurement of Angles

If the ordinary eyepiece of the measuring microscope with its fixed cross-wires is removed, and a special goniometer eyepiece substituted, it is possible to carry out direct measurement of angles in typescript. Even a relatively simple type of goniometer eyepiece, fitted with movable cross-wires, will enable an angle to be measured with an accuracy of about a fifth of a degree when a vernier is fitted to the angle scale on the eyepiece.

The Measurement of the Thickness of Paper

For the accurate measurement of small intervals, such as the thickness of paper, some form of micrometer is practically indispensable. For measuring the thickness of paper, it is possible to purchase direct-reading instruments designed for the paper-trade, but an engineer's micrometer screw gauge, being an instrument in general use in industry, is far cheaper, although a little less convenient to use.

Many patterns of micrometer screw gauge are available, but the smallest and simplest, with a capacity of an inch and reading to thousandths of an inch, is quite suitable. Unless the user is practised in the handling of these instruments, it is advisable to obtain one fitted with a friction head which limits the pressure which can be applied to the object being measured. The fine thread incorporated in a screw gauge affords such a great mechanical advantage that any but the most

Fig. 4–9. Cambridge Measuring Instrument with goniometer eye piece.

gentle turning effort imposes a crushing pressure on the object in the jaws. The friction head not only limits the force applied, but also allows any measurements to be made at a reasonably constant pressure; this is important when compressible material such as soft spongy paper is being measured.

Special Scales

Where great accuracy is called for, the measuring machine is essential, but many measurements on documents can be made more speedily with sufficient accuracy by using special scales. Scales of many sorts have been described in the literature, and there is no doubt that some of those devised for use with questioned typescript are well worth acquiring.

Scales made to order by engraving on glass are both expensive and fragile. Whilst the fragility of glass may be avoided by the use of plastic, the only plastic which approaches glass in transparency—perspex—is too soft for general use. Celluloid is tougher but is apt to discolour with age. Even if plastic scales are substituted for glass, they are certain to be expensive when engraved to special order. The scales in use in the author's laboratory are all made on the premises by photography. This scheme has the great advantage that once the master negative has been prepared, inexpensive copies can be made as required.

Production is simple. The initial stage is the preparation of a considerably enlarged drawing of the scale on a piece of white card. As some skill is required if Indian ink, the most suitable medium, is used, the lines are drawn with a special pencil which photographs well. (" Ferroprint " pencils made by the Royal Sovereign

Pencil Co.) The extent to which the scale is enlarged in the drawing depends on the photographic equipment which is available. The drawing is then copied on to the negative so that a scale of the required size can be made by contact printing.

The most satisfactory results are obtained by using a " Formalith " plate for both negative and final scale. The processing throughout should be designed to

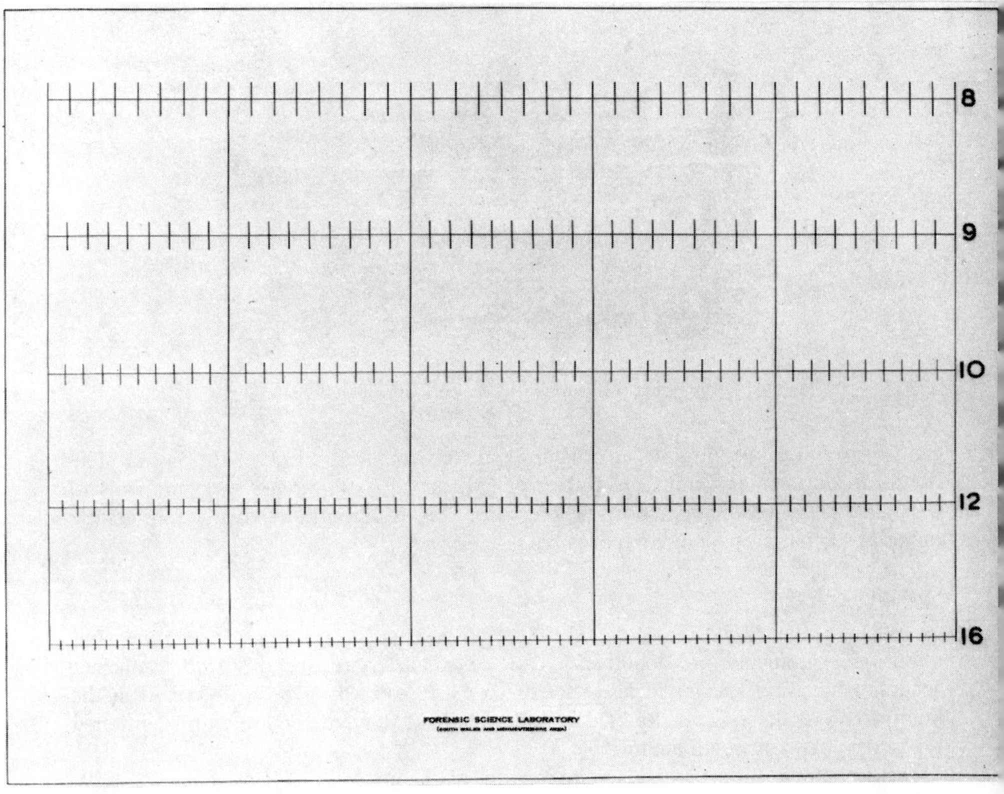

Fig. 4–10. Scale used for determining the letter spacing of typescript.

achieve the maximum degree of contrast between the lines of the scale and the background, and to this end the " fine line " technique discussed in Chapter 6 should be employed. If the processing is correctly carried out, there will be no need for any " cutting " of the final transparency, which will consist of a reduced copy of the original scale in jet black lines on a clear gelatine background on a thin sheet of glass.

The only fault possessed by scales made in this way is that after some considerable use, the gelatine surface becomes covered with a network of fine scratches which reduce the light transmission. Owing to their low cost, there need be no reluctance to discard scales which show appreciable signs of wear.

Once the negative has been made, scales of the highest quality may be prepared from it by a process worked out at the National Bureau of Standards Laboratory, Washington. In a Circular,[1] practical details are given for the synthesis of a phenol-formaldehyde resin which is made photo-sensitive by the addition of a small concentration of iodoform. After colouring with carbon black, this resin is coated on to the glass sheet on which the scale is to be reproduced, and after drying, exposed through the negative of the scale to a powerful source of light. The iodoform decomposes under the influence of the light to liberate iodine which catalyses the further polymerisation of the resin and renders it insoluble in the solvent which is used to wash away any resin unaffected by light. This treatment leaves the outline of the scale reproduced in lines made of black, insoluble resin with clear glass in between.

A valuable scale for use on typescript consists of a set of parallel lines about a half-inch apart. Each line is crossed at right angles by short intersecting lines at equal distances apart. Each long line is intersected at different intervals; the most useful spacings being those which are 9, 10, 12 and 16 to the inch as well as one of 2·6 mms. (See Figure 4–10.) This scale enables the spacing of most typescript to be ascertained at a glance. If the typescript fails to conform to any of the spacings which can be expressed as simple fractions of an inch, this will be an indication that the typescript is spaced on the metric system.

Another useful scale is covered with lines spaced at intervals of a sixth of an inch crossed at right angles with a similar set, so that a pattern of squares is formed. This scale is used for testing typescript, some of which is suspected to have been typed after the document has been taken out and then reinserted into the machine. It can also be applied to signatures which are suspected to be traced forgeries.

The co-ordinates of prominent points on one signature may be recorded so as to obtain a quick check of others which appear somewhat similar. This scale can also be superimposed and photographed over those signatures which have been traced from the same model to show how closely they coincide in all important particulars. This may save having to make photographic replicas to prove the case. (See Figure 11–11.)

When proportionately spaced typescript has to be tested for accuracy of alignment, the task can be greatly simplified by the use of scales similar to those described for the purpose by Ordway Hilton.[2] In these scales, parallel lines spaced at intervals of either one thirty-second or one thirty-sixth of an inch are crossed at intervals of one-sixth of an inch by other lines at right angles to the first, to form a series of narrow rectangles.

Another useful device to which the term " scale " can hardly be applied is a sheet of plastic such as " perspex " along which a fine straight line has been

1 Davis, R., and Pope, C. I., " Techniques for Ruling and Etching Precise Scales in Glass and Their Reproduction by Photoetching With a New Light-Sensitive Resist," U.S. Dept. of Commerce Nat. Bur. of Standards Circular 565, August, 1955.

2 Hilton, O., " A Test Plate for Proportional-Spacing Typewriter Examination," *Jour. of Crim. Law, Criminology and Police Sci.* 47, 2, July-August, 1956.

scratched. The sheet of plastic can be placed on a document so that the line is in actual contact with the paper. In this way, alignment tests of typescript and handwriting can be carried out without any risk of error due to parallax.

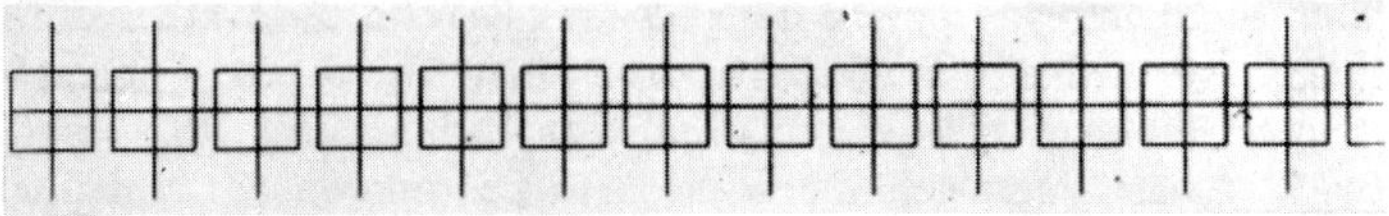

Fig. 4–11. Alignment scale for typescript.

Special Lighting Equipment

Sources of Infra-red Radiation

The sensitivity of photographic emulsions to infra-red is so low that powerful sources of radiation are essential if exposures are to be kept to a reasonable length. This puts out of consideration sources such as the Nernst filament or even the small infra-red lamps which have been recommended as convenient sources of radiant heat.

The only suitable source of infra-red for either photographic work or for use with the image converter is the 1,000-watt tungsten filament lamp. One of these units emits nearly as much energy in the form of heat as a small domestic electric fire so that, when one or two of these lamps have to be accommodated in a piece of apparatus, provision must be made for ample ventilation if a disastrous rise in temperature is not to be experienced.

It is unfortunate that the fluorescent lamp which is such a cool but powerful source of white light is useless as a generator of infra-red radiation; there is no theoretical reason why discharge lamps could not be developed to give a greatly increased infra-red output, but at the time of writing there seems little prospect of such a development.

Ultra-violet Light

Sources of ultra-violet light may be classified according to their power. The most convenient low-power source is the lamp of conventional bulb shape where the glass envelope also acts as a filter which, while absorbing the bulk of the visible radiation, allows the passage of light of shorter wave-lengths. These lamps find many commercial applications and are consequently reasonably priced; they are run off the mains and need no starting gear, although a special three-pin socket has to be provided for the lamp, and a choke inserted in the circuit to prevent excessive passage of current when the lamp has warmed up and the discharge through the mercury vapour has been initiated. These lamps are particularly useful for photography, for their low power can be compensated for by an increase in their number and in the time of exposure.

For the visual examination of documents, a more powerful source of ultra-violet light is needed, a demand which can be amply met by any of the many quartz mercury vapour discharge lamps which are in commercial production. In these lamps, the discharge takes place through mercury vapour contained in a tube of transparent fused quartz. Heat and visible light are generated along with the ultra-violet light; the heat is dissipated by providing adequate ventilation, and the visible light is absorbed in filters of nickel glass mounted independently of the discharge tube. A certain amount of control gear is needed to initiate the discharge and to prevent overloading of the transformer once it has been established.

Following the initiation of the discharge, these lamps emit radiation which ozonises some of the oxygen in the surrounding air. Although traces of ozone cannot be said to constitute a health hazard, some find the odour exceedingly irritating to the air passages. For this reason, the ventilation of the rooms where these lamps are used should be good enough to clear the air rapidly enough to prevent an unpleasant concentration of ozone being built up. As the lamp warms up, the intensity of the wave-lengths responsible for the ozonisation falls off owing to their absorption by the mercury vapour inside the tube, so that the rate of production of ozone soon falls below nuisance level.

In view of the physiological effects of ultra-violet light, certain precautions should be taken. The eyes should never be exposed to direct ultra-violet radiation and, as many surfaces are able to reflect these short wave-lengths, spectacles should be worn to absorb any stray ultra-violet light which might otherwise find its way into the eyes with most unpleasant consequences. On one occasion, after exposing some hundreds of documents to the rays of a powerful lamp, the author found that the tough and relatively insensitive skin on the back of the hands was becoming inflamed through excessive exposure to the rays. Since then, he has invariably worn gloves when working for any length of time with a powerful source of ultra-violet light.

The exceptionally powerful sources of ultra-violet light obtained when a heavy current is passed through mercury vapour in a narrow water-cooled quartz tube have no immediate application to the examination of documents.

For the reflection of ultra-violet light, ordinary glass mirrors are useless as the light is absorbed during its double passage through the glass fronting the reflecting surface. Either front-surfaced mirrors or polished aluminium should be used.

Very little light of the shorter wave-lengths is reflected from surfaces covered with lead paint. It is for this reason that the inner walls of the "Illuminator" described in the chapter on photography are painted with a lead-free coating, which acts as a reflector of diffused light on to the documents being photographed.

Discharge Lamps

The use of filters for isolating a narrow band of wave-lengths is referred to in the chapter on photography, but there is another method whereby a powerful source of light which is substantially monochromatic may be gained for experimental purposes. This is to employ discharge tubes containing the vapour of the appropriate element, supplemented where necessary by filters.

In the author's laboratory, the source of substantially monochromatic yellow light is a commercially-available sodium lamp developed for street lighting. A similar lamp containing mercury vapour is also in use, and from this a selection of wave-lengths may be obtained by the use of the appropriate filters. Both these lamps are reasonable in price and of high efficiency.

Discharge lamps of very much smaller light output, but of much greater cost, containing the vapours of other elements are also available as laboratory rather than commercial equipment. Among these may be mentioned the Xenon discharge lamp. As a very small but exceedingly powerful source of white light, these lamps have everything to recommend them but their price. This, with the control gear, runs into some hundreds of pounds, which puts them out of consideration for all but the most specialised applications.

Point Sources of Light

For many experiments, a point source of light is needed. This can be provided by a microscope lamp of the " Point-o-light " type wherein a tiny bead of tungsten is rendered incandescent to serve as the light source. These lamps, though effective for microscopic work, have a limited luminous output, are expensive and require special control gear.

An excellent substitute with a high light output can be fashioned out of a motor headlamp bulb of the type with a compact filament. Such a lamp may be run from the mains through a step-down transformer. By a judicious increase of the voltage applied to the filament, the luminous output may be increased at the price of a reduction in the life of the lamp. As a rough guide, it may be taken that a 10 per cent. increase in the voltage will nearly double the actinic value of the light. The bulbs cost but a few shillings and are available over a a range of from five to sixty watts. If one of the most powerful is mounted at the principal focus of a large condensing lens and over-run, a strong beam of parallel light may be obtained; this is invaluable for the photography of impressions.

Röntgen Rays

Röntgen or X-rays, as they are more generally known, are rarely used in document examination although very soft X-rays or Grenz rays, as they are sometimes termed, can be used for making transmitted light photographs to show up watermarks and any thinner places on the sheet such as the sites of erasures. These rays are so soft that they are partially absorbed by the paper, but as absorption of X-rays is roughly proportional to the density and mass of the absorber and not to its colour, they are little affected by any writing on the paper. This means that a much better transmitted light photograph of a watermark on paper which has been written over can be obtained with Grenz rays than with ordinary transmitted light.

These very soft rays may be generated by the direct impact on a target of slow electrons, produced and accelerated by comparatively low voltages or by secondary emission from a target bombarded by X-rays, which are sufficiently hard to produce the secondary emission.

Explosives are sometimes sent through the post in cardboard or thin wooden boxes and arranged to detonate when the parcel is opened. Any suspect parcel can be X-rayed before opening to detect the presence of metal objects such as wires and detonators.

It is unlikely that any laboratory would receive sufficient work of this nature to justify the installation of X-ray equipment but where, as in the case of the laboratory directed by the author, it happens to be available, good use may sometimes be made of it.

Oblique Lighting

It has already been mentioned that the most effective arrangement for the examination of a document by oblique lighting is a lamp in an opaque shade held in a fitting of the " Anglepoise " type, which can be worked by hand across the surface of the document. When photographs have to be taken, something more elaborate is required.

In one form of apparatus, strip lights are mounted behind a series of slits to provide a beam of light which is substantially flat. If a cylindrical lens can be mounted in place of one of the slits, the intensity may be greatly increased. No matter how carefully the light is adjusted it will be found impracticable to light more than a small area of the document at one time, because of the difficulty of maintaining the document in a reasonable state of flatness without temporarily sticking it to a mount, something which must be avoided if the impressions are not to be disturbed.

Every uneven area on the document will present varying angles to the incident light; some areas may even present negative angles and be in dark shadow. This difficulty caused by negative angles may be entirely eliminated by mounting the document on the curved surface of a cylinder which has its axis at right angles to the beam of light. The greater curvature of the cylinder will swamp the minor irregularities in the paper.

This scheme suffers from the disadvantage that at any one position of the cylinder, the portion of the document which is illuminated at grazing incidence will consist of but a narrow strip, so that this scheme is useless for visual examination.

If the cylinder is revolved about its axis, this will bring successive portions of the document into view until the whole surface has been illuminated. If, as the cylinder is rotated, a mechanical linkage results in the image of the illuminated strip travelling across a photographic plate, a photograph of the whole document in which the illuminated strips have merged into each other can be prepared. The simplest mechanical linkage which results in the illuminated strip travelling across the photographic plate in focus is achieved by allowing the cylinder to rotate along a plane which is parallel to the photographic plate in the camera. As each successive strip comes to the top as the cylinder rolls, it will form an image on a fresh portion of the plate. The only disadvantage of this simple scheme is that the lighting arrangements will have to travel with the cylinder in such a way that the upper strip is kept illuminated with light at grazing incidence as the cylinder rolls.

Examinations by Transmitted Light

In the description of the apparatus used for the preparation of photographs of documents by transmitted light, it was pointed out that the main difficulty was that of achieving even illumination. This problem does not arise when the apparatus is intended for visual examination when the objective is to attain sufficient luminous intensity to ensure a worthwhile transmission of light through a double layer of paper.

The apparatus is simple; in essentials it consists of a stout sheet of glass on which the document is placed with a source of light conveniently placed beneath it. A single 100-watt lamp backed by a metal reflector is suitable for most purposes. A refinement consists in using a 200-volt lamp on 240-volt mains. For normal use, a ballast resistance of about 80 ohms is left in circuit, but when extra light intensity is called for this resistance is shorted with a switch. This arrangement will shorten the life of the lamp but it is far more convenient than mounting extra lamps.

To eliminate eyestrain, the lamp should be housed in a box of which the glass sheet forms the top and a set of masks made of cardboard with apertures of different shapes and sizes should be available. These can be placed on the glass sheet to restrict the light to the required area, so that the operator is not dazzled by light which passes to one side of the document.

Infra-red Photoscopy

The development of the caesium-silver cathode photoelectric cell, which is sensitive to radiation in the infra-red, has made it possible for documents to be examined visually by infra-red. In this apparatus, the infra-red light which is reflected and diffused from the surface of a document is passed through a filter (which absorbs any visible light) on to a lens system which focuses the document on to a semi-transparent photo-cathode. The light distribution which makes up the image gives rise to a similar distribution of emitted electrons which are accelerated by the high potential applied between the cathode and an internal electrode, which takes the form of a cylinder whose axis is at right angles to the cathode. The beam of electrons is then focused by means of an electron lens on to a translucent screen.

The impact of the high speed electrons on the screen causes the emission of visible light which corresponds in its distribution with that of the original image, so that a remarkably correct reproduction of the original document, as revealed by infra-red, is seen on the screen. The electronic device which converts the original infra-red image into one which is visible is often termed an " image converter."

The caesium-on-silver oxide cathode has an excellent response to radiation whose wave-length ranges from 7,000 to 12,000 Å., which is roughly that which can be obtained with the range of infra-red sensitive plates at present available.

The electron lens referred to may be electrostatic, electromagnetic or a combination of both. With electrostatic focusing, the image converter tube can be expected to have a longer useful life than when the alternative system is employed.

The image converter tubes with which the author is familiar have a resolving power of about ten lines to the millimetre, which is sufficient for most purposes. It is also possible to achieve a certain degree of magnification of the image during the passage of the electrons from the photo-cathode to the translucent screen, but this cannot be taken to excess, for with high magnification, resolving power falls off and distortion increases.

At the present time, image converter tubes of the type described above are made in small batches for experimental purposes only. They are expensive, and, being magnetically focused, they are short-lived. If high resolving power and constant focus are to be maintained, it will be necessary to stabilise both the voltage on the tube and the current through the focusing coils. Whilst tubes vary in their requirements, it may be taken that about 2ma. at about 6,000 volts will be required for the anode, and if the power supply has a high impedance output, the ripple voltage will have to be kept below 2 per cent.

From the foregoing, it will be seen that the installation of apparatus of this type for infra-red photoscopy is not to be undertaken lightly, and unless a great number of examinations by infra-red have to be undertaken, it is far cheaper and simpler to employ photographic methods.

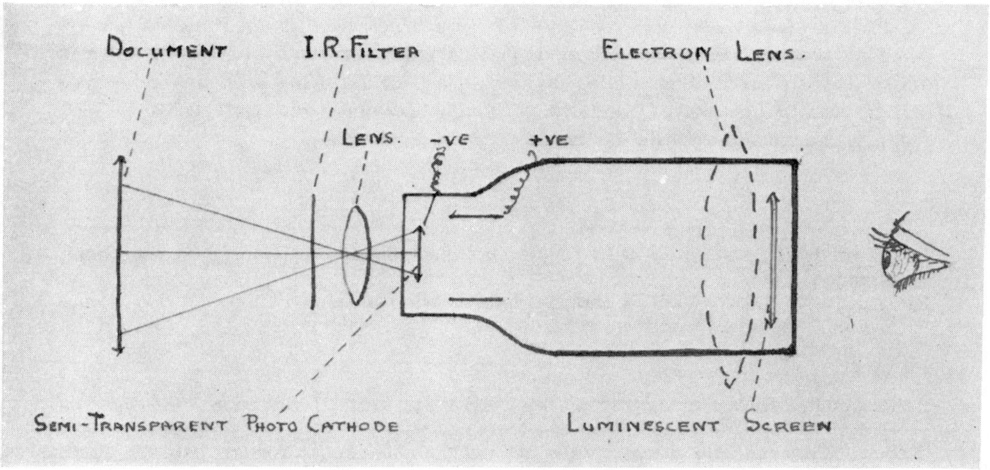

Fig. 4–12. Diagram of apparatus used for Infra-red Photoscopy using an image converter tube.

It is possible to improvise a fairly useful infra-red viewer by making use of a cell devised for use in military equipment (*sniperscopes*). This cell is much smaller in all its dimensions than that described above, but has a similar photo-cathode and translucent screen. No provision is made for focusing, but by placing the luminescent screen very near to the photo-cathode its brightness is controlled by the density of the electrons emitted in its neighbourhood.

To convert such a cell into a viewing apparatus, a lens and filter system must be employed to throw the desired infra-red image on to the cathode; a source of high voltage supplied most conveniently by a pile must be applied to the cell, and a magnifier arranged for viewing the translucent screen on which the visible image is formed.

Apparatus constructed on these lines will work in a satisfactory manner, but compared with the image converter tube described above, the resolving power is low, the area of both cathode and luminescent screen is small and the image is not very bright. Its main use is to determine whether there is anything on a document which is worth photographing by infra-red, relying on the photograph to give the resolution which is necessary for decipherment. Used in this way, this simple apparatus will probably save time and expensive photographic material.

Special Apparatus for Analysis

For the chemical analysis of minute amounts of materials fairly elaborate apparatus may be necessary. In the laboratory directed by the author, both the spectrograph and the X-ray powder camera are available for the analysis of traces of material removed from stains on documents, or of fragments of paper ash which are too minute to be dealt with by standard methods of analysis. These pieces of apparatus are both costly to purchase and difficult to house in a small laboratory; their fullest capabilities are realised only by those who are experienced in their use so that no good purpose would be served in describing either the apparatus or the way in which they are used. Suffice it to say that with their aid many problems in analysis can be successfully solved, and the document examiner who has access to such facilities can consider himself fortunate.

Bibliography

Lovibond, J. W., *Measurement of Light and Colour Sensations* (George Gill and Sons, London, 1893.).

Ross, K., "A Device for Developing Latent Impressions by Fuming," *The Police Journal,* October-December, 1957.

Image Converter Tubes

Edlin, C. H., "Infra-red Microscopy using Electronic Image Conversion," *International Criminal Police Review,* No. 96, March, 1956.

Lechat, "Infra-red Photoscopy," *International Criminal Police Review,* No. 69, June–July, 1953.

Morton & Flory, *R.C.A. Rev.,* September, 1946.

Morton & Ramberg, *R.C.A. Television Paper,* Vol. 11.

Pratt, "An Infra-red Image Converter Tube," *Journal of Scientific Instruments,* 24, 1947.

Pratt, T. H., *Electronic Eng.,* 20 (1948), 274, 314.

Veith, W., "L'Optique Electronique du Converteur d'Image," *La Revue Scientifique,* Vol. 86, 1948.

Solid State Amplifiers

Garlick, G. F. J., *Journ. of Sci. Instr.,* 34, 12, December, 1957.

Kazan, B., & Nicoll, F. H., *Proc. Inst. Radio Engrs.,* 43, P1888, 1955.

5

THE EXAMINATION OF SUSPECT DOCUMENTS IN THE LABORATORY

THE examination of a suspect document in the laboratory should supplement a preliminary examination conducted on the lines laid down in Chapter 3. In the laboratory, the visual methods employed for the preliminary examination are extended by the use of special apparatus and by chemical treatment of the document when such a course is necessary.

Laboratory methods of examination fall into two classes. The first, employing procedures which are purely physical, are generally preferred, because in their use there is little risk of the document becoming disfigured in any way. In the second class are grouped methods of examination which require, either the application of reagents to the document or the removal of material from it for testing elsewhere.

The resources of physical methods of testing should always be exhausted before any procedure which falls into the second class is applied to the document. No reasonable objection can be raised to a purely physical examination, for if it is carried out with care the document is unlikely to be changed in any way. On the other hand, whenever a reagent is applied to a document, no matter how carefully this is accomplished, or if any material however small in amount is removed, the document will have been disfigured to some extent.

Permission in writing should be obtained from the interested parties before any chemical testing involving mutilation of the document is undertaken. Even in the event of permission being given, a careful photograph of the document should be prepared before any test is carried out in case some serious harm is inflicted on it.

Within the confines of a single chapter, it is manifestly impossible to deal comprehensively with the laboratory testing of a document; for details specialist publications should be consulted. Whilst the brief notes on the various methods of examination do little more than outline the procedures which have to be adopted, an endeavour will be made to provide a fairly full evaluation of the practical significance of the various tests.

EXAMINATION BY ULTRA-VIOLET LIGHT

This should be carried out in a darkened room after the lamp has thoroughly warmed up so that it is giving its maximum output of ultra-violet light. The observer should be sure that his eyes have become fully adapted to the conditions before concluding that nothing significant is to be seen, for some fluorescence effects are very faint and need continued observation for full appreciation.

As ultra-violet light is highly actinic, the exposure of a document to a powerful source should be restricted to the minimum, for the dyestuffs in some coloured inks and in many typewriter ribbons are fugitive and may fade appreciably even during comparatively short exposures. This fading may have serious consequences for there may be no known procedure whereby the colour may be restored. If it is anticipated that a long exposure may be necessary, a mask of thick card should be used to restrict the exposure area under examination. Long continued exposure of the unprotected hands to a powerful source of ultra-violet light will produce a painful skin reaction akin to sunburn, so gloves should be worn if many documents have to be manipulated under the lamp.

The Fluorescence of Paper

The exposure of paper to ultra-violet light is a useful test when a document consists of several pages and the substitution of one or more is suspected. The forger may be able to match the general colour and appearance of an unwatermarked sheet as viewed under ordinary conditions of lighting, but unless a very similar paper has been chosen, it is unlikely to exhibit the same fluorescence in ultra-violet light.

It is extremely rare to find a paper which has no fluorescence in ultra-violet light, but both the colour and the intensity of the fluorescence are variable. The fluorescence of most undyed paper is faint and its colour is governed by the nature of the loading material, and the treatment the cellulose fibres have undergone during manufacture. If dyes have been added to improve the colour, it is generally the fluorescence of the dye which has the greatest influence. If one of the recently introduced " optical bleaches " has been used, its vivid blue fluorescence will mask that of the other constituents of the paper. Some papers contain a small proportion of differently dyed pulp which produces a speckled effect.

The pages of any suspect document should be exposed side by side and their fluorescence compared; no decision should be made until both sides of all the sheets have been examined, for the back and front surfaces may differ in their fluorescence. With a single page document, the actual colour of the fluorescence may have little significance, so that the attention should be concentrated on the discovery of places where there is some modification of either colour or intensity, for these may well be the sites of erasures.

Erasures

Erasure is effected either by abrasion, which results in the physical removal of the writing, or by chemical treatment, which has for its object the conversion of the colouring matter of the ink line into colourless compounds whose presence in the paper will escape notice.

If the paper has a good well-sized surface, any abrasion or chemical treatment to which it has been subjected will be almost certain to change, not only the reflectivity, but also the fluorescence of the area affected. On the other hand, if the paper is thick and its surface is matt, some abrasion may have taken place without any significant change becoming apparent in either reflectivity or in fluorescence. If the normal fluorescence of the paper is yellowish, the chemical eradication of the ink writing may often be accomplished without any noticeable modification of the fluorescence in the area affected.

These points are stressed because of the widely held belief that ultra-violet light will invariably expose an erasure no matter how carefully it has been effected; many a forged document has been given a cursory examination by ultra-violet light and then declared free from fraudulent erasure. Any suspect document, especially when yellow tinted with a matt surface, has to be given a thorough examination, which extends far beyond a visual inspection by ultra-violet light if erasures are not to go undetected.

Where the paper is other than yellow-tinted and the erased ink contained iron compounds, not only will the site of the erasure be revealed by the change in

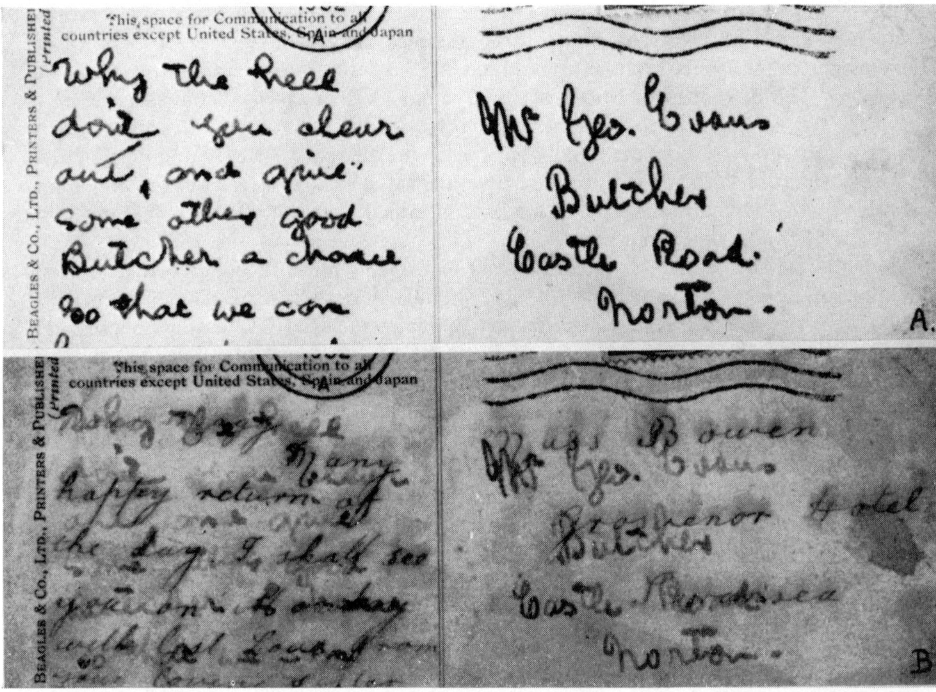

Fig. 5–1. The upper photograph "A" shows a photograph of a postcard bearing scurrilous writing. Examination and photography by filtered ultra-violet light "B" enabled a chemically erased original name and address to be deciphered.

fluorescence, but it may be possible to decipher the original writing. Unless the erasure has been thoroughly carried out and the surface of the paper removed, the residual traces of iron compounds will be revealed as yellow-brown outlines which can be picked out against the general fluorescence of the paper. When the paper itself is yellow, the ink residues will not be so readily apparent. This is one reason why erasures of ink writing on motor-vehicle log-books are so difficult to detect and decipher.

Areas exhibiting uneven fluorescence are not always the site of erasures, for such patches occur in ancient documents where an attempt has been made to remove " foxing " by chemical treatment. " Foxing " is the term applied to the brownish-yellow stains which arise from microbiological attack stimulated by the presence of traces of iron compounds. Surface repairs, not necessarily fraudulent, are yet another cause of uneven fluorescence in ancient documents.

Traces of oil which may be so slight that they are not apparent to the eye fluoresce vividly. The colour of the fluorescence depends on the nature of the oil. Mineral oil and petroleum jelly give a blue and oils of vegetable and animal origin a yellow fluorescence. The particular oil which is present cannot be identified by its fluorescence, for different samples of the same oil are found to vary in both colour and intensity of fluorescence. The presence of oil or grease may serve to link a number of sheets of paper, for sometimes pads of notepaper or bundles of envelopes or of labels become contaminated along the edges with smears of oil or grease. The discovery of traces of oil through its characteristic fluorescence may " place " a suspect envelope, label or sheet of paper among others of known origin which are similarly contaminated. Again, it may happen that all but one of the sheets which make up a multi-leaved document will exhibit traces of contamination with oil; this will throw suspicion on the unstained sheet should there be any hint of substitution having taken place.

Little can be learned from the ultra-violet examination of either pencil or iron gallotannate ink lines, but many of the dyestuffs in coloured inks, indelible pencils and wax crayons fluoresce in a distinctive manner. Red inks and pigments are generally used for outlining areas on plans which form part of a legal document; it is easy to fraudulently extend an area to include a wall or similar feature by a judicious thickening of the red line which indicates the boundary.

Several different dyes are available for the manufacture of red ink and coloured washes; some are so similar when applied to paper or parchment that no visual differentiation is possible. Even photography through filters cannot be relied upon to distinguish between them. Fortunately, it is often possible to distinguish between the original markings on a plan and any subsequent additions in a different ink by the different fluorescent properties of the inks.

Fluorescence of Adhesives

It is possible to distinguish between the three types of adhesive in general use by means of their fluorescence in ultra-violet light. The dextrins which form the adhesive layer on postage stamps fluoresce blue-white, gum arabic has little, if any, fluorescence whilst adhesives, such as glue, based on gelatine fluoresce yellow.

If an envelope has been opened by steaming and re-sealed with fresh adhesive or a stamp has been peeled off one document and stuck on another, a dual fluorescence will be apparent unless the new adhesive is the same as that originally used. When making an examination of an envelope, the bottom flap should be given the same scrutiny as the top; with a long envelope it is far more likely to have been tampered with.

Sealing Wax

Specimens of sealing wax which appear identical in ordinary light often exhibit differences in their fluorescence in ultra-violet light. A repair to a seal made with a different wax may easily be detected in this way. Incidentally, repaired wax seals are rarely encountered for there are methods for opening sealed envelopes and parcels which leave the original seals intact.

Safety Papers

Some safety papers undergo a marked change in fluorescence wherever their surface has been subjected to abrasion or the action of chemical ink eradicators. Others are protected by having their surface printed with a fugitive colour which is removed by abrasion or bleached by chemical. An erasure which will defy detection in ordinary lighting may be accomplished on this second class of safety paper if the lost colour is restored by careful tinting of the area of the erasure. The author has encountered specimens of so-called safety paper which has been tinted with a dye so resistant to the action of chemicals that ink writing can be bleached without any noticeable effect on the background.

In view of the foregoing, documents written on safety paper should never be omitted from the examination in ultra-violet light even when they appear to be in perfect condition. Repairs which defy detection in ordinary light and erasures of ink writing are almost certain to be revealed by the change in fluorescence in the affected areas.

Cancellation Marks

Cancellation marks are sometimes removed from valuable stamps, generally National Insurance stamps, by what is colloquially known as "washing" so that the stamps can be fraudulently re-used. If the "washing" is carefully done, nothing of the original marks can be seen on the most critical inspection. In marked contrast, examination in ultra-violet light will almost invariably reveal the nature of the fraud, by the change in the fluorescence of the surface of the stamps in the region of the erased cancellation marks.

Examination by Infra-red Radiation

Despite the claims made for apparatus incorporating combinations of filters and lights, infra-red radiation cannot be detected by the human eye. Either photography has to be employed, or the infra-red image cast by a lens on to a suitable photocathode has to be converted into a visible image on a screen by electronic means. This latter is the function of the "image converter" described elsewhere. Visual examination carried out with the image converter is termed "infra-red photoscopy."

Ultra-violet light finds its main application to document examination because of its power to excite fluorescence effects in the visible region of the spectrum; any "fluorescence" excited by the long wave-length infra-red radiation would necessarily be of even longer wave-length and consequently undetected by the eye. The examination by infra-red is unlikely to yield results similar to those achieved by ultra-violet light, for all that can be detected will be differences in the surface-reflectivity for infra-red radiation. Certain materials, such as graphite and iron compounds, are opaque to infra-red radiation whilst others, opaque to ordinary light, are quite transparent. This means that partially erased pencil writing overlaid by matter opaque to ordinary light can often be detected and possibly deciphered by infra-red photoscopy. This will also apply to postmarks and other markings in cancellation inks, the bulk of which contain free carbon.

Whilst the image converter is useful for the speedy examination of any suspect areas on a document, the resolving power of some of the more crudely constructed instruments which utilise war-surplus material is insufficient for really critical work. Unless a really efficient instrument, with a resolving power of about ten lines to the millimetre, is available it is safer to rely on infra-red photography for the examination of any suspect document.

Examination by Light of Different Wave-lengths

An efficient infra-red image converter is expensive to construct and maintain, and infra-red photography is both slow and expensive as regards negative material. As this is so, it is not surprising that considerable interest has been taken in claims which have been made for the invention of viewing apparatus supposedly duplicating the achievements of the image converter though employing nothing more than a few light-filters and a conventional source of light.

The inventor of the apparatus usually demonstrates its capabilities by producing an over-written signature wherein the original signature is completely hidden by the overlying writing. With this is shown an infra-red photograph of the over-written signature in which, as might be expected, the underlying signature is revealed free of the obscuring writing. When the over-written signature is placed in the apparatus, the underlying signature can be seen quite clearly as it appears in the infra-red photograph. From this striking demonstration is drawn the completely erroneous conclusion that the apparatus " views by infra-red " rather than the true lesson of the demonstration, that the differentiation between the inks of various colours achieved in the apparatus by the use of filters can also be accomplished by an infra-red sensitive photographic plate and its associated filter.

As the normal human eye is insensitive to infra-red radiation, any such radiation scattered from a document cannot be seen, no matter what wave-lengths are cut off by filters or any other device. In the experience of the author, when any of these filter-containing viewers are applied to a document bearing erased ink writing which can completely be deciphered by infra-red photography or by examination with the image converter, no trace of the erased writing can be seen.

The achievements of these " viewers " emphasise the fact that the examination of a powerfully illuminated document through coloured filters may yield results of some value quickly and easily. There is no need to purchase special apparatus; an over-run tungsten filament lamp, similar to the " photoflood," will provide ample illumination and the filters applied to the eye can be those used for photography.

Physical Measurements

A simple test of substitution of one of a number of sheets is the measurement of the thickness of the paper with a micrometer screw-guage, for one of the most surprising features of modern machine-made paper is its remarkable consistency in thickness; a variation of more than 5 per cent. is rare in paper of good quality. The test is very sensitive, for it will enable a distinction to be drawn between "28 lb." and "32 lb." paper of the same description. To anyone outside the paper trade, there will be little apparent difference between these two papers and the substitution of a sheet of the same paper but of slightly different weight might well be attempted by a forger who is ignorant of the differences. The substitution might also pass unnoticed by a document examiner who had not taken the precaution of measuring the thickness of all the sheets making up the document.

In the attempt to identify the source of a document, the examiner may have to compare the paper with a very large number of specimens. A preliminary sorting by thickness will probably be justified, for paper varies in thickness from just under one two-thousandth of an inch for thin tissues, to heavy note-paper which might be as much as seven thousandths. Typewriting paper varies from three to five, and Treasury notes are four thousandths of an inch thick.

If a special gauge, such as that used in the trade, is not available and a micrometer screw gauge is employed, the average of several determinations should be taken and if the instrument is not fitted with a friction head, care should be taken not to compress the paper by exerting too much pressure on the screw.

Measurement of Ruling Spacings

When an investigation appears imminent, fraudulent account books may be prepared to avoid disclosure of evidence of wrongdoing. Even when fraud on this scale is not attempted, pages may be removed and others substituted in existing account books, a device which eliminates the necessity of effecting erasures or alterations which might arouse suspicion. This substitution of pages may often be exposed by measuring the spacing of the rulings which are found in practically all account books.

Paper is ruled by passage through machines fitted with inked ruling discs which have almost wholly replaced the multiple-pen machines of an earlier age. The relative spacing of these ruling discs, whilst tolerably accurate, is by no means perfect. A certain sequence of values for the spacing will be characteristic of a particular setting of a machine. For every setting, thousands of sheets may be given an identical set of rulings so that any particular sequence will be characteristic of a batch of ruled sheets.

As with other machinery, adjustments to the disc rulers are made at intervals. These modify the exact spacing of the rulings, so that different batches of ruled paper can be distinguished from each other by careful measurement of the spacings of the lines. Where a completely new account book has been prepared, it *may* be possible to show that its rulings are characteristic of paper ruled long after the dates given to the entries, but it must be confessed that the possibility is remote. Where substituted pages are concerned, all that is required is the comparison of the rulings on the suspect pages with those of all the other pages in the account book. The demonstration that a different spacing sequence exists will constitute strong evidence that a substitution has been effected.

Because of the extreme accuracy demanded, a measuring machine will have to be used to make a number of determinations of the line spacing across the page so that an average value can be calculated. In view of the poor dimensional stability of paper, it is more satisfactory to calculate the ratio of successive spacings rather than to quote the actual values, which will be subject to alteration with change in the humidity of the paper. If ratios are used, they are unlikely to be significantly affected by dimensional changes in the paper.

Microscopic Examination

For the preliminary examination, a stereoscopic microscope with a low power pair of objectives should be used. Examination under high power should be reserved for anything of interest revealed by the stereoscopic instrument for which its low power has proved inadequate.

Really high magnification is rarely called for in the examination of a document. Excessive magnification brings many troubles in its train, the worst for the document examiner being the reduction in the field of view and the dilution of colour. With a magnification restricted to ten diameters, a circular area about a quarter of an inch across can be examined at a time, whilst the combination of a high power objective with a conventional eyepiece giving a magnification of a thousand diameters will have a field of view which is even smaller than a full stop on this page of printing. The higher the magnification, the more difficult it becomes to gain an accurate impression of the surface as a whole. High magnification tends to dilute colours, so that stains which are apparent at low magnifications may escape notice should excessive magnification be employed for the initial examination.

A heavy microscope should never be thrust carelessly on to a document, for the sharp edges of the foot may make impressions in the paper which will cause confusion in a subsequent examination. The document should either be covered with a sheet of cardboard with an aperture through which the examination may be made, or the base of the microscope shod with thick baize or sponge rubber, so that impressions are not made on a document no matter how heavily the instrument is placed on it.

If there is any possibility that the document has been trimmed, the edges should be examined with the microscope. The edge of a sheet professionally trimmed with a guillotine can be distinguished from that formed by folding and slitting with a knife; the notched edge which results from the use of scissors is, incidentally, also quite distinctive. The worn edges of a much-handled document present under the microscope a different appearance from those recently cut. Serrated edges should be examined for traces of adhesive; reference has already been made to a scheme for defeating the check supposedly provided by the counterfoil, by using adhesive or a thin strip of cellulose tape to make a temporary union between it and a forged paying-in slip. Where cellulose tape has been used, no traces of adhesive can be expected to remain near the perforations but with the better qualities of cellulose tape, the adhesive is so strong and firmly attached to the base that when it is removed from paper, it takes with it some of the surface fibres of the paper which is left in a characteristically roughened condition. These unmistakable roughened patches will often be found on envelopes which have been passed through the post bearing a paper strip on which the address is written, so as to obtain a blank envelope which has already been date-stamped—a preliminary operation for the perpetration of a fraud on a bookmaker who caters for the postal backer. The strip is often held in position with cellulose tape which leaves a roughened surface when it is removed.

The edges of holes should be scrutinised for evidence as to how and why they were formed. For example, a hole exhibiting an edging of iron-rust would indicate that the document had been kept on a rusty spike for some time. On occasion, holes ostensibly made for filing, have actually been made to remove inconvenient written or printed matter which cannot be trimmed off without removing something it is desired to retain. This is sometimes done with stamped paper, where the embossed mark which bears the date of stamping in tiny figures is often placed near the top left-hand corner of the sheet. A carefully sited hole may be counted on to remove the figures which refer to the day of the month, the month, or the year of stamping. If the punching of the hole has not been carefully done, sufficient of the red colouring matter may be visible on microscopic examination to indicate from its position the figures which have been removed. (See Figure 3–13 of Chapter 3.)

The edges of stamps should be examined for traces of adhesive on the top surface which might have escaped notice when scrutinised with the naked eye. The edges of all the flaps on an envelope should be examined for both traces of excess adhesive and torn paper fibres, which might indicate that they have been torn apart and re-sealed.

Official marks such as date-stamps and the like are often necessary to authenticate a document or some entry thereon. As a genuine stamping instrument is rarely available to the forger, they are generally made by hand. The correct type of cancellation ink is rarely used; burned cork, carbon paper and the artist's charcoal pencil are common substitutes.

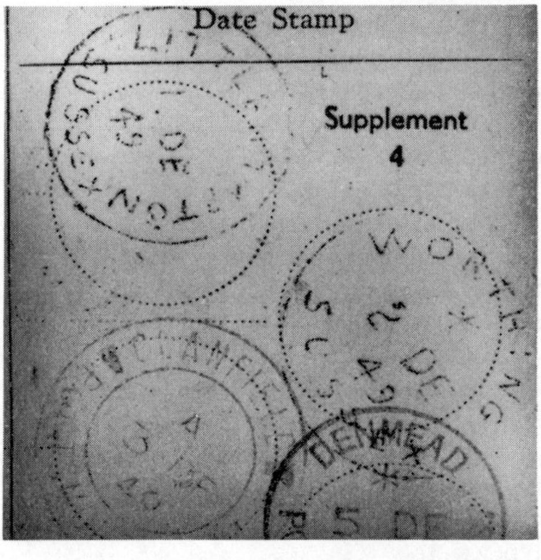

Fig. 5–2. The two upper date stamps taken on a Post Office Savings Book were forged by the application of burnt cork, using the point of a pin. The irregular outline of the two forged date stamps is in marked contrast with the even outline exhibited by the two lower genuine date stamps.

As these forged marks usually present a perfect picture to the unaided eye, every date-stamp or other official mark on a suspect document should be subjected to microscopic examination. Forgeries are generally exposed by the nature of the marking material, and by the imperfections in the hand-made figures and letters.

Printed data should be microscopically examined for signs of the removal or alteration by careful handwork of figures which refer to dates, telephone and street numbers, whose presence in the original state would expose the forgery.

Both sides of a sheet should be microscopically examined; special attention should be paid to any coloured smears on the back, for these may indicate that the document has been in contact with carbon paper. If the smeared document is known to bear a genuine signature, this should be followed up, as the genuine signature might have been used as the basis of a traced forgery on another document.

Typescript

Typewriter ribbons vary in their weave, with the result that the work of different ribbons of the same colour may sometimes be distinguished by determining the number of threads to the inch by microscopic examination of the typescript. The method is limited in its application, for with a well-inked ribbon it may prove impossible to distinguish the heavier impressions made by the threads sufficiently well to enable reliable measurements to be made. (See Figure 8–34, Chap. 8.)

The measurements are most conveniently made with a measuring machine, or failing this, an eyepiece micrometer. Several determinations should be made and an average value calculated for the ribbon. Evidence relating to ribbon thread spacing may be of value when it is suspected that additions to a typewritten document have been made on the same machine at a time subsequent to the original typing; any change in ribbon thread count will indicate that a different ribbon was used for some of the typescript.

It has already been stated that colours tend to pale under high magnification; advantage can be taken of this when intense colours, such as those of typescript, have to be compared for the detection of any difference which would indicate the use of a different ribbon. For this purpose, the comparison microscope will probably prove more convenient than the stereoscopic instrument. When a typewritten document is re-inserted into the machine for additions to be made, it is usual to actuate the stencil-cutting mechanism to keep the ribbon free of the typefaces until the adjustment of the position of the document is satisfactory. Trial impressions in the wrong places made by bare typefaces are not noticeable in the final effort because they consist of shallow impressions devoid of pigment. (See Figure 8–35, Chap. 8.)

Where re-insertion is suspected, these trial impressions should be sought for by low-power microscopic examination at the beginning of the suspect text. Care should be taken that impressions in the paper derived from its use as a backing sheet are not mistaken for trial impressions.

By the vigorous application of an eraser loaded with abrasive material it is possible to erase all traces of typescript, but no matter how vigorous the rubbing, the indentations in the paper associated with punctuation marks remain, and it is these which should be sought when evidence is required that typescript has been erased. The use of a template made from such indentations to identify the carbon copy of the erased typescript is described in Chapter 8, which deals with typescript.

Pencil Lines

A pencil line, so smooth and continuous to the naked eye, assumes a different appearance under the microscope; in its place appears a conglomeration of shining black, rather metallic particles lining a groove in the paper. In a line made with a hard lead, the haphazard grouping of the black graphite fragments will be disturbed by streaks (striations) running irregularly along the line. As these striations are absent in lines made with very soft pencils, they are probably caused by the presence of an appreciable proportion of clay in the harder leads.

It will also be discovered that some of the graphite fragments tend to pile up against one side of those fibres in the surface of the paper which lie across the pencil line. It will be found that the piling occurs against the side of the fibre which opposes the motion of the pencil point.

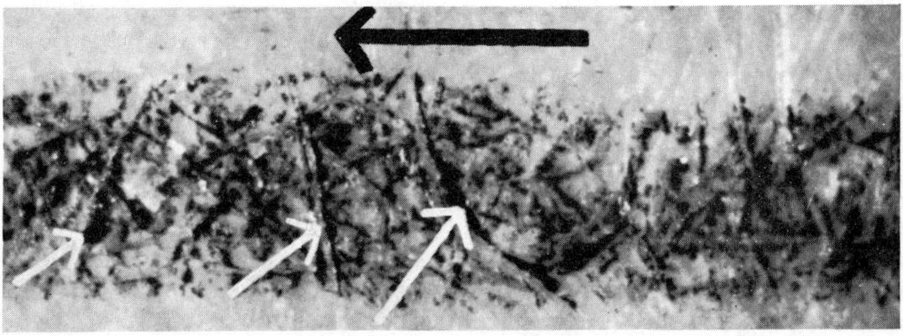

Fig. 5–3. The enlarged (times twenty) photograph of the pencil line shows heaping-up of the fragments of graphite to the right-hand side of transverse fibres indicated by the white arrows. This shows that the pencil moved in the direction indicated by the black arrow.

For reasons given in detail elsewhere, it is often difficult to find evidence on which a forged signature written in pencil can be condemned. Delicate retouching to improve outlines always indicates forgery; retouching may occasionally be revealed when it can be shown that in certain places the pencil has travelled in a reverse direction from that taken when the signature has been written normally.

Marks which Resemble Pencil

The surface of paper, with the soft cellulose fibres reinforced by both mineral matter and size is appreciably harder than many of the softer metals, which is why paper is able to abrade a soft metal which is rubbed against it. The detached fragments of the metals remain entangled in the surface fibres of the paper. As metals are optically dense, the most tenuous deposit can easily be seen as a greyish mark which might well be mistaken for pencil irrespective of the colour of the metal which gave rise to it. The term " lead " still applied to the core of a pencil is a reminder that soft alloys of lead were at one time used as marking materials.

It is sometimes difficult to determine whether a mark has been made by a metal or by a hard pencil. With silver, a freshly made mark will be seen to sparkle and catch the light, leaving little doubt as to its nature, but where the paper contains sulphur compounds such as ultramarine, the bright silver is soon converted into dark brown silver sulphide closely resembling the graphite-clay mixture of the lead pencil. A mark made by lead will appear black from the outset. A mark made by a metal contains many more fragments in a given area than a pencil line of the same depth of colour, but with a metal, the individual fragments are so much smaller than those of a pencil line, that although they are far more numerous, the total deposit on the paper is much less than with a pencil line of the same apparent density.

A chemical test may be required to identify the marking material. To bring metals or their sulphides into solution, powerful reagents are needed. As these should never be applied to a document, permission should be sought for the removal of a tiny disc of paper from the centre of the mark; the procedure is described elsewhere in this chapter. The tiny disc of paper is placed mark upward on a microscope slide and treated with warm nitric acid. Graphite from a pencil will be unaffected, but metals and their sulphides will go into solution. If the marking material disappears from the disc, spot tests should be applied to identify the metal. The presence of iron will not be significant because many pencil leads contain iron compounds as an impurity.

To the naked eye, the line made by a " liquid lead " ballpoint is indistinguishable from a pencil line, but under the microscope, its appearance is most distinctive; the line will appear to have remarkably little dark matter present when account is taken of its depth. The black particles will be seen to be extremely small compared with those of a pencil line; associated with these tiny particles will be seen a faint brownish streak consisting of carbon particles, too small to be resolved by the highest power of the microscope.

Indelible Leads

Where a high proportion of dyestuff has been incorporated in the lead to enable copies of the writing to be taken by the application of damp tissue paper, the iridescent appearance of the dyestuff in the " lead " enables the type of pencil to be identified on microscopic examination of the writing. When the proportion of dyestuff is low, which is the case with the " indelible " lead, the line will appear indistinguishable from that made with an ordinary pencil. If, whilst under the microscope, the line is touched with a tiny drop of water, the dyestuff will be seen to " bleed " from the line.

Wax Pencils

The line made by a wax crayon can be distinguished on microscopic examination from a pencil line, because the material abraded from the crayon appears as smears rather than discrete particles. The composition of the core of a wax crayon differs little from the wax coating of carbon paper, and there may be some difficulty in determining whether a line has been made with carbon paper or a wax crayon.

In some cases of attempted fraud on bookmakers, it may be necessary to show that carbon paper and not a wax crayon was used for preparing a betting slip. To accomplish this, the microscopic examination should be concentrated on the distribution of the wax-like colouring matter, with respect to those paper fibres which lie transversely to the line of writing. The deposit from the carbon paper having been formed by pressure at right angles to the surface of the paper, will be found to be equally distributed on both sides of the fibres, whilst that from the moving point of the crayon will tend to pile up against the sides of the fibres lying transverse to the direction of motion.

Ink Lines

If the presence of fraudulent additions is suspected, the whole of the ink writing on the document should be examined with a low power stereoscopic microscope to ascertain whether it presents the same appearance throughout. Ink which has been kept for some time in an open ink-well collects dust, and when it dries on a document, the dust particles can be distinguished as flecks in the ink line. If these flecks are present in the ink line of certain entries and absent from that of others, some explanation of this difference will have to be forthcoming before it can be assumed that all the entries were made at the same time.

Although the open ink-well is becoming obsolete, the microscopic examination of the whole of the ink line should not be neglected, for it may reveal the feathered edges which indicate that the pen has passed over the site of an erasure. (See Figure 3–9, Chapter 3.)

Overwriting

Any overwriting revealed by microscopic examination should be thoroughly investigated, for whilst certain types of overwriting carry no sinister implications it is often indicative of fraud. Overwriting may be nothing more than a manifestation of carelessness on the part of the writer who corrects a spelling error, alters a word or makes his writing more legible by overwriting rather than by crossing out and starting anew. Non-fraudulent overwriting of this type is boldly done and not only can the overwriting be easily distinguished, but the reason for its presence is equally obvious.

To be effective, fraudulent overwriting must be unobtrusive, and a searching examination may have to be carried out to determine its nature and extent. Fraudulent overwriting is found:

(1) when all the entries on a document, usually a cheque or receipt, are overwritten to hide fraudulent additions made in an ink the forger subsequently found failed to match the original ink. The addition of an extra line to all the entries is intended to smooth out and mask the difference between the new and the original writing;

(2) when strokes are added to alter the value of figures, such as 1 and 6 to 7 and 8, or words such as six and eight to sixty and eighty, the whole being overwritten to conceal the join;

(3) when a faint guide line is converted into a traced forgery;

(4) when a genuine signature has been used for making a traced forgery in the manner described in the chapter on forged signatures.

Overwriting can best be detected by paying particular attention to the centres of curved strokes and the ends of lines, for it is here that overlapping can be expected. Where an attempt has been made to conceal the fact that overwriting has been done, by erasing the original line, traces of this which have escaped erasure should be sought near the edge of the sheet; a thorough erasure is rarely made at the edge because of the risk of tearing the paper. If the erasure has been complete, an impression of the erased line may become apparent when the incident light is modified so that it strikes the surface at grazing incidence. (See the various illustrations in Chapter 11.)

Even when the overwriting is in ink of the same colour as the original writing, the two inks may have been formulated with different dyestuffs. In the attempt to differentiate between them, the microscopic examination should be carried out in ultra-violet light; if this fails, coloured light should be used, or to produce a similar effect, colour filters should be used between the eye and the eyepiece of the microscope.

The Nature of the Pen

Many unreliable statements have been made about the identification of the writing instrument by microscopic examination of the ink line. Contrary to popular belief, it is not always possible to distinguish the work of a quill, a fountain pen or even a ball-point.

The quill pen is stated to be unique, in that it makes a line wherein it is impossible to distinguish the tracks of the twin points of the nib, but a similar state of affairs will be found to hold for the writings of some fountain pens, especially with an alkaline ink. The conventional ball-point pen makes a coarse structureless line, characterised by abrupt thickenings on curves where the direction of rotation of the ball has been changed (see Figure 7–8), but the line made with the modified ball-point pen, which uses ordinary ink, shows none of these features, and may be difficult to distinguish from one made with a stylographic pen where the ink is fed along a fine wire.

Whilst it is not always possible to distinguish between the work of a fountain pen and the ordinary pen, sometimes referred to as the "dip pen," the presence of preliminary scratches will point to a fountain pen having been used. Where a considerable amount of writing is available for examination, signs of depletion of ink followed by recharging of the nib will suggest the use of a dip pen.

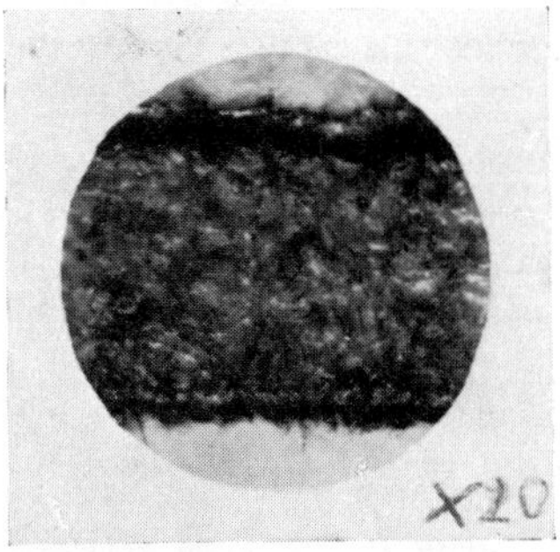

Fig. 5–4. A microphotograph of a portion of an ink line made with a worn pen. The two pen tracks are appreciably different in width.

Identification of the Pen with the Writing

The document examiner is often requested to identify a writing with a particular pen. This can be accomplished in only the most exceptional cases, although it is often possible to demonstrate that a specimen of writing could *not* have been written with a specified pen. In general it may be taken that only a very faulty pen can be identified with any certainty with the writing it produces.

Some inks are slightly acid in reaction and quickly corrode the ordinary steel nib. A badly worn or corroded nib will produce a line which, on microscopic examination, can be distinguished from one made by a nib in good condition. A line made with a steel nib in good condition is composed of two equally wide fine lines separated by a lighter area. The darker fine lines are the tracks of the points of the nib, and the lighter area is where the ink has flowed over the paper instead of being driven in by the ploughing action of the metal points. With an alkaline ink there will be an appreciable spread beyond the twin tracks.

Any uneven wear or corrosion of the points of the nib will have its influence on the nib point tracks in the ink line, and it is this which allows specimens of the work of the same faulty pen to be compared. Where the line reveals nothing outstandingly faulty in the nib which made it, nothing can be done to identify the pen with the writing.

Erasures

The site of an erasure can be discovered and outlined by testing the surface of the paper, which is invariably affected however the erasure was made.

The first test for change in surface reflectivity is best carried out by examining the reflection of light which is incident upon the paper at low angle. This test cannot always be relied on, for gentle abrasion has little if any effect upon the surface reflectivity of some matt-finished papers. The most reliable test for the presence of any roughening of the paper surface is carried out by allowing fine graphite powder to fall gently on the document. The graphite may be the finely divided powder used for fingerprint detection, or it may be prepared for the occasion by gently scraping the " lead " of a soft pencil held over the document. The document should be shaken to distribute the powder over its surface, before the excess is tipped off sideways. The graphite will leave the paper except where the surface has been roughened.

The areas outlined in this way should be noted before steps are taken to remove the graphite. As much as possible should be blown off with a strong blast of air, and the remainder should be removed by gently dabbing the document with lumps of plasticine softened by having been moulded in the hand. This treatment can be relied upon to remove all the graphite. No attempt should be made to remove the graphite by rubbing with an eraser. Rubbing will drive the graphite into the paper from which it will be impossible to remove it without causing serious damage to the document. Roughened areas revealed by the graphite test are not invariably the sites of erasures; they include places where cellulose tape has been removed from the paper.

It is sometimes possible to show that a sulphur-containing rubber has been used on a roughened patch on a document. The method depends on the fact that the considerable local rise in temperature at the surface of the paper when an eraser is vigorously applied, results in the volatilisation of some of the sulphur and sulphur-containing compounds in the rubber and their absorption into the paper. To detect these sulphur compounds in the paper, they are made to react with the surface of a heated silver plate which is applied to the document. The silver plate is cleaned with metal polish, swabbed with acetone to remove oil or grease, and then rubbed with a plug of cotton wool soaked in dilute nitric acid to expose a reactive silver surface, after which it is washed with distilled water and dried with filter paper. The roughened area on the document is pressed up against the prepared surface of the silver plate in a heated press; a dry-mounting press is ideal for the purpose.

Exposure to a temperature of about 100°C. for an hour causes any sulphur compounds in the paper to react with the silver to form brown stains of silver sulphide.

An eraser may be sulphur-free and the paper may be tinted with sulphur-containing ultramarine so that this test is not always applicable; if it yields a positive result it should be repeated on another area of the paper where there is no possibility of an erasure having been effected, to determine whether the discoloration of the silver plate when applied to the roughened area is significant, or whether it is due to a normal constituent of the paper.

The Deciphering of Erasures

Pencil Writing

A pencil line, unlike an ink line, lies wholly on the surface of the paper, and when it is thoroughly erased little is left except the impression made by the passage of the pencil over the paper. If there has been but a partial erasure, the residual traces of the lead will assist in the interpretation of the impressions. Photographic methods for the enhancement of faint residues from erased pencil lines are dealt with in the chapter on the photography of documents, but superior results may often be obtained by visual examination with a low power stereoscopic microscope.

The document should be manipulated under the microscope so that it is viewed by dim light which falls obliquely on it in an ever changing direction. The use of dim light is suggested because in such conditions, the eye can often distinguish faint markings which might otherwise be overlooked. The limited field of view with even the lowest powers of a microscope may prove a serious handicap when a large erasure is being deciphered, for it is sometimes easier to guess at a whole word rather than attempt to decipher it a letter at a time. Some magnification is desirable, and this may better be obtained by using a large reading glass or a desk-model magnifier fitted with a large plastic lens which allows both eyes to be used.

The back of the sheet should be examined, for if the erased writing was made with the paper resting on anything but a clean surface, sufficient dirt may have been picked up to form a faint mirror image of the writing on the back of the sheet.

When these methods have proved unavailing, further treatments can be applied to the document although the prospects of success are poor.

If the erased writing was written with a " lead " in which dyestuff had been incorporated, traces of the dyestuff may remain on the paper. These may be made more discernible by moistening the paper with alcohol, which will intensify the colour without causing it to spread unduly. Care should be taken in the application of the spirit; the safest method is to damp some filter paper with the spirit and then to press it into close contact with the site of the erasure. Sufficient spirit will diffuse into the paper to give the maximum intensification of the colour. When the spirit dries, the colour will fade.

The act of writing with a pencil will produce a local compression of the paper, which may result in the differential absorption of iodine from aqueous solutions of iodine in potassium iodide solution which has been loaded with the chlorides of other metals. The solution used for this purpose at the Laboratoire de Police Technique, Lyons, consists of an aqueous solution containing ·35% iodine, 13·3%

potassium iodide, 16·7% sodium chloride, 6·7% anhydrous aluminium chloride and 11·7% glycerine. Another similar solution patented in 1938 is made by mixing a solution of 50 gms. of magnesium chloride in 25 mls. of water with a solution of 10 gms. of potassium iodide and 0·4 gms. of iodine in 10 mls. of water. The author uses a solution of somewhat similar composition, which is much superior to both of the above, but is debarred from publishing its composition.

The general staining which occurs some time after these solutions have been applied to the paper rapidly obscures any effect produced by the differential absorption of the iodine, so the opportunity to photograph the area to which the solution is applied should be taken as soon as any writing appears. If the surface of the paper has been appreciably roughened by the erasure, the iodine solution should be applied to the back of the sheet. When nothing further is likely to be revealed, the excess solution should be removed by blotting, and the iodine stain decolorised by the application of a concentrated solution of sodium thiosulphate. As it is unwise to leave in the paper any sulphur compound which might become converted into sulphuric acid, the last traces of the thiosulphate solution should be decomposed by the application of mildly alkaline hydrogen peroxide solution.

These concentrated iodine solutions are unpleasant to work with, and it is certain that any document to which they and the clearing solutions are applied will be seriously affected, but as their use is vital to certain investigations they will probably continue to be employed, but only in the last resort when all other methods have failed.

Some pencil leads contain appreciable proportions of iron compounds as impurities. Therefore the sensitive chemical methods described below for the detection of traces of iron in erased ink writing can sometimes be successfully applied to erased pencil writing.

Erased Ink Writing

Ink writing may be erased by using an " ink rubber " which, being heavily loaded with abrasive, removes the surface of the paper, taking with it the coloured portion of the ink line. The more usual method is the use of a chemical ink eradicator which, if applied in accordance with the directions, will remove practically all inks with little apparent effect on the paper.

Chemical Ink Eradicators

Chemical ink eradicators are solutions of powerful oxidising agents which convert the dyestuff of the ink into colourless oxidation products, and any coloured compounds of iron or other metals into practically colourless soluble salts which are either removed when blotting off the excess solution or are diffused into the paper. Ink eradicators are the most harmful substances which are ever deliberately applied to a document; their use should be forbidden on any document it is hoped to preserve for more than a short period.

For an erasure to be made effective, as much as possible of the soluble metal compounds should be extracted from the paper by washing the area of the erasure with successive portions of distilled water, each of which is removed by blotting before the next is applied; otherwise the writing may appear as a faint yellow outline after the lapse of a few weeks. Any residual metal salts diffuse into the paper. When the attempt is made to decipher the erased writing by converting these residues into highly coloured compounds, the outlines are often so diffuse that extreme difficulty is experienced in their interpretation.

Identifying a Chemical Erasure

The existence of a chemical erasure may be discovered by physical tests, such as the examination of the reflectivity of the surface of the paper, and its behaviour in ultra-violet light. Where water or any aqueous solution has been applied to paper, the surface becomes slightly rippled on drying and the fluorescence in ultra-violet light is changed. If the paper is coarse and of a yellow tint, neither of these tests can be counted on to reveal a chemical erasure, so that, in this case, other methods have to be employed.

The simplest is to place the emulsion side of an unexposed photographic plate against the site of the erasure and leave them in contact in the absence of light for several days. Most chemical ink eradicators give off chemically active volatile products, so that any traces that remain in the paper will diffuse out and affect the emulsion which will show stains when developed. If this treatment has failed, or cannot be applied through lack of time, the document can be fumed with iodine vapour which will be selectively absorbed at the site of the erasure. After fuming, the document should be allowed to remain in a warm place until the iodine evaporates and leaves it ready for further testing. Fuming with iodine is preferred to the far more sensitive test with the iodine staining solution previously referred to. This solution, however, which should only be applied as a last resort, can be counted on to reveal every area on the document which has been interfered with, either by abrasion or the action of water or chemicals.

It is a common device to put an ink blot on the site of an erasure to hide the roughened or stained area, and incidentally to make it more difficult to decipher whatever was erased; consequently, blots should be scrutinised with care. With an accidentally caused blot, some attempt will usually be made to remove most of the surplus ink with blotting-paper, a course which is never taken with a deliberate blot which is allowed to dry naturally so as to attain the maximum density. (See Figure 5–5.)

The Decipherment and Restoration of Erased Ink Writing

The resources of physical methods of decipherment such as photography, examination by both ultra-violet and infra-red radiation (with the image converter) should be exhausted before any chemical reagents are applied to the paper.

Iron gallotannate ink writing, erased either chemically or by abrasion, can often be deciphered in ultra-violet light by the change in the fluorescence of the paper associated with the presence of traces of ferric compounds. Residual ferric compounds also affect the reflectivity of paper to infra-red radiation, which is why photography or photoscopy with the image converter often proves effective.

Where the erased ink has contained little iron, physical methods of detection often prove ineffective, so that recourse has to be made to chemical reactions which convert residues from the ink into highly coloured compounds. Unfortunately it has hitherto proved impossible to devise a treatment which will render visible the oxidation products of the ink dyestuff; the reagents in use are designed to react with residues from the iron compounds present in the ink, either as a main constituent or as an impurity. Many reagents have been suggested for this purpose, but in the opinion of the author, thiocyanic acid gas is unsurpassed. As it can be applied merely by exposing the document to the vapours which emanate from a vessel containing a mixture of potassium thiocyanate and dilute sulphuric acid, the treatment cannot increase the diffusion of the residual iron compounds and so decrease the legibility of the restored writing. This is always the danger when liquid reagents are applied to the site of an erasure.

The reddish-brown colour of the restored writing not only photographs well but enables it to be distinguished from any superimposed material, which is unaffected by the treatment. The only disadvantage of thiocyanic acid is that, like all gases, it is difficult to handle and must be prepared as required.

Fuming with hydrogen sulphide is often recommended but the poor results achieved by the use of this unpleasant and very poisonous gas rule it out of consideration.

Where it is not practicable to fume with thiocyanic acid, a simple treatment devised by the author should be tried. This is to moisten the site of the erasure with a solution of ammonium hydrogen sulphide in alcohol. This solution should be freshly prepared by saturating with hydrogen sulphide a small quantity of rectified spirit which has been made alkaline by the addition of a few drops of concentrated (·88) ammonia. The ammonium sulphide reacts with any iron salts in the paper to form the black iron sulphide, without the liberation of an equivalent amount of acid which would occur if hydrogen sulphide gas were used. The liquid does not stain the paper and can be removed by warming the document in a current of warm air. This treatment is employed when indecipherable traces of writing can be seen on examination by ultra-violet light. After treatment, the vague outlines are considerably enhanced.

This partial restoration of the writing as iron sulphide is not long-lasting, for the finely divided black iron sulphide soon becomes oxidised to the pale yellow sulphate. The colour may be restored by further treatment, but if a permanent record is required, it is preferable to photograph the restored writing as soon as possible.

In recent years, there has been considerable development of organic reagents which give highly coloured compounds with traces of metals such as iron, copper and vanadium. The author has tried out many of these for restoring the colour to bleached ink writings, but none can be recommended in place of thiocyanic acid. Any reagent recommended for use on a document should not only be sensitive to traces of iron, but also be of such a nature that its application will not result in the deterioration of the paper.

Many of the new reagents for testing for traces of metals have to be used soon after they are brought into solution. This may be taken as a sure indication that the reagents are reactive, and as their structures are often complex, they are almost certain to form coloured compounds on decomposition or oxidation on exposure to the air for any length of time. Before any of these new reagents are recommended for use on documents, they should be given long-term tests to determine whether any traces of the reagent which defy removal from the site of an erasure are likely to cause serious staining after a lapse of some time. Most of those tested by the author fail to pass this test for which reason they are not being treated here in any further detail.

The Restoration of Faded Writing

It should be stated at the outset that any attempts to restore ink writing are attended by a risk of causing such serious deterioration of the document that the last state will be worse than the first. It is preferable to prepare a photograph which enhances the contrast of the writing by employing the techniques described in the chapter on the photography of documents, and to file this along with the original document.

All the methods hitherto suggested for the restoration of faded ink writing involve the conversion of any residual iron into highly coloured compounds; there is no procedure known to the author which utilises the oxidation products of the dyestuff. From this it follows that the success which attends any attempt at restoration will be dependent upon the concentration of iron in the original ink. This is unfortunate, for the less iron an ink contains, the more likely is it to fade.

The document may be lightly sprayed with an aqueous solution of tannic acid, which will convert any iron compounds into products closely resembling the original ink, but an inconspicuous portion of the document should be given a preliminary treatment in case the reagent causes a general staining due to the presence of traces of iron as an impurity in the paper.

Potassium ferrocyanide solution has been suggested as a reagent for restoring faded or erased ink writing by the conversion of any residual iron compounds into an iron-blue. This procedure cannot be recommended, for not only is this reagent comparatively insensitive to traces of iron but is almost certain to cause serious staining.

Where no detectable concentrations of iron or other heavy metal are present in a faded or chemically erased writing, the problem of restoring or deciphering the vanished writing becomes far more formidable and in the great majority of cases little can be achieved.

Where circumstances demand that everything possible shall be done to effect a decipherment, and particularly where there is no objection to the document becoming defaced, it may be treated with reagents which reveal changes in the surface properties of the constituents of the paper caused by the presence of the oxidation products originally present in the ink. One of the best reagents for this purpose is the iodine-potassium iodide-metal chloride staining solution already referred to. On occasion, a differential staining along the ink line may be observed, but this occurs so rarely that no reliance can be placed on this method.

It has been observed that when paper is impregnated with certain fluorescent substances, the fluorescence is sometimes profoundly modified in certain areas because of slight differences in the state of the paper. In the course of experiments, therefore, the sites of erasures have been impregnated with solutions of fluorescent

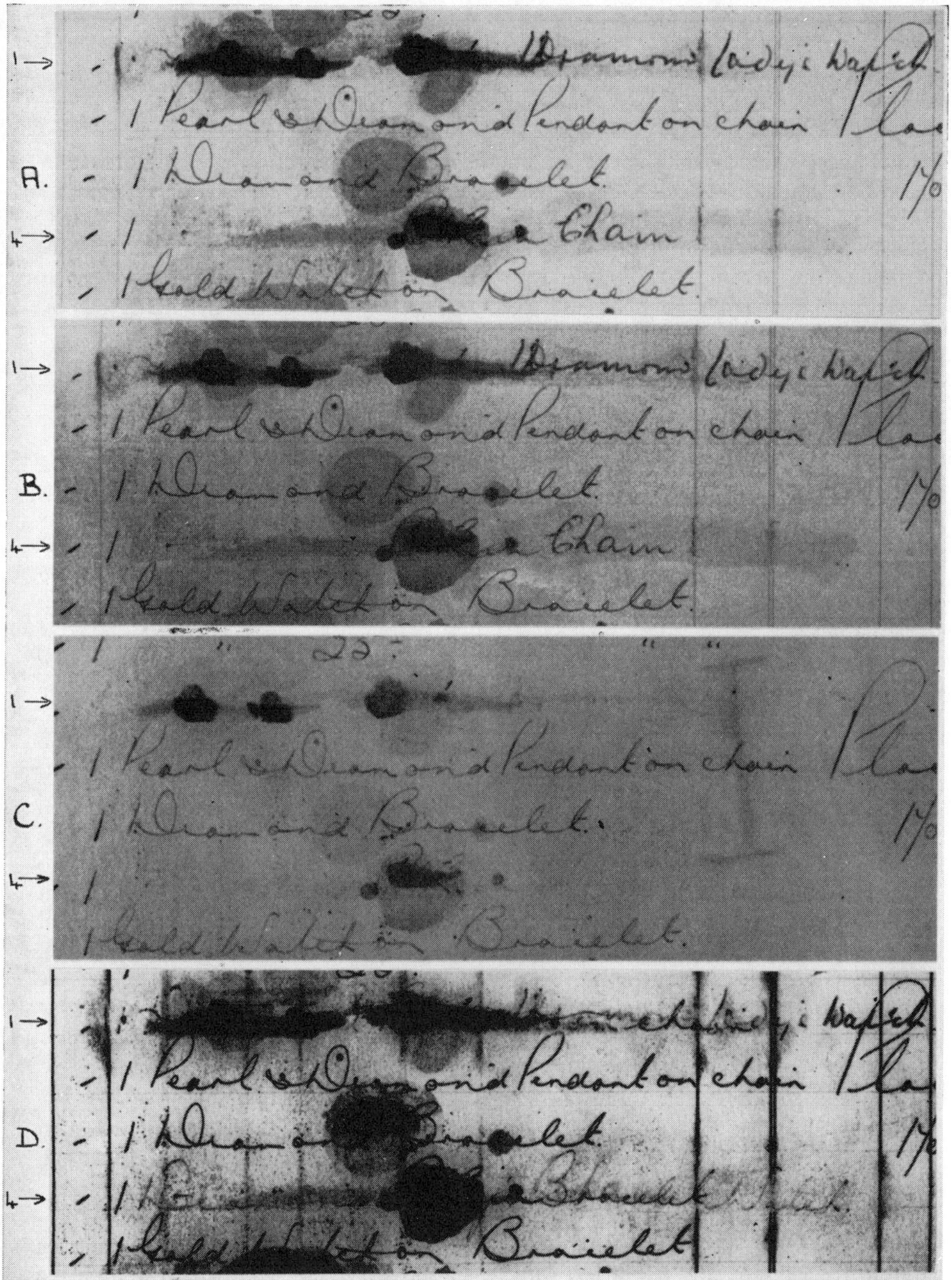

Fig. 5–5. *Decipherment of erasures by chemical treatment combined with Infra-Red photography.*
"A" is a photograph of a portion of a register where the original entries in lines 1 and 4 had been chemically erased, blotted and overwritten.

"B" is a photograph taken by Ultra-Violet light which merely makes more obvious the site of the erasure.

"C" is a photograph taken by Infra-Red. This has eliminated the overwriting but has failed to reveal the entries which were chemically erased. The document was treated chemically to render visible the original entry and then photographed by Infra-Red to produce "D." In this print the greater part of the original entries can be deciphered.

substances such as anthracine, anthranilic acid and eosin and then examined in ultra-violet light. On occasion, it has been observed that the erased ink line has become visible as a slight change in the fluorescence. Of the materials tested, eosin has given the most satisfactory results, but has the disadvantage of seriously staining the paper.

Further research may suggest more satisfactory fluorescent materials, but as the theory of the action is lacking, testing has to be done by trial and error.

Ball-point Pen Writing Erasures

The original ball-point pen inks were based on oil-soluble dyestuffs some of which faded very rapidly in strong light. The writing could be erased by the action of hypochlorite or permanganate solutions similar to those employed for erasing ordinary inks. The modern trend has been to improve the lasting qualities of the writing by incorporating dyestuffs of different properties into the inks. One dyestuff is chosen to ensure that the writing stands out boldly even when the supply of ink is restricted, whilst the presence of the other will confer resistance to fading.

A proportion of most ball-point inks can be removed from the paper by the action of solvents such as a mixture of equal parts of acetone and water. The residual writing is often changed in colour because of the differential removal of the dyestuffs present in the ink. The last traces of colour may be removed by treatment with a solution of an oxidising agent.

Little can be done to restore or decipher bleached or faded ball-point pen writing; this applies also to erasures effected by abrasion where the ink deposit is removed along with the surface layer of the paper. The problem is similar to that presented by the restoration of a faded or erased ink writing where insufficient iron is present to react with the vapour of thiocyanic acid. The compression of the paper along the track of the ball-point may alter its capacity to absorb iodine, in which case the iodine staining solution previously referred to may reveal the outline of the writing when it is applied to the paper, preferably to the back of the page.

The Deciphering of Charred Documents

Many of the methods for deciphering charred documents described in the literature on this subject have been tested by the author; with some, partial success was achieved, whilst others proved useless under the conditions of the test.

Practically all the charred documents with which the author has had to deal have consisted of warped and twisted fragile masses, which were far removed from the substantially flat sheets with which most of those who had written on the subject must have experimented. In the experience of the author, the essential preliminary has been to treat the twisted mass so that the individual sheets or fragments of sheets can be separated and flattened out for further treatment. This is more easily said than done, and it may be significant that this step is so often glossed over or not even mentioned by the majority of those who have written on the subject. The approach to the problem is obvious—the fragile and twisted

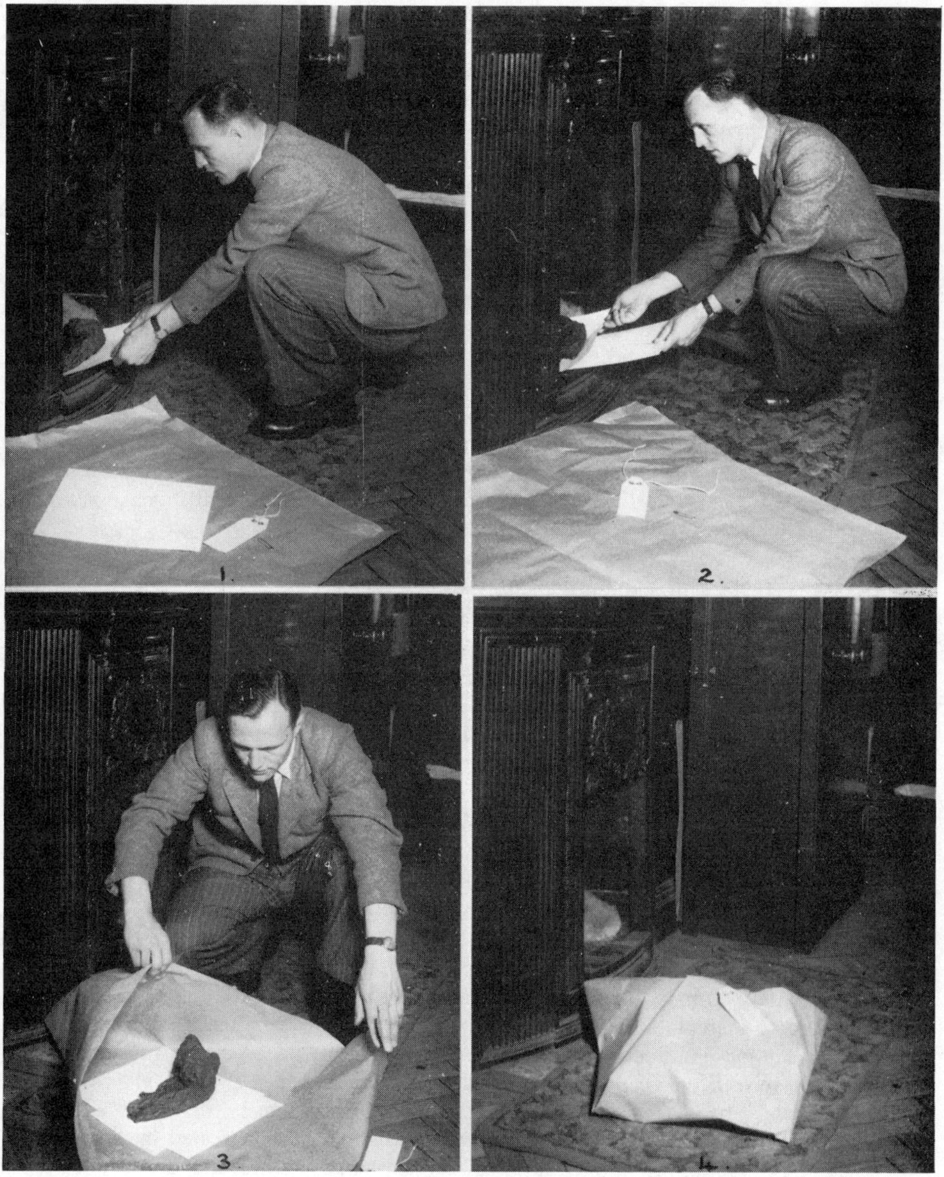

Fig. 5–6. *Transference of Charred Paper*

(1) A stiff sheet of paper is inserted beneath the charred mass in the fire-place.

(2) The charred mass is being withdrawn by pulling the paper and its burden on to a stiff sheet of cardboard, which is being thrust forward at the same time.

(3) The charred mass supported on the paper and the cardboard is being covered by drawing the corners of the sheet of brown paper together.

(4) The parcel is now ready for the transference of the charred mass to the laboratory.

material must be strengthened and made flexible so that it can be handled and flattened.

The choice of a suitable binder is restricted. It should be simple to apply and not require the use of a spray, for a spray is not always easy to control and is apt to deposit material where it is unwanted. The binder should readily be absorbed by charred paper, a condition which rules out the dilute gelatine solutions recommended by those who have obviously had little experience in their use. After treatment, the impregnated sheets should be sufficiently flexible to allow them to be flattened, but tough enough to permit them to be pulled apart. This last condition rules out gum arabic, another suggested binding material.

The author has made many trials of solutions of plastics in different organic solvents. For many years nothing superior to a dilute solution of cellulose acetate in acetone could be found, although it had a number of disadvantages. The solution was rather viscous and had to be sprayed; under some conditions it was apt to " bloom " and cover the charred mass with a white coating, but most serious of all it conferred too little plasticity on the treated sheets.

The position has changed with the introduction into commerce of polyvinyl acetate. A 3 per cent. solution of this plastic in acetone makes an ideal binding agent for laboratory use on charred paper.

The Transference and Stabilisation of Charred Paper

Charred paper, and even more so, paper ash, has little tensile strength, so that no attempt should be made to lift it with tweezers; instead, the charred mass should be moved by first insinuating a sheet of stiff paper beneath it (see Figure 5–6 (1)) and then drawing the paper and its burden on to a stiff sheet of cardboard or metal (see Figure 5–6 (2)). The whole should then be transferred into a box or on to the centre of a large sheet of wrapping paper (see Figure 5–6 (3)) the sides of which are drawn up around the charred mass to protect it from draughts (see Figure 5–6 (4)). Protected in this way, it can be taken by hand either to the laboratory or to a sheltered place for stabilisation, after which it may safely be passed through the post for further treatment at a laboratory.

Stabilisation

A solution of polyvinyl acetate in acetone is a powerful adhesive, and if used indiscriminately it may be found at a later stage that some of the treated char has become adherent to the support on which it was resting whilst being treated with the binding solution. To eliminate this possibility, the author stabilises the charred mass with the binding solution while it is resting on a sheet of glass which has previously been treated with a silicone water repellent.[1] Polyvinyl acetate shows little tendency to adhere to any surface which has been treated in this way. The binding solution is applied with a pipette, made by drawing one end of a three inch length of quill tubing into a capillary and fitting a rubber teat on to the other. The pipette is charged with the solution, and the end of the capillary is applied to the top of the charred mass. It will be found that the solution runs

[1] A 1 per cent. solution of Silicone Fluid M.S. 1107 (Hopkin & Williams) in petrol ether.

very readily from the capillary into the char. The acetone quickly evaporates, leaving a small area impregnated with solid polyvinyl acetate. The capillary is then moved on to an adjoining area, and the process repeated until the whole of the upper sheet has been treated.

The upper sheet may now be removed. It will probably be found that it tends to adhere to the rest of the charred mass at a number of places. No force should be applied to effect a separation, but fresh solution should be applied to each place in turn when there is any adhesion. The fresh solution rapidly dissolves the excess polyvinyl acetate which is responsible for the unwanted adhesion, so that the upper sheet may gradually be detached. The process is repeated until all the sheets have been stabilised and separated. Once the sheets have dried sufficiently to enable them to be handled safely, they can literally be pulled into shape with little risk of their tearing.

The minimum quantity of stabilising solution should be used, as a charred sheet enclosed within a thick cloudy layer of polyvinyl acetate is of little use for further testing.

As the last traces of acetone evaporate from the film, the extreme flexibility which distinguished it at the outset is reduced, but even when all the solvent has disappeared the film of absorbed polyvinyl acetate is sufficiently tough to enable the impregnated charred paper to stand normal handling. If the charred sheets are required in the flat state but free of the binder, they should be rested on sheets of glass in a shallow tray. If a slow current of acetone is allowed to flow over them, the sheets will become limp as the binder softens and finally dissolves in the acetone. The acetone is run off and replaced by fresh solvent to remove the last traces of binder. When the acetone has evaporated, the sheets of charred paper will be found to be firmly adherent to the glass, probably due to traces of binder adsorbed on the glass surface. If the charred sheets are desired free of the glass support, the glass should be treated with a silicone water repellent solution before use.

Charred documents may be preserved in a number of ways. The most satisfactory is to bind them between sheets of glass. Because of the fragility of glass, sheets of transparent plastic, such as perspex, would be more suitable but very much more expensive.

Deciphering Charred Documents

In the author's experience the most satisfactory, and in many instances the only, method of deciphering a charred document is to flatten it as described above and then to adjust the lighting so that the residue of any writing or printing thereon is rendered visible because the reflecting power of the surface is modified. If this simple procedure fails to reveal anything, there is little prospect of decipherment being accomplished by any of the chemical or other treatments which have been advocated.

If, without stabilisation, a charred document can be flattened against the emulsion surface of a photographic plate, the emanations from the charred paper and ink will slowly fog the plate, with some difference in the extent of the fogging where the ink or printing ink residues are in contact with the emulsion. On development, there is a chance that the writing or printing can be distinguished against the background. The method is slow and by no means certain. Success has also been reported from methods which involve the impregnation of the charred sheet with fluorescent materials, such as certain oils, which may show a differential absorption at the site of any writing or printing, which will be revealed when the impregnated char is examined in ultra-violet light.

In the experience of the author, nothing is so time wasting and frustrating as the attempt to decipher charred documents. After the fires caused in air raids during the Second World War, masses of charred account books were submitted to him for decipherment; success was achieved in cases which at first sight appeared hopeless, but many hours were wasted on what appeared to be but slightly charred documents from which not a single word could be deciphered.

The Chemical Analysis of Ink

Many documents are sent to a laboratory for " the ink to be analysed " or for " the ink on the document to be compared with that in the fountain pen, also submitted." These demands are often made for no apparent reason, and with very little conception of the difficulties of the analysis; neither is it appreciated that, in all but the smallest minority of cases, the results of the analysis would be valueless in the investigation. The meanings which can be associated with the term " analysis of ink " may best be apprehended by considering a few examples.

If an analyst were presented with a number of fairly large bottles of different brands of black or blue-black writing-ink and asked to compare them by chemical analysis, he would be in a position to furnish a considerable amount of information. By simple tests applied to small quantities of ink from each bottle, he could divide the inks into four groups. The first and largest group would consist of aqueous solutions of dyestuffs, and the second of iron gallotannate ink; there would be a few bottles of ink based on carbon, and the fourth group would be represented by a few bottles of the recently introduced alkaline quick-drying ink. With little further trouble, the analyst could sub-divide the second group of iron gallotannate inks according to their iron content. Certain of these inks—the " record " inks—would be found to have about double the iron concentration of the others—the " writing " inks.

To carry the distinction still further, the analyst could determine the nature of the dyestuff present in each of the inks. For this he would require a drop or so of each of the inks, together with samples of all the dyes used in the manufacture of ink as reference material. The dyestuffs in the inks would be separated and compared with the reference specimens by paper chromatography. It would soon be discovered that even when the dyestuff and iron-containing inks had been further sub-divided according to the concentration of iron and the nature of the dyestuffs present, each sub-group would still contain a number of different brands of ink indistinguishable from each other on the tests which had hitherto been carried out.

If the analyst were pressed to carry the analysis further, so as to distinguish between the inks in each sub-group, he would explain that as ink making is an ancient art, the period of experimentation in the manufacture of ordinary writing ink is past, and that it has become so standardised that there is often little difference between the products of different firms. For example, an aqueous solution of a dyestuff marketed as a washable ink by one firm hardly differs from an aqueous solution of the same dyestuff sold by another, especially as both ink merchants will probably buy the dyestuff from the same manufacturing chemist. On accepting this further assignment, the analyst would require a fair amount of ink from each bottle, perhaps as much as a cupful, so that he could extract from each of the inks, for subsequent identification, the impurities introduced with the water and any traces of materials such as wetting agents which are sometimes added to ink. Working in this way, with ample ink at his disposal, there is little doubt that eventually the analyst would be able to distinguish every ink from the others, so that at this stage it could fairly be claimed that every brand of ink represented had been identified by chemical analysis.

The foregoing account has been given at some length to remove any misconception of what is implied by the chemical analysis of ink *in bulk* to distinguish it from other inks of similar composition.

The analysis of the ink on a document presents a far more difficult problem than than that posed by its analysis in bulk, for at the outset there is the almost insuperable difficulty of obtaining sufficient ink for analysis, without seriously defacing the document. There is no " cupful of liquid ink " at the disposal of the analyst for the extraction of trace materials; the analysis has to be conducted on a fragment of solid material which can hardly be seen by the naked eye.

It is hard to realise how little solid matter is needed to form an ink line. Ordinary writing ink in bulk contains just over two per cent. of total solids, so that about thirty-nine out of forty parts of the ink transferred to the paper by the pen evaporate as water vapour, to leave behind an extremely small residue of solid matter. It has been estimated that a single ounce of ink solids can be spread out to give about six miles of unblotted ink line. Where the line is hastily blotted, the same amount of ink is spread over sixty miles or so of ink line. With the passage of time, the solids in the line slowly decompose to give a residue of less than half the original weight.

Any ink analysis involves destruction; if the ink on a document is to be analysed, some of the ink line must be sacrificed and the document suffer mutilation. The extent of this mutilation may be gauged by the fact that even if the whole of an average stroke about a half an inch in length is removed, the analyst will be fortunate if he succeeds in obtaining as much as forty microgrammes of material on which to work. With this literally microscopic quantity of ink solids, he is usually able to determine the type of ink and the nature of any metals present; he may also be successful in identifying the dyestuffs, and these may include as many as three or four out of the dozen or more commonly used in the manufacture of ink.

Applying the foregoing to the problems encountered in the examination of a suspect document, it may be concluded, at the price of some denudation of the ink of some of the thicker lines of writing, that:

(a) if inks of different type are present, say iron gallotannate and dyestuff, the analyst will have no difficulty in showing that this is so by identifying the type of ink;

(b) if two inks of the same class, but which contain different dyestuffs, are present, it will probably be possible to show that different inks are present; added to this, it might also be possible to identify the dyestuffs if they are those commonly used in the manufacture of ink;

(c) if two brands of ink of the same type incorporating the same dyestuffs are present, although it might be possible to distinguish between them when in bulk, it will probably prove impossible to distinguish between them on the document. There is no opportunity for determining the nature and amounts of impurities in microgramme amounts of material.

The analysis of the ink on a document should never be contemplated until every endeavour has been made to solve the problem by physical methods which leave the document unharmed.

The ink on a document may have to be tested:

(1) to gauge the accuracy of a description of its preparation. This may state that the ink used was the same as that on another document, or that the testator and witnesses signed with the same pen, etc., whilst there may be good reason to doubt the accuracy of the account;

(2) to give a limit of age to the writing. For example, a document drawn up with an alkaline ink containing vanadium is unlikely to be of any great age because this is a comparatively new ink;

(3) where subsequent additions are suspected, and it is thought that a different ink might have been used. It may happen that it can be shown that the suspect writings were made in an ink of the same class using different dyestuffs, or better still, in an ink of a different class which appeared identical because the same dyestuff was used in both.

The tests for ink on a document may be grouped under three headings:

(1) Physical tests such as the comparison of colour in light of different wavelengths which range from the ultra-violet to the infra-red, supplemented by photography through filters.

(2) Chemical tests for metals such as iron, copper, vanadium, chromium, etc., carried out on tiny fragments of the ink removed from the centres of the denser ink lines.

(3) Chromatographic analysis of the colouring matter of the ink. This may serve to show that different dyestuffs are present, and sometimes to identify the actual dyestuffs present. In the past, this was attempted by reacting extracts from the ink line with acids, oxidising and reducing agents, a procedure which could not be counted on to give conclusive results. Nowadays, the extracts are either examined with the spectrophotometer or are spotted on to strips of filter paper so as to separate their constituents, either by the action of an applied electric potential (electrophoretic analysis) or of a travelling solvent-front (chromatographic analysis). With these modern methods of analysis, separation of the coloured constituents of the inks facilitates their recognition.

No scheme for the differentiation of the inks in use at the time of writing is likely to be of indefinite application. When Mitchell published the third edition of his standard work, *Inks, Their Composition and Manufacture,* in 1924, research on the production of writing inks had been proceeding for over half a century. Many liquids had been tried as writing inks, but practically all had been discarded in favour of the iron gallotannate ink (Blue-black) and the dyestuff inks, which had then been in extended use for over seventy-five and fifty years respectively. The advent of a class of inks whose quick-drying properties are primarily due to their strongly alkaline character could never have been suspected by anyone writing at that time.

Again, it was held, and is still repeated, that all writing inks except those containing free carbon could speedily be bleached by the action of powerful oxidising agents such as permanganates and hypochlorites. At that time, however, copper and other metallic derivatives of stable organic compounds such as the phthalocyanines, which today are " tailor made " for incorporation into alkaline inks, by modification of the molecule, were not in existence. It is impossible to bleach inks containing these compounds by any treatment which does not destroy the paper.

The introduction of new colouring matters and the continued progress in the formulation of writing inks for special purposes forbid the blind application of any scheme for the identification and analysis of inks in the form given in any work of reference. The scheme should be modified and brought into line with contemporary practice, taking into account both the nature of the inks which may be encountered, and the methods of analysis.

Determination of the Type of Ink

In any standard book on ink there will be found a fairly long list of the different types of ink which have been invented, together with a number of " spot tests " for distinguishing between them. Most of these inks are now obsolete and are of interest only to the palaeographer. As this is so, there is no point in repeating this detailed information here, for it may be found in the standard works by Mitchell referred to in the bibliography at the end of this chapter.

At the present time, the only types of ink likely to be found on any but fairly old documents are, in order of popularity: (1) the dyestuff inks, (2) the iron gallotannate inks, and (3) the alkaline inks. In view of this, the tests to be described will be limited to these three types of ink.

Many writers advocate the careful addition of a drop of the appropriate reagent to the ink line on the document, followed by its removal with blotting-paper once the reaction has been noted. No matter how skilfully this addition and removal is carried out, the complete elimination of the reagents from the paper can never be guaranteed and even when no apparent damage has been done at the time, there is every prospect of the residual chemicals exerting a slow, but none the less steady, deleterious effect upon the paper. It is best to accept the fact that something will have to be sacrificed, and then ensure that the damage is limited to what is apparent at the time of examination.

A little of the dried ink can be removed on to a microscope slide for further examination, by scraping the centre of an ink line with the point of a scalpel. Alternatively, a tiny circle can be punched from the centre of a heavy ink line and the tiny paper disc manipulated on to a slide for the application of reagents, without any further risk of mutilating the document. The simplest method for punching the disc is to place the document on a thick piece of rubber into which the disc is pressed by piercing the centre of the selected line with a needle which has had its point ground off at right angles to its length. The removal of the disc will leave a tiny hole which is imperceptible, except when the document is viewed by transmitted light. Nothing will have been done to reduce the life of the document, the legibility of the writing or the characteristics of the handwriting.

When it is required to extract soluble material from the ink line by the action of distilled water or dilute acid, a loop of platinum wire, a hypodermic needle or, best of all, a fine glass capillary attached to a rubber teat, may be used for the transference. If a glass capillary is used, it should first be treated with a silicone water-repellent liquid, so that all the liquid which is extracted from the ink line can subsequently be removed from the capillary.

Reagents for the Determination of the Type of Ink

Many reagents have been suggested for testing contemporary blue or blue-black writing inks, but the following five solutions should suffice:

(1) a saturated aqueous solution of bromine;
(2) a saturated aqueous solution of bleaching powder;
(3) a 2-normal aqueous solution of sodium hydroxide;
(4) a 10% aqueous solution of stannous chloride;
(5) a 5% aqueous solution of potassium permanganate, whose action is followed by the application of a 10% aqueous solution of sodium sulphite which has been saturated with sulphur dioxide. A saturated aqueous solution of potassium metabisulphite may be used, if this latter solution cannot conveniently be prepared. These two solutions are extensively used in some countries as a chemical ink eradicator.

In a series of experiments carried out by the author, these reagents were tested on writing made with a representative selection of popular blue or blue-black writing inks; a carbon ink similar to Post Office cancelling ink, and the recently introduced alkaline ink "Superchrome Jade Green" were also included in the tests. Before use, all the inks were analysed with the spectrograph to determine what metallic elements were present. Common writing paper was used, although the type of paper was found to have little or no effect on the results of the tests; the writing was allowed to dry without the application of blotting-paper, and the sheets were stored in a warm room for some days before being tested.

The description of what was observed when the reagents were applied is deliberately given in general terms, because any mention of exact time-intervals is certain to be misleading. For example, a faint line might bleach very rapidly upon the application of a reagent, whereas another line on the same paper made with the same ink, heavily written, and allowed to harden in a warm dry atmosphere, would be certain to bleach more slowly, for more pigment would have to be destroyed before the underlying paper became visible through the residues from the bleached dyestuffs. In addition, a hard dry material reacts more slowly than one which can easily be penetrated by the reagent.

The Nature of the Inks Selected for Testing

Superchrome Blue-black. This is a quick-drying alkaline ink in which the sodium hydroxide reacts with ammonium vanadate to give an ammoniacal smell when in bulk. The ink owes its colour to the presence of a dark blue dye which has many of the properties of a direct-cotton dye. This dye has a strong affinity for cellulose which is assisted by the alkali present.

Spectrographic analysis showed the presence of vanadium, sodium and calcium together with traces of aluminium, magnesium, lead, strontium and silicon. Many of these trace elements owe their inclusion to their occurrence as impurities in the materials from which the ink is made; some may have been extracted from the container by the action of the strong alkali.

Superchrome Turquoise Blue. This is another quick-drying alkaline ink which owes its brilliant colour to the presence of a copper phthalocyanine derivative.

Spectrographic analysis showed the presence of copper, sodium and calcium with traces of aluminium, magnesium and silicon.

Superchrome Jade Green. This is the third quick-drying alkaline ink available on the British market at the time of writing. The green colour is obtained by the addition of a yellow dyestuff, probably an azo dye, to the Turquoise Blue ink with which it is otherwise identical.

" Quink " Permanent Blue-black, Stephens Blue-black, Swan Blue-black, Swan Blue. These four inks are all of the iron gallotannate type. Spectrographic analysis showed that all contained iron, sodium and calcium with traces of aluminium, silicon, magnesium and copper.

" Quink " Royal Blue Washable. This is a dyestuff ink substantially free of iron or other heavy metal. Spectrographic analysis showed the presence of sodium and calcium with traces of barium, iron, aluminium, copper, strontium, magnesium and silicon.

Cancellation Ink. Essentially, this consisted of free carbon bound in a varnish medium. The blue toner was an organic dyestuff which tended to " bleed " from the line. Spectrographic analysis showed the presence of traces of sodium, calcium, magnesium, copper, barium, iron and aluminium.

Reaction of Popular Inks with Reagents

Ink	**Reagent A**	**B**	**C**	**D**	**E**
Superchrome Blue-Black	*1*	*6*	*11*	*10*	*5*
Superchrome Turquoise Blue	*2*	*7*	*11*	*14*	*17*
Superchrome Jade Green	*3*	*7*	*11*	*14*	*17*
Quink Royal Blue Washable	*4*	*8*	*12*	*15*	*10*
Quink Blue-Black	*5*	*9*	*13*	*16*	*10*
Stephens Blue-Black	*4*	*8*	*12*	*16*	*10*

Ink	Reagent A	B	C	D	E
Swan Blue	*4*	*10*	*12*	*15*	*10*
Swan Blue-Black	*4*	*9*	*12*	*15*	*10*
Cancellation Ink	*18*	*18*	*11*	*18*	*18*

Reagents

A saturated aqueous solution of Bromine
B saturated aqueous solution of Bleaching Powder
C 2-Normal aqueous solution of Sodium Hydroxide
D 10 per cent. aqueous solution of Stannous Chloride
E 5 per cent. aqueous solution of Potassium Permanganate followed by a solution of Sodium Bisulphite or Metabisulphite.

Reactions

1 Turns brown immediately and slowly goes yellow
2 Darkens slightly at first and then turns to slightly paler blue colour
3 Unaffected at first but later acquires a blue tint
4 Turns dark green and then bleaches to a pale yellow grey
5 Slowly bleaches
6 Turns brown and then bleaches
7 Unaffected at first and then bleaches to a pale green-blue
8 Turns yellow and then bleaches
9 Turns yellow-grey and then bleaches to pale yellow
10 Bleaches rapidly
11 No action at first, followed by slow bleeding of the colour
12 Instantaneous change to reddish-brown
13 A brownish tinge is superimposed on the black line
14 Slowly blackens
15 No immediate action except some bleeding of the colour
16 Bleeding of colour followed by partial bleaching
17 Very slow bleaching with very resistant vestiges of colour
18 No action.

Coloured Inks

With the exception of the alkaline quick-drying inks, coloured inks are generally simple aqueous solutions of synthetic dyestuffs. In the past, in the endeavour to identify the dyestuffs, a whole series of reactions, better suited to ink in bulk than to the traces which could be scraped from a document, had to be undertaken with the ink.

These tests are now obsolete; with the development of chromatographic analysis, it is far simpler and more effective to extract a little of the colouring matter from the ink line and then to " run " it with a suitable solvent or mixture of solvents along with specimens of dyestuffs known to be used for the manufacture of inks of that colour. If the ink contains more than a single dyestuff, a separation will be effected during the chromatographic analysis. To make a final comparison between the separated coloured constituents of the inks and those comparison dyestuffs which behaved in the same way, the spots on the filter paper can be extracted and the absorption spectrum over the range of 7,500 to 24,000 A. determined with the spectrophotometer.

Comparison of Inks

Inks which cannot be distinguished by the spot tests given above because they are of the same type may be compared by separating and then identifying the dyestuffs present, either by electrophoresis or by paper chromatography. If the inks produce chromatograms which are obviously different, then there need be no hesitation in concluding that they contain different dyestuffs and are consequently quite different. The difficulties arise when the chromatograms are either similar or show differences which are not great enough to be outside the range of variation which might be expected in this type of separation. In such cases, the dry chromatograms can be examined by ultra-violet light. This will sometimes reveal the presence of fluorescent constituents in one of the inks which are absent from the other.

If examination in ultra-violet light fails to reveal any significant differences, the next step should be to extract the various spots of colour from any chromatograms and to determine the absorption-spectrum of each in the spectrophotometer. Whilst such a determination may allow a definite distinction to be drawn, a suitable spectrophotometer, which is a very expensive instrument, may not be available. Where this is the case, an attempt should be made to obtain chromatograms which are less equivocal, by repeating the separation on fresh specimens of the inks using a different running fluid. Should all attempts by chromatography fail to reveal any significant differences in the inks, electrophoretic separation should be attempted. Should this fail, it may safely be assumed that the inks are similar, if not the same ink. It does not necessarily follow that they are the same brand, for neither chromatography nor electrophoresis applied to microgramme quantities of dried ink can be counted on to reveal the nature of the minor constituents.

Whenever possible, the colouring matter in an ink line should be removed by taking it up in tiny drops of distilled water, but dilute hydrochloric acid may have to be used with a well-matured iron gallotannate ink. If acid is used, any residue on the document should be neutralised with dilute ammonia.

Neither water nor dilute acid are likely to prove effective for removing ball-point inks, although dilute ammonia will remove some from paper. For ball-point inks based on olein, organic solvents such as petrol ether, methylene chloride and ethyl acetate are effective, but some of the modern inks are extremely difficult to remove in their entirety. Acetone, acetone-glycerol and acetone-acetic acid-water should be tried, but in many cases it will be found that the solvent, whilst removing some of the dyes, leaves others firmly bound to the paper. This difficulty experienced in the removal of the dyes is a serious obstacle to the analysis of ball-point inks. It is to be hoped that the development of the micro-spectrophotometer will, in the near future, enable the absorption spectrum of the ink to be determined without having to remove it from the document. The obstacles to this development are practical rather than theoretical, and work in this direction is already being prosecuted.

Chromatography

Reference has been made to application of chromatography to the micro-analysis of ink removed from a document. The theoretical background to this method of analysis is still obscure but its practice is deceptively simple.

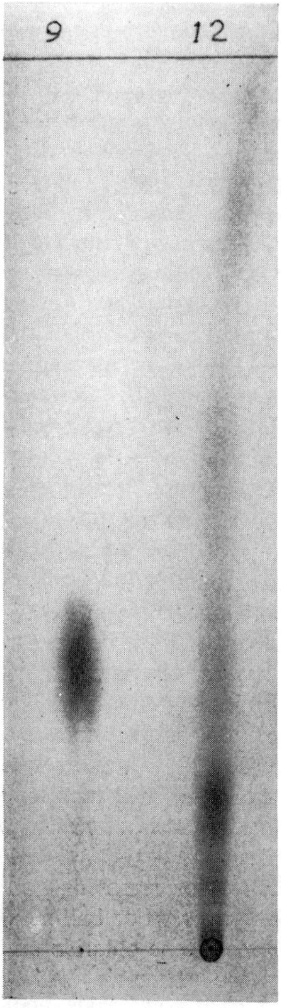

Fig. 5–7. A chromatogram of two inks which appeared identical to the naked eye. The constituents of ink No. 12 travelled with the solvent to give a long tailed trace showing the presence of two major and three minor constituents. No. 9 travelled a short distance to form a single spot indicating the presence of but one major constituent.

From the published descriptions it would appear that all that has to be done is to spot the various inks to be analysed and compared, side by side near one end of a strip of filter paper about a foot long. This filter paper is then hung inside an enclosure, so that the end near the spots of ink is bent over a support so that it dips into a vessel which contains the running fluid. This slowly diffuses up into and then down the strip of filter paper, carrying with it the various constituents of the inks which are spread out along the filter paper as a series of spots. (See Figure 4–4a.) The position of the spots enables the inks to be compared, and in some cases, the various constituents of the inks to be identified.

In practice, things are often quite different; no difficulty is experienced in spotting the inks or in setting up the apparatus, but instead of a well-defined series of spots, the chromatogram will probably consist of a number of vague streaks extending for some inches along the paper.

The failure of the procedure to effect a clean separation of the constituents of the ink may be due to the filter paper—that specially prepared for the purpose should be used—but it is more likely to be an unhappy choice of running fluid. Although the efficiency of any separation depends largely on the choice of a suitable running fluid, there is little theoretical guidance to be obtained in the present state of knowledge, and all that experience teaches is that the most effective fluids are those in which the materials to be separated are but slightly soluble. Apart from the meagre amount of assistance given by this general rule, running fluids have to be chosen by trial and error. Research on suitable running fluids for the analysis of inks has shown that a fair degree of success may be obtained by the use of butinol-ammonia and phenol-water solutions.

In spite of the apparent simplicity of the procedure, textbooks dealing with chromatographic analysis in general, and the research papers on the application of chromatography to the analysis, should be consulted before any experimental work is begun. Before any attempt is made to analyse case material, proficiency should be obtained with material removed from unimportant documents; it will probably be found that the efficiency of the separations which are obtained will show considerable improvement with practice.

It should not be forgotten that blank tests are as important in chromatographic analysis as in analysis conducted by classical methods. Many papers are dyed to improve their appearance; there is always a possibility that dyes and optical bleaches which are present in the paper will be removed with the ink, and form part of the chromatogram. In view of this, an aqueous extract from the paper itself should be run alongside the extract from the ink line, to show which features of the ink chromatogram are derived from the paper.

Circular Papers

Effective chromatograms of ink may be prepared more conveniently on circular filter papers than on the long strips already described. The apparatus, which can be improvised very easily, is described in Chapter 4 which deals with the equipment of a document laboratory. (See Figure 4–4b.)

The solutions of the inks to be analysed are spotted along the circumference of a small circle at the centre of the filter paper. Through the centre projects a paper thimble into which is poured the running fluid; the filter paper is gripped along its circumference between two pie dishes, while the fluid, streaming from the centre to the edge of the paper, carries with it those components of the ink which are less strongly absorbed by the filter paper. The spots broaden into short bands as they approach the circumference of the paper. A run with the long filter paper strips usually takes several hours for a good separation to be effected, but the apparatus needs little attention once it has been set up. With the circular filter paper, the separation is generally more speedy.

The chromatograms themselves may be

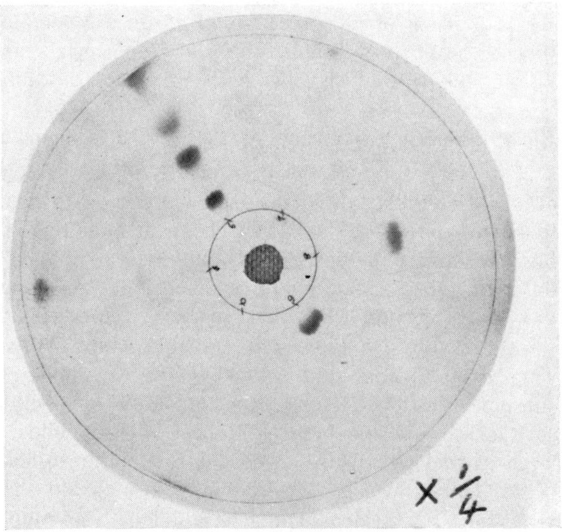

Fig. 5–8. This is a reduced photograph of a circular chromatogram. " 5 " is a red ink which has been resolved into four separate components. The scarlet spot nearest the centre is in the same position as the spot from dyestuff No. 9, Naphthalene Ink Scarlet 4R125. The next brick-red spot corresponds with the spot of the same colour No. 8—Croceine Scarlet 3BS. The third diffuse yellow spot is an unidentified component of the ink. The diffuse bright red spot nearest the circumference corresponds with No. 4, Eosine. This chromatogram enabled three of the four dyestuffs present in the ink to be identified in a single run. The unidentified yellow spot is probably an impurity in one of the dyestuffs used in the ink.

presented as evidence. If this is contemplated, they should be soaked in molten paraffin wax to exclude dust and moisture. If coloured inks have been separated, they should be preserved between cardboard sheets to exclude light.

Aged Ink

As an ink ages, the dyestuffs therein slowly decompose, until nothing but a crust of ferric oxide remains. At this stage, the chromatogram of anything which can be extracted from the ink line will bear little resemblance to that derived from the original ink. It might appear, therefore, that the age of an ink writing might be determined from the appearance of the chromatogram, but experiments have shown that, as long as the ink has not decomposed, the chromatogram is not appreciably affected.

There is a possibility that further work will result in a useful separation of the ferrous and ferric iron present, in which case chromatography might be used to compare fairly recently written entries on the same document. It would be a fair assumption that the writing showing the greater proportion of ferrous iron was the more recently applied. It is to be feared that any method which depends on the iron in the ink will have an increasingly limited application in the future, for the proportion of iron-free writing ink in use is certain to increase. It may well be that in the not too distant future, with the improvement in stability of dyestuffs, all writing ink will consist merely of an aqueous solution of a stable dyestuff.

Electrophoretic Separation of the Constituents of Inks

The separation of the constituents of ink by chromatography depends mainly on slight solubility differences and different partition ratios. When the compounds to be separated are similar in chemical, and possibly physical, properties, a satisfactory separation may not be achieved no matter how the changes are rung on different solvents and mixtures of solvents as running fluids. Different principles may have to be applied to achieve a satisfactory separation.

Many substances give rise to electrically charged particles when dissolved in water or in aqueous solutions of dilute acids or alkalis. Aqueous solutions of simple substances such as ferrous sulphate contain relatively simple charged particles known as " ions," whereas more complicated compounds, such as dyestuffs, form much larger particles known as " micelles " which owe their electric charge to the presence of simpler ions which have become associated with them.

When an electric potential is applied to a solution containing ions or micelles, these electrically charged particles will migrate under the influence of the field, in accordance with the rule that positively charged particles will move towards the negative electrode and vice versa. The speed of movement and consequently the distance travelled in a given time, will depend on a number of factors; the potential gradient, the size and charge on the particles, and the viscosity of the solution being the more important. From this it follows that if the electric potential is applied for any length of time, the differential movement of the charged particles will tend to separate them. In bulk solution, this tendency towards separation is opposed by factors such as convection and diffusion which tend to equalise concentrations throughout the solution. To achieve a useful separation, measures must be taken to minimise all those factors which tend to equalise concentrations.

The most simple and effective means is to absorb the solution on filter paper when convection currents can be eliminated and diffusion reduced. As diffusion cannot entirely be eliminated, a relatively high potential must be used so as to increase the speed of the particles, but any increase cannot be carried to extremes because the higher the potential, the greater the heating effect of the current. In practice, potentials of the order of a few hundreds of volts are used; as the experiment is carried out in a matter of minutes, diffusion effects are minimised.

The apparatus which must be used for the electrophoretic separation of the constituents of ink is described in Chapter 5. The ink is removed from the line, and spotted on to the centre of the strip of filter paper in exactly the same way as for the chromatographic separation, but where distilled water has been used for extraction the ink extract should be slightly acidified to ensure that its constituents are given every opportunity to become charged either through direct ionisation or through absorption of ions from the acid to form micelles. It is fortunate that the electrophoretic separation of the constituents of ink does not depend on a nice adjustment of the acidity, which is the case with many other materials to which the method is applied. The current is carried through a buffer solution in which the paper is soaked. The ends of the paper dip into troughs of the same buffer solution, which communicate by means of strips of moistened filter paper with similar troughs of buffer solution in which the electrodes are placed. (See Fig. 5–5 for a sketch of the apparatus.) Good results may be achieved by the use of practically any of the buffer solutions described in the literature.

To effect a good separation, attention must be given to a number of practical details. After the ink has been spotted on to the centre of the paper strip, the ends are soaked in buffer solution so that the paper is wetted almost up to the ink spot. At the last moment, when everything has been made ready, the buffer solution is brought right up to the ink spot by careful use of a small brush. To prevent any gravitational flow of the buffer solution along the filter paper strip, the levels of the solution in all four troughs should be adjusted by momentarily connecting the troughs either by a submerged tube or by an inverted U-tube filled with solution. Once the liquids have been levelled, the connecting tube is either closed with a tap or removed. As the separation is fairly speedy, its progress can be watched and the action stopped when sufficient separation has been effected. The filter paper strip should be dried and examined as though it were a chromatogram.

When a number of inks have to be compared, they should be spotted side by side on the same strip of paper, so that they can be subjected to the same conditions. As with chromatograms, specimens of dyestuffs can be spotted alongside the inks; if different separation patterns are exhibited by the inks, it is a fair assumption that they are different in composition.

Electrophoresis supplements rather than supplants chromatography in the analysis of traces of ink; whilst both procedures are essentially simple, considerable practice is needed before consistent and useful separations can be obtained with the traces of ink which can be spared from the average document.

Fingerprints on Documents

Whilst fingerprints on polished surfaces may often be detected without prior treatment, it is rare for a fingerprint on any but the glossiest of paper to be visible before development. Latent—the term applied to the fingerprint before development—fingerprints are formed by the absorption into the paper of the perspiration and oily matter secreted by the sweat pores in the skin, together with any grease or dirt derived from the finger-tips.

The methods which have been suggested for the development of fingerprints on paper fall into three groups. These are methods based on:

(1) the alteration in the surface of the paper caused by the absorption of the perspiration, etc., from the finger-tips;
(2) the detection of the chlorides or amino-acid-like substances in the absorbed perspiration;
(3) the reactions of the fatty matter in absorbed perspiration.

The classical methods for the development of fingerprints are included in the first group. The paper is treated with coloured solids, liquids or vapours, in the hope that along the pattern made by the secretions there will occur a differential fixation or absorption of coloured material, which will result in the print being outlined in sufficient detail to allow of its being identified. Trials have been made with innumerable powders, and it is probable that any highly coloured powder which is both finely powdered and amorphous would prove effective, as its only function is to adhere more strongly to the slightly sticky print than to the remainder of the paper.

Finely powdered graphite is in general use for developing prints on light coloured surfaces and there is no reason why it should not prove effective for fresh prints on documents. The powder should be dusted on, and the surplus lightly swept off with a soft brush so that the graphite adhering to the print is not dislodged. Once the fingerprint has been photographed, the graphite can be removed by dabbing with plasticene. On a paper with a non-absorbent surface, a print may be developed in this way after a lapse of some weeks, but with ordinary paper, the sticky layer which causes the powder to adhere is rapidly absorbed into the paper.

Because of the inevitable lapse of time between the insertion of an anonymous letter into its envelope and its treatment for fingerprints, the powder method is rarely worth a trial, especially in view of the greatly superior methods of detection which rely on other principles. The presence of a fingerprint not only makes the surface of the paper slightly sticky but also alters its absorptive powers for certain liquids and vapours.

The document may be fumed with iodine vapour by holding it over a dish in which a few lumps of iodine are heated. The method is very sensitive, and will often reveal the presence of prints when dusting with powder has yielded no positive results. The fingerprints develop rapidly but the colour is unsatisfactory for photography. Unless treated, the prints fade very rapidly. They may be rendered more permanent by being sprayed with a suspension of starch containing a little dissolved potassium iodide to convert them into the blue iodine-starch complex known as starch iodide. Mitchell has suggested the use of mercuric iodide vapour, which, although less sensitive than iodine, yields prints which are more stable. The mercuric iodide vapour is obtained by heating together a mixture of five parts of iodine and four of mercury. The prints are red when first formed, but soon change to the yellow of the alternative form of mercuric iodide.

Fingerprints may often be detected by application of the iodine-potassium iodide-metallic chloride staining solution previously referred to. This solution is a sensitive reagent but has little else to recommend it. The fingerprints developed are quickly merged in the general staining which attends the use of this reagent.

Reactions with the Chloride of the Latent Print

Perspiration contains an appreciable amount of chloride which cannot evaporate, and which is unlikely to diffuse very far from where it was deposited on the paper, so that the effective life of a latent fingerprint, developed by virtue of its chloride content, is probably all that can be desired. The main disadvantage of the method is that the chloride is rendered visible by treatment with a dilute aqueous solution of silver nitrate, which reacts to form white silver chloride, whose position in the paper is revealed by exposing the document to highly actinic light, which will blacken the chloride more readily than the excess nitrate.

Silver nitrate is a reagent which should be applied to an important document with extreme reluctance, for it can be counted on to produce a general staining which is difficult to prevent and impossible to remove. Again, it is not every paper which is sufficiently free from chloride derived from the water used in its manufacture to allow the method to be applied without causing general staining.

Reactions with the Fatty Matter of the Latent Print

A greasy surface will repel aqueous solutions, and this is the basis of the iron-tannin and osmium gallotannate ink-brushing methods referred to by Mitchell. The prints are outlined by their reluctance to absorb the coloured solutions. These treatments are as inapplicable to important documents as that with silver nitrate.

Far less objectionable is the development of the latent print with osmium tetroxide vapour, which reacts with the fatty matter present to give a dark deposit of osmium metal which forms a permanent print. Unfortunately, the method lacks sensitivity, and an impression has to have more than the usual proportion of fatty matter present before it yields an identifiable print.

Reactions with the Amino-acids of the Latent Print

When heated with microgramme quantities of amino-acids, "ninhydrin" (1, 2, 3, indantrione hydrate) reacts to form what is generally described in the literature as a blue colour, but which appears to the author to be more of a reddish-purple. This forms the basis of what is by far the best method for the development of latent fingerprints on paper. The print is developed by the application to the document of a freshly prepared 0·3 per cent. solution of ninhydrin in acetone. There has been some controversy as to whether it is better to brush or to spray this solution on to the document, but in the author's laboratory, the use of a fine spray has been found to give better results. Once the document has been evenly coated with the reagent, it is heated for twenty minutes in an air oven maintained at 80°C. At the end of this period, any fingerprints will be revealed as faint purple-red outlines which photograph well, especially if a green filter is used to enhance the contrast.

Once the document has been sprayed, it is in a very sensitive condition, for if handled with the bare fingers, the fingerprints of the operator will slowly develop without any further heating.

Provided the document contains no written matter which is affected by acetone, the excess ninhydrin can be removed by several washes with acetone once the prints have been developed. The acetone is without action on the reddish-purple colour of the developed prints but care should be taken before acetone is applied to a document bearing ball-point pen writing.

A spray of good quality, preferably made of glass, should be used, and the spraying carried out in a good fume cupboard. Ninhydrin is poisonous, so that the acetone solution should not be allowed to remain on the hands if by any chance they have become wetted with it.

Whenever it is proposed to treat a document with any vapour or liquid, two things should be borne in mind:

(1) that any new procedure may have been tested and found to be harmless on but a limited range of papers and inks; and

(2) that new materials are constantly being pressed into service for the manufacture of paper and other writing materials, so that even a procedure which has been in use for many years may cause serious staining when applied to a paper in which some new material such as an optical bleach or surface treatment has been incorporated.

The ninhydrin process for developing fingerprints is a case in point. The ninhydrin solution may be applied with impunity to the bulk of papers encountered because the sizing material employed is devoid of protein breakdown products. Ninhydrin will form coloured compounds with amino-acids derived from any source, so that any paper sized with protein or related material will be stained wherever the solution is applied. Some of the highest quality papers are sized with gelatine, so that before the ninhydrin spray is applied, a test should be made on an inconspicuous portion of the surface with a tiny drop of the reagent. If no stain appears on warming, it will be safe to apply the reagent, provided again that the acetone used as a solvent has no effect on any written or printed matter on which a separate test should be made.

What has been said about the risks of treatment with ninhydrin applies with equal force to other reagents intended for general application to a document. A test on a small scale should invariably be carried out, for it is easier to avoid damaging a document than to attempt to put matters right after the damage has been done.

The search for fingerprints on anonymous letters is almost invariably fruitless, and it is only in recent years, since the introduction of the ninhydrin process, that identifiable prints have been developed on such documents. If a print is deliberately made by pressing the finger firmly on to a sheet of paper, it will probably be developed by any one of the methods outlined above, but it is possible for a document to be handled by someone whose finger-tips are clean and dry—especially when the paper is soft and absorbent—without acquiring a single fingerprint which is recognisable after the lapse of a few hours.

Fingerprints in Dust

Fingerprints are sometimes found on a document outlined in dust. If the colour of the dust contrasts with that of the paper, and the prints are on an area devoid of any writing or printing, it is preferable to photograph them *in situ* without further treatment, for any brushing, fuming or spraying is almost certain to spoil the outlines. If, for any reason, it is impracticable to photograph the print as it stands, it should be removed from the document by some procedure which can be counted on to preserve its outlines unchanged. Lifting with the special foil which has been devised for the purpose can be attempted, but in its absence, a process devised by the author many years ago will prove simple and effective.

The transfer material is prepared by " fixing " a sheet of unexposed bromide paper in a solution of sodium thiosulphate (not acid hypo) and then washing thoroughly to remove all traces of silver salts and residual hypo. The gelatine surface of the paper is softened and made absorptive by being soaked for a minute or so in water made alkaline with either a little ammonia or borax. After removal from this solution, the sheet is drained and all excess liquid removed with fluffless blotting-paper. Before it can become dry, the gelatine surface is pressed into contact with the print, care being taken to prevent slipping. On lifting the paper, the fingerprint will be seen to be firmly adherent to the gelatine layer, which can then be hardened by drying.

If the dust is dark, the paper is used as it comes from the alkaline bath, but where it is of a colour which contrasts badly with white paper, the gelatine layer can be dyed after the removal of the silver salts, to provide a more suitable background to the print. If a black background is required, this can be provided by exposing the paper to light and developing before fixing.

As with all transfer processes, there will be a lateral inversion of the prints which must be taken into account when comparisons are made with prints taken in the conventional manner.

Examination of the Paper

Fibre Identification

To identify the fibres of which a paper is composed, it is of little avail merely to peer at its surface through a microscope, no matter how high the magnification. On the rare occasions when such an investigation has to be conducted, it is necessary to sacrifice a fragment of the paper. This is then boiled with sodium hydroxide solution which will attack the sizing and allow the fibres to be separated. With some types of paper this digestion with alkali is ineffective, in which case disintegration may be brought about by boiling with moderately concentrated acid.

When disintegration is complete, the pulp is washed free of the digestion liquor and a bunch of the fibres is spread out on a microscope slide and covered with a cover slip. The structure of the fibres is examined under fairly high power. To an experienced worker, this is usually all that is necessary, but, on occasion, the fibres will be found to have been so extensively disintegrated during the manufacture of the paper that they cannot be identified from what structure remains. When this is so, the identification can be facilitated by the application of one of the staining reagents which have been developed for this purpose. These staining reagents, the majority of which consist largely of solutions of zinc chloride and iodine, give characteristic colour effects with the different fibres, but considerable experience is needed before any colours which are observed can be interpreted with any confidence. The presence of mechanical wood-pulp in a paper can be easily demonstrated by the development of colours when certain chemical solutions are applied to the paper itself.

The identification of the fibres which constitute the furnish of a paper is more than adequately treated in the standard works on paper technology; for this reason, no details of the microscopic appearance of the principal paper-making fibres, stains or staining techniques are given here.

It must be emphasised that fibre identification is by no means simple and straightforward, and that no one can expect to determine the furnish of a paper by comparing what he sees with a microscope with pictures in a book, no matter how lavishly it may be illustrated. To acquire skill in this work, papers of known furnish must be acquired and examined as described in the textbooks until the appearance of the more important fibres and their behaviour with staining solutions are familiar to the investigator. It is only then that the examination of papers of unknown furnish should be embarked upon. Whilst, in the past, fibres were derived from comparatively few sources, today the net of the paper-maker is widely cast to discover new cellulosic materials from which paper may be made. As this is so, the discovery of exotic fibres may provide evidence of both the place of manufacture and the maximum age the paper is likely to have.

Rags still form a fair proportion of the raw material, and it may happen that some of the newer synthetic fibres may find their way into paper from this source. Rayon fibres fail to survive the beating process as recognisable entities, and are unlikely to be recognised as such in a paper. However, some of the more recently introduced fibres are far more resistant to disintegration, and the possibility exists that these may be found in a paper under investigation, in which case the dating value of such a discovery would be considerable. Any such discovery would almost certainly be accidental, because the search through a mass of ordinary paper-making fibres would be time-consuming and it would be difficult to identify such exotic fibres when isolated. The most one could hope for would be the discovery of a very sensitive staining test for the presence of new polymers, which could be applied to the paper as a whole, when the fibres could be identified by their colour *in situ*.

Analysis of Paper Ash

The analysis of paper ash is necessary when the excuse of " accidental burning " has been advanced for the disappearance of sums of money. Very few people have ever seen bank-note ash and noted how fine and silky it is. In the author's experience, on every occasion, a heap of crude heavy ash has been produced as all that remains of a bundle of bank-notes " accidentally set on fire." By analysis of the ash it is often possible to identify the burned material with other paper at the scene.

The modern practice of inserting a metal filament in the paper on which British Treasury notes are printed has made this type of fraud less attractive, but one can always look forward to meeting the enterprising operator who will add his own specially prepared metal filaments to the pile of ash, to " give an air of fact and verisimilitude to what would otherwise be a bald and uninteresting narrative."

Where only small quantities of ash are available, microchemical methods may not be sufficiently sensitive to demonstrate whether two specimens of ash are identical or not. The ash may be spectrographed to identify the metals present, but the most satisfactory procedure is to prepare an X-ray " powder photograph." The procedure is simple, although the apparatus is expensive. A few milligrammes of the ash are powdered and rotated in the path of a collimated beam of X-rays which is substantially monochromatic. The X-rays are scattered in their passage

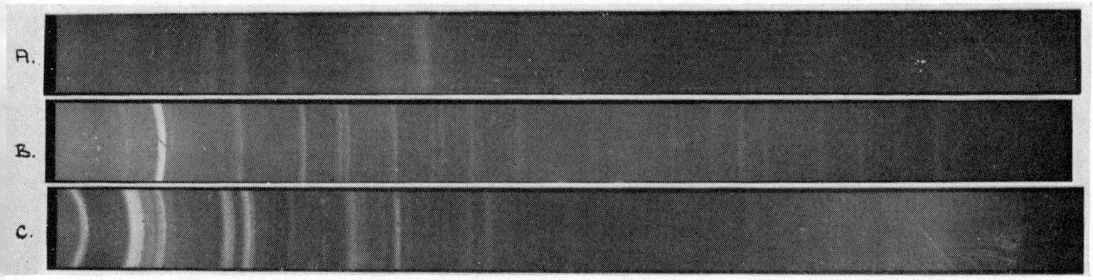

Fig. 5–9. A, B and C are three prints produced from negatives made in an X-ray diffraction powder camera. A is of the ash derived from Treasury notes, B of the ash from a paper loaded with Titanium Dioxide and C from Kaolin—a common loading material. Only the stronger lines are reproduced in the prints; the original negatives exhibit a large number of fine lines which it has not proved possible to reproduce. Even so, there is no possibility of confusing the different spectra.

through the ash, and the diffracted beams are received on a strip of photographic film which is placed around the ash so as to intercept the scattered radiation.

On the photographic film will appear a series of lines whose relative spacings are proportional to the spacings of the atoms of the compounds in the ash. From the relative spacings and the intensities of the lines it is possible to identify the compounds which are present. Specimens of ash of similar papers will give identical X-ray spectra.

The presence of appreciable proportions of copper in the ash would probably point to the paper having been tinted by one of the phthalocyanine derivatives of copper; this would indicate that the paper was of comparatively recent manufacture.

Analysis of Sizing Materials

To analyse the sizing, enough has to be stripped from the paper to allow identification by microchemical techniques. The analysis is comparatively simple, but some of the paper has to be destroyed.

Analysis of the size need be undertaken only when an abraded patch at the site of an erasure has been re-sized to enable it to take ink without showing a feathered edge to the new writing, or when it is thought that a treatment with synthetic resin, with some significance for dating, has been applied to the paper.

The Measurement of Colour

In the course of an investigation into the age of an iron gallotannate ink writing, which, as described in Chapter 7, undergoes a series of colour changes as it ages, colour measurements may have to be made.

As a general rule, the only evidence which is likely to have any real bearing on the problem is the proof that rapid colour changes are taking place in writing which is alleged to be of some considerable age. The best demonstration of this would be the production of a series of dated colour photographs which could be compared with each other, but at the time of writing, no colour process has been developed to the stage where accurate and consistent reproduction of dark blue tones can be looked for, so other means of recording the colour of the ink must be sought.

The colour of an object is determined by the spectral distribution of the light which is reflected from it. This depends on two factors; the first is the nature of the light which is incident upon it, and the second is the reflecting and absorbing properties of its surface. The spectral reflectivity of a surface is a measure of the fraction of incident light which is reflected from it for each band of wave-lengths as the visible spectrum is traversed from deep violet to dark red. Except for white or neutral grey objects, this fraction will change as the wave-length of the incident light alters. For example, with a red object, the fraction of the longer wave-lengths reflected will be greater than for light at the other end of the spectrum.

Where colour is concerned, the eye is easily deceived, for objects of widely differing spectral reflectivities may appear to be of the same colour in white light. The matching would be less close if the colour of the incident light were changed, for then the objects would no longer give " reflectivity pictures " which would have the same effect on the eye. This is why filters sometimes enable a discrimination to be made between objects which appear of the same colour to the unaided eye.

Although the spectral distribution of the light reflected from an object determines its colour, it has been shown that there is no need to embark on this rather tedious determination in order to make a record of its colour, for any colour can be matched in terms of three specified colour stimuli.

With the subtractive " Lovibond " colour measuring system, the colour to be measured is matched by building up a series of coloured glass slips in front of a " standard white " object, usually a block of magnesium carbonate. Where the colour of a small object such as an ink line has to be recorded, the simplest method is to bring an image of both line and " standard white " into the eyepiece of a comparison microscope. In the apparatus used by the author, the slips of coloured glass are fixed in sliding racks in increasing depth of colour to facilitate matching. (See Figure 4–8 of Chapter 4.)

For reproducible results, both ink line and standard white must be lit by light which approximates closely to what is termed " North Daylight." This may be attained by working at a window which faces north, or more simply and reliably by the use of a suitably tinted electric lamp.

The three primary colours are used for the glass slips, so that the colour of an ink line can be expressed in terms of a value for each component colour. As an ink line darkens, this will be reflected in a rise in the value of the red component.

Secret Writing

The problem posed by secret writing is not that it cannot be deciphered by a thorough and systematic investigation, but that its presence may be unsuspected. It is for this reason that the preliminary examination of any suspect document as outlined in Chapter 3 should never be neglected.

Over the centuries, many methods of increasing complexity have been devised for secret writing. These have ranged from the simple trick of moistening the paper before covering it with a sheet of waterproof material and writing the message with a metal stylus to compress the fibres, the use of vegetable juice or a convenient body fluid such as saliva as the " ink," to elaborate photographic techniques which impress a latent photographic image on the paper. With the rise in international tension, considerable effort has gone into the search for secret inks which are easily portable and usable with conventional writing equipment, and yet are simple to develop when required. It is certain that an equal effort has been put into the search for methods which would enable secret writing to be detected and deciphered, preferably without leaving any indication that this had been accomplished.

Many accounts have been given of the use and detection of secret inks, but it is very unlikely that any procedure which has been described in print is still in serious use in espionage, since it would be against public policy to reveal current methods of detection. However, it has been considered desirable to deal very briefly with the general run of secret inks and methods of detection, because criminals may become acquainted with some of the better publicised methods for secret writing and be tempted to put them to use.

Practically any colourless fluid which does not evaporate too readily may be used as a secret ink if there is no objection to the writing having a comparatively short life. The extreme example of this is distilled water; a writing in distilled water will affect the cellulose fibres and also the sizing which become wetted by it, so that even when the water has apparently dried off, those portions of the paper surface which have been wetted will differ from the remainder in the rate at which they will absorb iodine or other coloured substance from solution. If any non-volatile substance were dissolved in the water, this would have a more permanent effect on the power of the affected portions of the surface to absorb coloured material.

As a general rule, it may be assumed that, in the absence of any treatment designed to protect the surface of the paper from the action of such reagents, *any* secret writing can be developed by the application of the iodine-potassium iodide-metallic chloride stain previously referred to.[2] Instead of this very unpleasant solution, it is possible to use a dilute solution of a dye in either water or alcohol to give a more permanent development which does not disappear as the staining becomes

[2] See p. 104 for details of the preparation of this reagent.

general. It is no secret that by an appropriate treatment, the surface of the document can be " protected " against development by either iodine or dye solutions, but the methods which have been published, sponging with ammonia solution and the like, are of doubtful efficacy. No good purpose would be served by giving any details of methods which are really effective.

The simplest secret ink, a dilute aqueous solution of cobalt nitrate, dries on the paper as a very pale pink outline which is imperceptible if the paper is carefully chosen. On gentle heating, the pink hydrate loses water to form the intensely blue anhydrous salt and so the writing becomes visible. On damping the paper or simply by leaving it in a damp atmosphere, the pink hydrate is re-formed and the writing disappears. Reference is made to this children's plaything because attempts have been made to utilise this reaction as an alternative to the starch-iodide blue as the basis of a swindle based on a " disappearing ink."

The secret inks most favoured by criminals are the body fluids such as saliva, urine, and milk or vegetable juices from the lemon or onion. With the exception of saliva, all these char at temperatures too low to darken paper, a reaction which enables them to be developed. In practice, the paper is pressed with a hot domestic iron to bring up the writing as a brown line. This development is non-reversible, for the writing remains when the paper cools. Writing in saliva cannot be developed by heating, but as one of the constituents of saliva catalyses the oxidation of iron gallotannate ink, when the sheet is brushed over with a very dilute solution of this ink, the secret writing is revealed as a dark line on the pale blue background.

Some secret inks can be developed by wetting the sheet, when the writing becomes visible because of the change in translucency. The pressure-writing referred to above is developed in this way. A similar effect is produced when the secret ink consists of a solution of bismuth nitrate in dilute nitric acid, or a fixed oil such as castor or linseed dissolved in alcohol.

To provide secret inks for espionage, the resources of governments are mobilised. An effective secret ink can be developed only by the application of a very restricted range of reagents and then the process is non-reversible. The secret writing with such an ink should defy detection by any of the routine tests which are applied to suspect documents and, if possible, the " ink " should be one whose presence in the possession of the agent should be capable of innocent explanation.

Secret inks which fulfil the majority of these conditions have been devised, but little or nothing authentic has been published about them. According to some reports, very dilute solutions of pharmaceuticals were made use of during both World Wars; any chemist could suggest a list of organic compounds of some pharmaceutical value which would react with other reagents to give highly coloured products, but considerable research would be required to discover the most effective combination. The best of secret inks are of little practical value unless used with discretion. To pass without undue scrutiny, a document bearing secret writing would have to appear normal in every respect: wide margins, large blank areas and widely separated lines of writing immediately arouse suspicion, no matter how cursory the examination in the course of a routine inspection. To this end, secret inks are best applied where a casual inspection is unlikely to reveal their presence—under stamps and along the adhesive areas on envelopes.

Photocryptography

Reports of the extreme condensation of typewritten matter into a minute area by photography were received with some scepticism after the Second World War, but when it is realised that a maximum-resolution emulsion will resolve about a thousand lines to the millimetre, it is not surprising that a long typewritten message may be condensed into an area about the size of a full stop and yet be decipherable on microscopic examination.

Whilst a message rendered invisible by extreme condensation can be deciphered once sufficient magnification is applied, inspection by the highest magnification alone is of no avail should the message be applied to the document in the form of a latent photographic image. The first effect of light on a photosensitive emulsion is to form a latent image consisting of a most tenuous deposit of silver. After exposure, it is possible to remove all the other components of the emulsion, leaving behind nothing but the latent image whose presence can hardly be demonstrated by the most sensitive test for silver. If the paper bearing the latent image is treated with a developer containing silver salts similar to that employed for the physical development of photographic negatives, sufficient silver will then become deposited upon the latent image to render it visible.

Whilst unduly large white areas on a suspect photograph are regarded with suspicion if there is any chance of its bearing a secret message, these bare spaces are not essential, for by a further refinement of technique, a latent image may be impressed on a photographic print after development and washing, but before fixing. When the secret message is to be developed, the obscuring photograph can be bleached out as a preliminary to the decipherment. This method of impressing a latent image on a photograph is not one which can be undertaken in a hurry from the meagre description given above. Conventional methods of developing and fixing cannot be applied, and anyone who wishes to pursue the matter should study the properties of the latent image in one of the larger textbooks on the theory of photography. The method is mentioned to give some idea as to what is possible by the application of special techniques. It is because the ordinary criminal who uses secret ink is not supported by the resources at the disposal of the spy, that comparatively simple methods can be counted on to reveal any secret messages written by the average wrongdoer.

Detection of Secret Writing

As with other examinations on documents, physical methods should be exhausted before any chemical tests are applied. The paper should be examined with light at grazing incidence, especially any spaces between the writing, for the presence of pen impressions, which, although indecipherable in themselves, will point to the position of the hidden writing. This examination should be followed by inspection in ultra-violet light which can be counted on to expose many of the more common secret inks. If nothing is discovered in this examination, the document should be inspected with the image-converter when flooded with infra-red radiation.

If any trace of secret writing is revealed during these examinations, it will probably prove possible to decipher the whole by photography.

The effect of heat should be tried over a number of small areas. A thermostatic domestic iron with the control set at " rayon " may be used or, more conveniently, the document can be shielded with a thick card in which is cut a small aperture, through which the heat rays from an infra-red lamp can be directed on to its surface while the effect is being watched.

At this stage, it is permissible to try the effect of lightly dusting the surface of the document with a fine, highly coloured powder. If the secret ink is slightly sticky or if it has roughened the surface of the paper as it dried, powder may adhere to the secret writing when the excess is tipped off. Care must be taken not to rub the powder into the surface of the paper from which it may prove impossible to dislodge. Any powder which cannot be removed by blowing should be dabbed with a ball of plasticine. Any highly coloured amorphous powder such as graphite or red lead may be used; the only essential is that it must be easily adherent to paper.

If the foregoing physical methods have failed to reveal any secret writing, other treatments must be applied. The document should be moistened in places and examined by transmitted light, in case the method of writing has been to change the translucency of the paper when wet.

The iodine staining solution should be reserved to the end, as its application is liable to render the document useless for further tests. A less drastic, but also less sensitive, treatment is to fume the document with iodine vapour as recommended for fingerprints. (See p. 126.)

When physical methods have failed to reveal any hidden writing, and it is essential that the document should exhibit no obvious signs of having been tested, an effort should be made to induce the secret writing to diffuse from the document into the surface of another sheet of paper to which a variety of treatments can be applied without risk to the original document. To accomplish this, a sheet of photographic bromide paper should be fixed and well washed without being exposed to the light; this will conveniently provide a sheet of good-quality paper covered with an even layer of gelatine a few thousandths of an inch thick. The gelatine layer is then softened by being soaked in a dilute aqueous solution of ammonia for a few minutes before being washed in distilled water and drained and blotted to remove excess moisture.

This prepared sheet is pressed with its gelatine surface against the suspect document for some hours; any water-soluble material in the surface of the document will slowly diffuse into the gelatine layer. It may happen that the surface reflectivity of the gelatine layer will have become affected by the secret ink, so that it should be examined by light at grazing incidence before any reagents are applied. A variety of reagents should be drawn across the gelatine surface as narrow stripes, in an endeavour to discover a reagent which will react with any of the secret ink which has been absorbed into the gelatine.

The reagents should include: solutions of indicators which will reveal any change in the pH of the gelatine caused by the presence of the secret ink; ferric chloride, which will form coloured compounds with many pharmaceuticals; ammonium sulphide, which will react with salts of most heavy metals to give black sulphides, and general-purpose organic reagents such as dimethylaminobenzaldehyde.

BIBLIOGRAPHY

Examination of Paper

Graff, J. H., *A Color Atlas of Fiber Identification* (The Institute of Paper Chemistry, Appleton, Wis., 1940).

Graff, J. H., *Pulp and Paper Microscopy,* 2nd ed. (The Paper Institute, Appleton, Wis., 1942).

Grundy, J. G., "The Identification of Colours on Dyed Paper," *Proc. Tech. Sect. P.M.A.*, 14 (1), 233, 1933.

Pitt, T. M., *Microscopic Methods used in Identifying Commercial Fibres* (National Bureau of Standards, 1939).

Ultra-violet Light

Hilton, O., "Pitfalls in the Use of Ultra-Violet Examination to Differentiate between Writing Papers," *Journal of Criminal Law and Criminology,* Vol. 40, No. 4, November–December, 1949.

Mitchell, C. A., "Erasures and Ultra-Violet Light," *Analyst* 58, 1933.

Mitchell, C. A., "Ink and Ultra-Violet Light," *Analyst* 55, 1930.

Mitchell, C. A., "The Use of Invisible Rays in Criminology," *The Medico-Legal and Criminological Review* 3, 1935.

Infra-red

Edlin, "Infra-red Rays in Criminal Investigation," *Police Journal,* VIII, p. 458, 1935.

Grant, J., "Deciphering Charred Documents," *Analyst* 67, 1942.

Lechat, "Infra-red Photoscopy," *International Criminal Police Review,* No. 69, June–July, 1953.

Stedry, W., "Infra-red in Criminalistics," *Kriminalistik,* 11 (1), January, 1957.

Erasures

Edlin, C. H., "A Case of an Altered Document," *Police Journal*, 11, 1938.

Hilton, O., "Restoring Erased Ink Writing," *Police Journal,* October–December, 1956.

Longhetti, A., and Kirk, P. L., "Restoration and Decipherment of Erasures and Obliterated or Indented Writing," *Journal of Criminal Law and Criminology,* Vol. 41, No. 4, November–December, 1950.

Mellet, R., and Bischoff, M. A., "Application du phénomène de teinture à la revivification de textes laves," *Comptes Rendus des Séances de l'Académie des Sciences,* Vol. 181, November, 1925.

O'Neill, M. E., "The Restoration of Obliterated Ink Writing," *Journal of Criminal Law and Criminology,* Vol. 127, No. 4, November–December, 1936.

Charred Documents

Baker, G. W., Report of the Government Analyst for the Year 1938, Palestine, *Analyst* 65, 1940.

Bendikson, L., "Charred Documents," *The Library Journal,* March, 1933.

Davis, R., "Action of Charred Paper on the Photographic Plate," *Scientific Papers of the National Bureau of Standards,* Vol. 18, October, 1922.

Doud, D., "Charred Documents, Their Handling and Decipherment," *Journal of Criminal Law, Criminology and Police Science,* Vol. 43, No. 6, March–April, 1953.

Jones, G. A., *Nature* 147, 1941.

Matthews, C. G., "Treatment of Parchments Damaged by Fire," *Analyst* 49, 1924.

Mitchell, C. A., "The Deciphering of Scorched Documents," *Discovery* 5, 1924.

Mitchell, C. A., "The Examination of Charred Documents," *Analyst* 50, 1925.

Murray, H. D., *Nature* 148, 1941.

Taylor, W. D., and Walls, H. J., *Nature,* 147, 1941.
Tyrrell, J. F., "The Decipherment of Charred Documents," *Journal of Criminal Law and Criminology,* Vol. 30, 1939.

Finger Prints on Documents

Fruh, W., and Hofmann, W., "A Critical Evaluation of the Iodine, Silver Nitrate and Ninhydrin Process," *Archiv. für Kriminologie,* Vol. 118, pp. 89–98.
O'Neill, M. E., "Decipherment of Latent Fingerprints on Paper," *Journal of Criminal Law and Criminology,* Vol. 28, No. 4, November–December, 1937.

Chromatography

Balston, J. N., and Talbot, B. E., *Guide to Filter Paper and Cellulose Powder Chromatography* (H. Reeve Angel Co., R. and W. Balston, Ltd., London, 1952).
Brackett, J. W., and Bradford, L., "Comparison of Ink Writing on Documents by Paper Chromatography," *Journal of Criminal Law and Criminology,* Vol. 43, No. 4, November–December, 1952.
Brown, C., and Kirk, P. L., "Horizontal Paper Chromatography in the Identification of Ballpoint Pen Inks," *Journal of Criminal Law and Criminology,* Vol. 43, September–October, 1954.
Coldwell, "The Comparison of Inks and Writings by Paper Chromatography," *Analyst,* 80, 1955.
Martin, "Further Developments in the Chromatographic Analysis of Dried Ink," *International Criminal Police Review,* No. 91, October, 1955. "Chromatographic Microanalysis of Dried Ink," *International Criminal Police Review,* No. 81, October, 1954.
Pollard, F. H., McOmie, J. F. F., Banister, A. J., and Nickless, G., "The Separation of Ferrous and Ferric Iron," *Analyst* 82, December, 1957.
Somerford, "The Comparison of Writing Inks by Chromatography," *International Criminal Police Review,* No. 59, June–July, 1952.
Williams, T. I., *Introduction to Chromatography* (Chem. Publishing Co., Brooklyn N.Y., 1947).

Chemical Analysis

Lucas, A., "Chemical Tests for Adhesives," *Forensic Chemistry* (Arnold, 4th ed., 1945), p. 323.
Mitchell, C. A., "Copying Ink Pencils and the Examination of their Pigments in Writing," *Analyst* 42, 1917.
Sannie, C., "Recherches sur l'analyse de l'encre des documents manuscripts," *Revue de Criminologie et de la Police Technique,* Vol. 6, No. 2, 1952.
Ward, T. J., "The Microchemical Identification of Ink in Handwriting," *Analyst* 59, 1934.

Invisible Ink

Aston, Sir G., *Secret Service.*
Boyer, J., "German Spies and Invisible Writing," *Conquest* 3, 1921.
Erikson, G. L., "Invisible Ink," *Typo Graphic,* 41, January, 1956.
Felstead, T. S., *German Spies at Bay,* 1920.
"The Lovibond Colour System: A Spectrophotometric Analysis of the Lovibond Glasses," *Scientific Papers of the National Bureau of Standards,* No. 547, 1927.
Yardley, H. O., *The American Black Chamber.*

6

PHOTOGRAPHY OF DOCUMENTS

PHOTOGRAPHY plays an essential part in document examination and without the improvements in photographic apparatus such as cameras, lenses, filters, lighting equipment and emulsions, many of the modern techniques would never have been originated. Photography has to be applied to so many aspects of the work of the document examiner that the modern document laboratory may be said to be built around its studios and dark rooms.

Whilst everyone is prepared to pay lip-service to the importance of photography in document examination, there are many laboratories which include the examination of documents among their functions which are so poorly equipped—although with the most expensive apparatus—that its full potentialities are never realised. This means that many a problem which the photographic process is particularly competent to solve remains a mystery

It is not sufficiently realised that photography in a document laboratory has a number of distinct although occasionally overlapping functions, and that the apparatus, sensitive material and procedures best suited to one aspect of the work are not necessarily satisfactory for another. It is for this reason that this chapter which deals with the application of photography to the examination of documents has been written. No attempt is made to deal with the fundamental theory of the photographic process or with the action of a lens system in forming an image, but it will be assumed that the reader has a general acquaintance with the theory and practice of photography. If not, it is suggested that an elementary treatment of the subject, such as that given in the *Ilford Manual of Photography,* should be studied before reading any further. A list of books suitable for more general reading is given at the end of this chapter.

In document examination, photography is utilised in the conventional way for its ability to record, duplicate and enlarge, but application is also found for its sensitivity to radiations invisible to the eye and its facility for distinguishing between colours which appear to be identical to the eye, as well as for its power to integrate and render noticeable small luminous effects which might otherwise be overlooked.

PHOTOGRAPHY FOR RECORD

Deficiencies of Conventional Photographs

A photographer may possess considerable technical skill and yet fail to prepare a photograph of a document which is entirely satisfactory for production in court. Why this is so is best discussed by taking an actual example.

Supposing one were to prepare what might be described as a conventional photograph of a document which had received a fair amount of handling so that it had become creased, without, however, the surface becoming soiled in any way. The final print would probably be an excellent reproduction of any handwriting, typescript or printed matter shown up clearly against the lighter background of the paper. As an indication of the general appearance of the document, considered as an object, or even as a record of the information contained thereon, it is unlikely that any exception could be taken to such a photograph; it is only when the attention is turned to other aspects of the photograph that its failings become apparent, especially when the original document is compared with it.

Although the paper of the original document can be seen to be clean and of the same tint throughout the whole of its area, this is unlikely to be so in the case of the photograph. Instead of the paper being represented throughout as a uniform white or pale grey tone, the appearance of the paper in the photograph will vary from bright white patches devoid of any detail, known colloquially as " hot-spots " to grey areas which are appreciably darker than the average. At first sight the

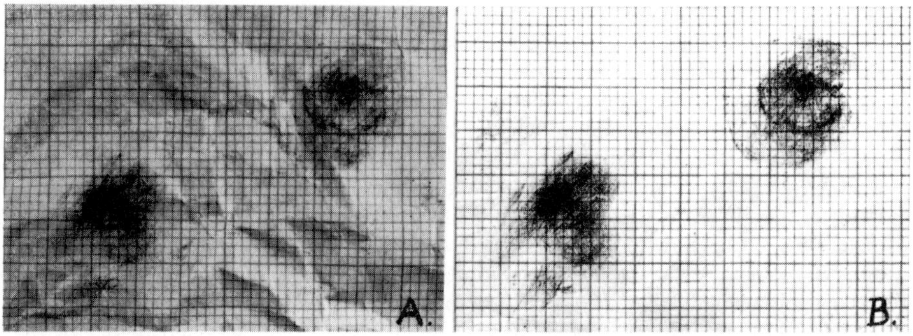

Fig. 6–1. The unevenly lit photograph " A " shows dark marks which are due to shadows, in addition to those due to stains on the paper. In places the fine lines have been imperfectly reproduced owing to excess of light—" hot spots." " B " is a photograph of the same sheet taken in the Illuminator. It is devoid of " hot spots " and shadows and the dark marks are all due to the presence of stains on the paper.

photograph had appeared to be a satisfying representation of the document, but it is now apparent that as a faithful presentation of the surface of the document it falls far short of perfection.

There is no mystery as to why there is this considerable difference between the appearance of the paper in the original document and in the photograph. The appearance of the paper surface in the photograph depends entirely upon the lighting, for the varying angles presented by different areas of the creased sheet of paper to the incident light will cause different amounts of light to be reflected into the camera lens. Where the maximum amount of light has been reflected into the lens " hot-spots " will occur, whilst other areas such as the bottoms of the creases, although actually no darker than the remainder of the paper, reflect less light, and will consequently be reproduced in darker shades of grey. It is thus apparent that if a document is photographed without special precautions being taken about the lighting, a most artistic and faithful reproduction of how it appeared from a certain point of view may be obtained, but the photograph may prove misleading and consequently of little use in a court of law.

The real objection to such a photograph is that a stained document would be reproduced with dark areas due to staining which might be difficult if not impossible to distinguish from those caused by uneven lighting. Stains, especially those faint stains which are best revealed in photographs, are often of great evidential value, but much of their value would be lost if there were any uncertainty whether a dark patch on the photograph represented either a stain, or an unstained area of low reflectivity caused by its orientation with respect to the main direction of the incident light.

The foregoing does not mean that there is no place for the ordinary photograph. The conventional photograph of a document, with its different registration of tone, possesses somewhat of a three-dimensional quality which enables the general condition of a document to be readily appreciated. This is of value when it is desired to record and possibly to emphasise the presence of any impressions or creases which are considered to be significant.

Essentials of a True Photograph

From the foregoing it will be seen that for court purposes, something quite distinct from a mere photograph of the document as a whole is required. What is needed is best described as the " photographic representation of the surface of the document."

When properly prepared, this latter type of photograph will present an appearance which is quite different from that of the ordinary photograph. The document will appear substantially two-dimensional, as all the effects of light and shade will be absent, and any creases will hardly be noticeable unless the surface of the paper in their vicinity has been affected in some way. If the print shows a dark patch on the surface of the paper, one can be sure that in this region the paper has been stained or treated in some manner which reduces its reflectivity. If there is a gap to be seen in the line of writing, the gap will have a real existence in the writing on the document, and not be a spurious effect produced by excessive reflection of light which has more than counterbalanced the absorption of light by the colouring matter in the line. Furthermore, any variation in the intensity of the colour of any of the ink lines may confidently be expected to be found in the original writing and not be caused by uneven lighting. The production of a true photographic representation of the surface of a document demands the skilled use of specialised apparatus, and because of its importance it is dealt with in detail below.

Non-specialist Apparatus

For many purposes a far less accurate reproduction of a document is all that is required, and for this a number of different processes have been devised.

Reflex Copying

This is one of the simplest processes yet devised for the copying of documents.[1] No camera is required, as the sensitive materials are exposed to light whilst they are

[1] O'Connor, F., " Copying in Reflex," *American Photoengraver*, 39, 1945.

in intimate contact with each other or with the surface of the document being copied. Exposure and processing can be carried out in a dark room or in a room dimly lit with tungsten filament lamps. Reflex copying is of great value for the copying of faded documents because of the enhanced contrast the process is capable of affording.

The first stage is the preparation of a paper negative by pressing the emulsion surface of the reflex paper which is a slow high-contrast bromide paper, into intimate contact with the face of the document being copied and then passing light through the back of the reflex paper into the emulsion. If the document being copied has any markings on the other side, the effect of these is neutralised by putting a sheet of paper of similar colour into contact with the back of the document. The resultant print is a negative, reversed left-for-right, which can be read by viewing its reflection in a mirror or by holding it before a strong light and reading through the back. Right-reading positives may be made by printing through this paper negative on to another sheet of reflex paper or any other desired sensitised material. To do this, the paper negative and the unexposed material are placed face to face and the light is allowed to print through from the back of the negative.

The theory of the process is interesting.[2] As the light passes through the reflex paper, it tends to fog the emulsion evenly all over. When the light emerges from the emulsion, it is absorbed by any dark areas on the surface of the document being copied, but where the paper is clear, it is both scattered and reflected back into the emulsion. The amount of light reflected is governed by the absorbing light power of the surface of the document and by the amount of scattering which takes place. The net result is that those areas of the reflected paper opposite the lighter portions of the document receive more light, and consequently fog to a greater extent, than those opposite the darker places.

When the special reflex paper is used with a carefully controlled exposure, development with an energetic developer containing a high concentration of bromide will produce a useful paper negative of far higher quality than might be expected from the crude nature of the process.

Filters in Reflex Copying. Unlike the original reflex papers, the modern material needs no yellow filter before the light source when negatives are being prepared, although when copying old faded documents or documents with blue markings, a yellow filter may be used to advantage in order to increase contrast. When making positives, there is no need to use a filter of any sort.

Apparatus. To obtain satisfactory results, (1) the reflex paper must be kept in intimate contact with the document being copied, and (2) the lighting must be even. It is fortunate that light from a tungsten filament lamp is sufficiently actinic to activate the emulsion. The source of light in most forms of commercial apparatus is a group of these lamps arranged to give substantially even illumination. When a yellow filter is employed, a sheet of yellow dyed cellulose acetate is used. Some idea of the exposure required may be gained from the statement that with a single 60-watt lamp, at a distance of about two feet, thirty-five seconds exposure is required

[2] Murray, H. D., "Theory and Practice of Reflex Copying," *Photographic Journal,* 84, 1944.

for negatives and about three times this for printing positives from the paper negatives.

If the document is fairly small and uncreased, the weight of a heavy sheet of glass through which the exposure can be given is sufficient to ensure the essential contact between document and reflex paper. With larger or stiffer documents, special printing boxes may be necessary. In these, good contact is ensured by pressure through sponge rubber pads. For the largest documents, vacuum frames have been devised, but these have their main application where large plans have to be copied in drawing offices.

Direct-positive Papers. If only a very limited number of copies of a document are required, the reflex process can be simplified by the elimination of the preparation of a negative by the use of direct-positive papers. (" Inverpos," Ilford and " Autopositive," Kodak.)

Direct-positive papers are handled and processed like reflex papers, but their speed is but a fiftieth of that of reflex papers. This means that the illumination for exposure must be much more intense if abnormally long exposures are to be avoided. Photoflood lamps or mercury vapour discharge lamps are the most suitable light sources, but with these the exposure must be made through a suitable yellow filter. If an unexposed direct-positive paper is developed, an all-over black image will be formed. This is because the paper has been evenly fogged all-over during manufacture. This latent all-over fog-image is destroyed by the action of intense light, so that when the document being copied is pressed up against the direct-positive paper, the initial fog-image on the paper is destroyed opposite the white areas on the document.

Direct-positive paper may be printed in any one of a number of ways depending on the nature of the document being copied and the result which is required. If the document is single-sided and the paper is sufficiently translucent to ultra-violet light, the print-through method may be used. In this, the document is laid face up on the direct-positive paper which is also face up, and the light is passed down through the document. This will give a copy which is a facsimile of the original. If the document is creased or on a non-uniform base, or if the paper is optically denser than the direct-positive paper, it is better to place the emulsion surface of the direct-positive paper on a sheet of white paper and to lay the document face down on to the back of the direct-positive paper. The light is then passed down through the document into the direct-positive paper. The white paper reflector serves to increase the image-destroying effect of the white areas on the document. If the document to be copied has markings on the back or is on opaque paper, then a reflex method must be employed. The document and the emulsion side of the direct-positive paper are placed together and the light is passed through the direct-positive paper. The print obtained in this way has correct tones but is reverse-reading. A right-reading print can be obtained from this reverse-reading copy by treating it as a translucent original and printing through on to another sheet of direct-positive paper.

After exposure, direct-positive prints are processed in the conventional way. A high-contrast-producing metol-hydroquinone developer is generally used, as one of the most satisfactory characteristics of direct-positive paper is its enhancement of contrast which enables good copies to be made of faded originals. The processing of direct-positive paper has been simplified to such an extent that, in one commercially developed process, quite satisfactory prints can be obtained within a short period of the exposure. The print is developed simply by sponging with developer held in a viscose sponge. When development is complete, the print is not fixed and washed in the conventional way for this is normally a time-consuming process; instead, the development is stopped and, by sponging with a solution of a " stabiliser," the residual silver salts in the emulsion are converted into compounds which are both colourless and stable to light. After blotting, the prints can be dried in a current of warm air for immediate use.

A copy prepared in this way cannot be expected to have the permanency of one processed by fixing and washing, but, if not exposed to broad daylight, it may be expected to have a useful life of some years. At any time, the print may be fixed in hypo and washed so as to increase its expectation of useful life.

For merely recording the information contained in a document, the reflex process has much to recommend it, and when the simplicity and comparative crudity of the method are borne in mind, the results are surprisingly good. Any image formed by the reflected and scattered light can never be as sharp as that produced by a lens of even medium quality so that copies made by any reflex process, useful though they may be, fall short in many respects when they are compared with photographs prepared in the conventional manner where the image is formed by a lens of good quality. In particular, the details of the structure of the ink line, which are all important where forgery is suspected, are but poorly represented in a print produced by any reflex process. This lack of sharpness and the absence of fine detail means that reflex methods of copying cannot be employed for anything other than the recording of the general appearance of a document. (See Figure 6–2.)

Of necessity, reflex copies are approximately natural size and neither reduction nor enlargement can be effected. This puts a limit on the size of the document which can conveniently be copied on most commercial copiers, which in general will accommodate documents up to fourteen by eighteen inches. Other processes for the copying of documents without the use of camera or other projection equipment have been devised but they all work on reflex principles and differ only in the nature of the coatings on the papers.

Photostat copying

This is a quick, cheap and effective method of making a photographic record of a document which has become so well known that the trade mark " Photostat " and the term " Photograph " have become so confused in the minds of many that the term " Photostatic copy " is often applied to any photographic reproduction of a document, irrespective of the process by which it has been produced.

A true " Photostatic " copy is made by projecting the image of the document on to sensitive paper contained inside a large camera specially designed for the purpose. As a lens is used, enlargements or reduced copies can be made at will. The characteristic feature of the process is that a reversing prism is used before the lens so as to produce on the sensitive paper a tone-reversed image which is correctly orientated. Development, fixing and washing of the exposed paper is carried out in the conventional way. As a result of the tone reversal, the black areas on the original document are represented as white areas on the print and vice versa.

For many purposes these single-stage reproductions are all that may be required. If the tone reversal is objected to, all that has to be done is to copy the reversed-tone print in the same apparatus to effect a further reversal, which will produce a final print with correct tone as well as the correct orientation. Whilst excellent for purposes of record, photostatic copies usually suffer from excessive contrast, and also lack the fine detail and the correct rendering of details which are characteristic of carefully prepared photographs. (See Figure 6–2.)

Fig. 6–2. (A) is an enlarged photograph of a signature. (B) is a reflex copy, whilst (C) is a photostat showing tone reversal. The structure of the ink line is admirably shown in the photograph (A) but is absent from the reflex copy (B). The photostat has a quality which falls between that of (A) and (B).

Conventional Photography

There is no question that, at the present time, the only satisfactory method of making a photographic reproduction of the surface of a document is to use a lens to project the image of the document on to conventional negative material, either plates or films. Beyond this, there is little further agreement among photographers of documents, and the question of the most satisfactory apparatus and the choice of sensitive materials is invariably the subject of debate whenever document photographers foregather. The fact that wide differences of opinion have existed for years among experienced workers, is probably an indication that little depends on the exact size of camera, the make of lens, or whether plates or films are used. Excellent photographs of documents have been prepared on cameras which range in size from the 35mm. miniature to enormous instruments accommodating large areas of cut film, whose cost is prohibitive to those who have to work on limited budgets.

The 35mm. devotees point to the precision construction of their tiny cameras and to the wide range of lenses and sensitive material which is available to them. They are quite content to be absolutely dependent upon the large degree of enlargement which is necessary to prepare prints from their tiny negatives. On the other hand, the users of the very large cameras bring forward theoretical considerations which they contend prove that all enlargements should be effected by the taking-lens during the preparation of the negative which can then be printed by contact. Also, there is a wide difference of opinion as to whether plates or films make the better negative materials; but in this case the division of opinion seems to be governed largely by nationality. In the United States of America, glass plates are regarded as obsolete curiosities, whilst in Great Britain, in spite of long continued advertising campaigns to enhance the sale of cut film, plates are still used extensively for scientific purposes. Fortunately there is general agreement on the subject of lenses and emulsions, for there is usually abundant visual proof of the adverse effects on the final print of the use of an unsuitable lens or the incorrect type of photographic emulsion.

The author is constantly receiving requests for advice on the choice of photographic apparatus and sensitive material for use in the photography of documents. As this is so, some discussion of these matters may not be out of place, although it is realised that nothing is likely to shake the faith of those who already practise photography to any great extent in the instruments and photographic materials they are accustomed to use.

Cameras

Miniature Cameras

There is no question that the modern miniature camera is a precision scientific instrument which, at its best, is capable of producing photographs of documents whose quality can hardly be surpassed by any other form of camera. The convenience of these light-weight cameras, the wide range of excellent lenses available for use with them and the low cost of negative material need no stressing here, for this is chorused by the devotees of these fascinating instruments.

The foregoing tribute should not be read uncritically for it has been carefully worded. The emphasis is on the words " is capable of producing " which must not be regarded as synonymous with " which invariably does produce " or even " will generally produce." Some of the most unsatisfactory photographs of documents ever perpetrated have been produced on expensive miniature cameras, and if it happens that only one out of a dozen negatives proves to be satisfactory, much of the economy associated with the small size of the negative disappears.

Anyone who contemplates using a miniature camera for document work must first resign himself to a very heavy initial expenditure on the camera, the lenses and the wide range of accessories which must be acquired if the full capabilities of the instrument as a document camera are to be realised. Money spent on a cheap miniature camera is usually wasted, useful though such an instrument may be outside a laboratory. A high initial outlay of money does nothing to guarantee good results, for the camera must be used, and the sensitive material processed, by a skilled and conscientious technician who must constantly be on guard against carelessness or any relaxation of vigilance. It is unwise to contemplate photography of documents using miniature equipment with a semi-skilled laboratory staff, as there appears to be no half-way house; results with miniature cameras are either near perfect or completely unacceptable.

For the production of prints of reasonable dimensions, the miniature negative must be enlarged to a considerable extent. This not only necessitates the use of a precision enlarger, but results in any blemishes on the negative becoming very prominent in the final print. Consequently, the negatives must be perfect to stand the extreme enlargement they must undergo.

The other criticism of the miniature camera, that it is virtually impossible to retouch the tiny negatives, has no force when such cameras are used for document photography, when no retouching or interference with the negative should ever be contemplated.

Large Cameras

With a large camera an enlarger is not necessary, as all printing is done by contact. As it may occasionally be necessary to prepare document photographs which measure up to eighteen by twelve inches, a camera which can take negative material of these dimensions so that contact prints can be made therefrom must of necessity be a substantial piece of equipment.

These large cameras are both cumbersome and expensive, and the long focal-length lenses which must be used with them are also very costly. It is true that the expense and the complications involved in the provision of an enlarger are saved, but the appetite of these cameras for negative material is insatiable. As this is the case, it is not surprising that these monsters are found only in laboratories maintained by wealthy organisations for whom heavy expenditure on photographic material is regarded as a secondary consideration.

Whilst, like all other photographic apparatus, the working of a large camera demands some skill and experience, good photographs may be obtained with these large instruments by workers who could not hope to achieve the same results with miniature cameras.

It is often argued by those who, in spite of its manifold disadvantages, pin their faith to the large camera, that perfection of definition and maintenance of contrast can only be obtained by the passage of the light through a single lens system, and not a two lens system, which is the case when the negative has to be printed by projection through the enlarger. Whatever might have been the merits of this argument in the past when lenses had not reached their present state of perfection, there is little doubt that this position cannot be defended today. The extra distortion or loss of contrast produced during the enlarging process, is for all practical purposes non-existent if apparatus of the highest quality is skilfully used throughout the operations.

Cameras of Medium Size

In the author's laboratory, a compromise has been effected between the two extremes which have been mentioned; the greater part of the straightforward work on the photography of documents is carried out on half-plate negatives.

These measure six and a half inches by four and three-quarter inches. (16·5 cms. by 10·9 cms.) Negative material of this popular size is readily available and can easily be handled and stored. Processing can be done with conventional commercial equipment which is easily available, and only a moderate degree of enlargement is required for the largest print which is likely to be required.

The lenses required for half-plate work are listed by all the best manufacturers and are very reasonable in price compared with those which have to be used with the larger cameras. This size of plate is ideally suited for use with the exceptionally high quality process lenses of the shortest focal length which is available commercially—nine inches.

Half-plate negatives are not prohibitively expensive, and the problem of " grain " which often plagues the miniature worker never arises where half-plate negatives are concerned. This means that for any problem, the most suitable emulsion and developer can be chosen without having to consider the possible occurrence of grain, which is ever uppermost in the mind of the " miniature " worker who has to make use of an extreme degree of enlargement in the preparation of his final print. Also, cameras for use with half-plate negative material are reasonable in size so that they can conveniently be accommodated in any laboratory.

A camera of medium size has one great advantage for those who have to work on a limited budget, for although no one would ever contemplate the " home construction " of a miniature camera, it is a comparatively simple matter to construct a laboratory document-copying camera for use with half-plate negatives. The proof of this contention is that the document-copying camera at the author's laboratory, though constructed on the premises at comparatively small cost, has given every satisfaction in use.

Negative Material

Plates or films? The best advice on this vexed question is to use the type of negative material which is most easily available, for excellent results may be obtained with either. In places where ample supplies of both films and plates are to hand, a decision must be made on other grounds.

In the laboratory under the direction of the author, both plates and cut films are used but generally speaking, plates are regarded as superior to films for precision work.

Plates are truly described as heavy, bulky and fragile but they have certain solid advantages which far outweigh these drawbacks. Weight and bulk mean nothing when neither the negative nor the camera has to leave the laboratory, and the fragility of glass is greatly overstressed by those who advocate the use of film. All sensitive material should be treated gently and even film can be scratched and rendered useless when mishandled. There is an unsurpassed degree of permanence in a correctly processed and packed photographic plate which is not shared by the nitro-cellulose or other plastic film, which is always a source of danger as a potential fire hazard in a laboratory. In the camera or the enlarger, the rigidity and flatness of the glass plate is something which is inherent in itself and not dependent on the proper functioning of some stretching mechanism, so that with plates one subtle source of trouble often experienced with film is eliminated at the outset.

Again, whatever may be the case in the future, there is no doubt that at the present time, a wider range of emulsions can be obtained on plates than on film, for the plate user has open to him the whole of the excellent range of special emulsions made for scientific purposes, such as astronomical and spectrographic recording, all of which are not available on film. The only advantage in this direction for the film user is the availability to him of colour-film of a number of different makes.

Finally, for those who work on a limited budget, it is well to know that plates are usually appreciably cheaper than cut film of the same size.

Lighting

A correct photographic reproduction of the surface of a document can be produced only under suitable conditions of lighting.

In some favoured parts of the world it is possible to use daylight. If the document can be exposed to an even well-diffused north light, then little difficulty should be experienced in making a negative in which the white surface of the document is reproduced in an even tone without " hot-spots " or darker patches where the lighting has been uneven. Unfortunately, in most other places, document photography has to be carried out in artificial light. This is far more difficult to adjust for evenness of illumination than daylight, but artificial light has certain advantages which more than compensate for the extra trouble involved in its use.

It is true that an even tone to the paper may be obtained, at the expense of every other quality in the photograph, without taking care to ensure satisfactory lighting. This is accomplished by under-exposing the negative and then printing on to a paper of the highest contrast. A price has to be paid for the even background achieved in this way, for an appreciable proportion of the handwriting on the document will be missing from the photograph. Fine lines will disappear altogether and the details of the structure of those ink lines which happen to be represented in the final print will be grotesquely distorted. The handwriting will bear a most unnatural appearance, and the comparison of such a travesty of a photograph with the original document will immediately reveal the poverty of the reproduction.

Many commercial firms supply lighting equipment which is supposed to, and occasionally does, provide the flat, even, lighting which is essential for the critical photography of a document. The most efficient commercial solution to the problem is to provide a multiple source, at least four lamps, mounted some distance away from the document so that the light falls nearly normally on to its surface. If the lamps are carefully balanced, such a system will often provide good, even, illumination but there is always the possibility of the negative showing " hot-spots " where an undue amount of light has been reflected back into the camera lens.

Testing Lighting Systems

A good test of any system which purports to give even illumination over a considerable area is to prepare a negative of a glossy sheet of graph paper which has been ruled with fine lines in a violet-blue ink. If the system of illumination being tested results in the production of a negative with all the lines evenly reproduced, with the paper background rendered in the same pale grey tone throughout, every confidence may be felt in it. This test is so searching that few commercial systems tested by the author have given results which are at all satisfactory.

It would be a good thing if every document which is photographed for court purposes were surrounded by strips of this graph paper. If these were perfectly reproduced in the final print, it would be a guarantee that the lighting was even and the processing satisfactory. It is to be feared that if this were insisted on, the number of document photographs produced in court by the numerous unskilled practitioners who pose as expert document examiners would be considerably reduced. The strips of graph paper would have another function; they could be used as scales from which the dimensions of anything shown in the photograph could be determined by the use of dividers.

Fluorescent Lighting

Another arrangement which is now coming into favour is the use of banks of fluorescent tubes as the light sources. These tubes, which emit light over the whole surface of the tube, form powerful sources of fairly well diffused light. Their adjustment to give even illumination is consequently much simpler than that of the substantially point sources formed by the bunched filaments of tungsten lamps.

The advantages are not all on the side of the fluorescent lamp. Unless the high voltage type is utilised, the lamps take some time to " strike," and like other fluorescent devices, they do not develop their full light output until they have been in action for some minutes. This precludes the control of exposure by switching the lights on and off, which is such a useful feature of the tungsten filament lamp. With fluorescent light-sources, exposure must be controlled by means of a lens-cap or shutter associated with the lens. It should be remembered that the light from ordinary fluorescent tubes is deficient in infra-red radiation, so that they cannot be substituted for the high-power tungsten filament lamps which are still essential for infra-red photography.

Various systems of " open " illumination have been tried out at the author's laboratory, but for the routine photography of documents all have been abandoned in favour of what might be termed a " closed " system which has proved a complete success. This system is simple, and once set up requires no further adjustment to ensure the perfectly even illumination of a document however creased it may be. The system has the further advantage that, by the simplest of manipulations, it may be used for preparing a conventional photograph of a document when it is desired to throw into prominence any folds and creases thereon. In the laboratory, this apparatus is generally referred to as the " Illuminator," as its primary function is to illuminate the document for photography.

The Illuminator

In its essentials, this apparatus is very simple and may easily be constructed by any handyman who can do simple work in wood and iron; the apparatus at the author's laboratory was made on the premises in a comparatively short time. Whilst it is devoid of the gleaming mahogany surfaces and chromium plate of commercial photographic equipment it is nonetheless effective for its purpose.

In essentials it consists of a large wooden box about five feet in length and about three feet square in section, which rests on one of its larger sides on a stout table of convenient height. As the laboratory where it is housed consists of a brick-built building, erected on a very heavy slab of concrete surrounded by peaty soil situated a fair way from any source of shock or vibration, no special precautions have been found necessary to eliminate vibration from the apparatus. If there is any risk of vibration, the box should be rested on a thick felt pad on the table. If this fails to insulate the apparatus from shock, the recommendations given below should be followed.

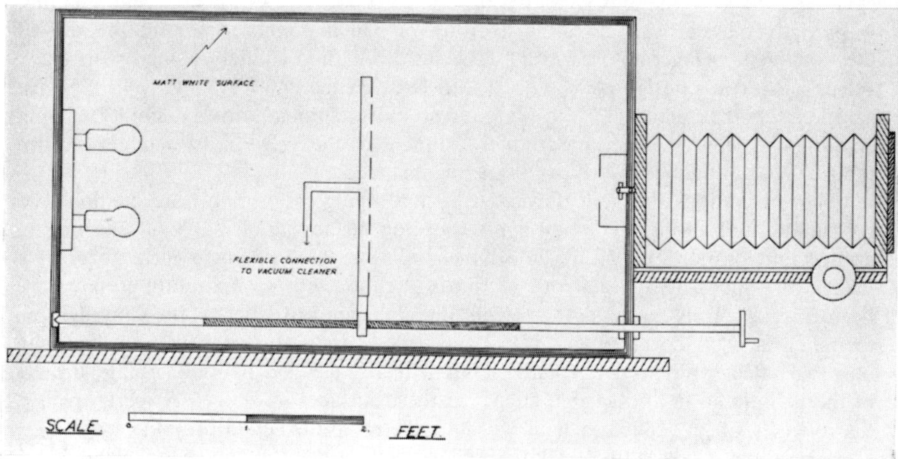

Fig. 6–3. Diagrammatic representation of the illuminator designed for document photography.

Light Source. The source of light for making the exposure consists of a group of four sixty-watt, coiled-coil, tungsten filament, gas-filled lamps, mounted close together inside the box at the centre of one of the ends so that they project into the box. These comparatively small-wattage lamps provide an intensity of illumination which necessitates exposures of about twenty to thirty seconds. This is an advantage, for, with an exposure of this length of time, no shutter need be provided for the lens; control can be exercised by switching the lights on and off. The heat given off by these four lamps is so small—about 50 cals./sec.—that no special ventilation of the box is called for.

Ample access to the inside of the box is provided by an arrangement which allows one of the long sides of the box to slide open.

The camera lens is fixed inside the box at the centre of the end which faces the light source. In the apparatus used by the author, this end of the box also forms the lens panel of the camera proper, but a satisfactory alternative arrangement is to have the lens of an independent stand camera " looking into " the box through a hole in the end. The lens must be " bloomed " to cut down the internal reflections from the glass-air surfaces of the components of the lens which are responsible for the formation of flare spots, and which reduce contrast by general veiling of the image.

As every effort must be made to eliminate anything which tends to reduce contrast by veiling or fogging of the image, an essential step is the provision of a really effective lens hood. This is designed to prevent the entry into the lens of any light other than that reflected from the surface of the document, and possibly a small surrounding strip of the surface on which it is mounted.

Lens Hood. A most satisfactory form of lens hood was made from a cylinder of metal about six inches in diameter and about four inches long. One end of the cylinder is fixed to the lens panel that is formed by the end of the box, and the other is partially closed by a stop, the aperture of which is chosen to suit the size of the document being photographed. The inside of the cylinder is lined with black velvet. With this design of lens hood, little extraneous light can enter into the lens. The lens hood is made of large diameter so as to eliminate any possibility of light entering the lens by reflection from the surface of the velvet, which might happen if any powerful light-rays strike it at grazing incidence.

The precautions to avoid unwanted light reaching the negative are continued in the camera body itself. The best light-absorbing surfaces are capable of reflecting an appreciable proportion of any light which falls on them at angles near to grazing incidence, which is why a narrow tight-fitting bellows, however carefully it may have been blacked on its inside surfaces, will often be found to reflect some stray light on to the surface of the negative. If a large bellows is used, then any stray light can only be reflected on to the negative after it has struck the light-absorbing surfaces of the bellows at an appreciable angle. If these surfaces have been properly treated, the intensity of any reflected light will be reduced to negligible proportions.

The use of an abnormally large bellows will mean that the back plate of the camera will also be considerably larger than the negative. This will prove advantageous because any " excess image " formed by the lens will strike the back plate outside the bounds of the negative and be absorbed there, instead of just grazing the folded edges of the bellows and spilling onto the negative. These precautions are taken because any veiling of the negative by unwanted light reflected from either the lens or the inside of the camera is certain to be serious, especially when faint markings are photographed in an effort to render them more apparent.

Document Holder. So far, little more has been described than a large box with a group of lamps at one end facing a camera lens, which looks into the box through an oversize lens hood. To complete the apparatus, a movable document holder is suspended in the box so that it is parallel with the two ends carrying the lights and the lens. The document holder is opaque and is sufficiently large to obstruct any light-rays which would otherwise fall from the lamps directly on to the front surface of the lens. The construction of the movable document holder presented a number of problems which now have almost completely been solved.

For photography, a document should be held as flat as possible. The simplest way of doing this, namely, by pressing the document flat under a sheet of glass, is never used in the author's laboratory because spurious effects may be produced by photographing a document whilst it is under a sheet of glass.

On one occasion, the author was asked to pass an opinion on some questioned signatures. In the enlarged photographs which were supplied, the ink line appeared to be defective, especially in some of the thicker strokes, as though a certain amount of scraping and patching had been done. When the original document was later submitted for examination, it soon became obvious that the peculiar violet-green ink line was perfect throughout the whole of every signature. It was thought that the original photographs had been badly prepared so others were taken with the thick document held flat under a heavy sheet of glass. The final prints closely resembled the original defective prints in every respect, and no solution to the problem of why the photographs showed something which was not apparent on microscopic examination could be discovered by examination of either the document or the photographs. It was finally realised that the nature of the ink line was responsible for the peculiar effect seen in the photograph. The signatures had been written in a very iridescent violet-green ink and the tiny crystals in the dry ink line showed an unusually high reflecting power. To test the theory, fresh photographs were made *without* the sheet of glass. These new photographs showed intact ink lines similar to those observed on microscopic examination of the actual signature on the document.

It was then evident that multiple reflections had occurred between the dyestuff crystals in the dried ink and the surfaces of the glass sheet to produce a concentration of highly actinic light at the centre of the heavier ink lines. On the negative, this produced a darkening about equal to that produced by light reflected from the surface of the paper, so that in the final print from this negative, the centre of the ink lines was recorded as being as bright as the paper. This brightness was, not unnaturally, interpreted as the paper surface showing through the centre of the ink line. This, incidentally, is an example of the failure of the black and white photographic process to make a faithful reproduction of the surface of a document, for the confusion would never have arisen if the photographs had been prepared in colour. In a colour print, the centre of the thicker lines would have been recorded as bright green-violet which could not have been mistaken for white paper showing through.

The foregoing is an instance why original documents should be examined whenever possible, and the minimum reliance placed on even the most carefully prepared photographs which may be offered as substitutes.

As the documents should not be held flat against the document holder with a sheet of glass, some other method which does not involve mutilation had to be sought. Pins and adhesive are unsatisfactory, for the pins make holes and cast shadows, while adhesives will generally be found to adhere better to the document, from which they can be removed only with difficulty, than to the document holder.

The simplest solution, and by far the most satisfactory, is to hold the document against its vertical support by atmospheric pressure. To do this, the document holder is made in the form of a rigid shallow box. The central space is connected to a suction apparatus via a long corrugated rubber tube similar to that used by dentists to administer nitrous oxide. Whilst the back and the sides are solid, the front of the holder is covered with a stiff wire gauze or sheet of perforated metal suitably reinforced, so that it remains flat when a partial vacuum is applied to the central space. The wire gauze is covered with a loosely woven sheet of cotton or linen cloth. If this is carefully chosen for its porosity, a document of any size has merely to be placed against it for it to be held so firmly that there is no danger of its falling off. At the same time it is held loosely enough to allow of its position being adjusted by gentle pulling. When the partial vacuum produced by the suction apparatus is relieved, the document falls away from the holder. Whilst the atmospheric pressure is just sufficient to hold the document firmly in place, any creases and folds are unaffected.

A domestic vacuum cleaner provides sufficient suction, but as these pieces of household equipment are not designed for long hours of running under full load, a more substantially built centrifugal exhausting system is more likely to prove satisfactory. Any exhausting system is sure to be noisy so it is best established on the other side of a thick wall. The tube or tubes from the exhaust system should be so long and flexible that there is no possibility of their transmitting vibration from the exhaust system to the document holder, and to avoid pulsations in the exhaust, a large reservoir should be placed between the exhaust pump and the flexible pipes leading to the document holder.

The document holder at the author's laboratory is just over two feet square, and is held symmetrically in the box so that a gap of about nine inches exists between its four edges and the sides of the box. It should be apparent from this that the only light which can fall on the face of the document is that which has been scattered and reflected at least twice from the sides and ends of the box.

Treatment of Reflecting Surfaces. As no direct light should fall on the document, the walls of the box are so treated that they scatter rather than reflect the light. A suitable matt scattering surface can most simply be prepared by painting with a zinc-white or titanium-white paint. Paint which is prepared for undercoating —flatting—gives an excellent matt surface which can be renewed cheaply and easily should it become discoloured and lose some of its reflectivity.

Focusing arrangements. As the lens is fixed, both the back panel of the camera and the document holder must be capable of movement to permit focusing. The position of the camera back can be adjusted by a conventional rack focusing mechanism, but something has to be contrived which will allow the document holder to be moved from outside the apparatus whilst the focusing is being carried out.

In the apparatus at the author's laboratory, the document holder runs on rails fixed to the bottom of the box, and its position is adjusted by rotation of a square-threaded rod which terminates in a handwheel placed just below the camera, thus enabling the position of the document holder to be altered while the camera is being focused. The dimensions quoted for the size of the box are ideal for the photography of normal documents on to a half-plate negative using a lens of about nine inches focal length.

The movement of the document holder is restricted to a distance of about half the length of the box, symmetrically arranged about its centre; this prevents the holder being placed so near either the lamps or the lens that the conditions of even illumination are disturbed. With a nine-inch lens, this range of movement enables negatives to be made with a degree of reduction from approximately unity to about four times. If a five-inch lens is substituted, this degree of reduction can be approximately doubled.

In practice, these values of focal length for the lenses have proved most satisfactory, for they match the characteristics of most commercial enlargers. This is important because some enlargement is usually necessary to obtain prints of a size suitable for production in court.

If a " normal " photograph of a document is required in which are recorded all the creases and other irregularities in its surface, the exposure is made with the sliding door in the open position. This produces sufficient disturbance of the symmetry of the lighting to give enough light and shade in the photograph, and to give an excellent impression of the general appearance of the document. The lighting of the surface of a document achieved in this rather primitive and bulky apparatus is so even and well distributed that no difficulty is ever experienced in making negatives entirely free from either " hot-spots " or shaded areas, even when the document is large enough to cover the whole of the holder—an area of over four square feet. Very few " open " systems of lighting enable this to be accomplished without considerable trial and error.

The apparatus described above has been copied by many who have seen it in use and has given every satisfaction. The dimensions can be varied to suit the size of a document and the focal lengths of the available lenses. The only feature which should not be varied is the design of the lens hood; a really efficient lens hood which admits no stray light is essential. The reason for this is that the lens projects into the box and receives light of some intensity over the whole solid angle subtended by the walls of the box and the document holder. The only light which is used in the formation of the image is that which falls on the lens from the surface of the document; any other light must either be blocked off by the lens hood or absorbed by the blackened surfaces inside the lens mount. The blackening of these surfaces cannot be relied on to absorb powerful rays of side light, so that in order to cut these off and avoid the formation of flare spots and general veiling of the image, a really efficient lens hood must be fitted.

As the lens is not always used at full aperture, and as it is advisable that focusing be done with the taking stop, extra illumination should be provided for focusing. This extra illumination, which is of great value when focusing through a dense filter such as the tri-colour red, is obtained from four tungsten filament lamps mounted alongside the lens so that they shine directly on to the document. These auxiliary lamps are of course switched off when the exposure is being made.

In the form in which it has been described, the apparatus is not suited for the entire range of document photography. Whilst photographs may be made with coloured light by masking the light source with a large gelatine filter of the required colour, exposures by ultra-violet light tend to become unduly long. This is because the most convenient source of ultra-violet light—the lamps which are used commercially with the filter incorporated in the glass envelope—have a low luminous output. Also, few paints are efficient reflectors of ultra-violet light, so that a document is but feebly lit even if an increased number of ultra-violet lamps be employed. The apparatus is also unsatisfactory for infra-red work because of the difficulty experienced in mounting and ventilating the powerful light sources which are essential for this work. Direct illumination of the document is essential with either ultra-violet or infra-red.

Use of Light Meter to Test Illumination

When documents which are too large to be accommodated in the Illuminator have to be photographed, they are best fixed to a wall and illuminated by a number of lamps placed well behind the camera. The use of a simple form of light meter, made by connecting a selenium photo-electric cell to a microammeter through a resistance of about a thousand ohms, will facilitate the preliminary arrangements of the lights. If a photo-electric cell with an area of approximately one square inch is coupled to a fifty-microampere meter, a convenient value of deflection should be obtained. The lights are adjusted until the same reading is obtained on the micro-ammeter wherever the cell is placed on the document in such a way that it faces the camera.

This adjustment with the light meter cannot be guaranteed to give a good negative free from shadow patches and "hot-spots," so that test negatives should be made and the position of the lights adjusted after each exposure, until the required result has been obtained. A conventional stand-camera can be used providing it is steady. The greatest difficulty will be experienced with a document which has a shiny surface, such as a highly glazed photograph bearing writing across it. A solution to this problem is suggested below.

It is difficult to photograph a page from a thick book with the suction type holder described above; the most practical solution is to hold the book open in the desired position in the Illuminator by the aid of retort stands and clamps resting on the floor of the box. This at its best is a makeshift device; on the whole, therefore, it is preferable to dispense with the Illuminator for any documents other than those which can be held up against the face of the document holder by suction, and to use an open system of illumination which is adjusted for even lighting by trial and error.

Other Devices for Producing Even Illumination

If difficulty is experienced in obtaining an evenly lit photograph of a document, in the absence of apparatus such as the "Illuminator" described above, it is possible to extemporise an effective lighting system from a few wooden or metal rods and a length of muslin or cheese-cloth.

The rods are lashed together to form the outline of a box which is slightly larger in cross-section than the document to be photographed. The length of this box-like frame should be slightly less than the distance the camera lens will have to be placed from the document in order to prepare a negative with the required degree of reduction. The muslin should then be wrapped around the frame so as to make an open tube. The document is placed against a convenient wall or other support, against which one of the open ends of the tube is also placed so that the document is framed therein. The camera is fixed so that it "looks in" at the document from the other open end of the tube. A number of lights are arranged to shine on the outer surface of the muslin walls so that all four appear to be equally illuminated when observed from the position to be occupied by the camera lens. A lens-hood should be fitted.

A few trial negatives will show what readjustment of the lights is necessary to produce a photograph of the required freedom from both shaded areas and " hot spots."

Vibration

Unsuspected vibration is the cause of poor, unsharp negatives for which good lenses are often unjustly blamed.[3] Whilst it is often easy to show that vibration is the cause of the trouble, the cure of the condition is by no means straightforward.

Wherever possible, vibration should be dealt with at the source; it is advisable to shut down any noisy machinery which may be in the neighbourhood of a camera or enlarger when a long exposure is being made, unless it is known that it causes no harm. If this cannot be done, the photographic apparatus should be sited in a room where vibration is at a minimum. Generally speaking, a cellar is better in this respect than an attic, and a room remote from traffic preferable to one which is adjacent to a road carrying heavy vehicles.

The apparatus itself should be as rigid as possible. Struts and other supports should be liberally provided, and in its construction, material should never be stinted, because weight and bulk will tend to reduce the amplitude of any vibration. Resilient materials, such as sponge rubber, make poor transmitters of vibrational energy, so that when vibration cannot be controlled by other methods, the effect of resting the apparatus on a thick bed of latex sponge should be tried.

To cope with exceptionally bad conditions, it may be necessary to utilise one of the proprietary anti-vibration beds for photographic equipment which are on the market. These consist of a very heavy iron casting suspended from a rigid frame by a set of springs. The frame rests on the floor and the casting carries the photographic equipment. The period of the springs is related to the weight of the casting so as to minimise the amplitude of the vibration transmitted to the apparatus.

The reduction of any appreciable degree of vibration to negligible proportions is rarely a straightforward matter, and it may be that a certain amount of experiment and trial of different arrangements will have to be carried out before the results are satisfactory.

Lenses

Every photographer has his favourite make of lens, so that the only advice which is called for is to buy the best which can be afforded. It is a waste of time and money to attempt to produce good results with an inferior or unsuitable type of lens. In this connection, it is sometimes forgotten that the best lenses are designed and corrected for specific conditions of use. For example, when a landscape lens or one for general photography is designed, the curvatures of the various components are chosen and arranged with respect to the direction of the incident light, to minimise the various aberrations which affect lens performance for the conditions under which it is likely to be used—the photography of fairly distant objects.

[3] " The Vibration Insulation of Photographic Equipment," *Kodak Data Sheet* EQ.6.

Even if the most expensive lens of this type were used for copying a portion of a document full size or with a slight degree of enlargement, the negative might not be as satisfactory as if a much cheaper lens designed specifically for such work were employed.

It is indeed fortunate for the document examiner that the graphic industries demand lenses of the highest quality which have been designed to work under the very conditions met with in document photography. Since this is so, there is a wide choice of excellent lenses at prices which are extremely reasonable considering the remarkable qualities of the lenses.

The lenses best adapted to the copying of documents are generally known as " process " lenses. They are supplied in focal lengths which range from nine inches upward. Whilst they are not designed to work at the wide apertures common among ordinary landscape lenses, they are quite fast enough to permit of exposures which are not unduly long. The best of these lenses, generally termed " apochromatic " lenses, are corrected for three wave-lengths widely spaced in the spectrum, so that all colours are brought to substantially the same focus. These lenses are particularly useful for work in the infra-red, for, unlike achromatic lenses, they can be focused visually by using a filter such as the Ilford " tricolour red " which passes light in the extreme red. This setting will be found to be quite satisfactory when the infra-red filter is substituted in readiness for the actual exposure.

The many components necessary for the construction of these highly corrected apochromatic lenses were, in the past, liable to cause flare spots and a loss of contrast by the multiple reflections which took place at the numerous air-glass surfaces, but this fault has been largely eliminated by the development of the " blooming " process. The modern bloomed lenses give a degree of contrast equal to that which could formerly be obtained only with a lens of few components and consequently less well corrected for aberrations.

In spite of its relatively high cost, a modern bloomed apochromatic process lens is the lens of choice for the critical photography of documents. Not only are these lenses adequately corrected for all types of aberration, but their resolving power is all that is ever likely to be required, and indeed is equal to that of any photographic emulsion at present on the market. If the document examiner makes use of such a lens by any of the world-famous optical firms he may confidently look elsewhere for the source of any defects in his photographs.

Care of Lenses

Many poor photographs of documents are constantly being made with expensive lenses which have seriously deteriorated in use. A photographic lens must be treated with care if it is to retain its efficiency and give long service. When not in use, a lens should be capped on both ends and kept in a dry dust-free atmosphere, for both heat and humidity can cause serious deterioration. Considerable research has been carried out by the war departments of a number of governments into methods for the protection of lenses, especially those which have to be used in tropical conditions.

There is no known procedure which, under all conditions, can be guaranteed to give complete protection from the moulds which are able to live and multiply on the glass surface of optical instruments, but the investigations have all pointed to extreme cleanliness being the first essential. If the camera lens is kept scrupulously clean from perspiration or other deposits and is preserved in an air-tight jar when not in use, it should come to little harm. As an additional precaution, when conditions of high humidity are experienced, the air inside the jar should be kept dry by the use of a colour-coded activated silica-gel desiccant. Ordinary silica-gel may be used, but the colour-coded variety changes in colour when it requires re-activating by heating. This drives off the absorbed moisture and restores its ability to remove water vapour from the air.

If a lens is allowed to suffer an appreciable rise in temperature, which may very well happen when it is being used in an enlarger equipped with a high-wattage tungsten filament lamp, the cement joining the individual glasses in the lens will probably break down and the lens be rendered useless. To avoid any chance of this happening, care should be taken to prevent powerful beams of white light from passing through any photographic lens except when absolutely necessary; the lens should be given time to cool if ever it becomes warm to the touch. It is fortunate in this respect that recent developments allow of the substitution of the white light from the tungsten filament lamp by the highly actinic radiation from mercury vapour discharge lamps. Not only is the duration of the exposure considerably reduced, but the radiation is practically devoid of light of the longer wave-lengths which produce heat in their passage through the lens and are of little photographic value.

The foregoing are what might be termed the long-term or permanent troubles which affect lenses, but even with a new lens, the surface may become contaminated with a layer of grease, dust, or condensed moisture. Should this happen, some of the incident light will be scattered to form halos around the highlights on the negative which is another "short-term" reason why the surface of the lens should be kept clean. The condensation of moisture on the surface of the lens, liable to occur whenever a lens is brought into a warmer more humid atmosphere, is often the unsuspected cause of mysterious defects in negatives for which no good reason can be found when the matter is investigated. By the time the faulty negative has been discovered, the condensed moisture has evaporated and the lens is once more in good working order.

Cleaning of Lenses

Optical glass differs from ordinary glass in that it is far more susceptible to the influence of grease, moisture or chemicals.[4] This is another reason why the glass surface should never be touched with the fingers, but as complete protection of the lens is impracticable under working conditions it is sometimes necessary to clean the lens surfaces. Any cleaning should be restricted to the outer surfaces, for the components of a lens should never be separated. Once a lens has been taken apart there is little likelihood that re-assembly by anyone other than the makers will recreate the original separation of the components; failure to accomplish this will ruin the lens as a high grade objective.

[4] Barcham, J., *Lens Cleaning Manual* (Green, Ltd., Maidstone, England).

The first step in the cleaning process is to remove all abrasive dust by blowing with clean dry air or by dusting with a soft clean artist's brush. The brush should be used only for lens cleaning, and should be stored in a dust-free container. When dust-free, the lens surfaces should be wiped with a folded piece of special lens-cleaning tissue which is marketed for the purpose. Only one side of the tissue should be used, so that nothing is transferred from the fingers on to the lens surface. If this special tissue is not available, a well-washed soft dust-free linen or cotton cloth may be used.

Salt spray or any other water soluble material should be washed off with distilled water, and not tap-water which might contain harmful chlorine compounds, and the lens dried off with tissue. Grease may be removed by gentle swabbing with the tissue or soft cloth impregnated with either benzene or petroleum ether, but, before using any solvent on a lens, the liquid should be tested for the presence of nonvolatile matter by dropping a small quantity on to a clean glass sheet. If any residue remains after the solvent has evaporated the liquid is unsuitable for use on any lens.

Cleaning Bloomed Lenses

The coating on a bloomed lens is extremely thin—about four-millionths of an inch, *i.e.*, about one-thousandth of the thickness of a banknote. Although the coating materials are fairly hard, they should be treated with extreme care because any alteration in thickness is almost certain to render them ineffective. Some coating materials have an appreciable solubility in water, so that any cleaning will have to be restricted to organic solvents. Those most generally used for this purpose are rectified spirit, xylene, or a mixture of acetone and ether. It is best to purchase any of these solvents in what is known as the A.R. (analytical reagent) quality, because the commercial solvents are almost certain to be unsuitable for use on a valuable lens.

Certain non-flam solvents contain chlorinated compounds which, when exposed to light in the presence of moisture, suffer a partial decomposition to form hydrochloric acid and other reactive chlorine compounds. Any solvent which does not smell sweet should never be used on a lens or other photographic equipment. It is far safer to choose one of the solvents named above, because they contain neither chlorine nor any other element which is liable to form corrosive compounds.

Definition

For scientific purposes, the value of a photograph depends largely upon the way in which the fine detail in the object photographed has been recorded. Many people are under the mistaken impression that this depends mainly on the degree of magnification shown in the final print. This is not so, for if a poor negative is enlarged, the final print, however large, will enable no extra detail to be distinguished, since all that the enlargement accomplishes is to render larger the blurred details in the original negative.

It is often said that a satisfactory photograph of a document should exhibit good "definition." "Definition" used in this sense is difficult to define strictly and quite impossible to measure. It is best described as the " degree of distinctness " in the outline of the image formed by a lens or reproduced in a photograph. Definition is affected by many factors, the most important being the combined resolution of the lens and of the photographic emulsion employed, the sharpness of any boundaries in the photograph and the " graininess " of the silver deposit on the final print.

Resolution

The resolution of a lens is its ability to form separate recognisable images of objects which are very close together. " Resolving power " is the term used when a numerical value is given to the resolution of the lens; it is usually expressed as the reciprocal of the smallest separation of lines which can be observed in the image. There has to be some latitude in this way of expressing " Resolving power " because the figure for any given lens will vary according to a number of factors, one being the wave-length of the light by which the image is formed.

It is well known that if a sharp boundary between black and white areas is photographed, it is impossible for any lens to produce a perfectly sharp boundary in the image, because light is a wave phenomenon and consequently suffers spreading or " diffraction " at the edges of an obstacle or sharp boundary. This is why a set of sharp-edged black and white lines can never be reproduced in the image with equally sharp outlines, although the departure from perfection may not be easily apparent. If, in the image of a test object of black and white lines, it can be seen that any two adjacent lines can be observed as separate images, the lines are considered to be resolved, although their edges are unlikely to be perfectly defined because of diffraction effects and residual errors in the lens system.

Resolving Power. If the distance between the centres of the two separate images of adjacent lines is one hundredth of a millimetre, then the resolving power of the lens for the conditions of the experiment is said to be one hundred lines per millimetre.

Measurement of Resolving Power. On theoretical grounds it has been calculated that the maximum resolving power in lines/mm. of a theoretically perfect lens for yellow-green light is 1,430 divided by the stop number of the lens. This means that the maximum resolving power will be about 360 lines/mm. at f. 4, dropping to 16 lines/mm. at f. 90. These figures apply to regions near the axis. At an angle of 25° they are reduced to something approximating to three-quarters of these values. These values increase with decrease in the wave-length of the light.

Lens Aberrations. In every lens there will be found certain inherent faults, generally referred to as aberrations; there are two axial aberrations—chromatic and spherical—together with five oblique aberrations—coma, astigmatism, field curvature distortion and lateral chromatic aberrations.

The skill of the lens designer is shown by the extent to which he has balanced his glasses and curvatures to reduce these sources of error to the minimum, but complete elimination is not possible and the residual aberrations reduce the resolving power of the lens from that which is theoretically possible.

Testing Lens Quality. As there is no satisfactory method of calculating the overall quality of a lens, the best method of assessment is to determine its performance, and to some extent that of the associated equipment, by photographing test charts under specified conditions. Many different types of test charts have been proposed, but no one type of chart has any outstanding advantage over the others. Lens-testing in this way has been rendered comparatively simple for the document examiner through the work of the U.S. Department of Commerce National Bureau of Standards, who, in 1940, issued a Circular entitled " A Test of Lens Resolution for Photographers " (Circular C. 428), together with a set of charts for carrying out the tests described.

Whilst the Circular deals in some detail with the general problem of the choice of criteria for the performance of a lens, the section of greatest interest to the document examiner is that dealing with quality of definition.

The test charts are ruled with groups of line-patterns placed at right angles to each other. Each line is separated from its neighbours by a distance equal to its width. The widths of the lines, and consequently that of the spacings, are different in various parts of the chart, and the ratio between the width of any line and those next to it in size is as one to the square root of two.

It is obvious that if the resolving power of a lens is to be judged by the quality of the photograph of a test chart it produces, then the printing of the test chart must be of the highest possible quality. Those supplied by the National Bureau of Standards are printed from an intaglio plate engraved on a dividing engine, and are reproduced by methods identical with those employed for the production of postage stamps. When test charts are used in an endeavour to assess the performance of a lens, a great deal depends on the way in which they are set up for photography. The Circular should be consulted on this as well as for information bearing on the examination of the negative and the interpretation of the results.

When the charts are set up and photographed at the recommended distance from the camera of twenty-six times the focal length of the lens, the lines reproduced on the negative will correspond to a range of from 3·5 to 56 lines per millimetre. These figures for line spacing are well within the resolving power of any good lens and of most photographic emulsions, for even fast plates will resolve about 50 lines/mm., whilst process plates will resolve about two to three hundred lines/mm.

Degree of Resolution Necessary. The eye can resolve about 8 lines/mm. at the normal distance for viewing—ten inches (25 cms.)—so that all photographs will appear equally sharp if they show a resolution of eight lines or better to the millimetre. This means that if the largest print likely to be required in court is about a foot square, the half-plate negative from which it is made should show at least twenty-five lines to the millimetre so as to allow for some falling off during enlargement. This is well within the power of a process lens even when the resolution of the emulsion has also to be taken into account.

If miniature cameras are used, it will be necessary for the negatives to show a minimum resolution in excess of a hundred lines to the millimetre if large prints are to be made from them. The figure of twenty-five lines to the millimetre quoted for half-plates is far more easily realised than one which runs to more than a hundred; the use of a miniature camera consequently requires a high standard of both focusing and processing of the negative.

Resolving Power of Photographic Emulsions. The resolving power of an emulsion is limited because of the nature of the materials of which it is composed. A photographic emulsion contains opaque grains of silver halide which scatter and diffract the incident light, and this results in the destruction of the finest details of the image. A fast emulsion will resolve about 50 lines/mm., a process plate emulsion about 200 lines/mm. and the Formalith and Kodalith materials mentioned below, about 800 lines/mm.

Resolving Power of Lens-Emulsion Combination. The resolving power of a lens-emulsion combination is always appreciably less than the resolving power of either taken by itself. Some idea of the combined resolving power of the combination may be gained by the statement that the reciprocal of the resolving power of the combination is equal to the sum of the reciprocals of the resolving power of the lens, when forming a visual image, and that of the emulsion. Thus a lens with a resolving power of 250 lines/mm. working with an emulsion with a resolving power of 200 lines/mm. will produce a negative with a resolving power of about 110 lines/mm.

The effect of Stopping-Down. It is well known that stopping-down decreases the effect of the residual aberrations of the lens, but the process cannot be continued indefinitely. As a rough approximation, it may be said that when a lens is stopped down for about two stops from the maximum aperture, the most perfect definition along the axis is obtained. Further stopping-down will often improve the general focus at the price of a slight loss of definition along the axis. Excessive stopping-down will bring into play two factors which will more than negative any further improvement in definition. The first is the drop in resolving power, which is proportional to aperture, and the second will be the softening of the image. This second effect is due to the phenomenon of diffraction which has already been referred to as one cause of poor definition, and the smaller the stop the greater is the deleterious effect of diffraction on the image. This rules out for critical photography careless focusing followed by excessive stopping-down to increase the depth of focus so as to compensate for imperfections in focusing.

The Effect of Exposure on Definition. In spite of the considerable exposure latitude of many emulsions for general purposes, the maximum resolving power of an emulsion is only achieved when the exposure is correct. Under-exposure is more harmful than over-exposure, as it is certain to result in loss of detail. With the Formalith negative materials referred to later, a slight modification in exposure will often have a profound influence on the final result, so that a certain amount of trial and error may have to be indulged in to obtain the maximum sharpness in the image.

The Effect of Development on Definition. The resolution of an emulsion is affected by the composition of the developer, the temperature and the time of development. As might be expected, fine-grain development gives better resolution than coarse-grain development because of the reduction in grain size. Any appreciable departure from the optimum temperature range for development will result in loss of resolution. The influence of modifications in the scheme of development in the production of " sharpness " as distinct from " resolution " is dealt with below when Formalith materials are discussed.

Other Factors which Affect Definition. The use of a lens of low resolving power with an unsuitable emulsion is certain to result in the production of photographs of poor definition, but this does not mean that if a lens of high resolving power is used with an emulsion of equal quality, photographs of good definition are certain to result. The calculated resolving power of the lens and emulsion combination is only one of the factors involved.

The condition of the surfaces of the lens is all-important. Any " blooming " must be perfect and not have been removed in patches through careless cleaning. Any grease or condensed moisture on the lens will be certain to cause diffraction effects which will reduce resolution. During exposure, the lens must be protected from any strong extraneous light which will cause veiling of the image or the production of flare spots, as it is inadvisable to rely on the blackening of the inside of the lens mount to absorb all the unwanted light which falls on to the lens.

Even when the condition of the camera and lens is all it ought to be, definition may suffer through loss of contrast and diffusion of the image; this may take place in both the emulsion of the negative and that of the final print. Methods for the reduction of this unwanted diffusion which results in loss of sharpness in the final image is dealt with when " Fine Line " development is discussed.

Focusing

Judging from some of the photographs of documents which are produced in court, too little regard is paid to the problem of ensuring good focus. The best of lenses will produce results which are inferior unless they are correctly focused; this is the first essential if the finest detail is to be registered on the negative.

It may be of some interest to record that as the result of work on the preparation of graticules for use in optical instruments by photographing a greatly enlarged drawing of the graticule on to a " maximum resolution " plate, it has been discovered that a movement of a thousandth of an inch in either direction from the optimum position of the plate will produce a serious falling off in the quality of the graticule.

It is not suggested that it is either practicable or desirable to focus documents to an accuracy of a thousandth of an inch, but this finding indicates that care spent on focusing will be amply repaid in the quality of the negative, especially as the resolving power of a lens is dependent upon accurate focusing.

There is no excuse for anything which falls short of perfection where photographs of documents are concerned. The document lies in one plane so that the problem of ensuring sufficient depth of focus does not exist and there is also full control of both lighting and exposure. A photograph which is not critically sharp and evenly illuminated is of no more use than the much cheaper reflex or photostatic copy.

Most document photographers are content to use the ground glass screen for focusing. Except for the preliminary operations of adjusting the size of the image and obtaining a rough focus, the ground glass screen is far too coarse for critical work.

Parallax focusing

Precision in focusing can best be ensured by the adoption of a coincidence method of parallax focusing. This may be carried out in several ways. Probably the simplest is to have the conventional ground glass screen rendered transparent in the centre of the field, either during manufacture of the screen or by cementing a thin circular cover-glass to the ground-glass surface by means of Canada balsam. A cross should be marked on the ground glass before the cover slip is cemented in position, or if the centre portion has been left clear during manufacture, a cross should be marked on the glass surface with a suitable marking pencil.

The only other accessory is a magnifier. To make this, a lens should be mounted in a tube so that it brings into focus any area against which the end of the tube is placed. A short-focus camera lens of fairly wide aperture is excellent for this purpose and the tube may be of metal, plastic or even strong cardboard.

To use the device, the image of the document should be focused on to the ground glass as carefully as possible. When this has been done, the magnifier is applied to the clear centre of the ground glass, when it should be possible to see both the cross on the ground glass and the image of the centre of the document at the same time. If the image is exactly in focus, that is, when it is in the same plane as the cross which has been marked on the surface of the ground glass, movement of the eye will not result in movement of the image of the document relative to the cross. If, however, the image of the document and the cross are not in the same plane, then some degree of relative movement of cross and image will be perceived. Whichever of the two—image or cross—is farther from the eye, will appear to move in the same direction as the eye—the parallax effect. The focus should then be adjusted until all relative motion appears to cease as the eye is moved.

With the conventional method of focusing on to a ground-glass screen, the eye is called upon to judge the sharpness of the image whilst the focus is being adjusted; in the parallax method, not maximum sharpness but the absence of relative motion must be looked for—a task which most observers find much easier to accomplish.

Alteration of Focus with Change of Aperture

Whilst some makers state that their best lenses are free from this defect, there is no doubt that the focus of the majority of lenses is appreciably if only slightly affected by alteration in aperture. Unless the lens which is being used is known to retain its focus unchanged by alteration in aperture, it should be made an invariable rule to focus at the aperture at which the lens will be used for making the exposure.

It is bad practice to use too small an aperture, for a first-class lens is usually designed to work with its aberrations at a minimum somewhere near its full aperture. Apart from this, the use of a tiny aperture does little to improve sharpness, and indeed it can be expected to produce a number of undesired diffraction effects which have a bad effect on the image.

The most careful focusing is rendered of little avail if the camera construction does not allow the sensitive surface of the negative to be sited in the same plane as that previously occupied by the inner surface of the focusing screen. If there is any reason to suspect that failure in this respect is the cause of unsharpness, a test should be made by taking three separate negatives of the same document, preferably a test chart. The first is taken with the camera accurately focused, the second with the screen racked slightly towards the lens, and the third after the screen has been moved slightly farther back than the position of best focus. If the siting of the negative is all that can be desired, then the first negative should exhibit the sharpest focus. If either of the others is in sharper focus than the first, the nature of the alteration to the camera which is required can be determined and the necessary correction applied.

Neither achromatic nor apochromatic lenses are fully corrected for photography with either ultra-violet or infra-red radiation. With an achromatic lens, the approximate focus for infra-red can be determined by focusing first with white light and then increasing the extension of the camera by about one-half per cent. The final adjustment can only be made by trial and error. With an apochromatic lens, a good approximation to the correct focus can be made by visual focusing with a deep red filter such as the tri-colour red.

For the ultra-violet, no simple rule can be given. For the best results, preliminary focusing should be done through a blue filter, and the distance of the plate from the lens reduced a little at a time until a trial exposure produces the most satisfactory result. This procedure is necessary only when the photograph is being taken by ultra-violet light. When the visible fluorescence produced by ultra-violet light is being photographed and a filter is used before the lens to exclude any reflected ultra-violet light, focusing must be accomplished visually in the normal manner.

Light Sources for General Photography of Documents

As already stated, gas-filled coiled-coil tungsten filament lamps are used as the light sources in the Illuminator. These lamps are very suitable for general purpose document photography, as the exposure can be controlled by switching them on and off provided it is longer than about ten seconds. Unlike most discharge devices, the light from these lamps covers the whole spectrum, from the near ultra-violet to the far infra-red, so that they may be used with suitable filters throughout the whole of the visible range.

One serious disadvantage of the tungsten lamp is that the actinic value of the light emitted is very dependent upon the voltage; a drop of about five per cent. from the normal rating will result in a loss of about forty per cent. of the actinic value of the light. In the absence of any system of voltage control, this will render meaningless any records of exposures, and as the lamp ages, particularly when it has been slightly over-run, the gradual thickening of the deposit of tungsten on the inside of the bulb steadily reduces its light output.

At the author's laboratory, to avoid the difficulties in regulating exposures caused by fluctuating mains voltages, lamps rated at 210 volts are run off the nominal 230–240-volt supply. The voltage applied to the lamps is kept steady at 205 volts by the use of a rheostat and voltmeter. The mains voltage rarely drops as low as

205 volts, and the fluctuations over the short time required for even the longest exposure are sufficiently slow to permit of manual control. The slight under-running of the lamps ensures that they have a long life at fairly constant light output.

There would be little difficulty in constructing an electronically operated voltage stabiliser, but the extra expense and trouble would not be justified; experience has shown that the simple arrangement described allows exposures to be adjusted and controlled sufficiently well for most purposes. This under-running of the lamps to keep their light output fairly constant has one serious disadvantage. When a blue filter has to be used, it will be found that the drop in running voltage has resulted in such a serious depletion of the blue and violet components of the light, that the normal exposure has to be increased by a factor of about forty. This will result in very lengthy exposures being necessary for any but the fastest plates.

Unless it is realised that the deliberate under-running of the lamps increases the exposure through a blue filter so considerably, large numbers of negatives are likely to be wasted through being under-exposed.

Exposures

Exposure tables are of little use in document photography, and in the majority of cases exposures have to be determined by trial and error. It is surprising how near to the correct exposure the first estimate will become with experience, and it is in the most exceptional circumstances that there will be any appreciable waste of negative material in determining the optimum exposure.

Fluorescent Lighting

There is no reason why fluorescent tubes should not be used for the general photography of documents. These light sources give a highly actinic light from a comparatively large luminous area so that little diffusing is necessary. The light is comparatively poor in red radiation, so that the tubes neither run hot nor do they appreciably warm the object being illuminated. They are comparatively simple to instal and the intermittent character of the light is no disadvantage. The one serious drawback to their use is that they do not reach their full intensity until they have been working for about ten minutes, which means that difficulties might be experienced with the timing of exposures; it follows from this that they cannot be used for control of exposures by switching on and off.

The use of daylight for general photography of documents has already been mentioned, but even in the most favoured parts of the world, its quality varies so rapidly with conditions that difficulties are sure to arise with the timing of exposures. It is sometimes very difficult to duplicate conditions, and in this respect artificial light has much to recommend it, even when it might be possible to do all the necessary photography by daylight.

In the author's laboratory daylight is never used for document photography. This is because accurate records are kept of every negative which is prepared; with controlled voltage and under-run lamps, exposures can be compared or duplicated in a way which is not possible if daylight were the illuminant.

Photography in Colour

Practically all photographs of documents are reproduced in monochrome, usually shades of grey which range from white to black. Toning is rarely resorted to, except as a measure designed to confer long life and freedom from colour degradation on to a photograph which is being kept for record.

In view of the striking advances made in colour photography, it might be thought that colour would greatly extend the value of photography applied to the examination of documents. When, however, the matter is considered in the light of all the facts, it will be found that colour photography—as practised in 1958—has far less to offer to the document examiner than might at first be supposed.

In the first place, it is agreed on all sides that no practical system of colour photography at present in use, or even contemplated, pretends to give anything but an imperfect rendering of the colours of the original. Whilst it is admitted that modern colour photographs can be most pleasing in appearance, and may carry more information than photographs in monotone, the only reason they appear so satisfactory is that few people have a true memory for exact shades of colour. If a scene is photographed in colour and the finished product is viewed some days afterwards, there is no opportunity of comparing it, tint for tint, with the original, so that the deficiencies in the colour rendering in the photograph are not apparent. The author has made colour photographs of groups of postage stamps. When compared with the originals, no matter what process was used, the inaccuracy of the colour rendering was most apparent.

One of the reasons for the comparatively poor rendering of colour is that the colours in all contemporary systems of colour photography are produced by dyestuffs. The dyestuffs available to the photographic chemists are by no means infinite in number, and those which are used in colour photography have been selected as the result of compromise. Any particular dyestuff actually in use may not give the best possible rendering of colour, but it has probably been chosen because it is superior to others of more satisfactory hue but which might be too fugitive, or possess other failings which more than counterbalance their superior colour rendering.

It is unfortunate for the document examiner that the dyestuffs which would have to be used to reproduce the dark blue-violet tones of ink lines are by no means ideally suited for correct colour rendering, for true colour photographs of ink lines would be certain to be of considerable value in some fields of document examination. At the time of writing, there is *no* colour process which can be relied upon to reproduce accurately the various shades of colour through which an iron tanno-gallate ink line changes as it ages.

What has been said about the reproduction of the exact shades of colour of an ink line also applies to the photography in colour of the faint stains found on paper in the region of a chemical erasure. Slight differences in colour are of such significance in the examination of a questioned document that any colour process would have to be capable of reproducing, not only the general coloration of a document, but also any delicate shadings of the main colours present. There are other difficulties which would be likely to attend the use of colour, apart from the inability of any commercial process to give tolerably exact colour renderings. For presentation in a court of law, all the copies of any one photograph must be so alike that no differences are distinguishable between them. With monochrome photography, photographic materials are so standardised and reliable that if one takes the precaution of using both the printing paper and the negative material from the same packages, no difficulty is likely to arise in producing identical copies.

On the other hand, at the present time, there is no certainty that any two copies of a colour photograph will be identical, or even so similar that differences are not immediately apparent when they are placed together for comparison.

Availability of Colour Material

The term " resolution " can hardly be applied to colour film,[5] but it is another source of difficulty that the most satisfactory colour film for the reproduction of fine detail is supplied only in the 35 mm. size and has to be sent to the makers for processing after exposure. This seriously limits the apparatus with which this film can be used, and it also poses other problems such as that of security or exposure of evidence, which must be ever present in the minds of those who work in government laboratories.

It is possible to purchase cut-film which can be processed " at home " with the special chemicals supplied by the makers. This cut-film is available in a wide range of sizes, and quite pleasing colour photographs of documents have been made in the author's laboratory. In the present stage of development these colour photographs are regarded more as coloured illustrations than as scientific exhibits for court use.

No details of lighting, exposure or development are given here for the production of colour photographs. The literature supplied by the makers should be consulted by anyone who wishes to undertake this work. Absolute cleanliness, careful control of temperature, close adherence to the instructions during processing and a long purse, are the essentials if colour photographs of documents are to be prepared as a routine procedure.

Filters

A photographic filter is a simple device which is used to absorb light of some wave-lengths, but to transmit that of others. Filters play a most important part in the photography of documents, and it is extremely fortunate for the document examiner that an exceptionally wide range of filters is commercially available. A filter may take the form of a glass or plastic cell with parallel sides filled with a suitable coloured liquid, but more often the effective component consists of a dyed film of gelatine or transparent plastic. The coloured film may be used in the form of an unsupported sheet, but is more often found cemented between thin sheets of specially worked glass. When cemented between sheets of glass, the coloured film is rarely more than a tenth of a millimetre in thickness with a variation in thickness of about one per cent.

[5] " Resolving-Power Measurements on Colour Film," *British Journal of Photography*, Vol. 101, July, 1954.

Whilst the interposition of even the most perfect filter between the lens and the object being photographed causes a slight increase in the residual aberrations of the lens, in practice this is unlikely to be appreciable, and the gain in the scope of the photographic process by the use of filters is more than enough to offset this slight disadvantage. Any alternative position for the filter, such as between the lens components or between the lens and the negative, is ruled out because the inevitable distortion produced by the filter is least when it is placed in front of the lens.

With very precise work, where the least effect upon the performance of the lens is desired, the thin unsupported film should be used alone, because this causes the least alteration in the optical length of the paths of the light-rays entering the lens. However, because of the obvious objections to the use of the fragile unsupported film, except for special work, glass-protected filters are used almost exclusively in document photography.

Glass-protected Filters

Glass-protected filters are usually supplied in two qualities. The cheaper " B " filters, to use the Wratten nomenclature, use glass which has been rendered plane-parallel in the sheet, and are quite satisfactory for most document photography. The more expensive " A " class filters are individually surfaced to the same degree of accuracy as a good quality lens. The use of these high-class filters is justified only when the lens is of long focal length and is being used at large apertures, or when the utmost perfection is desired in the rendering of the finest detail in copy work. With other makers of filters such as Ilford, the scheme of lettering is reversed so that the " A " quality is the cheaper. Ilford list four grades of filter. " A " quality refers to filters which are cemented between glass of ordinary quality. They are quite suitable for examining documents visually, but not for photographic work of any precision. " B " quality filters are cemented between optically worked glass and are suitable for all photographic purposes except when the highest precision is required. The other two classes are—

Optical Flats

These are cemented between glass worked to optical flatness with a precision greater than that used for most lens manufacture. These are suitable for work of the highest precision but their general use is ruled out because of cost.

Lamp Filters

These are coated on glass and are protected by a second sheet of glass, a mode of construction similar to that used for dark-room safe lights. They should never be used as part of an image-forming system.

Some filters are made entirely of special glass such as the ultra-violet transmitting filter No. 828 of Ilford. These are finished to " B " quality and are about 3 mm. thick.

Combinations of Filters

Filters may be used in combination but this course should never be taken unless it is unavoidable. If more than one filter is used, the definition will be adversely affected by the scattering of light which takes place at the various surfaces, as well as by the accumulated errors of the many sheets of glass through which the light has to pass.

Focusing must be done with the filter in place, because if the filter is in the preferred position between the lens and the document, this will bring the document optically nearer to the lens with consequent alteration in focus. Dummy filters of glass enclosing a film of undyed gelatine are available to facilitate focusing when exposures have to be made through very dense filters.

There is no theoretical reason why the filter should not in some instances be used between the source of light and the document so as to avoid the deleterious effect on definition when the filter is used at the lens. There are, however, certain practical difficulties in that large filters will probably be necessary, and some bleaching of the dyestuff incorporated in the gelatine may be anticipated if powerful beams of light are transmitted by the filters for long periods. The quality of the glass used for the protection of these large filters which do not enter the optical path of the lens need not be high, and for most purposes ordinary sheet is quite satisfactory.

A good example of the filter being used at the light source is the Woods glass filter, which is fixed before a source of ultra-violet light to prevent the passage of visible light. This arrangement has the added advantage that a filter of different characteristics may be used before the lens of the camera to supplement the effect of the filter at the source of light.

Care of Filters

When not in use, filters should be kept in the dark so as to minimise the fading of the dyes in the coloured film. The glass surfaces should be treated with the same care as the surfaces of a lens.

If a filter film consists of dyed gelatine, it is imperative that the filters be protected from moisture or humid conditions which would cause the film to swell and consequently to separate or deform the protecting sheets of glass. This would ruin the filter for practically every purpose except visual inspection. Gelatine or plastic film filters unprotected by glass may be varnished with a solution of celluloid in a mixture of amyl acetate and acetone which will give a certain amount of temporary protection. It should be remembered that this varnish film will slowly yellow with time especially if it is exposed to strong light.

It is probable that a solution of polymethylmethacrylate in chloroform would provide a softer but more permanent protection, as this plastic is relatively unaffected by light. The problem of the protection of film filters is not very serious, because the bare film is very reasonable in price, so that the filters may be replaced when they become unserviceable.

Damp gelatine is subject to rapid microbiological attack whether loose in the form of sheet or held between glass plates. This is certain to ruin any filter, so that in humid conditions great care should be taken to keep filters both cool and dry.

In photography which is undertaken purely for purposes of record, filters are used to compensate for the deficiencies of the negative emulsion or for the conditions of lighting. The use of filters for special examinations will be considered at a later stage.

No details are given here concerning the range of wave-lengths covered by commercially available filters and the emulsions and lighting sources for which they have been designed. The large photographic material makers issue literature which gives the fullest up-to-date information about the filters they market, and there is no point in duplicating the information for it would probably be out of date within a very short period.

Care should be taken to attach the filter very securely to the front of the lens of the camera; many of the commercial attachment devices are too flimsy in construction to remain reliable with use. It is also important to see that the filter surface is at right angles to the optic axis of the lens, for if it is placed at any other angle the distortion created will be appreciably increased.

The large lens hood described for use with the Illuminator allows ample space for the fixing of the filter to the front of the lens, well inside the body of the lens hood.

PHOTOMICROGRAPHS

The Illuminator and its associated equipment will serve admirably for making negatives with a degree of reduction of from just over four times, to approximately normal size when the nine-inch lens is used, and the half-plate negative can be enlarged about five times in a commercial enlarger so that a magnification of about six times linear is all that can be expected of this combination. If a greater degree of magnification is required, a lens of a shorter focal length than nine inches can be used, but the limit to the magnification is imposed by the length of the camera bellows and the fact that illumination of the document becomes uneven if the document holder in the Illuminator is brought too near the lens.

If a lens of slightly shorter focal length is also used in the enlarger, it is possible to attain a maximum magnification of about ten times linear using the Illuminator and an ordinary enlarger.

Grain

If a greater degree of enlargement is sought by using a lens of much shorter focal length in the enlarger, the problem of grain would have to be faced.

Although the individual particles of silver in an emulsion are exceedingly small, they tend on development to aggregate into clumps. If a greatly enlarged print is made from a negative where there has been any considerable tendency for this to happen, the final print will lack definition and be most unpleasantly spotty, an effect known as " graininess."

It is, of course, quite possible to effect a considerable degree of enlargement of the negatives from miniature cameras, but a restricted range of emulsions and special fine-grain developers must be used. Not only this, but there is little, if any, latitude in the condition of processing if the negatives are to be capable of making enlargements in which the grain has been restricted to reasonable proportions.

Micro-cameras

There is no doubt that the most satisfactory method of producing greatly enlarged photographs of portions of a document is to effect most of the enlargement during the preparation of the negative. Here again, the document examiner is fortunate in that there are commercially available, lenses of high precision which have been designed to give enlarged images in the camera, so that all that is necessary for the preparation of direct enlargements on to the negative is a camera with sufficient extension to accommodate one of these lenses and a suitable system for the lighting of the document.

The lighting should be fairly intense to allow of both easy focusing and exposures which are not too long. At high magnification, the area being photographed is necessarily small so that no difficulty should be experienced in obtaining level as well as intense illumination.

The simplest system of illumination is to project an intense beam of light on to the document from a point just behind and to one side of the camera lens. A microscope lamp similar to the " Point-o-light " does very well for the purpose, but if a satisfactory lamp of this type is not available, it is easy to improvise a substitute. Many excellent photographs have been prepared by lighting the document with a 36- or 48-watt motor-car headlamp bulb mounted behind a simple lens such as a " Bull's Eye " or even a spectacle lens, so as to throw a rough image of the filament on to the document.

While this simple system is quite effective, the most efficient general-purpose arrangement for the lighting equipment is that used at the author's laboratory. In this, the camera lens protrudes through the centre of a motor-car headlamp reflector. The reflector itself is pierced to allow four 12-watt 12-volt lamp bulbs to project symmetrically through it. The bulbs are mounted in holders fixed to the outside of the reflector. With the assistance of the reflector, these bulbs throw an even flood of light just where it is required—about an inch or so in front of the lens.

A lens of a focal length of about three inches will accomplish practically every task for which this apparatus is suitable. The selection of the lens is important. A landscape or general-purpose lens is not satisfactory because it has been corrected for forming a small image of a large object. This is the very reverse of what is required in a lens for producing direct enlargements on to the negative. If the circumstances do not permit or justify the purchase of a lens which has been corrected for this work, a general-purpose lens may be used if it is mounted back to front so as to have the back of the lens facing the document. This arrangement of the lens will minimise the distortion it would produce if it were mounted in the conventional way.

With a three-inch lens fitted in a camera with a reasonably long extension, a magnification ranging from about twice to six times linear can conveniently be obtained on the negative without any appreciable trouble being experienced from vibration. If higher magnification is needed, the rigidity and precision focusing mechanism associated with microscopical equipment are essential to ensure worthwhile negatives.

It is often possible to adapt a vertical enlarger for use as a micro-camera. The short-focus lens is substituted for the projection lens, and the lamp house and condenser, if any, are removed to allow the substitution of a camera-back which accommodates the focusing screen and the dark slide holding the negative.

The vertical position for the bellows is most convenient, for the document may be rested on the table of the enlarger.

With a magnification of about six times on the negative, which can be followed by a further four or five times in the enlarger, the majority of the extreme enlargements which are required can be made with the apparatus just described, but there may be occasions when considerably greater enlargement is called for. When this is so, a conventional microscope must be used for providing the greater part of the enlargement, the camera portion of the apparatus being used merely for recording the image produced by the microscope.

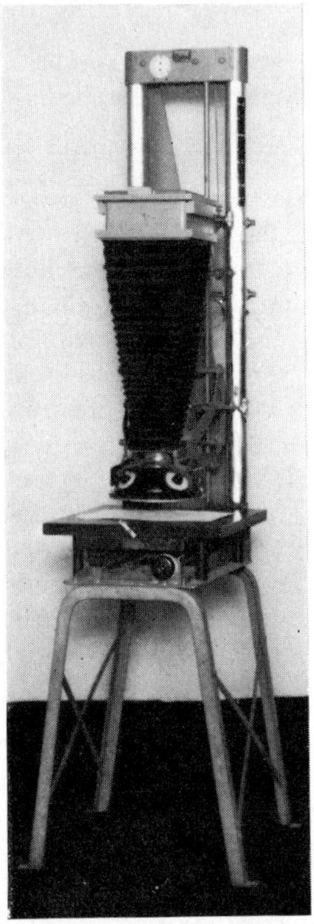

Fig. 6–4. Micro-camera improvised from a vertical enlarger. The document illuminator fixed to the lower part of the bellows consists of a reflector through which protrude four motor-car headlamp bulbs.

Most modern microscopes can be fitted with camera attachments which can record photographically the image as it is observed in the microscope. In document examination, the use of high-power objectives is rarely necessary, and most of the work can be covered by objectives of a sixth of an inch and longer focal length. As this is so, the use of a microscope with a built-in camera attachment is not essential, for it is possible to use a conventional microscope coupled to a camera of the focusing type used for making ordinary photographs.

Improvised Apparatus for Preparing Photomicrographs

Many schemes have been devised for using a conventional microscope in conjunction with an ordinary camera for the preparation of photomicrographs. Whilst they differ in detail, the principle is the same in every case. The magnification is obtained from the microscope objective as this is designed for producing a large undistorted image of a small object. Either the eyepiece lens of the microscope, the objective lens of the camera, or, in some arrangements, both, are then used to throw the enlarged image formed by the microscope objective on to the plate in the camera.

The simplest arrangement is to remove the lens from a camera fitted with a ground glass focusing screen. The eyepiece of the microscope is placed so that it is up against or just inside the gap left by the removal of the camera lens. After a light-tight joint has been made between the microscope and the camera, all that remains to be done is to focus the objective of the microscope so that the enlarged image is in good focus on the ground glass. The degree of enlargement can be controlled by the selection of the microscope objective and the extension of the camera. The main difficulty is that of accurate focusing, for the light transmitted is so limited that the image on the ground glass is very dim.

An arrangement which dispenses with the need for focusing the final image is first to focus the object at infinity with the microscope (refer to any book on microscopy for details) using both eyepiece and objective. The camera is then focused at infinity and its lens applied to the eyepiece of the microscope. This will give an image in good focus in the camera, which need have neither detachable lens nor focusing screen.

The exposure has to be determined by trial and error because too many factors are involved to allow of its being estimated with any degree of certainty.

Quite satisfactory results may be obtained with any of these simple arrangements, because document examination rarely demands the use of the higher powers of the microscope; a linear magnification of about twenty on the negative is sufficient for most purposes. Should more extreme degrees of enlargement ever be required, the only satisfactory procedure is to make use of conventional photomicrographic apparatus.

Enlargement

Unless cameras accommodating large sizes of negative material are employed, the problem of ensuring that there is no loss of quality on enlargement must be faced by any document examiner who wishes to supply photographs of reasonable size to illustrate and justify his findings.

The miniature worker is well served with a number of excellent enlargers, some of which are marketed by the firms which make the cameras, so that all that he has to do is to purchase the best instrument which he can afford from a first-class maker and then to use it strictly according to the instructions. An enlarger which is capable of producing acceptable results from a miniature negative is necessarily an expensive precision instrument, so that the purchase of a cheap enlarger is little more than a waste of money.

With a fair-sized negative, such as a quarter- or half-plate, the degree of magnification usually required is about three times linear. With reasonable care this should be accomplished with ease without any risk of graininess in the final print. It is only in the most exceptional circumstances that a higher degree of enlargement is necessary with a half-plate negative, but to cover all requirements the enlarger chosen should be capable in the last resort of producing an enlargement of about five or six times.

In spite of these relatively modest requirements, the half-plate worker is poorly served by the commercial firms. It is true that the market abounds with enlargers of a sort, whose prices range from a few pounds to many hundreds. For enlarging negatives of landscapes or portraits, many of these instruments can be counted on to give satisfaction, but when a precision enlargement of a photograph of a document from a half- or quarter-plate negative up to a size of twelve by fifteen inches is demanded, the position is quite different. Very few of the commercial enlargers which have been examined by the author have proved capable of this achievement, the main faults being uneven lighting and distortion at the edges of the print.

Requirements in an Enlarger

Any enlarger should be thoroughly tested before purchase. The first test is to determine whether the negative, and consequently the final print, is evenly illuminated. Many enlargers fail in this respect and produce prints wherein the centre of the field has to be appreciably over-exposed to avoid serious under-exposure at the edges. A test for even lighting is easily carried out. At the outset, the enlarger should be set to give the maximum degree of enlargement of a negative of the size which is in greatest use, on to a sheet of white paper which is substituted for the printing paper. The negative is then removed from the enlarger and the intensity of the light falling on the paper is measured at various points in the field, with special attention being paid to the centre and the edges. The measurement of the intensity of the illumination can best be carried out with a light-meter. The selenium photoelectric cell coupled to a microammeter, to which previous reference has been made, is ideal for the purpose, but an exposure meter such as the S.E.I. (Salford Electric Company, marketed by Ilfords) is also quite suitable. In this instrument—and in others which work on the same principle—an adjustment of a built-in lamp is made until a bright patch in the field of view just merges into the background when the instrument is directed at the place whose luminosity is being measured.

If the illumination is even, the reading of the microammeter in the first instrument mentioned, or the adjustment of the lamp in the second, should remain constant whatever portion of the paper is examined. The test is repeated at the position of minimum enlargement and at an intermediate position. It is surprising how many enlargers fail to pass this test for even illumination.

The second test is far more searching and is mainly concerned with the quality of the lens of the enlarger. The normal type of lens supplied with even the most expensive instrument, a simple anastigmat, is quite useless for precision work, but its shortcomings cannot be realised by testing its powers on a negative of a landscape or portrait. The best test-negative is one made specially for the purpose from the test charts for testing lens resolution previously referred to. (See p. 162.)

To prepare a test negative, four charts should be set up in the middle of the field and the others arranged so that they appear along the edges of the test negative. A process lens should be used in the camera and a high contrast emulsion such as Kodalith or Formalith selected for making the negative. If this is correctly exposed and developed in a vigorous developer, a negative with practically clear gelatine separating dense black lines at both the centre and the edges should result; no reduction, intensification, or other treatment of the negative should be necessary. When thoroughly dry, the negative should be examined all over with a low-power microscope to confirm that the edges of all the lines are sharp, and that the widths of the lines and spaces in the finest groups are not noticeably different from each other.

The test negative is placed in the enlarger, which is set to give its maximum degree of enlargement, and the lens is opened to its fullest aperture. The image is focused on to a sheet of white paper so that the maximum degree of definition is achieved in the centre of the field. With many enlargers it will immediately be noticed that the definition at the edges of the field is vastly inferior to that in the centre, and that only the coarsest groups can be recognised as distinct lines and spaces, the others appearing as grey blurs. An improvement in the definition at the edges of the field will almost certainly be obtained by some adjustment of the focus, but this will almost certainly result in a serious loss of definition in the centre. If the lens is stopped down, a general improvement of the focus over the whole field may be obtained by compromise focusing.

Very few enlargers will give really good definition at both the centre and at the edges of the field at a reasonable lens aperture, unless they have been fitted with lenses far superior to the quality of the usual enlarger lens. In the experience of the author, the only lens which can be expected to give definition of the quality which is essential for document examination is a process lens, and it is this very expensive type of lens which he uses at his laboratory.

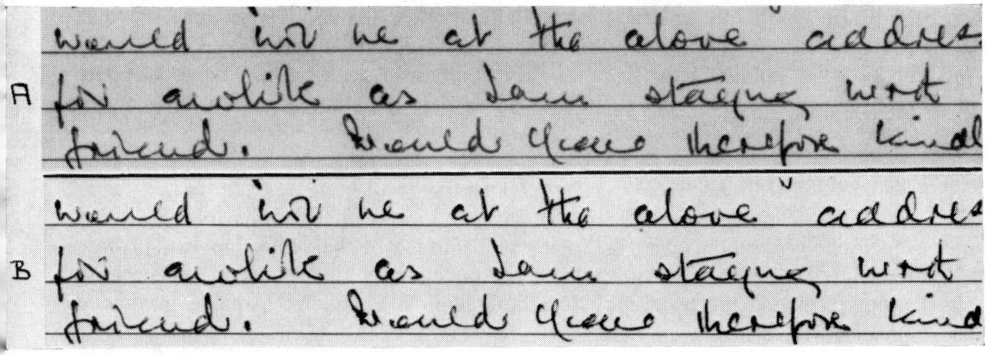

Fig. 6–5. " A " and " B " are prints from the same negative, on paper of the same degree of contrast, prepared in two different enlargers. The enlarger used for " A " had a diffuse lighting system whereas that used for preparing " B " had a condenser system. The increase in contrast shown by " B " over " A " is a striking demonstration of the influence of the lighting system.

In an enlargement of an ordinary photograph, all that is required is fair definition at the point of interest; any slight falling off elsewhere might even add to the artistic quality of the picture. This device of ensuring the best definition at one place on the print cannot be applied to a photograph of a document, for if a page of typescript is photographed, the observer of the final print will expect to find the typescript at the edges of the print reproduced with the same accuracy as that in the centre.

If the enlarger is to take advantage of the high quality of a process lens, it must be strongly and, above all, rigidly constructed with all essential parts guarded against any possibility of relative motion due to vibration. Automatic focusing saves time but is a luxury which can well be dispensed with for scientific work. What is essential is a system of construction which allows the corners of the negative to be adjusted relative to the lens, so that the whole can be accurately focused on to the printing paper. Some enlargers are not capable of adjustment in this respect, and if they become distorted in any way, they are no longer capable of producing a well-focused print; an enlarger which can only bring one edge of a negative into sharp focus at a time is useless.

An electronic timer is a justifiable expense when numerous copies of any one print are required, for once the optimum exposure has been determined, the timer can be set to ensure that the same exposure is automatically repeated as often as required.

A good test of the camera-enlarger combination is to photograph the whole of a sheet of newspaper on to the size of negative which is in normal use, and then endeavour to make a full-size copy of the original in the enlarger. The final prints should then be compared in detail with the original with special attention being paid to the edges. If the results of this test are entirely satisfactory, the apparatus is suitable for copying documents in general. If not, the source of any deficiency should be ascertained so that it can be eliminated by the appropriate action. An even more searching test is to photograph an ordnance map and then to reproduce it full size or slightly enlarged. No matter how well this may be done, the final result is much less impressive than the original. The difference stems from the liberal use of colour in the map, and the comparison with the monochrome photograph shows how badly a reliable system of colour photography is needed by the scientific worker.

Light Sources for Enlargers

On theoretical grounds, it is necessary to have a point source of light which is focused by the condenser on to the rear surface of the projection lens in order to obtain the ultimate in the faithful reproduction of the details of the negative. Except for some precision miniature enlargers, little attempt is made in practice to realise this ideal.

A true point source of sufficient power is not commercially available in a form which can conveniently be built into an enlarger lamp-housing, and even if it were, a very expensive condenser of considerable size and weight would be necessary to cover a large negative in anything like an adequate fashion. This is the reason why the majority of large commercial enlargers are fitted with diffuse light sources, which, indeed, have much to recommend them for general purpose work.

Diffuse Light Sources

If diffuse illumination is secured by the simplest means, by a number of spaced-out tungsten filament lamps placed behind a sheet of ground glass, an efficient and light-proof ventilating system must be incorporated into the apparatus. This is because a considerable proportion of the energy output of the lamps takes the form of heat and of light of too long a wave-length to affect the emulsion of the bromide paper used for making the enlargement. Unless this excess heat is removed it will affect the negative and possibly the lens as well should the exposure be unduly prolonged.

The most recent development in achieving substantially even diffused illumination of a large negative is the application of the cold-cathode fluorescent tube in a coiled or grid-like form. These discharge tubes, which vary in length from about ten to thirteen feet, and in diameter from one third to one half of an inch, are actuated by leakage-reactance transformers. Although initial striking voltage of about two to three thousand volts falls to half when the discharge is passing, it is still sufficiently high to be dangerous which is why the apparatus must be both well insulated and well earthed. The wall temperature of the tube rarely rises above about 35°C., so that the luminous coil can be sited close to the negative without fear of causing damage by overheating. The fluorescent coating in these discharge tubes which is most favoured for photographic purposes is either the standard " daylight " powder or one based on calcium tungstate, which emits a highly actinic bluish light.

All diffuse-lighting systems tend to cause reduction in contrast in the enlarged image, which is why they are not entirely satisfactory for work in enlargers for document photography. Some improvement in contrast may be obtained when using a cold-cathode grid, by placing a single plano-convex lens between the grid and the negative with its convex facing the grid. If this is done it must be borne in mind that the positioning of grid, lens and negative with respect to each other is a matter for critical adjustment, otherwise the results with the lens may be inferior to those without it; incorrect adjustment will result in uneven illumination and the consequent production of " hot-spots." This is why cold-cathode sources are sometimes unjustly condemned when the faults are in the housing and not in the source itself.

Temperature affects the functioning and the light output of cold-cathode grids. Indeed, at very low ambient temperatures the tube may fail to strike until it has been warmed by external means. At ordinary temperatures the tubes deliver no more than about eighty per cent. of their maximum light output when first switched on. The output slowly rises as the tube warms up and after a period of a couple of minutes under normal conditions it reaches a steady state.

For accurately timed exposures, a shutter or safety filter must be used after the tube has been given enough time to reach a steady state, but with fairly long exposures, provided the tube has been allowed to warm up and is not given sufficient resting time between exposures to cool off, an on–off switch may be used to time the exposures.

Compromise Point Sources

The best compromise between the impractical completely-focused point source and the contrast-reducing diffuse lighting system is a comparatively small light source which is given a certain degree of focusing by means of a reflector.

As a tungsten filament lamp produces too much heat and non-actinic light to be entirely satisfactory, a mercury vapour lamp of the " Osira " type is utilised. A lamp of this class, rated at 125 watts may be substituted for a 1,000-watt tungsten filament lamp. This will be more convenient and result in a lessening of the running costs. The combination of a mercury vapour lamp of this type with a reflector, permits the construction of an enlarger light source which is entirely satisfactory for any but the most exceptional purposes.

The mercury vapour lamp is run at mains voltage with a choke in series to limit the current. Like all discharge lamps there is a lapse of some time before it reaches its full luminous output, so exposures have to be made with a shutter or filter after the lamp has reached a steady state. Although the electric discharge through the mercury vapour excites radiation of a number of different wave-lengths, for photographic purposes the light from a mercury vapour lamp may be regarded as substantially monochromatic. Whilst this light is highly actinic, it falls unpleasantly on the eye and some difficulty in focusing may be experienced. This is perhaps the only serious failing of this very efficient light source.

Degree of Enlargement of Documents

Some discussion of the degree of enlargement which is required for the general run of document examinations may be of assistance when apparatus has to be chosen.

If half-plate ($4\frac{3}{4}'' \times 6\frac{1}{2}''$) negative material is used, most documents will be copied on to the negative with a reduction of about two to three diameters, for which the Illuminator previously described will prove suitable when used with a nine-inch lens. If full-size copies are required, this negative must be used with an enlarger adjusted to give an enlargement of from two to three diameters.

If the purpose of the photograph is to illustrate evidence concerning authorship of handwriting, an enlargement of two diameters is advisable, for handwriting in its natural size is almost invariably too small for critical examination by the inexperienced. This degree of enlargement is well within the scope of the Illuminator and the enlarger.

An appreciably greater degree of enlargement is necessary where forged signatures are concerned, for many forged signatures pass muster in their original form because the disjointed individual elements of which they are so often composed are too small to be appreciated as separate factors in the make-up of the signatures. For these individual pen movements to be seen in their true perspective, an enlargement of four diameters or even more may be necessary. For this degree of enlargement the Illuminator is less suitable, so that it is best to employ the " semi-microcamera " with the three inch lens. The signature can then be photographed on to the negative with a magnification of about two to three diameters, so that the final print can be obtained with a magnification of up to as much as ten diameters, should this be necessary, without demanding too much of the enlarger.

If the forgery contains subtle retouchings associated with abnormal pen stops and lifts, an even greater degree of magnification may become necessary. In such cases a microscope should be used for obtaining the greater proportion of this enhanced magnification. A one-inch objective is usually sufficiently powerful to obtain the required magnification, but as most microscope camera attachments take small negatives, the enlarger may be required to give the little extra degree of magnification necessary to make a print of reasonable size.

Certain other investigations such as those concerned with the appearance of the intersections of ink lines may require even higher magnification, but anything over ten diameters is rarely called for.

With typescript, an enlargement of about two diameters is convenient where the evidence is to be on alignment characteristics, with a slightly greater magnification when defective typefaces are illustrated.

At first sight, an enlargement of ten diameters may not seem very impressive. Actually it means that the enlargement is no less than a hundred times the area of the original feature which was photographed. A postage stamp enlarged ten diameters would be slightly larger than this page of print.

Processing of Sensitive Material

Unlike photographers in other fields, who are at the mercy of conditions, the document photographer is in the fortunate position of being able to adjust both the intensity of the lighting and the duration of the exposure to secure negatives which are perfectly exposed. As this is so, development of negatives of documents taken purely for purpose of record should follow along conventional lines.

The makers of photographic material are in the best position to give advice, therefore their recommendations with respect to developers and time and temperature of development should be adhered to, for it is very unlikely that they can be improved upon. As this is so, any advice given here with respect to the processing of sensitive material would be superfluous.

Many makers of photographic materials issue special pamphlets and data books which are kept up to date by the issue of new data. It should not be forgotten that research on photography is vigorously prosecuted, and that from time to time new materials are placed on the market and improved techniques devised. Every document examiner should endeavour to become acquainted with new developments, because he may well find that some process which has been introduced to meet a need in some branch or science or art remote from document examination, may be adapted for his own purposes in a way not visualised by those responsible for its introduction. An example of this is the Kodalith and Formalith negative material which will be referred to below. These emulsions of high contrasts, which were introduced for the benefit of the photomechanical trades have revolutionised certain aspects of the work of the document examiner, and with their aid, faint markings which were previously undecipherable may now be reproduced in a way which could not be approached with more conventional materials and methods.

Photography for Purposes other than Record

Filters

Few photographs are taken without a filter. Whilst the general function of the filter is to correct the emulsion characteristics for the lighting employed, in the specialised photography which plays such a large part in document examination, filters have additional roles to play, and the success of the photographic section of a document laboratory is largely bound up with the skill which is brought to bear on the selection of the appropriate filter from the wide range which is now commercially available. The way in which filters are utilised for specialised photography of documents may best be dealt with by considering the functions which they are called upon to perform.

In the treatment which follows, principles rather than practical details are stressed, and only the broadest description is given of any filter which is mentioned. It is only on rare occasions that a particular filter is given an identifying symbol, and no attempt is made to describe individual filters or to give any detailed information about their characteristics. There is good reason for this; research work on filters is proceeding apace and a steady improvement in filter characteristics is being realised. Many of the filters which were popular with photographers a generation ago have been superseded by greatly improved types, and as their manufacture has ceased specific recommendations may become meaningless.

A document photographer should keep himself abreast of developments in this field and the current literature of the manufacturers should always be to hand.

From this may be drawn all the necessary information concerning filter characteristics with every assurance that full use is being made of the latest discoveries.

At the time of writing, practically all photographic filters depend upon the light-absorbing power of glasses or of mixtures of dyestuffs and related compounds. It may be that in the future, improved filters based on different principles, such as the interference of light, will become available to the photographer.

Photography by Ultra-violet light

It is not generally realised that there are two distinct procedures for the photography of documents by ultra-violet light.

The first may be referred to as "direct" photography.[6] In this, the photographic plate records the differences in the reflectivity of ultra-violet light at various places on the document, in exactly the same way as light and dark areas in the visible spectrum are recorded by conventional methods of photography. The eye is not sensitive to radiation in the ultra-violet, which is why any differences in reflectivity have to be recorded photographically. To accomplish this, any visible light which emanates from the surface of the document must be eliminated by means of a filter, so that the ultra-violet effects are not swamped by light of longer wave-length.

Whilst the range of ultra-violet radiations which can be used without employing a quartz lens system is restricted, because optical glass has little transmission for radiation of a wave-length less than 3,500 A., a useful band extending from 3,500–4,000 A. is available. This includes the powerful 3,650 A. line radiated by the mercury-in-quartz lamp. The best filter is one with characteristics approximating to those of the Wratten 18A (Ilford 601 or 828) which has a transmission band which extends from 2,580–3,950 A. to 395 mu. An emulsion of high contrast such as that of a process plate should be used.

The focal length of a lens to ultra-violet light is shorter than it is to visible light. To surmount this difficulty the lens should either be stopped down to increase its depth of focus, or the exact focus found by a process of trial and error.

Some photographic lenses have a distinct yellow tint; these should not be used as it is very unlikely that they will transmit very far, if at all, into the ultra-violet.

The exposure which will give the best results must be determined by trial and error, because it is impossible to take into account all the variables if an attempt is made to estimate its value.

The other procedure for photography by ultra-violet light is more correctly termed "Fluorescence Photography."

Fluorescence Photography

In this, no ultra-violet light is allowed to reach the negative, as it is stopped by a filter before the lens. What is recorded is the visible fluorescence which is excited when the ultra-violet light falls on the surface of the document.

Some fluorescence effects are sufficiently powerful to be distinguished by the naked eye, but others are so weak that they pass unnoticed. It is with these

[6] Svedberg, T., and Anderson, H., "Fluorescence Photography by Means of the New Wratten U.V. Filter," *The Photographic Journal*. LXIII, No. 1, Jan., 1923

weak fluorescence effects that the integrating power of the photographic process finds an important application. As it is visible light which must be recorded, it is necessary to use a panchromatic plate, unless the fluorescence is blue or green, when an orthochromatic plate will be equally suitable. The most satisfactory filter is one which is similar to the Wratten 2B or Ilford 102. The filter should be colourless so as to pass fluorescence of all colours, but should be opaque to ultra-violet light because a small leakage of this highly actinic light would be certain to veil any weak fluorescence effects.

One problem associated with this type of photography is the maintenance and, if possible, the enhancement of contrast. This can best be achieved by increasing the time of development of the negative by as much as 50 per cent.

The exposure which will give the most satisfactory result must be ascertained by trial and error. Whilst the ultra-violet light itself is highly actinic, the light excited by fluorescence is generally weak, and exposures may be very lengthy especially when the fluorescence is feeble and at the red end of the spectrum.

Infra-red Photography

In recent years, photographic emulsions sensitive to radiations in the infra-red have been extensively used in document photography. These emulsions are even more sensitive to light of shorter wave-lengths, so that they have to be used with filters which are opaque to visible radiation.

If it can be contrived that a document is " illuminated " by infra-red radiation from which all visible light has been removed by passage through a suitable filter, such as a thin sheet of ebonite, then a satisfactory photograph may be obtained without any filter before the lens of the camera being necessary. In practice it is found that the powerful metal filament lamps which are the only convenient source of infra-red radiation are very inefficient as generators of infra-red radiation, so that the remainder of their energy output appears in the filter as unwanted heat which has to be dissipated—often a matter of some difficulty.

By far the most convenient solution to the problem of infra-red photography is to use a filter which will pass only infra-red radiation before the camera lens. The problem of focusing when the infra-red filter has to be used has already been dealt with. (See p. 158.)

Background Suppression

Filters are of considerable use in document examination for the suppression of unwanted backgrounds. This is best accomplished by using a filter which is of the same colour as the unwanted background. A preliminary choice may be made by visually examining the document through those filters which experience suggests should be of the required hue, and then picking out those which appear to give the best suppression of the unwanted background. This visual test should not be regarded as final, because the sensitivity of the photographic emulsion is almost certain to be appreciably different from that of the eye. Therefore photographs should be prepared with a range of similar filters until the most favourable result is obtained.

It often happens that the unwanted background is multicoloured, when it would be unreasonable to expect a single filter or even a combination of filters to effectively suppress all the different colours. A procedure known as " Photographic Masking " is described below for dealing with this problem, but a much simpler partial solution may be attained by making the required material stand out from the unwanted background by the use of a contrast filter.

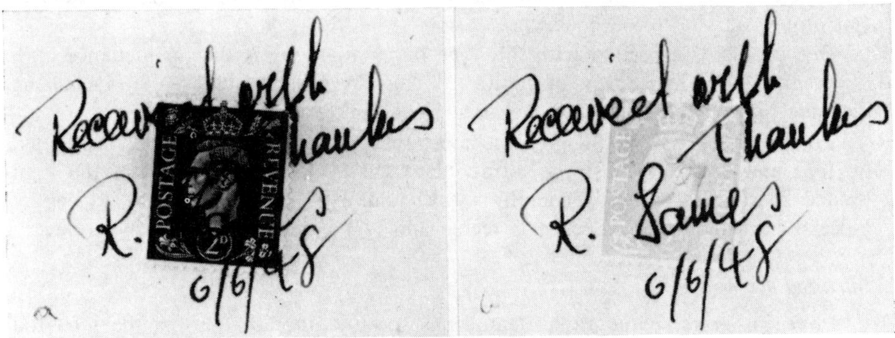

Fig. 6–6. In (a) the details of the signature cannot be distinguished against the stamp. In (b) the interference from the stamp has been suppressed by the use of an orange filter.

Contrast Filters. The general rule for the selection of a contrast filter is to try the effect of a filter of the complementary colour. The following table may serve as a guide:

Colour of Marking	*Contrast Colour*
Red	Blue Green
Orange	Violet
Yellow	Blue
Pink	Deep Green
Purple	Light Green

This table may be used in reverse.

As with the suppression of background, a number of experiments may have to be performed before the most suitable filter is discovered.

Contrast enhancement by the use of filters finds another important application as a most effective means of making a satisfactory record of faded writing or faint stains on documents.

Discrimination with Filters

Filters have considerable application as aids to discrimination. Two colours may appear identical to the eye although their spectral make-up may be quite different. In these cases it is sometimes possible to differentiate between them by visual examination through a succession of narrow-pass filters whose action is to remove light of a certain spectral range. If the two colours have a different spectral make-up, they are unlikely to be modified in the same way and to the same extent when viewed through the filters so that a difference in colour is apparent, when, without the filter, no difference could be seen.

If visual examination with a filter reveals no differences, it may happen that photography through the same filter will prove effective, for the photographic

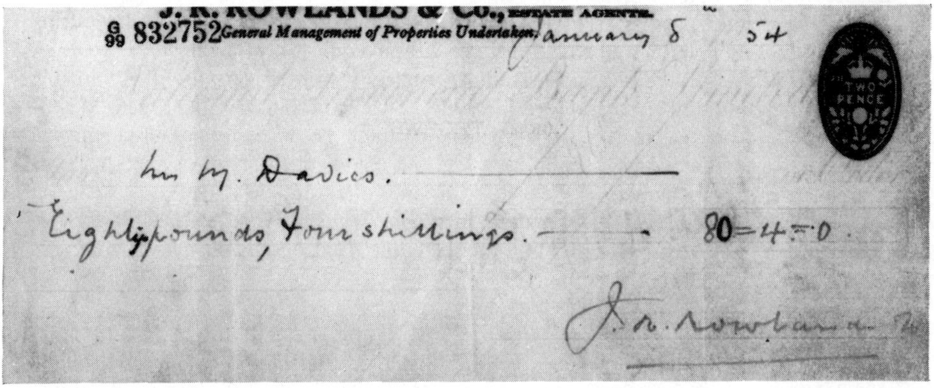

Fig. 6–7. Discrimination between inks by photography through a filter to show that a " y " has been added in a different ink to " Eight " and a " 0 " to " 8 " to " raise " the cheque.

emulsion will be unlikely to have the same spectral sensitivity as the eye. The filter may very well have affected the colours in a region to which the emulsion but not the eye is sensitive, in which case some discrimination is achieved in the photograph.

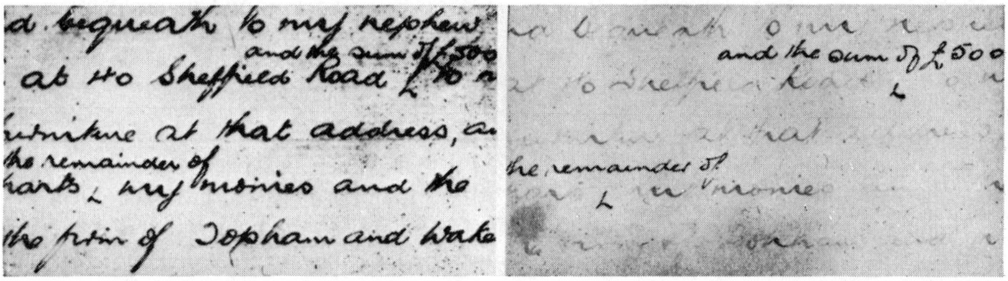

Fig. 6–8. Differentiation of inks by photography by infra-red. Whereas the whole of the ink writing appeared to be similar when taken with a panchromatic plate as shown on the left, photography by infra-red (shown on the right) shows quite clearly that the additions were made in an ink which had a greatly increased absorption for infra-red.

Improvised Filters

The commercial range of filters is so wide that practically all the demands of the document examiner are well catered for, but it may happen that a special filter will be called for at short notice to eliminate an unwanted background stain.

If the nature of the material causing the stain is known, an effective filter can often be specially prepared from the same material. The simplest way to do this is to fix and wash some unexposed photographic film and then to soak it in a concentrated solution of the staining material. This will give a filter consisting of a strip of cellulose nitrate or acetate with a coloured layer of gelatine on each side. Exposed film which has been bleached and washed is less satisfactory than unexposed film, because the gelatine layer is hardened during processing and becomes less absorbent of the colouring matter.

If this simple process does not yield a satisfactory filter, or if the colouring matter is not soluble in water or dilute alcohol, a liquid filter might be improvised. For this purpose a cell with sides made of optically worked glass is filled with the coloured solution and placed before the lens. This rather inconvenient method is of more general application than the dyed gelatine filter, because any coloured solution which does not attack glass can be used and the colour of the filter may be made as deep as necessary by increasing the concentration of the solution.

Liquid filters were extensively used in the past when dyed gelatine filters were not commercially available, so that there should be no difficulty in obtaining a suitable cell for holding the liquid.[7]

Filters used in Combination to enhance contrast

The action of a filter may be modified by alteration of the colour of the light which is used to illuminate the document. As a filter is characterised by its ability to pass light of certain wave-lengths and to suppress others, if light of some of the wave-lengths normally passed by the filter is removed from that which is incident on the document, then for all practical purposes, the action of the filter will have been modified.

In practice the colour of the incident light is often modified so as to assist the filter which is in use before the lens. When a contrast filter is being used to bring into prominence any particular markings, some of the background material may be made less obtrusive if the light by which the document is being photographed is passed through a filter of the same colour as the background it is desired to suppress.

In a similar way, the action of a contrast filter might be enhanced and the exposure shortened if the document is lit by light which has been passed through a filter of similar colour to that used with the camera. This will have the effect of brightening the background without adding appreciably to the light which is reflected from the markings it is desired to record on the negative as lighter areas.

Coloured Lighting

Coloured lighting is generally obtained by passage of white light through a suitable filter, usually a sheet of dyed gelatine, but monochromatic light, or light which is almost monochromatic, may best be obtained by the use of a discharge tube filled with the appropriate gas. Filters are rarely used with these sources of radiation except when it is desired to transmit substantially monochromatic light for physical measurements. The pink neon light is well known, but other discharge tubes such as the sodium tube for the D line are also available. Whilst small in size, some of the high pressure units have a considerable luminous output. At the author's laboratory, street lighting discharge lamps are used to good effect.

7 "Liquid Filters," *Kodak Data Sheet* F.T.5.

Polarisers

These may be regarded as filters of a special type which discriminate according to the plane of polarisation of the light rather than its wave-length or colour.

A polarising filter or " polar screen " as it is usually termed, consists of a sheet of special plastic which is bound between glass plates in much the same way as a dyed gelatine filter. The plane of polarisation of the light which is passed unaltered through the screen is generally marked on the screen mount. If two polar screens are arranged so that their polarising planes are at right angles, they should theoretically pass no light. In practice, owing to the failure of the plastic film to deal adequately with light at the extreme ends of the spectrum, a little reddish-violet light will still be passed even when the planes of polarisation are at right angles.

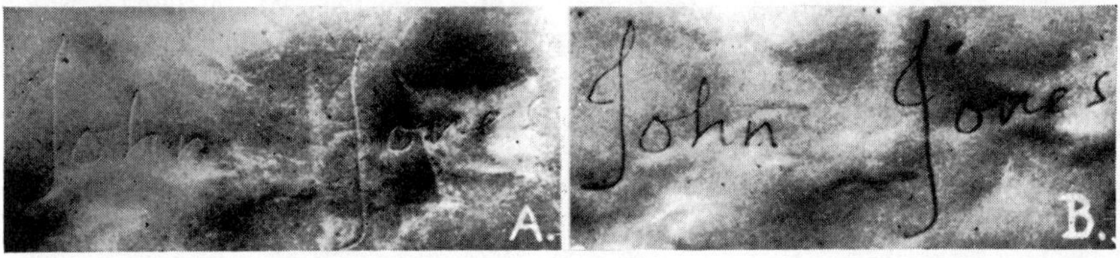

Fig. 6–9. " A " is a photograph of pencil writing on dark brown paper. The reflection of light from the surface of the pencil is greater than that from the surface of the paper. In " B " the reflected light from the pencil writing has been eliminated by means of a polarising filter so that the pencil records darker than the background.

In photography, polar screens have their greatest application in cutting out reflected light. Ordinary or scattered light will pass through a polarising screen to an extent which is unaffected by the orientation of the screen because it has no preferred plane of polarisation. On the other hand, a fair proportion of reflected light is polarised, so that it is often possible to adjust a polarising screen to effect an appreciable absorption of unwanted reflected light.

In the photography of a discoloured document, reflected light will often cause trouble when faint writing in pencil or in an ink whose colouring matter is highly reflecting is involved. It may happen that the light which is reflected into the camera lens from the reflecting surface of the line is about as intense as or even more intense than that reflected and scattered from the discoloured surface of the document. Under these conditions, the line of writing would photograph lighter than the surrounding paper, or might even merge into the background. The effect of the reflections may be sufficient to render the writing practically invisible in the final print. The cure for this condition is to adjust a polarising screen so that the polarised component of the reflected light is preferentially absorbed. In this way the normal contrast is preserved in the photograph instead of being reduced or even reversed.

Polarised light is reflected unaltered from a polished surface but is depolarised when scattered from a matt surface. Advantage may be taken of this when a very glossy document has to be photographed. A polarising screen is placed before the light sources so that the glossy document is lit with polarised light. Any reflected light from the surface of the document remains polarised and can be prevented from entering the lens by the interposition of a second polarising screen which is correctly orientated. Any direct reflection from the surface of a document militates against the production of a satisfactory photograph so that the loss of any directly reflected polarised light is desirable. On the other hand, the details on the surface of a document are best reproduced by the light which is scattered from that surface. As this scattered light is no longer polarised, sufficient will pass through the polar screen to register on the negative. Useful as this method may be, it is not the only way in which a photograph of a glossy surface may be made, for several other methods are described below.

It may be of interest to record that photography by polarised light is the basis of several schemes which have been devised for the production of three-dimensional effects in a single print. In these, photographs from the two separated positions are taken and printed together on special material. When the final print is viewed with spectacles fitted with polarised glasses, each eye is allowed to see only the appropriate image so that a stereoscopic effect is produced.

Photography of Matter on Highly Reflecting Surfaces

It occasionally happens that writing on a mirror or on some highly reflecting surface has to be photographed. If the camera is placed in the normal position before such a surface, a reflection of the camera may well appear in the photograph. To avoid any unwanted reflections appearing on the negative, the best procedure is to line up the reflecting surface before the camera in the normal fashion and then to tilt it slightly about one edge so that the camera no longer appears in the reflection.

Once the foreshortened image has been roughly focused, a sheet of paper or card of a colour which affords the maximum contrast with the matter it is desired to record is placed in such a position that it is this sheet which is reflected into the camera. As this is so, the matter it is desired to record will then stand out on a background of contrasting colour.

The camera lens is stopped down to increase the depth of focus and thus bring all the desired matter into focus at the same time. The distorted negative can be made to give an undistorted print by careful adjustment of the negative in the enlarger. To simplify this correcting procedure, two paper scales are stuck on to the reflecting surface at right angles. One scale is preferably fixed along the edge about which the sheet is turned, and the other is placed at right angles to the first.

When in the enlarger, both the negative and the paper holder are tilted so as to make the scales appear of the same size in the print. When this is done, an undistorted print free of all unwanted reflections will be obtained.

Photography by Transmitted Light

To photograph a document by transmitted light, all that need be done is to place the document between two sheets of glass and then to pass a beam of diffused light through the document which is photographed in the usual way. The only difficulty is in ensuring even illumination.

If the area of the document is small, then the light-beam may be diffused by placing a sheet of ground glass between the document and a tungsten filament lamp. A more satisfactory scheme is to place a tungsten lamp at the principal focus of an enlarger condenser lens which is large enough to cover the document, and then to rest the document on a sheet of ground glass which is placed against the condenser.

If a fairly large document has to be photographed by transmitted light, it is fixed to a sheet of glass behind which a sheet of glossy white card is placed about a foot or so away to act as a source of reflected light. The sheet of glossy card is lit as evenly as possible by shining lights on to it from the side. A fair amount of trial and error will probably be necessary before sufficiently even lighting is achieved.

Fig. 6–10. The cheque shown on the left was written above the fraudulently obtained signature, on a blank sheet of paper. The stamp was fixed over the original "Lena" and this name was then written on the stamp. (a) A photograph by ordinary lighting. (b) A photograph by transmitted light showing both "Lena"s. (c) A photograph by transmitted infra-red light to which the ink of the original "Lena" was opaque, and that of the "Lena" on the stamp transparent. Note the watermark on the stamp.

The illuminators designed for viewing radiographs make admirable light sources for transmitted light photography. The illumination is not only fairly even but is sufficiently powerful to allow of reasonable lengths of exposure. The scattering of the transmitted light may be minimised by the use of a yellow or even a red filter before the light source. If a yellow filter is used, orthochromatic negative material will have to be used. With a red filter, a panchromatic emulsion will be necessary.

It may sometimes happen that a straightforward photograph by transmitted light is unsatisfactory. This will be the case when the writing to be deciphered has been obscured by a gummed strip of paper which itself bears writing and in the circumstances cannot be removed; in such a case the negative will record both the overwritten and the original writings.

Where the two writings have been made in different types of ink, it may be possible to eliminate the interfering writings by the use of filters. An infra-red sensitive plate should be tried, for many dyestuff inks are transparent to infra-red which, on the other hand, is absorbed by both carbon and iron-containing inks.

If the interfering writing cannot be eliminated by the use of filters, it will be necessary to resort to photographic masking, a procedure which is treated in some detail below.

Increasing the Translucency of Paper

As a preliminary to photography by transmitted light, paper may be rendered more translucent by replacing the air in its interstices with a medium whose refractive index is near to that of cellulose (approx. 1·5). This will reduce the scatter of the light which passes into the paper.

The most effective liquid for this purpose is benzyl alcohol (refractive index 1·5396 for the D line). It evaporates slowly, and there is little risk of fire, but difficulty will be experienced in the removal of the last traces from the document, which will have to be kept in a current of warm air for some hours once the photography has been completed. A more convenient liquid is petrol ether, but this evaporates so quickly that the paper may have to be fed with fresh liquid during a long exposure. The vapour is also extremely inflammable, so that precautions against explosion and fire have to be most thorough when this liquid is used.

Paper is also treated in this way when it is being examined for traces of adhesive and the fragments of paper left behind at places where stamps have been removed. These stand out clearly on the more translucent paper where they may very well be overlooked on the untreated sheet.

Neither benzyl alcohol nor petrol ether will have any deleterious effect upon either pencil or ink writing, but certain ball-point pen inks are affected by these solvents. Before applying either liquid to a document, a test should be made on the writing with a tiny drop. The action should be watched with a microscope, and if there is any sign of the dyestuff running, some other liquid should be tried. There is a wide range of organic liquids with a refractive index of about 1·5, and it should be possible to discover at least one which has no effect on the ball-point pen ink in question.

Photographic Enhancement of Faint Markings

It is often desirable to be able to decipher markings on documents which either through accident (fading) or design (erasure) have become so faint that they are hardly discernible.

A substantial increase in legibility may often be achieved by conventional photographic procedures which result in the production of prints in which the contrast between the markings and the background has been appreciably increased; the use of contrast filters, special emulsions and control of lighting to this end has already been considered.

Where these conventional methods fail to achieve the desired result, recourse may be made to the employment of high-contrast negative material processed in an unorthodox manner.

Conditions Governing Intelligibility

Increased contrast alone is not always sufficient to confer any appreciable increase in legibility; indeed, too great an enhancement of contrast may well result in a considerable reduction in intelligibility. Consider a faint passage of typescript which contains characters showing considerable variation in intensity. Increase of contrast carried to extreme will cause the already considerable difference in intensity to increase. If the object has been to suppress the background, it may well happen that some of the fainter characters will be entirely suppressed along with the background.

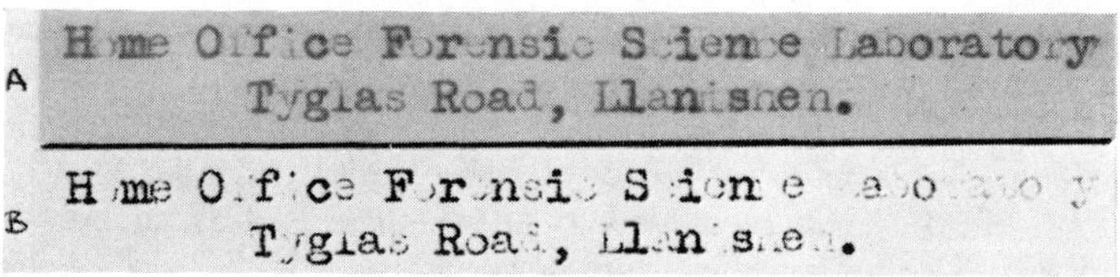

Fig. 6–11. A negative was made of a specimen of imperfect typescript on brown paper. " A " is a print on soft paper. " B " is a print on hard paper in which the contrast has been deliberately increased. Whereas the tint of the background has been suppressed in " B " and more heavily printed characters made more legible, the excessive increase of contrast has resulted in a loss of detail in the fainter characters, some of which are hardly reproduced at all.

In the same way, a faint handwriting characterised by relatively heavy downstrokes connected by appreciably weaker lines, which is not uncommon, will appear in the final print as a series of disconnected vertical strokes almost certainly less legible than the original of the photograph.

Even where the lines in the final print are rendered as intense black deposits of silver, a writing may remain indecipherable if the blackest of lines shade and merge slowly into each other and into the background; in spite of their high density, it may prove impossible to define and interpret the outlines because they are too diffuse for discrimination. On the other hand, in another print, the writing may be quite legible in spite of its being reproduced in a pale grey tone but little darker than the background. The difference lies in the fact that in this second print the edges of the lines, although faint, are crisp and sharp with little merging or shading into each other or into the background.

Experience has shown that legibility depends more on the attainment of this crispness than on either absolute density or contrast with the background. Crispness, which is the abrupt change in tone when passing from the line to the background, can be achieved by the combination of critical focus, the control of exposure and development and, most important of all, the selection of the appropriate negative emulsion.

When light falls upon a light-sensitive emulsion some is absorbed but the remainder is scattered throughout the emulsion, largely due to the turbidity caused by the presence of the particles of silver halide. It is this scattering of the incident light which is reponsible for the spread of the image, which can easily be seen where there has been considerable over-exposure. This means that unless steps are taken either to reduce this light scattering or to prevent its effects appearing upon development, the photograph will necessarily appear less sharp than the aerial image formed by the lens.

In the very slow Lippmann-type emulsions used for graticule production, the amount of scatter is reduced by employing a very dilute suspension of extremely finely divided silver halide particles. In this way, extreme resolving power of approximately a thousand lines to the millimetre may be obtained, largely because of the fineness of the halide particles and the lack of any perceptible scatter when the light passes through the emulsion. These maximum resolution emulsions are too slow and of too great a contrast for use with documents, so recourse must be made to negative material which relies upon a development procedure that largely eliminates the effect of the scattered light upon the final image.

Suitable negative material was introduced in 1952, primarily for photo-mechanical work, and is marketed under a variety of trade names (Kodalith by Kodak, and Formalith by Ilford).[8] At the present time it is marketed as an orthochromatic emulsion of exceptionally high resolving power and fine grain, which is capable of yielding images of very high contrast and extreme density. Incidentally, the statement by the makers that these plates are suitable for line-reversal by conventional etch-bleach methods should be borne in mind, for it means that positive images of exact size may be obtained without preparing a separate negative.

Kodalith and Formalith Negative Material

Whilst these emulsions have a resolving power which approaches that of the maximum resolution Lippmann-type, they have the great advantage that they are sufficiently fast for all ordinary purposes. Both these emulsions are similar in resolving power and speed, but at present the spectral sensitivities are not quite the same. Kodalith has its highest sensitivity in the violet and blue, whilst Formalith has a greater sensitivity in the green. The yellow sensitivity of both emulsions make them very suitable for the copying of writing on faded yellow documents, and their good qualities in this respect can be further enhanced by the use of a yellow filter.

[8] Hepher, " The Kodalith Plate," *The Penrose Annual*, Vol. 46, L.952.

The strongly alkaline hydroquinone developers used with process plates to obtain extreme contrast are unsuitable for Kodalith or Formalith plates which need a hydroquinone-formaldehyde developer.

When extreme resolution is required to ensure that the edges of the image are as sharp as possible, the effects of the scattered light may be minimised by the employment of a special technique for development, known as "Fine Line" development.

Fine Line Development

This has to be carried out with a special developer supplied by the makers of the plates, in conjunction with the "still bath" technique, as it is generally termed.[9] For the initial stages of the development, no departure is made from conventional practice, for the negative is placed in the dish, flooded with the developer and agitated until the image begins to appear. When this stage is reached, all agitation is stopped, the dish is covered and the negative allowed to remain in the still liquid until development is complete; this is determined in the usual way from considerations of time and temperature.

Various explanations have been given for the excellent results achieved in this way.[10] One is that the products of the development process itself appear to play the part of an accelerator in the initial stages, so that over a certain range of times development is almost an all-or-nothing process, leaving either a dense black image or clear gelatine to give increased contrast and a hard boundary between exposed and unexposed areas. (Ilford Technical Publication).

Another explanation is that during normal development with agitation and circulation of the developer, the end-products of development are steadily and continuously being removed from any areas where the image is being developed, and replaced by a constant stream of fresh developer. With the still-bath technique, development products accumulate around any areas of high density on the negative and restrain the development of those parts of the emulsion which border on them. This means that the light which has scattered into the emulsion at the edges of these areas is unlikely to be developed and represented as silver deposits in the negative by the time the development is brought to a close. In those parts of the negative where little development is taking place, there is an absence of any high concentration of developer end-products to restrict development which proceeds unhindered. This explanation accounts for the production of images whose edges are sharp and crisp.

There is no doubt that neither of the above explanations for the production of sharp crisp outlines by the fine-line technique can be considered entirely satisfactory, but whatever may be the true reasons for the effects produced, it is beyond question that the document examiner can achieve results with either of these new emulsions which but a few years ago would have been regarded as beyond any prospect of realisation.

Exposure times are critical if the fullest use is to be made of the fine-line technique, and when photographing faint markings, the document examiner must

[9] "Fine-Line Technique," *Kodak Data Book* PH–2.

[10] Yule, "The Kodalith Mechanism," *Journal of the Franklin Institute,* Vol. 239, No. 3, March, 1945.

resign himself to a fair amount of trial and error. With conventional negative material, the times of trial exposures are usually advanced in a geometrical progression, but with Kodalith or Formalith emulsions, once the approximate exposure has been determined, it may save time in the end if the intermediate exposures are made with increases based on arithmetical, rather than geometrical, progression.

Manipulation of Negative after Development

If " Kodalith " or " Formalith " negative material is not available a great deal can still be done to enhance contrast with ordinary process plates if they are given correct development and an appropriate after-treatment. A very full development in a vigorous hydroquinone developer should be followed by reduction with ferricyanide to reduce fog. A further improvement in the contrast of the negative can sometimes be effected by a careful intensification subsequent to the cutting with ferricyanide.

Some workers make a print on a paper of highest contrast at this stage, and then re-photograph the print in an effort to gain more contrast, but in most cases any improvement which results from this elaborate treatment is more apparent than real.

If the markings on the negative are very faint, care should be taken to ensure that nothing further is lost during the printing. If the printing is to be done by contact, the light should not be unduly bright, and in some cases an appreciable improvement may be obtained by the use of very feeble light indeed. If the printing is to be by projection, the preferred type of enlarger would be one where a small light source is utilised in conjunction with a carefully adjusted condenser, since this arrangement is ideal for the maintenance on the print of all the detail and contrast of the image on the negative.

Except for a small degree of reduction to improve printing quality, there is little to be gained by further work on the negative when the Formalith or Kodalith emulsions have been used.

Other Methods for the Improvement of Vague Outlines

When, in an effort to discover what has been erased, the site of an erasure is investigated whether by chemical or photographic methods, or a combination of both, there is usually little difficulty in demonstrating that *something* has been erased and it is generally possible to prepare a photograph which gives a vague impression of the original matter. With this photograph available, it appears at first sight that there should be little difficulty in deciphering what is shown thereon. However, when this is attempted it usually happens that the writing or typescript shown in the photograph seems to represent a different set of letters every time it is studied. After a fair period of study the outlines seem so protean in nature that it is quite impossible to read anything definite into them.

The erased matter as a whole can be seen quite easily, but as the various letters or figures merge gradually into each other and into the background, it becomes increasingly difficult to say exactly where the boundaries of any stroke should come in the writing, and without any definite guidance about this, the exact shape of any letter must remain a matter for speculation.

It has already been mentioned that it is not only the darkness of the photographic image, for this can be increased at will by increasing exposure, but its contrast with its immediate surroundings which is of the greatest importance when the boundary of a line has to be determined. Purely photographic methods of increasing the useful contrast have already been mentioned. These include the exclusion of all extraneous light which would veil the image, the use of photographic material of high contrast and special methods of development such as the " fine line " technique used with Kodalith and Formalith emulsions.

Occasionally all these are of little avail. When this happens, it is worth while trying any method which might give a line image which possibly can be deciphered, in exchange for a continuous tone which cannot be made to yield a recognisable letter pattern.

It is well known that it is possible to treat a continuous tone photograph in such a way as to produce a negative which will give a print which has much of the appearance of a line drawing. This interesting process was devised to permit the photo-mechanical reproduction of illustrations without the use of a half-tone screen.[11]

The final print is made from a composite consisting of the negative combined with a positive of nearly equal contrast. (This is not the same as, and must not be confused with, the production of a pseudo-relief effect by printing from a negative and a positive slightly out of register with each other.) In this case when a positive and a negative which exactly match each other in size and contrast are fixed together back to back, they exactly neutralise each other's tone values *except at the boundaries of the image.* If from this composite, a print is made by projection on to a high contrast material, a line image will be formed at the edges of areas of continuous tone.

The foregoing is but a brief account of the rather involved process which is necessary to make an acceptable conversion of a continuous tone subject into something similar to a drawing, but it should point the way to the possible improvement of vague outlines that cannot be deciphered by conventional methods. The practical details are as follows. From the negative of the more or less continuous tone image it is required to improve, there should first be made a positive transparency. This should be made by contact using a fine grain film, and the lighting should be derived from a point source. This positive transparency should be bound up against the negative and a print made by contact, using a light which is rotated above the printing frame so as to penetrate into each " edge " where the tones of the negative and positive have not quite neutralised each other. If a paper of high contrast is used, it may be possible to produce a decipherable print from this composite.

There is no guarantee that any real improvement will be effected in this way, but there is always the chance that the substitution of lines for merging tones will give a worthwhile increase in legibility.

11 " Kodak Tone-Line Process," *Kodak Data Book* PH–6

Spectral Sensitivity of Negative Material

The visual range of the human eye is about one octave, extending from about 4,000–7,000 Å. At the present time the document examiner has at his disposal a range of photographic emulsions whose sensitivity extends from the far ultra-violet (about 2,400 Å.) to the far infra-red (beyond 11,500 Å.). This extension into the infra-red is beyond that of the image-converter which is described elsewhere and which is used for "seeing" into the infra-red, for the silver-caesium cell employed as the detector of the infra-red in this instrument is unaffected by radiation of a wave-length greater than about 10,000 Å. Negative material with a sensitisation in the extreme infra-red finds little application in document photography and this is as well, for not only are these plates difficult to obtain, being made only to special order, but they have a short shelf-life even when stored in a refrigerator. They are also very expensive.

It is generally agreed that very little advantage is gained by using wave-lengths longer than about 8,000 Å. The tungsten filament lamps, which are by far the most convenient sources of infra-red radiation, have their maximum emission at about this wave-length and suitable plates are readily available, reasonable in price, and have a fair shelf-life when stored in a cool place.

A further advantage of working in this region is that with an apochromatic lens, focusing can be done visually if a filter such as the Wratten 91 or the Ilford Tri-colour Red is used. These filters transmit sufficient of the visible spectrum to enable quite sharp focusing to be carried out. When the exposure is to be made, the focusing filter is replaced by the infra-red filter. With the Ilford infra-red plate, the Ilford 207 filter is the most satisfactory; for Kodak plates the Wratten Infra-red filter is advised.

Special Emulsions

It should be borne in mind that most photographic firms list their negative material under a number of different headings. The usual practice is to distinguish between material sold for use in the arts and industry which makes up by far the greater proportion of their output, and that described under a title such as—to quote Kodak—"photographic emulsions for scientific use."[12] Many photographers are unaware of the existence of this second classification which includes emulsions of great interest to the document examiner.

The "Scientific" plates are supplied in a wide range of emulsions each with a range of different sensitivities. A few examples should suffice to illustrate the wide choice of negative material included in this special category.

If a very fast infra-red sensitive plate to cover the range 7,700–8,400 Å. were required it would be found that, as such a plate is not in general use, there would be no mention of it in the ordinary catalogue. If, however, the search is prosecuted in the list of "scientific" plates, one which would answer the purpose admirably will be found among the Kodak spectrographic plates, with what is described as the "N sensitisation."

To cover the deeper range from 8,600–9,600 Å., the "M sensitisation" plate from the same range would be satisfactory. Incidentally, these plates with the M

[12] "Kodak Scientific Plates," *Kodak Data Booklet* SE–3.

sensitisation can be supplied in two grades, either as fast plates with high sensitivity and medium contrast (M.I.), or with low sensitivity and very high contrast (M.IV.). These special emulsions are not supplied on film, which is another reason why plates are considered by many to be superior for scientific work.

It has already been stated that infra-red sensitive plates have a short shelf-life unless stored in a cool place. They are best stored in a refrigerator after being sealed to keep out moisture, but even under the best storage conditions, these plates suffer a steady deterioration in sensitivity, so that they should be tested before being used. The simplest test is to expose a fresh plate covered with a thin sheet of ebonite bearing a thin metal strip to light from a 1,000-watt tungsten lamp. The exposure is made in steps by shielding with a sheet of metal which is advanced in steps across the ebonite. When developed, a test negative showing the effect of the various exposures will be available for comparison with other plates tested under the same conditions. The ebonite sheet will allow the passage of infra-red radiation but not light of other wave-lengths. The metal strip will keep a portion of the negative clear of radiation of any wave-length, so that any general fogging of the negative will not be mistaken for sensitivity to infra-red radiation.

When cold negative material is brought into a warm humid atmosphere, it may become covered with a deposit of dew. To avoid this, after cold storage, it should be allowed to reach room temperature before being taken from the waterproof wrappings in which it should have been kept.

Whilst metals are opaque to infra-red radiation, the same cannot be said of many of the other materials used in the construction of cameras and dark slides. As already stated, ebonite will transmit infra-red radiation freely, and some woods as well as many of the materials used for fabrication of camera bellows, may allow sufficient leakage of infra-red radiation to cause serious fogging. Before infra-red is used for serious work, a test of the light-proofing of the apparatus should be carried out.

The elimination of undesired backgrounds and the penetration of stains by the use of filters combined with special lighting has already been dealt with in some detail. When these conventional methods have proved to be unavailing, recourse should be made to infra-red photography, for many dyestuffs and other coloured, and some opaque, materials, irrespective of the appearance they present to the eye, are transparent to infra-red. On the other hand, pencil writing, or indeed any markings made with carbon-containing pigments, such as those found in post office cancellation inks, are opaque to infra-red radiation. Most iron-containing inks are also opaque to infra-red, so that faint markings made with pencil, cancellation inks and iron-containing inks obscured by overlying matter can often be recorded free of any interference by infra-red photography.

Faults in Photographic Materials

Photographic materials marketed by firms with a reputation to maintain can generally be relied upon to give consistently good results if they are properly stored, handled and processed according to the makers' instructions. Occasionally, a defective plate or even a whole box of defective plates may be encountered. The most common failings are the occurrence of pinholes in thin-film negative material, and the appearance in finished negatives of striations and vague markings for which no explanation can be given.

In commercial half-tone work for which thin film half-tone material is generally intended, the occurrence of a few extra black spots is almost certain to pass unnoticed, and even in general photography they can be removed by a little attention to the negative or by touching up the finished print.

When it is handwriting which has been photographed, extra spots on the print may very well be mistaken for part of the handwriting, so that the defective photograph will not constitute an accurate record of the handwriting on the original document. Any " spotting " or other handwork on the negative is naturally out of the question, so that it is of the utmost importance that no document should be released from the laboratory before the dry negative has been inspected and found to be free of pinholes or other defects which would render it useless. Any neglect of this precaution will cause serious inconvenience if not worse if the defects are discovered only after the documents have left the laboratory.

Positive Materials

Coarse matt-surfaced printing papers have no part in document photography; maximum detail can be reproduced only on paper with a smooth surface. The degree of contrast of the printing paper is also of some importance. To obtain the most effective print, the contrast of the printing paper should be chosen to suit both the negative and the subject of the photograph. It is fortunate that most documents can easily be accommodated within the tone range of printing paper which is readily available.

The question of the matching of the contrast of the paper with the negative and the class of photograph required is dealt with in great detail in all the standard works on photography, so that there is nothing to be gained by any detailed discussion here. One warning may be given. In an endeavour to hide the faulty lighting of the original document, and to produce a final print wherein the whole of the document surface is rendered as white rather than as a melange of grey patches of widely differing density, some incompetent photographers resort to very questionable practices. Instead of using a paper of the appropriate contrast, they print on to papers of the highest possible contrast, and what is more, both under-expose and under-develop in order to suppress the background. In this way, an even white background to the writing is obtained, but in the prints obtained by these dubious methods, the finer strokes of the handwriting will be missing and the thicker heavier strokes, which alone appear in the final print, will be shown as devoid of structure as though they had been made with a stylo instead of a pen.

Mounting

For the temporary mounting of prints on card or other rigid mount, it is best to use either rubber solution or a liquid known as " Paper Flat " (Ilford). With either of these, the print may be peeled off with ease at any time and all traces of adhesive removed from the print by gentle rubbing between the fingers.

For permanent mounting, there is nothing superior to dry-mounting tissue, which has a resinous basis and which unites the print with the mount when heat and pressure are applied. When but a few prints have to be mounted, a domestic iron may be used for this purpose, but when the amount of work justifies the cost, a special heated press should be used.

Dry-mounting has completely superseded the use of starch and similar pastes for permanent work. If the dry-mounting has been correctly carried out, the prints will never peel from the mount although they may be removed by controlled heating followed by careful peeling.

Photographic Masking

The application of photographic masking is one of the problems encountered in the photography of documents by transmitted light and has already been referred to, but this device has a more extended use than that already described.

It sometimes happens that a photograph is required of some writing which is either partially or wholly obscured by markings of several other colours. An example of this occurs when a particular piece of writing on a well-used piece of blotting-paper has to be photographed free of the other multi-coloured markings which are also present.

These unwanted markings are often of so many different colours that the conventional method of elimination or suppression by the use of a filter cannot be applied with any expectation of success. In many cases, a single glance is sufficient to show that it is unlikely that any single filter or combination of filters would eliminate more than a small fraction of them. If *the required markings are substantially of one colour,* the problem may be solved by the application of the masking technique described below.

To start with, a negative should be made using a panchromatic plate and a filter to suit the lighting. The function of this filter is not to eliminate any of the markings but merely to ensure that every marking on the blotting-paper is properly represented on the negative.

Once this negative has been made, a series of experiments should be carried out with filters and different negative emulsions until a second negative can be made which shows up everything *except the required markings which should be completely eliminated from this negative.* If possible, the unwanted markings should be reproduced as fully as they occur on the first negative.

From this second negative, a positive transparency should be prepared on film so that it is exactly the same size as the first negative. This positive transparency which ideally should not bear any trace of the required markings, is then bound into intimate contact with the first negative. Provided (1) the two negatives reproduce the unwanted markings with the same density on both, and (2) the contrasts of the first negative and the transparency from the second have been fairly well matched, then the positive transparency will block out and prevent from printing everything in the first negative which appears in the positive transparency.

As there should be nothing in the positive transparency which prevents the required markings from printing through, when a print is made from the composite, the required markings alone will be reproduced thereon.

The composite is best printed by projection, the most satisfactory results being obtained by using a printing paper of the highest contrast; this will not record the

A

B

C

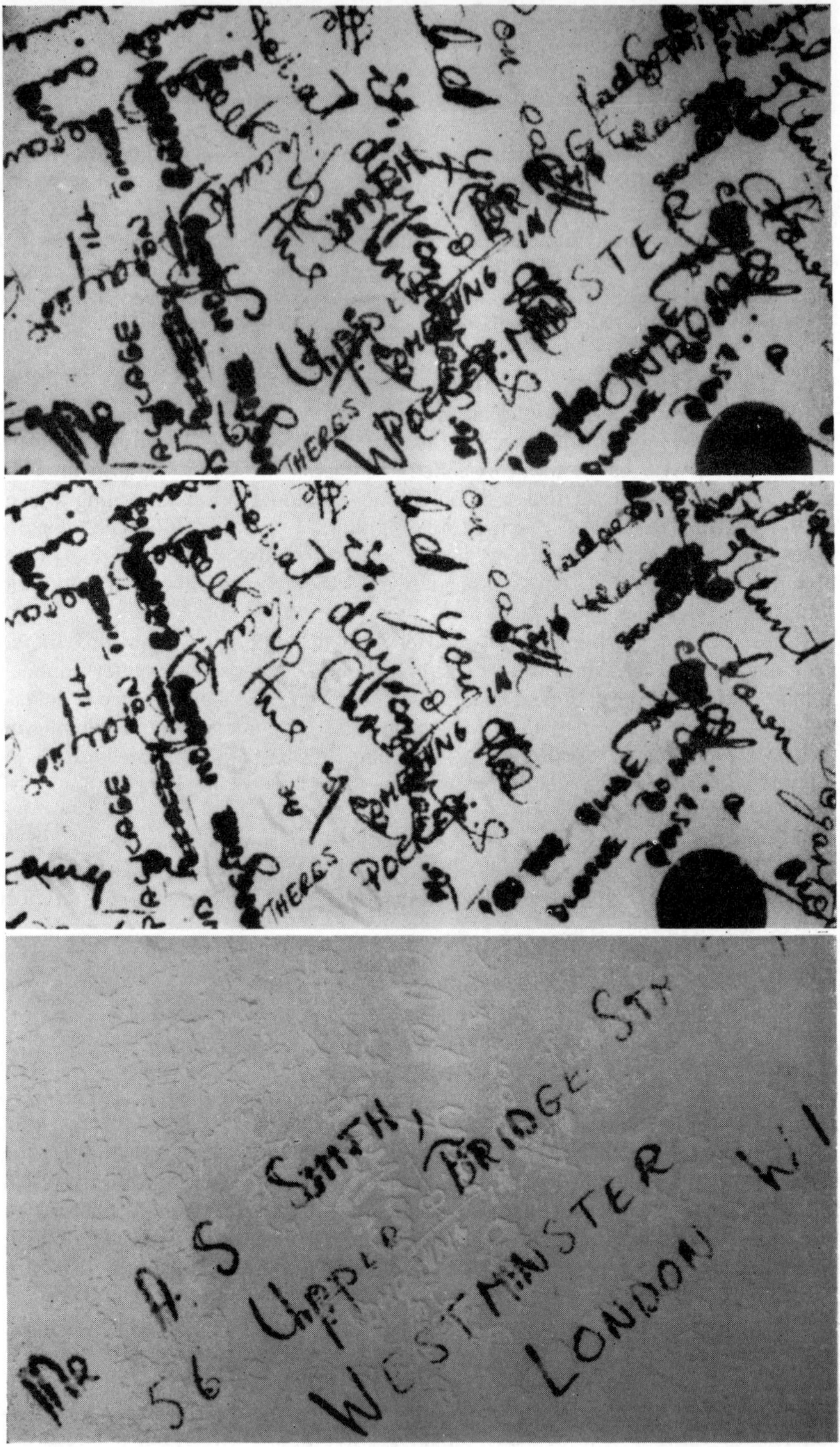

Fig. 6–12.

faint light transmitted from any unwanted markings which have not been completely masked by the positive transparency.

If an exact registration is not achieved, the unwanted markings appear in the final print in a vague form with a suggestion of bas-relief. Fortunately, this does little to obscure the required markings which print through very heavily.

From the theoretical point of view, the method has many imperfections. In the first place, whilst it may be possible to obtain a filter which will remove the required markings quite effectively in the preparation of the second negative, this filter will not be without its effect on the reproduction of some of the unwanted markings also. When this occurs, the positive transparency cannot be expected to mask these particular unwanted markings as effectively as the others on which the filter had no effect.

Fig. 6–13. *Photographic Masking*

The left hand photograph taken by infra red shows that the erased entries which have been revealed are obscured by the new entries made on top of the erasure. In the right hand print these new entries have been eliminated by photographic masking and this has enabled the original erased entries to be deciphered.

This happens in practice, which is why a certain amount of experimental work has to be undertaken with different combinations of filters and emulsions until the most favourable compromise is reached. The use of paper of excessive contrast

---

Fig. 6–12 (opposite). *Photographic Masking*

The name and address shown in " C " was represented on the piece of blotting paper " A," in red ink. The other markings on the blotting paper were in black, blue and green. " B " represents a positive transparency made from " A " using a filter which eliminated the required name and address. The positive transparency " B " was bound into contact with the negative from which " A " was made. When this composite was printed, the print " C " was produced. Owing to slight imperfection of register some of the unwanted markings can be seen in bas-relief on " C." All three photographs have been reversed to render them legible.

will usually take care of any partial failure to mask out unwanted material, for only those portions of the composite which have a low density will print fully on such paper. The results of this technique in practice are far superior to those which might be expected on theoretical grounds alone.

Stereoscopic Photography

This may play an occasional part in document examination especially if the perspective can be exaggerated to render more obvious the phenomena to be recorded. It is only by the use of stereoscopic photography that a full record can be made of what can be observed when a stereoscopic microscope is used for the examination of such features as the intersection of ink and pencil lines, etc.

A special stereoscopic camera capable of taking simultaneous photographs is not essential because, as the document is stationary whilst it is being photographed, the two exposures which are necessary need not be made simultaneously. In practice, it is preferable to move the camera between the exposures rather than the document because for the recording of phenomena which are best rendered stereoscopically, a preponderance of side lighting is generally required. If the document has to be moved, it might prove difficult to maintain the same conditions of lighting for both exposures.

Theoretically, the camera should be given a lateral movement of about two and a half inches, which is the average separation of the human eyes, but in practice, this movement may be increased so as to exaggerate the stereoscopic effect.[13]

The prints should be viewed in a stereoscope for it requires a certain knack and much practice to obtain a stereoscopic effect by observing the two prints with the unaided eyes.

A number of methods of preparing photographs which enable a stereoscopic view to be obtained from a single print have been devised. One method which employs polarised light is capable of producing most convincing stereoscopic views from a single print which is viewed by polarising spectacles, but the process is fairly expensive and time-consuming. Stereoscopic views of a document have to be recorded so seldom that there is little point in equipping a laboratory with special apparatus and material to meet a contingency which occurs so infrequently.

Dimensional Stability of Photographic Materials[14]

Glass is a most stable substance whose dimensions are unaffected by either the chemical treatment or the wetting and drying involved when a photographic emulsion thereon is being processed. The plastic film base, either cellulose nitrate or cellulose acetate, also suffers but little dimensional change.

The recently introduced (1957) polystyrene base shows a marked improvement over both cellulose nitrate and acetate. For a 20 per cent. change in relative humidity, there is but a ·05 per cent. change in linear dimensions.

Whilst it is true that the gelatine layer, which holds the silver halide, swells to a considerable extent when wet and shrinks on subsequent drying, it is fortunate

13 Shnitka, T. K., " Photomicrography with a Stereoscopic Microscope," *Medical Radiography and Photography*, 1956, 32 (2).

14 Ray, A. A., " Dimensional Stability of Sensitised Photographic Material," *Photographic Journal*, Nov.–Dec.. 1947.

that practically all these changes in dimensions take place at right angles to the support. This means that the dimensional stability of a photographic emulsion either on glass or on film is high, and advantage is taken of this in many branches of science to make accurate measurements on photographs based on glass or film.

In document examination, it often happens that fairly accurate measurements are required of small distances which cannot conveniently be determined directly without using a travelling microscope which might not be available. In these circumstances, it is permissible, even if rather expensive and time-consuming, to prepare a highly enlarged negative by direct photography and to make the measurements on this. If the degree of enlargement is known, dividers may be used with an ordinary metal scale. Alternatively, an accurate scale can be introduced into the photograph in the same plane as the object to be measured, and the dividers used with the reproduced scale on the photograph. This will have the advantage of being a direct reading and independent of the exact degree of enlargement.

It might be thought that a simple extension of this idea would be to project the enlarged negative on to a sheet of printing paper so as to obtain an even greater degree of enlargement, with the added convenience of working on paper instead of on glass or film. Unfortunately, this procedure cannot be guaranteed to give anything like accurate results.

Unlike glass or film base, the dimensions of a sheet of paper and consequently of anything adhering closely to it, are dependent upon the treatment it has received when wet and also on the amount of water it contains on drying. What is worse is that the expansion it undergoes when wetted is not the same in all directions along the sheet, paper being anisotropic in this respect. This prevents a scale on the print being used for making the measurements. It must be accepted that unless a special metal-interleaved paper is used, it is impossible to obtain a processed and dried print which has preserved unaltered the exact dimensions of the image projected thereon by the enlarger.

Waterproof Papers

As a compromise between the use of ordinary bromide paper, which suffers appreciable change during processing, and the compound aluminium-foil-containing paper, which is practically unaffected, the use of the waterproofed bromide paper may be considered. This is an ordinary bromide paper which has had the paper base coated on both sides with a waterproof nitro-cellulose lacquer. The dimensional stability of this paper is comparable with that of film, and although its response to changes in atmospheric humidity is slightly greater than that of film, it is much less than that of paper.

As the paper base does not absorb any appreciable amount of water from the processing solutions, it has appreciable wet-strength. As the absorption of water is almost entirely occasioned by the emulsion, which like that of ordinary bromide papers is extremely thin, it can be dried very rapidly after washing.

Degree of Enlargement

When stating the degree of enlargements made on ordinary printing paper, the document examiner should bear in mind the dimensional instability of paper, and refrain from quoting a value which is given to more significant figures than are justified by the facts. It is better practice to state that an enlargement is approximately two diameters than to give a false impression of extreme accuracy and precision by quoting an enlargement of 2·04 diameters, which in the circumstances is meaningless.

Photographic materials are usually well standardised, but slight differences occur in different batches. When identical copies of photographs have to be prepared, it is best to use material—either negative or positive—from the same box. If this is given identical conditions of exposure and processing, there need be no apprehension that differences will arise through variations in its quality.

Stains on Photographic Materials

Occasionally the document examiner will have to deal with photographs, negatives and positives, not always of his own making, which are disfigured with stains, some of which have only appeared on storage. It will be necessary to diagnose the cause of a stain before it can be treated in the rather unlikely event of amelioration proving possible. This may be a matter of some difficulty if the document examiner has to rely solely on his own efforts.

Fortunately, stains on photographic material have been the subject of considerable research, and the best source from which information can be sought is in the publications of the larger manufacturers of photographic materials. The pamphlet issued by the Eastman Kodak Co., entitled "Stains on Negatives and Prints" will be found to be a mine of information and it is very unlikely that any improvement on the techniques described therein will be discovered by the average photographer.

The trouble most likely to plague the document examiner with negatives and prints of his own making are the tiny spots due to pinholes in the negatives. When this has occurred nothing can be done except to make another negative using more satisfactory negative material. Other spots due to dust on the negative, air bells in the developer or grit in the wash water, are the result of carelessness and the photographer has merited the inconvenience they cause.

Mould Growth on Photographic Material

If photographic materials are stored for any length of time in an atmosphere having a relative humidity above sixty per cent., moulds will tend to grow on any unprotected gelatine surfaces.[15]

If unprocessed material is attacked, the mycellium of the mould will cause a thread-like pattern to appear on the image. Nothing can be done to cure a fault of this nature because it has become part of the photographic image. A cure is impossible; prevention of the trouble is essential. This is best accomplished by storing any photographic material which is not packed in a vapour-tight sealed package, in a desiccator. This may take the form of an air-tight container in which the air is kept dry by the colour-coded activated silica-gel desiccant widely used for the purpose.

15 "The Prevention and Removal of Mould Growth on Photographic Materials," *Kodak Data Sheet* RF–9.

With the advent of the new water-resistant packing films such as polythene and pliofilm, some of which can be heat-sealed, the problem of storing sensitive materials in unfavourable atmospheres should be appreciably eased.

Mould attack on processed material is not so speedy, and if the attack is slight, it may be possible to remove the mould before it causes serious damage to the image or can etch or distort the gelatine layer.

No attempt should be made to remove moulds by the action of either water or aqueous solutions, because the first action of a mould is to cause the gelatine to become water-soluble through degradation of the molecule. Any mould should be cleaned off by gentle rubbing with a plug of cotton wool moistened with carbon tetrachloride, petrol ether or rectified spirit. If it is available, one of the commercial brands of film cleaner will probably prove even more suitable.

Processed plates which have been thoroughly dried may be given a measure of protection from microbiological attack by being varnished. Shellac dissolved in alcohol or gum dammar in benzene may be used. The method of varnishing glass negatives, a widespread practice in a more leisurely age, is described in detail in many of the older books on photography. A useful piece of research would be to try the long-term effect of dissolving a small amount of pentachlorphenol in the varnish before application, because this very efficient fungicide might very well confer a considerable degree of immunity from attack. This treatment cannot be recommended without a trial because there is always the possibility of the impurities, which occur in all commercial chemicals, attacking the image if the commercial fungicide were used, even if the pure pentachlorphenol itself had no deleterious action.

The Permanence of Photographic Records

Prints and negatives must be preserved under reasonable conditions of storage if their useful life is not to be curtailed through the deleterious action of heat, humidity, impure atmospheres and the inevitable sequelae to these conditions—microbiological attack.[16]

Methods for ensuring the maximum life for photographic prints and negatives have been the subject of considerable research by makers of photographic materials, and should there be any reason for ensuring the maximum life for certain prints or negatives, or any doubt about the suitability of the conditions under which they are to be stored, the exhaustive data which have already been published should be consulted.[17] If through special conditions any question still remains, inquiry should be made of the research departments maintained by the manufacturers of the material.

The recommendations upon which all instructed opinion is agreed are summarised below.

The first essential is the control of humidity. The maintenance of too dry an atmosphere so that plates or prints become desiccated is certain to cause cracking should they be handled at all carelessly in the dry state. Conditions of high

[16] Scribner, B. W., " Summary Report of Research at the National Bureau of Standards on the Stability and Preservation of Records on Photographic Film," *National Bureau of Standards Miscellaneous Publication* M. 162, May, 1939.

[17] " The Storage of Photographic Materials and Photographic Records," *Kodak Data Sheet* RF–6.

humidity are even more dangerous in that there will be a serious risk of sticking or of microbiological attack.

Kodak base their recommendations on the basis of three degrees of permanence, namely:

(1) Short term — the records lasting for a few years.
(2) Moderate term — an anticipated life of up to twenty years.
(3) Archival permanence — the longest possible life—possibly running into centuries.

For each term there are given the appropriate recommendations concerning processing, temperature and humidity control, and storage conditions.

These may be summarised thus:

(1) *Short Term*

The usual processing should be carried out, taking care to ensure thorough fixing by the use of two hypo baths followed by efficient washing. It is only under tropical conditions that any further action to remove all traces of residual silver compounds and thiosulphates need be taken.[18 19]

Dry mounting is at all times preferred to the use of starch pastes or similar adhesives.

In storage, any sulphur-containing gases must be regarded as harmful as they attack both the silver image and adversely affect the paper base.

Photographs, more than other documents, should be protected from atmospheres contaminated with sulphur compounds.

In temperate climates, photographs may be stored safely at room temperature and humidity which should be kept within the range 25 to 60 per cent. relative humidity. Under adverse conditions of temperature and humidity, the humidity should be controlled rather than temperature if a compromise has to be made.

(2) *Moderate Term*

To ensure a life of about twenty-five years for a negative, whether on glass or film, research has shown that the residual thiosulphate content should not exceed a value of 0·005 mg. per square inch. No residual thiosulphate at all should be allowed to remain on a print and as this cannot be achieved by washing alone, chemical methods of removing the last traces must be utilised. This is usually accomplished by oxidation with a suitable reagent such as hydrogen peroxide rendered alkaline with ammonia.

After the removal of all thiosulphate, the absence of residual silver compounds must be proved by spot-testing with a solution of a soluble sulphide, which will give a yellow discolouration with any residual silver salt which may be present.

In storage, high temperatures must be avoided, and if the humidity is likely to

[18] Crabtree, J. I., Eaton, G. T., and Muehler, L. E., " The Elimination of Hypo from Photographic Images," *Journal of the Photographic Society of America* 6, Oct., 1940.

[19] Crabtree, J. I., Eaton, G. T., and Muehler, L. E., " The Removal of Hypo and Silver Salts from Photographic Materials as affected by the Composition of the Processing Solutions," *Journal of the Society of Motion Pictures of England* 41, July, 1943.

exceed the range given in the preceding section, both negatives and prints should be sealed in airtight containers.

(3) *Archival Permanence*

To achieve this, the processing should follow the lines already indicated and the storage temperature maintained within a range of 60°–70°F. preferably at 70°F.

The air should be rendered free from acid gases and there should be no opportunity for the ingress of impure air.

If suitable metal cans with loose lids are not available for holding the negatives and prints, envelopes may be substituted.

The paper from which the envelopes are made should be free of harmful compounds, such as the sulphur-containing ultramarine which is sometimes added to paper as a whitener. The adhesives should not contain sulphur compounds or yield acids on microbiological attacks; synthetic resin adhesives are safest in these respects.

The image side of the negatives and prints should face away from the seams of the envelopes, which should be arranged so that the records stand on edge and are not subjected to pressure.

Bibliography

Adams, J., "Miniature Lenses. The Quest for Fine Definition," *The Photographic Journal,* Vol. 195, Sec. A, September, 1955.

Bowen, E. J., *Chemical Aspects of Light* (Clarendon Press, Oxford, 1942).

Clark, W., *Photography by Infra-red* (Chapman and Hall, London, 1946).

Clerc, L. P., *Photography Theory and Practice* (Pitman, 1937).

Dalgoutte, W. C., "Miniature Stereo Photography and Projection," *Photographic Journal,* 96, September, 1956.

Dudley, L. P., *Stereoptics* (Macdonald, London, 1952).

Dunn, J. F., *Exposure Meters* (Fountain Press, London, 1952).

Greenwood, H. W., *Document Photography* (Focal Press, 1943).

Hilton, O., "Photographic Methods of Deciphering Erased Pencil Writing," *International Criminal Police Review,* No, 85, February, 1955.

James, T. H., & Higgins, G. C., *Fundamentals of Photographic Theory* (Chapman and Hall, 1948).

Lerich, L., "Photography in the Detection of Forgery by Addition," *International Criminal Police Review,* No. 84, November, 1954.

Mees, C. E. K., *Theory of the Photographic Process* (Macmillan, 1942).

Radley, J. A., *Photography in Crime Detection* (Chapman and Hall, London, 1948).

Rawlings, *Infra-red Photography* (Blackie, London, 1933).

Stevens, G. W. W., *Microphotography* (Chapman and Hall, 1957).

Ward, T. J., "The Photomicrography of Ink Sediment in Pen Writing," *Analyst,* 55, 1930.

Anon., "Deciphering and Photorecording of Indented Writings," *Royal Canadian Mounted Police Gazette,* Vol. 18, No. 8, August, 1956.

Anon., *Document Copying with Ilford Materials* (Ilford, Ltd., Ilford, London, 1955).

Anon., "Materials for the Construction of Photographic Processing Apparatus," *Eastman Kodak Co. Data Book.*

Anon., "Photographic Copying of Documents," *Kodak Data Sheet,* DC–1.

Anon., "Stains on Negatives and Prints," *Kodak Data Sheet,* PR–12.

Anon., "Wratten Light Filters" (Kodak, Ltd.).

7

DATING PROBLEMS

It is easy to be wise after the event, and this is the reason why many documents advanced to support a cause have been fraudulently prepared for the occasion or have been added to or altered in some material particular at a date much later than is alleged. This explains why a fair proportion of the problems with which a document examiner has to deal are concerned with the dating of documents or of some of the entries thereon.

Problems concerned with dating fall into one of two categories. In the first, the absolute age of the document or an entry has to be determined, whilst in the second relative ages or times of writing are all that are required.

The determination of absolute age, or, in its most usual form, the establishment of the maximum age a document is likely to be, is usually demanded when the whole document is suspected to be a fabrication, whilst the determination of relative ages, or more usually of relative times of writing or typing, is required when there is reason to believe that the whole of a document has not been prepared at the one time, or that significant alterations were made at some time subsequent to the preparation of the original document.

Establishment of a Limit of Age

The majority of dating problems are difficult if not impossible to solve in a manner which is completely satisfactory, so that every factor which might have some bearing on the matter must be taken into consideration. Evidence must be sought from the paper itself, from any printed or typewritten matter thereon as well as from any handwriting or other markings which are present; even the design of a paper fastener or the nature of any trace of adhesive present may very occasionally be taken into consideration.

Ancient Documents

Where really ancient documents are concerned, dating is the province of the palaeographer and the methods used will not be considered here. Practically all the documents concerned in legal proceedings are of comparatively recent origin. Occasionally, however, reputedly ancient documents, such as charts which purport to reveal the whereabouts of mythical treasures on the strength of which large sums are extracted from the pockets of the credulous, are submitted for examination as a preliminary to the prosecution of swindlers. In almost every instance these ancient documents are so obviously spurious that little difficulty is experienced in proving them to be of modern origin.

Evidence from Paper

It is generally when the suspect document is alleged to be of some antiquity, for example dating from the nineteenth century, that the paper itself is likely to be the source of valuable evidence of its true age.[1] In the examination of the paper, the fibre make-up, the nature of the filler, the size and even the exact nature of the dyestuff used for improving its colour, all have to be taken into consideration. In marked contrast, with but few exceptions, where contemporary documents are concerned it is rare for the examination of the paper to yield any significant data from which its age may be deduced. The reason for this will become apparent when the history of paper-making is considered.

It was only during the latter half of the nineteenth century that any extensive changes were made in the materials and methods of manufacture of paper; before and since that period, fundamental changes have been few and of comparatively small importance where dating is concerned.

Until approximately the middle of the nineteenth century, linen and cotton rags were almost exclusively used, and with these fibres the only problem of any interest in dating, and then only to the palaeographer, is the significance of the presence of cotton in papers reputedly earlier than the twelfth century. The rising demand for paper and the impossibility of increasing the supply of linen and cotton rags inspired experiments on other vegetable materials in an endeavour to discover new and less limited sources of paper-making fibres.

Straw Papers

The first date of interest is 1800, when the first rather crude papers containing fibres derived from straw were manufactured. Little success was achieved, and until 1860 straw was used in conjunction with rag fibre in the manufacture of paper used for wrapping rather than writing. Straw has proved to be a difficult material to handle, and it is only in comparatively recent years that the problems associated with its use have been solved so that it can take its place as a constituent of good quality writing paper. The Second World War gave great impetus to its use owing to the shortage of other sources of cellulose fibres, and it may be fairly safely assumed that a writing paper of reasonable quality which contains appreciable proportions of straw must date from the nineteen-forties; it is unlikely to be much older.

Esparto Papers

The large-scale manufacture of paper from esparto dates from 1861. Until the middle years of the twentieth century it was safe to assume that an esparto paper probably originated from the British Isles, but about that time the manufacture of esparto paper on a large scale was started in other countries which had easy access to the raw material—esparto grass.

The presence of appreciable proportions of esparto fibre in paper has been cited as a proof that a number of publications bearing dates prior to 1860 are

[1] Carter, J., Pollard, G., *An Enquiry into the Nature of Certain Nineteenth Century Pamphlets* (1934).

forgeries produced at a much later date, to take advantage of the high prices realised by first editions of well-known literary works. Esparto forms a light bulky paper which takes printing ink exceptionally well, so that this fibre is more often a constituent of book paper than of writing paper.

Wood Pulp Papers

Paper of comparatively poor quality was made from wood by the Soda Process in the years following 1856; this enables a limit of age to be placed on any paper containing fibres derived from wood. Very few spurious " ancient documents " are entirely free from traces of wood pulp, the presence of which will serve to expose them as forgeries. The Soda Process was improved by the substitution of sodium sulphate for the carbonate, which facilitated the manufacture of very strong dark coloured papers known as " Krafts." Since about 1930, it has been possible to make " bleached krafts " of good colour. Whilst a bleached kraft will make a good writing paper, its other qualities result in its employment for purposes where strength is all-important, so that the document examiner is unlikely to find a suspect document written on one of these distinctive modern papers.

Apart from rags, which are still used for the very best qualities, most writing paper is based upon sulphite wood pulp. Production of this widely used material began a few years prior to 1872, but the paper can be said to date from this year, which was when quantity production was commenced in Sweden.

The cheapest papers, such as newsprint, are made directly from ground wood. This " mechanical " wood pulp, as it is sometimes termed, was invented as far back as 1843, but it was not until 1869 that it was produced in any quantity.

Papers made from Mixtures of Fibres

It is rare for a paper to be made from a single class of fibre. The paper maker will combine the various fibres which are at his disposal to take advantage of their different properties in order to make the best paper at the lowest price. The identity of the fibres in a mixture may itself provide valuable dating evidence, especially for papers reputedly made during the latter half of the nineteenth century. For example, a paper containing either esparto alone or mixed with rag was almost certainly made during the period between 1861 and 1890. After this date, esparto has almost invariably been used along with chemical wood pulp.

Practically every source of cellulose has, during the past century, been tried out as a source of paper-making fibres, so that a paper may be found to contain a variety of fibres from various sources. These usually have but little significance for dating, although they may throw some light on the country where the paper was made.

Recent Developments

Apart from the advent of the bleached krafts, marked changes in the fibre make-up of paper have been few. Practically the only other change with dating significance has been the utilisation of chemical pulps derived from hardwoods towards the middle of the twentieth century. The woods mainly used for paper-making are termed " softwoods," a term which has nothing to do with the physical quality of the wood, but which is related to the type of leaf on the tree. Softwood yields a pulp of long fibre length which renders it very suitable for paper making.

For many years, efforts have been made to utilise the " hardwoods," derived from trees with broad leaves, as a source of paper-making fibres; but it is only in recent years that any appreciable proportion of hardwood fibre has been found in writing paper of good quality.

Fillers

Clay-like materials of natural origin such as kaolin have been added to paper from the earliest times. A more recent development, but one dating back more than a century, is the use of a synthetic substitute known in the trade as " Blanc Fixe." The only filler which is of significance in a modern paper is titanium white.

The presence of this filler in a paper is easily demonstrated, for very delicate tests are known for titanium compounds. If titanium white is present, it may be assumed that the paper is unlikely to be older than 1930, the year this loading material was introduced.

Colouring Matters

Most papers, even those which appear white, contain colouring matter which has been added to improve their appearance, even when the paper is not noticeably tinted. Where it is possible to identify the colouring matter, it will be possible to give a limit of age to the paper.

The commonly used " iron-blues " date from the early eighteenth century, and the other common additive to white paper, ultramarine, was first produced on a commercial scale in 1828, so that the presence in a paper of either of these substances is likely to be of interest only to the palaeographer.

Synthetic dyestuffs were first marketed in the later years of the eighteenth century, so that any paper containing one or more of these colouring matters can be given a more restricted limit of age. If it proves possible to identify the actual dyestuff present, an even finer limit may be given by ascertaining when that particular dyestuff was patented. Dyestuffs for the improvement of the colour of paper are being continually improved, and some of the blues based on the phthalocyanines are of very recent introduction, so that this method of giving a limit of age may have some application to contemporary documents.

Optical Bleaches

A post-war development is the marked improvement in the appearance of a paper by the incorporation of a minute proportion of colourless fluorescent materials, referred to in the trade as " Optical Bleaches." These substances absorb the shorter wave-lengths of the light incident upon the paper and fluoresce with a bluish glow. The paper appears much whiter and brighter than otherwise, especially when viewed by daylight. At the present time about a half-dozen different compounds are used as optical bleaches; the presence of any one can easily be established, and may be regarded as a certain indication that the paper is a post-war product.

Surface Treatment

Surface treatment of paper with plastics and synthetic resins, which has been an outstanding modern development in the manufacture of paper for special purposes, is rarely indulged in where writing paper is concerned. The only exception at the present time is the treatment of cartridge paper with melamine resin, which would enable the paper to be dated as post-1945. It is to be hoped that this practice will spread and simplify the task of the document examiner with respect to modern papers.

Watermarks

Whilst a sheet of paper may sometimes be given a useful limit of age by virtue of its watermark, too much reliance cannot be placed on this source of evidence. Apart from the fact that the greater part of modern paper is unmarked, it is often difficult to accomplish the preliminary stage of dating the paper, that is, the identification of the paper-maker.

Most paper trade directories afford some information about the watermarks used by various manufacturers, but few deal at all adequately with the products of paper

Fig. 7–1. This illustrates four watermarks with dating significance. The upper photograph is of a watermark giving the year of manufacture—1957. The left hand lower photograph shows the key letter K placed under the gateway. In the centre the K is shown misplaced owing to the use of a faulty dandy roll, whilst the right hand lower photograph shows an imperfect W owing to the use of a damaged dandy roll.

makers outside the countries in which the directories circulate. To trace a particular watermark on a modern paper, it will probably be necessary to consult not only paper trade directories but also registers of trade marks and similar publications. Even when every available book of reference has been consulted, success is not certain, for it is often overlooked by writers on this subject that a paper may be watermarked at the request of a customer whose property the watermark happens to be, so that the same watermark may be found on many different papers emanating from a wide variety of paper-mills.

In view of this, it is often preferable to concentrate on tracing the dandy-roll used for forming the watermark, for while paper makers are many, dandy-roll manufacturers are comparatively few. In even the most highly industrialised country, all the dandy rolls in use will probably have been made by only one or two manufacturers whose identity may be determined by inquiry at any paper-mill. Most dandy-roll makers keep records of their products, and from these it may be possible to trace the mill which made the paper in question. Once the paper-mill has been traced, it may be discovered that the watermark has been " keyed " to indicate the year of manufacture. Sometimes the actual date forms part of the watermark, but it is more usual to make some inconspicuous change in the watermark. (See Figure 7–1.) Where a watermark is unkeyed, paper with an unchanged watermark may be produced over a long period of years. When this is the case, the watermark should be scrutinised for defects.

On rare occasions, the dandy-roll maker will produce a dandy-roll bearing a defective design, an error which might well escape notice until a quantity of defectively marked paper has been produced. Alternatively, and far more frequently, a dandy-roll may become damaged in use, with the result that paper with a defective watermark will be produced until the defect is remedied. In a well-conducted paper-mill, a record of the dates of production of such defectively marked paper may well be available, so that the presence in a paper of a defective watermark may serve to date a paper even when the watermark itself has not been keyed to indicate the year of manufacture.

Type Design

Many documents bear printed matter which may serve to give a limit of age. The design of printers' type is subject to modification; from time to time new founts are introduced or modifications made in conventional letter designs to improve appearance and efficiency. The dates of such introductions are known in the trade, and such evidence may be brought forward to show that a document has been given a date which is earlier than that indicated by the design of the printed characters it bears. Many fraudulent " first editions " have been exposed by evidence of this nature.

Fig. 7–2. Modified forms of " j " and " f." The curved-back forms were first introduced in 1880–1883.

Adhesives

The conventional envelope is a surprisingly recent invention, as it first came into use in 1839. The adhesives used may also have some dating significance. For many years they were based on natural products such as gum, gelatine and starch, but whilst such products are still in extensive use, improved adhesives incorporating rubber, both natural and synthetic, plastics and synthetic resins have been developed for use where their special properties justify the extra cost.

It is only since the end of the Second World War that these newer adhesives have come into general use, so that the presence of an adhesive based, say, on polyvinyl acetate on an envelope bearing the date 1929 would be an anachronism which would throw serious doubt on the accuracy of this date.

A torn document is sometimes repaired by the use of the transparent cellulose adhesive tape commonly known as " Scotch tape." This, again, is a material of comparatively recent development, since the modern variety consisting of a strip of reconstituted cellulose with an adhesive based on rubber or plastic was first marketed in 1930, and did not come into extended general use until some years after that date.

Paper Fasteners

The common paper fastener can take many forms, for great ingenuity has been exercised in the search for a cheap effective device which can be counted on to hold together several sheets without damaging the paper. Although an arduous task, it is possible, by combing the patent literature and the index of registered designs, to determine the earliest date on which any particular form of fastener could have been purchased. It must be admitted that the possibility of obtaining any significant estimate of age by means of a paper fastener is remote in the extreme, but the possibility is mentioned here to emphasise that in the endeavour to establish a limit of age to a document, nothing is too trivial to be overlooked.

The Dating of Bound Books

Where the questioned document takes the form of a bound book such as an account book, it is often possible to trace the stationer responsible for its production. Even when a certain type of book has been on the market for a number of years, from time to time the printing or the make-up is subjected to modification, so that it becomes possible for the stationers to put a limit of age on any particular form of book.

The author was once concerned in a case where a fraudulent duplicate set of account books was hurriedly prepared to meet an investigation into the affairs of the firm. The fraudulent entries purported to go back a number of years, so before any attempt was made to date the ink writing, the stationers who marketed the books were traced. They were able to show that the particular form of account book produced was first made available to the public some months *after* the dates given in the earlier entries.

Dating Evidence from Printed Headings

Many forgeries are prepared on paper bearing printed headings. Even when no new or modified information such as changes in addresses or telephone numbers has to be included, it is sometimes found necessary to prepare new blocks for a

CONSTRUCTIONAL ENGINEERS
THE CEDARS COWLEY MIDDLESEX
TELEGRAMS AND TELEPHONE UXBRIDGE 1151

Fig. 7–3. Notepaper with this heading was first supplied 9.1.41 but bore agreements dated between 22.12.40 and 4.1.41.

fresh printing. Whilst the new blocks may closely resemble the old, careful scrutiny will generally reveal definite, if slight, variations in the design or the arrangement of the printed matter.

Such changes have led to the undoing of more than one forger who has made use of headed paper which was not in existence on the date given to the forgery.

The Dating of Written Matter

Pencil Writing

Little difficulty is experienced in distinguishing, on microscopic examination, between a mark made by the primitive pencil consisting of a sawn strip of natural graphite held in a wooden holder, and one made by a modern pencil with a " lead " compounded of a baked mixture of graphite and clay. Unfortunately, the ability to accomplish this feat is of interest only to the palaeographer, for the modern pencil came into use during the first decade of the nineteenth century.

Whilst pencils of different qualities make marks which are appreciably different on microscopic examination, it is impossible to determine either the make or the date of production of the pencil by any examination which can be applied to the line. It is unfortunate that synthetic graphite, the date of whose commercial production is known, is inferior to natural graphite, so that it plays little part in the manufacture of pencils.

Different pencils contain varying amounts of iron as an impurity in their leads, but whilst the presence of this iron will sometimes allow of the chemical intensification of a partially erased pencil line, the amount which is present has no dating significance.

If the paper on which it appears is allowed to remain undisturbed, a pencil line will undergo no alteration with time because of the extreme stability of the materials of which the " lead " is composed. The only change with age in the appearance of a pencil line is that it may become diffuse when the surface of the paper is subjected to abrasion, such as that which occurs when a diary is carried in the pocket. This change is of some significance when recently added pencil entries in a diary have to be distinguished from those originally present.

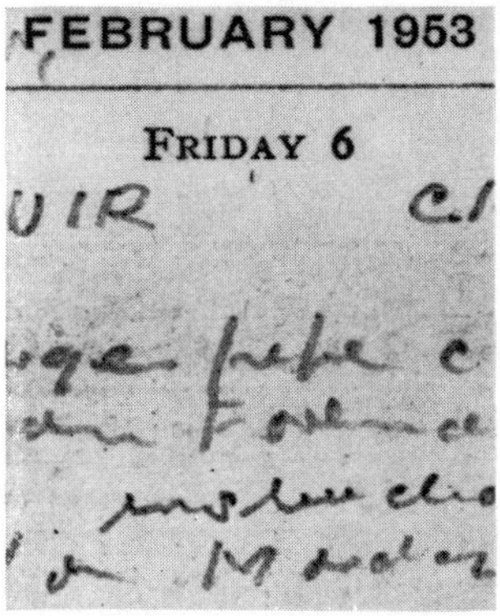

Fig. 7–4. The whole of the pencil entries were alleged to have been written at the same time in a diary. The suspect entry—the penultimate line—shows none of the signs of smudging exhibited by the other entries.

Liquid-lead Ball-points

The only recent development in the manufacture of writing instruments for the production on paper of a line consisting essentially of graphite, is the introduction in January of 1955 of the " liquid-lead " ball-point writing instrument. In the following year there followed the liquid-lead ball-point fitted with a spring-mounted ball, which enabled some degree of shading to be introduced into the writing.

To the naked eye, there is little difference between a line made with a conventional pencil and one formed by the liquid-lead ball-point, but there is little risk of confusion if the examination is made with a microscope. Any writing made with a liquid-lead can confidently be dated as post-1954, and if it is well shaded as well, it will probably be more recent than early 1956.

Copying Pencil

Both copying and indelible pencils are more recent inventions than the conventional pencil, because their successful commercial production waited on the availability of synthetic dyestuffs of sufficiently high tinctorial power. Suitable dyestuffs were first marketed in the last quarter of the nineteenth century, so that any writing in an indelible or copying pencil can be given a limit of age. If it is possible to identify the dyestuff present, a slightly narrower limit may be drawn by reference to the patent literature.[2]

Similar remarks apply to writings made with wax crayons or coloured chalks. Whilst writings in either are rarely encountered, they may be met with on disputed maps and charts.

Writing Inks

Carbon Ink

As carbon inks have been in use for some thousands of years, it might, at first sight, appear to be a hopeless task to attempt to give a limit of age to a writing made with a simple mixture of amorphous carbon and glue. Fortunately, as described elsewhere, the brownish tone of the carbon is generally corrected by the addition of blue colouring matter.

Suitable blue colourants are few, and are identical with those already mentioned for the tinting of paper. As this is so, suspect writing to which a great age is attributed should be tested for the presence of a blue toner which, on identification, will allow a limit of age to be given to the writing.

Tests should also be applied for the presence of a binder other than hide glue. If borate is found, this will indicate that a solution of shellac in borax has been used to bind the carbon. This will prove the writing to be modern and a limit of age may be given by discovering from the patent literature when Indian ink was first made in this manner.

As a binder for the carbon, shellac solution leaves much to be desired, and it may well happen that it will be superseded by solutions or suspensions of plastics or synthetic resins of more recent introduction. As this is so, a chemical test of the binder should be carried out whenever it is suspected that the writing is of recent origin.

Carbon inks undergo little change with the passage of time. Carbon itself is one of the most stable of substances and the only change is likely to be in the toner. Ultramarine is susceptible to acid fumes and the iron blues to alkaline conditions, whereas the copper phthalocyanines are extremely stable to both. Even if the toner decomposed entirely, the only change would be a slight browning of the ink unrelated to the time it had been on the document.

Ball-point Inks

Whilst the concept of a rotating ball as a writing instrument is by no means modern—references to this principle may be found in the patent literature of the early years of the nineteenth century—the commercial exploitation of the principle

[2] *Aniline Dyes in Ink,* B.P. 2235, 2972—1861–62.

awaited on the development of machinery which could ensure the mass-production of both precision-made balls and the appropriate housings, as well as the progress in industrial chemistry which alone has allowed the development of suitable inks. Even today, whilst the mechanical problems have been largely overcome, research continues apace, for the perfect ink has yet to be evolved.

It is difficult to fix the date when the first practicable ball-point pen was marketed [3]; it is said that some twenty-five thousand ball-points were sold in Europe some time before 1935, but whether any of these pens were of any real use is a moot point, but owing to the fact that a fair number were undoubtedly distributed, a writing in ball-point could possibly date from that period.

The " Biro " ball-point, a reasonably practical writing instrument, had a limited distribution in the Argentine in 1943, and by 1945 similar pens were being sold by the million. From the foregoing, it is fairly safe to assume that any tolerable writing with a ball-point pen is almost, but not quite, certain to have been made subsequent to 1943.

The age of a ball-point writing may be estimated more accurately as the result of chemical tests on the ink. The first successful inks developed for use with the Biro pen were all based on olein. Whilst such inks have been superseded by improved products in the better pens, they are still being used in the cheaper pens.

Inks based on olein were discovered to have many defects, one of the more important being the limited range of dyestuffs suitable for incorporation in an oily medium. In the improved inks, the olein has been replaced by ethylene glycol polymers; instead of the oil-soluble dyestuffs, a more satisfactory range of colouring matters similar to those used in the steam-setting printing inks is available.

Pens charged with these improved inks were first placed on the market during 1952, which means that any writing in these polyethylene glycol-based inks must have been written some time subsequent to 1951.

It is a simple matter to determine whether an ink is of the olein or polyethylene glycol type, because one is oily in nature whereas the other is based on an aqueous solution. The addition of a tiny drop of petroleum ether to the line will cause an olein ink to run in marked contrast to its very limited action on a line made with the newer ink. The author has used the ink test to show that a signature on a will dated 1946 was actually written in the newer type of ink, that is, some time after 1951, a finding which was later confirmed by a confession.

Recent developments in the formulation of ball-point inks have led to the incorporation of more than a single dyestuff in the ink. One dyestuff is present to give an intense colour to the faintest writing trace, whilst the function of the other is to give a greater degree of permanence to the writing. With writing made with these complex inks, the colour will generally be found to change appreciably when it is treated with a solvent such as a mixture of equal parts of acetone and water, which has the effect of removing the less permanent dyestuff from the paper. It is interesting to note that many inks which appear to be of the same colour show marked differences of behaviour when treated with this or similar solvents.

[3] " History of Ballpoint Pen," *Fortune*, July, 1946; *Readers Digest*, December, 1946; *New Yorker*, February 17, 1951.

It is a matter of some difficulty to keep track of the changes which take place, and it is almost impossible to establish the date of the first appearance of a modified ink. The patent literature is not as helpful as might appear, for sometimes a long period will elapse between the issue of the patent and the marketing of the product described therein.[4]

Ageing of Ball-point Writing. Many of the early ball-point inks faded rapidly, especially when they were exposed to direct sunlight; the reds and greens were noteworthy in this respect. Not only were the inks liable to fade, but some, especially those containing Victoria blue, were found to " strike " very badly.

Unfortunately, it is impossible to estimate the age of a writing by the fading or the degree of striking it exhibits, for both are dependent on the nature of the paper and the conditions of storage of the document. On the other hand, additions to a writing which showed marked fading or striking can be distinguished from the original writing, provided the examination is carried out within a short period of the making of the additions. If too long a period is allowed to elapse before the examination, the additional entries will themselves exhibit both fading and striking which will be difficult to distinguish from that shown by the original writing.

The better ball-point pen inks are strongly resistant to both fading and striking, so that additions may be made to existing writing without there being any definite indication that all the writing was not written at the same time.

Dyestuff Writing Inks

Apart from the strongly alkaline quick-drying inks, practically all dyestuff writing inks are composed of materials which have been used for the purpose since the last quarter of the nineteenth century. Whilst any writing in such an ink must be of comparatively modern origin, it is impossible to estimate its age by chemical or any other methods.

The only change of the writing with time is a slow loss of brightness of hue, complete fading being rarely found except with the violet, red and green inks which have been exposed to bright light. Any attempt to estimate the age of a writing by controlled fading tests is certain to prove abortive. Even where the same ink and similar paper is available, fading is so dependent upon light intensity and quality that the experimental error in any series of experiments would be so great as to render the results meaningless. The estimation of the age of a dyestuff writing is one of the urgent unsolved problems confronting the document examiner.

Blue-Black Iron Gallotannate Ink

Inks based upon the highly coloured compounds formed when soluble iron salts react with tannins are of considerable antiquity, and there is no certainty as to when they were first brought into use. It might be thought that chemical analysis would provide the answer, but no one can be sure that ancient writings in inks which can be shown to contain appreciable proportions of iron compounds, were indeed made with iron gallotannate inks. Some carbon inks of poor quality are

[4] Biro Pens—British Patents. 546,172 1944. 573,747 1945. 609,817 1948. 629,226 1949. 629,283 1949. 625,359 1951.

known to contain appreciable amounts of iron as an impurity. However, this is a problem for the palaeographer rather than the document examiner, and is mentioned here to emphasise that the results of even the most exact chemical analysis require correct interpretation before accurate conclusions can be drawn from them.

Whilst the first use of an iron-containing ink dates back into the remote past, the incorporation of a dyestuff to give a temporary colour is a comparatively recent development. The first inks based on this principle were marketed in 1830, although the idea had been suggested many years previously. The early inks contained indigo as the temporary colour, but this was replaced by other more suitable dyestuffs during the last quarter of the nineteenth century.

Ageing of Iron Gallotannate Ink Writing. An iron gallotannate ink line exhibits an interesting series of colour changes as it ages, and it is largely because of this that many think that it is possible to determine the age of an ink writing from the colour.

A freshly prepared and unoxidised solution of the reaction-products of a soluble iron salt and a tannin is practically colourless in the concentration which is used for writing fluids and as the ink contains sufficient acid to retard its oxidation whilst in bulk, the colour of newly-made writing is due almost entirely to the dyestuff present. The temporary colour is usually a bright blue that contributes little to the final colour which is slowly developed as the writing ages.

The application of the ink to the paper greatly increases its specific surface, so that the absorption of oxygen from the air is greatly facilitated. Should the paper have incorporated with it either loading or sizing material which tends to reduce the acidity of the ink, this will further accelerate its oxidation. As the ink oxidises, the colourless and water-soluble ferrous compounds originally present are converted into black insoluble ferric compounds which mask the temporary blue colour of the ink line. Under normal circumstances, the oxidation is slow and the ink will take something like two years or so to reach the fully oxidised state, when it will be jet black in colour and so slightly soluble that the writing will be relatively unaffected by the action of water.

Under reasonable conditions of storage, a well proportioned ink formulated with the optimum concentration of iron compounds will remain black for a number of years, possibly for centuries. Eventually, a slow but inevitable process of fading will set in, due to the decomposition of both dyestuff and the organic iron compounds, until all that is left of the line is a faint trace of ferric oxide. Ferric oxide is yellow in colour, which is why inks tend to yellow as they age.

In view of this colour change from blue through black to yellow, it might be thought possible to date iron gallotannate ink writing by virtue of its colour, and there have been many who consider themselves capable of accomplishing this feat. Unfortunately, experience has shown that the rate of oxidation, and hence the development of both colour and fading is influenced by many factors other than the passage of time. All chemical reactions are profoundly influenced by change in temperature; a rise of only 10°F. is sufficient to double the rate of most chemical reactions, and the oxidation and fading of ink are both photosensitive and affected by the acidity of the ink after it has been in contact with the paper.

Many writing papers have a slight acid reaction, generally due to the presence of alum added during manufacture, and on an acid paper the ink line may remain noticeably blue for some years. On the other hand, an alkaline loading in the paper will cause its acidity to fall, with a consequent acceleration of the oxidation, so that an ink line may become appreciably blackened in a matter of days.

There are also substances small traces of which will accelerate the oxidation of ink. One of these is saliva, which owes its use as a secret ink to this property. A little saliva added to the ink can be counted on to cause it to blacken in a very short time.

The darkening of an ink line is a complex process. Although the blue surface colour of a newly written ink line may appear to change little in the course of a day or so, experiments made by the author, using a photoelectric cell as the receptor to avoid the errors inherent in any subjective estimate of opacity, have shown that there is an appreciable increase in the opacity of the ink line from the moment the ink is applied to the paper. The rate of increase of opacity is very great as the ink line dries, but falls off exponentially during the first forty-eight hours after application, after which opacity slowly increases to a maximum value which is not attained until many months have passed.

These experiments afford some justification for the belief that measurement of the *rate of increase of opacity* would serve to give a fairly accurate estimate of the age of a newly written writing in iron gallotannate ink. Even if this proved to be the case, it would leave the major problem unresolved, for the majority of the problems concerned with the dating of ink writings reach the laboratory long after the ink has been applied to the paper, when the rate of change of opacity is too slow to enable any reliable estimate of the age of the writing to be given.

It is generally admitted that in certain circumstances, valuable information relating to the age of an ink writing may be adduced by making observations, not of the colour of the ink lines as such, but of the rate of change in colour over a short period of time. In practice, this change is best demonstrated by quoting the increase in the red component of the colour as measured on the Lovibond scale.

It is not uncommon for a document such as a receipt, or entries in an account book which purport to be several years old, to be fabricated in a hurry to meet an investigation. If a blue-black ink is used, the bright blue tint of the ink lines may arouse suspicion, but this in itself is no proof of recent fraudulent fabrication. If, however, a record of the colour of the ink is made on the Lovibond system as described elsewhere, and the document is then kept for a short period in conditions not widely divergent from those in which it is alleged to have been kept, it will be possible to make a series of observations which will indicate how the colour of the ink is changing with time.

With a genuine document several years old, the colour of the ink will show no appreciable change over a week or so, but any darkening as shown by an increase in the red component will afford conclusive evidence that the writing is more recent than alleged.

Estimates of Age Based on Solubility. If water is spilled on to freshly made gallotannate ink writing, the ink will run and the writing become smeared. This is because some of the ink solids in the writing are still in the unoxidised, and consequently water-soluble, state. Once the ink writing has become fully matured, the effect of water upon it will be relatively slight, the dyestuff is still water-soluble but is bound up in the insoluble iron compounds from which it will leach with difficulty.

From time to time, claims are advanced for ways of determining the age of a gallotannate ink writing by observing the rate at which the dyestuff diffuses out from the line of writing upon the application of water, or in the case of a well-matured ink, dilute solutions of acid. The acid may be either hydrochloric or oxalic.[5]

It cannot be gainsaid that as an ink line matures, the slower will be the attack of water or aqueous solutions of acids, and that the extent to which the dyestuff diffuses out of the line in a given period will be some measure of the rate of attack, but it must be borne in mind that what is being measured is the degree of oxidation of the ink. It is this oxidation which is the cause of the colour change, and it is hard to see why estimates of the age of ink writing based on solubility changes should be any more reliable than those derived from colour changes.

The factors which render estimates of age based on colour unreliable operate with equal force where solubility is concerned, and the only advantage possessed by the solubility test is that it may be applied to inks which have become so darkened that their colour is practically indistinguishable from that of the fully matured ink.

It is agreed that any estimate of absolute age based on solubility or any of its manifestations cannot be more than approximate, although the test may have some application when it is required to determine whether two entries in the same ink on a document were written at the same time or not. If the attack of the chosen reagent on the two entries differs widely, then, in the absence of any good reason to the contrary, it will be safe to assume that the entry which shows the greater diffusion of the colouring matter out of the ink line is the more recent. With such a test, the ink lines selected for examination should be equal in width and of the same depth of colour.

Nothing is gained by comparing the effect of the same reagent on both the suspect writings and those of known age, for the assumption that writings which are contemporary will necessarily exhibit the same effect, or the converse, will have little justification. Such comparisons are justified only when the comparison writings are made with the same ink on similar paper, and stored under the same conditions as the documents under examination.

Age Determination from Ion Migration. Iron gallotannate inks contain low concentrations of sulphate or chloride ions derived from the iron salts or acids used in their preparation. Once the ink has been applied to the paper, there will occur a steady diffusion of these ions from the ink line into paper. If the document is stored in anything but damp conditions, this process of diffusion will be very slow and its extent will be some function of the age of the writing. Therefore, this phenomenon would appear to form the basis of a method for the determination

[5] Mitchell, C. A., " Estimation of the Age of ink in writing," *Analyst* 45, 1920.

of the relative ages of different writings on the same document, and possibly the absolute age of a writing stored under known conditions.[6]

At the outset, certain advantages of this method over the others which have been considered are apparent. Diffusion, being a physical process, is less dependent upon temperature than chemical reactions. Added to this, the diffusion, unlike colour and solubility, is independent of the state of oxidation of the ink when it is first applied to the paper. Unfortunately, it has been established that the rate of diffusion of both chloride and sulphate ions is influenced by changes in the humidity of the paper, which itself is largely dependent upon the humidity of the atmosphere in which the paper is stored. This means that the extent of the diffusion is dependent upon the history of the document, and unless this is known it will be impossible to make the necessary allowances when the age of a writing is being assessed from its " diffusion picture," as it will be termed.

A most pertinent objection to the application of the method to the writing on an important document is that the methods in vogue for the development of both chloride and sulphate " diffusion pictures " are such that the test involves the literal destruction of the document in the neighbourhood of the lines being tested. It may well happen that further research will yield a solution to the problem of developing the " diffusion picture " without injury to the document, but even when this can be accomplished, any estimate of the age of a writing from the extent of the diffusion of the ions contained in the ink is certain to be unreliable for the reasons given above.

The Development of the Diffusion Picture. In brief, the document is subjected to chemical treatment which has the effect of bleaching the colouring matter of the ink line and of converting all the sulphate and chloride present into insoluble salts of lead and silver respectively. As both these compounds are white, their position in the paper is made manifest by converting the lead sulphate into the black sulphide by treatment with a soluble sulphide, and blackening the silver chloride by exposing it to actinic light. The result of this treatment is that the original ink line is completely destroyed, and in its place will have been developed black deposits which outline the extent of the diffusion of the sulphate or chloride from the ink line.

From this brief description of the treatment which has to be applied to the document for the development of either the chloride or sulphate diffusion picture, it is apparent that the document concerned is unlikely to be other than seriously mutilated. It is not surprising that it is recommended that the successive operations should be carried out on strips of paper which have been cut from the document at right angles to the ink lines being tested.

Such a procedure constitutes a serious mutilation which is by no means comparable with the removal of a small quantity of the colouring matter from the centre of an ink line, which is recommended when tests on the nature of the ink have to be carried out. It is unlikely that permission would ever be forthcoming

[6] Mezger, O., Rall, H., and Heese, W., " The Chloride Test," *Zangew Chem.* 44, 649, 1931; Heese, W., " The Chloride Test," *Arch. Kriminol,* 98, 13–17, 1935; 101, 7–37, 1937 (1935); *Analyst,* 60, 338; Finn, J., and Cornish, R. E., " Chloride Migration," *Ind. Eng. Chem. Anal.,* 10th ed., 524, 1938; Cornish, R. E., Finn, J., and McLaughlin, W., " Age of Inks by Chloride Test," *Ind. Eng. Chem. News,* 12th ed., 315, 1934.

for the removal of strips of paper from any document which was to play an important part in legal proceedings. For this reason, no details of the chemical procedures are given; if required, they can be found in the original papers on the method.

The author has carried out some work on an alternative method for the development of the chloride or sulphate diffusion picture, which has the advantage that no mutilation of the document is involved. The scheme is to induce the chloride, sulphate or any other negatively charged ions derived from the ink to migrate at right angles to the surface of the paper into a soft gelatine layer pressed into intimate contact with it. For convenience, the gelatine layer is coated on either metal foil or stout paper.

If this diffusion of the ions could be made to occur with only a negligible disturbance of the original pattern of diffusion, then the diffusion picture could be developed into the gelatine layer on its backing sheet without any harm coming to the original document, which, once it had yielded its ions to the gelatine, would play no further part in the test when parted from the gelatine. If necessary, the migration of the ions from the paper into the gelatine could be accelerated by applying an appropriate electric field.

The appearance of the document tested in this way would be unaltered, and the only change it would suffer would be the disappearance of the invisible chloride and sulphate ions previously associated with the ink lines. Although this may be considered a technical mutilation, it would have no apparent effect on the legibility, so there is little reason why such a procedure should not be permissible for even the most important documents.

Once the "diffusion picture" has been rendered visible, irrespective of the means employed, there still remains the problem of its interpretation. As a guide to the absolute age of an ink line, it has to be interpreted in the broadest terms; an ink line which exhibits no great diffusion of ions which can be seen to have been present in the ink line itself in fair concentration, cannot be of any great age, and the converse is also true. Beyond such generalities it is unsafe to venture.

On the other hand, there is little doubt that the "diffusion picture" may be used with advantage when the problem is the determination of the relative ages of ink lines on the same document.

It must be emphasised that the development of an ion diffusion picture is dependent upon the presence of relatively mobile ions in the ink. The only common inks to which this criterion applies are the iron gallotannate inks which are rapidly being superseded for ordinary use by the non-corrosive relatively ion-free dyestuff inks; the quick-drying alkaline inks, also ion-containing, are unlikely to supplant any of the other inks in common use, because of the expense and the fact that they are unsuitable for use with the majority of makes of fountain pen.

Alkaline Quick-drying Ink

As the first alkaline quick-drying ink to achieve even a limited commercial success was made available to the public as recently as 1927,[7] any writing in such an ink is unlikely to be of any great age. This original alkaline ink may be regarded

[7] *Alkaline Ink,* U.S.P. 1,645,117, 1927; *Quick Drying Ink,* B.P. 619,972, 1946; B.P. 351,611, 1930.

as an alkaline version of the ordinary dyestuff ink, from which it differed only in its alkaline reaction and the presence of an azo dyestuff, resistant to light and oxidation in alkaline solution, as the colouring agent.

The modern commercially successful alkaline inks, containing compounds of vanadium or copper, are a much more recent introduction.

While the original patents covering the manufacture of these inks date from 1933,[8] those disclosing the use of copper and vanadium compounds were granted in 1949,[9] so that any writing in one of these "Superchrome" inks must have been made some time after this year, because of the delay between patent protection and commercial exploitation. These inks were not available in England prior to 1954, and until 1955 only the black and turquoise inks were on the market, although other colours such as jade-green and red were then available in North America.

Nothing has yet been published on methods which might be used to date writing made with these inks, or to determine the relative ages of entries on the same document. The only method which seems to hold out any promise is some modification of the ion diffusion procedure suitably modified to deal with the different ions present in these inks.

The alkaline inks undergo no oxidative changes with age, for in many respects they resemble the dyestuff inks. In the blue and green inks, the copper phthalocyanine derivatives which are present are certain to confer great stability of colour because of their resistance to both oxidation and reduction. This means that there will be little hope of associating any colour change with the age of the writing.

The present position with respect to the dating of writing, whether in ink, ballpoint or pencil is that, in spite of the claims which have been made from time to time, there is no known procedure which can be relied upon to give an absolute age to a writing unless the nature of the ink enables a useful limit to be stated. The most that can be done is to give a rough indication as to whether the writing is fairly recent or not, provided it is possible to apply either the ion diffusion technique or tests based on colour and solubility.

Carbon Copies

It is only occasionally that a carbon copy will be submitted for dating. Before any tests are applied to the carbon itself, all other sources from which evidence of age may be obtained should be exhausted.

The fact that a carbon copy is in question will indicate that the document is not of any great antiquity, for it was the invention of the typewriter in the latter half of the nineteenth century which gave the impetus to the development of a practicable carbon paper.

The only tests applied to the carbon copy which are likely to be of any assistance are those designed to identify the blue toner, which is often added to improve the colour of the carbon. The toner can be released for identification by careful treatment of the line with a powerful wax solvent, such as methylene chloride or chloroform. If one of the iron blues or ultramarine has been used for this purpose,

[8] *Vanadate in Ink,* U.S.P. 1,932,248, 1933; Ottley, *Quick-drying Ink,* U.S.P. 1,987,071, 1933.
[9] *Stable Blue Dye for Alkaline Ink,* Reynolds, U.S.P. 2,489,463, 1949; *Alkaline Writing Inks,* U.S.P. 2,528,390, 1950.

the evidential value of the nature of the toner will be nil, as these compounds were in common use long before the invention of carbon paper. If the blue toner happens to be copper phthalocyanine or any related compound, this will indicate the carbon copy must have been made after the expiration of the first quarter of the twentieth century.

Evidence of Date from Stamps

Many documents, such as envelopes which have passed through the post, receipts for sums of money, legal agreements, etc., bear stamps from which significant data concerning the date of the document can often be derived.

Everyone is aware that the design of postage stamps is subject to periodical change, but what is rarely appreciated is that from time to time, more subtle variations may occur. An excellent example of a subtle change concerns the British orange-coloured twopenny stamp which was in current use in 1939. The colour of this stamp was changed to brown on March 3, 1951, and both colour and design were changed on September 1, 1953. These colour changes were obvious, but what passed unnoticed by more than one forger was that after October 6, 1941, the orange shade was lightened as an economy measure to conserve wartime stocks of printing ink. More than one ostensibly pre-war receipt has come to the notice of the author where the presence of this paler version of the stamp has exposed it as a forgery. The war, with the consequent destruction of records, accidental by enemy action, and deliberate for salvage, greatly facilitated the production of forged receipts to support inflated claims for compensation for loss of property.

The value of the watermark for dating a stamp is well known to the philatelist, but this source of evidence is not always available to the document examiner, for it is difficult if not impossible to observe the watermark on a stamp without removing it from the document, a procedure for which it is not always possible to obtain permission. (See, however, Chap. 6, Fig. 6–10.)

Because of the difficulty in obtaining unused copies of obsolete stamps, the forger may be forced to remove a suitable stamp from an existing document for use on the forgery. In view of this, every stamp on a document which might have some dating significance should never be taken at its face value, but should be scrutinised to see whether any such transference has been effected.

Problems Limited to the Determination of the Relative Ages of Entries on the Same Document

In favourable circumstances, it is possible to carry the determination of the relative ages of entries on a document much further than might be expected from the meagre success which so often attends the methods of absolute dating to which reference has already been made.

The most successful methods are those based on the phenomena associated with intersections. The intersections are generally those occurring between lines of writing, but the intersections of lines of writing with folds and creases in the paper may also be pressed into service. From the appearance of the intersection, it is often possible to prove the order of writing or of writing and folding.

A great deal that is vague, and in some instances quite misleading, has been written on the interpretation of the phenomena observed with a microscope at the intersections of lines with other lines and with folds and creases in the paper, but in the opinion of the author, the following observations are soundly based.

(1) *Appearances are generally if not invariably deceptive*

The fact that truth is rarely what appears " obvious at a glance " can be demonstrated by considering the well-known optical illusion—that, of two intersecting lines, the darker invariably appears to have been written over the lighter, irrespective of the true state of affairs.

Also, the groove made by a line which happens to lie athwart the main direction of the incident light will appear both deeper and better defined than another similar groove of equal depth which lies at an acute angle to the light.

To quote yet another example of misleading appearances; if an ink line has been written over a pencil line, and the incident light is arranged so that it is caught and reflected by the fragments of graphite which form the pencil line, an inexperienced observer will be convinced that he can clearly see the fragments of graphite from the pencil *resting on the surface* of the dried ink, from which it is fatally easy to reach the conclusion that the ink line was written first. On mature consideration, however, it might be more correctly decided that, as the fragments of graphite which make up a pencil line must invariably lie on and amid the surface fibres of the paper, in marked contrast to the action of the ink which sinks into the paper, the apparent relative positions of ink stain and pencil fragments is likely to be unaffected by the order in which they are applied to the paper.

(2) *The Absence of an Effect Produced by a Certain Sequence is no Proof of the Sequence having been Reversed*

An excellent example of this important principle occurs at the intersection of an ink line with a fold or crease in the paper. If, on microscopic examination, some of the ink from the line can be seen to have seeped out of the track of the pen into the disturbed paper in the region of the fold (see Fig. 7–13), this will constitute good evidence that the fold must have been in the paper *before* the ink line was written across it, otherwise the surplus ink would not have spread into the very region to be *later* disturbed by the act of folding.

If, however, an ink line can be seen to cross a fold in the paper without there being any seepage of ink from the pen track into the fold, this must not be taken to mean that the fold must necessarily have been made after the ink line had dried, although it is quite possible that this is what had happened. There are a number of good reasons why there should be no observable seepage from an ink line into a previously existing fold across which it is written. For example, there may have been no excess ink in the line available for lateral spreading, for all that was delivered from the pen point might have been absorbed into the paper immediately under the pen nib as it travelled over the paper.

The foregoing example must not be taken to mean that it is never possible to show that an ink line was made before an intersecting fold, for there are other considerations which can be taken into account when the sequence has to be established even in the absence of any lateral spreading.

(3) *An Effect may be Produced in More than One Way if Conditions are Altered*

If, by trial and error, with intersecting lines or lines and folds, it is found possible to duplicate the effect found in the document under examination, it must not be assumed that this effect was necessarily produced in exactly the same way.

This is because the experimenter can rarely be sure that in his experiment he has duplicated all the conditions originally associated with the effect found in the document under examination. Even the duplication of the writing materials is certain to present difficulty.

The term " writing ink " includes liquids of widely differing properties. Writing inks range from the strongly alkaline quick-drying inks through the neutral dyestuff inks to the decidedly acid record inks. The alkaline inks readily soak into and spread on the surface of most papers, whilst the record inks are repelled by the slightest trace of greasy contamination of the paper. It is not surprising that the behaviour of these inks in similar circumstances is as different as their compositions.

In view of this variability in the nature of writing ink, it is unwise to make any dogmatic pronouncement as to the interpretation of the different phenomena observed at intersections, without taking into consideration the nature of the ink, the pressure on and the speed of the pen, and the quantity of ink with which the nib was charged.

Even if a preliminary investigation has disclosed the nature of both ink and paper so that they could be duplicated for the experiment, there will be no certainty that when the experiment is carried out the paper will be in the same state as when the intersection under investigation was made. To take but one factor; the humidity of the paper is certain to have a profound influence on the way it will take an ink, and the humidity of any paper is subject to change according to its condition of storage.

(4) *The Phenomena Observed at Intersections are often Poorly Defined*

Any worthwhile treatment of the phenomena observed at intersections has to be illustrated with photographs. From the majority of the photographs which have been published it would appear that the effects observed on microscopic examination are invariably clear-cut and incapable of being confused with, for example, the imperfections which may be discovered in any line, whether written with conventional pen, ball-point or pencil. It is sometimes lost sight of that these illustrations are carefully selected to exhibit the phenomena in the most favourable and least equivocal manner. There is no harm in this, provided it is understood that the photographs illustrate cases which are the exception rather than the rule, and that in practice the effects are sometimes so poorly defined that even the most experienced operators may have some difficulty in deciding whether the modifications in the character of the line at the intersection are indeed significant and capable of unequivocal interpretation. It is only a document examiner capable of gross self-deception who is prepared to express definite opinions about the order of writing at every intersection he is called upon to examine.

The Intersection of Ink Lines

When two ink lines intersect or are joined whilst the ink is still wet, the excess ink in both will merge at the intersection, so that when dry, there will be no evidence from which the order of writing can be determined. This is emphasised because claims are sometimes made that the order of writing at such an intersection can be determined by microscopic study of the pen tracks. Such evidence is almost invariably subjective and has little existence outside the mind of the observer.

Elaborate and detailed conclusions supposedly drawn from the microscopic examination of the intersection and joining of wet ink lines are the stock-in-trade of the charlatan who is prepared to " prove " any questioned signature to be either genuine or forged, according to the demands made by those who are availing themselves of his services.

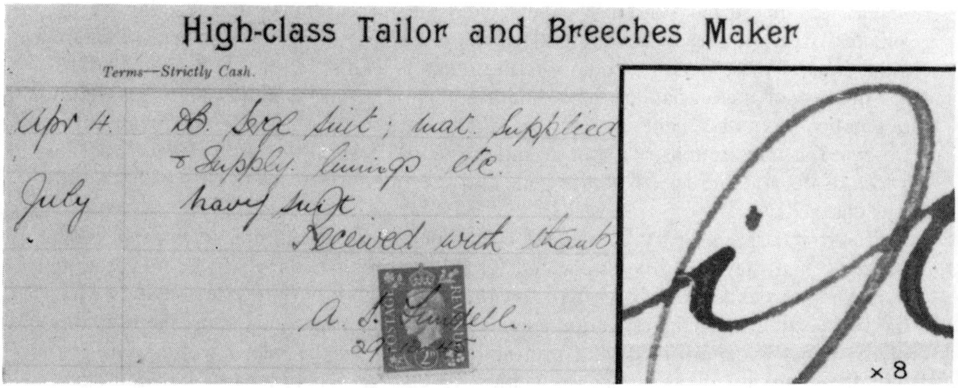

Fig. 7–5. The last item on this account was added after it was receipted. The " R " of " Received " intersects the " i " of " suit." The photomicrograph shows how the ink from the " i " has run into the " R."

If an ink line, well charged with ink, crosses another which, although no longer moist, has not yet dried hard, there will almost invariably be a flow of ink from the new line into the old. This overflowing ink will dry with a well-defined edge which can be observed on microscopic examination. This flow of ink can easily be distinguished from the mingling which occurs when two wet lines intersect or join, for here the flow will have a diffuse edge rather than one which is well-defined.[10]

When two ink lines intersect, there is not necessarily either a merging of the ink or a perceptible flow of ink from one to the other. If the second line is sparsely inked there will, of course, be no surplus of ink to flow into the other. Even when there is ample ink in the second line, should the first consist of thoroughly oxidised and insoluble iron gallotannate ink, there will be little tendency to spread.

[10] Mitchell, C. A., and Ward, T. J., " The Sequence of Strokes in Writing," *Analyst*, 52, 1927.

These two examples illustrate how different effects can be produced at a line intersection. (See Figure 7–6.)

Where no flow has taken place at the intersection of two ink lines, it is tempting to make an effort to determine the order of writing by microscopic examination of the tracks in the paper made by the points of the nib. When side lighting is used to throw the nib tracks into greater prominence, it will often seem that one pair of nib point tracks appears to cross the other without being interrupted at the point of intersection. This is often interpreted as evidence that the ink line exhibiting the uninterrupted tracks must have been written after the other.

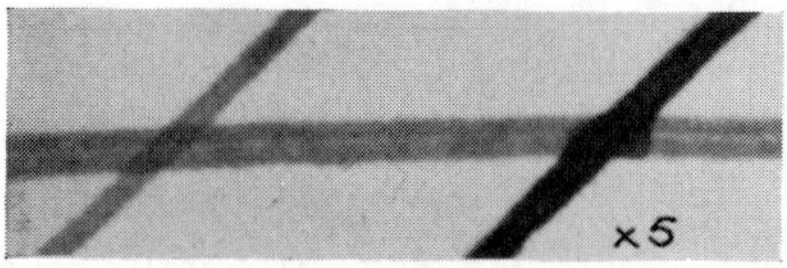

Fig. 7–6. Although both diagonal strokes were written in the same ink across the pre-existing horizontal ink line the intersection phenomena are different. The flow of ink from the right hand diagonal stroke into the horizontal line is most apparent but there has been no corresponding flow from the left hand diagonal stroke. This is because of different conditions of writing. The right hand diagonal stroke was made with a well charged nib before the ink of the horizontal stroke had fully dried. The left hand diagonal stroke was written with a nib sparsely charged with ink after the horizontal stroke had fully dried.

Working in this way, the observer can expect to be right in half the cases he deals with, for this is the percentage of success achieved by guesswork! Almost invariably, the observer merely imagines the effect he thinks he is observing; with a slight change in the lighting, an equally convincing set of observations could be made for the other pair of tracks.

The Effect of Blotting at an Intersection

The tiny area covered by both lines at an intersection is usually darker in colour than either of the lines, because it has received a double application of ink, provided of course that the second line was written after the first had dried fairly hard. On occasion, it will be observed that this doubly inked area is actually lighter in colour and less rich in excess ink than the darker of the two intersecting lines.[11] This may at first sight appear to be inexplicable, but on further examination it will almost certainly be noticed that one of the lines was blotted very soon after writing. If it happened to be the second of the two lines which was blotted, this would provide the reason for the lightening of the colour of the doubly inked region. The blotting paper would remove, not only the greater part of the ink from the newly written line but also some from the original line which had been loosened at the intersection by the application of the fresh ink. As ink is a dilute aqueous solution, its effect on an established ink line is very similar to that of water. (See Figure 7–7.)

Fig. 7–7. Some of the colour from " D " has been removed when " f " was blotted. This proves that " f " was written after " D."

If this explanation can be seen to apply to the

[11] Osborn, A. S., " Sequence of Strokes in Blotted Writing," *Analyst*, 53, 1928.

intersection under examination, it may safely be concluded that, (a) the line which had been blotted must have been written last, and (b) if an iron gallotannate ink was used for the first line, the ink solids had not had time to become oxidised and so insoluble that they were relatively unaffected by the action of the fresh ink. This means that the second line was probably written within a few years of the first.

This unexpected lightening of the area crossed by both ink lines at the intersection is but a single example of the curious effects which are sometimes observed. It should serve to emphasise that, before any attempt is made to interpret the phenomena which are observed at intersections, other portions of the intersecting lines should be given the same close scrutiny. In the absence of this further examination, it will not be possible to distinguish between those effects which are peculiar to the intersection and the others which are characteristic of the line itself.

It is not uncommon for an ink line to be characterised by places where the ink has gathered to form patches of appreciable thickness and irregularity of outline.

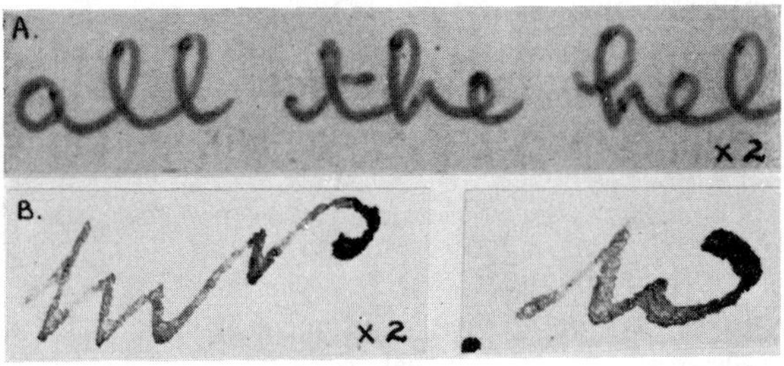

Fig. 7–8. (A) The thickenings in the line are characteristic of the writing of the ball-point pen and are caused by a change in the direction of rotation of the ball. (B) The thickenings are due to irregular flow of ink from the pen.

Slight variations in the condition of the surface of the paper and some unevenness in the flow of ink from the pen will cause the line to present a mottled appearance on microscopic examination. If one of these thickenings happened to coincide with an intersection erroneous conclusions might be drawn concerning the order of writing, unless the examiner had noted that the thickenings were a line rather than an intersection phenomenon. (See Figure 7–8.)

Paper is by no means an isotropic material, and from place to place the surfaces of some papers vary considerably in their physical properties. The presence of a trace of grease or of oily matter will cause lines made with most inks to shrink in width because of the reluctance of dilute aqueous solutions to spread over a greasy surface. Exceptions to this general rule occur, for a greasy surface on which a neutral or slightly acid ink would take with difficulty would probably offer little hindrance to the spread of an alkaline ink. This shrinkage in the width of an ink line when it crosses a greasy area is referred to because it has an important bearing on the interpretation of the phenomena observed at the intersection of ink lines with marks made with carbon paper, printing ink and typewriter ribbons.

Additions and Alterations to Ink Lines

Much that has been said concerning the intersection of ink lines will apply also to those additions and alterations which are of significance when suspect signatures are being examined.

If an ink line is partially overwritten, added to or altered whilst the ink is still wet, there is no possibility of the examiner being able to decide the order of writing of the several strokes, although the fact of alteration or addition is patent.

Unless a strong grip is kept on the imagination, it is possible to examine a melange of intersecting ink strokes and find confirmation of any theory which might have been formed about the order of writing. Almost invariably the evidence is subjective and has no basis in reality. Even when the examination is carried out with an open mind, optical illusions and the direction of the incident light will be largely at the root of any conclusions which are arrived at.

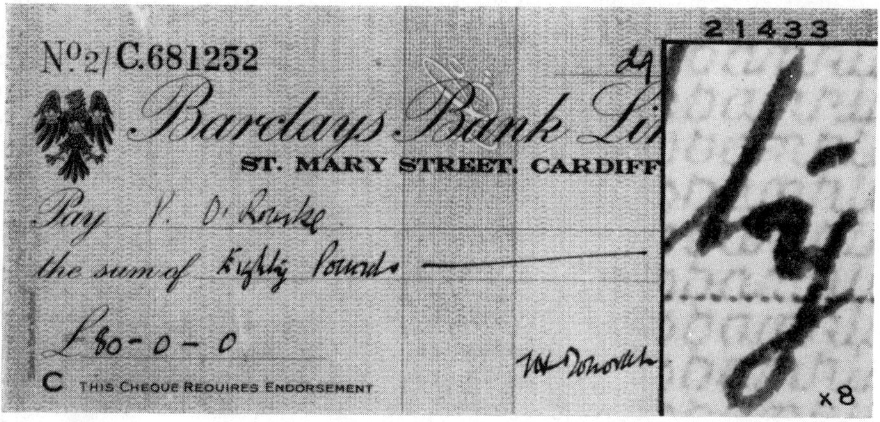

Fig. 7–9. The photomicrograph illustrates the abrupt boundary between the " t " and the added " y " of the " raised " cheque.

Some stress is laid upon this matter because evidence is often recklessly tendered that genuine signatures are fraudulent because the witness has formed the opinion that the sequence of strokes in certain of the letters, generally the capitals, differs from that characteristic of the genuine signatures, whereas in point of fact the witness is unable to determine the order of writing in either suspect or genuine signatures.

This must not be taken to imply that the presence of retouching in a forged signature cannot be demonstrated; it is the order in which the strokes are made which cannot be determined, and this matters little, for any stroke added to improve an outline must have been written subsequent to the stroke it is designed to modify.

Once the original ink has dried, the order of writing of any additional strokes can be settled, because of the nature of the outline between the ink of the original stroke and that subsequently added. This enables the fraudulent nature of " raised " cheques, where sums such as six and eight pounds are increased to sixty and eighty, to be demonstrated. If the addition is made at the time of drawing the cheque, there is a merging of the ink which is absent from the cheque which is " raised " after the original ink has dried. (See Figure 7–9.)

The Intersection of Ink and Pencil Lines

As the final stage in the preparation of the " lead " of a modern pencil is its boiling in tallow, the fragments of the graphite-clay mixture which make up a pencil line are unlikely to become wetted by any ink which is subsequently applied. This is one reason why, when a pencil-ink line intersection is microscopically examined, the fragments of the " lead " are seen to stand out quite clear of the ink which has soaked into the underlying paper.

The inexperienced observer is apt to conclude, irrespective of the true state of affairs, that any intersecting pencil line has been written subsequent to that made with ink.

It is only in the most exceptional circumstances that it is possible to state the order of writing of a pencil-ink intersection. If the passage of the pencil point has resulted in a serious disturbance of the surface of the paper, and a strongly alkaline ink is then used for making the intersecting line, there may occur a definite spreading of the ink along the track made by the pencil. The inference to be drawn from this is that the pencil line must have been on the paper when the ink was applied. Such special cases are rarely encountered, so that for all practical purposes it may be assumed that it is impossible to determine the order of writing of intersecting pencil and ink lines. This sometimes leads to difficulties when a crudely made signature, written in ink, is found closely associated with a faint pencil line. The problem is whether the signature is a crudely written genuine signature which has been used as the basis of a traced forgery, or whether it is a traced signature incorporating the guide line used in its production. This problem cannot usually be solved by microscopic examination alone, and other criteria have to be sought.

The Intersection of Lines in Ink with Others in an Oily Medium

Unless the ink is strongly alkaline, an ink line crossing one made with a " liquid lead " ball-point will probably exhibit a discontinuity at the intersection because of the water-repellent nature of the " liquid lead " medium. On the other hand, the presence of dry ink is no obstacle to the deposit of a layer of the " liquid lead," so that it is possible to determine the order of writing at a " liquid lead "–ink intersection, unless the ink happens to be strongly alkaline. (See Figure 7–10.)

This latter proviso is yet another example of the importance of taking all the factors into consideration before reaching any conclusion.

The strong alkali in the modern quick-drying inks tends to swell cellulose. When a line is drawn with either a " liquid lead " ball-point or with an ordinary pencil, and heavy pressure is employed, a well-defined groove will be found associated with it. If such a groove is crossed with a line made with an alkaline ink, the swelling of the cellulose will cause the groove to become much less definite at the intersection with the ink line. Under these circumstances, it may be possible to show that the pencil line was drawn before the ink was applied to the paper.

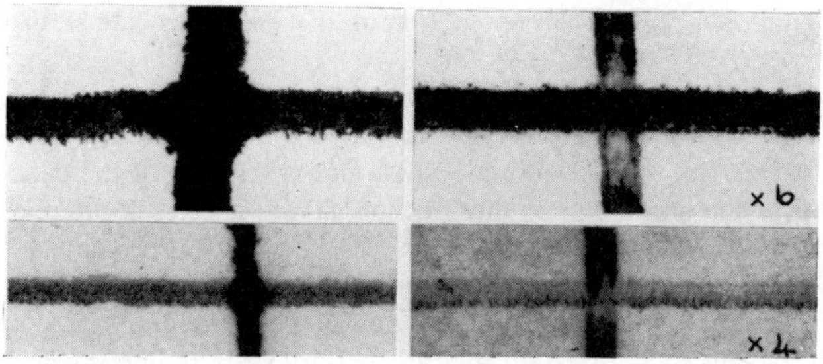

Fig. 7–10. The upper horizontal stroke was made with carbon paper, the lower with a " liquid lead " ball-point. The left-hand vertical intersecting line is an alkaline ink, the right-hand line being ordinary blue-black ink. The alkaline ink spreads into the horizontal lines whose greasy nature causes a partial interruption of the ordinary ink line.

The Intersection of Ink Lines with Typescript

It is often stated that it is possible to determine whether an ink line which intersects typescript was written before or after the typing. The theory is simple; most typewriter inks are greasy, and an ink line tends to shrink in width as it passes over a greasy place on the paper. If, indeed, an ink line is observed to suffer a distinct reduction in width every time it intersects the typescript, it may safely be concluded that the ink line was written after the typescript.

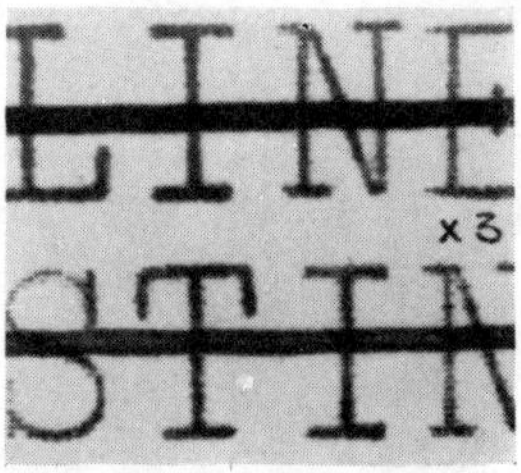

Fig. 7–11. The typescript was made after the upper, but before the lower ink line was drawn. Little difference is apparent.

In practice, however, ink lines written across typescript are rarely seen to suffer any appreciable shrinkage in width, since the amount of oily medium transferred from the ribbon to the paper is rarely sufficient to have any effect. Indeed, if the ink happens to be alkaline, surplus ink, instead of shrinking, may spread out into the typescript to increase the width of the ink line at the intersection. In this case, the proof that the ink followed the typescript would be the presence of a swelling rather than a shrinkage.

Experience has shown that it is rarely possible for any definite opinion as to the order of appearance on the paper for intersecting ink lines and typescript to be justified on the meagre amount of evidence which is generally available.

A similar state of affairs will be found to hold for carbon paper and wax crayons, which have much in common with typewriter ribbons in the way the marks they make on paper react with intersecting ink lines.

The Intersection of Ink Lines with Cancellation Ink

It is sometimes necessary to examine envelopes with suspect date stamps in the investigation of certain types of fraud. When the cancellation mark on the envelopes partially overlaps the address, there exists the possibility of determining which of the two first appeared on the envelope. This is of great interest in cases where it is suspected that the address was not written on the envelope until it had been passed through the post in order to obtain the required date-stamp cancellation mark.

The majority of official cancellation inks are of an oily nature, very like printing ink and the ink with which typewriter ribbons are impregnated. This opens up the possibility that an ink-written address which intersects part of the cancellation mark would exhibit some shrinkage of the ink line should it cross a previously impressed cancellation mark. This is sometimes seen to occur, but, unfortunately, envelopes are usually made from paper of poor quality, so absorbent that the oily medium of the cancellation ink rapidly diffuses into its substances, reducing the concentration of oil on the surface to such an extent that a superimposed ink line is generally relatively unaffected.

Therefore, it is only when the cancellation mark has been heavily impressed on a paper with a low tendency towards oil absorption that shrinkage of a subsequently written ink line can confidently be expected.

The Intersection of Pencil Lines

The detached fragments of " lead " which form a pencil line tend to become heaped against those surface fibres of the paper which happen to lie across the direction of motion of the pencil. This means that it is possible to determine the direction in which a pencil line was made.

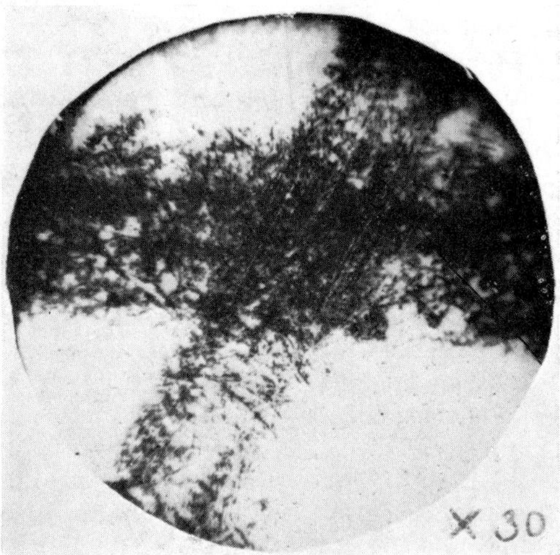

Fig. 7–12. *Intersection of pencil lines.* The striations associated with the vertical line may be seen to continue uninterrupted across the horizontal line. This may be taken as proof that the horizontal line was written first.

If the pencil is graded HB or harder, the line is also characterised by longitudinal striations which, provided the light is carefully adjusted, can be detected on microscopic examination. These striations often enable the order of writing of two intersecting pencil lines to be determined, although this is of very infrequent interest to the document examiner. It stands to reason that the line which exhibits striations which pass uninterrupted through the intersection must have been written after one whose striations have been interrupted. When the pencil is so soft that well-defined striations are absent, this method cannot be applied. (See Figure 7–12.)

It is sometimes possible to determine the order of writing by microscopic examination of the grooves in the paper surface made by the passage of the pencil points. Before any conclusion as to the order of writing is reached, the evidence for the existence of an uninterrupted groove for the more recently written line must be unequivocal; above all its appearance of continuity must be independent of the direction of the incident light. If the pencil marks are faint, the microscopic evidence is almost certain to be inconclusive; great caution should be observed in expressing any opinion, and the influence of optical illusions fully taken into account.

The Intersection of Lines with Folds and Creases in the Paper

When a sheet of paper is folded, and particularly when it is heavily creased, considerable stress and strain will be imposed on the paper in the neighbourhood of the fold. The consequent disturbance of its surface condition will be governed by a number of factors—the thickness of the paper and the nature of the fibres, the extent to which it has been loaded and, above all, the sharpness of the creasing. A great deal will also depend on the surface treatment it has received. A writing

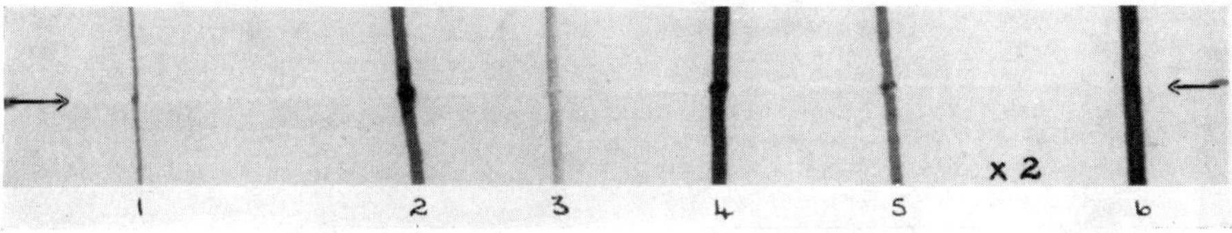

Fig. 7–13. The crease indicated by the arrows is crossed by various lines: (1) lightly written dyestuff ink; (2) heavily written dyestuff ink; (3) pencil; (4) alkaline ink; (5) ball-point; (6) dyestuff ink (before folding). The fold has had little effect on the pencil line (3), and none on the ink line (6). The lateral spreading of the ink into the fold is most marked with the alkaline ink (4).

paper of good quality, tubsized with gelatine, may be little affected by a treatment which might well cause the splitting of a sheet of poor quality paper which has been surface loaded with a thick coating of mineral matter.

Whatever the quality of the paper, any disturbance of the surface will facilitate both the absorption and spread of ink. It is for this reason that an ink line written across a fold in the paper will often exhibit a certain degree of lateral spreading of the ink into the fold. Once an ink line has dried, no amount of folding will give rise to this lateral spreading of the ink, so that this phenomenon may often be used to determine the order of writing and folding where line and fold intersect. Such evidence may be important when later additions to a folded document, such as a will or agreement, are suspected. (See Figure 3–1 of Chapter 3.)

As the lateral spreading is generally small in extent, examination by the naked eye even when supplemented with a hand lens should never be relied on; a stereoscopic microscope adjusted to give a linear magnification of about ten times should be used. If the paper is of good quality and the ink line has been lightly written across the fold, there may be no lateral spreading of the ink; instead, careful examination of the ink line at high magnification may reveal the presence of a transverse dark stripe in the ink line itself where it crosses the fold. This dark stripe is caused by the increased absorption of ink where the disturbance of the paper surface is at its maximum, that is, in the fold itself. This dark stripe may be seen even when the line has been made with a ball-point pen or liquid-lead pencil.

In the neighbourhood of a fold, not only is the absorbency of the paper for ink increased, but a considerable departure from flatness may persist in the neighbourhood of the fold even after the paper has been opened out for writing. This residual curvature of the paper will often affect any ink line written across the fold. This is most noticeable when a ball-point pen has been used; when the ball-point sinks into the trough of the fold, there will be a distinct tendency for the line to widen as the ball housing makes a momentary contact with the far side of the trough. The ball housing is often encrusted with excess ink which has been wiped off the ball on to its contact surfaces, which is why an occasional doubling of the line may be found in signatures when the ball-point pen has been given an excessive slope.

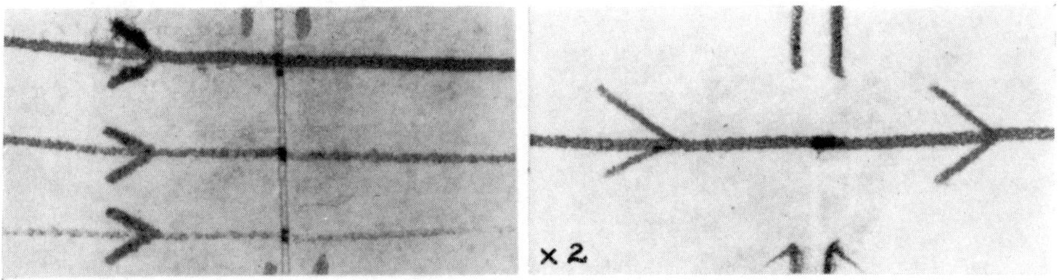

Fig. 7–14. (a) As the ball-point ploughs through the raised crease in the paper, the sides of the ball are wiped to cause a thickening of the line. If the pen is lightly held, it jumps the paper after passing over the crease to produce a discontinuity in the line. (b) As the ball-point falls into the hollow of the crease, the ball is wiped to cause a thickening of the line on the far side. The arrows indicate the direction of writing and the pencil lines flank the crease.

Not only does the widening of the line show that the pen point passed over a pre-existing fold but the position of the widening shows which way the pen was travelling, for the widening must occur on the far side of the fold. (See Figure 7–14.)

If the fold has been made in the reverse sense, so that the pen point has to traverse not a trough but a hump in the paper, a different effect is seen. If the pen, either conventional or ball-point, is lightly held, there will often be a hiatus in the line through the pen point having jumped the paper after passing over the raised edge of the fold.

There should be no difficulty in interpreting any positive indications such as the foregoing when the order of folding and writing is being investigated; doubt can arise only when an ink line is seen to cross a fold with no apparent change in its appearance. Such negative evidence must always be considered with care. It is unsafe to conclude, solely because no extra absorption, lateral spreading or hiatus can be seen, that the fold must have been made subsequent to the writing of the line. It is true that this absence of any noticeable effect on the character of the line is what is likely to be seen when the fold is made after the line, but a few experiments will show that it is sometimes possible to make ink lines across folds in the paper without there being any positive evidence that the fold was made before the ink line. From this it should not be implied that in no circumstances is it possible to show that an ink line has been made before an intersecting fold, for other circumstances can be taken into account.

For example, the ink may be one of the modern quick-drying alkaline inks which have a strong tendency to spread beyond the limits of the pen points. With one of these inks, it is practically impossible to write anything but the very faintest of traces across a fold without leaving some evidence that this has been the order of writing. Since this is so, it is quite safe to assume that a bold line in one of these inks which crosses a fold without suffering any alteration in character must have been written before the paper was folded.

In other instances, it may be possible to show that similar ink lines on the document are affected in their passage across the fold, in which case the absence of any change may be taken as proof that the folding followed the writing. Again, if a well-inked line is seen to cross a sharply creased fold where the surface of the paper has obviously been disturbed, the absence of any spreading or localised increased absorption can be interpreted in only one way—the line must have been written before the folding took place.

Difficulties are most likely to occur when the lightest of lines traverse gentle folds in the paper. A lightly made line contains little if any surplus ink, and the surface of a paper which has been gently folded is little affected, so there is unlikely to be any intersection phenomena of evidential value, whatever the order of writing.

It must be repeated that too much reliance should never be placed on the results of experiments designed to reproduce phenomena similar to those under investigation, for there will be no certainty that the original conditions have been duplicated. For example, the effect produced on a sheet of paper by creasing will be governed to a large extent by its humidity. A crease which would sever a sheet which is bone dry would have little effect on the same sheet when damp. Similarly, a crease on a sheet of paper which has become desiccated through storage in hot, dry conditions will behave towards an intersecting ink line in a very different manner to that exhibited towards the same ink line, should the paper become damp and limp. Ink will rapidly sink into a dry sheet of indifferently glazed paper, whereas with an ink line of the same depth on the same sheet saturated with moisture, excess ink may lie for some time on the surface of the paper.

The Effects of Folds on Typescript

Typescript is relatively little affected by the alteration in the surface of the paper in the vicinity of a fold, but where the folding has produced a definite ridge in the paper, some of the ink will be wiped off the ribbon as it is driven into the raised portion of the surface. This will cause a regional broadening of the imprint when the ridge has become flattened by the impact of the typeface. A somewhat similar effect will be seen when a soft pencil point has ploughed through a ridge in the paper; light graphite smears will be rubbed from the sides of the lead to cause a local thickening of the pencil line. (See Figure 7–15 for examples of these effects.)

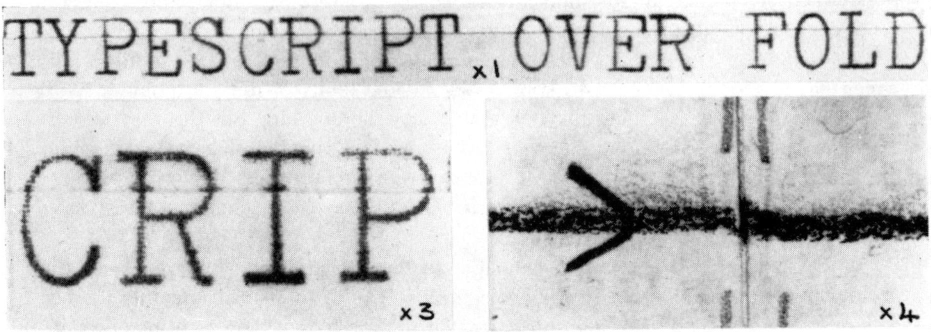

Fig. 7–15. (a) The type-face forces the ribbon into the raised crease in the paper to cause thickening at the intersections. (b) The soft pencil ploughs through the raised crease to cause a thickening of the line.

Dating Typescript

In Chapter 8, which deals with the examination of typescript, it is shown how it is sometimes possible to quote a narrow interval of time during which a particular specimen of typescript must have been produced. Briefly, this is accomplished by comparing the imperfections in the typescript under examination with those exhibited in specimens typed on the same machine at known times. The method involves, first, the identification of the actual machine which was used, and secondly, suitable specimens of typescript typed on that machine both before and after the typescript in question.

In many of the problems in which the date of typing is in question, there is no possibility of identifying the machine which was used, so that the method is no longer applicable.

Many are aware that even if the actual date of typing cannot be determined, it is possible to give a limit of age to a specimen of typescript by taking into consideration the style or fount of the type employed, the details of its design and, to a lesser extent, certain other features of the typescript which derive from what might be termed the " mechanical features " of the machine concerned.

It should be made clear at the outset that here, as in many other activities, there is a wide gulf between what is theoretically possible and what is likely to be accomplished when a document examiner is asked to give a limit of age to a specimen of typescript chosen at random. The reason for this will be appreciated when consideration is given to the manner in which dating based on this principle has to be accomplished.

Establishment of a Limit of Age to Typescript

As the first successful commercial typewriter—the Remington—was marketed about 1874, it follows that any specimen of typescript is very unlikely to be older than this, a fact which, in itself, is of little use. Where he is able to determine the make of the machine, the document examiner is able to be a little more explicit, for the different makes of typewriter now on the market made their first appearance over a period of something like fifty years.

The Remington was followed by the Smith Premier in 1889, the Barlock 1891, the Oliver 1894, the Underwood 1896, the L. C. Smith 1903, the Royal 1906 and the Woodstock (now the Allen) as recently as 1914. The Imperial, which began its existence as the Moya, was first marketed in 1908. This does not complete the story, for in the years just preceding the Second World War, the Electromatic, now the I.B.M., was introduced.

This list of dates alone is unlikely to be of any practical value, for very few specimens of questioned typescript date back to the last years of the nineteenth century or the early years of the twentieth, but, fortunately, factors other than the make of the machine can be pressed into service.

Once the typewriter appeared to have a commercial future, not only were new makes of machine put on the market, but improvements directed towards simplicity of operation, improved appearance of the typescript and ease of manufacture and maintenance were introduced into existing machines. Some of these improvements, such as those designed to reduce friction or to simplify operation, were purely mechanical and cannot be utilised as dating characteristics where the typescript is all that is available. Where the actual machine can be examined, mechanical improvements may serve to establish the model and consequently the date of introduction. Some mechanical improvements, such as the introduction of the shift key which enabled the Model 4 Remington to print lower case as well as capitals and the bi-colour ribbon of the 1909 Underwood, are reflected in the work of the machine. Another mechanical improvement, the introduction of proportionate spacing, with its obvious effect on the typescript, became a reality in the 1930s.

From the standpoint of dating, the most significant changes are those in the appearance of the letter designs. From the first Remington, which printed only capitals, to contemporary machines with their bewildering varieties of type styles or founts, which range in size from six to sixteen characters to the inch, the story has been one of steady development and increasing complexity. Not only have the different type styles made their appearance in the makers' catalogues at different times, new styles being added almost annually, but, with one important exception, all the important manufacturers have introduced modifications into certain of the letters of the ever-popular pica and elite styles. The exception is the Imperial, who have retained their pica style virtually unaltered since it was first introduced.

In view of this there is no doubt that, provided the machine responsible has not been extensively repaired or rebuilt, it should be possible to give a useful limit of age to any specimen of typescript. Whilst this is the theoretical position, in practice it will soon be discovered that many specimens of typescript can be given a limit of age in only the most general terms. The reason for this is simple—the necessary information and reference material is not available to the document examiner.

This should occasion no surprise, for as explained in Chapter 8, even the identification of the make of typewriter from the typescript cannot be guaranteed, because to do this would require specimens from every make and model of typewriter which had been put up for sale anywhere in the world. The assembly of sufficient comparison material of known date, so that a limit of age could be given to any specimen of typescript which might be submitted for examination, would be an even more formidable task. It might be argued that once the make of the typewriter had been established, even if the necessary data was not immediately available, the manufacturers could supply the necessary information. Whilst many manufacturers would do their utmost to answer queries, the necessary records might not be in existence. It might well happen that the makers were responsible only for the production of the machine, the type having been made by a specialist firm, and perhaps only fitted to the machine after it had left the factory. In the case of many machines still in use, the manufacturers have gone out of business.

It is true that details of schemes for the identification of the make and age of machines through the medium of a small number of key letters have been published,[12] but whilst they may lead to a number of identifications, they are applicable only to pica and elite styles of typescript drawn from popular machines of American manufacture. Another disadvantage for any scheme of identification is that it is necessarily limited to those type styles which were in existence when the scheme was being drawn up, which might be some time before publication. Any scheme must be subject to periodical revision as new material is brought on to the market.

From a variety of sources—and in this connection he wishes to acknowledge the generous assistance of his fellow members of the American Society of Questioned Document Examiners—the author has been able to acquire a considerable amount of comparison data which can be used for the identification and the dating of the machine used from the typescript, but experience has shown that the collection is less than adequate for dealing with all the dating problems which are presented to him. A fundamental difficulty which arises when dating problems are submitted to a laboratory which deals almost exclusively with matters arising from criminal investigations is that of proving the accuracy of the comparison material to the standard required in a criminal prosecution.

If there occurs in a questioned document a style of type which the document examiner discovers from his records to have been initially issued to the public in a certain year, he may have little hesitation in assigning a limit of age to the typescript. However, if such evidence is then tendered for the prosecution in a serious criminal charge it is sure to be challenged on a number of grounds.

The first test will be that of accuracy; it will be suggested that the type style in question might have been issued in another part of the world at a date much earlier than it was first noticed by the document examiner; alternatively, that it might have been issued as a special design to private order some time before it was made generally available. This latter suggestion cannot be dismissed as fantastic because this actually happens.

If the witness has guarded against this line of attack by seeking information on these points from the manufacturers, any statement to this effect will be objected to on the grounds that it partakes of the nature of hearsay. It is probable that the

12 Hilton, O., "Identification of the Make of Typewriter," *International Criminal Police Review*, Oct.–Nov., 1951.

only acceptable testimony as to the age of the typescript would be that of a representative of the firm who made and marketed the original type. This is almost certain to be difficult if not impossible to arrange, especially if the firm concerned had gone out of business.

For these reasons, the dating of typescript from the style of type, etc., will be considered no further here, except to repeat the warning that it is improbable that any document examiner will be in the position to date any but pica and elite typescript drawn from American machines.

Bibliography

Bessemans, A., "Triple Verification of the Age of a Questioned Document," *International Criminal Police Review,* No. 84, January, 1955.

Casey, R. S., "Writing Ink," *Encyclopaedia of Chemical Technology,* Polytechnic Institute of Brooklyn, Brooklyn N.Y.

Lockwood Directory of Paper Manufacturers (an annual publication).

Lucas, A., *Forensic Science and Scientific Criminal Investigation* (4th ed., 1946, Arnold, London). *History of Ink,* pp. 79–88.

Margival, *Les Encres* (Gauthier-Villars, Paris, 1912).

Reynolds, W. B., "The Development of Quick-drying Writing Inks," *Chemical and Engineering News,* April, 1946.

Waters, C. E., "Blue Dye as Evidence of the Age of Writing," *Industrial Engineering Chemist and Chemistry,* 25, 1034, 1933.

8

TYPESCRIPT

MANY who readily admit that much may be learned from the comparison of handwritten documents consider that typescript, being the product of a mass-produced machine, in no way lends itself to scientific examination for evidence of its age, origin and the identity of the typist. If this were true, the scope of the work of a document examiner would be increasingly limited, for the introduction of the typewriter less than a hundred years ago has revolutionised the production of all documents except those of a personal nature.

This is reflected in the fact that an increasing proportion of the documents submitted for examination at the author's laboratory are typewritten, although many are still unaware of what evidence can be adduced by the examination and comparison of typescript. While to the casual observer all typescript appears to be identical, the only apparent difference being in the colour of the ribbon which has been used, some little consideration will show that this is by no means the case.

Typewriters are manufactured in all highly industrialised countries by many makers who have made individual approaches to the problem of producing a reliable and effective machine. The typewriter is, despite its simplicity of operation, a most complicated piece of mechanism, for it is assembled from approximately two thousand parts which require something like twenty thousand different operations to manufacture. Not only are typewriters assembled from many components, but their action is the resultant of a number of interlocking adjustments which have to be made before the machine can be taken into service. When a typist is typing at a rate of sixty words a minute, he or she motivates about two hundred working parts a second, so that the creation of a line of typescript is the end product of many motions of a multitude of tiny pieces of mechanism, each unique in size, shape and action.

Once a machine is put into use, it suffers wear which has an increasing effect on the work it produces, although it is rarely that a typewriter can be considered to be worn out. A machine may be discarded for high-speed work in a busy office, but it may have a useful life of many years in private hands where a low standard of performance is acceptable.

From the foregoing, it may be anticipated that a great deal may be learned from the examination of typescript, but as document examination is a practical subject, actual specimens of typescript must be examined to discover whether these expectations are confirmed by experience.

TYPESCRIPT FROM DIFFERENT MAKES OF MACHINE

If typescript from machines of different manufacturers is compared, certain differences in the design of the typefaces will be apparent, because few manufacturers have identical views on what is the most pleasing and serviceable design for typewritten characters. This means that in some cases, at least, it will be possible to identify the make of the machine used for a particular specimen of typescript by taking into consideration the design of the type. Evidence such as this will often

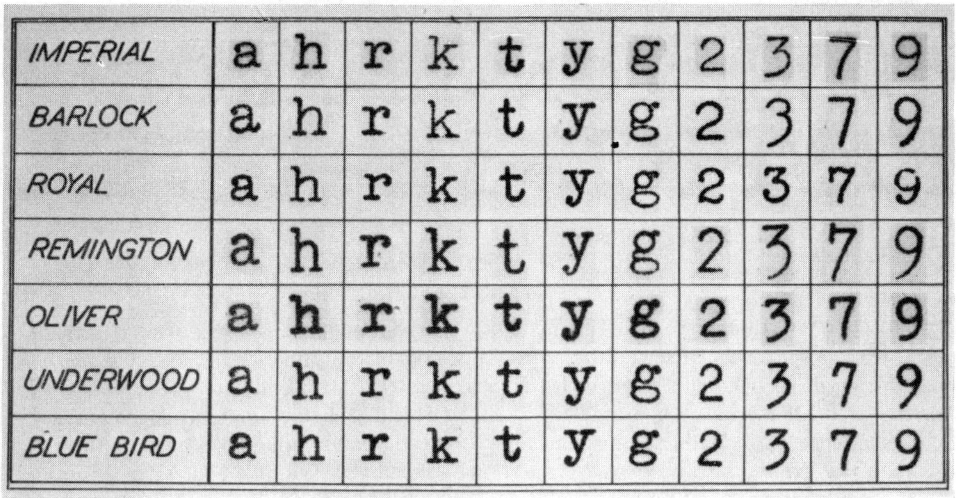

IMPERIAL	a	h	r	k	t	y	g	2	3	7	9
BARLOCK	a	h	r	k	t	y	g	2	3	7	9
ROYAL	a	h	r	k	t	y	g	2	3	7	9
REMINGTON	a	h	r	k	t	y	g	2	3	7	9
OLIVER	a	h	r	k	t	y	g	2	3	7	9
UNDERWOOD	a	h	r	k	t	y	g	2	3	7	9
BLUE BIRD	a	h	r	k	t	y	g	2	3	7	9

Fig. 8–1. " Pica " designs from a number of popular machines. The variation in design is greatest with the numerals and letters such as " g " and " t."

narrow the search for the author of a typewritten anonymous letter. This identification of the make of machine from the design of the type will be considered in more detail at a later stage.

Different Sizes of Type

If the catalogue of a large manufacturer is consulted, it will be found that a machine may be fitted with any of a bewildering variety of type styles. These vary in size from six to sixteen characters to the inch, and in design from what is termed shaded type, which has something of the appearance of incised letters, to designs which bear some resemblance to ordinary handwriting. The most popular style is that known as " pica," which runs ten to the inch; next in popularity comes " elite," which is slightly smaller, running twelve to the inch, although this type may

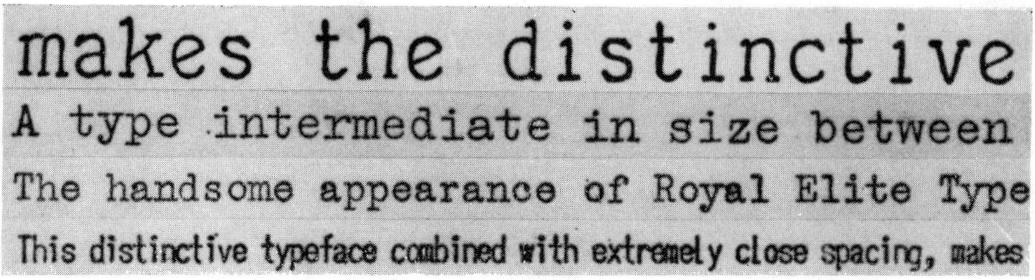

Fig. 8–2. This illustrates the variation in size and appearance of typescript. The magnification is approximately 1½ times linear.

be had spaced ten to the inch as with pica. As well as what might be termed conventional type styles, special designs are provided for use by those who require an individual style for business purposes or for typing mathematical formulae, etc.

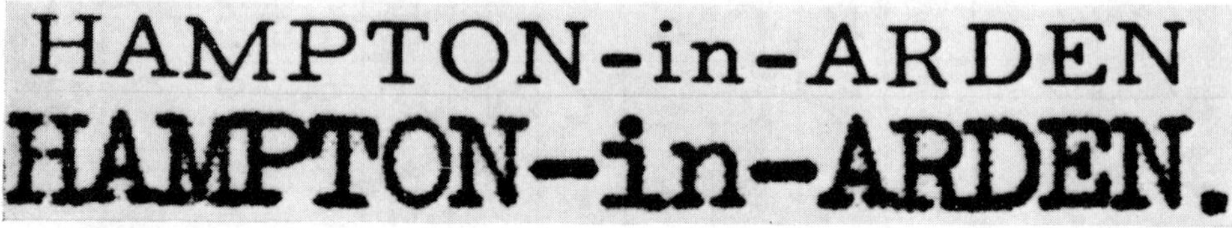

Fig. 8–3. A comparison of typescript derived from an I.B.M. proportionate-spacing machine imprinted through carbon paper, with fixed-space typescript from an Imperial machine imprinted through a woven carbon (not to scale).

The majority of type styles examined, it will be found, are designed so that every letter, irrespective of its width, is accommodated in the same space along the line, which will be one-tenth of an inch for pica, one-twelfth for elite, etc. If type from the I. B. M. machine [1] is examined, it will be found that this simple arrangement is not adhered to. With this machine, the space allotted is adjusted to the width of the letter, commonly known as " proportionate spacing." With the I. B. M. machine, each letter is allotted from two to five units of space. The unit is usually either one thirty-second or one thirty-sixth of an inch. Another thing which is noticeable about the typescript from this machine is that, unlike most other typescript, it has a clear-cut outline. This is because the I. B. M. machine in the example shown above has printed through carbon paper, whereas the other machine is fitted with a woven cloth ribbon, the threads of which produce the ragged outline of the type.

Some typescript will be found to be rather indistinct, so that whilst it may be read without any difficulty, it will prove impossible to distinguish the details of type design. This is the case when a large number of carbons have been taken, particularly

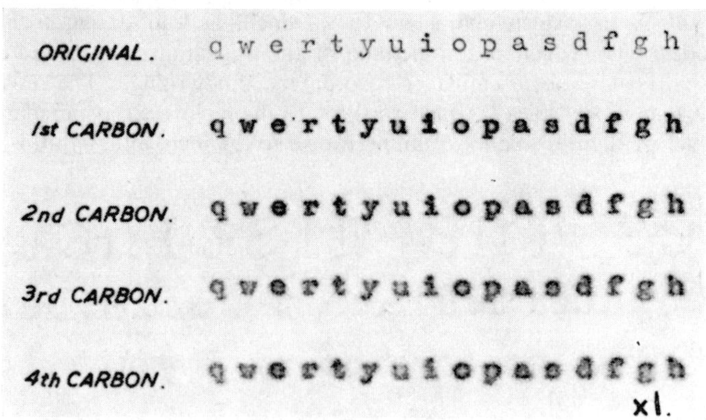

Fig. 8–4. A chart to illustrate the falling off in quality and definition of outline with an increasing number of carbons.

[1] A recently introduced Olivetti machine will also print proportionately spaced typescript.

when a soft platen and unsuitable paper have been used. Where a machine is fitted with a relatively hard platen (which is the name given to the roller around which the paper is wrapped in the machine) and good quality carbon paper is used, it is sometimes very difficult to determine whether the typescript is indeed a carbon copy or not. A quick test which is effective in the majority of cases is to examine the back of the sheet. With an original, punctuation marks tend to punch through the paper, something which is rarely found in a carbon copy.

Occasionally, traces of different colours may be found at the bottom edge of the typescript. This happens when a bi-colour ribbon is used in a defective machine.

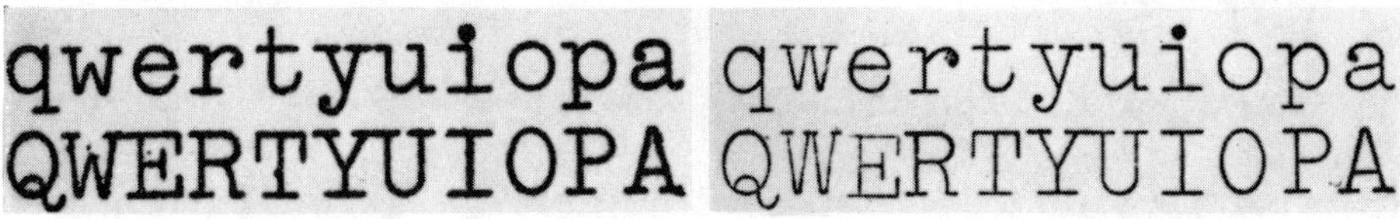

Fig. 8–5. This illustrates a change in design of Royal " pica " type which took place in 1950. The specimen on the left is the more recent of the two. (× 2½.)

If the pica style fitted to a contemporary Royal typewriter is compared with the pica style fitted to these machines a few years ago, a considerable difference in design will be apparent. This change in design is not peculiar to this make of machine, for most manufacturers introduce changes in design from time to time. The extent to which this practice is indulged in varies with the manufacturer. Underwood has introduced many changes in the pica style over the past twenty years, whilst Imperial, with true British conservatism, has kept this style of type virtually unchanged since its introduction over thirty years ago.

These changes in design are of great significance to the document examiner, because thereby he is able to put a limit of age on any typewritten document, provided, of course, that he has the necessary reference data. This is referred to in greater detail elsewhere.

Worn Machines

If an examination is carried out on specimens of typescript from well-worn machines, it will be observed that in some of the specimens every example of certain

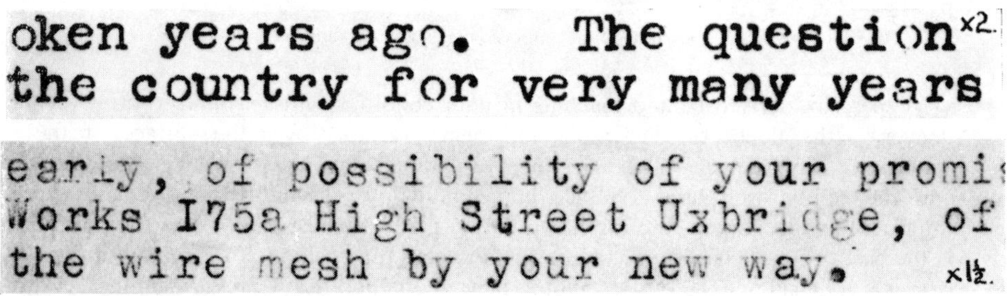

Fig. 8–6. The upper specimen of typescript is characterised by a " y " with a broken serif. The lower specimen of typescript is characterised by an abnormally large period (full stop). This defect was caused by the owner of the machine filing the type face to enlarge the period so as to avoid making holes whilst cutting stencils.

letters or figures will be found to be defective. Portions of the character will be found to be missing altogether, or there will be obvious distortion of the outline. These imperfections in the typescript are due to wear or damage to the typeface, which imprints the character through the ribbon. On occasion this damage may have been deliberately caused. In one case in the author's experience the full stop had been filed to enlarge its area, so as to reduce the tendency for it to be struck through the paper by a heavy handed typist; in another case the type had been filed to alter the characteristics of the machine when a request was made for it to be delivered for examination during an investigation into the origin of certain libellous typewritten letters.

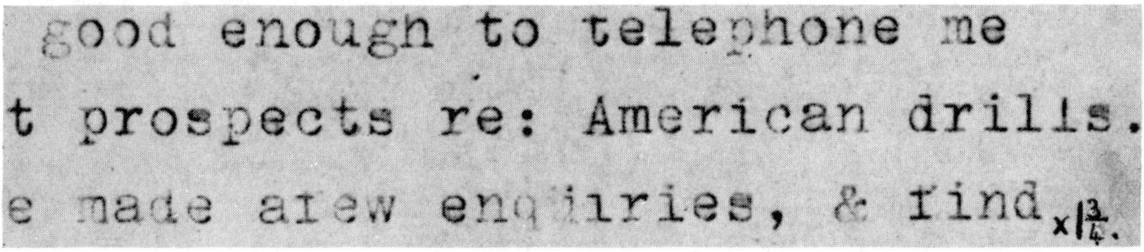

Fig. 8–7. This specimen of typescript exhibits faulty impressions stemming from the use of an imperfect ribbon. Compare the various examples of " l," some are perfect whilst others are faulty.

A defective character may be found in one line of typescript, whilst it will be found to print perfectly in the very next line. This defect cannot be caused by a broken typeface, so other reasons must be sought for its presence. The most likely is that the ribbon is defective in places, for without an evenly inked ribbon, it is unreasonable to expect perfect reproduction of the typeface. Another cause is a well worn and indented platen. To obtain a perfect impression of the typeface, the platen must present a smooth unbroken surface to the rear surface of the paper.

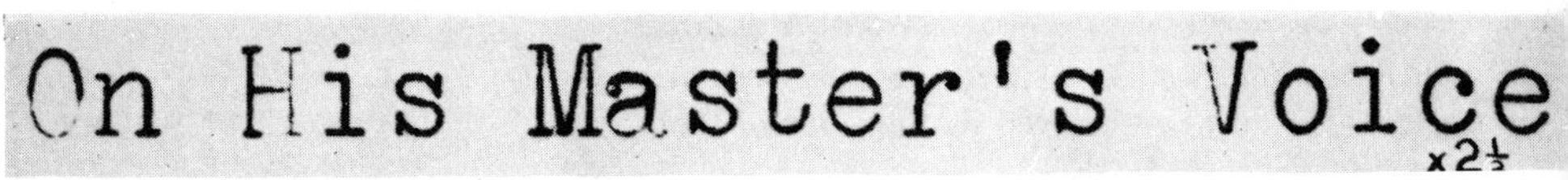

Fig. 8–8. The uneven depth of impression is caused by badly aligned typefaces.

Typescript derived from a machine in poor condition will be found to print very unevenly, the depth of the impression being variable over the surface of the character. This defect will be the more apparent when the touch has been light and the ribbon well used. Some characters will be found to be more heavily imprinted at the bottom, the top being hardly visible, whilst with others the reverse is the case. Other characters may be found where the position of maximum impression is at one side or the other. With a new ribbon and heavy pressure on the keys, these defects may be much less apparent. Sometimes practically the whole of a specimen of typescript will be found to have printed unevenly, the defect being that the position of maximum impression is at the bottom of every character. This is caused by faulty alignment of the platen to the type as a whole, a machine defect which might have been caused by the use of the wrong size of platen or by maladjustment of the machine.

Fig. 8–9. Example of typescript showing gross errors in horizontal alignment. (× 2½.)

When the line of type is inspected as a whole, it will become apparent that not all of the imperfections in the typescript are associated with the manner in which the outlines of the characters are reproduced. One of the most obvious defects is the occurrence of errors in the lateral spacing of the typescript along the line. These "errors in horizontal alignment," as they are termed, are most noticeable because any crowding of the characters is associated with neighbouring gaps which throw the overcrowding into relief.

Fig. 8–10. This illustrates examples of gross errors in vertical alignment. The "t" prints consistently above, and the "e" below, the line of type.

Examples of characters which print either above or below the line are less obvious. With an old machine, the extent of these errors in vertical alignment is governed to some extent by the speed with which the type-bar carrying the typeface has been moved. With worn bearings, centrifugal force tends to lift a character above the normal typing position.

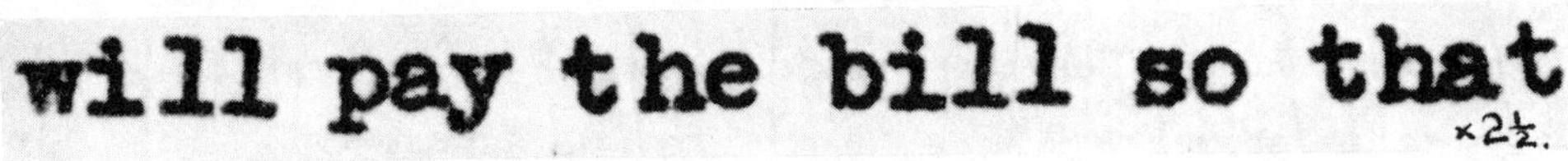

Fig. 8–11. This illustrates examples of slope misalignment. The "t" slopes backward and the "l" forward.

If the typescript has been derived from a machine which has been subjected to considerable abuse, some of the characters will be found to exhibit consistent slope-alignment defects because they lean either backwards or forwards.

When typescript from a well-worn machine is examined, it may happen that in one word a character will be reproduced with a particular alignment error, whilst in another word this error will either not occur or be exhibited in the reverse sense. The explanation for this mutability is that this particular character is loose and the manner in which it prints is fortuitous.

Finally, it must not be assumed that all variation in alignment characteristics is due to wear and loose bearings, for lack of rhythm on the part of the typist may be responsible, more especially for variation in horizontal alignment characteristics. For

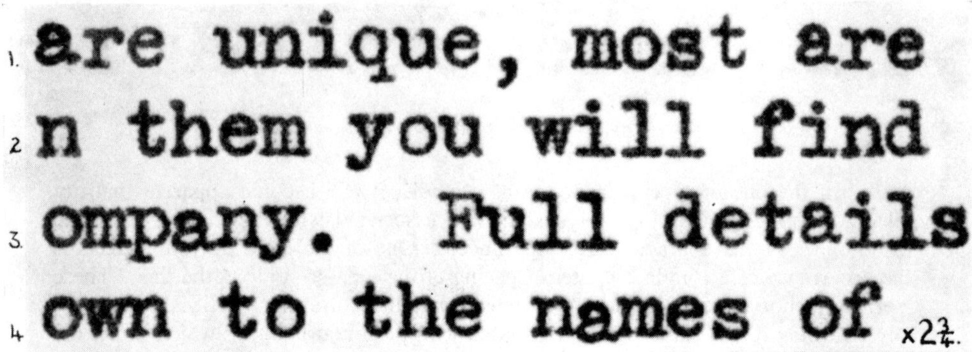
1. are unique, most are
2. n them you will find
3. ompany. Full details
4. own to the names of ×2¾.

Fig. 8–12. The typewriter responsible for this specimen of typescript had a loose " a " which resulted in this letter printing well above the line of type in the top line and appreciably below in the bottom line.

example, if the keys are pressed in rapid succession before the carriage has had time to complete its movement, a certain degree of cramping of the letters may be caused.

Machines with gross defects in alignment and obviously defective type are not supplied in this state from the factory; therefore it follows that every gross defect must make its appearance at some time during the working life of the machines. If

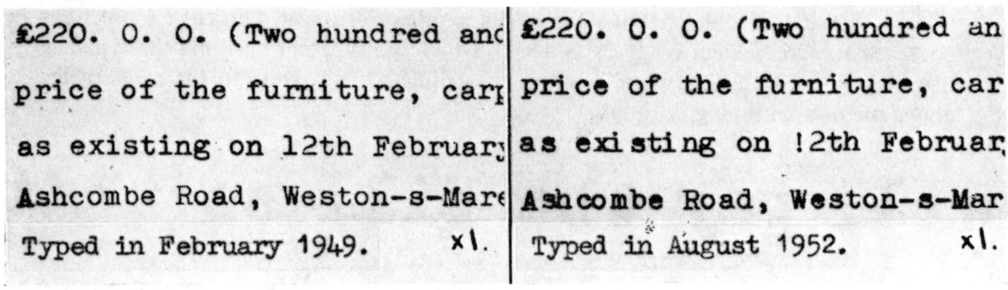
£220. O. O. (Two hundred and | £220. O. O. (Two hundred an
price of the furniture, carp | price of the furniture, car
as existing on 12th February | as existing on !2th Februar
Ashcombe Road, Weston-s-Mare | Ashcombe Road, Weston-s-Mar
Typed in February 1949. ×1. | Typed in August 1952. ×1.

Fig. 8–13. The same machine was used for typing both specimens. The defects present in the 1949 specimen are also represented on the 1952 copy which exhibits other defects which have appeared in the interval.

dated specimens of the work of the machine are available, it is possible to date the appearance of any particular defect. This affords yet another way in which typescript may be dated.

Marginal Defects

When the typescript is considered as a whole, a number of other defects may be noticed. A comparatively common defect in typescript is the presence of an irregular left-hand margin. Sometimes this irregularity may be general, because the typist had neglected to set up the margin stop but returned the carriage by eye to approximately the same position at the commencement of each new line of typing. When, however, the majority of the lines begin at the correct place and there is an occasional insert of a single space, the cause is most likely to be a defective margin stop.

On occasion, piling of the letters at the right-hand extremity of the line may be noticed. This is generally due to the imperfect action of the stop, which should prevent any printing once the carriage has ceased to move.

The irregularity of the left-hand margin may be confined to a comparatively few lines of typescript. This may have nothing to do with the action of the machine, but may be due to the sheet having been removed from the machine and then replaced for further typing. When this is the case, the lines of typescript may exhibit noticeable departures from parallelism as well.

Other Defects in Typescript

Very rarely, the typescript will be found to consist of two or more columns, separated by vertical strips equal to the width of one letter where a space has been jumped by the carriage at the same place in every line.

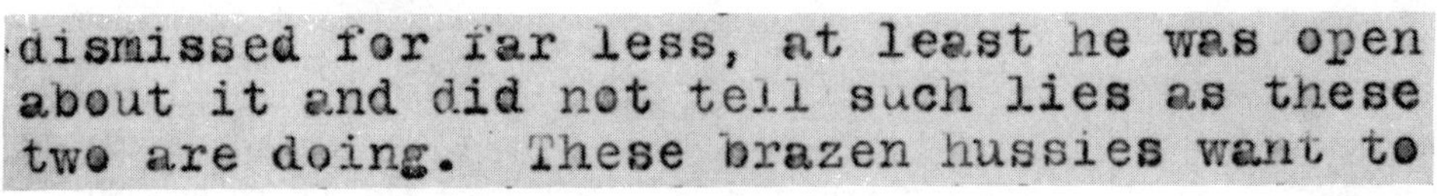

dismissed for far less, at least he was open
about it and did not tell such lies as these
two are doing. These brazen hussies want to

Fig. 8–14. Example of typescript showing partially filled ovals of " a," " d," and " o " caused by clogged type faces.

Unless cleaned at regular intervals, the hollows in the typefaces of certain letters such as " o," " e," " p," " d," etc., become filled with debris from the ribbon. This condition of a typewriter is liable to change rapidly so that the production of " filled " letters cannot be regarded as more than a temporary characteristic of the machine. This condition may have considerable evidential value when typescript has to be dated. If a typewriter can be shown to be producing " filled " characters immediately before and after the date given on a suspect document, it is only reasonable to expect the typescript thereon to show the same feature. If it fails to do so, this is prima facie evidence that the document is incorrectly dated.

Fig. 8–15. Examples of doubly struck characters caused by faulty machine action.

The typescript from some machines will exhibit a double impression whenever certain of the characters are firmly struck. The cause and significance of this defect is considered in some detail below.

Identity of Typist

It is well known that those who work closely with a small group of different typists are able to determine who was responsible for typing any passage of reasonable size, even when all the available machines are used in common. This more or less unconscious recognition of the authorship of typescript depends partly on the fact that, although a typewriter is a mechanical device, the way in which it is operated is reflected to some extent in the work it produces. More detailed consideration will be given at a later stage to the problem of determining the authorship of typescript, but for the present it will be sufficient to state that something positive in this direction can often be accomplished.

The foregoing account of what may be observed when typescript is examined is by no means exhaustive, but should indicate that, although typescript is the product of a mass-produced machine, it can have an individuality which is in no way inferior to that of a specimen of handwriting.

The Determination from the Typescript of the Make and Age of the Machine

Some of the foregoing characteristics of typescript will now be considered in greater detail, so that some estimate may be made of their value as evidence that a specimen of typescript was typed on a particular machine by an indicated typist.

At first sight this may appear to be simple and straightforward, for, in theory, all that has to be done is to compare the design of the typescript in question with that derived from machines of known age and manufacture. In practice, difficulties arise and it may happen that it will prove impossible to identify either the make or the age of the typewriter used; there are a number of reasons why this is so.

In the first place, especially with machines manufactured outside the United States of America, not every differently named typewriter is fitted with its own distinctive style of type. Sometimes whole groups of machines have identical

MINERVA.

German. 1912. Also known as the RIVAL, MERCURIUS, REGENT, LEMCO, WATERLOO, KOMO, LIBRA and HACOBA.

Fig. 8–16. Portion of card from " Machine Index " showing the various names under which the " MINERVA " typewriter is sold.

typefaces, and it may happen that different names merely represent the titles under which the same machine is sold at different times or in different countries.

To such an extent has this taken place that at the author's laboratory it has been found necessary to compile a special index of the different names given to the same machine. If the fullest information on this is not made available to the investigating officer, a promising line of inquiry may be caused to be abandoned.

Secondly, it is not unknown for new machines to be delivered from the factory already fitted with a competitor's typefaces. This remarkable practice is indulged in when, for example, a firm which uses a large number of typewriters wishes to make a gradual change in the make of typewriter it employs, but finds it advisable to retain the same design of type on all the machines so that a number of typists can be simultaneously engaged on a task where variation in the style of typeface would detract from the appearance of the finished typescript.

Thirdly, when severely damaged machines are rebuilt, it is not always possible to replace damaged typefaces with replicas; extensive rebuilding often results in the production of a hybrid machine, in which case it is impossible to ascertain the original make from the typescript.

Finally, if the typefaces are badly worn, or the document is a poor carbon copy, or has perhaps been copied by the hectograph process or through a worn stencil, it may prove impossible to distinguish sufficient of the details of the type design to make identification possible. This limitation also applies when but a small amount of typescript is in question.

Apart from the foregoing difficulties, the establishment of a comprehensive collection of comparison typescript of known origin is no mean task, and continuous effort is needed to keep such a collection up to date as new machines and different styles of type come onto the market.

Any experienced examiner of documents will agree that no typewriter ever becomes so worn and ineffective that somebody cannot find a use for it, so that efforts have to be made to accumulate specimens of typescript from the most ancient machines. Many pre-1914 typewriters are still in active use in England, and a fair proportion of anonymous letters are regularly being typed on these ancient relics.

In the U.S. the problem of identifying the make of the typewriter from the typescript is comparatively simple where the most popular styles of type such as pica and elite are concerned, for it is unlikely that the work of any but American-made machines is likely to be encountered.[1a]

In Britain, the problem is far more difficult; besides machines of domestic manufacture, there are considerable imports from America and the continent of Europe. Not only this, but the influx of foreign nationals during the past twenty-five years has resulted in the introduction into the country of many practically obsolete machines of foreign manufacture. Typescript encountered by the document examiner in Britain may have been derived from any of the typewriters produced anywhere in the world during the past fifty years. The availability of a host of different designs and sizes of type complicates the problem of ensuring comprehensive comparison data. To make matters worse, some makers are ready to cut type to any special design which might be submitted to them, and it has happened that a style of type originally cut for one customer has eventually been listed among those generally available. This practice may pose a pretty problem in dating, as the first appearance of this style in the general catalogue of type designs may occur many years after it was first supplied to special order.

The difficulty of making a reference collection is increased by the fact that some

[1a] O. Hilton in *Scientific Examination of Documents* lists about half a dozen makes of imported machines.

makers introduce various modifications in design intended to improve legibility, appearance or ease of manufacture at irregular intervals of time (see Figure 8–5). For example, during the past thirty years, pica type marketed by Remington, Underwood, L. C. Smith and Royal has undergone modification on about eight, eight, five and five occasions respectively. Whilst these modifications are of great value when a limit of age has to be given to typescript, they add to the difficulty of assembling a reference collection which has any pretensions to being comprehensive. With pica type made by Imperial, few if any modifications have been made since the typewriter was first manufactured. This causes difficulty when it is desired to date typescript derived from this make of machine.

The Reference Collection of Typescript

The raw material of any reference collection of typescript must consist mainly of specimens of typescript, preferably in the form of a keyboard run-off, taken from typewriters in use. This can be supplemented by material derived from advertising literature supplied by the manufacturers to illustrate the work of their contemporary models and the type styles which are available. Whenever possible, specimens should be derived from new machines, because with these the typefaces are unlikely to be damaged or worn so that clear-cut impressions may be obtained. With a new machine there is little risk of obtaining a reference specimen adulterated by the presence of "foreign" type included as the result of repair or rebuilding. At the same time it is possible to determine the date of marketing of the machine.

Where obsolete or well-worn machines are all that are available, the best must be made of the material. The deleterious effect on the impressions caused by a pitted platen can be overcome by the use of a stout backing sheet; the ribbon should be thrown out of action or removed, and the specimen taken on a paper with a glossy surface through a new sheet of "record" carbon paper which, as it contains carbon black, is unlikely to fade.

Once the keyboard run-off has been obtained, the typefaces should be examined. In most instances in the space between the upper- and lower-case outlines on a typeface there will be found a letter or group of letters. These markings, which do not reproduce on the typescript, have been placed on the typeface by the manufacturer as an identifying symbol. If all the typefaces on the machine bear the same manufacturer's mark, this provides good ground for the assumption that "foreign" types are absent. If any are present, a note to this effect should be made on the sheet. An inquiry should always be made about any repairs or renovations undergone by the machine.

Fig. 8–17. Photograph of a type face. The makers' mark can be seen lightly impressed near the centre of the type face. (× 5.)

The number of the machine should also be ascertained and entered on the sheet for from the manufacturer's number it is possible to determine the year the machine was marketed.

The sheets containing specimens of typescript are too fragile and valuable for everyday use, so when they are being prepared, an extra example of the keyboard should be taken, conveniently arranged for making photographic copies. To do this the keyboard should be typed about nine letters to the line with single spacing between the lines. This will give a compact block of typescript which can be copied on to a quarter-plate negative with a linear magnification of approximately twice. This will provide a convenient photograph for the working collection.

Valuable dating information can be obtained from the confidential publications of the various Typewriter Trades Federations who issue booklets to their members giving such information in connection with the recommended part-exchange allowances. These are confidential, but are supplied to document examiners engaged in an official capacity.

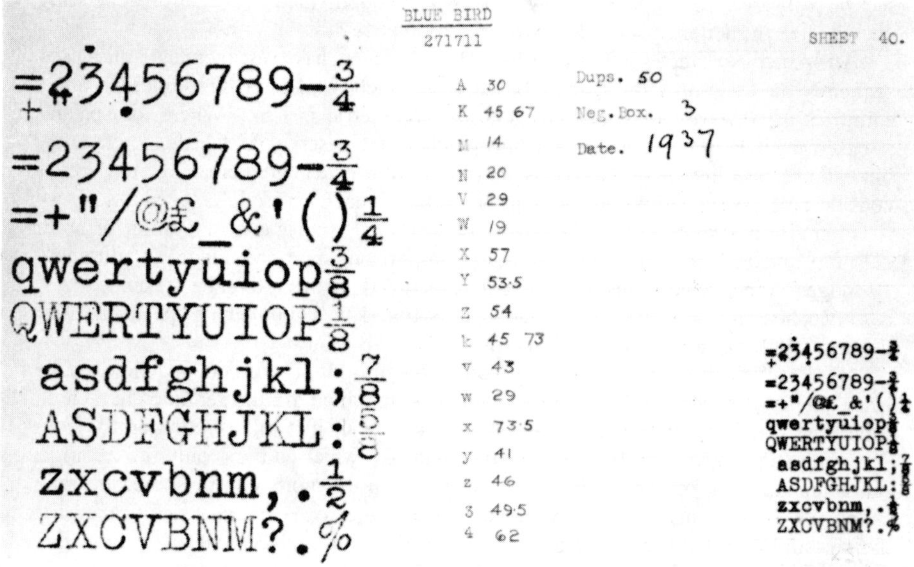

Fig. 8–18. Photograph (reduced) of a typical card from the Cardiff Laboratory "Type Style" index. At the bottom right the typeface is reproduced natural size. On the left-hand side, it is reproduced with a magnification of approximately 2½ times to facilitate comparison. The centre line of figures refers to the angles between the straight lines which make up the characters.

In the author's laboratory, each specimen of typescript is allotted a card which is seven by five inches. To each card is fixed a photograph of the typescript of approximately natural size, also another photograph with a linear enlargement of about twice to enable the details of type design to be seen without eyestrain. On the card is written the name of the machine, its date of issue, and any other information which might be of interest. Each card is given a number and then filed in its appropriate section along with others of the same make. It has been found convenient to divide the reference collection into three sections. The first, and by far the largest, is termed the "pica" section. This includes all those specimens which print approximately ten characters to the inch, and which do not diverge appreciably from the conventional pica design. About eighty per cent. of typewriters in use at the present time are fitted with type of this description.

The second section is termed the "elite" section. This includes all those typefaces of conventional design which are slightly smaller than pica, and which are spaced about twelve characters to the inch. In this section is included elite type which is spaced at ten characters to the inch, for the small size of the type is regarded as more significant than its spacing.

The third section includes all the typescript which cannot be included in either of the other sections.

At the present time, when the collection contains approximately a thousand distinct type styles, this subdivision is satisfactory, but in the near future the pica section will have to be broken down. It will be subdivided into groups depending on whether the letter spacing is based on the metric system or not.

All American and some English-made machines have escapements and consequently the letter and line spacing based on the inch, whilst machines made in other countries usually base their letter spacing on the metric system. Where the spacing is based on the inch, the letter and line spacing of typescript is of little significance, but where the alternative system is employed, the exact letter spacing may be of considerable assistance in determining the make of machine used.

Every opportunity should be taken of obtaining specimens of typescript from old and uncommon machines, so that comparisons may be made to eliminate "foreign" type, which may have become included in the reference specimens. It is only when the same design of character is found in a number of specimens that it can safely be assumed to be characteristic of the machine.

Until sufficient specimens of the keyboard run-off of obsolete machines have been obtained to allow a decision to be made as to which are the genuine characters, each new specimen of typescript should be filed, even if it differs but slightly from those already in the collection. Extra material which differs only in a single character may make the reference collection a little more cumbersome, but the changed character may be discovered at a later date to have some significance for dating, and not be present merely as a result of a replacement of a damaged character.

To keep a collection up to date, specimens should be taken from current models at fairly frequent intervals to ascertain what modifications in design have taken place. These changes are of the greatest significance when typescript has to be given a limit of age.

Using the Reference Collection

When a collection of type styles is in the early stages and is limited in extent, the simplest way of making use of it is to take the typescript in question and compare it with each individual specimen in the collection, but when something like a thousand specimens are represented, it is no longer practicable to search through every specimen in the collection of typescript. There are many schemes intended to facilitate searching which at first sight seem to have much to recommend them but they often break down in practice.

Schemes which rely upon the use of punched cards often appear very impressive until an effort is made to put them into practice; others depending on the use of key letters work quickly and well, until a limited specimen of questioned typescript or one containing " foreign " or damaged typefaces is encountered. Practically every scheme which has been published is restricted to pica and elite type, no effort being made to include any style of type which falls outside this classification.

In the opinion of the author, after more than twenty years of experience with all sorts and conditions of typescript, the more rigid and detailed the scheme for identification, the less use it is in dealing with the poor and ill-defined typescript which is submitted for identification to any laboratory dealing essentially with criminal investigations. Also, it is certain that no collection of reference material, however comprehensive, or any scheme of classification, however ingenious, is of any real use unless it is reinforced by the flair of an experienced operator.

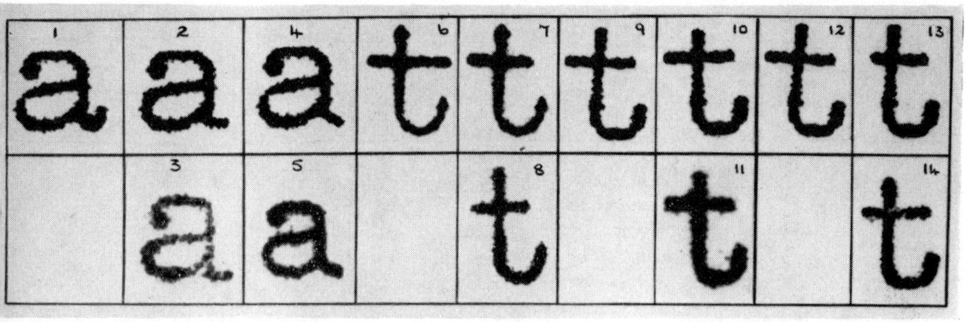

Fig. 8–19. In the upper line examples " 1 " and " 6 " show the normal outlines of " a " and " t." Wear and tear may well result in these becoming modified to the outlines shown in numbers " 2," " 4 " and numbers " 7," " 9," " 10," " 12 " and " 13 " respectively.

Should this happen these damaged outlines may be mistaken for numbers " 3 " and " 5 " and numbers " 8," " 11 " and " 14 " in the lower line, which are examples of other undamaged type designs. This means that any scheme of identification based on the letter designs shown in the lower line would probably break down.

This flair becomes important when the questioned typescript contains examples of foreign or defective typefaces, either of which is calculated to throw out of gear any elaborate scheme using punched cards. An experienced operator can often pick out " foreigners " and defective outlines at a glance because typefaces are generally designed by men of artistic ability, and " foreign " type rarely seems " to belong "; he also knows where and how typefaces are liable to be broken and distorted so that this source of error may be minimised.

At the author's laboratory, the scheme adopted for the use of the reference collection is to delay reaching any conclusion as to the make of machine until the whole of the typescript has been explored. " Key letters " are not used, and no one character is given any greater consideration than another.

A " character index " has been compiled from the main type-style collection, by reference to which every make of typewriter which is fitted with a character of similar design to that of the questioned typescript can quickly be determined.

Certain characters such as "o," "O," "e," "u," etc., are of little diagnostic value, so that these have not been included in the index.

The search is begun with letters such as "a," "g," "t," "r," which are chosen because of the wide variation in design which is encountered in different makes of machine. The numerals too are of great assistance in facilitating the search. As a rule, by the time half a dozen characters have been compared, the number of possible machines will have been so reduced that direct comparison between the questioned typescript and a comparatively limited number of keyboards from the main collection will be possible. This method of work allows for the presence of damaged and foreign typefaces in the machine on which the questioned specimen was typed, for care is taken to include in the preliminary list every possible make

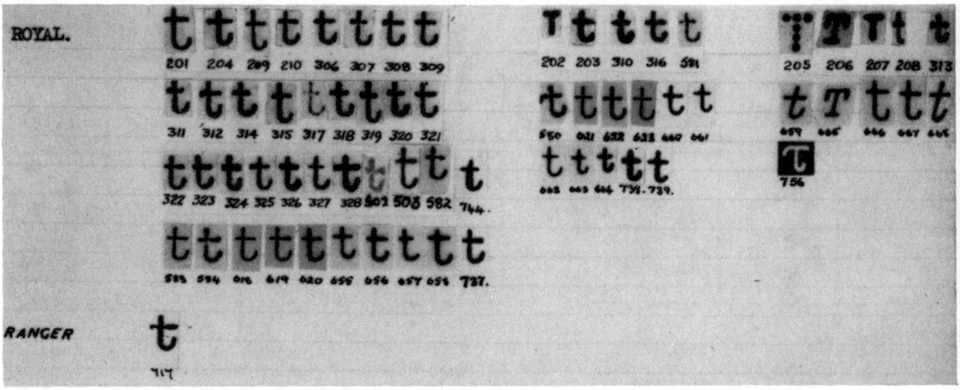

Fig. 8–20. Portion of a card from the "letter index" at the Cardiff Laboratory. The subscript figures refer to the card in the "Style Index" from which the extract was taken.

of machine when allowance has been made for damage to the typefaces. This is in marked contrast to those schemes of selection which rely on the presence of spurs, which may become altered in shape or even broken off when the machine is ill-used.

Even where a machine has been extensively rebuilt, this method will often allow a fairly reliable guess to be made about the identity of the original type.

When a number of makes of machine have been fitted with identical styles of type, it is impossible to name the actual machine used, but another index has been made which gives a list of those makes of machine which have the same type style.

Where the spacing of the type along the line is based upon the metric system, an accurate measurement is made of the type spacing, for this may be of considerable assistance in limiting the number of possible makes of machine, especially when the amount of questioned typescript is limited.

In the experience of the author, positive identification of the type has been possible in about ninety per cent. of the cases which have been submitted to his laboratory, which is a very gratifying result when it is considered how wide is the range from which the questioned typescript is drawn—machines fitted with a multitude of type-styles drawn from all over the world.

Defects in Outline

It has already been stated that imperfections in outline are a comparatively common feature of typescript, especially that derived from well-used or abused machines. These imperfections fall into one of two classes. The first includes defects caused by faulty, worn or damaged typefaces, whilst imperfections of the second class arise from the use of a faulty ribbon, a pitted platen and maladjustment or non-rhythmic operation of the machine.

Defects Caused by Faulty Typefaces

The first stage in the manufacture of a typeface is to cut a pattern in brass on a greatly enlarged scale. By means of a pantograph the outline of an appropriately reduced copy is traced by an engraving tool which reproduces the design in a block of steel. When the cutting is complete, this reproduction or " die " is hardened before being fixed in the machine for rolling the typeface.

The typeface which is to be fitted to the typewriter is made from a tough alloy steel blank which is rolled into intimate contact with the die. Under the influence of the extreme pressure the metal flows into the cavities in the surface of the die and takes on the required profile. After formation, the typeface is toughened and surface-hardened to enable it to stand up to its arduous work. Typefaces are usually soldered on to the ends of the type bars which actuate them in the machine, although other methods such as riveting or fixing by means of a shank may be employed. Riveting is used in machines of the " noiseless " type in which, instead of the conventional swinging type-bar, a girder-like rod bearing the typeface at its extremity is thrust towards the ribbon by a toggle-joint mechanism.

A gap in the outline of a typewritten character which is invariably present throughout the typescript is caused by a depression of the metal of the typeface. Such a depression may arise from one of two causes. The first, a rare occurrence, is because a particle of grit has become embedded at the bottom of the die from which the typeface has been rolled. This grit, which may consist of metal or oxide detached from an earlier typeface, will cause each succeeding typeface rolled while it is still in position, to have the same defect. Usually such defective typefaces are rejected on inspection, but if the fault is comparatively inconspicuous it may be passed over, so that a number of machines of the same batch will include similarly imperfect typefaces.

The second and more usual cause of a depression appearing in the metal of the typeface is wear and tear, especially the striking of the typeface against a hard object such as another type-bar when two keys have been depressed at the same time, or the metal grips which hold the paper in position. Whilst it is unusual for a piece of metal to be completely detached from the typeface during the accidental clash of typebars, a portion of the raised outlines may become flattened to such an extent that a gap occurs in the printed outline. A gap caused in this way is often associated with a distorted outline. When this is the case, it may safely be assumed that the gap is due to an accident during the working life, and not to faulty rolling of the typeface during manufacture.

When a typeface suffers damage through impact, the force of the blow may be insufficient to flatten the typeface so as to invariably cause a gap in the printing; in fact a partial flattening may cause a thickening of the outline. This is the explanation of a curious effect which sometimes may be observed. If the depression caused by impact is slight, typing with a light touch combined with an exhausted ribbon may result in the production of a gapped character, whilst a heavy touch coupled with the use of a well-inked ribbon may result in the production of a complete outline, associated with a thickening of the outline in the neighbourhood of the gap formerly observed.

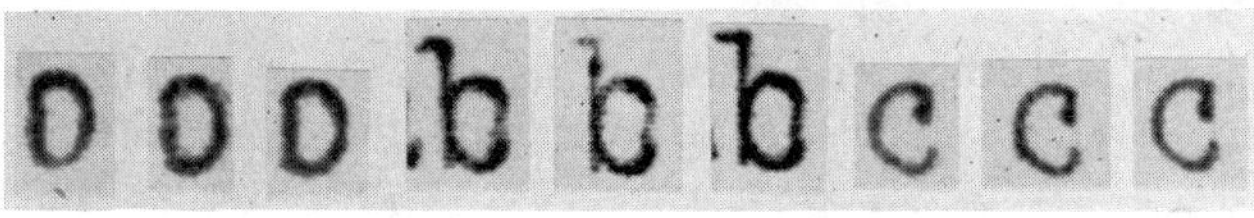

Fig. 8–21. Examples of defective letter outlines caused by damaged typefaces.

Flattening of the outline on a typeface is generally caused by a blow which falls normally on to its surface; if the typeface is struck at an angle, distortion of the outline rather than flattening is likely to be the consequence. The portions of the typeface liable to become damaged in this way are the serifs, which may be bent, and the curved outlines of the ovals of such letters as " g," " a," " d," etc., which become unsymmetrical.

Sometimes the damage to the outline is confined to the serifs—the tiny strokes which occur at the extremities of the main strokes in many designs of type. When a serif is seen to be either bent, or twisted, there can be no doubt that the typeface is faulty, but where the serif is not reproduced in the printed character, it cannot lightly be assumed that this is due to the outline of the typeface being defective.

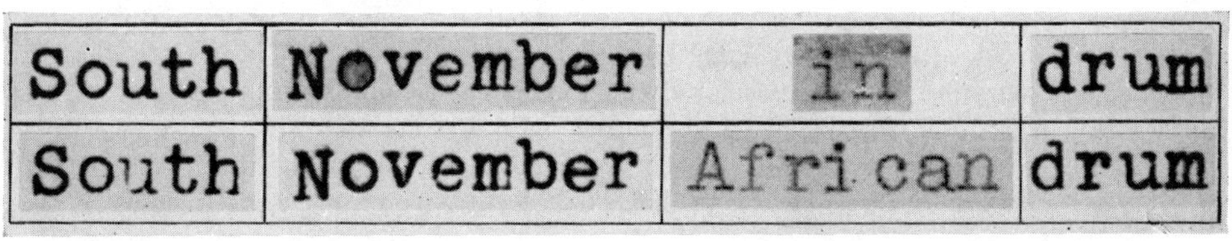

Fig. 8–22. In the lower line, the serifs from the " h," " m," " i " and " d " are missing. This is not due to their being absent from the typefaces concerned because they are all present in the typescript of the upper line. The absence of the serifs in the lower line is fortuitous and is probably caused by a weaker blow being delivered by the typefaces.

The absence of a serif in a position where it is normally found may be due to the design of type being one where the omission is deliberate on the part of the manufacturer. An example of this is the omission of the serif from the bottom of the middle stroke of the " m " in the current (1956) Royal pica style.

The serif on one side of a wide character such as " m " or " w " may fail to print in spite of its being present in good condition on the typeface, if the typeface has become twisted so that it prints more heavily on the one side than the other.

If the degree of twist is considerable and the character has been lightly typed through a ribbon which has become impoverished of ink, the serif on the lightly printed side may fail to be recorded anywhere in the specimen of typescript under examination. This means that it is unsafe to regard a typeface as being characterised by a defective serif, *unless the stroke from which the serif is missing is seen to have been deeply printed without any trace of the serif being apparent.* Missing serifs are far more common than other defects such as gaps in the outline, and consequently are of less evidential value in characterising the work of a typewriter.

Missing Characters

A character may be missing from a specimen of typescript. One explanation may be that the character is not included in the keyboard, a simple example being the attempt to type a passage in French using a standard English keyboard which includes neither acute nor grave accents.

If, however, the missing character is a vowel which is common to all European languages, then its absence may be due either to the typeface having become detached or to a failure of the mechanism to print that particular letter. In either case, this would be a feature of great evidential value, for typewriters are rarely allowed to continue for long in such a state. If a character is missing from a short passage of typescript, a more likely reason for its absence is stiffness in the mechanism of the machine or carelessness on the part of the typist.

Uneven Impression

To ensure an even impression, once the machine has been assembled individual adjustment of the typefaces is carried out. Any gross unevenness caused by defective soldering is easily dealt with, but there may be other causes of error which cannot entirely be eliminated. On occasion, the hardening process to which the type is subjected after rolling results in the distortion of the typeface. In this distortion, the lower-case character may be unaffected, the defect occurring only in the upper-case or capital letter. When this has occurred, no manipulation by the typewriter adjuster can be expected to result in an even impression being produced by both the characters carried by the typeface.

Lateral Unevenness of Impression. Lateral unevenness of impression usually makes its appearance during the working life of the machine. It is generally caused by the clashing of the type bars when two keys are pressed simultaneously. This lateral unevenness is practically unaffected by any wear in the bearings, so that once occasioned, it remains fairly constant until aggravated by a further clashing of the type bars. Speed of operation of the machine has little influence on either its nature or extent, although when a heavily inked ribbon is associated with a heavy touch, there may be some difficulty in establishing the fact that there is unevenness in the strength of the impression.

Vertical Unevenness of Impression. When a typewriter is being adjusted before it is released for sale, care is taken to ensure an even impression at both the top and bottom of every character, by ensuring that the curvature of the typefaces matches that of the roller and that at the moment of impact the centre of curvature of the typefaces coincides with the rotational axis of the roller. This perfection of positioning is not necessarily held throughout the working life of the machine, for any alteration in the curvature of the type-bar will result in a displacement of the centre of curvature of the typeface from the ideal position. This will result in an unevenness of impression. Again, any wear or looseness in the bearings will cause the character to rise above its normal position when the key is heavily struck, because of the increased centrifugal forces which come into play. This will displace the centre of curvature of the typeface from the ideal position, with a consequent failure to print an even impression. Therefore, with a worn typewriter, the extent of any vertical unevenness of impression will be governed to some extent by the way in which the machine is operated.

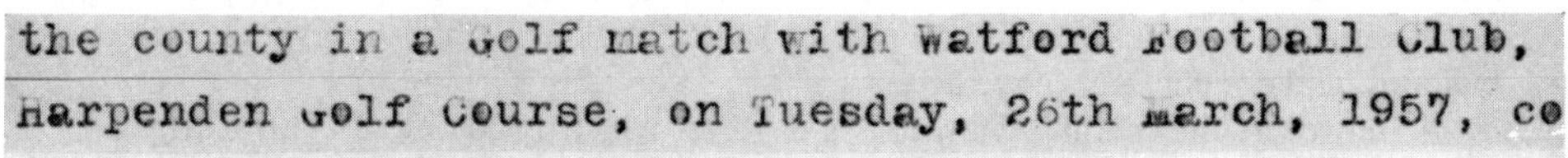

the county in a Golf match with Watford Football Club,
Harpenden Golf Course, on Tuesday, 26th March, 1957, co

Fig. 8–23. The upper portions of *all* the capital letters are poorly reproduced. This is not a fault of the individual typefaces but is caused by faulty operation of the shift-key mechanism.

If a roller of incorrect diameter is substituted, or if the adjustment of the rotational axis of the roller is unsatisfactory, there will be unevenness of vertical impression which can be distinguished from that due to distortion of a typeface, for it will be common to the whole of the typescript from the machine.

The final cause of unevenness of vertical impression is the fitting of replacement typefaces which have the incorrect degree of curvature. This is most likely to happen when type designed for a standard machine is fitted to a portable, and vice versa. No matter how the typeface is twisted it is impossible to ensure an even impression, as at the moment of contact there is no position in which the whole of the typeface can embrace the paper-covered roller with a force which is equal throughout the area of contact.

Unevenness due to Ribbon Defects. It should not lightly be assumed that all inequality of impression has its origin in either faulty typefaces or defective adjustment of the machine. Sometimes a ribbon will fold along its length, and produce unequally inked typescript until the ribbon feeds through the machine and presents a normal appearance once more. The temporary nature of the defect and the fact that it applies to all the characters gives a clue to its cause.

In some specimens of typescript, occasional characters will be found to print unevenly. This usually happens when the ribbon is nearing the end of its useful life (see Fig. 8–7). The defective impressions will have been printed through the holes in the ribbon, the residual ink on the typeface being responsible for the faint portions of the uneven outline. The discovery of such a defect in a specimen of typescript may prove important, for it is reasonable to suppose that a ribbon holed in one place may well be defective elsewhere, so that other defects in the typescript may reasonably be ascribed to a faulty ribbon rather than to a defect in the mechanism.

When a bi-colour ribbon is in use, it may happen that certain characters will show traces of the second colour. This is a defect which is generally associated with certain models and makes of machine,[2] so that its value as an identifying feature should be considered in the light of the make of the machine involved.

If the ribbon ceases to move through the machine through failure of the feed or of the reversing mechanism, the typescript will grow progressively paler until the fault is rectified. This fault therefore should be ascribed to inattention on the part of the typist; it is unlikely to be a permanent feature of all the work of that machine.

Constant and Sporadic Defects in Typescript

When a typeface is imperfect, a corresponding defect must occur in every printed character made while it is in this condition. As already pointed out, defects in the outline of the printed character are occasioned by factors other than faulty typefaces. Many of these factors, such as a faulty ribbon, are temporary, whilst others, such as those due to a pitted platen, are sporadic in their influence on the outline of the printed characters. The test of consistency must be applied before any defect in outline can be attributed to a faulty typeface.

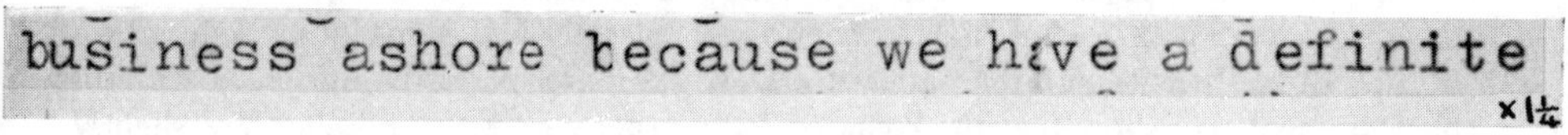

Fig. 8–24. The defects in both " b " and " a " are more apparent than real. The original sheet is thin and has become creased. In the photograph the creasing is not apparent. This shows the inadvisability of working entirely from photographs of questioned documents.

Even when a defective outline is found to be present throughout the typescript, the position of the defect must be taken into account before it is considered to be indicative of a damaged typeface. For example, it has already been stated that defective printing of the tops or bottoms of characters may be due to gross maladjustment of the typeface with respect to the rotational axis of the roller. Another example is the failure to print serifs on badly twisted characters. (See Fig. 8–22.)

Great difficulty in determining whether a defect occurs throughout a specimen of typescript may be experienced when slight defects are the subject of investigation. A grossly defective typeface will print what is obviously an imperfect character whatever the state of the ribbon, but where the defect is slight, such as the flattening of one side of an oval, it may not be possible to distinguish the faulty printing if the ribbon is so well inked that the defect is swamped in the thickened impression.

The test of consistency cannot be applied when only a limited amount of typescript is in question, for few, if any, other specimens of the characters with defective outlines may be available for comparison. All that can be done in these circumstances is for the document examiner to use his judgment. If the ribbon appears to be in good condition and the outlines of the other letters are well reproduced, he may safely conclude that any defect is unlikely to be due either to a pitted platen or a faulty ribbon, and thus exclude two of the usual reasons for the printing of

[2] At one time the Underwood tended to exhibit this defect when out of adjustment.

defective outlines by perfect typefaces. If, on the other hand, the ribbon is obviously at the end of useful life or the platen shows signs of wear, he will be very reluctant to attribute a single example of a defective outline to a defective typeface, and conclude therefrom that all contemporary typescript drawn from that machine will exhibit the same defect.

In many instances, where small amounts of typescript are in question, the document examiner will find himself in the same position as when he has to deal with small amounts of handwriting; there may be insufficient evidence to justify any definite expression of opinion.

Alignment Defects

Although the average typewriter consists of about two thousand parts, they are all mass produced and then assembled in jigs. It might be concluded from this that new machines of the same model should produce identical typescript. The fact that the last stage of manufacture is the manual adjustment of the typefaces to ensure the production of an even line of typescript should indicate that this condition does not hold.

If a line of typescript from a new machine is examined, it will seem that all the characters, with the obvious exception of capitals and some other letters, are of the same height and that all vertical strokes are perfectly upright. Careful measurement will show that the rounded letters such as " o," " e," etc., are slightly taller than letters such as " i," " l," etc., and that letters such as " t," " f," " j," etc., are anything but perfectly upright. If they were, the letter as a whole would appear to slope towards the curved portion because of an optical illusion.

The time allowed for these adjustments in slope and the correction of errors in horizontal, vertical and slope alignment is limited by economic factors, so that the typescript of even a brand new machine cannot be expected to show perfect alignment. Whilst the alignment defects in new machines are almost imperceptible they have the great advantage of being constant. During the working life of the machine, there are added to these original defects, others, often far more obvious, caused by wear and abuse.

A typewriter is capable of a considerable amount of adjustment, so that when the various defects have increased to such an extent that the typescript has been rendered unacceptable, the machine may be restored to working order by adjustment of the various movements and re-alignment of the typefaces. This means that the typescript produced is characteristic of a machine for only a particular period of its working life. The length of this period before the characteristics change appreciably is governed by the treatment the machine receives. With a well-built machine, carefully maintained and infrequently used, this period may span several years, but with another machine of lighter construction which is much used and abused, the appearance of the typescript it produces may alter appreciably in a matter of days.

Imperfect Lateral Alignment

On careful examination, most typescript will be found to possess errors in the lateral alignment of the characters, or, as it is often termed, imperfect " horizontal alignment." These errors, especially when they are slight, are not necessarily characteristic of the machine, for they will often be found to be variable and not always associated to the same extent with the same letter throughout the script. When this is the case, they are either due to wear in the bearings or to non-rhythmic operation of the machine.

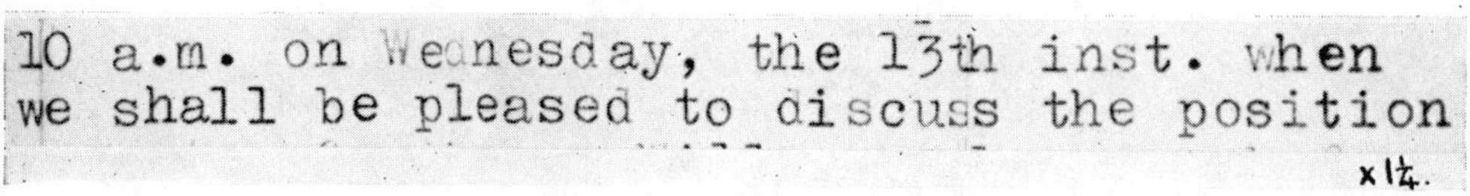

Fig. 8–25. This illustrates examples of apparent faulty alignment caused by improper action of the machine. Compare the well-separated " th " in " the " in both upper and lower line with the joined up " th " in the upper line in " 13th."

A rapid succession of blows associated with the typing of familiar letter combinations will often result in the printing of the characters while the machine is vibrating, and before the escapement mechanism has served to position and halt the moving carriage. If the machine is not firmly supported, excessive vibration can be set up by non-rhythmic actuation, and this can be counted on to destroy the alignment of the work from a machine in excellent condition.

If the machine is badly worn, the alignment of the characters suffers, for the exact position of imprint is the net result of a number of variables. Worn bearings are often associated with damaged typefaces and gross errors in alignment, so that any variability superimposed on gross errors causes little difficulty. If, however, the machine is repaired and re-aligned by a skilled mechanic, and nothing is done to correct the effect of the worn and loose bearings, all the gross errors are eliminated. With a machine in this condition, it is sometimes impossible to find sufficient *consistent* errors in alignment to enable the work of the machine to be characterised in this respect. It is only when an appreciable and consistent lateral misalignment persists throughout a specimen of typescript that this particular error may safely be regarded as characteristic of the machine. Some authorities go so far as to declare that errors in horizontal alignment are practically useless for identifying the work of a machine, but in the experience of the author this is not the case, and to neglect the presence of any consistent errors in this respect is to disregard evidence which may prove of the greatest value, especially when small amounts of typescript are in question.

Vertical Misalignment

Departures from perfection in vertical alignment where characters print either above or below the line of type are less obvious to the eye than errors in horizontal alignment of similar magnitude. For this reason, the work of new typewriters may be characterised by such errors because there is less reason for their elimination during the manual alignment of the type at the end of the manufacturing process.

This defect in typescript may arise in several ways. Gross errors are usually the result of careless operation of the shift key. If the typist fails to depress this sufficiently when a capital letter is required, or strikes a key after the operation of the shift key before the carriage or the type basket has had time to resume its normal position, a substantial error in vertical alignment is certain to result. There is very little likelihood of an experienced examiner attributing such an error to a machine defect, because it will invariably be associated with the use of the shift key either for the misaligned character or that immediately preceding it.

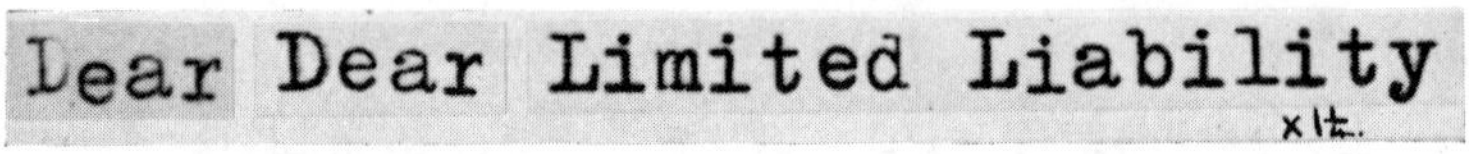

Fig. 8–26. Examples of vertical misalignment of letters typed after the use of the shift key. Both examples of " Dear " came from the same document. The alignment is defective in the first but perfect in the second. In the word " Liability," the alignment of the first " i " but not that of the others in this word is faulty. This fault does not necessarily follow the use of the shift key because in the word " Limited " the alignment is good throughout although the same machine was used.

With a worn machine, the sporadic and variable rise of a character above the line of type may be caused by the action of centrifugal force, which has already been referred to as the cause of an uneven vertical impression in typescript derived from a worn machine. When this is the cause of the error, the extent of the rise will often be found to be proportional to the depth of the impression, for a heavy impression results from high speed of the typeface at the moment of impact. This high speed will give rise to increased centrifugal force on the typeface and so cause it to rise on its worn bearings.

Fig. 8–27. This is an example of variation in vertical alignment defect caused by increased centrifugal force acting on worn bearings. Increased speed of the typeface results in the letter being printed above the line. This is well shown in the various examples of the ' s."

If, for any particular character, the displacement above or below the line of type is found to be constant, then the cause of the error is either the alteration in the curvature of the type bars bearing the typeface, due to the constant hammering they have experienced, or to faulty fixing of the typeface on its type bar. Both of these are mechanical faults, and in this case the vertical alignment error in the typescript is characteristic of the machine which produced it.

Most typewriters have two characters on each typeface, so that in the majority of cases both characters will exhibit the same error. On the very rare occasions when this relationship is not found, the explanation is that a foreign typeface has been fitted whereon the separation of the two outlines differs from that on the other typefaces. When such a crude repair has been effected, the mechanic finds it impossible to align both characters; the course usually taken is to align that character in more common use, rather than to compromise and have both characters incorrectly outlined. The presence of a foreign character of this nature is an identifying feature of great value.

Occasionally, a typeface will become loose at the end of the type bar, when it will be found to register irregularly as it moves from one position to another.

Errors in vertical alignment are extremely useful in characterising the work of a machine, especially when it is electrically operated so that the force applied to the printing operation is outside the control of the operator, or when the machine is of the " noiseless " type where type bars are pushed rather than swung, and so are uninfluenced by centrifugal forces.

Slope Misalignment

If typescript from a worn machine is examined, certain of the characters will be found to be appreciably out of the vertical. This error in alignment must not be confused with the deliberate slope of a degree or so, given to such characters as " t " and " f " to correct the optical illusion which would make these characters appear to slope if they were adjusted to be perfectly upright.

Obvious and consistent defects in slope are caused by the twisting of the type bars, which causes them to depart from their correct alignment and consequently to print a character with an incorrect slope. Slope misalignment due to this defect is outside the control of the typist, so that constant errors of this description enable the work of the machine to be characterised. Like other alignment defects, errors in slope are affected to some extent by the presence of wear in the bearings, but as the effects of wear are unmistakable, allowance can be made for variation caused in this way.

Deliberate Misalignment

On more than one occasion, the author has received for examination specimens of typescript exhibiting gross errors in alignment. In each case it soon became apparent that these were not caused by faulty action of the machine, but were the result of deliberate action on the part of the typist. In one case the paper was left loose in the machine, being given a slight tug after each character had been typed, and in the other the back-spacing key was used to destroy the horizontal alignment of the letters. The object in both cases was the same—to prevent identification of the typewriter used. The ruse was unsuccessful, for in the first case the typefaces fortunately happened to be very defective, and in the second the use of the back-spacer left the numerous defects in vertical alignment, slope alignment and position of maximum impression unaffected.

With a machine whose typefaces are in good condition, the use of a loose sheet which is moved after every character is typed may defeat any attempt to identify the machine, but typing in this way is so slow and laborious that it is unlikely to become a popular device for concealing the identity of the typewriter used.

Other Faults in Typescript

Double Impressions

If a key is depressed very slowly, it will be noticed that the curved surface of the typeface bearing the outline of the character stops short of the paper, no matter how hard the key is pressed. If the key is sharply struck in the normal manner, the momentum of the heavy typeface will cause the thin steel type-bar to bend when its motion is arrested, so that the typeface follows on to deliver a single sharp blow to the ribbon which has been thrust between it and the paper.

The vibration of the type bar which occurs at the moment of impact does not, if the machine is in good condition, result in a second fainter blow being struck, because the vibration takes place at the rest position which is just short of the paper surface (see Fig. 8–15.) If the machine is defective and the rest position is practically touching the paper, a second impression may be approximately superimposed on the first. As this double impression is the consequence of a mechanical fault, it is characteristic of all the work of the machine whilst it is in this condition. As this fault is comparatively rare, the presence of a double impression is an identifying feature of some importance.

Irregular Margins

The extremes of motion of the carriage are controlled by margin stops which can be thrown out of action by pressure on the appropriate release keys. Sometimes the carriage will tend to rebound from the stop which controls the left-hand margin, in which case some of the lines of typescript will be found to start one space to the right.

When the motion of the carriage is stopped by the right-hand stop, this should lock the keys so as to prevent any further characters being printed. With a defective machine this may not happen, so that the lines of type will exhibit a number of superimposed letters at the extreme right. This is another example of a mechanical defect betraying itself in defective typescript.

Letter and Line Spacing

Where the letter spacing along the line is based on the inch, which is the case with all American- and some British-made machines, a quick test with a graduated scale or the application to the typescript of one of the special scales previously described will be all that is necessary to determine the letter spacing, which is invariably some figure between six and sixteen letters to the inch. When based on the metric system, the determination of the letter spacing is more difficult.

It is hardly worth while making special scales except for a spacing of 2·6 mms., which is very near to and can easily be mistaken for pica (2·54 mms.). The simplest way to carry out the measurement is to select a line of typescript which contains the same letter with a well-defined vertical stroke such as " I," " i," " l," " L," etc., near both the beginning and the end of the line. The distance apart of the vertical strokes is measured to the nearest millimetre with the graduated scale, and then divided by the number of letter spaces included. It is as well to make a practice of counting both the reference letters and then subtracting one from the number. This procedure should be repeated with another pair of different letters in another line, in case the first pair chosen happen to be loose.

Letter spacing along the line is governed by the escapement, which in turn governs the movement of the carriage, provided this is in good order and is unaffected by the way in which the machine is operated. When the escapement is faulty or the actuating spring is weak, a number of alignment defects such as crowding and irregularity of the type may become evident, so care must be taken to avoid making measurements where such imperfections are present.

Whilst typefaces on a machine may be quickly and easily changed, any interference with the escapement is a major operation which is rarely undertaken except for the repair of a badly damaged machine. As this is so, where specimens of typescript differ in their letter spacing, this may be taken as an indication that they were typed on different machines.

Pitch

The spacing of the lines of typescript is often referred to as the " pitch " of the machine, although the same term is sometimes applied to letter spacing along the line.

The majority of machines fitted with pica type have a pitch or line spacing of six spaces to the inch; machines based on the metric system often have line spacing which is standardised at six mms., which is about five per cent. less.

While letter spacing along the line is a fixed characteristic of the machine, this is not true of line spacing. Line spacing is governed by the ratchet fixed to the roller around which the paper is wrapped; it is the degree of rotation of the roller which is fixed, so that the amount of paper which is unrolled for every advancement of one tooth on the ratchet is proportional to the diameter of the roller. Whilst the diameter of the roller itself is fixed, the use of a backing sheet will increase its effective diameter and so increase the pitch of the typescript.

The thickness of ordinary typing paper varies from about four to ten thousandths of an inch, whilst that of a special backing sheet may be appreciably greater. This means that the interlinear space on any machine will vary by about a hundredth of an inch according to whether a backing sheet is used or not. If a number of carbons are being cut, a comparatively thick wad of paper may be introduced into the machine. This will have a proportionately greater effect on the interlinear distance. The difference in interlinear distance for a pair of lines is only appreciable when an accurate estimate of the line spacing is made with a measuring machine, but where a whole sheet of foolscap is concerned, a perceptible difference may be seen between one specimen typed without a backing sheet and another which is the top copy when several carbons have been cut.

From the foregoing it may be concluded that very slight differences in interlinear spacing between two specimens of typescript do not necessarily indicate that the work of two different machines is concerned. It is only when the two specimens are found to have interlinear spacings which are appreciably different that two different machines must have been involved. An exception to this rule occurs when a replacement roller has been fitted, a not uncommon repair for a well-used machine. Usually care is taken to substitute a roller of the correct diameter, but this is not always done. It is possible to detect the substitution of a roller of incorrect diameter by the unevenness of the resulting type impression, so that this exception need not make the rule hazardous to apply.

Hitherto it has been assumed that the ratchet mechanism was used to rotate the roller, but it is possible to throw this out of action and turn the roller by hand.

When this is done, a marked irregularity in the interlinear spacing will be observed, as the most careful hand operation of the roller will fall far short of the regularity achieved by the use of the ratchet mechanism.

Obtaining Typescript for Purposes of Comparison

To determine whether a specimen of typescript was typed on a particular machine, it must be compared with adequate specimens of typescript derived from the suspect typewriter. The term " adequate " must be stressed because, in the majority of investigations, the document examiner is expected to work with standards which are far from suitable either in amount or in the nature of the material. Very often, all that is submitted in the way of comparison material is a keyboard run-off, or the sentence that " now is the time for all good men to come to the aid of the party." Whilst such standards may enable a document examiner to exclude the machine in question as the source of the typescript under examination, it is extremely unlikely that he will ever be able to implicate a machine on such inadequate standard material.

Comparison typescript falls into two categories. The first comprises specimens of typescript made specifically for the investigation; this will be referred to as " prepared " standard material. In the second category is included material typed on the machine in question in the ordinary way of business, sometimes over a considerable period of time. For want of a better term, this will be referred to as " random " standard material.

Whilst the form and content of a " prepared " standard are within the control of the investigator, the disadvantage of all prepared standards is that they must, of necessity, be made subsequently to the typing of the questioned typescript. In the interval, which in some instances may amount to months or even years, considerable changes may take place in the condition of the typewriter; these changes may even include those consequent upon major repairs. (See Fig. 8–13, which shows how the work of a machine may change.)

These deficiencies may be made good by the use of random standards which include specimens of typescript contemporary with the questioned material, although this advantage is sometimes nullified by the random standards being unsatisfactory in form, in character or in amount.

Whether standards be random or prepared or both, they must be of such a nature that a complete assessment of the state of the machine at the material time can be made by the document examiner. In the case of random standards, this means that as a general rule, a couple of pages of typescript are the minimum with which an effective comparison can be carried out, and it may well happen that in some cases this amount of typescript may have to be considerably increased.

Random Standards

If there is no possibility of a prepared standard being available, as much random material as possible should be accumulated. No document examination is ever hindered by a surplus of comparison material, although the contrary applies all too often. The best comparisons are made between like materials, so that specimens of typescript which resemble the questioned document in nature and which are as near contemporary as possible should be the first to be sought. These can be supplemented by others, so that every aspect of the condition and behaviour of the machine can be studied. Without suitable standards, the document examiner is working under a handicap which may prove fatal to his chances of expressing and justifying any definite opinion.

Great care should be taken never to rely on any random standards whose authenticity cannot be proved; in the event of proceedings, it may very well happen that the very standards on which the comparison is based are found to be inadmissible because of uncertainty concerning their origin.

Sometimes, top copies are not available and carbon copies have to be used. If the carbon copies have been properly prepared and the outlines of the typewritten characters are clear, they may prove quite satisfactory; the author has presented at court more than one case in which all the standards were carbon copies, with complete success, so this source of standard material should not be neglected. On the other hand, faint carbons made with sub-standard carbon paper in which the letters can hardly be deciphered are completely unsuitable.

" Prepared " Standards

When a prepared standard consists of a keyboard run-off, together with a phrase such as " the quick brown fox jumps over the lazy dog," or " now is the time for all good men to come to the aid of the party," it is practically useless when a piece of conventional typescript is in question, for it is obviously impossible to prepare a comparison table for production in court on the basis of such a standard. As the best comparisons are made between similar texts, the most suitable standard is a copy of the questioned material prepared on similar paper, with the ribbon in a similar condition, and with a touch which does not depart widely from that used for making the questioned typescript.

If three copies of the questioned text are made with a light, medium and a heavy touch respectively, the document examiner will have all that he requires. Normally a backing sheet will be used for preparing the specimen, but if there is evidence, in the form of " scrappy " reproduction of the character outlines in the questioned typescript, that it was typed without a backing sheet on a machine with a pitted platen, then an extra copy should be made without a backing sheet to test this point.

If certain of the characters are found to print unevenly, these should be separately typed at the end of the text with a gradually increasing pressure, in order to determine how their reproduction is affected by the degree of pressure employed.

If the questioned typescript is on rough-surfaced paper, it is of some importance that at least one specimen is prepared on similar material, otherwise the imperfect impressions which are often found on such paper may be attributed to the machine instead of the paper. The production of a specimen on rough paper should be additional to and not in lieu of a specimen typed on smooth paper, which will produce the most perfect impression of the typefaces.

The appearance of typescript is governed to a considerable extent by the condition of the ribbon. As the use of a heavily inked ribbon may cause slight defects in the outlines to become buried in the thickness of the impression, a lightly inked ribbon is preferable if the details of any imperfections in the outlines of the characters are to be rendered effectively.

If the typewriter has not been cleaned and the typefaces are found to be clogged, a specimen should be taken before any cleaning is attempted. If a complete study of the outlines of the typefaces is required, it will be necessary to clean them thoroughly before a second specimen is taken. This cleaning should be done by means of a stiff brush charged with a cleaning fluid such as benzene, and no attempt should be made to pick out the clogging material with a metal tool which might have the effect of damaging the outline of the typefaces.

If a suspect machine is discovered very soon after the typing of the questioned material and the ribbon is in a new condition, it is worth while unrolling the ribbon to see whether the impressions relating to the questioned material can still be read thereon. This is by no means a forlorn hope, because in one case in the author's experience, this was actually accomplished. The letter sequence of a number of obscene words which were included in an anonymous letter could still be easily recognised. It was found impracticable to make a satisfactory photograph of the impressions, so the ribbon itself had to be mounted and examined by light at grazing incidence.

If the ribbon is in very bad condition, it is best to make one copy of the suspect text through a piece of carbon paper after the ribbon has been thrown out of action or removed from the machine. Good carbon paper can be counted on to furnish an excellent impression of the typefaces which is superior to that produced with the best ribbons. (See Figure 8–3.)

Every specimen of typescript should be adequately identified with the make and number of the machine, the name of the typist and the date, and if it was necessary either to clean the type or to use carbon paper, a note should be made on the sheet. Unless there is some mechanical defect on the machine, it is rarely necessary to convey the machine itself to the document examiner, provided that the specimens are properly prepared in accordance with the above suggestions.

When the specimen of typescript has been completed, the typefaces should be inspected for the presence of " foreign " type as previously described. If a typeface has been substituted in the course of a repair between the typing of the questioned and standard specimens, this will cause a consistent difference to appear in the typescript which will need explanation. The discovery of a foreign typeface associated with this difference will provide a good explanation for its presence.

Comparison of Typescripts

To determine whether or not two specimens of typescript were typed on the same machine, the examination should be systematically carried out in definite stages to ensure that no significant feature is overlooked, and that the minimum of time is spent on the comparison. Whilst the early discovery of significant differences may prove that different machines were involved, the conclusion that both specimens of typescript are the work of the same machine can be reached only after a full consideration of the whole of the evidence; short cuts are liable to lead to erroneous conclusions.

Comparison of Letter Design

The examination should be commenced by comparing the details of the design of the numerals and then such letters as " a," " r," " y," " f," " g," which are chosen because these characters exhibit the greatest variation. If no differences are found with these letters, the comparison should be extended to every other character which is represented, not forgetting the punctuation marks.

If several characters show differences in design, this should terminate the examination, for it may then safely be assumed that different machines are involved. There is little likelihood that even a major repair will involve the substitution of several characters.

If but a solitary character shows a difference in design, it will be unsafe to assume from this alone that different machines are involved. The examiner has to consider whether the difference can be accounted for by an accident. In this connection, the worn and damaged characters shown in Figure 8–19 should be studied. If this possibility can be discounted, the possibility that there has been a substitution of a character of different design in the course of a repair must be taken into consideration. The safest policy is to carry on with the examination, because if two machines are involved, there is certain to be additional evidence of this at a later stage in the examination.

Comparison of Letter and Line Spacing

The next step is to measure the letter spacing, for any difference is sufficient to rule out the possibility of both specimens having been typed on the same machine, unless one of the documents has been wetted and stretched. The nature of the surface of the paper will enable this point to be tested. The interlinear distances should then be determined, and the measurements interpreted in the light of what has already been said about the influence of backing sheets and carbon copies.

Examination for Defective Outlines

If both specimens of typescript have passed all the foregoing tests for similarity, it may safely be concluded that both have been typed on machines of the same model if not on the same machine. It is as well at this stage to determine the make of the machine so that the type designs can be compared with those from the standard collection. This is to enable the presence of any " foreign " type to be distinguished. If any are found they will constitute identifying evidence of the greatest value.

Fig. 8–28. The missing serif from the " m," the abruptly bent stroke of the " r," the absence of a serif on the " R " and the bent vertical stroke on the " G " are not defects but design characteristics.

The next step is to examine the outlines for the presence of consistent defects such as missing serifs, irregular ovals, gaps and broken spurs. It should be borne in mind that an unusual appearance is not necessarily due to a defect in the outline. For example, in the contemporary Royal pica type the serif which occurs in most designs of type on the mid-stroke of the " m " is missing, and the " r " on the Olympia is furnished with an extremely short cross stroke. To the inexperienced, these features might be regarded as due to damage to the typeface, and consequently of some evidential value. To guard against such mistakes and so as not to overlook any broken spurs, a copy of the type style should be available for comparison. Punctuation marks should not be overlooked. In one case, the author found that the full stop had been deliberately enlarged by filing to prevent its penetrating a stencil, an identifying feature unique in his experience and consequently of great evidential value. Any consistent thickenings of the line should also be noted, as in some circumstances a gap may appear where they occur. The reason for this has already been discussed in the section on defective outlines.

Defective Impressions

The next step in the comparison is likely to prove difficult, for it demands the comparison of letters which exhibit markedly uneven depth of impression. For the first time, the influence of the ribbon becomes important, and it may prove impossible to make an effective comparison if the two specimens of typescript were typed on ribbons whose condition was considerably different. With a ribbon which is practically exhausted, there is little difficulty in observing the position of maximum impression, something which is extremely difficult to accomplish when the ribbon is new and heavily charged with ink. In this case, it is sometimes possible to make an estimate of the position of maximum impression on a top copy by making a microscopic examination of the character when it is obliquely illuminated. Unfortunately, with a carbon copy this cannot be done.

If differences in the evenness of vertical impression are found, these should not necessarily be interpreted as showing that the two specimens of typescript must have been typed on different machines, for the differences should be considered in the light of what has already been stated about the action of centrifugal force on the depth of impression when the bearings of the machine are worn.

Some idea of the relative alignment of the centres of the typefaces and the rotational axis of the platen may be gained by the state of the impression for the typefaces as a whole. If a difference in this respect is noticed in the specimens of typescript, it should be remembered that it is often possible to cure a machine of this fault by a relatively simple adjustment of the mechanism.

Before the study of the impression is regarded as complete, a search should be made for examples of double impression caused by vibration of the typeface when in contact with the paper. Examples of these double impressions are illustrated in Figure 8–15. A double impression caused by a defect in the adjustment of the machine is characteristic of the work of the machine until it is repaired.

Alignment Characteristics

These are the final subject for consideration. The simplest and most reliable are any obviously faulty slopes in letters such as " I," " T," " t," " f," etc. The term " obviously faulty slope " is used because many characters are slightly sloped so as to make them appear perfectly upright. If a character has a variable slope it can safely be characterised as " loose," an identifying feature of some value.

A refinement is to determine the angle of slope of any characters misaligned in this way. This may be accomplished by one of several methods. A simple method is to use a special protractor, which consists of a number of lines ruled at slopes of one, two, three, four and five degrees to a base line. The protractor is placed so that the base line falls along the line of type. The easiest way of doing this is to align the base line of the protractor with the bottoms of two examples of letters such as "i," "f," "l," etc., which occur a fair distance apart in the line. It is by no means easy to measure the exact angle of slope, so that the best way is to estimate it by determining which angle on the protractor is definitely greater and which is definitely smaller than the slope being measured. The gap between these figures is narrowed as much as possible and the mean taken.

Another method is to use the measuring machine with a goniometer eyepiece. To get over the difficulty of obtaining a datum line, the paper is placed under the machine in what is thought to be the correct position, and the angle of every vertical stroke is measured as the microscope is passed along the line of type. A number of letters will be found to have the same reading, so that the required value of slope misalignment for the obviously misaligned letter will be the amount it differs from this common value.

If no precision measuring equipment is available, then an enlarged photograph can be taken of the typescript and lines drawn on the print to represent the base line and also the slope of the misaligned character. The angle these two lines make with each other can then be measured with an ordinary protractor.

Obvious errors in vertical alignment should next be the subject of consideration, bearing in mind what has already been said about the influence of centrifugal force when the machine has worn bearings.

Measurement of the degree of misalignment may be made with the measuring machine, but where it is desirable to illustrate the misalignment, enlarged photographs on which lines representing both the base line of the typescript and the bottoms of the misaligned type are drawn should be prepared.

It is only when the foregoing investigations have been completed that the attention is directed to errors in horizontal alignment. The reasons why the attention should be restricted to those which are both well marked and consistent have already been dealt with. It is most convenient to consider first the errors consistently shown by the same pairs of letters in both specimens of typescript.

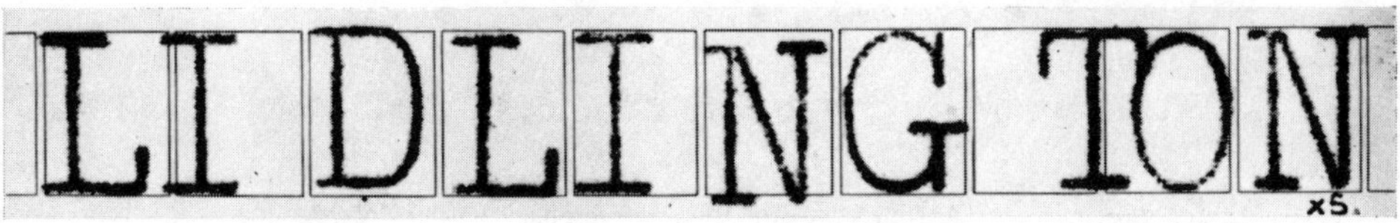

Fig. 8–29. The various alignment defects of a specimen of typescript can be demonstrated both quantitatively and qualitatively by superimposition of a transparent scale of rectangles similar to those described in Chapter 4.

It is difficult to measure errors in horizontal alignment because of the difficulty in obtaining a datum line. The most effective demonstration of the presence of such errors is to photograph several successive words in a line under a scale which allows a square for each character. If this scale is fitted over the type so as to frame the majority of the letters, any of them appreciably out of alignment will be seen to project beyond the outline of the square into which they should fit, if correctly aligned.

Other Identifying Characteristics

On comparatively rare occasions the beginning of each line of typescript will be seen to be deeply imprinted, but as the carriage moves, the typescript will grow progressively fainter. Both this and the reverse effect have nothing to do with the way the machine has been operated, but are due to misalignment of the carriage. Therefore, the presence of this fault in a machine will characterise all the work done on it until the fault has been corrected.

Some machines are characterised by faulty operation of the stops or of the release keys connected with them, so that when the carriage is brought back to the margin stop it sometimes fails to stay in position and rebounds a single space along the line. If the fault passes unnoticed by the typist, the typescript will present an uneven left-hand margin. The same machine, used by a more careful operator aware of the defect, would produce work in which the left-hand margin was no longer irregular. In a similar way, the operation of a defective right-hand margin release will sometimes cause the carriage to move an extra space, with a corresponding defect being produced in the words at the ends of the lines whenever the margin release has been improperly operated. These are examples of how the characteristics of a machine may be modified by the skill and care of the operator. As this is so, such differences in the typescript do not necessarily indicate that more than one machine has been used for the typescript being compared.

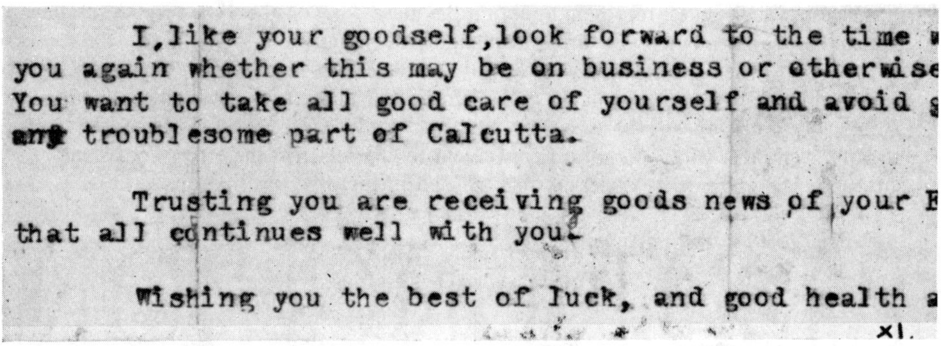
I,like your goodself,look forward to the time
you again whether this may be on business or otherwise
You want to take all good care of yourself and avoid
troublesome part of Calcutta.

Trusting you are receiving goods news of your
that all continues well with you.

Wishing you the best of luck, and good health
x1.

Fig. 8–30. Specimen of typescript which exhibits variable blocking of the "e." In some examples, the letter is clear cut whilst in others, where increased pressure was used on the key, the loop is completely blocked.

Another characteristic of typescript, which is transient and dependent upon the care taken by the operator in the maintenance of the machine, is the presence of blocked letters. Even in the same specimen of typescript, differences may be apparent in this respect. If the typeface is but partially clogged, the degree to which the letter is blocked will depend upon the strength of the blow given to the key. The debris which clogs the typeface may increase in bulk during the operation of the machine and obviously may disappear when the typefaces are cleaned. Whilst the presence of blocked characters is of little significance when the identity of a machine is in question, it may prove valuable when typescript is being dated. This is considered in greater detail below.

When the comparison of two specimens of typescript has been completed, the examiner must sum up the evidence in order to form his conclusion as to whether both were typed on the same machine or not. His task is almost invariably complicated by the fact that typewriters are subject to variation; it is extremely unlikely that any two specimens of typescript, even when derived from the same machine at the same time, are ever perfect replicas, and when an interval elapses and the effects of wear, misuse and repair have to be taken into account, they may differ superficially in many respects. Any information which might be forthcoming concerning the interval which has elapsed between the typing of the two specimens, which is the older, the amount of use the machine receives, and any repairs which may have been effected, will be of considerable assistance, so that efforts should be made to provide enlightenment on these points.

The examiner finds his greatest difficulty when he has to assess the significance of consistent differences in the two specimens of typescript. Some he may safely attribute to the condition of the ribbon, the state of the platen and the nature of the surface of the paper. Others he may dismiss as being due to the way in which the machine was operated, but when this has been done, there will often remain some dissimilarities for which there is no easily demonstrable explanation.

If the two specimens of typescript have little in common in the way of outstanding characteristics such as broken and defective typefaces, gross errors in alignment or obviously defective impressions, it may be that these slight differences indicate that two different machines of the same model and not a single machine are concerned. If both specimens of typescript are of good quality, and there is but a short interval of time between the typing, this may very well be the case. Where small quantities of typescript devoid of any obvious defects are concerned, the document examiner may not be in a position to carry the case any farther.

When the two specimens of typescript have a number of outstanding characteristics in common, the document examiner is not justified in assuming that what might be termed the "residual" differences indicate that different machines are involved, for he has to investigate the possibility that the differences are due to change in the characteristics of the one machine in the interval between the typing of the specimens.

A useful rule which has to be applied in these circumstances is that, in the absence of repair, errors tend to multiply and increase in magnitude with time. If the later specimen of typescript exhibits all the imperfections of the earlier specimen of typescript, possibly with some aggravation, then it is probable that both specimens were typed on the same machine. If, on the other hand, the later specimen does not include the errors characteristic of the first, it will be unsafe to conclude that one machine alone was used, as the possibility of defects vanishing with use is remote in the extreme.

If the machine has been repaired or overhauled in the interval, it is very unlikely that there will be any conclusive evidence that the same machine was used for both specimens, as adjustment and realignment can be counted on to change the characteristics beyond recognition.

It will now be apparent that the comparison of typescript to determine the machine of origin is not invariably a simple operation. In many cases the document examiner has to rely on his experience when assessing the significance of any dissimilarities which become apparent on close examination. The comparison of typescript is by no means a matter of balancing similarities and dissimilarities; a single consistent dissimilarity, for the presence of which no reasonable explanation is forthcoming, will more than outweigh a series of the most striking similarities in misalignment or imprint. In this respect, therefore, the comparison of typescript has much in common with that of handwriting.

Erasure, Decipherment and Restoration of Typescript

Typescript is difficult to erase without removing the surface of the paper, because of the affinity of the dyestuff in the ink on the ribbon for the cellulose fibre of the paper. The total erasure of typescript calls for drastic action with a rubber loaded with abrasive, such as carborundum, so that while the site of an erasure is easily discovered, it is generally found impossible either to restore or decipher what has been erased.

On occasion, erased typescript may partially be deciphered by bringing into prominence any residual impressions in the paper, by lighting the document at

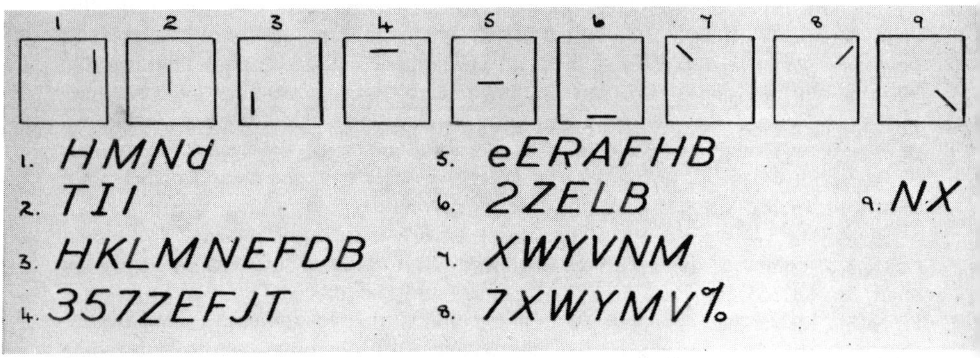

Fig. 8–31. The positions of any fragmentary impression will afford a clue to the character of which it formed part. The nine rectangles illustrate the different positions where impressions of typescript may be found. In the table below are given some of the characters which would be likely to give rise to impressions in these positions.

grazing incidence. Generally it will be discovered that capital letters and wide characters, *e.g.*, " m " and " w " will probably have vanished without trace, whilst letters with small outlines such as " i " and " l," and punctuation marks in particular, have been so deeply impressed that recognisable traces remain.

The interpretation of residual impressions is facilitated if the area is subdivided into spaces, each of which would be occupied symmetrically by a single character.

If this is done, the position of but a slight impression will yield a clue as to the identity of the character which gave rise to it.

There is no procedure known to the author which can be used to restore the colour of erased typescript. The oily medium associated with some typewriter ribbons will soak into the paper and defy erasure, but it will prove far too diffuse for a colour restoration to be built thereon.

If a carbon copy of the erased typescript was made using defective carbon paper, or if the document was typed on a machine with a dirty platen, faint impressions of the erased typescript may be discernible on the *back* of the sheet.

Where a carbon copy has been erased, any attempt to decipher the residual smudges is almost certain to prove a waste of time.

Faded Typescript

Unless record ribbon containing free carbon has been used typescript is apt to fade, especially on exposure to sunlight. There is no method known to the author which holds out any prospect of restoring the colour. The only practical treatment is to prepare a photographic copy of the faded typescript by methods which have been described in some detail elsewhere.

Identification of Erased Typescript with its Carbon Copy

If a carbon copy of erased or completely faded typescript is known to be in existence, this, once properly identified, will furnish a complete solution to the problem of deciphering what has been erased. The difficulty lies in the selection of the appropriate carbon copy which might have to be sought from a multitude of documents, and in the identification of the selected copy with the erased typescript. The possibility of accomplishing this lies in the fact that it is practically impossible to erase all traces of the impressions left by punctuation marks, which are usually driven right into the paper. The author has devised a procedure which takes advantage of this fact and which facilitates the search for the required carbon copy.

A sheet of tracing paper, or preferably celluloid, is placed over the site of the erasure and the exact position of every punctuation mark is outlined with a tiny circle. If ink fails to take on the plastic, a wax crayon may be used for making the circles. The marked sheet of transparent material will form a template which can speedily be applied to any carbon copies which are available for comparison.

Once a carbon copy has been discovered in which the punctuation marks coincide with the centres of the circles on the template, there should be little prospect of this being other than the required carbon copy, for the odds against two documents having punctuation marks in exactly the same relative positions are extremely great. Once the carbon copy has been discovered, it can be positively identified with the erased original by relating such letters as "i," "l" and "f" with residual traces in the site of the erasure.

Additions to Typewritten Documents

The forgery of a typewritten document by the addition of a sentence in a convenient gap in the typescript or in the form of a postscript, is far more common than the forgery of a complete document. The forger is usually scrupulous to use

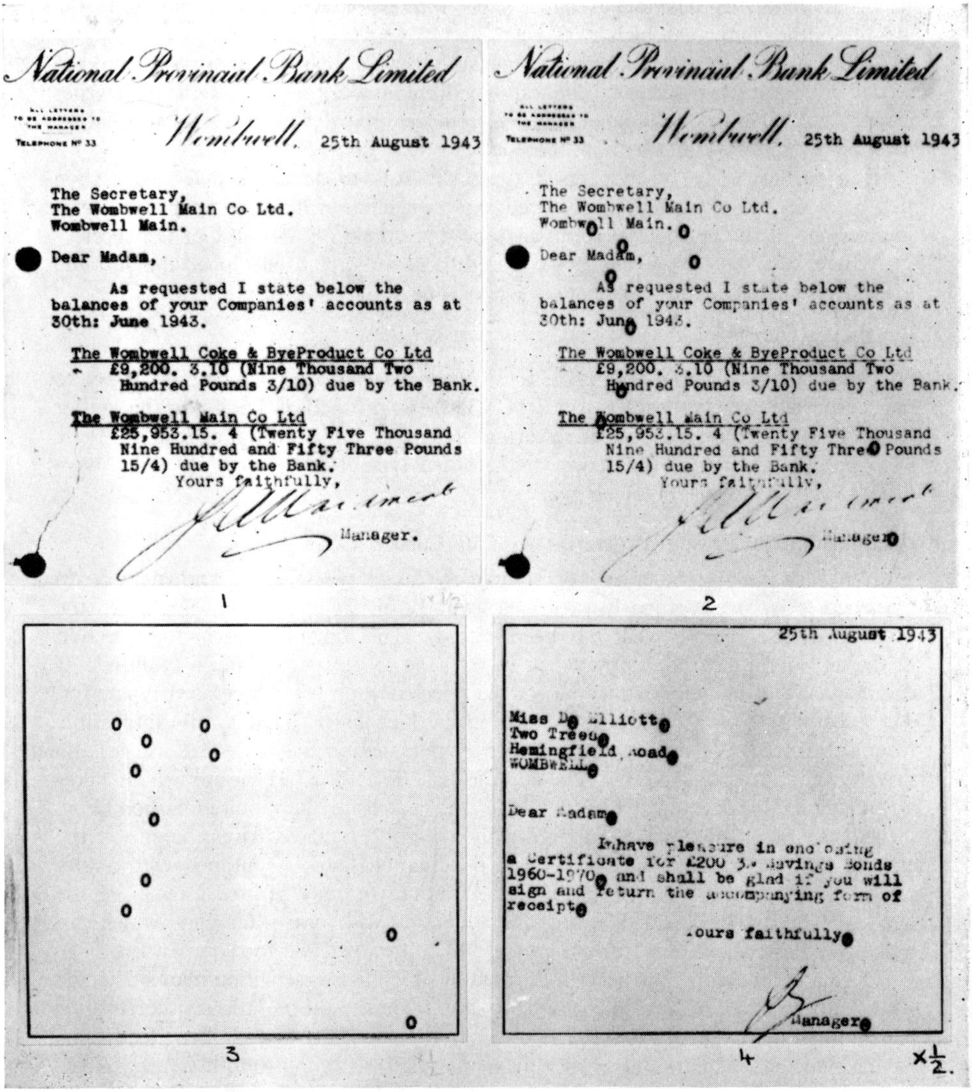

Fig. 8–32. *Identification of Carbon Copy with Erased Original*

(1) The document which has been typed over an erasure.

(2) A sheet of plastic was placed over the document bearing the traces of punctuation marks whose position was marked with circles on the plastic.

(3) The sheet of plastic used as a template.

(4) The template in position over the carbon copy of the original document showing how the punctuation marks on the carbon copy are aligned with those partially erased on the original document.

a machine fitted with type which does not differ appreciably in appearance from that of the original machine and a ribbon of a similar colour; precautions which are unnecessary when the original machine is available.

In this latter case, the only difficulty is that of inserting the document in the machine so that the added matter is correctly aligned with that already on the machine. A skilled typist is able to accomplish this with such accuracy that a convincing demonstration that material has been added is rendered very difficult.

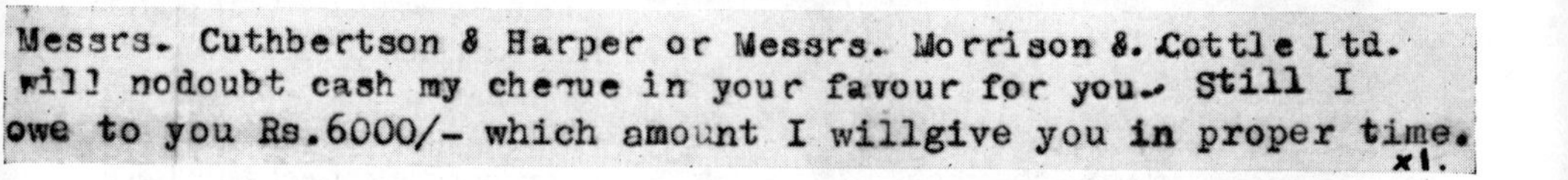
Messrs. Cuthbertson & Harper or Messrs. Morrison &. Cottle Ltd. will nodoubt cash my cheque in your favour for you. Still I owe to you Rs.6000/- which amount I willgive you in proper time. xl.

Fig. 8–33. The above is a postscript to a letter which formed the basis of a claim for 6,000 Rupees on the executors of the estate of the signatory. The final sentence of the postscript was proved to have been typed on a different machine. The designs of "t," "a," "s," "r" are obviously different.

Many other indications that a different machine was used for this sentence are also apparent.

Whenever fraudulent additions are suspected, the document should be considered as a whole and a note made of any words, figures, or clauses whose presence has modified the sense of the remainder of the text. Examples are the word "not," figures referring to dates, and quantities of material, sums of money, short clauses at the beginning or the ends of sections or at the bottom of sheets. The document should be examined for any words or phrases which appear to be cramped or which have been typed with a ribbon in different condition from the remainder of the typescript. Any short phrases which appear to have been typed with a different rhythm should also be noted for further examination.

The initial examination of any suspect typescript involves the comparison of its letter design with that of the remainder, for it is surprising how often a forger will use a machine fitted with type which differs widely in appearance from that of the original. Punctuation marks, commas in particular, should be taken into consideration, as differences here may have escaped notice by the forger.

If no obvious differences in letter design are apparent, the search must be continued for differences in the other characteristics of typescript such as defects in outline, impression and alignment. At the same time, an examination should be made of the quality of impression of the typescript, which depends on the condition of the ribbon and the cleanliness of the typefaces. These transient characteristics are often of great significance when the same machine has been used within a comparatively short period.

If certain characters such as "e," "a," etc., are found to be blocked in the suspect passages whilst clear in the remainder of the typescript, this will constitute valuable evidence that there was a significant time interval between the typing.

Ribbon Colour

In machines which are in constant use, ribbon changes have to be made at comparatively short intervals. The colour of the typescript should be tested both by eye and by photography through filters which might disclose some difference not apparent to the naked eye. If possible, a count should be made of the ribbon threads by means of a microscope fitted with an eyepiece micrometer.

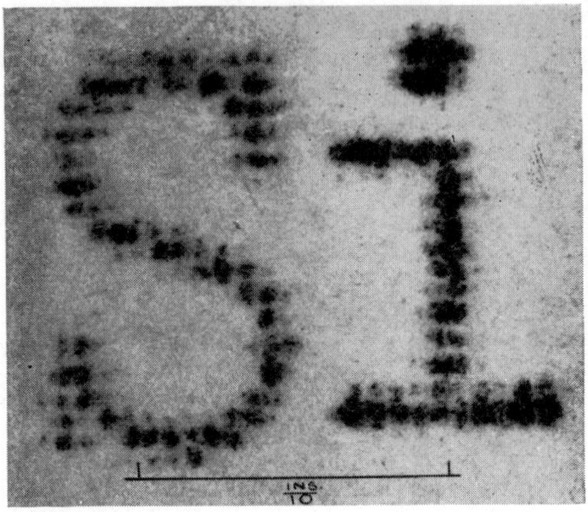

Fig. 8–34. Enlarged photograph of typewritten character showing ribbon thread marks.

For this, a lightly typed character should be selected. On one occasion, the author was able to show that a vital portion had been added to a document by demonstrating that the pigment in the ribbon was soluble in an organic solvent (ethyl acetate), whilst the remainder of the typescript on the document was unaffected by this reagent. The use of chemicals should be restricted to those cases when all else has proved of no avail.

If the foregoing examination has failed to reveal any evidence that the whole of the typescript in question was not typed at the same time, differences in the alignment of the remainder of the suspected typescript should then be sought.

When re-inserting a document into a typewriter, a skilful typist will follow a routine which is calculated to disturb the alignment as little as possible. The sheet is first adjusted so that the line of type runs horizontally in the correct position in the machine. This is important, because any marked convergence of the lines of the new and the original typescript is most unacceptable to the eye. Nothing like the same care has to be taken with respect to vertical alignment.

The next step is to throw the ribbon out of action and to strike against the existing typescript with the bare typefaces so as to leave faint impressions on two or three. The position of the paper is adjusted until the impression coincides with the printed character. Once the paper is in position, some of the added matter is typed in with the ribbon still out of action. The faint impressions are inspected, and it is only when the typist is satisfied that everything is in order that the ribbon is brought into action and the added material completed. If the operation has been carefully carried out, the results may appear excellent. If the machine is in poor condition and the paper is inclined to move in its guides, it may prove impossible to demonstrate that the paper has been reinserted into the machine, especially if the added material is at the bottom of a sheet where the paper grips often fail to function properly.

The first step in the investigation of the alignment of any suspect typescript is to test the accuracy with which the main body of the typescript has been imprinted. With a worn machine, it is of great importance to know what error can be expected in normal typescript produced on the machine, due to wear of the paper-gripping mechanism, before any significance can be attached to any misalignment of the suspect matter.

A typewriter in fair condition is a precision instrument, and the typescript it produces is aligned both horizontally and vertically. Each character falls into alignment not only with those on the same line but also with those in the corresponding position in the lines above and below.

The preliminary measurements can best be made with the measuring machine, but perhaps the best demonstration of the errors is accomplished by means of enlarged photographs. It is best made with photographs on to film because of the dimensional changes which take place when paper is wetted, but where the errors

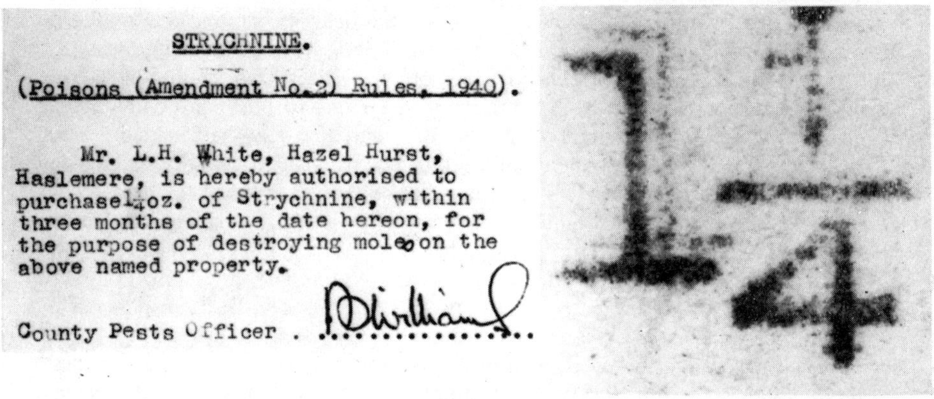
STRYCHNINE.

(Poisons (Amendment No.2) Rules, 1940).

Mr. L.H. White, Hazel Hurst, Haslemere, is hereby authorised to purchase1¼oz. of Strychnine, within three months of the date hereon, for the purpose of destroying moles on the above named property.

County Pests Officer . ...

Fig. 8–35. In the permit the original amount of Strychnine $\frac{1}{4}$ oz. has been increased to $1\frac{1}{4}$ oz. by the addition of another character. Careful measurement of the 1 showed that it is of a different size from the other 1's in the document, proving that a different typewriter was used. The enlarged photograph on the right hand side shows the trial attempt made to position this character with the ribbon thrown out of action. The typeface was stained with ink from its previous contact with the ribbon and this has made the trial position more obvious than was intended by the forger.

are gross, waterproofed bromide paper is quite satisfactory. Lines may be drawn on the enlarged photograph to show the departure in alignment so that the eye can more easily perceive the errors.

Proportional-space typescript can be treated in the same way although, in this case, units which are smaller than the smallest letter's space must be chosen. With the I.B.M. machine, which is the most popular using proportional spacing, the characters occupy a space whose width varies from two to five units. The unit may be either one thirty-second or one thirty-sixth of an inch. When the work of one of these machines is concerned, it is best to prepare a suitable scale which can be superimposed on the typescript and an enlarged photograph prepared.[3]

When a typewritten document has been reinserted into a machine with fraudulent intent, it is rarely that there will be only one source of evidence to show what has taken place. Even where the same machine has been used, the altered state of the type will be made to appear more significant when errors in alignment are also

[3] Suitable scales have been described by O. Hilton in *Journal of Criminal Law, Criminology and Police Science,* Vol. 47, No. 2, July–August, 1956.

shown to be present. Also, additions fraudulently made are rarely typed with the same freedom and rhythm as the remainder of the document, and this fact alone will often serve to direct attention to any added matter. Ribbons change far more rapidly than might be supposed, and it is extremely difficult to match the exact ribbon condition of the remainder of the document. This is another factor which tends to bring into prominence any added material.

Identification of Typist

In many investigations, information is sought concerning the identity of the typist. Whilst a considerable amount of help may sometimes be afforded to the investigator in this direction, it must be admitted that where the field is wide and the quality of the typewriting average, or above average, there is little hope of indicting the typist with any degree of certainty. The training of typists has been standardised to a considerable extent, and the work of trained typists has so much in common that there is very little variation upon which any differentiation may be founded. With a partially trained or a self-taught typist, sufficient personal peculiarities or deviations from conventional practice are usually present in their work to indicate the most probable author of an extended specimen of typescript, providing satisfactory standard material is available and the number of possible typists is limited.

The evidence from the typescript *per se* is generally limited, and consists largely of such features as habitual errors in the use of the shift key, the transposition of commonly occurring pairs of letters, carelessness in the return of the carriage at the beginning of a line and the overtyping of errors instead of erasing. Added to these are the qualities of rhythm and depth of impression. Some typists type very heavily or very lightly throughout, whilst others vary the depth of the impression from word to word, or even from letter to letter.

The evidence concerning the identity of the typist drawn from the matter which has been typed is more far-reaching, because to some extent it reflects both the educational standard and the artistic ability of the typist. Educational standards govern the punctuation and division into paragraphs, spelling, the division of words into syllables, when they are too long to be completed on the line, and the way in which abbreviations of titles are written.

Artistic ability or taste governs the arrangement of the matter on the sheet, the width of the margins at the sides and at the top of the sheet, the division of a word into syllables, or the reluctance to do this by leaving a space and beginning the word on the following line, and the extent to which the paragraphs are indented. Included in this is the practice with respect to the omission of spaces after punctuation marks, initials, etc.

Occasionally, a typist will be bound to use an unconventional character such as the " I " instead of the " l " on a machine which has no figure 1.

Duplicated Copies of Typescript

Instead of an original, the document examiner is often presented with a duplicated copy of typescript. The commonly encountered copies are those made with carbon paper, and the examination of these follows closely on the principles which have already been laid down. With good carbon copies, little difficulty is experienced, and the examination may be carried out with much the same degree of certainty as with original typescript. With a poor carbon copy the scope of the examination may be restricted because of lack of definition of the characters. Some carbon copies are so deficient in this respect that they are practically indecipherable. With these poor copies, there is little which can be done to identify them with the machine of origin, simply because the necessary evidence cannot be distinguished in the vague letter outlines which are all that the examiner has to work with.

Sometimes the problem is to relate a carbon copy with the original. This is not always such a simple task as might appear, especially when the machine is worn and the sheets of paper are apt to change their relative positions as they are fed through the machine. In such cases, mere super-position is insufficient to prove that one document is a carbon copy of the other, for it will be found that the two are by no means coincident when they are tested in this way. In these cases, the only resource is to compare the alignment of selected pairs of letters. If these letters are loose so much the better, for it will only be a carbon copy which will exhibit the same variations in relative letter alignment as the original.

The number of copies which can be produced as direct carbon copies is severely limited, so that when a large number of copies is required, other methods have to be employed. Four methods of making relatively large numbers of copies of a typewritten document are in common use. Each has its own advantages and defects, and each poses its own problem to the document examiner.

The simplest employs a development of the hectograph process, which has been in use for many years for the duplication of handwritten documents. Special hectograph carbons are all that is needed if typescript is to be duplicated, instead of manuscript written with hectograph ink.

Copying with Hectograph Carbons

A hectograph carbon, which differs from the conventional carbon in that its coating contains a very high concentration of special dyestuff, is placed so that the active surface faces the back of the thin, strong sheet of paper which is to form the master copy. When the required matter is typed on the face of this sheet, with the ribbon removed or thrown out of action, the carbon forms a reversed copy on the back. To prepare the copies, the paper on which they are required is moistened with a mixture of carefully chosen organic solvents and pressed into intimate contact with the master copy. The solvent present moistens the typescript of the master copy, so that a little of the dyestuff is dissolved to diffuse on to the copy paper and forms a correctly orientated copy of the original typescript. If a good carbon is used, several hundreds of copies may be made in this way.

The problem of relating a hectograph copy with the machine which produced the master copy is almost certain to prove difficult in the absence of obvious defects in letter outlines or gross errors in alignment. In the first place, as the master copy is made by typing through the substance of the paper, the outlines of the characters will be less clearly defined than with ordinary typescript; they will resemble a first carbon copy in their general lack of definition. The moistening of the text with solvent is certain to result in some degree of lateral diffusion of the dyestuff of the master copy, and the further diffusion of the dyestuff on to the copy paper causes even greater loss of definition.

In the majority of instances, all that can be done is to search the typescript of the copy for gross errors in outline and alignment which can be matched with ordinary typescript produced in the suspect machine. If such are absent, there is little prospect of linking a hectograph copy with the original machine.

The Mimeograph Process

This process is typical of those which produce copies on an absorbent sheet of paper from the ink which has seeped through the outlines of typescript that has been cut in a stencil. The stencil consists of a fibrous base, generally a long-fibred paper, impregnated with a plasticised nitrocellulose. The nitrocellulose coating is carefully compounded so that the impact of the typeface breaks up its physical structure to such an extent that the stencil becomes permeable to the thick viscous ink employed, without the fibrous base being cut through. A special ink has to be used, one which is without effect on the stencil and will readily pass through the fibrous base, and be immediately absorbed by the absorbent paper. A properly prepared stencil will make several hundreds of copies before it breaks down.

Any obvious impairment of the outline of a character and gross errors in alignment or slope will be reproduced on the stencil and will consequently find their way into the copies, so that in these respects the copies may be matched with the original machine. Stencil cutting is an art, and a defective stencil and consequently defective copies may be made by an unskilful operator on a good machine. The powdered " wax," as the impregnating material is often referred to, tends to fill up the hollows in the typefaces, and then when the effects of this combine with local failures on the part of the stencil medium to remain intact after cutting, it is quite possible to obtain copies which exhibit wholesale defects in the letter outlines from a machine in perfect order. With such copies, although it may be possible to state they could not have been derived from a particular machine, it is usually impossible to associate them with the machine of origin.

Multilith Process

This is a more recently developed process, whereby a very large number of excellent copies may be obtained. A special ribbon impregnated with a greasy ink is used to type the matter to be duplicated on to flexible metal plates for long runs, or on to special paper plates if fewer copies are required. The plates are used in the conventional lithograph printing machine. The contrasting properties of greasy ink and wetted metal or paper background are used to influence the attraction or repulsion of printing ink in its application to the paper on which the copies are to be made. The copies produced by this process are excellent, and may be compared almost as easily as direct typescript with standard specimens to identify the typewriter concerned in their production.

Forgery of a Typewriter

Reference has already been made to the final alignment of the type before a machine leaves the factory, and to the fact that a general overhaul of a machine may completely alter its characteristics.

As it is manifestly possible to change the identifying characteristics of a machine, the question arises whether it is also possible to change the characteristics of a carefully selected machine to make them coincide with those of another machine so that their work is indistinguishable. In other words, is it possible to forge typescript in the same way that manuscript is sometimes forged?

This question is of some importance, because it has been raised in more than one case where convictions have been obtained largely by proving that certain documents emanated from specified machines. If it were shown that such a feat is possible, it would tend to cast doubt on every conviction based on evidence of the origin of typescript, and incidentally upset the theory underlying the comparison of typewritten documents.

Very little consideration is needed to make it quite clear that the copying of handwriting and the selection and adjustment of a typewriter so that it can be made to produce typescript with certain very narrowly defined characteristics, have little in common.

In every advanced community the majority of adults have been taught to write, so that the fundamental skill needed by the forger, the ability to hold a pen and form a selected outline, is possessed by the greater part of the population. The only apparatus needed by anyone who sets out to forge handwriting is a pen and ink, and if this is backed by a certain degree of manual dexterity, all the conditions for tolerably efficient forgery are present. In view of this, there should be no surprise that forgery is relatively common, and that occasional examples of considerable success in this field are encountered.

Where the forgery of typescript by the modification of a selected machine to imitate the characteristics of another is concerned, the case is different. Despite its simple mode of operation, it must not be forgotten that the efficient functioning of a typewriter is dependent upon a considerable number of interlocking adjustments carried out after the assembly of the machine in the factory. The skill, training and experience demanded of anyone who wishes to make a successful adjustment of such a sensitive machine as a typewriter is such that the field from which possible forgers can be drawn is limited to but a few individuals in a million in even the most highly mechanised community.

Even if one of this very limited class were willing to prostitute his skill, a number of other severely limiting conditions would have to be complied with before the successful modification of a machine would become remotely possible.

The question as to whether a skilful forger who found all the conditions in his favour could modify a machine so that it would produce typescript which could not be distinguished from that of a specified machine by the most skilful document examiner has often been debated but it is extremely unlikely that the question will ever be capable of a definite answer.

Any practical test is unlikely to yield results of sufficient value to justify the expense and trouble involved. It could always be argued that with a different machine or with different personnel any results obtained might be quite different.

A considerable amount of light was thrown on this problem by certain developments in the case of Alger Hiss, a former high official in the State Department of the United States Government at Washington, who in January, 1950, was found guilty of perjury and sentenced to a term of imprisonment. The case of Hiss excited interest on both sides of the Atlantic, and the two trials and the events which led up to them have been more adequately dealt with from more than one point of view.

The most deadly testimony Hiss had to face was that presented by a document examiner from the Federal Bureau of Investigation who demonstrated to the court by means of enlarged photographs that a Woodstock typewriter on which Mrs. Hiss had admittedly typed three of her private letters was the machine used for typing copies of forty-seven of the secret documents Hiss was accused of betraying to the Communists.

At neither trial was there any serious challenge of the conclusion that the private letters and the copies of the secret documents were typed on the same machine; the efforts of the defence were concentrated on the attempt to show that the machine had passed out of the possession of Hiss at the material time. Nevertheless, on the day he was sentenced, Hiss declared that one day evidence would be forthcoming to show that forgery of the typewriter had been accomplished.

Shortly after this, it appears that representatives of Hiss approached a man named Tytell, an experienced typewriter mechanic, and asked him to attempt the task of modifying a typewriter so that it would produce typescript which was indistinguishable from that of the incriminating documents.

Tytell has given an account of the work he had to undertake to accomplish what he himself considered to be a successful forgery of the typewriter. Whilst there is no agreement as to the measure of his success it is worthy of notice that a substantial fee had to be paid for the work, which took over two years. At the end of this time, efforts to free Hiss failed and he was not released until he had served his sentence.

Whilst the story of the efforts made to show that Hiss might have been the victim of a forged typewriter has done nothing to throw light on the question as to whether a typewriter can be forged, there is no doubt that it has shown that there is little chance of its ever being accomplished in any but the most exceptional circumstances.

Bibliography

Bliven, B., *The Wonderful Writing Machine* (Random House, New York, 1954).

Brown, C., Kirk, P. L., "Identification of Typewriter Ribbons," *Journal of Criminal Law, Criminology and Police Science,* Vol. 46, No. 6, March–April, 1956.

Cassidy, H. E., "Chemical Reactions from Typewriting," *Journal of Criminal Law and Criminology,* Vol. 33, No. 2, July–August, 1942.

Current, R. N., *The Typewriter and the Men who Made It* (University of Illinois Press, Urbana, 1954).

Gayet, J., "Complete Forgeries," *International Criminal Police Review,* No. 75, February, 1954.

Gayet, J., " Efforts at Disguise in Typewritten Documents," *Journal of Criminal Law, Criminology and Police Science,* 46, No. 6, March–April, 1956.

Gayet, J., " Individual Identification of Typewriting Machines," *International Criminal Police Review,* Nos. 42, 43, 44, November, December, 1950, January, 1951.

Gayet, J., " The Identification of Makes of Typewriters by their Script," *International Criminal Police Review,* Nos. 26, 27, March, April, 1949.

Hilton, O., " A Systematic Method for Identifying the Make and Age-Model of a Typewriter from its Work," *Journal of Criminal Law and Criminology,* 41, January–February, 1951.

Hilton, O., " Identification of Make of Typewriter," *International Criminal Police Review,* No. 51, October, 1951.

Mares, C., *The History of the Typewriter* (Guilbert Pitman, London, 1909).

Tilghman, R. G., *Typewriters* (H.M.S.O., London, 1948).

9

HANDWRITING

ALL handwriting exhibits identifying features which will hereafter be referred to as its "characteristics." The characteristics of a handwriting fall into two classes. These are:

(1) those derived from the general style to which the handwriting conforms, termed "style characteristics," and

(2) those which have been introduced into the handwriting, whether consciously or unconsciously, by the writer. These will be referred to as "personal characteristics."

STYLE CHARACTERISTICS

These are taught to the child when learning to write. The style of handwriting which is acquired by the learner is that which is fashionable at the particular time and place. In the United Kingdom, at the present moment, the child will become acquainted with either "script" or the semi-upright cursive handwriting which is commonly known as "Civil Service" handwriting. In other ages and in other countries, handwriting styles which differ widely in general appearance would be the subject of study.

As the majority of children are nowadays taught to write from printed copybooks which have been produced in large numbers from the one master copy, it follows that any really popular style of handwriting will be taught to and acquired by literally millions of people. From the standpoint of the identification of handwriting, this is unfortunate, especially as the style characteristics are often the most obvious features of a handwriting, especially in the eyes of the inexperienced observer who encounters the style for the first time.

For example, it is the angular nature of the handwriting almost exclusively employed by European women during the greater part of the nineteenth century which makes the greatest impression on an observer accustomed only to the general appearance of "Civil Service" handwriting, with its rounded curves and long connecting strokes between the letters. An inexperienced observer, presented with a number of specimens of the handwriting of different persons all written in this unfamiliar angular style, might well mistakenly conclude that all were by the same hand, because they would appear to have their most outstanding characteristics in common. In his ignorance, he would be unaware that the unfamiliar features which caught his attention were common to the handwriting of everyone who had adopted this style of writing, and were consequently of little value as identifying features of an individual handwriting.

Nationality Characteristics

Although many countries employ written alphabets which derive from a single source from, for example, the block capitals of Roman times, few have identical letter designs. This means that although style characteristics are useless for the identification of a handwriting, they may be used to determine the nationality of the writer, or, more correctly, the country where he was taught to write. This is of some importance in a country such as the U.S.A., where there has been a recent influx of immigrants from many lands, as the determination of the nationality of an unknown writer may materially narrow the search.

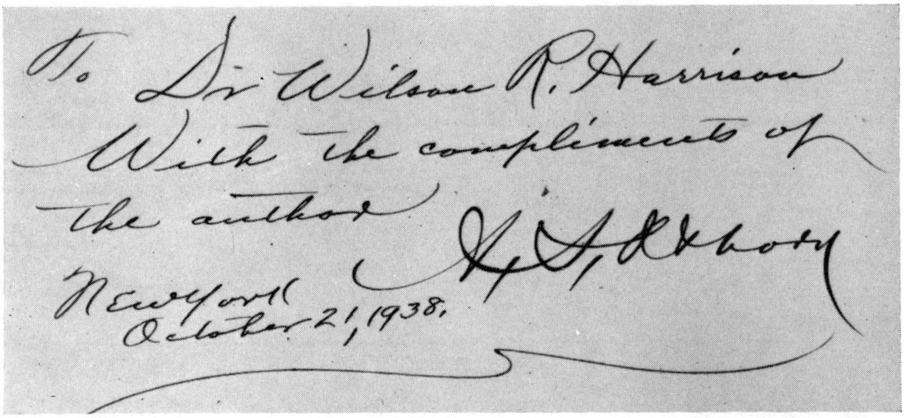

Fig. 9–1. Specimen of contemporary American handwriting. The ornate capitals are style characteristics, whereas the long bars to the "t's," placed well above the letter, are personal characteristics. Another personal characteristic is the use of the Greek "E" of "New" and the joining of the "w" to "Y" in "New York."

Dating Characteristics

There are fashions in handwriting; in all countries and in all ages a particular style of handwriting will be found to gain adherents until it is practically universally accepted, but, after a lapse of time, its popularity will wane as it becomes superseded by a new style, which itself will pass through the same cycle.

The effect of this is that the recognition of the style of a handwriting will sometimes enable a rough estimate to be made of the period when the writer learnt to write. Such an estimate cannot by itself be conclusive of the age of the document, for if a document is found to be written in an ancient style, there is no certainty from this fact alone that the document is as old as the style of writing, for there is nothing to stop a skilled penman of the present acquiring the style of a bygone age. Point is given to this by the fact that many English children habitually write in a style prevalent in England during the Tudor period.

On the other hand, a document written in a contemporary style bearing a date 1700 is very unlikely to be as ancient as this, for our contemporary styles of handwriting had not been developed at that time. Many forgers are unaware of this pitfall, for the author has had submitted for examination a number of allegedly ancient documents written in a modern semi-upright hand. One purported to be a chart disclosing the whereabouts of treasure buried by Captain William Kidd the pirate (hanged in 1701). The suspicions aroused by the presence of handwriting employing contemporary letter formations were confirmed by the discovery that some of the ink contained a dyestuff first manufactured in 1879.

A.

B.

C.

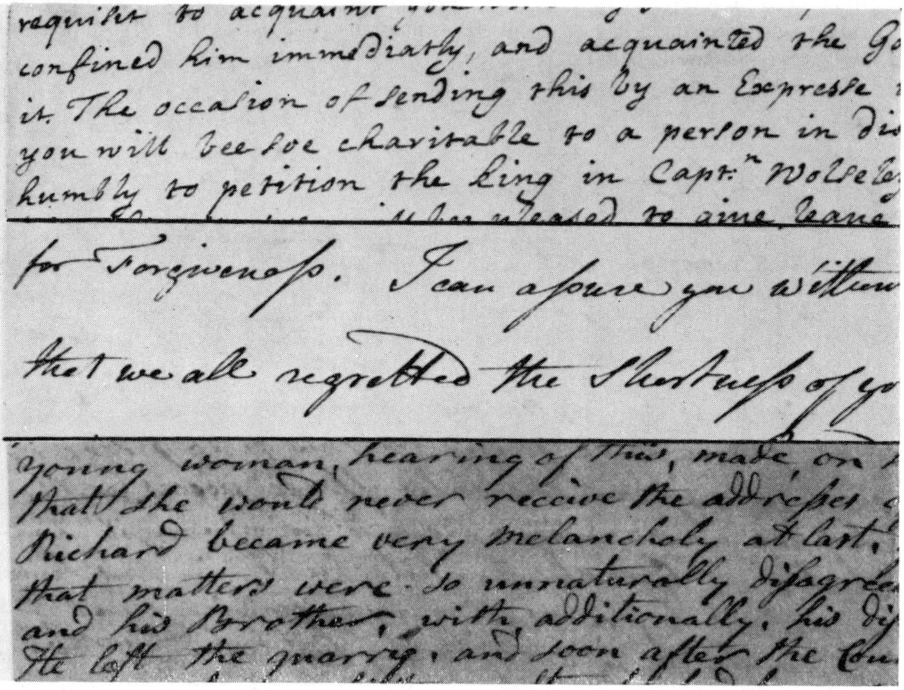
confined him immediatly, and acquainted the Go
it. The occasion of sending this by an Expresse
you will bee soe charitable to a person in di
humbly to petition the king in Captn Wolsele
for forgiveness. I can assure you without
that we all regretted the Shortness of yo
young woman, hearing of this, made, on
that she would never receive the addresses
Richard became very melancholy at last,
that matters were so unnaturally disagree
and his Brother, with additionally, his di
He left the quarry, and soon after the Cou

Fig. 9–2. *English Handwriting*

" A " is an extract from an autograph letter (1688) of Thomas Herbert, Earl of Pembroke and Montgomery. " B " is an extract from an autograph letter (1755) of John Ewer, Bishop of Llandaff. " C " is an extract from an autograph letter (1797) of the literary forger, Edward Williams (Iolo Morganwg).

Personal Characteristics

Personal characteristics, in the form of obvious deviations from normal practice, are sometimes due to deliberate action on the part of the writer who is endeavouring to give his handwriting a marked individuality. This may take several forms.

A common affectation is the incorporation of alien letter designs, one example being the use of the Greek " ϵ " instead of the conventional form of this letter. The substitution of the terminal " d " by the Greek delta " δ " is somewhat rarer.

Some writers deliberately distort certain features of their letter designs; the lower loops often suffer in this respect, some being developed into rubrics. (See Figure 9–40.) Others retain the conventional forms of the letters, but render their handwriting more individual by the introduction of an abnormal degree of shading produced by wielding a flexible nib with appreciably greater pressure on the down-strokes or, on occasion, on the horizontal strokes.

Fortunately for the document examiner, deliberate action on the part of the writer accounts for only a minority of those departures from strict copybook practice which constitute the personal characteristics of a normal handwriting; the great majority of these come into existence gradually, and often imperceptibly, from the

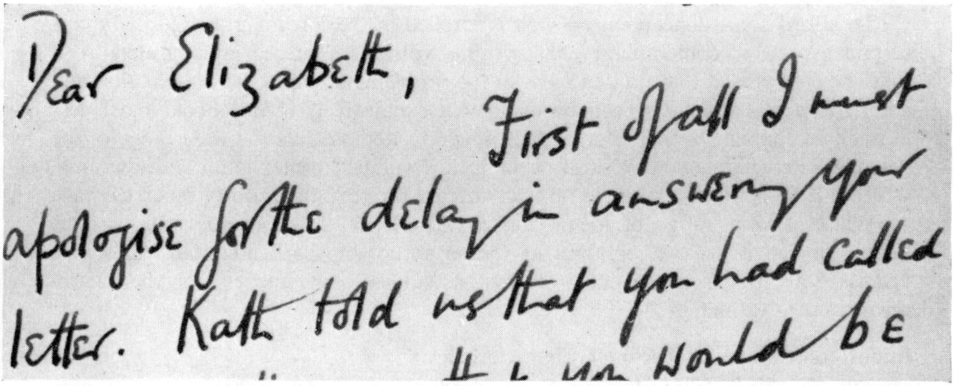
Dear Elizabeth,
First of all I must
apologise for the delay in answering your
letter. Kath told us that you had called
would be

Fig. 9–3. Specimen of handwriting characterised by (i) the existence of script forms of "b," "p" and "s"; (ii) the use of a Greek "e"; (iii) a block letter form for the "K" and (iv) the joining of words in spite of the fact that many of the letters in the words themselves are not joined.

moment the child forms his first "pothook" in his copybook. An account of this gradual process of modification is given below, when the development of handwriting is considered in some detail.

The Basis of Handwriting Identification

Experience has taught us that the possibility of a handwriting being identifiable depends on the developed handwriting of any individual being the structurally complex product of a long period of modification of the copybook form and adaptation to his needs and abilities. Such a handwriting is characterised by a multitude of departures from normal or copybook practice, which enable it to be identified beyond reasonable doubt. Unlike "style characteristics," which are usually obvious on the most cursory examination, the majority of "personal characteristics" are inconspicuous and have to be diligently sought for, even by those experienced in the critical examination of handwriting. The comparison of handwriting is dealt with in some detail at the end of this chapter, but it can be stated here that it cannot be accomplished by mere inspection and comparison of letter designs. Whilst there is no need for the would-be document examiner to be endowed by nature with any special sense or innate ability, he must acquire the ability to:

(1) distinguish clearly between the *style* and *personal* characteristics in any handwriting;

(2) distinguish between those characteristics of a handwriting which are *natural* and those which are due to *disguise*;
(3) make allowance for the existence in all handwritings of natural *variation*. The subject of variation is treated in some detail below;
(4) assess the *significance* and consequently the *evidential value* of the characteristics his examination has disclosed. This can best be acquired by the intensive study of handwriting contemporary with that under examination.

To afford some conception of what is implied in the foregoing list of conditions, certain aspects of contemporary handwriting will be considered in some detail. It must be emphasised that no treatment of the problems posed in the examination and comparison of handwriting can be dealt with exhaustively in one book, much less in a single chapter, but an effort will be made to demonstrate the wide range of the personal characteristics which can occur in a developed contemporary handwriting, whether it be connected, cursive or disconnected script in the form of block capitals.

Where a wide range of identifying characteristics exists, identification can be largely objective, so that opinions as to the authorship of handwriting cannot be dismissed as guesses or, to put it crudely, as subjective " hunches " on the part of the document examiner.

Initial Acquisition of Personal Characteristics

The departure from the copybook standard of perfection begins at the very outset of the learning process. Handwriting has to be taught to very young children in easy stages; the child has to be shown how to hold the pen so as to take advantage of the separation of the points of the nib when the pressure is increased, for control of this separation is essential if a shaded handwriting is to be acquired. Some seem to acquire this control instinctively, and produce well-shaded strokes exhibiting a smooth transition from the thin to the thicker lines. Others fail completely, and throughout life their handwriting is characterised by abrupt changes in line structure.

Improved control of the pen is achieved as the child masters the formation of the small number of fundamental forms—strokes, loops, troughs and arches—which can be combined to form figures and the letters of the alphabet. When these simple forms have been learned, complete letter designs are attempted.

It might well be thought that at this early stage, the work of the class would present a substantial degree of uniformity, but experience shows that this is rarely the case. Already, certain inborn tendencies in the pupils make their presence felt, and an experienced teacher can not only distinguish the work of individuals, but forecast with some accuracy which children are likely to become fluent writers, as well as those who are unlikely to attain much proficiency in the art, however much they may labour to perfect their performance.

Even where letter formations are being learned by the inking-in of faint guide lines, there will be considerable variation in the way in which this extremely simple task is performed. Some will exhibit a complete control of the pen, and produce smooth well-shaded letters accurately superimposed upon the guide lines; others painstakingly follow the guide line, but the concentration and mental effort demanded is apparent in the unshaded, uneven and laboured appearance of the line; and a few either through incapacity or carelessness, seem quite incapable of following the guide-line provided.

The level of intelligence seems to bear little relation to writing ability, for it will frequently happen that some of the more intelligent children will be numbered among the poorer writers. This is often the case when the child is particularly good at arithmetic. It is noteworthy, but not surprising that those who have talent in drawing are often good writers.

Acquisition of Slope

Once the guide lines in the copybook have been left behind, the differences in the writing of the pupils becomes more marked because, for the first time, the slope

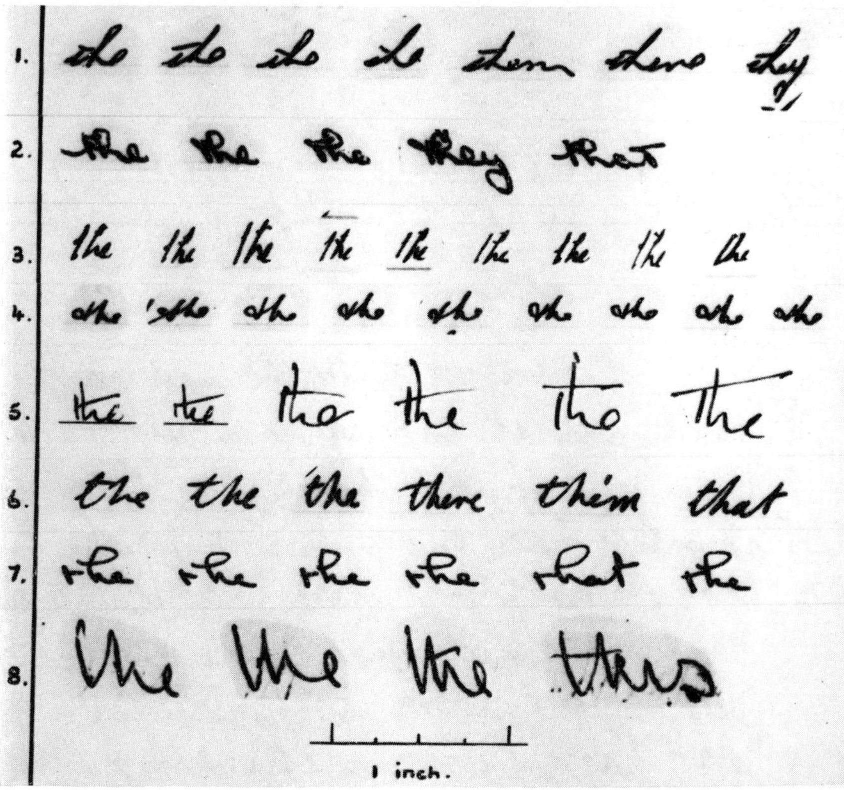

Fig. 9–4. Specimens taken from the handwriting of eight persons to show the range of handwriting habits with respect to the writing of the very common word "the." Compare the relative heights of the "t" with the "h" in specimens 1 and 8, the size of the loops in specimens 7, 2, 3, 6 and 8, and the size of the eyelet of the "e" in 1, 2, 3 and 4. The length of the "t" crossings in 5 and 7, the length of the final stroke of the "e" in 1 and 7 and the design of the "t" in 3, 4 and 8 and the slope in 2 and 6. The above by no means exhaust the variants which can be found in these eight writings.

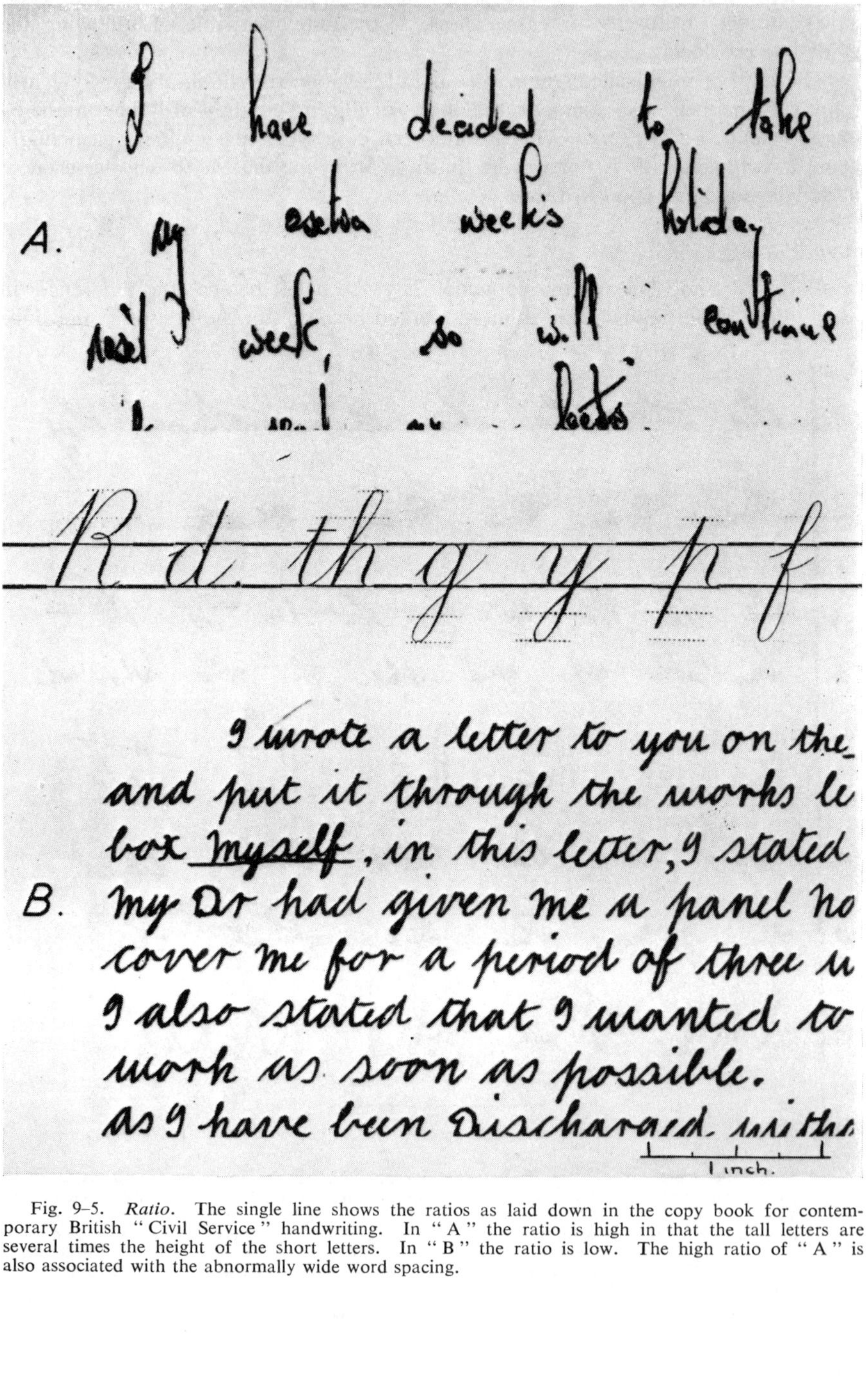

Fig. 9–5. *Ratio*. The single line shows the ratios as laid down in the copy book for contemporary British "Civil Service" handwriting. In "A" the ratio is high in that the tall letters are several times the height of the short letters. In "B" the ratio is low. The high ratio of "A" is also associated with the abnormally wide word spacing.

of the writing has to be controlled whilst the letters are being outlined. Some find little difficulty in establishing a reasonably constant slope, whilst others find this beyond their capacity and produce unevenly sloped handwriting to the end of their days.

Even those who succeed in establishing a constant slope do not always adopt that illustrated in the copybook, so that in time, the handwriting of the class will be found to vary in slope from a little forward of the copybook style to a distinct backward inclination. Once fixed, the slope remains fairly constant and becomes a feature of the handwriting, which can be deliberately altered only at the expense of rhythm and fluency.

The Size of Handwriting

In the early stages, the formation of a comparatively large script is prescribed to facilitate the construction of accurate letter designs; it is only in the later stages that any attempt is made to reduce the size of the letters to that which is conventional for adult writing.

Those who are likely to become good writers experience little difficulty in controlling both the absolute and the relative sizes of their letters, but others, generally those who show lack of skill in pen control, will exhibit a marked lack of consistency in both respects.

This variation in the relative sizes of letters and parts of letters plays such an important part in the comparison of handwriting that it will be considered in some detail below.

Letter Design

Throughout the preliminary stages in learning to write, the pupil will conform to the letter designs laid down in the copybook, because any obvious failing in this respect is immediately apparent to the teacher, who can point out the error and ensure its correction. On the other hand, the teacher is practically powerless to cope with those departures from good practice which are attributable to lack of muscular skill and co-ordination, or of concentration on the task in hand, such as the maintenance of even slope, shading and line quality. For the most part these pass uncorrected unless the divergence from the ideal is extreme.

Increased practice in careful writing may be prescribed, but whilst this may effect some slight improvement, no amount of practice can be counted on to ensure that any particular individual will eventually be capable of writing a smooth, fluent and rhythmic hand.

Handwriting has slowly developed over the ages; the original forms of the letters from which most Western alphabets have been developed were designed by the Romans for simplicity in cutting into stone. Whilst these original letter designs were well adapted to their medium, there is little doubt that the modern connected cursive handwriting into which they have been modified has little to recommend it for speed of writing. This becomes patent when its letter formations are compared with the corresponding outlines which form the basis of any modern system of shorthand. (See Figure 9–6.)

Shorthand letter outlines have been designed to ensure that, as far as is practicable, the writing-point travels in a forward direction with any interruption of this forward motion reduced to a minimum. Whilst it is true that the adoption of phonetic spelling and of simple formations which represent whole word-groupings, endows the writer with great speed, the fundamental improvement over conventional handwriting lies in the flowing nature of the script resulting from the elimination of abrupt changes in direction.

On the other hand, handwriting bristles with formations which not only halt the forward motion of the pen, but actually demand the reversal of its motion to form the retraces which are an essential feature of many letter designs.

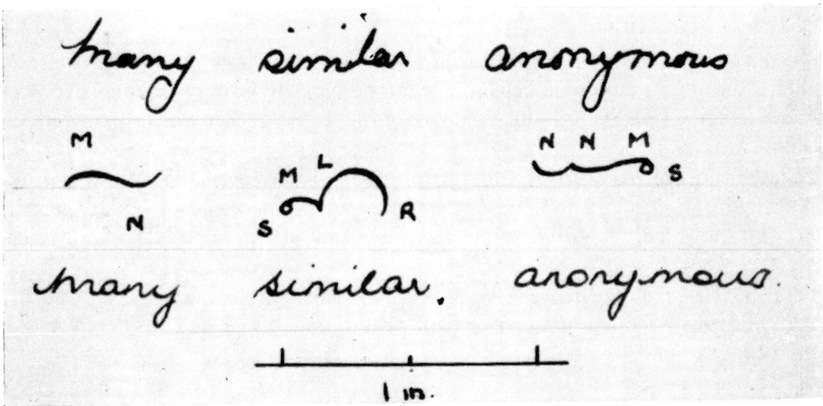

Fig. 9–6. This contrasts the frequently reproduced letter structures of conventional handwriting with the smooth flowing curves of the shorthand equivalents. In the lower specimen of handwriting the connecting strokes are practically horizontal, which indicates that the writer was originally taught disconnected-stroke handwriting. A further indication that this is the case is given by the many pen lifts in this handwriting compared with the upper specimen, in which each word has been written without lifting the pen.

It is consequently not surprising that when the pupil sets out to apply his newly acquired handwriting to practical purposes, he feels impatience at the relatively slow pace of this handwriting as his pen point slowly traces out the elaborate outlines of the letter designs he has been taught. Little time is lost before this impatience is given an outlet by the deliberate slurring of parts of certain letter designs and the modification of others, with the object of both speeding and easing the production of the written script. (See Figures 9–13, 9–14, 9–23.)

This means that once handwriting is used for practical purposes, gross deviations from the copybook letter designs are introduced to add to the lapses from perfection already present.

Generally speaking, about forty letter designs (taking into account both capital (upper case) and small (lower case) letters) are in regular use, and as most people have their own methods of simplifying and speeding their writing, it is apparent that there is considerable scope for variation in handwriting, solely from the point of view of letter design. By the time adolescence is past and the handwriting has assumed the character it will almost certainly retain until senility or ill-health take their toll, it may well be that comparatively few of the letters will conform at all closely to the original copybook designs.

Modification in letter design is not invariably the result of efforts to make writing simpler and easier. Some writers, in the endeavour to attain a highly individual hand, experiment with various modifications in letter design until they have hit on those which appear to them as worthy of incorporation into their handwriting.

If the rough notebooks of a class of adolescent girls are examined, many will be found to contain specimens of handwriting wherein the effects of various modifications have been tried out before being incorporated into the handwriting. Some of the letter structures tentatively adopted can be seen to have had but a limited period of favour, whilst others have been incorporated into the style of handwriting finally assumed. The examination will also afford evidence that copying from other members of the class has been indulged in, although whether this is conscious or unconscious it is difficult to say. Copying is probably one reason why the handwritings of close relatives and of those who have lived together for a long time often have so much in common.

The protean nature of the handwriting of the average adolescent, in particular the adolescent girl, is one reason why the greatest caution should be exercised in expressing any opinion on the authorship of such handwriting. The handwriting of some adolescents change with bewildering rapidity, and with the ever-present possibility of copying, the document examiner should insist on being provided with ample specimens of the handwriting of everyone concerned, written over a fair period of time, before he ventures on the expression of opinion as to the authorship of a disputed writing.

Variation in Handwriting

Everyone is aware of the different appearance presented by his carefully executed handwriting, compared with that of a scribble dashed off in haste. Apart from any question of haste or lack of care, the physical state of the writer is not without its effect, for it is well known that fatigue and a poor state of health can have a most deleterious effect upon handwriting, even if it is written with the greatest of care. Again, not only the health of the writer but the physical conditions under which the act of writing is carried out can severely modify the appearance presented by the script. For example, handwriting done standing up, without any real support for the paper, will differ in many respects from that written at a desk with everything favourably disposed for the writer. To go one stage further, even the nature of the writing instrument will have an effect on the handwriting, especially if it is in any way defective. (See Figure 9–33.)

In view of this, it is not surprising that, when specimens of the handwriting of one person written under different conditions are compared, there should be a doubt expressed that one individual was responsible for writing all the scripts, so different do they appear.

This mutability of handwriting extends even further, for when specimens of the handwriting of any person which at first sight appear to be identical are compared, careful scrutiny will reveal differences which need no microscope to make them visible. It is possible to go further, and to state that the handwriting found in consecutive sentences in the same passage will be found to vary in a number of respects.

Even the signature, which on account of its identifying function, is the one word which every writer endeavours to execute in a fixed fashion, is not immune from variation. It is very exceptional to find two examples of a signature comprising more than a few letters, which are so similar that they can justly be described as perfect replicas—unless, of course, one has been copied from the other by some mechanical process such as tracing. (See the chapter on Forged Signatures for further discussion on this point.)

The existence of this mutability of handwriting, or " natural variation " as it will henceforth be termed, need occasion no surprise, since human beings cannot be expected to function with the precision of machines whenever pen is put to paper. It is this natural variation which is pointed out by those who, knowing little or nothing of the principles on which they are based, question the reliability of conclusions as to the authorship of handwriting derived from consideration of the personal characteristics.

Although it can be shown that the existence of natural variation in handwriting does not justify scepticism as to the reliability of his conclusions, there is no doubt that the validity of any document examiner's opinions on the authorship of handwriting, will depend largely on his ability to determine whether the differences shown in the writings can safely be discounted as due to natural variation or whether they indicate that more than one writer is concerned. The experimental approach alone will allow the rules which govern the nature and occurrence of natural variation in handwriting to be determined in a manner which admits of neither doubts nor reservations.

The Determination of the Nature and Extent of Variation

It will be necessary to have available for detailed examination, extended specimens of the handwriting of a number of persons written under diverse circumstances.

The handwritings chosen for the examination should vary in quality; they should include both good and bad handwriting, and, if possible, handwritings influenced only slightly by the conditions in which they were made as well as others which have been considerably modified by such conditions. Lecture notebooks make an excellent source for such raw material, since the writing therein will have been written at different times under different conditions. Some of the notes will have been made while the writer was fresh, whilst others made at the end of a lecture given towards the end of the course will probably have been written when the writer was feeling jaded. Some of the writing will have been written a few words at a time with ample opportunity for rest in the intervals between the writing, whilst a large proportion is almost certain to have been taken down with the writer under pressure.

The writing of a single person should be selected for attention, that of the others being allowed to remain unexamined until the first has been dealt with. There is good reason for this advice, because it is only when the attention is concentrated on the handwriting of a single individual that the writing becomes sufficiently familiar to the examiner for him to perceive more than its most obvious characteristics.

In this handwriting, the " a " should be singled out for detailed examination. This letter is suggested because it will be found to have been written under a variety of conditions; some examples will be written in detached form as the indefinite article, whilst in many of the words it will be found as an initial, medial or, occasionally, as a terminal letter.

Whenever any particular letter in a series of handwritings is being studied, the attention can best be concentrated on the details of its design, by the examiner making a slightly enlarged sketch of each example as it is encountered. In this way, the salient points of its design become fixed in his mind.

When all the examples of the detached " a " have been studied, two points will have been brought home to the examiner. The first is that the general design of this letter has almost certainly departed in some respects from the ideal or copybook form. The second is that very few, if any, of the specimens studied are so exactly alike that no differences can be perceived. The departure of the general design of the letter from that laid down in the copybook will occasion no surprise, since the reason for this has already been considered. The fact that few, if any, of the examples of the detached " a " are exactly alike is an example of the occurrence of the natural variation being studied.

The next step is to consider all the detached " a's " as a group. It will be discovered that, with very few exceptions, all will exhibit a strong " family likeness " in spite of differences in some details of design. Another way of expressing this is to say that all these detached " a's " conform to what might be termed a " master pattern " for this letter. The rare specimens which fail to conform to this master pattern are generally termed " accidentals." Accidentals occur as the result of some interference, either physical or mental, with the normal formation of the letter. An example of the occurrence of an accidental is where the writer's mind outpaces his pen, so that he starts to form some letter which is to appear at a later stage, but, suddenly realising his error, alters the partially formed letter to something which may be interpreted as the letter which should have been written. An accidental written in this way may bear little resemblance to the usual form of the letter.

In an undeveloped handwriting, the master pattern for the " a " may bear a close resemblance to the copybook form, in which case the letter design must be regarded more as a " style " than a " personal " characteristic. As such, its evidential value would be slight. If, however, the master pattern differs widely from the copybook or conventional form, it can no longer be considered purely as a " style " characteristic, for it will stem more from the mind and the writing habits of the writer than from the copybook. A widely divergent master pattern can properly be considered to be a " personal " characteristic of the handwriting in which it occurs.

When the other groups of handwritings by different individuals are examined in the same way as the first, a similar state of affairs will be discovered; the handwriting of each individual will be found to be characterised by the presence of its own master pattern for the detached " a." It is, however, unlikely that every handwriting

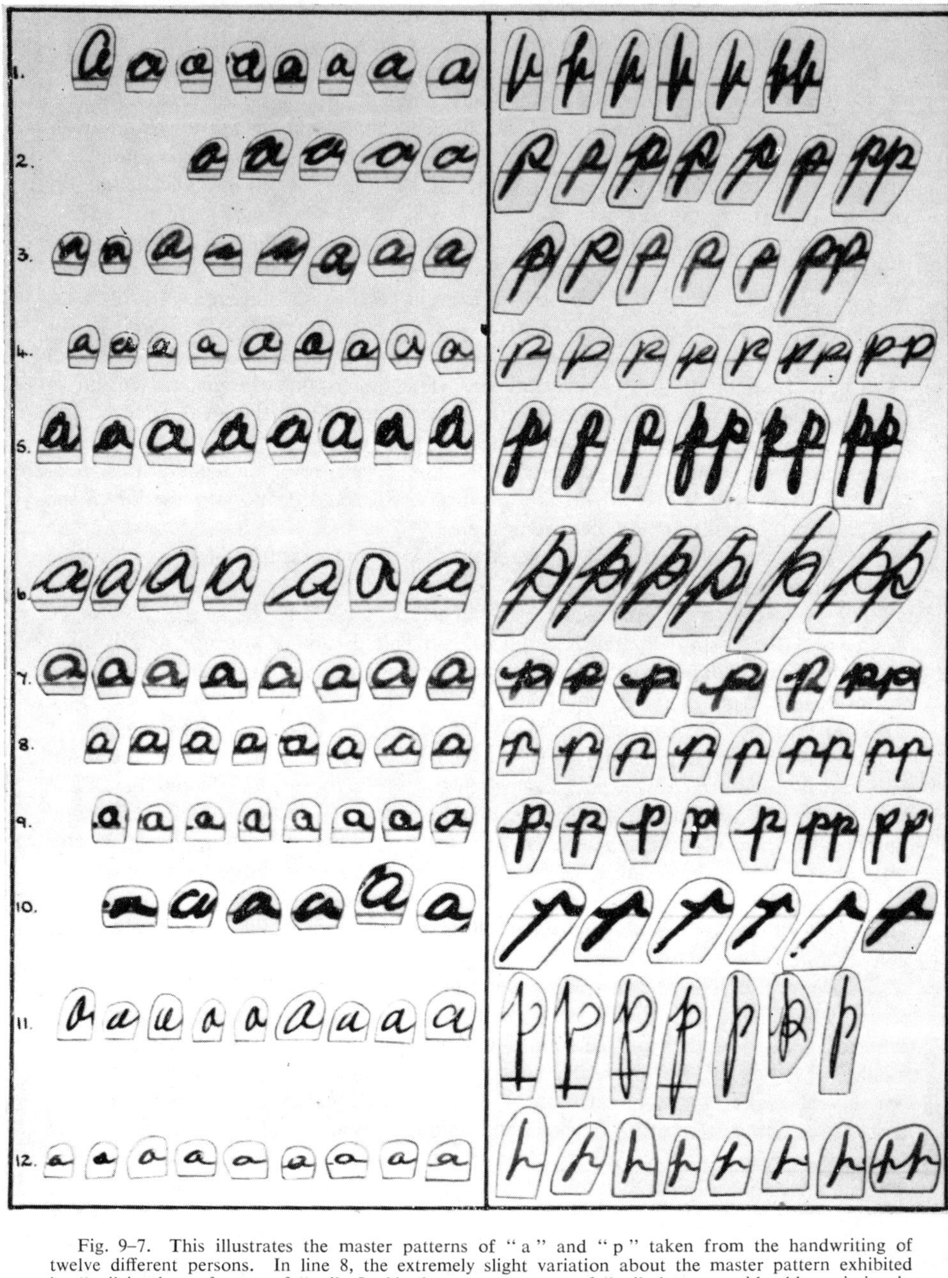

Fig. 9–7. This illustrates the master patterns of " a " and " p " taken from the handwriting of twelve different persons. In line 8, the extremely slight variation about the master pattern exhibited by " a " is also a feature of " p." In 11, the master pattern of " a " shows considerable variation in size. The " p " illustrates the same feature. In 6, the " a " is characterised by the presence of an eyelet which is employed to simplify retracing. A similar feature may be seen in connection with the " p."

will be found to have a different design of master pattern, especially if the specimens examined include a number of relatively undeveloped handwritings.

Range and Nature of the Variation in Letter Design Around the Master Patterns

Once the master pattern for the detached " a " has been determined, the writing should be re-examined to ascertain the nature and the extent of the variation in individual letter design around this master pattern. It will be found that the handwritings of different persons vary considerably in this respect. In one handwriting it may prove that the range of variation is small and is concerned largely with the size of the letter, whilst in another, the variation may be considerable and consist in variations in the design of the letter.

The value of this determination of the nature and extent of the variation around the master pattern will become evident when two handwritings which have similar master patterns for any particular letter are considered. Although similar master patterns are employed, it is unlikely that both handwritings will display the same variation. From this it may be concluded that a handwriting may be characterised, not only by the form of its master patterns but also by the nature and extent of the variation around the master patterns exhibited by each of the individual letter designs.

Therefore, it is instructive to see how variation in handwriting which some critics mistakenly regard as fatal to any conclusion as to authorship, can actually be turned to good account as an extra identifying feature.

Once all the information concerned with the writing of the detached " a " has been gleaned, a similar investigation should be carried out on the initial, medial and terminal examples of this letter. It may prove to be the case, and it is certainly so with many handwritings, that the position of the letter in the word, and sometimes the nature of the letters which flank it when in a medial position, has a considerable influence on its design. (See Figure 9–9 for extreme examples of this.) In some handwritings, it may prove advisable to regard some of the letters as conforming to three different master patterns, according to whether they are initial, medial or terminal letters.

Some defending counsel endeavour to discredit testimony that two specimens of handwriting are by the same hand by demanding that the witness compare initial specimens of a particular letter in one passage of handwriting with medial or, more likely, terminal specimens in the other. This is done to obtain an admission that the structures are obviously different, which might well be true. Such an admission is followed by the suggestion that the admitted difference in design is indicative of the handwritings being by different persons. The fallacy of such an argument is that effective comparisons can only be made when the letters are similarly placed in the word; initial letters should only be compared with initial letters, terminal with terminal, and medial with medial.

Once the " a " has been studied, the other letters should be subjected to the same investigation; when the examination is complete it will be found that the " a " is no different from the other letters in its adherence to a master pattern, and the dependence of its design on its position in the word. The most important discovery

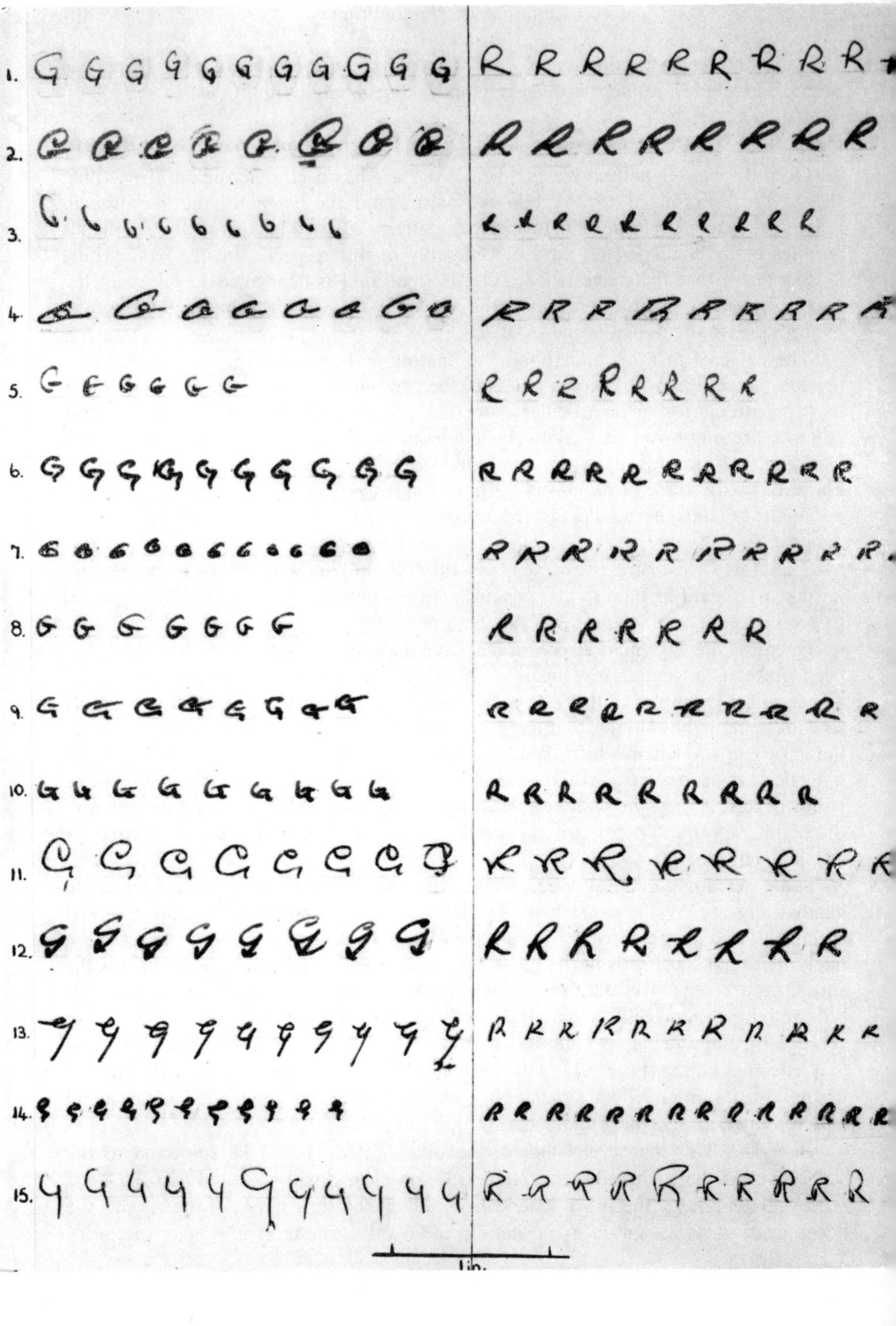
1.
2.
3.
4.
5.
6.
7.
8.
9.
10.
11.
12.
13.
14.
15.
1 in.

which will be made in the course of this investigation is that, irrespective of the general appearance of the different specimens, all the handwriting of any individual will be characterised by the same master patterns for the letter designs which remain essentially unaltered. This will be the case whether the handwriting has been carefully or carelessly written, whether the writer is alert or fatigued and whatever the nature of the writing instrument which has been used. In Chapter 10, which concerns disguise, a number of illustrations are shown in which the master patterns for writing of different appearance by the same author can be seen to be identical.

Fig. 9–9. Examples of the variation in design of the letter " t " according to whether it is an initial, medial or terminal letter in the word.

From the foregoing, it becomes apparent that the natural variation, which is an ever-present feature of handwriting, is not in any way haphazard, and that the differences in letter design which appear on close examination are, to use an expression drawn from music, nothing more than variations on the same theme—the master pattern—which runs virtually unchanged throughout the whole of the handwriting of any individual. There is no reason why a handwriting should not be characterised, in part perhaps, on its letter design, provided that (1) the existence and nature of variation is recognised, and (2) the characterisation is based, not upon the design of any single letter but upon the master pattern to which all the examples of any letter conform.

Dependence of Range of Variation in Letter Design upon the Complexity of the Letter Structure

As might be expected, the range of master pattern designs found in contemporary writings is not the same for all letters. Where the letter is of extremely simple design—" o," " i," " e " the range of master patterns will be limited. The

---

Fig. 9–8. *Variation* (opposite)

Specimens of " G " and " R " from the handwriting of fifteen persons show that

(1) there is a wide range of designs employed for these letters;
(2) in the handwriting of every person there is some variation in the exact form of the letter; no two specimens being perfect replicas of each other;
(3) in each handwriting the nature and range of variation found in the " G " is also characteristic of the " R."

In specimens 4, 5, 12 and 15 the size of the " G " is variable. The same characteristic is also found in the " R."

In specimen 4 the design of the " G " is very variable; this is also the case with the " R."

In specimens 1, 6 and 10 the design and size of the " G " shows little variation; a corresponding narrow range of variation is found with the " R " of these writers.

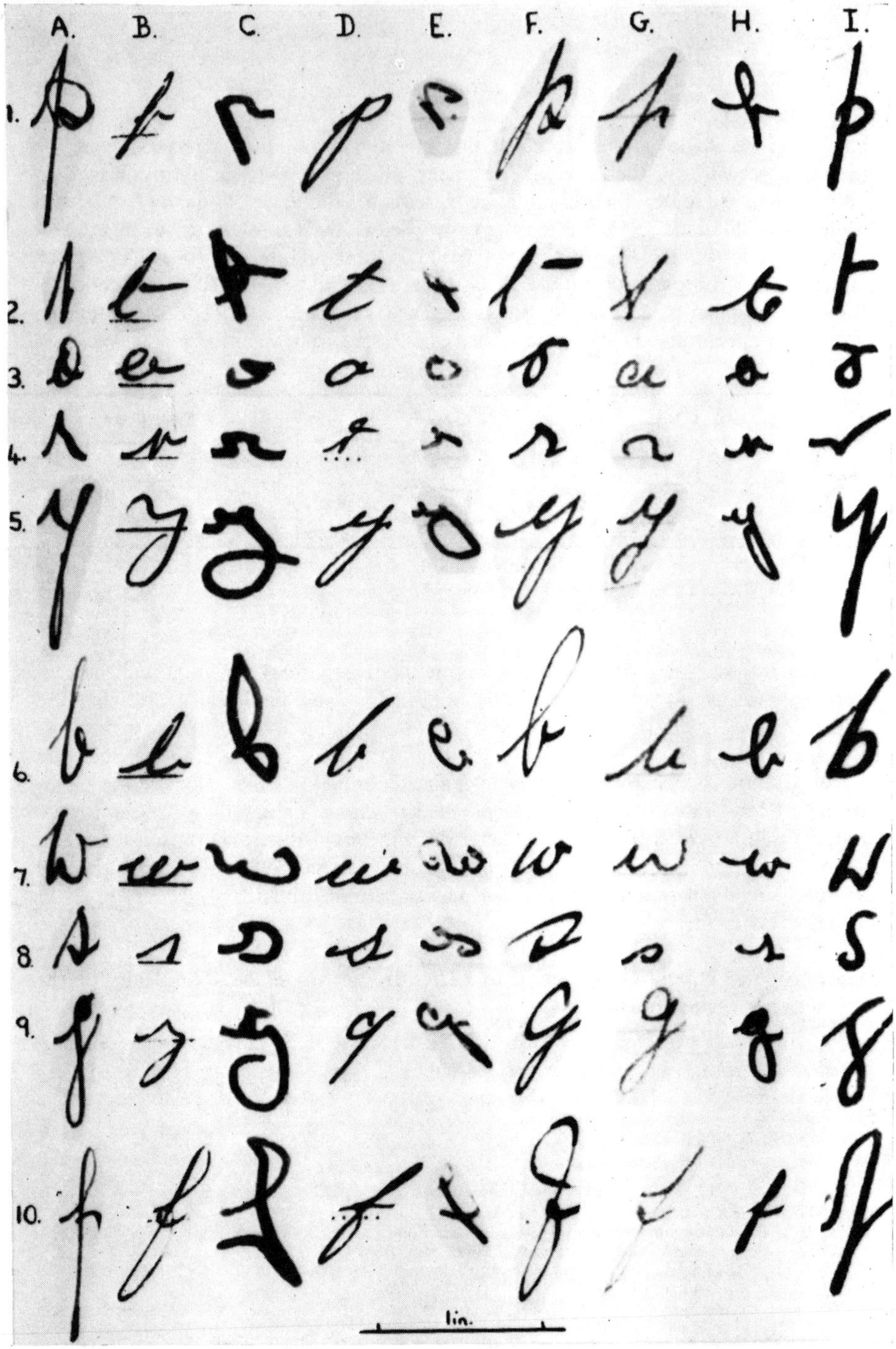

Fig. 9–10. *Variation in letter design.* This illustrates letter designs taken from the handwriting of nine different persons. Complex letters such as " p " and " f," lines 1 and 10, as might be expected show the greatest range of letter design, but even simple letters such as " t," " o " and " s," lines 2, 3 and 8 show considerable variation.

essentially simple letter design limits the range, because any appreciable modification of the design would be likely to render the letter illegible. For such simple letters, it might be thought that the number of distinct master patterns encountered would be limited to about two or three, but a little consideration will show that this cannot be the case. Consider two of the simplest letters, " i " and " e."

Even where the " i " is written correctly, it is sometimes written so that it appears very tiny compared with the letters which flank it. This is a deviation from copybook practice which converts the master pattern into a personal rather than a style characteristic. In other hands, the design is varied so that it is written with a small loop rather than a retrace, so that it tends to resemble the " e " of the copybook. In yet other hands, this variation in design may be combined with small size, so that three major variants have been shown to be possible.

This by no means exhausts the lists of variants, for the diacritic must now be taken into consideration. In this, considerable variation in shape and position may be found. (See Figure 9–39.) The diacritic may be omitted, or it may be written as a dot, comma, horizontal or vertical stroke or even as a small circle; and it may be positioned near the staff of the letter, well above it, behind or before it.

The effect of the foregoing is that even with a simple letter such as " i," about half a dozen distinct master patterns are likely to be encountered in every hundred handwritings examined.

It might be thought that there is little scope for variety in the writing of " o," as this consists of but a single oval. In spite of this simplicity, the range of variation in design is by no means negligible.

In the first place, the oval may be rounded or elongated, very small or relatively large, and the join, to use shooting parlance, may occur anywhere from nine to three o'clock. Furthermore, the oval may be written in either direction and either or both of the retraces may take the form of eyelets. On occasion, the oval may be left incomplete so that this letter may be mistaken for " u."

If letters of simple design such as " i " and " o " can be shown to exhibit a range of master patterns which can amount to double figures, it is not surprising that with letters of more complicated design, such as " p," " f " and " k," the number of distinct master patterns in common use may well run into dozens.

The Individuality of Handwriting

In spite of the fact that millions are taught to write from identical copybooks, it should now be apparent that, from the standpoint of letter design alone, there is ample scope for individuality in handwriting. In contemporary handwriting, employing something like forty distinct letter formations, considering capital letters as distinct from their lower case counterparts, and neglecting such uncommon letters as " X," " Z," " x " and " z," the number of distinct and distinguishable handwritings which are possible on the basis of letter design alone must reach astronomical proportions. Assuming that the master patterns for the letters range from about five for simple letters to about a dozen for more complicated designs, which is a very modest estimate, some students of the subject, with more optimism than knowledge of the subject, assert that on this basis the number of possible handwritings must range between a figure of five raised to the fortieth power and

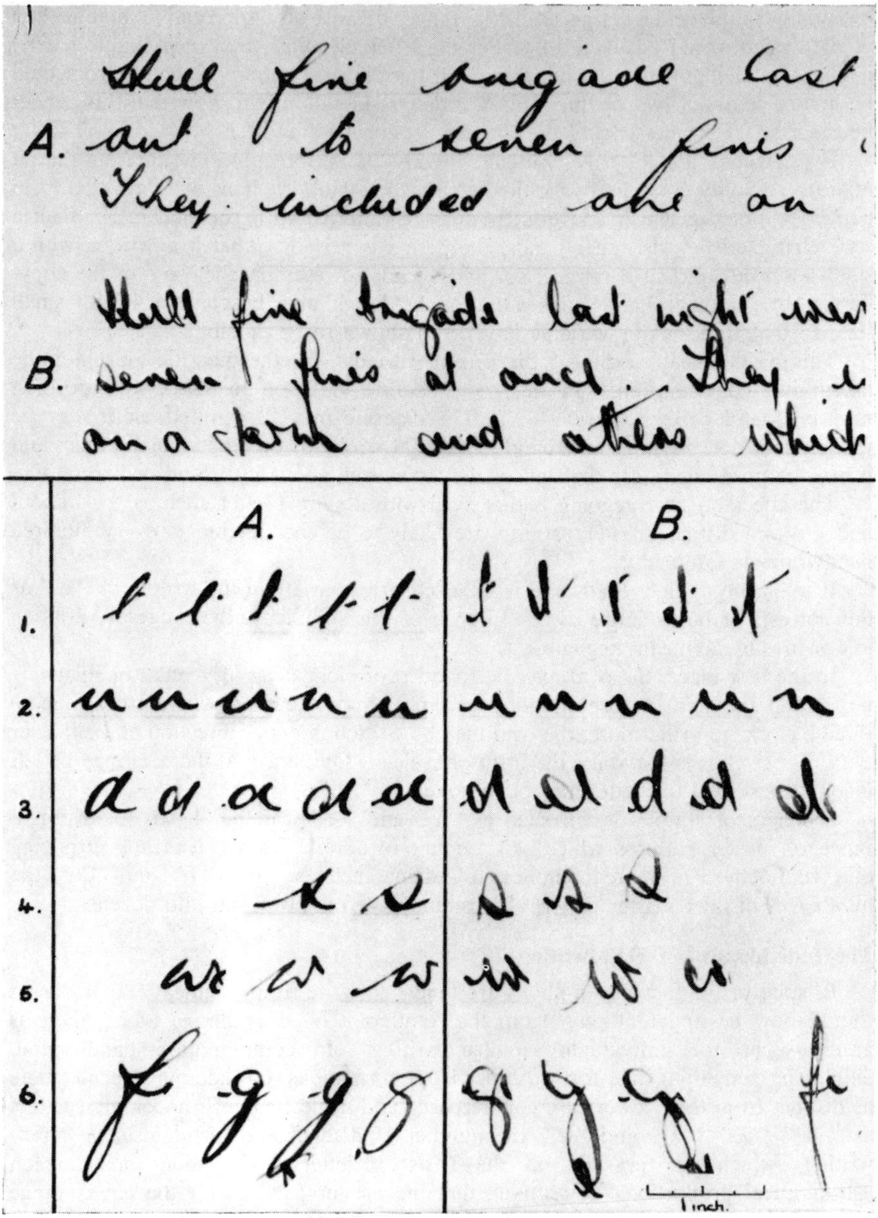

Fig. 9–11. " A " and " B " are specimens of the handwriting of the same person which appear at first sight to be dissimilar. Six characters have been chosen for detailed comparison: " t," " u," " d," " s," " w," " g " with a single specimen of " f." Examples of these letters have been placed in juxtaposition to form a comparison table. From this it will be seen that the master patterns governing the structure of both specimens of handwriting are the same.

one of twelve raised to the same extent; figures which are both astronomically great and equally absurd.

This crude application of the mathematics governing permutations would be justifiable only if it could be shown that the master pattern governing any particular letter design is not in any way influenced or related to that of any other letter. This is a state of affairs which anyone who has studied the structure of handwriting will know can never apply, since, far from being independent of each other, the master patterns to which the letters of any handwriting conform are very closely related. This close relationship is an expression of the internal consistency of a handwriting, and assumes great importance when the question of disguise in handwriting is considered. (See Chapter 10, in which this subject is discussed at some length.)

In spite of this severe limitation to the number of different handwritings which are theoretically possible, there is no doubt that on the basis of letter design alone, the number of distinguishable handwritings is virtually unlimited for all practical purposes.

Factors which Govern the General Appearance of Handwriting

In spite of the fact that the handwriting of any individual is based on a number of master patterns governing letter design, which are present substantially unaltered in all specimens of his writing, some of these specimens may at first sight appear to have little in common. On the other hand, the handwritings of different people may appear to bear a marked resemblance to each other, although, on analysis of the structure, the master patterns can be shown to be quite distinctive and unlikely to be confused. In view of this, the question may well be asked why this should be so, and why the general appearance of a handwriting is little guide to its fundamental structure.

The answer to such questions is simple, and is bound up with the way in which a great many people accomplish the reading process. A very young child will read either manuscript or printed matter a letter at a time, studying each character as it is encountered with a view to its identification before its subsequent synthesis into a complete word. As facility in reading is attained, this slow and unnecessarily exact procedure is discarded, to be replaced by a method of reading in which first the shorter and more familiar words, and finally all but the longest and most difficult letter groupings, are quickly scanned to be perceived as a whole. When this adult reading procedure has been mastered, the attention is no longer directed to the structure of the individual letters, unless the word is unfamiliar to the reader or has been obviously mis-spelt.

Very rapid readers go further; they pay little attention to individual words, but scan and absorb the meaning of groups of words and phrases as a whole. It is this method of reading " by eye " which makes the presence of dialect or unusual words in the text such a hindrance to rapid reading. In spite of its apparent simplicity, a passage in phonetic spelling is practically illegible to the practised reader, although it would probably give a young child little difficulty in its interpretation.

The " group " method of rapid reading is usually necessary for the deciphering of much contemporary handwriting, for it is rare to find a script which is so legibly written that every letter of every word can be deciphered without reference to its context. With many handwritings decipherment can only be carried out by running the eye backward and forward over word-groups to take into account the context, the length of the words and the position therein of the few letters whose identities can confidently be guessed at.

In view of this, it is not surprising that it is the *general pictorial effect* of a handwriting which makes the greatest, and often the only, impression on anyone giving it little more than a superficial examination. It is by the impact of the pictorial impression that most people are able to recognise the handwritings with which they are familiar. The fact that recognition is carried out at a glance is a proof that the examination is superficial in the extreme.

Experiments in connection with disguise show quite conclusively that the general pictorial effect of a handwriting is the sum of a small number of factors, of which slope and rhythm are by far the most important.

It can be shown that whenever the slope of a handwriting is altered appreciably, this fact, coupled with the consequent loss in rhythm and facility in letter formation, is generally sufficient to make the handwriting unrecognisable by many who would experience little hesitation in recognising the normal handwriting at a glance. The structural details, many of which are unobtrusive, whilst all-important for the characterisation of the handwriting, rarely have any marked effect on the general appearance of the script. This explains why handwritings of markedly different structure may at first sight appear to be very similar.

Legibility

As a handwriting may, to some extent, be characterised by its legibility, this is a sufficient reason for the discussion of this most desirable quality. Many are surprised to discover that legibility is sometimes unrelated to the artistic quality of the script, for many an elegant and fluid handwriting will prove difficult to decipher; whilst another, which is irregular and lacking in rhythm, may be read with ease, although it may afford little pleasure to the eye of the beholder.

Whilst a handwriting which conforms closely to copybook practice is invariably legible, this quality of close adherence to conventional formations is not an essential condition. There are many handwritings which are easily legible to those acquainted with them, although the master patterns, to which the designs of the majority of the letters conform, depart widely from copybook practice. When such handwritings are analysed, it will generally be found that two conditions hold good. In the first place, the extent of the variation of the letter designs around the master patterns will be found to be slight, and secondly, although the master patterns themselves may prove to be eccentric in design, they can easily be distinguished from each other. This latter condition is all-important, for it means that once any master pattern has been recognised and interpreted, there is little possibility of its being confused with another. This, added to the general consistency of the letter design, ensures that once the initial difficulties have been mastered, the writing is extremely legible.

Whenever a handwriting exhibits a wide range of variation around the master patterns, reading is certain to be slow and laborious, because each time an extreme variant in letter design is encountered, there will be both mental stress and delay while it is being deciphered, unless its identity can be guessed from the context. Extreme variation brings another evil in its train, for it is certain to cause confusion between letters of similar outline, such as the pairs " a " and " o," " e " and " i," etc., because of the similarity of extreme variants of these letters.

Slope may also affect legibility. The eye is accustomed to read handwriting with a slight forward slope, so that the use of a pronounced back slope will introduce a feature which is foreign to normal experience. The eye can readily interpret the changes in letter design which result from an enhanced forward slope, but it does not regard with the same tolerance those consequent upon the adoption of a slope in the reverse direction.

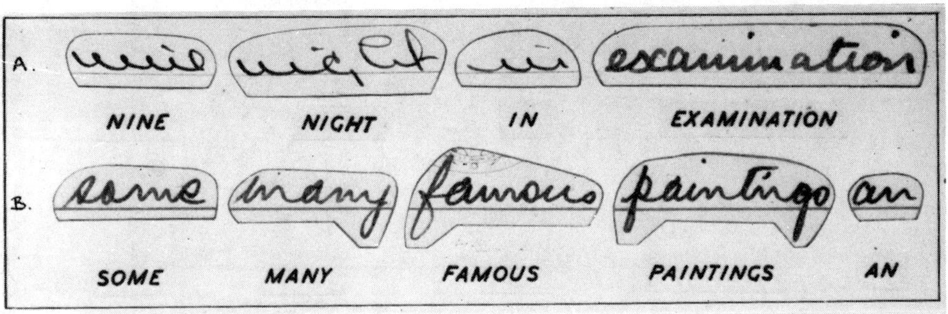

Fig. 9–12. " A " is an example of a garlanded writing. " B " is an example of an arcade form of handwriting.

The illegibility of certain handwritings which are by no means devoid of artistic merit sometimes springs from the adoption of an affectation which is far too popular at the present time. The form taken by this affectation is best appreciated by considering the fundamental structure of contemporary handwriting, which can be said to be largely formed from a series of troughs and arches. When the copybook forms are adhered to, there can be no confusion between the troughs, which make up such letters as " u," " v " and " w," and the arches, which form letters such as " n," " m " and " r."

Some persons prefer making arches to troughs to such an extent that they modify their letter designs to allow letters which are essentially of trough formation to be written as a series of arches. As a result, in such handwritings, troughed letter formations such as " u," " v " and " w " are written in practically the same fashion as " n " and " m." These " arcaded " writings as they are termed are often quite illegible, as many of the words are written as a series of arches, so that their meaning has to be guessed from their length and the presence of a few odd letters which cannot conveniently be converted into an arch.

Those with the opposite tendency, where all the arches are converted into troughs, produce a handwriting which is equally difficult to decipher; such a handwriting is termed " garlanded." Whilst this practice is taken to the extreme by comparatively few, a fair proportion of hands can be seen to favour either the arcaded or the garlanded style. This is why most schemes for the classification of handwriting incorporate this feature as an essential part of the scheme.

The most general cause of illegibility is lack of skill or gross carelessness in the formation of the letters, many of which are represented by little more than a wavy line. This type of illegibility is most prevalent in word endings such as -tion, -ing, etc. (See Figure 9–14.)

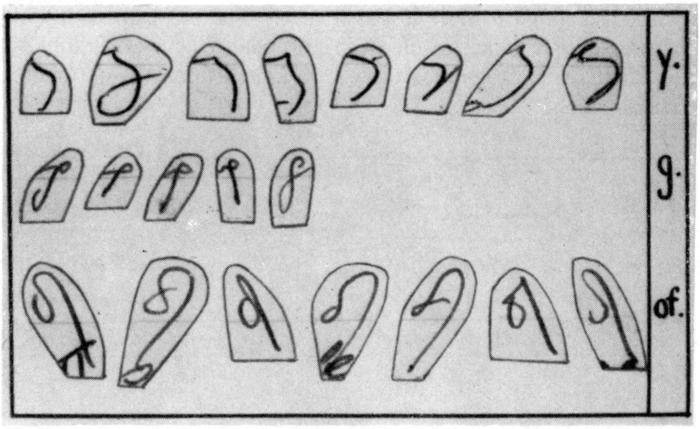

Fig. 9–13. Examples of the slurred forms for individual letters.

In these positions, slurred letters cause little harm, which is more than can be said of the slurred letters which are a common feature of the terminal portions of many signatures. Anyone who writes a signature an appreciable part of which is slurred, is making the forger's task unduly simple. All that he has to do to write a detection-proof forgery is to master the reproduction of the first few letters, and then to finish his task by drawing a wavy line to represent the remainder.

The Size of Handwriting

In the early stages of instruction, the construction of fairly large letters is insisted on; in this " Largehand," as it is termed by the publishers of copybooks, " short " letters such as " a," " e," " o," etc., have to be written between lines spaced about 8 mm. apart, and it is only after some facility has been attained in the production of such large letters that the pupils pass on to copybooks where the spacing between the lines has been reduced to about half this figure.

Some pupils resist the influence of these more advanced copybooks and keep their handwriting comparatively large, a habit they retain for life. It is perhaps noteworthy that these genuinely large handwritings are often modified to such an extent that the letter designs verge on the eccentric, whilst many are written with a pronounced back slope.

Other writers continue the reduction in the size of the handwriting until it reaches almost microscopic proportions, and unless carefully written with a fine pen, becomes difficult to read. The majority of those who write extremely small retain the copybook form of letter designs; eccentricities are rarely encountered.

When a ball-point pen is used for extremely small writing, the details of letter design are often submerged in the broad, often irregular, trace made by the rotating ball, so that the writing tends to become illegible. It may well happen that the growing popularity of this imperfect writing instrument will result in the elimination of very small handwriting except when it is used as disguise.

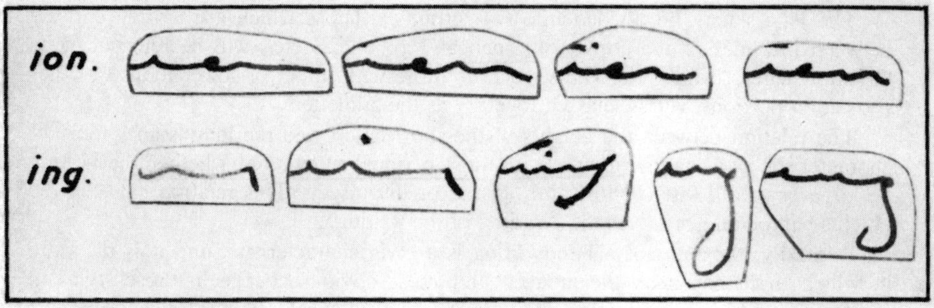

Fig. 9–14. Examples of the slurred form of the endings " ion " and " ing." The presence of these slurred forms is generally indicative of excessive speed in writing.

The size of a handwriting taken as a whole cannot be regarded as an identifying feature of any great value, for whilst the majority of people have a preferred size which they normally employ when space is not limited, nearly everybody is capable of altering the absolute size of his handwriting when circumstances call for some modification. This is readily brought home to anyone who has to examine large numbers of official forms, many of which call for the inclusion of a great deal of information in a limited space. Again, most people are capable of writing abnormally large letters when occasion demands, although this process proves so tiring that there is a distinct tendency for the handwriting to revert to its normal size.

Change in the size of a handwriting is sometimes used as a measure of disguise, in which case, if a considerable amount of handwriting has to be done, there will be a strong tendency for the writing to revert to the usual size, whether the disguise takes the form of either increasing or decreasing the size. A change in the size of a handwriting from the beginning to the end of a specimen should not invariably be interpreted as a failure to maintain disguise, for it may well be due either to a change in speed or the onset of fatigue.

When a writer tires, the size of the writing will often be reduced, but this cause of reduction in size will be confirmed by other signs—parts of words or even whole words or groups of words are omitted, and the writing tends to become slurred, especially at the word-endings. An excellent example of this type of slurring is the use of a short horizontal stroke which terminates in a vertical stroke extending below the line, instead of the three-letter syllable " -ing."

The reduction in the size of writing, which is the usual consequence of increase in speed, depends on the fact that the size of writing in the vertical direction is governed by the extent the pen point moves in a direction at right angles to the line of writing. Any abrupt motion at right angles to the line of writing tends to impede the forward motion of the pen, so that when the emphasis is on speed, the height of the writing tends to be reduced.

Ratio

The letters may be divided into two groups. Those which are written entirely between the lines of the copybook, such as " o," " a," etc., will be referred to as the short letters, whilst the others, such as those with upper or lower loops or other projection portions, will be classed together as the tall letters.

The relation between the heights of the short letters and the long is an important characteristic of a handwriting, as it tends to remain unaltered whether the writing be large or small, fast or slow and normal or disguised. This relation between the heights will be referred to as the " ratio " of the writing.

Primarily, the ratio of a handwriting is a style characteristic, and it is the ratio in which there has been the greatest and most obvious change in those styles of handwriting which have been in vogue in the English-speaking world during the past two centuries.

According to the dictates of the contemporary " Civil Service " style of handwriting, the loops of all the letters, with the exception of the upper loop of the " f," should extend above or below the line to an extent which is a little greater than the height of a short letter. The extension of the upper loop of the " f " should be a little less—about the height of a short letter. The lower extension of the staff of the " p " should be slightly less than that of a lower loop, but the upward extension of the " d," " t " and " p " should be only half that for an upper loop. Capitals should be written the same height as the tall letters.

If these proportions were universally retained, ratio would remain a style characteristic and consequently of little use for identification of a handwriting, but whilst the child is forced to conform to the ratio dictated by the copybook, this is one of the features of copybook practice which is subjected to early and very considerable modification once the copybook fetters have been discarded. The lessons of the copybook with respect to the finer details of ratio are soon forgotten, and it is doubtful whether any adults not engaged in teaching handwriting are aware of the exact proportions of the ratios quoted above.

A handwriting in which the ratio approximates to that prescribed by the copybook will be termed " normal "; if the tall letters have loops which are longer than the short letters are high, the ratio will be described as " high," whilst where the opposite is the case, the ratio will be considered to be " low." (See Figure 9–5 for examples of handwritings of widely differing ratio.)

In even a small number of handwritings, a wide range of ratio will probably be discovered; some writings will exhibit such a low ratio that it will appear that there was some reluctance on the part of the writer to venture either above or below the line of writing, so that the " d " and " e " are indistinguishable from " a " and " l," whilst the lower loops are so abbreviated that they are practically non-existent. In other writings the loops will be found to extend above or below the line to an extent which may be as much as several times the height of a short letter.

Once fixed, the ratio of a handwriting is very seldom altered, and experiment has shown that it is extremely difficult deliberately to effect a consistent change without a complete loss of fluency.

It is generally possible to assess the ratio when only a limited amount of handwriting is available for examination. This is important, because the test of ratio may generally be applied to the comparatively small amounts of handwriting which appear on the majority of printed forms. Whilst two specimens of handwriting of similar ratio cannot from this fact alone be considered to have common authorship, it is fairly safe to surmise that two specimens of widely differing ratio are unlikely to have been written by the same person.

The Relative Sizes of Letters

According to the copybook, not only should the short letters be of the same height, but those of similar construction such as " o," " e," " u," " a," etc., should be of approximately the same width as well. The examination of a comparatively small number of different handwritings will suffice to show that this rule is rarely observed in practice.

Abnormally large letters are frequently encountered; in some handwritings, the " c " is written so that it exceeds all other small letters in size (see Figure 9–15) whilst in others it will be the " a " which is written in this way.

As might be expected, other handwritings will be found to contain specimens of abnormally small letters. In some, the " i " has degenerated into a notch on the stroke which connects the letters which flank it, whilst in others the " e " has lost its loop and become almost indistinguishable from a tiny " i." Another letter which often suffers a distinct reduction in relative size is the " o "; this is frequently the case where block lettering is concerned, so much so that a specimen of this style of script in which the " O " is correctly proportioned may be regarded as exceptional in this respect.

In some hands, contrary to what is laid down in the copybook, the " t " is written appreciably taller than the " h," to give the very common letter grouping " th " a most unusual appearance. (See Figure 9–4.)

It sometimes happens that whilst the letter as a whole is normal in size, a part may appreciably be enlarged so that the letter stands out in the handwriting. This is often the case with " k "; whilst the letter as a whole is no taller than the " l " and the " h," the lower portion has been so exaggerated in size that this malformed letter may well be mistaken for a capital form which has strayed into the word.

It has already been stated that the absolute size of a handwriting may vary according to the circumstances in which it is written, but this variability rarely extends to the *relative sizes* of the letters. This is a feature of handwriting which remains remarkably constant. As few handwritings preserve the constancy of size laid down by the copybook, the relative proportions of the letters may be regarded as a useful characteristic of a handwriting. This is especially so when the handwriting contains a fair proportion of letters which are not of normal size.

The warning should be given that a fair proportion of "accidental" forms are abnormal in size, so that care should be taken to ensure that any letter considered to be of abnormal size is truly characteristic of the handwriting, and that conclusions are not being drawn from the fortuitous appearance in the handwriting of one of these formations.

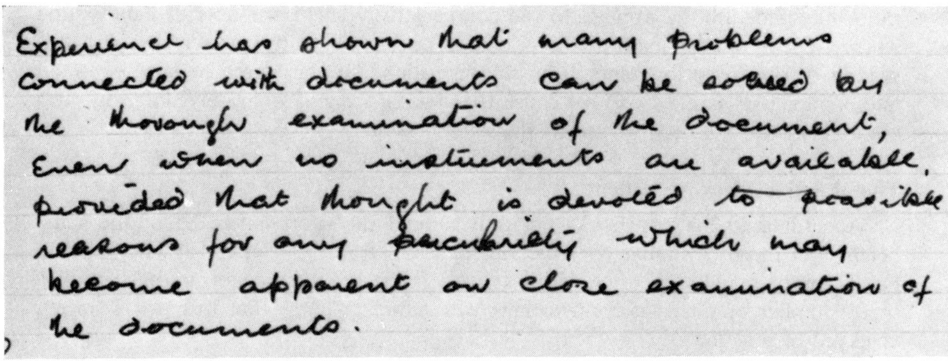
Experience has shown that many problems
connected with documents can be solved by
the thorough examination of the document,
Even when no instruments are available,
provided that thought is devoted to possible
reasons for any peculiarity which may
become apparent on close examination of
the documents.

Fig. 9–15. An example of connected cursive handwriting showing (i) the inclusion of script forms of the letters "b," "f," "p," "t" and "x"; (ii) Greek forms of "e" and "d"; and (iii) abnormally large "c."

It may happen that in a handwriting in which the relative sizes of the letters taken as a whole are remarkably constant, one letter, possibly "r," will be found to vary appreciably in relative size. This will generally indicate that the writer is unused to the construction of the particular form of this letter employed; in this connection it should be borne in mind that the use of an alternative form for letters such as "r," "e," "s" and "p" is a common characteristic of disguised writing. The effect of disguise on the relative sizes of the letters is dealt with in some detail in the chapter dealing with disguise.

Constancy in the relative sizes of the letters is lost when the writer is under the influence of either mental or physical restraint. When, for example, the slope is being deliberately changed to disguise the handwriting, the constancy of the relative sizes of the letters will suffer because the rhythm of the handwriting is being disturbed. When an even more difficult task, the use of the unaccustomed hand, is essayed, the relative sizes of the letters is subject to considerable modification. This is because the control of the pen with the unaccustomed hand is difficult, so that the attention has to be concentrated on the production of recognisable outlines for the letters. It is perhaps noteworthy that in these circumstances, irrespective of the normal writing habits, both ratio and the relative sizes of the letters tend to approach that of the copybook. It may be regarded as a general rule that any handwriting written under difficulty tends to lose its individuality and revert to the original copybook standard.

Initial Strokes

The copybook prescribes initial strokes to the majority of the initial letters of a word, but in some handwritings these are often omitted. Initial strokes are peculiar in that they form an exception to the general rule that the relative proportions of letters in a developed handwriting are fairly constant. Different specimens of the handwriting of some individuals exhibit numerous examples of initial strokes which vary from being relatively long to abnormally short, or even absent, according to the whim of the writer. Therefore, the fact that one specimen of writing is completely devoid of initial strokes does not mean that it cannot have been written by the author of another specimen which is liberally garnished with abnormally long examples of this formation.

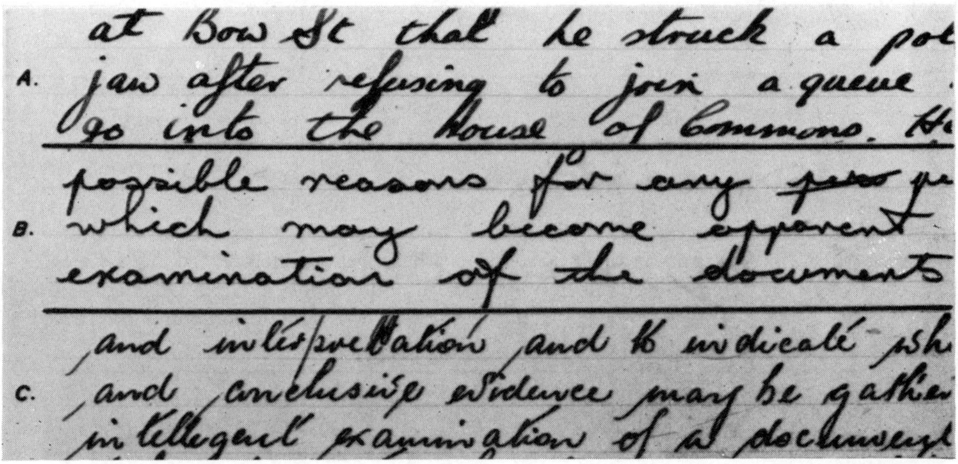

Fig. 9–16. " A " is devoid of initial strokes. In " B " the initial strokes are short and integral with the writing. In " C " the initial strokes are abnormally long and in many instances do not form an integral part of the following letter.

Terminal Spurs

In marked contrast to the initial strokes, the terminal spurs associated with such letters as " o," " w " and the arcade form of " r " are remarkably consistent in length. If a writer is found to use long spurs to these letters, then similar long spurs are almost certain to be present in every contemporary specimen of his handwriting. A similar constancy is found in the use of the more rarely encountered short spur, which approximates to little more than a " tick."

In general, it may be safely assumed that if a writer is in the habit of omitting the final spurs from letters such as " o," " w " and " r," he is unlikely to be the writer of a contemporary specimen of handwriting in which these letters are invariably spurred. The word contemporary is stressed because the spurring habit is sometimes the subject of long-term modification. A minority of writers will be inconsistent in the spurring of their letters, but in such cases it will generally be found that any passage of reasonable length will exhibit examples of both spurred and unspurred letters.

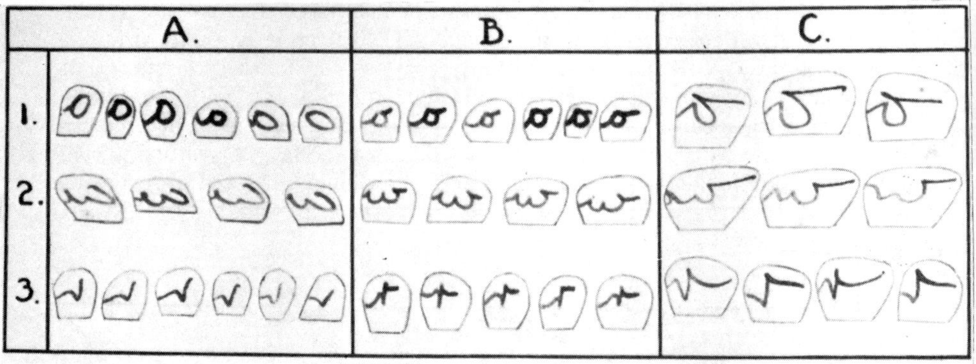

Fig. 9–17. The handwriting " A " is characterised by the absence of terminal spurs. In " B " the spurs are of medial length, whereas in " C " they are abnormally long.

Terminal Strokes

For contemporary " Civil Service " handwriting, the copybook prescribes upward-sloping terminal strokes of some length for letters such as " d," " t," " l," etc., when in the terminal position in a word, but should a child be taught the " script " hand derived from the Tudor period, he will acquire structures for these

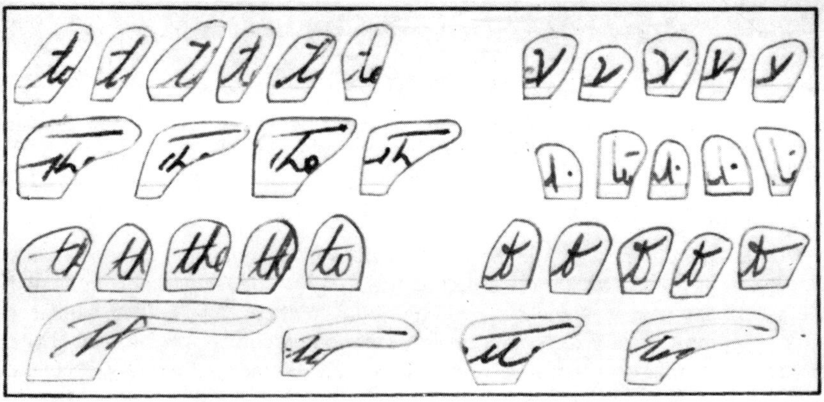

Fig. 9–18. This illustrates the extreme variation found in the size and position of the " t " crossing (bar), which can vary in length from a tiny stroke approximating to a dot to a long stroke. The position can vary from the extreme top of the staff to somewhere near the bottom of the letter. The stroke may be almost entirely to the left of the staff, through the staff or well to the right. Another variant often found in the terminal " t " is the bar being made continuous with the final up-stroke.

letters which differ from the " Civil Service " formations in that they are never terminated with relatively long upward strokes. When a connected hand is eventually acquired by those who were originally script writers, the influence of the original teaching will almost certainly be apparent in the omission of these upward terminal strokes to the terminal letters of the words.

Unlike initial strokes, terminal strokes are important for the characterisation of a handwriting, because their relative proportions tend to remain constant. If a writer is known to be in the habit of applying long terminal strokes to his letters, he is unlikely to be the writer of specimens of handwriting which exhibit markedly short strokes in these positions.

The slope of the terminal strokes may have some significance as an identifying feature of a handwriting, for not all slope upward as prescribed by the copybook; some are practically horizontal, whilst in rare cases the terminals may extend below the line of writing.

Another stroke which exhibits considerable variation in length is the " t " crossing, or " bar " as it is more correctly termed. The length of this stroke will often vary appreciably in different specimens of the writing of the same person, because it is one of the few handwriting characteristics which suffer appreciable modification with change of speed; increase of speed will generally result in the lengthening of the bar.

Relative Sizes of Letters in Block Lettering

The relative size of the letters is usually an important feature of a specimen of block lettering, for even when care is taken to reproduce the exact copybook forms of the letters, few writers are able to maintain a constant size for the different formations. The usual departure from constancy of size is where the writer follows

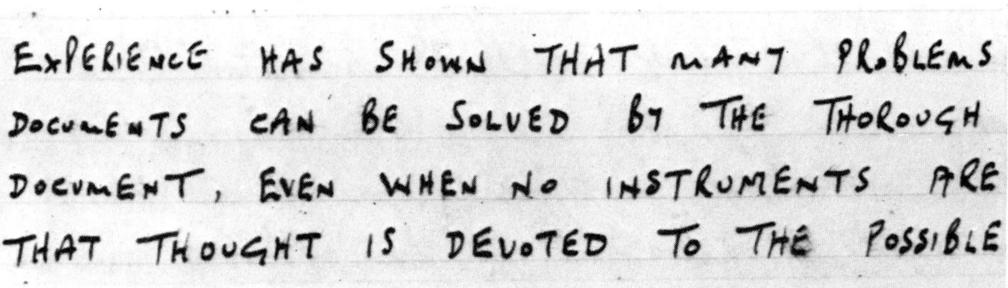

Fig. 9–19. Example of block lettering showing the variation in the height of the letters. Throughout the specimen the " O," " U," " N " and " M " are short, whereas the " T," " R," " B " and " P " are tall.

the practice of cursive handwriting, and makes the initial letters of proper names and of words which begin a sentence appreciably taller than the others. In some specimens of block lettering, the initial letter of every word will be appreciably taller than those which follow it.

Even in the medial position, some letters are written appreciably taller than the others. The most usual example of this is the " C," which in many specimens of block lettering appears most outstanding because of its size. The " T " is often written appreciably taller than the other letters, the reason probably being to enable the upper horizontal stroke to clear the letters which flank it in the word.

For some reason which is obscure, both the " O " and " I " are frequently made appreciably smaller than the other letters. This is so common that the existence of both " O " and " I " of the correct size in a block lettering is a characteristic of some considerable evidential value so rarely does this occur.

In many specimens of block lettering the " I " is given an unnecessary diacritic.

With block lettering, even more than with cursive handwriting, the relative widths of the letters may prove important. It is rare to find a specimen of block lettering wherein at least a few of the letters do not take up far more space along the line than is prescribed by the copybook. Common offenders in this respect are the letters " E," " H," " F " and " T," where it is so easy to increase the relative width of the letter by lengthening the horizontal strokes.

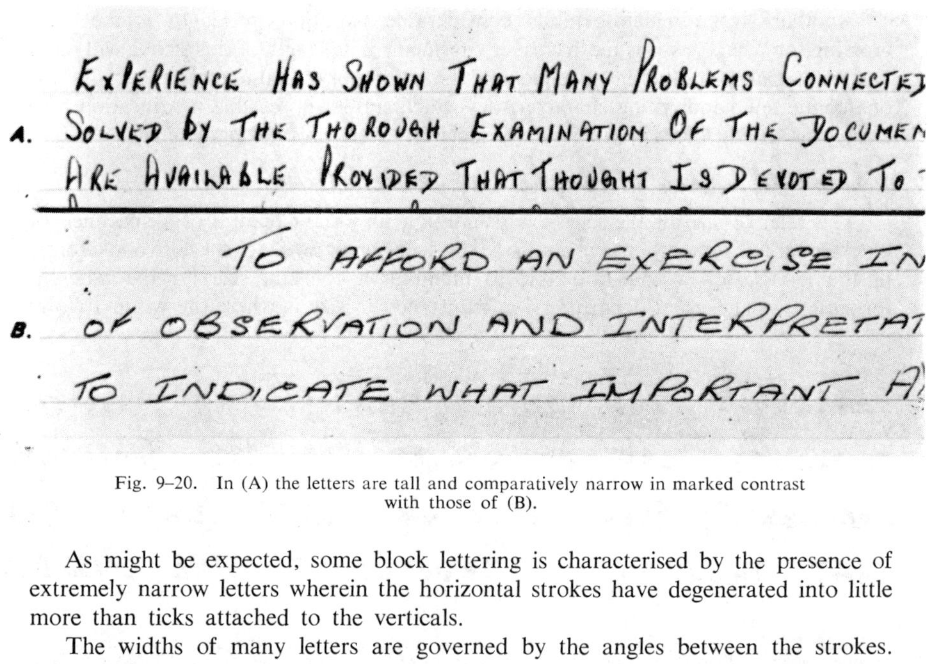

Fig. 9–20. In (A) the letters are tall and comparatively narrow in marked contrast with those of (B).

As might be expected, some block lettering is characterised by the presence of extremely narrow letters wherein the horizontal strokes have degenerated into little more than ticks attached to the verticals.

The widths of many letters are governed by the angles between the strokes. Where the block lettering is characterised by the use of acute angles, the relative widths of letters such as " X," " Y," " M," etc., are reduced and vice versa. It is noteworthy that the angle values remain fairly constant, even when an effort is made to disguise the block lettering by the introduction of modified letter designs.

Connecting Strokes

As long as writing was restricted to the chiselling of inscriptions on stone, there was no justification for the use of connecting strokes between the letters. In later ages, when modifications of the same letters had to be rapidly applied to paper with a pen, with many of the straight lines transformed to the more easily written cursive, the scribes found that writing could be made both quicker and easier if the pen had not to be lifted away from the paper after the tracing of each individual letter. The pen could be allowed to remain on the paper, provided the presence of connecting strokes was tolerated. As connecting strokes have little effect on legibility, there could be no real objection to their inclusion in the writing, so that what was originally a device on the part of the scribe to ease his task has become an integral and, to the document examiner, a most interesting feature of the modern cursive hand.

As might be expected, there are always those who can be trusted to deplore any modification of ancient practice, however well justified it may be, so that it is not surprising that from time to time attempts are made to " purify " handwriting by the elimination of these modern interlopers—the connecting strokes.

Fig. 9–21. Development of handwriting from Roman block capitals.

The first successful effort in this direction was the practice, originating in England in the early years of the twentieth century, of teaching beginners to write disconnected letters in a fashion reminiscent of Tudor handwriting. More recently there has been founded a society for the encouragement of the writing of another largely disconnected hand which reaches even further back into the past. This is an Italian hand of the 13th-14th century; well executed this beautiful script has an artistic appearance which is unequalled by any modern style of writing, but it is relatively slow to write and comparatively easy to forge.

In contemporary " Civil Service " writing, the connecting strokes are curved (unlike the straight angular connecting strokes of the American " Business " hands) as well as being relatively lengthy because of the abnormal separation of the letters in the word. This is perhaps the most noticeable feature of contemporary English handwriting, and it is this which serves to distinguish it from the older " Round Hand " from which it has been derived.

If the connecting strokes are written strictly according to the copybook, a considerable amount of retracing will be entailed. When writing at speed, abrupt changes of direction are resisted by the pen point, so that the most abrupt of all, the retrace, is subject to considerable modification wherever this is possible. A good example is found in the speedy writing of the medial " o." The two complete reversals of direction prescribed by the copybook are a hindrance to the attainment of speed, so that some writers reverse the direction of writing and convert the letter into a clock-wise written loop.

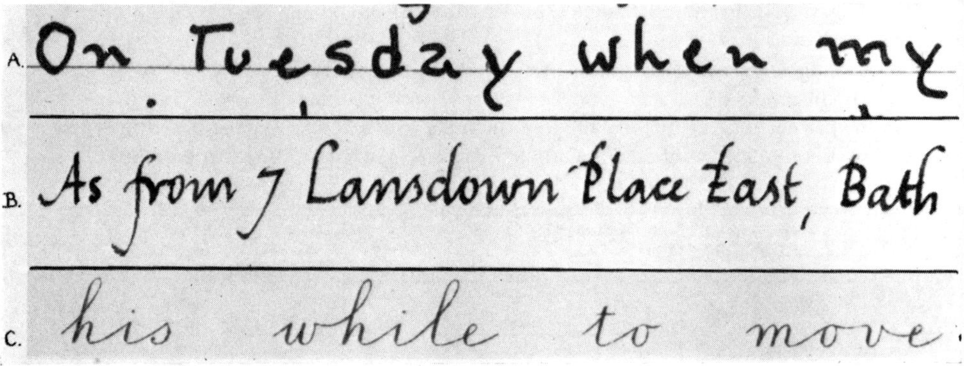

Fig. 9–22. (a) Disconnective script writing similar to English Tudor handwriting. (b) Modern hand based on italic handwriting of the thirteenth century. (c) Contemporary " semi-upright " or " Civil-Service " handwriting.

Another less radical change is the substitution of the retraces by eyelets, which sometimes approach the main oval in size, so that the letter has but a remote resemblance to the copybook form.

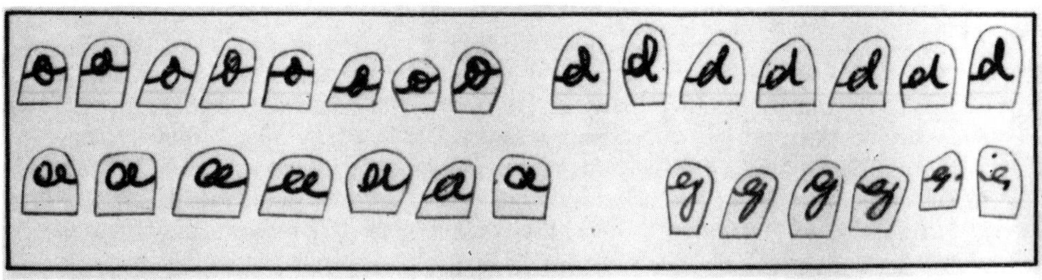

Fig. 9–23. This illustrates the use of eyelets rather than retraces in certain of the letters, notably the " a " and " g." The use of an exaggerated eyelet has reduced legibility in that the " a " may be mistaken for " ee " or " ei " and the " g " for " ej."

A similar replacement of retraces by eyelets can be found in other letters, such as " s," " d," " g," etc.

It may well be that the hesitation to form a retrace is at the bottom of the common habit of lifting the pen and starting anew, whenever a letter such as " c," " d," " g," etc., is encountered; a practice which accounts for the presence of many hiatuses in what are mainly conventional connected cursive hands, which have not been derived from an earlier practice of writing " script."

Whilst those who were originally taught to write a connected hand know the conventional methods for the formation of the connecting strokes, the unfortunate child who learns disconnected " script " often has little idea how these strokes should be made when, like the scribes of old, he finds that he must keep his pen on the paper if he wishes to write at speed. Many erstwhile " script " writers in this predicament experiment until they have derived a scheme of connection which suits their purpose, which is why the connected handwriting of those originally taught script will almost invariably exhibit many personal characteristics in the formation of these strokes. In this conversion of a script hand to connected writing some of the difficulties are side-stepped by dropping the script forms of letters such as " a," " s," etc., which are the most difficult to fit into the new style, but many of the letters, especially " p," " r," " t " and " b " are retained in their original form.

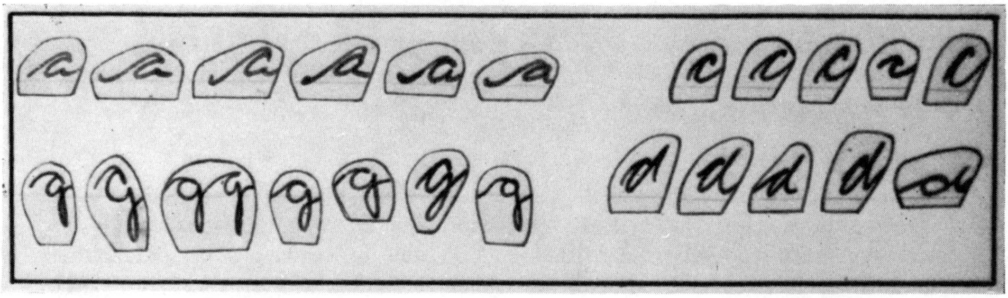

Fig. 9–24. The connections to the " a," " c," " g " and " d " tend to be written over the tops of the ovals. This is an excellent example of internal consistency in handwriting.

In view of the difficulty in the forming of connections, many connected hands produced by the modification of script will exhibit a high proportion of pen-lifts and gaps in the words. Some of these hands present a most unconventional appearance in that the connections to letters such as " r," " t," etc., take the form of horizontal lines which abruptly join on to these letters near to the base line of the writing. Connections of this type may be seen in Figure 9–6 in the lower specimen of handwriting.

Most writers have fixed habits with respect to the nature and placement of their connecting strokes, which means that these strokes, especially when they diverge widely from copybook forms, are of considerable value for the characterisation of handwriting. As this is so, it is fortunate that a wide range of variation will be found for the length, curvature and placement of the connecting strokes in contemporary handwriting. The length of these strokes is governed by the letter spacing, but the placement, which varies from horizontal lines joining the bottoms of the letters to strokes which are written separately over the tops of the letters (see Figure 9–24 for an extreme example of this tendency), is dependent only on the whim of the writer.

Whenever there is reason to suspect that a handwriting is a copy, the connecting strokes will amply repay close investigation. Almost invariably it will be found that whilst the copyist may have succeeded in reproducing the more obvious features of letter design, little care has been taken to introduce connecting strokes which will pass muster. One of the greatest difficulties experienced in dealing with the authorship of writings employing disconnected letters stems from the fact that such handwritings are devoid of connecting strokes.

Connected Words

Whilst the copybook permits the whole of a word, however lengthy, to be written in a single stroke, there is no sanction for the joining of words, however short, by any form of connecting stroke. This practice is sometimes found in contemporary handwriting, even when of good quality and not written in undue haste. Figure 9–3 illustrates a handwriting in which some of the words are connected, but whose most surprising feature is a frequent lapse in the connection of the letters in the word. There appears to be no reasonable explanation for the presence of these two features in the one handwriting.

It is curious how those who connect their words seem unable to discard this tendency, even when they are writing slowly and carefully. This feature can sometimes be found remaining in handwritings which have otherwise been most carefully disguised.

Pen-lifts and Hiatuses

The connected hand prescribed by the copybook admits of no gaps (hiatuses) in the words, a rule, like many others, more honoured in the breach than the observance. Consequently, the existence of hiatuses in words is a personal rather than a style characteristic and, being an obvious feature, is regarded by the inexperienced as more significant than its importance as an identifying feature merits.

Those who attach an undue importance to the presence of a hiatus in a handwriting are unaware that the writing habits of most people regarding the inclusion of hiatuses in their handwriting are by no means fixed; even the speed of a writing may have a pronounced effect on the number and the position of hiatuses. It is by no means uncommon to find a slowly written specimen of a particular handwriting liberally garnished with gaps in the words, whilst another written shortly afterwards is practically devoid of pen-lifts much less hiatuses.

Even where it can be shown that a handwriting is invariably characterised by the presence of a hiatus, the evidential value of this will depend largely on the letters between which the gap occurs. A hiatus before letters such as "c," "d," "g" or "o" is by no means uncommon, and many writers habitually leave a gap after "s"; even the "p" may habitually be followed by a complete break in the writing when this letter is written with a closed loop after the fashion of the "script" form of this letter. In all these examples, the reason for leaving a hiatus is the reluctance on the part of the writer to form the very full retraces which would be necessary if the words were to be written in a fully connected form.

On the other hand, a hiatus before such letters as "i," "e" and "v" is of less frequent occurrence, so that when truly characteristic of the handwriting, is a feature of some evidential value.

A hiatus occurring after "w" is an identifying feature of some value, for in the conventional form, this letter is furnished with a terminal spur which forms an ideal connection especially to such letters as " e," " b," " l," etc., where the loop of the succeeding letter can be written as a natural extension of the spur. A writer who fails to take advantage of this convenient mode of letter connection is rare, hence the considerable evidential value of a hiatus in this position.

The " v " is interesting in this respect; written according to the copybook, it will be furnished with a spur similar to that of the " w," which will prove equally advantageous for connection to the succeeding letter. On occasion, a variant will be found in which this letter terminates, not in a spur, but in an upward extension of the right-hand stroke of the trough. With such a variant, there can be no connection to the following letter whatever form it may take, so that a hiatus will appear in the writing.

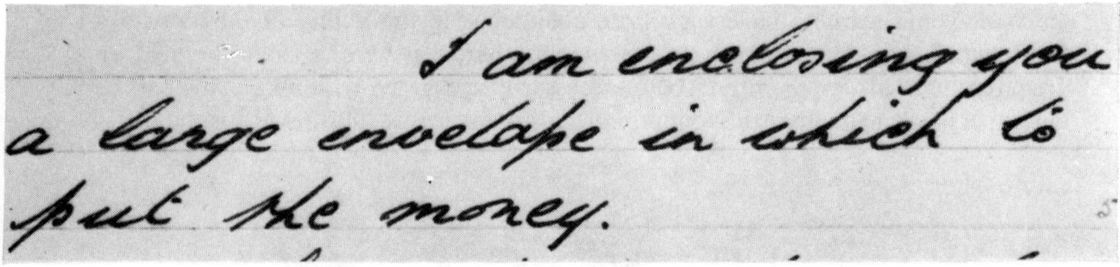
I am enclosing you
a large envelope in which to
put the money.

Fig. 9–25. Extract from a blackmailing letter illustrating connective, cursive handwriting characterised by the many hiatuses.

Where a word incorporates a capital letter, in certain instances, even the copybook will allow of a hiatus between it and the next letter. Not all capitals are treated in this manner, for an appreciable proportion may be joined quite satisfactorily to the next letter. Where the very common practice of using a block letter in the place of the cursive capital is followed, a hiatus is almost invariably left in.

The habit of leaving numerous gaps in the word has its counterpart in those handwritings where the penmen have gone to extraordinary lengths to ensure that every word is written as a connected whole. On occasion, a handwriting will exhibit the curious spectacle of the spur of the " W " being looped downward, practically to the line, in an effort to connect with a letter such as " e " or " i "; even block capitals, whose design lends little encouragement for the insertion of connecting strokes, are sometimes found joined in the most ingenious ways. These are features which give individuality if little else to a handwriting; they are noted with satisfaction by the document examiner.

In considering a hiatus as a handwriting characteristic, its width as well as its position in the handwriting has to be taken into account. This will be found to vary in different handwritings from a narrow gap which is barely perceptible to a space equal to, or slightly greater than, the average width of a letter. It is noteworthy that most writers closely adhere to a fixed width for the hiatus, which is rarely altered, even when some care has been taken to disguise both slope and letter design.

The spacing of the initial capital letter of the signature is often of the greatest significance, especially when the scrawled signatures of semi-illiterate people on printed forms are in question, for this is one of the few features in which such persons exhibit consistent writing habits. A wide range of variation is encountered, for whilst many writers cramp the remainder of the signature hard up against the capital letter, others go to the other extreme and invariably leave a space into which two or more letters could be written.

Pen-Lifts

The hiatus may be regarded as a special form of pen-lift, distinguishable in that a perceptible gap appears in the writing. The pen may be lifted during the writing of a word for a multitude of reasons; it is rarely for the purpose of recharging the nib with ink, because pen-lifts are nearly as common in writing made with a ball-point or fountain pen as with the simple dip pen.

It is probable that the habit of introducing unnecessary pen-lifts is acquired early in life. Some learners have such little confidence in the ability of their pen-nib to hold sufficient ink for more than a few letters that their writing has to be held up at frequent intervals for the nib to be unnecessarily recharged with ink. This bad habit often persists when either the fountain or ball-point pen is substituted for the dip pen.

Fig. 9–26. *Pen-lifts.* An example of a signature which is characterised by an abnormal number of pen-lifts.

Pen-lifts in general are of little use for the characterisation of a handwriting, for their frequency and positioning is often largely governed by the conditions in which it is written. With the writer carefully considering what is being slowly and carefully written, the pen may be lifted at frequent intervals, but with the same person writing at speed, pen-lifts, except those at the ends of words, may be completely absent from the script.

The foregoing rule applies to writing in general, but for the very specialised handwriting, the signature, many persons have fixed habits with respect to the occurrence of pen-lifts.

The subject of pen-lifts in signatures is treated in some detail in the chapter which deals with forged signatures, so that it will suffice to mention here that, as might be expected, a forged signature will often contain more pen-lifts than the genuine because, as signatures are generally forged a letter at a time, the forger tends to lift the pen as he takes stock at the conclusion of each copied fragment of the signature.

Whilst a hiatus is obvious on mere inspection, the presence of a pen-lift can often be established only on microscopic examination of the ink line. Whilst it is difficult to lift a pen from the paper and start again without leaving some trace when ordinary fluid ink is used, it is not always possible to demonstrate the presence of a pen-lift in either a ball-point pen or pencil writing, provided great care has been taken to ensure that the new line merges with the old. Another difficulty is often encountered when a ball-point pen has been used. When these pens are not in good working order the flow of ink to the rotating ball will be uneven, so that the line is characterised by a multitude of hiatuses which might be misinterpreted as pen-lifts when in reality the pen had never left the paper.

In some instances where this has occurred, it is possible to show that the irregular line is associated with a continuous impression made by the passage of the ball-point, even where it has ceased to transfer ink to the paper.

Hesitations

A hesitation is the term applied to the irregular thickening which is formed when the writing slows down or stops whilst the penman takes stock of the position. Hesitations are found, not only in forgeries, but in the handwriting of the illiterate. In a forgery, they are found, not only at the ends of strokes, where they leave the line with a club-shaped instead of the tapered appearance found when the pen travels fairly fast as it comes on to or leaves the paper, but also in the middle of curves. With the writing of the illiterate, the clubbed ends to the lines are a common feature, but the thickened curves are comparatively rare. (See Figure 9–41 for excellent examples of the clubbed ends of the downstrokes of the " d "s.)

When a ball-point pen or a pencil is used, it is difficult if not impossible to detect the places where the writing point has paused in its motion.

Pen-lifts in Detached-letter Scripts

In any style of handwriting based upon detached letters, pen-lifts have their importance only when an individual letter is constructed of separate strokes, because the pen is almost invariably lifted between letters.

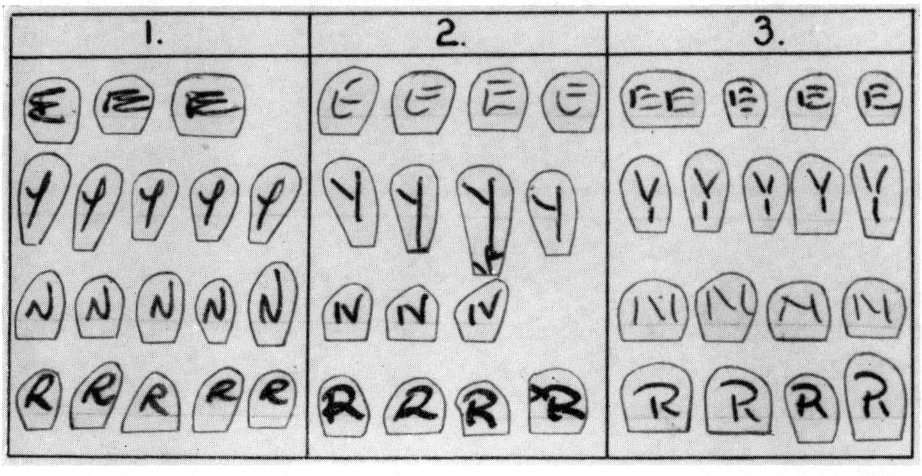

Fig. 9–27. In " 1 " all four block letters are written with a single stroke. In " 2 " a more normal practice is followed in that the letters are made with two or more strokes. " 3 " illustrates an uncommon style of block lettering in that all the letters are made with separate strokes

Many block-letter formations can conveniently be constructed without either pen-lifts or retraces, but some, notably " E," " Y," " H " and " X," are difficult to write in one continuous stroke. Writing habits vary, and block lettering may to some extent be characterised by the frequency and positioning of the pen-lifts. Some writers make all their block letters from separate strokes—even such simple structures as " V," " N " and " O " which could well be formed with a single continuous stroke. Others prefer to take liberties with the design of the letter to avoid lifting the pen. The " E," which can conveniently be constructed from a choice of two, three or four separate strokes, is made of a single continuous stroke by writing the central horizontal stroke as an exceedingly narrow " V." Retracing, sometimes so crude that a distinct double line is left, is also found in a small proportion of hands, especially when such letters as " Y," " A," " G " and " H " are formed with a single continuous stroke.

SPACING

Letter Spacing in Detached-letter Scripts

The copybook prescribes that the individual letters in a connected cursive hand shall be fairly equally spaced along the line. It is instructive to note that when block letters carefully outlined by a skilful writer seem to be equally spaced, this appearance of even spacing is an illusion, for letters placed at exact intervals would

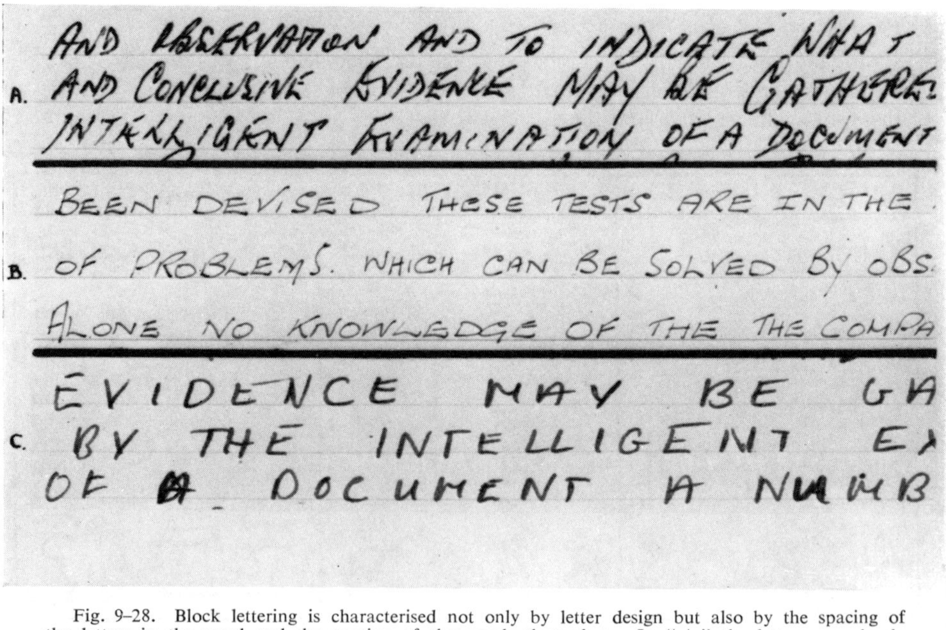

Fig. 9–28. Block lettering is characterised not only by letter design but also by the spacing of the letters in the word and the spacing of the words themselves. In " A " the letters are closely spaced in the word but the word spacing is normal. In " B " the letters are well spaced with word spacing normal. In " C " the letters are widely spaced whereas word spacing is only slightly greater than that which is normally found.

appear to be anything but evenly spaced. When block lettering, especially that used for disguise, is examined, it will be found that few examples exhibit even spacing, but this unevenness is more the consequence of carelessness and lack of skill than any calculated departure from equal spacing.

Experience shows that the most marked unevenness in spacing is generally associated with particular letter groupings; it is common to find the letter-pair " OU " very closely spaced, whilst the three letter group " ING " will often be comparatively widely spaced when it occurs as a terminal group. Many other examples could be quoted, and it is fair to state that an appreciable proportion of hands may be characterised by the abnormal spacing of certain letter groups.

The general spacing of the letters will be found to exhibit a considerable range of variation. For a given height of letter, some writers will put twice as many letters into a given space as others; the evidential value of an extreme fashion of spacing is considerable because it is a relatively strongly fixed characteristic.

Letter Spacing in Connected Cursive Hands

Fundamentally, letter spacing is a style characteristic; the comparatively wide spacing of the letters in the handwriting of the average Englishman today is derived from the copybook from which he learned to write. In spite of the influence of the initial teaching, handwritings are encountered wherein the letter spacing, already considerable, has been further increased so that it is over double that which is normal to the style. In marked contrast, other handwritings are so cramped that at first sight, the words appear as solid blocks of intertwined ink lines. Where these extremes occur, the letter spacing may safely be regarded as personal characteristics of some value, as the writers retain their abnormal spacing habits even when care is taken to disguise other features of the handwriting.

As with block lettering, unevenness of spacing will be discovered with particular letter groups. These latter are important when a handwriting is copied, for whilst the forger will pay attention to the details of letter design and the general spacing, he will rarely observe and include in the forgery the abnormal groupings which are also characteristic of the handwriting.

It is where forged signatures are concerned that the relative spacing of the letters is often of paramount importance, so this subject is treated in some detail in the chapter which treats of forgeries.

Spacing of Initials and of Titles such as Mr., Mrs., Dr., etc.

The spacing of initials and titles exhibits a wide variation, ranging from a gap equal to the width of two or more letters to virtually connected writing. The

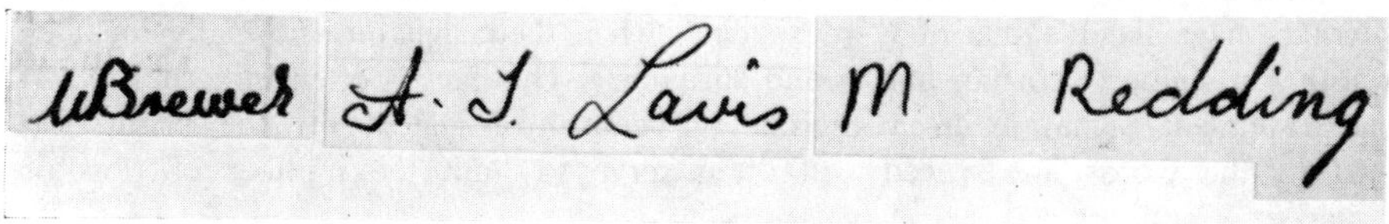

Fig. 9–29. Examples of variation of the spacing of the initials associated with a signature.

evidential value of extreme variants is considerable, more especially as habits remain fixed over many years; even where the handwriting has been disguised, it is rare to find that any alteration has been made in this respect.

Word Spacing

One of the difficulties experienced in reading ancient manuscripts written in disconnected script is that little if any extra space is left between the words; in some contemporary handwritings, the pendulum has swung so far the other way that little over half the space along the line is occupied by the writing. Today, the space which is left between the words varies from something greater than the width of four or five letters to practically nothing.

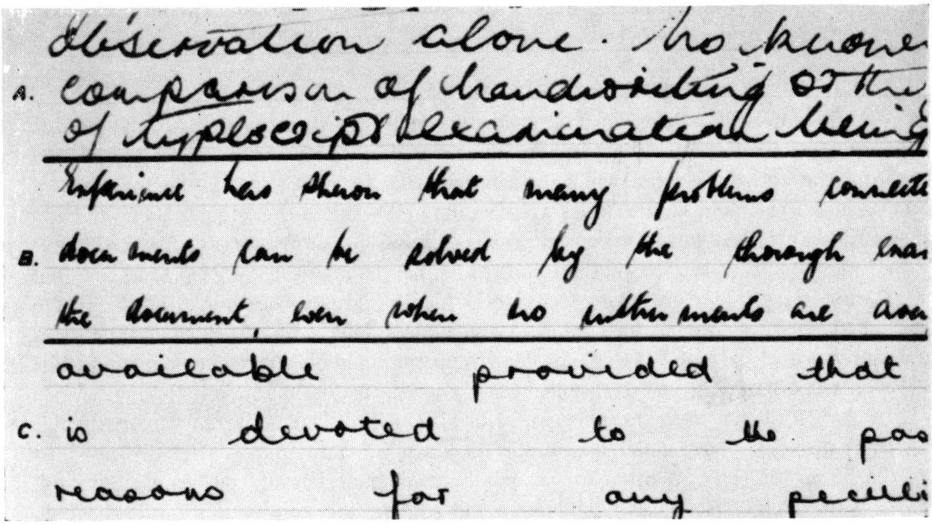

Fig. 9–30. *Word spacing*. In " A " the word spacing has been reduced to a minimum although the spacing of the letters in the word is normal. In " B " the letters are closely spaced but the words are comparatively widely spaced. In " C " both the letters and the words are abnormally widely spaced.

Word spacing is often a valuable identifying feature of a handwriting, for it tends to remain constant even when the handwriting is disguised or has to be written in a limited space; some writers prefer to reduce the size of their writing to near-illegibility rather than depart from the usual word-spacing habit. Many writers have fixed habits of word spacing, when their signature normally includes both fore-name (Christian name) and surname. This fact is often important when a fraudulent signature in a register is being investigated, for the manner in which the words are spaced will often serve to limit the number of possible suspects.

As with other spacing, distances should always be expressed in " letter-widths," rather than as so many millimetres or fractions of an inch. This precaution will take care of the reduction in the actual dimensions of the spaces when the overall size of the writing is reduced.

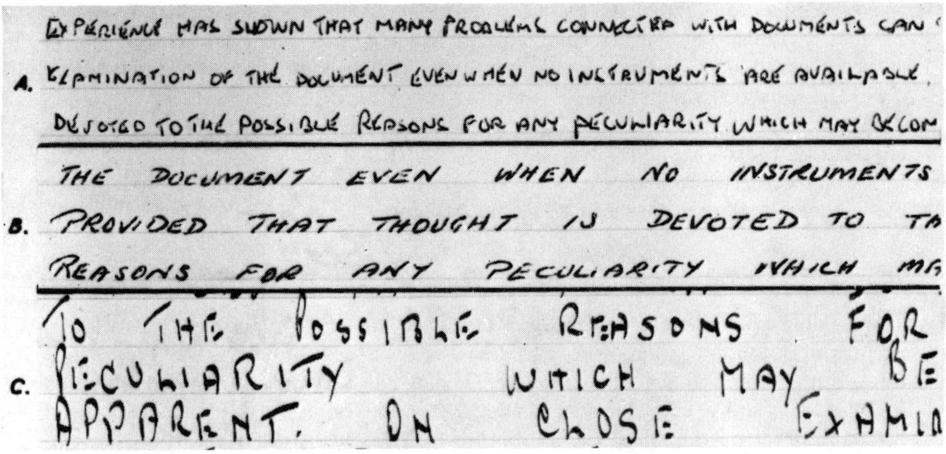

Fig. 9–31. *Spacing of letters and words.* In " A " not only are the letters written very closely together, but the words themselves are separated by extremely narrow gaps. In " B " both the letter and word spacing is normal. In " C " the letters are widely spaced and the words themselves have abnormally wide spacing corresponding to the width of 3–4 letters.

Slope of Handwriting

A regular slope, or as it is termed by some writers, slant, is an essential feature of a pleasing handwriting. The acquisition of a reasonably constant slope by the learner has already been referred to; during adolescence, the slope will be subject to modification, but once fixed in adult life will remain substantially unaltered.

In contemporary handwriting, slope will be found to vary through a range of about fifty degrees, from a pronounced forward slope, appreciably greater than that prescribed by the copybook, to a back slope of perhaps ten degrees beyond the vertical.

In a former generation, when the possession of a legible hand was not only a matter of pride but also of some economic importance, the great majority of educated people wrote with a constant well-defined slope. As experiments have shown that it is virtually impossible for the average penman to write fluently in a slope which is consistently slightly different from that which is normal to him, it is not surprising that the past generation of writers on the identification of handwriting attach considerable importance to slope and its measurement, for this was rightly regarded as an identifying feature of some value.

In his *Questioned Documents*, written nearly half a century ago, A. S. Osborn deals with this aspect of handwriting, particularly with its measurement, at some length. His treatment is not only exhaustive but is also very sound, so that anyone interested cannot do better than to consult this famous book.

Today, with the general marked decline in the quality of handwriting, handwritings which exhibit a slope which is sufficiently marked and constant to justify its being considered an identifying feature are in a small minority. The greater part of the handwriting received for examination at an official document laboratory is so irregular in slope that any measurements would be meaningless. Even the modern goniometers, which have superseded the engraved glass scales of an earlier generation of document examiners, are useless in the face of a handwriting devoid of any consistent slope.

Whilst the measurement of slope has lost its former significance in the characterisation of a handwriting, it is still important when disguised handwriting is the subject of examination, so for this reason a fuller treatment is included in the chapter dealing with disguise in handwriting.

Shading

The flexible split nib enables the width of the line to be controlled by variation in pressure; this variation in line width is known as shading. (See Figure 6–2 for examples of well-shaded writing.) The " Civil Service " style of handwriting is characterised by fairly heavily shaded downstrokes, formed by the pen being held at right angles to the line, as the downstrokes are written with an excess of pressure. As might be expected, considerable variation exists with respect to both the extent and the positioning of the shading; some hold the pen in a manner which is quite different from that taught to the beginner and produce handwriting in which the horizontal rather than the vertical strokes are thickened.

As the extent and the position of the shading is dependent upon the manner in which the writer manipulates the pen, shading may be used to characterise a handwriting.

What is of even greater importance is that any worthwhile imitation of a well-shaded handwriting must be written with the pen held and manipulated in a manner similar to that adopted by the original writer, which may not be that best suited to the forger. The consequences of this are treated in some detail in the chapter on forged signatures.

Many styles of handwriting, among them the modern American " Business " hand, employ little if any shading, and with the wide adoption of the ball-point pen with which the width of the line is practically unaffected by alteration in pen pressure, well-shaded handwriting is becoming increasingly rare. This is to be regretted, for with the virtual elimination of shading, a valuable characteristic which has served to individualise handwriting and make the task of the forger more difficult will have departed.

Line Quality

In any discussion of forged signatures, the expression " line quality " is certain to appear. Whilst this term is difficult to define, its meaning may be made clear by considering how a handwriting which can be said to exhibit good line quality, differs from that of poor line quality. If the natural handwriting of a skilled penman is examined, it will be found that practically all the curved strokes are smoothly written; they exhibit few, if any, abrupt changes in curvature, except where these are called for in the design of the letter. Again, whilst the width of the ink line may vary, a feature which distinguishes shaded from unshaded writing, these variations are smooth and continuous; the actual line will rarely exhibit " lumpiness." A stroke may start as an extremely thin line which gradually widens and deepens in tint before once again becoming thin and pale, but this alteration is continuous, with no abrupt change in width or depth of impression that is unrelated to the design of the letter.

Such a handwriting is described as being a good line quality, and is usually produced when the writer is concentrating his attention on what he is writing rather than on how the pen-point is moving. To produce handwriting of good line quality, the pen must be controlled by what are largely reflex movements of the muscles of the hand and arm.

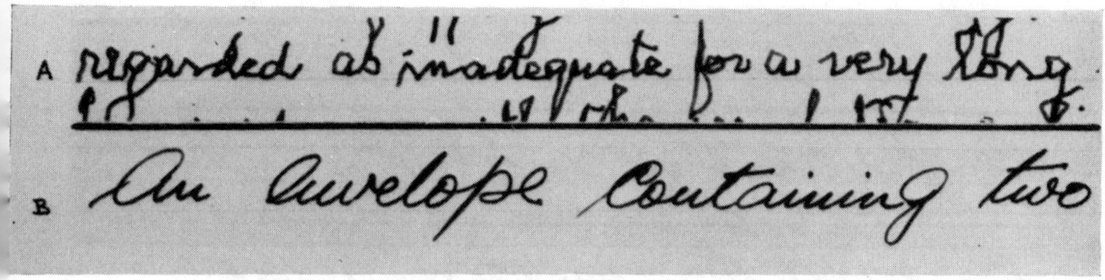

Fig. 9–32. " A " is an excellent example of handwriting of bad line quality. " B " is an example of handwriting of good line quality.

The unpractised, unskilful writer has to concentrate his attention on the movement of his pen point, with the result that reflex movements of the hand and arm muscles are ruled out, the pen being controlled largely by the fingers. Writing accomplished in such a manner will consist of strokes where both the pen pressure and direction of movement are anything but smooth and continuous. The writing will lack fluency, and the line will be both irregular and " lumpy." A writing which is characterised by this irregularity of line, haphazard change of curvature, and lack of a smooth transition from stroke to stroke is said to exhibit poor line quality.

Influence of the Writing Instrument

The question as to what extent handwriting is influenced by the nature of the writing instrument is often asked, because it is sometimes impossible to obtain handwriting written with a similar writing instrument for comparison with that of anonymous letters or other suspect documents. It is obvious that the writing instrument must have an effect which extends beyond that of mere difference in appearance; a fine flexible pen can be used to produce handwriting characterised by a clear outline, marked shading and the reproduction of the finest details of letter design, no matter how small the scale on which it has been written. On the other hand, a blunt pencil will defeat the efforts of the most skilled to include either shading or fine detail in the construction of the letters. The limit is reached when a ball-point pen is used; this implement has all the faults of the blunt pencil together with others peculiar to itself.

As at present constructed it cannot be used to form well shaded writing, for the width of the trace is practically unaffected by the pressure which is applied; as the refill nears the end of its useful life, the line will be both uneven and broken in spite of the ball-point having been kept on the paper. A rotating ball is hardly the instrument of choice for the reproduction of the finer details of letter design, and to add to this failing, the ball-point adds curious abrupt circular thickenings to the line when swept around a narrow curve. (See Figure 7–8.)

With some ball-point inks, the dye diffuses into the paper to cause an appreciable thickening of the line with consequent loss of definition.

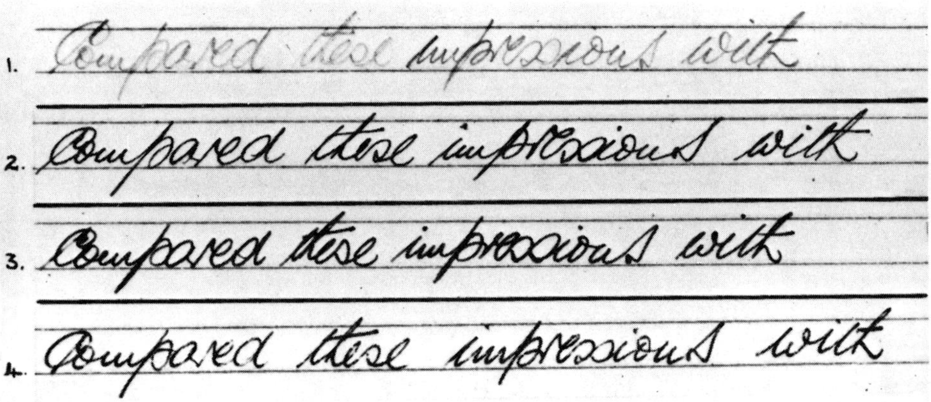

Fig. 9–33. *Influence of writing instrument*

Four lines of handwriting: (1) pencil; (2) ordinary dip pen; (3) fountain pen; (4) ball-point pen. It is apparent that the fundamental quality of the handwriting is unaffected by the nature of the writing instrument. The uneven line caused by the use of a defective ball-point pen is apparent in No. 4.

Fortunately for the document examiner, the brain which controls the hand remains the same, irrespective of the nature of the writing instrument. Therefore, the fundamental structure of the handwriting stays unaltered, and it is only the general appearance of the handwriting and the amount of detail which is present which is affected by the nature of the writing instrument. Provided that the specimens are sufficiently comprehensive for him to establish their structure, an experienced document examiner should be capable of making effective comparisons, irrespective of the writing instruments employed.

Contrary to general belief, it is often impossible to determine whether writing has been written with a fountain or a dip pen, so that comparison of handwriting written with a fountain pen with that made with a dip pen presents no difficulty from the point of view of the writing instrument. Writing made with a blunt pencil or a ball-point pen will be devoid of many of the finer details which can be seen when a pen has been used, but provided the examiner is familiar with ball-point pen writing, and is able to discount the presence of those features of the handwriting which stem from the use of a rotating ball, sufficient handwriting characteristics remain to enable an effective comparison to be made.

As is pointed out in some detail in the chapter on forged signatures, the use of the ball-point pen makes the detection of forgery much less certain, for here the finest details of handwriting structure are all-important.

Alignment

The term " line of writing " should be understood as the imaginary line to which the general trend of a handwriting conforms, so that it will be correct to speak of the " line of writing " even when the paper is unruled. When the " alignment " of a handwriting is being considered this term is not restricted to any one manifestation; the alignment of the words, the relative alignment of the letters in the word and even the relative alignment of parts of a letter have to be taken into consideration.

Relative Alignment of Parts of Letters

Where letters are concerned, the relative alignment of the simple structural forms which are combined to form the letter is strictly laid down by the copybook, but in spite of this, developed hands in which the rules are ignored are comparatively

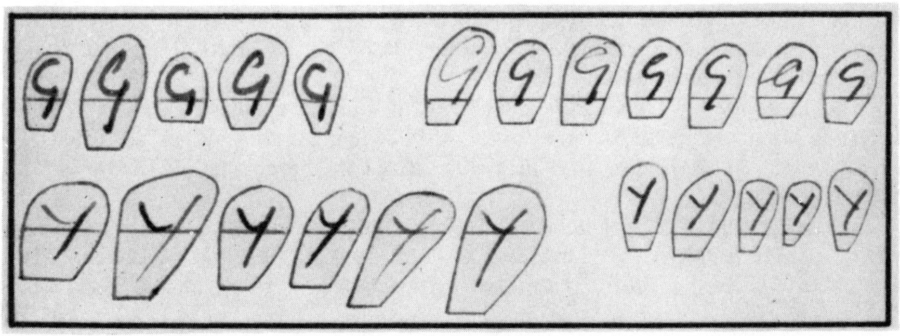

Fig. 9–34. Examples of different positioning of letters relative to the line.

common. In some hands, the lower loops of some of the letters, instead of projecting downward in practically a vertical direction, will be turned back so that they stretch nearly horizontally below the preceding letters, whilst in others, the trough of " y " will be suspended well above the line of writing. Figure 9–34 illustrates other comparatively common deviations from copybook alignment practice, all of which have considerable value for the characterisation of the handwriting in which they occur.

Relative Alignment of Letters in the Word

When letters, whether connected cursive or separate block capitals, are combined to form a word, convention controls their alignment with respect to each other and to the line of writing. In practice, even when ruled paper is used, it is rare for the alignment to approach perfection. Some handwritings are characterised by a general failing in this respect, but in others there will occur departures from accurate alignment associated only with certain letters or groups of letters.

The most common example of this occurs when terminal letters such as " s " and the Civil Service form of " r " are written well above the other letters in the word. Another instance, much less common, is where a terminal group such as " -tion " or " -ing " tends to sink well below the line of writing.

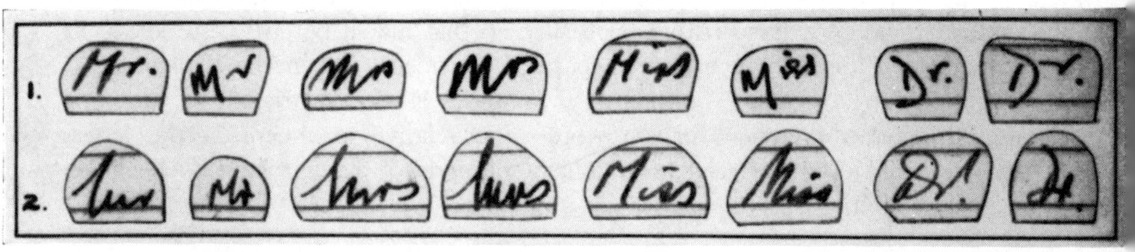

Fig. 9–35. Examples of the relative positioning of letters in abbreviations of titles.

The relative alignment of the letters in the word assumes the greatest significance when the word is a signature. Generally speaking, the signature is written in a more florid style than the remainder of the writing, and this is often associated with a greater degree of relative misalignment of the letters. In the majority of signatures, errors in the relative alignment of the letters persist and are often highly characteristic of the signature.

The necessity for copying the alignment as well as the designs of the various letters is often overlooked by the forger, so that many a forgery has been detected in this way. (This is discussed in greater detail in the chapter which deals with forged signatures.)

The alignment of the letters which follow the capital letter in abbreviations, such as " Mr.", " Mrs.", " Dr.", etc., is also capable of some variation. Most writers have a fixed form for these abbreviations which is rarely altered, even when the handwriting has been most painstakingly disguised; few seem to be aware of the fixity of their writing practice in this respect, which is probably why it is left unaltered.

Whilst, in general, the alignment of the words runs parallel with the line of writing, examples are sometimes found where the line of writing is horizontal, whilst that of the individual words is decidedly sloped. Generally the slope of the words in these rare specimens is downward, each word being begun well above the line of writing only to finish below it; still more rarely, the opposite tendency is seen. Such types of misalignment are personal characteristics of some value. Errors in alignment are not invariably an identifying feature of a handwriting, for sometimes, especially with rapid writing on unlined paper, the whole text will be found to have been split into groups of words which form arcs, with their concavity toward the bottom of the page. This type of misalignment cannot be considered a personal characteristic of the writing, for it is most frequently associated with a free arm motion in the act of handwriting, and would be absent in the writing of the same person made under conditions where arm movement is restricted.

Alignment of Writing as a Whole

It is not unusual to find that writing on unlined paper has a distinct slope. The general alignment of handwriting on unlined paper is considered to be of great significance by many graphologists. In the experience of the author, however, a pronounced slope to a handwriting, whether up or down, merely indicates that the

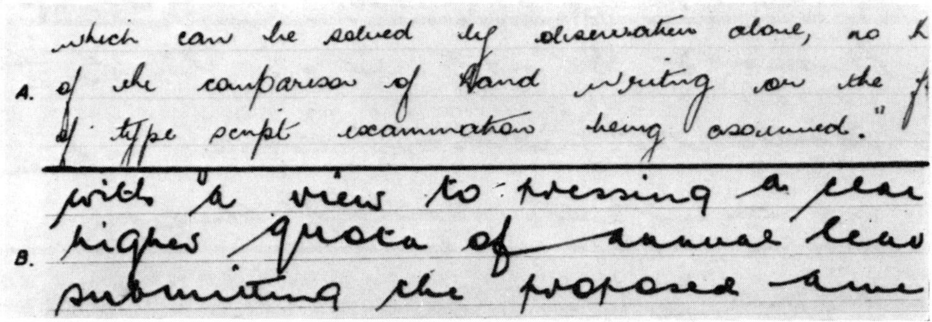

Fig. 9–36. *Word Alignment.* In specimen " A " each word is sloped upward compared with the general direction of the writing. This is probably caused by the position of the arm during the writing. In " B " the words tend to slope downward—this is a comparatively rare feature and is more likely to be a characteristic of the writing and independent of the arm position.

writer has had little experience in the use of unlined paper, for he has often observed how a little practice has made nearly perfect the alignment of a handwriting which originally exhibited a variety of faulty slopes sufficient to delight the heart of any graphologist who relies on such trivialities to justify his speculations.

When lined paper is used, only a minority write accurately upon the guide lines. The majority write just above the line, some write midway between the lines, whilst a small minority write through the line. The use of lined paper brings into prominence any errors in word alignment relative to the writing as a whole.

Irrespective of the conditions, even when writing has been thoroughly disguised, its alignment relative to any lines ruled on the paper stays constant, so that this alignment habit may be regarded as a relatively fixed characteristic of a handwriting; unfortunately, as there are only a few ways in which the writing can be aligned with respect to any rulings on the paper, this characteristic is of greater value for the *exclusion* of a certain percentage of possible writers than for the positive identification of the probable author.

Line Spacing

Writing should be spaced, provided the conditions permit, so that there will be no risk of the upper loops of the writing on one line clashing with the lower loops of the writing on the line above. Spacing habits vary widely. Some writers restrict the spaces between the lines to such an extent that the loops of one line intersect

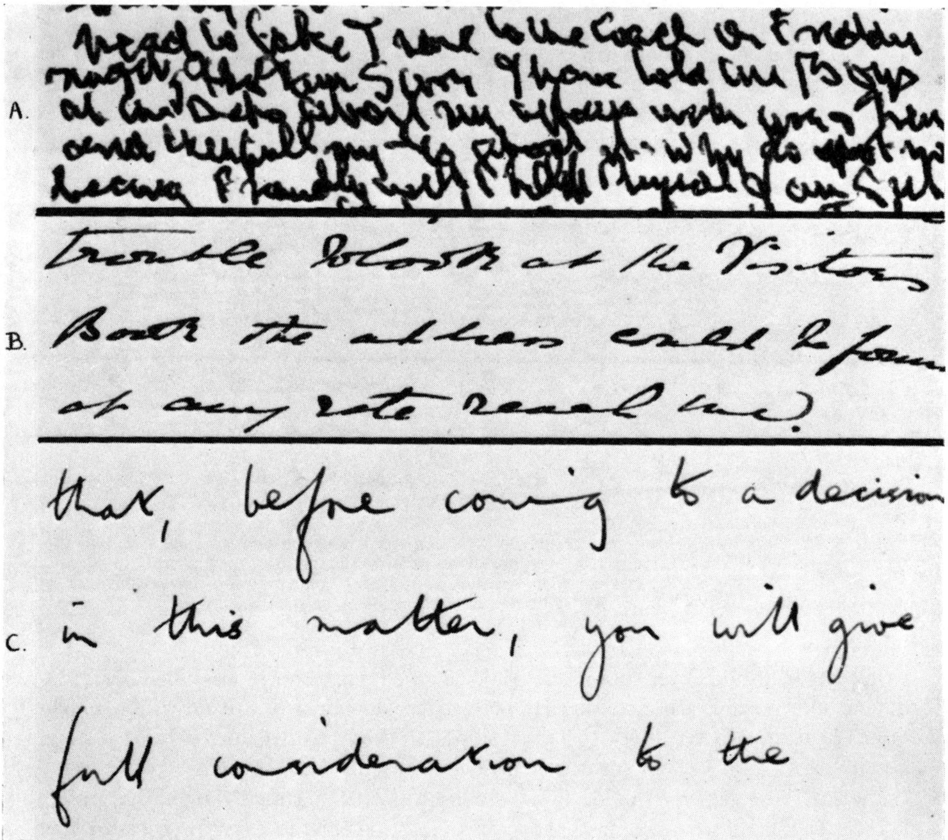

Fig. 9–37. Specimen " B " illustrates normal line spacing wherein the lower loops of writing of one line do not clash with the upper loops of the writing of the line below. In " C " the line spacing is abnormally wide. In " A " the line spacing is so close that the extended loops clash with the writing of the lines above and below. It will be seen that the word spacing in all three examples tends to follow the pattern of the line spacing.

the writing on that which is adjacent, whilst others leave spaces which are more than ample to avoid any possibility of overwriting.

When writing under what might be described as normal conditions, most people maintain a fairly constant line spacing, but when space is limited, they never hesitate to decrease this line spacing rather than decrease the relative spacing of the words along the line. This preference is probably exercised because word spacing, which is done after writing an average of about five letters, is practically a reflex action, whereas the commencement of a new line of writing, particularly when space is limited, is a more deliberate act and consequently more likely to be influenced by the circumstances in which the writing is made.

Arrangement of Handwriting on Envelopes

As the average envelope has more than sufficient area to accommodate the longest name and address, there is ample scope for variation in the manner in which the writing is arranged. As the addressing of an envelope is a comparatively common task, it is not surprising that, as the attention of the writer is devoted more to ensuring legibility than to the arrangement of the writing, most practised writers acquire a style of addressing envelopes from which they rarely depart.

This is fortunate for the investigator, for often it has been possible to select for further investigation a small group out of a large number of possible suspects, solely because of the arrangement of the often heavily disguised handwriting on the envelope of an anonymous letter.

Arrangement of Handwriting in General

If one carries out the experiment of dictating a letter of medium length to a group of average people provided with identical sheets of paper, there is certain to be considerable variation in the appearance of the dictated copies, in spite of the conditions having been the same for all.

In the first place, there is certain to be a marked divergence of opinion about the way in which the text should be divided into paragraphs. Some, probably a small minority, will correctly paragraph the dictated material, others will make no use of this device for rendering the information more readily intelligible, whilst the rest will divide it with little reference to the context. On further investigation, it will be found that the skill displayed in the paragraphing reflects the educational status of the writer and is unlikely to be equated with anything other than the punctuation and possibly the spelling; there is little likelihood of its being related to the artistic quality of the handwriting.

It will probably prove possible to correlate with the artistic quality of the handwriting the general arrangement of the writing on the sheet, the choice of margins, the degree to which the paragraphs are inset and the spacing of the words and the lines, for all these depend upon artistic skill which seems to be inborn and unrelated to educational status. It is more than likely that it is this general appearance of a handwriting which is utilised by the more successful graphologists, for when presented with a well-balanced script they may safely draw the conclusion that the writer is possessed of a certain measure of taste and artistic ability, qualities which are often associated with other personality traits.

When disguised handwriting is under investigation, it is always a safe deduction that the writer must be capable with his normal handwriting of producing an artistic result which is equal to, if not superior to, that displayed in the disguised script. This fact will often serve to limit the number of possible suspects when an anonymous writing displays a fair standard of artistic merit. This is especially so with the addressing of envelopes; anyone who habitually exhibits poor taste with respect to the arrangement of writing on an envelope is unlikely to be responsible for others displaying a fair standard of artistry in the way in which they have been addressed.

Marginal Habits

Whilst the actual width of a left-hand margin will often be influenced by the width of the sheet, those in the habit of leaving a relatively generous margin will continue to do so however narrow it may be. However, if the writer is not in the habit of leaving a well-defined margin, he will continue to write from the edge of the paper, even when little has to be written on a large sheet. On the other hand the practice of a writer with respect to the right-hand margin is generally of far greater evidential value, for here there is far more scope for variation.

Comparatively few writers leave such an ample margin on the right that they never face the necessity of dividing words between two lines; the majority write close up to this edge of the paper so that the problem of fitting in words has frequently to be faced. Habits differ: one writer will continue to the very edge of the paper, finishing the word on the next line so that its division is governed by the available space rather than its natural division into syllables, which would be the practice of a better educated writer; another will recoil from any splitting of the word and will reduce the size of his handwriting to accommodate it in the available space, or, more rarely, will abruptly slope the line of writing downward so as to gain enough extra space.

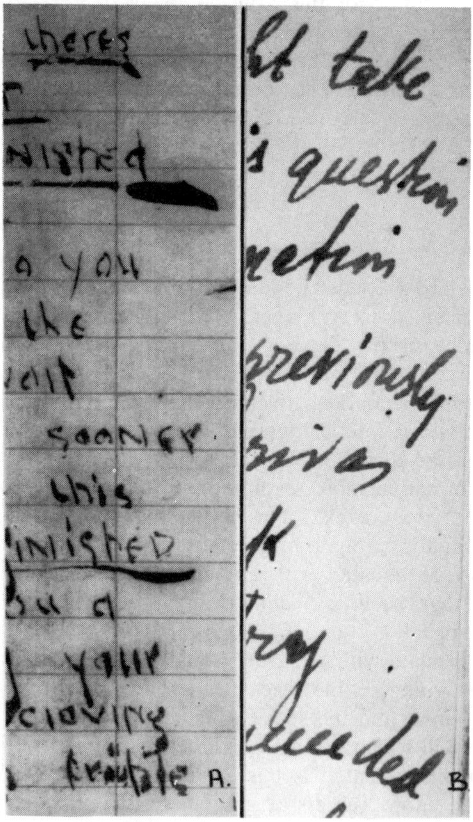

Fig. 9–38. *Marginal Habits.* A is an extract from a blackmailing letter in which the handwriting had been written across the crease so that it trespassed from page 2 on to page 3 of the letter. This was a common habit of the writer and assisted in his conviction. B is an example of all the final letters of a word being cramped and bent downwards at the edge of the sheets so as to avoid splitting the word.

The margins left at the top and, more particularly, at the bottom of the sheet are more variable in size and consistency than those at the sides; they are, to a great extent, governed by the amount of space available and are consequently less characteristic of the writer.

Folding Habits

Notepaper used for private correspondence is usually folded once to provide two pages with four sides for writing. The four pages may be written on in a number of different sequences, and it is worth noting that many writers have fixed habits in this respect. More than one series of anonymous letters has been traced to its source by the investigator noticing that the writer exhibited an uncommon practice with respect to folding or sequence of use of the pages.

Rhythm in Handwriting

Like good line quality, good rhythm in handwriting is more easily recognised than defined, for it is the regular rhythm of a handwriting which makes it acceptable as a pleasing hand which falls easily on the eye of the reader. One handwriting may be composed of letter designs which adhere closely to copybook standards to form a most legible script, and yet be regarded as inferior in appearance to another which is difficult to decipher, but which possesses the regular recurrence of stress and structural elements known as rhythm. Regularity in slope, size and curvature are the three essentials of rhythm in handwriting.

A handwriting rarely possesses good rhythm unless it has been written fluently and to an appreciable extent by reflex action. When some thought has to be exercised in the endeavour to produce a handwriting which differs in any material respect from that which is usual to the writer, there results an immediate loss of rhythm, for rhythm is even more influenced by the circumstances of the writing act than line quality. It follows from this that no handwriting which is disguised or copied can be expected to approach the standard of the rhythm shown by the normal hand; as this is so, a fluent, rhythmic script of good line quality is extremely unlikely to have been either forged or disguised.

Tremor

In a handwriting of poor line quality, straight lines are rarely free from deviations, and curves are neither smooth nor continuous in direction, and when this deterioration in line quality is carried to extremes so that deviations and discontinuities are frequent, the writing is described as exhibiting " tremor."

Tremor may arise in one of two ways. The first, and by far the most common, is where the handwriting has been formed in an unusual fashion, for example, in an effort to disguise the writing of the penman or to imitate that of another. This is tremor due to strain or, as it is more frequently termed, the " tremor of forgery." The other circumstance in which a tremulous writing is formed is when there is loss of muscular control of the pen. This type of tremor is found in the handwriting of those who have either inherited or acquired some physical disability: it is most often found in the handwriting of the sick and aged. As might be expected, the question of tremor looms large in any discussion of forgery, so that this aspect of handwriting is treated in some detail in the chapter which deals with forged signatures.

Punctuation Marks and Diacritics

Compared with some languages, English demands the use of few of the modifications to letter designs known generally as " diacritics," which are of some assistance in characterising a handwriting.

The simplest diacritic is the dot which, according to the copybook, should be placed over the main downstroke of the " i." It should consist of a small solid circular mark placed vertically over and near the downstroke, but in point of fact few dot the " i " in this position, and it is surprising how wide is the range of variation found in contemporary handwriting.

Fig. 9–39. Examples of variation in " i " dotting.

Some rarely, if ever, dot the " i," whilst with others the size of the dot varies from the microscopically tiny spot to large blackened areas whose presence gives the handwriting the appearance of having been splashed with ink-blots. Short strokes or commas may be used instead of dots, and these are also variable in size; they may be sloped in any direction from the horizontal to the vertical. On occasion, more complex forms such as wedges or hollow circles are encountered.

The diacritic is most commonly placed slightly to the right of the downstroke, but its position may vary from somewhere slightly to the left of the downstroke to a distance equal to the width of several letters to the right. The height is also variable, and in some cases search has to be made for the diacritic among the letters of the line above.

Whilst both the shape and the position of the diacritic is affected by the speed of writing, a handwriting may often be characterised by the nature and positioning of the " i " dot; incidentally, as this is such an inconspicuous feature, it is rarely altered in disguised handwriting.

The " t " crossing, or " bar," is best regarded as an integral part of the design of this letter, so for this reason there is little point in dealing with the range of variation presented by this feature of a handwriting.

Although strictly speaking they are neither diacritics nor punctuation marks, both the rubric and underlining included for emphasis may well be considered here.

Some of those who wish to emphasise their views underline words and phrases rather than reframe the sentence. Once they have acquired this insidious habit many find it difficult to write an extended passage which fails to include some underlining, even in an anonymous letter in which the handwriting has been carefully disguised.

The rubric may be regarded as a special form of underlining restricted to the signature. It may consist of a separate stroke or it may be generated from the downstroke of the final letter. In a genuine signature, the rubric is written with a flourish so that it displays quite a different appearance from that carefully and painstakingly drawn beneath a forgery.

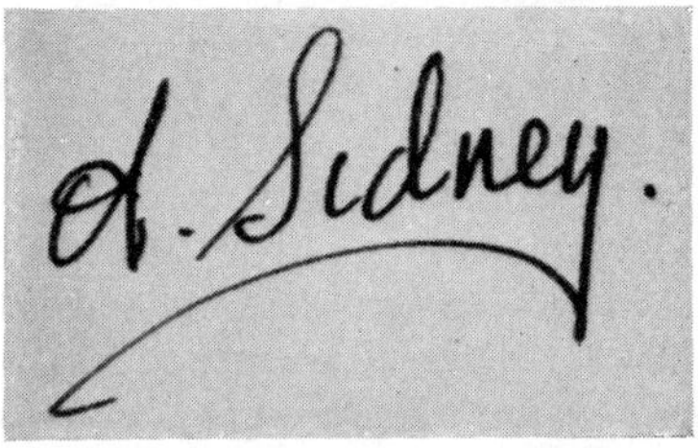

Fig. 9–40. *Terminal "y."* The terminal "y" has been converted into a rubric.

Punctuation

The sole function of punctuation is to aid understanding. The use of the period (full stop), together with certain other marks such as inverted commas, is governed by fairly strict rules, the breach of which will indicate that the education of the writer has been defective. Sometimes the correct use of inverted commas is associated with gross errors in grammar and in the spelling of simple words. This indicates that the writer is endeavouring to hide the fact that an educated person is the author.

The use of other punctuation marks, such as the comma, is governed largely by taste; some writers use commas liberally whilst others seem able to write without ambiguity, using them most sparingly.

The size, positioning with respect to the line, and also the design of punctuation marks and abbreviations, such as the ampersand, occasionally may serve to characterise a handwriting. Again, being inconspicuous features, they are rarely disguised as their significance is not appreciated.

The punctuation marks on envelopes are often of great evidential value, for nothing very definite is laid down as to what punctuation marks, if any, are to be associated with each line of writing, so that practice varies considerably. With some, the whole of the matter on the envelope is written without punctuation marks of any kind, whilst with others, periods are placed at the ends of all the lines, after initials, associated with abbreviated titles, and even after the number of the house in the street. In some cases, commas are partially or even wholly substituted for the periods.

The punctuation habits in the addressing of envelopes are rarely varied, even when great care has been taken to disguise both the handwriting and the spelling to convey an impression of illiteracy.

The Comparison of Handwriting

Theoretical Considerations

From the foregoing, it may fairly be assumed that a developed handwriting, being the product of a long period of modification and adaptation to the needs and abilities of the writer, will be peculiar to the individual; in view of its complexity, the probability of any two persons having handwritings which are so similar that the presence of one or more consistent dissimilarities cannot be demonstrated, is extremely small.

Although this is so, it does not follow that the comparison of various specimens of handwriting to determine whether or not they have been written by the same person is necessarily simple and straightforward, even when there is no possibility of disguise having been introduced. The comparison of handwritings can never be accomplished mechanically as though pieces of a jig-saw puzzle were being compared with the spaces which remain to be filled. Human beings never function with the regularity and precision of machines, which is why natural variation will be a characteristic of every specimen of handwriting which is the subject of examination and comparison. The influence on handwriting of this natural variation has already been considered in some detail, but it must be repeated that because of it, one is unlikely to encounter passages of handwriting or even individual words which are perfect replicas, even when they have been written under similar conditions by a practised penman.

It follows from this that because two specimens of handwriting, even when written by the same person, can never be replicas, a measure of judgment is called for on the part of the examiner when he has to decide whether:

(1) the differences in the handwritings being compared can be regarded as being due to variation, or if they are indicative of different authorship;
(2) in the absence of any consistent differences which cannot reasonably be attributed to natural variation, the sum total of resemblances in letter design and in details of structure uncovered by the examination can be explained only on the grounds that the writings are of common authorship, and that the possibility of the resemblances occurring by chance can be discounted.

As a measure of judgment is called for, it follows that the comparison of handwriting must be, in part, a subjective process and consequently liable to human error. As in any scientific process there is an invariable tendency to shrink from conclusions which are not entirely objective, it is hardly surprising that efforts have been made to reduce, if not to entirely eliminate, the subjective element in the comparison of handwriting.

The schemes which are simplest in conception are those in which each handwriting specimen is broken down on the basis of its general characteristics, such as ratio, angularity, shading, artistic quality, etc., so that it can be given a "code number," a process which has much in common with the procedures used for the classification of handwriting. The most enthusiastic proponents of such schemes claim that if this breaking-down process is carried sufficiently far, all specimens of handwriting which bear the same code number must be of common authorship. On the other hand, more cautious advocates prudently assert that their main merit is to enable a rapid preliminary sorting to be accomplished when a large number of suspect handwritings have to be dealt with. They maintain that such schemes select for further examination a comparatively small number of handwritings which might very well be of common authorship. Whilst it is difficult to quarrel with this point of view, the original difficulty remains, for no suggestion is made as to what purely objective principles any final process of selection must conform.

Other comparatively simple schemes are given a pseudo-quantitative basis in that a system of scoring is suggested. Where similarities are recorded during the examination, positive points on a sliding scale of values are awarded, whilst dissimilarities are acknowledged by the scoring of negative points. If the final result is overwhelmingly positive, it is concluded that the handwritings are of common authorship; a large negative result is interpreted as indicating more than one writer; anything in between is regarded as inconclusive.

The most elaborate and time-consuming schemes are those based on graphometric principles. Graphometry, as the name implies, is a method of characterising a handwriting by proportionate values for the angles and ratios for the heights and widths of the letters. It is claimed that the characterisation of a handwriting achieved in this way must be wholly objective and divorced from the personal idiosyncrasies of the examiner, and that, theoretically, the same classification should be arrived at for a handwriting irrespective of the personality of the operator.

One criticism which immediately springs to mind is that, whatever the theoretical merits of the scheme, the measurements which form the basis of the classification are certain to be influenced by the person responsible for making them. Absolutely straight lines are characteristic of few handwritings, and the angle between two short curved lines will probably be given as many different values as there are operators to measure it, so that ratios calculated from measurements subject to personal bias in interpretation can hardly claim to be free from the personality of the operator.

The above list by no means exhausts the suggestions which have been made for decreasing the subjective element in the comparison of handwriting, and nothing is to be gained by more detailed description or criticism of schemes for the comparison of handwriting based on measurement, on general features or on some system of scoring points for and against. All such schemes are worthless because they fail to take into account the fundamental rule which admits of no exception when handwritings are being compared. The rule is simple—whatever features two specimens of handwriting may have in common, they cannot be considered to be of common authorship if they display but a single consistent dissimilarity in any feature which is fundamental to the structure of the handwriting, and whose presence is not capable of reasonable explanation.

This rule must not be applied blindly. For example, the dissimilarity must be present in some feature which is known to the examiner to be fundamental to the structure of the handwriting. The presence of initial strokes to some of the letters of one specimen of handwriting and their absence in the other is not fatal to an expression of opinion that they are of common authorship, for the experienced examiner is aware that many writers vary their habits with respect to the initial strokes to certain letters. On occasion, a handwriting will be liberally garnished with such strokes, whilst in a specimen written by the same person under different circumstances, initial strokes may be sought for in vain.

Again, the dissimilarity must be truly consistent; the presence of a few accidentals should never be interpreted as denoting the existence of a consistent dissimilarity not capable of reasonable explanation. The dissimilarity must clearly be shown to be a natural feature of the writing.

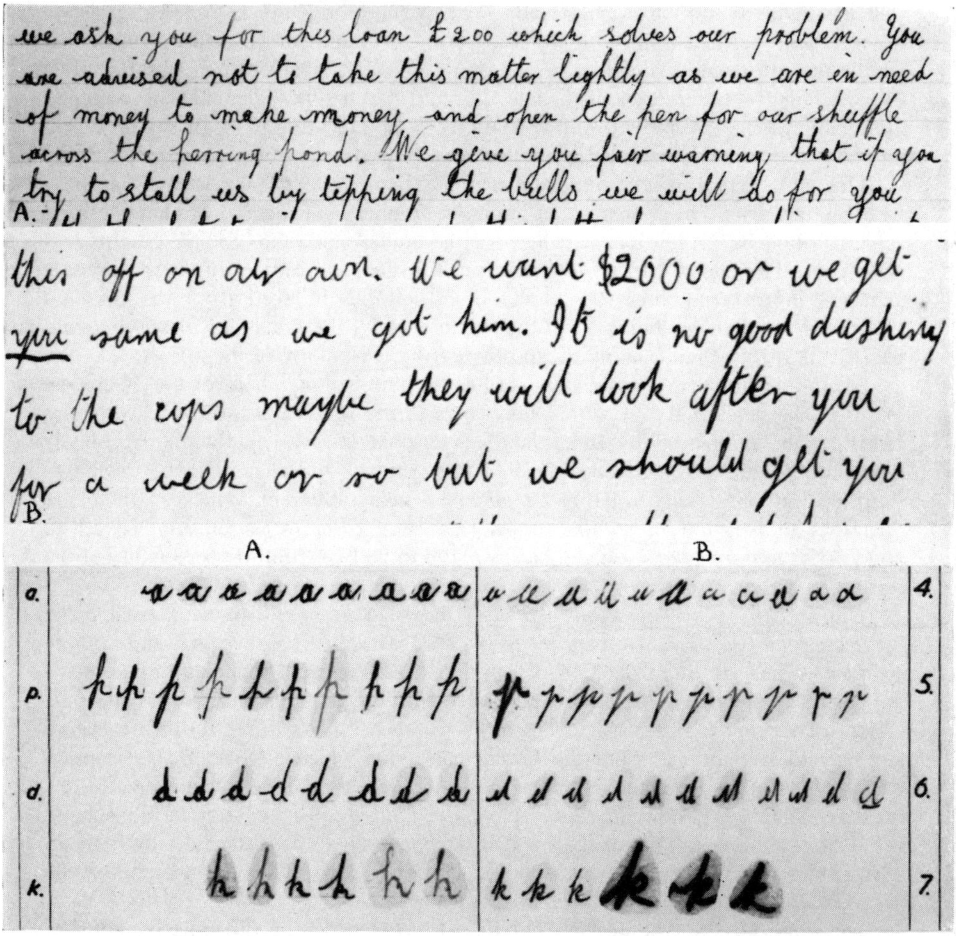

Fig. 9–41. There is a strong general resemblance between the handwriting of the specimen " A " and that of a blackmailing letter " B " which led to a wrongful conviction (*R.* v. *Binney*). The lower comparison table shows that there are consistent differences between the designs of the letters " a," " p," " d " and " k " which should have shown conclusively that " A " and " B " were not written by the same person.

The consistent dissimilarity need not be such an obvious feature of the handwriting that its presence obtrudes itself on the eye. Too obvious a feature of a handwriting is invariably regarded with some suspicion by the careful document examiner, because there is always the possibility that it has been deliberately introduced to confuse the issue. The type of dissimilarity which is regarded as most significant is that which has to be sought for in the *structure* of the handwriting and whose presence may well be overlooked by those inexperienced in the critical examination of handwriting. There is little chance of such inconspicuous dissimilarities having been deliberately introduced as disguise.

It has been stated that a consistent dissimilarity may be disregarded as negativing common authorship if there is some reasonable explanation for its presence, but it must be emphasised that the grounds for its passing-over must be real and not fanciful. The evidence on which any exclusion is based must be concrete; it is never sufficient merely to assume that variation or deliberate disguise is responsible. Practically all the well-publicised errors made by former generations of " handwriting experts " have arisen through consistent differences, which should on the evidence have indicated different authorship, being brushed aside as due either to disguise or variation without sufficient evidence, simply because their presence has conflicted with a preconceived idea about authorship.

Apart from disguise and variation, there are a number of " reasonable explanations " for the appearance of consistent dissimilarities in specimens of handwriting written by the same person. These are generally concerned with the conditions under which the writing act was carried out. The physical conditions, such as the nature of the pen and other writing materials as well as the position taken up by the writer, play their part to say nothing of the physical and mental state of the writer himself.

The rule that a single consistent dissimilarity, irrespective of the number and nature of the similarities which are demonstrable must exclude any possibility of common authorship may seem harsh, but in practice, it is exceptional for handwritings by different authors to be found to differ in but one material particular.

Once suspicion has been aroused that two handwritings, which at first sight appear to bear an exceedingly strong resemblance to each other, are unlikely to be of common authorship, because of a consistent dissimilarity fundamental to the structure of the handwriting, it is curious how rapidly others of similar import are observed, once the attention has been diverted from the similarity of the handwritings to the search for confirmatory evidence of different authorship.

Where the examiner is presented with reasonable amounts of the handwriting of different persons, he usually experiences little difficulty in finding sufficient evidence to satisfy himself that the work of more than a single writer is concerned. Difficulties are more likely to arise:

(1) where the handwritings under examination are under-developed in that they have been written letter by letter in an endeavour to reproduce outlines but poorly memorised, instead of in an instinctive and reflex manner, with the attention concentrated more on what is being written than on the control of the writing act;

(2) where the handwritings being compared are limited in amount.

In the first case, where undeveloped handwritings are concerned, the examiner has to make a realistic approach to the problem. He must bear in mind that the principles which have been laid down for, and any experience he may have acquired, in the examination of handwriting which has been written with such little thought for structural detail that writing has practically become a reflex habit, cannot be applied in their entirety to the comparison of undeveloped handwritings which may be little more than crude drawings of dimly recalled outlines. In the worst of these cases, the examiner should have no hesitation in realising his limitations, and confessing that the problem is beyond his skill; " conclusions " based on insufficient evidence are nothing other than guesses.

In the second case, where the handwritings are limited in extent so that the examiner is unable to study the range of variation in letter design, the examiner, in the absence of obvious dissimilarities which unequivocably indicate different authorship, has to weigh the evidence in an endeavour to decide whether the differences are due to variation or are indicative of different authorship.

Qualified Opinions

If the examiner can find nothing which definitely indicates that different persons are concerned, this does not necessarily mean that he can safely conclude that the specimens are of common authorship, even if they have a number of features in common—generally referred to as similarities. Some similarities are of copybook origin and consequently have little evidential value—these are the " style characteristics " previously referred to. Others which take the form of deviations from copybook practice may be indicative of common authorship, but where the amount of handwriting is limited and the deviations from copybook practice which are common to all the specimens of handwriting, are neither numerous nor outstanding in their rarity in contemporary handwriting, the chance of their appearing fortuitously must be taken into account. In such cases, the examiner may be unable to find sufficient evidence to resolve his doubts on this score so that he will be forced to express a qualified opinion. This may take the form that whilst he can find nothing which definitely points to the handwritings being of different origin, there is insufficient evidence to prove that they are the work of a single person, although they have in common a number of deviations from normal copybook practice which would be consistent with their being by the same hand.

In the courts of some countries, qualified opinions are not accepted, and the examiner is expected either to express a definite opinion as to authorship or hold his peace. In the opinion of the author, this is hair-splitting, for the most definite opinion expressed by any document examiner is subject to the unspoken qualification " as far as my skill allows," for unless he saw a specimen of handwriting being written, he is unable to *swear* to its authorship however skilled he may be.

In questions of personal identification, there is rarely any objection raised to a witness describing the general appearance of someone he has failed to identify, for even a piece of evidence which in itself is not conclusive may prove of some assistance to the court, so why should the document examiner be debarred from expressing qualified opinions?

Practical Considerations

When two passages of handwriting are to be compared, a certain amount of preliminary work has to be undertaken before any detailed comparison of their characteristics is embarked upon. The writing should be read, re-read and studied until the examiner is so familiar with its appearance that he is able to interpret any word at a glance. Great care should be exercised in the interpretation of doubtful letter formations, and the possibility of there being examples of mis-spelling or of the inclusion of unfamiliar proper names should be borne in mind, otherwise the examiner may be confused by some of the letter designs.

On one occasion the author encountered the comparatively rare surname "Janes" in a badly written anonymous letter. When this was interpreted as "Jones," an exceedingly common name in South Wales, where his laboratory is situated, because the poorly written "a" resembled an "o," some difficulty was experienced in the comparison with the known handwriting of the suspect. Further inquiry revealed the true spelling of the surname, so that the difficulty was resolved.

If the handwriting is anything but clearly written, it is advisable to prepare slightly (× 2) enlarged photographs which can be referred to. Where the language is unfamiliar or the writing is highly illegible, the interpretation of each formation should be typed or clearly written just above the writing on the enlarged photographs. This will greatly facilitate the comparison and reduce the possibility of erroneous reading of the writing. Where faint pencil writing is concerned the preparation of enlarged photographs in which the contrast between the writing and its background has been enhanced, is an essential preliminary to the comparison.

Before anything else is attempted, each passage of handwriting should be examined to discover whether there is any evidence of its being the work of more than a single writer. It will sometimes be discovered that dates, numbers or notes, such as those giving the time of receipt, have been added in a different hand; it is as well to block out all such writing on the enlarged photograph. It should also be borne in mind that there is always the possibility that a blackmailing letter may be the composite achievement of more than a single writer, with words or groups of words written alternately.

Where several specimens of handwriting have been submitted as the work of a suspect, these should be intercompared before they are accepted as the work of a single person. That this precaution is sometimes well justified is shown by the experience of the author, who has, on occasion, been supplied with the work of no less than four individuals attributed to a single suspect. Each passage should next be tested for evidence of copying or disguise. The principles on which copying can be detected and the effects of disguise eliminated are dealt with in the chapter on "Disguise."

By the time this stage has been reached, the examiner will have become fairly familiar with the general appearance of the handwritings under examination, but no attempt should be made to anticipate the conclusions as to authorship, for these can only be reached after a complete analysis of the structure of the handwriting has been carried out. This is best accomplished by studying each specimen of handwriting letter by letter, fixing the details of the letter design in the mind by drawing rough sketches. No attempt should be made to draw accurate outlines; on the contrary, the sketches should be distorted so as to emphasise the salient features of the letter designs with clear indications of the way in which the letter formations depart from conventional copybook practice. In the sketches, care should be taken to indicate how any letter is connected to those which flank it in the writing.

When the master patterns governing letter design and the nature and the extent of the variation associated with them have been fixed in the mind, the general characteristics of the writing as a whole are studied. This will include such features as the relative spacing and alignment of the letters and words, marginal habits, etc.

It is only when the examiner has a mental picture of each specimen of handwriting as a whole that he will turn his attention to the problem of summing up the evidence which points to common authorship, provided that the discovery of some consistent dissimilarity, fundamental to the structure of the handwriting, has not already led him to the conclusion that different writers are concerned.

Bibliography

Bruning, A., "A Genuine Counterfeit," *International Criminal Police Review,* No. 72, November, 1953.

Day, C. D., *Alphabets Old and New* (Charles Scribner's Sons, New York, 1910).

Fry, R., and Lowe, E. A., *English Handwriting* (S.P.E. Tract No. XXIII, London, 1926).

Hewitt, G., *Handwriting. Every Man's Craft* (Kegan Paul, London, 1938).

Hilton, O., "Characteristics of the Ballpoint Pen and its Influence on Handwriting Identification," *Journal of Criminal Law, Criminology and Police Science,* Vol. 47, No. 5, January–February, 1957.

Hilton, Ordway, "Proper Evaluation of Dissimilarities in Handwriting," *International Criminal Police Review,* 105, February, 1957.

Karpisek, Karl, "Identification of Suicide Notes," *Kriminalistik,* 10 (2), 50–53, February, 1956.

Lee, C. D., and Abbey, R. A., *Classification and Identification of Handwriting* (Appleton, February, 1923).

Maguinness, I., *Rhythm in Handwriting* (W. Heffer & Sons, Ltd., Cambridge, 1928).

Malespine, E., "Graphology and its Applications," *International Criminal Police Review,* No. 51, October, 1951.

Malley, R., "Identification and Handwriting," *International Criminal Police Review,* No. 94, January, 1956.

Mather, J., "Ballpoint Pens and Expert Appraisal of Written Documents," *International Criminal Police Review,* December, 1950.

Mitchell, C. A., "Handwriting and its value as Evidence," *Journal of the Royal Society of Arts,* 81, 1923.

Neves, N., "Similarities in Handwriting of Relations," *International Criminal Police Review,* No. 77, April, 1954.

Piggott, R., *Handwriting. A National Survey* (Allen and Unwin, London, 1958).

Sellars, Clarke, "The Handwriting Evidence against Hauptmann," *The Journal of Criminal Law and Criminology,* 27, 1937.

Sjoegren, Tore, "Handwriting Comparison and Probability," *International Criminal Police Review,* No. 92, November, 1955.

Smith, Stanley S., "A Method of Comparing Written Documents," *International Criminal Police Review,* No. 80, August–September, 1954.

Anon., "Expert Examination of a Shorthand Text," *International Criminal Police Review,* No. 52, November, 1951.

10

DISGUISE

Because of the existence of natural variation, the comparison of handwriting to determine authorship cannot be regarded as a simple and straightforward task, but the difficulties are increased when the writer has deliberately departed from his usual style of handwriting. A deliberate departure from normal handwriting habits, generally referred to as " disguise " can be expected whenever:

(1) the handwriting is that of an anonymous letter which the writer has no desire to have traced back to him by recognition of the handwriting;
(2) the signature of a fictitious person is fabricated on a receipt or other similar document;
(3) the signature of a real person is carefully copied from a genuine signature;
(4) the handwriting, or more often the figuring, of another person is copied in an endeavour to place the blame elsewhere.

Whenever there is any reason for suspecting that the handwriting under examination is disguised, the document examiner must proceed with caution if he is not to fall into serious error.

In the first place, his suspicions may be unjustified, the handwriting being free of any deliberate alteration. Where disguise is confidently expected he will run the very real risk of making an incorrect identification of the writer by lightly dismissing as disguise any consistent dissimilarities which otherwise he would have attributed to different authorship. This facile tendency to shrug off any differences as due to disguise lies at the root of most of the notorious errors of judgment made by some of the " handwriting experts " of a former generation.

Although it occurred in the very early years of the twentieth century, the case of Adolph Beck is regularly resurrected as a justification for the refusal to accept any opinion as to the authorship of handwriting. Here, the obvious differences between the handwriting of Beck and that of the real swindler were wrongly attributed to disguise, when in reality they were a clear indication that the handwriting of two different persons were concerned.

The second danger is that the document examiner may not realise that he is dealing with a disguised handwriting, and so may fail to make a positive identification. This will happen if he regards dissimilarities which have occurred as a result of disguise as indicating different authorship. Whilst a failure to make a positive identification may not result in a serious miscarriage of justice, it may thwart the investigation by drawing the investigating officer away from a promising line of inquiry.

The identification of handwriting embodying even the simplest consistent disguise is certain to present the document examiner with a stern test of his skill, and it should be made clear at the outset that anyone who guarantees to penetrate the disguise of every specimen of disguised handwriting which might be submitted to him, is suffering from self-deception. There is no doubt that many people, provided they are willing to take the trouble, are quite capable of writing a few lines of handwriting which has been so thoroughly disguised that its identification by comparison with the normal handwriting is virtually impossible. Fortunately, for reasons which will be made clear, most of the disguised handwritings encountered in the course of criminal investigations are only superficially disguised; the identification of many disguised handwritings will cause an experienced document examiner little more difficulty than is presented by the comparison of normal, but rather variable, handwriting.

The Recognition of Disguise

The recognition of those features in a handwriting which can correctly be attributed to disguise is dependent upon the application of certain fundamental principles, which can only be derived from the study of very many specimens of disguised handwriting. The assembly of a number of specimens of disguised handwriting sufficiently large to enable valid general conclusions to be drawn has proved a formidable task, but thanks to the invaluable co-operation of the Police Forces of England and Wales, in particular that of the West Riding of Yorkshire, the author has been able to acquire an almost unlimited quantity of experimental material.

As a result of the detailed study of this mass of disguised handwriting, allied with the experience gained over many years spent in the examination of handwriting in general, he regards certain general principles as being firmly established. These are:

(1) Most Disguise is Relatively Simple in Nature

To those who have little more than a nodding acquaintance with disguised handwriting, this statement may occasion some surprise. It is, however, no new discovery, for reference to this fact has often been made in the past. There are two reasons why this should be so, and both are capable of experimental verification.

The primary reason for the essential simplicity of most disguise stems from the manner in which everyone, with the exception of the document examiner, identifies a familiar handwriting. The recognition is at a glance, and is based upon an awareness of the "general pictorial effect" of a familiar handwriting. As previously pointed out, this general pictorial effect is almost entirely a function of a few features such as slope, shading, fluency and rhythm, coupled with some of the more obvious features in letter design.

Any deliberate marked change in any of these features, particularly an alteration in slope, will have a profound effect upon the appearance of the handwriting. Where the slope is changed, the effort demanded of the writer endeavouring to maintain the slope to which he is unaccustomed will be reflected in a loss of much of the fluency and rhythm normally associated with the handwriting. If the writer extends the disguise by introducing alternative forms for the capitals and for letters such as " r," " p," " e," etc., the resulting handwriting will have become so changed in its general appearance that it will no longer be recognisable at a glance by anyone familiar with it in its normal state.

As comparatively simple modifications can produce such a profound effect upon the general appearance of a handwriting, the would-be writer of a disguised hand who himself uses the general pictorial effect as the basis of his recognition of a familiar handwriting rarely considers it necessary to go to any further trouble when effecting a disguise. In many cases a profound alteration in slope is considered all that is necessary to render a handwriting unrecognisable.

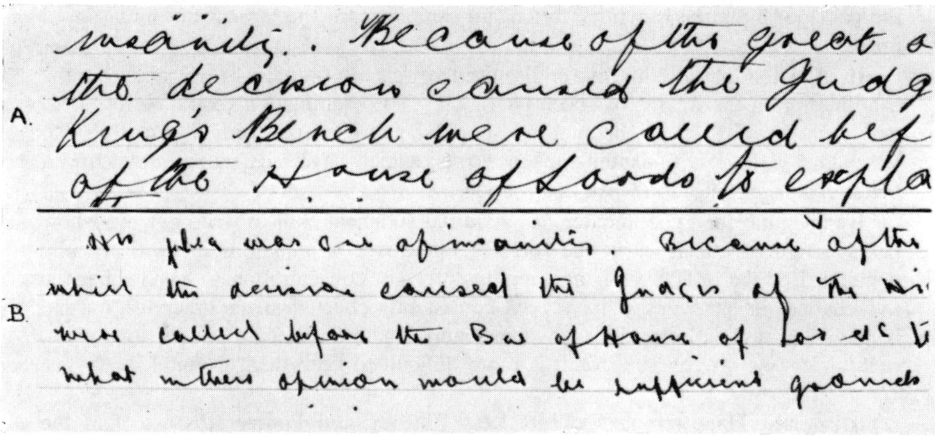

Fig. 10–1. Two specimens of handwriting by the same person (a) normal and (b) disguised. The disguised handwriting has been more deliberately written with a back slope which has caused the alteration in pictorial effect. Note that the uncommon writing habit of joining certain of the words has persisted into the disguised specimen.

The second reason for the prevalence of a simple rather than of a complicated scheme of disguise is that, where more than a few lines of disguised writing have to be written, the intense concentration which is essential for the maintenance of any complicated scheme of disguise is beyond the capability of the average person. To prove the truth of this assertion and to gain some insight into what is involved in the production of disguised handwriting, a simple experiment in the writing of a disguised hand should be essayed. The aim is the writing of a passage of handwriting which is normal in all respects, except for the letter designs of the vowels, for which different forms are to be substituted.

The experimenter should first study about a dozen lines of his normal handwriting in order to ascertain how he forms the vowels. To help in this study, enlarged drawings of the vowel designs should be made on scrap paper. These should be repeated until the details of the design of all the vowels are firmly fixed in the mind.

When this has been accomplished, a new and quite distinctive design for each vowel should be invented; these new designs are to constitute the disguise which is to be introduced into the otherwise normal handwriting. To fix these new vowel designs in the mind, a few examples of words in which they occur should be written, at first slowly, and then more rapidly until the normal speed of writing has been attained. The next step to to copy about fifty lines from a newspaper, taking care to introduce the new vowel designs to the complete exclusion of the normal formations. The handwriting is then carefully examined to ascertain whether any of the normal vowel designs have been included in the disguised handwriting. This is best carried out by working backwards through the script, otherwise the attention may become diverted by the " message " carried by the writing, instead of remaining concentrated on the letter designs. If any undisguised vowel designs are discovered, the passage should be re-written and again examined for the presence of undisguised forms.

If, after the first attempt, no undisguised vowels are found, it is probable that the examination of the writing has been uncritical. The examination should be repeated, and each vowel as it is encountered should be crossed out with a pencil stroke. When the passage is re-examined, any vowels which have escaped scrutiny stand a better chance of detection when this is done.

By the time the experimenter has acquired sufficient skill to write out the whole passage free of all lapses in the form of alteration or omissions, he will be fully convinced of the difficulty of maintaining sufficient concentration to ensure that the five changes in letter design have been consistently effected in the otherwise normal hand. The task is more difficult when letters which are not all of the same class, such as vowels, are chosen, for it is more difficult to keep them in mind.

(2) Disguised Handwriting Exhibits Less Fluency and Poorer Rhythm than the Normal Hand

By definition, it follows that it is the " normal " hand in which any writer has become most practised and in which he has had the greatest opportunity to become fluent; there cannot be anything like the same fluency and rhythm associated with a hand which is written deliberately in any style to which the writer has not become accustomed. A handwriting can exhibit its best rhythm only when it has been executed to a great part as a reflex movement, without conscious thought having to be given to the details of its structure. This is well shown in those illustrations of disguised handwriting shown alongside that which is normal to the writer; a feature which is common to every specimen of disguised handwriting is the marked falling off in the rhythm and fluency.

If the experiment on the insertion of modified vowel formations was carried out, it will be instructive to compare the rhythm and smoothness of the successfully disguised handwriting with that of the normal hand; it will be found that the greater the effort and concentration necessary to form the disguised script, the greater will be the extent to which it has departed from its original fluency and rhythm.

A forged signature is an excellent example of a specialised type of disguised handwriting, and it has already been mentioned (see Chapter 9) that one of the features most characteristic of a forgery, no matter how carefully the letters have been copied from the genuine signature, is the poorer rhythm and complete absence of fluency exhibited by the forgery when compared with the original.

In any discussion of fluency and rhythm in handwriting, it is the average man who is referred to; exceptions have to be made in the case of the professional signwriter or expert in artistic lettering, who is invariably a man of high innate artistic ability who has mastered a number of styles of handwriting and printing in the pursuit of his profession. Fortunately, these men are in a small minority, and the number who use their talents illicitly even smaller, so that their existence has little practical effect on the application of the principles concerning the effect of disguise on the rhythm and fluency of handwriting in general.

(3) Any Change in Slope Introduced as Disguise is Rarely Constant

The author has had the opportunity, enjoyed by few, of having been able to make a detailed examination of some thousands of specimens of handwriting which had been disguised solely by the deliberate alteration of the slope, sometimes termed the " slant," of the writing. From this extensive survey some important principles have been derived. Apart from their theoretical interest, these are of practical value because, as already mentioned, gross alteration in slope is by far the most favoured device for the disguise of handwriting in criminal cases.

One fact which emerged was that a pronounced change from a forward to a back slope was more than seven times as popular as a change of slope in the reverse direction. The reason for this is not far to seek. Most handwriting is written with a slight but quite perceptible forward slope and any increase in the forward slope would have little effect on its general appearance. If the change is from a forward to a back slope, this will affect the " sense " as well as the extent of the slope, with a consequent profound effect on the appearance of the handwriting. A change of slope in a forward direction would profoundly alter the general appearance only of those handwritings characterised by a back slope in the normal condition. These are in a minority, because a " style characteristic " of most contemporary handwriting is the adoption of a forward slope.

Another fact which was established was that, whilst most writers were able to begin writing with a slope appreciably different from that to which they were accustomed, comparatively few were able to maintain a consistent false slope for any length of time. With the majority of those tested, it was found that as soon as the attention flagged, the slope tended to revert to that which was normal for the writer, but was changed back to the revised slope as soon as the reversion had become sufficiently marked to be noticeable to the writer.

This must not be taken as the justification for deeming every handwriting which exhibits a variable slope to be disguised. Many handwritings of poor quality exhibit marked changes in slope, but in such cases, other failings will almost certainly become apparent on close examination. Where variable slope is accompanied by variation in size, spacing and design of the letters, it is more than likely that it is caused by incompetence rather than design.

It was also apparent that few attempted, and still fewer succeeded, in writing consistently with a slope which was only a few degrees different from that normal to their handwriting. This is no new discovery, for Osborn in his *Questioned*

Documents[1] refers to the same point. Osborn goes even further, and expresses the opinion that a consistent small difference in slope (less than 15°) between two specimens of handwriting is unlikely to be due to disguise, but must be interpreted as evidence of different authorship.

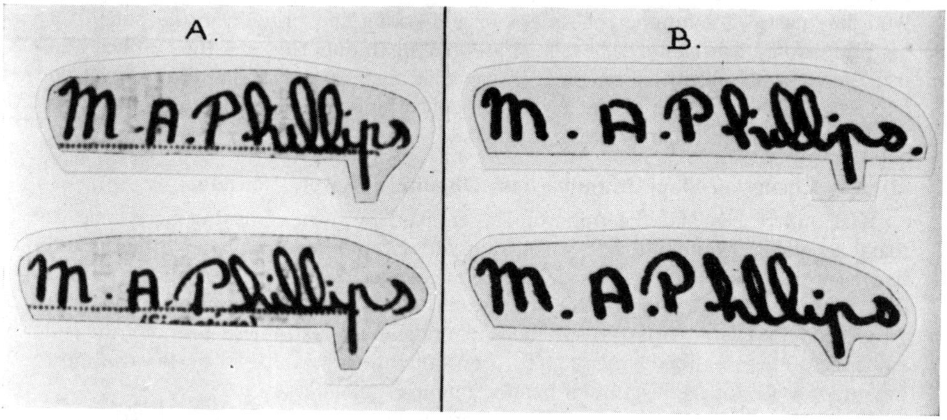

Fig. 10–2. The two signatures in column " B " are normal, whereas those in " A " are disguised with a view to repudiation. The slope of the signatures in " A " has been altered but the normal tendency to write a pronounced back slope has been too strong for the writer. Note that all four signatures show similar spacing for the capital letters.

In general, this opinion is probably correct, but the influence of speed has to be taken into account. A fast undisguised handwriting will often exhibit a small consistent increase of forward slope compared with a slow handwriting made by the same person. As with many other aspects of handwriting, bald statements concerning the significance of changes of slope cannot be made without some degree of qualification.

(4) Disguised Handwriting Often Contains Altered Letter Designs

Altered or modified letter designs are quite common in handwritings which are undisguised, but in almost every case, the most cursory examination will reveal some good reason why the alteration has been made. In a clear and legible script, alterations are made in an effort to correct spelling mistakes, etc., whilst a poor writer will touch-up his handwriting in an attempt to improve its legibility. It is quite common to find scripts where the wrong word has been started and the writer has preferred to over-write rather than to strike out the incorrect letters and start again.

When there is reason to suspect that a handwriting has been disguised, a thorough search should be made for alterations in letter design. Some which are discovered will immediately be explicable on reasonable grounds, such as those referred to above, but for the presence of others there may be no immediately apparent justification. For example, there is no good reason why anyone should

[1] 2nd ed., at p. 149

first write a Greek "e," and then take pains to change it into one of the conventional design. Still less will there appear any reason for converting one or two examples of the arcade form of "r" into the alternative "Civil Service" form, for either of these designs may be employed indiscriminately throughout a handwriting with a loss of neither legibility nor elegance.

The reason for such apparently pointless alterations becomes patent when it is realised that about 20 per cent. of those who wish to disguise their handwriting do so by substituting alternative forms for certain of their letter designs. They consider that if in their normal handwriting they make use of a particular form of a letter such as "r" or "e," the substitution of the alternative form in a disguised handwriting will ensure that its authorship will never be attributed to them.

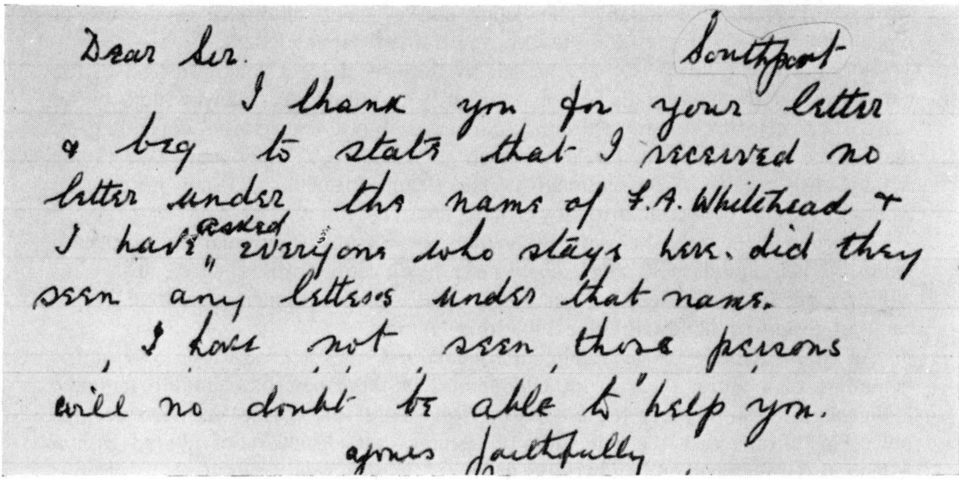
Dear Sir. Southport
I thank you for your letter & beg to state that I received no letter under the name of F.A. Whitehead & I have asked everyone who stays here. did they seen any letters under that name.
I have not seen those persons will no doubt be able to help you.
yours faithfully

Fig. 10–3. In this specimen of disguised handwriting the Greek "ϵ" has been introduced instead of the normal form. In "Whitehead" the normal form has inadvertently been written and has remained undetected by the writer. In the word "able" in the penultimate line the normal form has been written and then converted into a Greek "ϵ." The Civil Service form of "r" has also been introduced into the disguised handwriting. In "Southport" the original type of "r" has been partially converted to the alternative form.

Whether such optimism is justified need not be considered at this stage, but it is far less simple than it might appear to carry out any substitution of letter designs consistently throughout a fairly long passage. At the outset, the substitution seems an easy task, but as the attention is relaxed, the forms of the letters which are normal to the handwriting creep back unnoticed. When, during the writing, or in the course of any subsequent checking, the unwanted normal form of the letter is seen to have been inadvertently inserted, few writers can resist the temptation to alter it by careful overwriting, rather than to play for safety by rewriting the whole passage. However, these alterations do nothing to render the disguise more perfect, for their presence will indubitably reveal the fact that an attempt has been made to disguise the handwriting by the substitution of alternative forms of letter design.

Alternative forms of letter design are often sought from outside the connected cursive style of handwriting; for example, designs emanating from the disconnected Tudor " script " are freely incorporated as disguise. Especially favoured are the script forms of " b," " s " and " p."

The occurrence of " script " forms in a connected writing does not necessarily indicate disguise, because many who were originally taught this style retain some of the characteristic letter formations when they change over to a connected handwriting.

It is by no means unusual to find the block letter form of " K " or even " R " in the middle of a word written in connected handwriting, in spite of the fact that block letters do not readily lend themselves to incorporation as alternative forms in cursive handwriting, because of the difficulty in making suitable connecting strokes. This lack of suitable connecting strokes is no hindrance to the use of block letters as substitutes for the cursive form of capital letters.

A handwriting which is characterised by the use of block letters instead of the cursive forms of the capitals is not necessarily disguised, for many writers prefer these simpler forms; others use either cursive or block letter forms depending on their mood. Furthermore, for letters such as " A," " C," " S " and " W," some writers dispense with conventional capital letter formations, using instead an enlarged version of the small or lower case letter.

A writer in the habit of using either the cursive form or an enlarged lower case letter for his capitals will often substitute a block letter form when disguising his handwriting; the survey carried out by the author showed that no less than 10 per cent. of disguised handwritings exhibit this feature.

As capital letters are relatively infrequent, and almost invariably occur at the beginning of a word, there is little likelihood of there being any failure to make a thorough substitution of the alternative form once this course has been decided on. This means that there is little prospect of the discovery of altered capital letters in a specimen of handwriting disguised in this way.

The document examiner cannot hope to discover enough evidence to enable him to decide whether the particular forms of capital letters he finds in a suspect handwriting are those favoured by the writer when writing normally. Fortunately, this matters little, since few writers remain faithful to any particular style of capital letter over long periods of time, for taste in capitals is more capricious than in most other features of handwriting. Consequently, when handwritings are being compared, the safest and simplest course is to leave out of consideration the *style* in which the capitals are written, and not jump to the conclusion that, because one specimen of handwriting is embellished with cursive capitals and the other has only the more pedestrian block letters, they have necessarily been written by different persons.

It is futile to attempt any detailed comparison of block letters used as capitals in one specimen of handwriting with cursive capitals taken from another because such letter designs have little in common. Apart from a few generalisations based on the degree of writing skill exhibited in each case, nothing further in the way of comparison should be attempted.

If a fair amount of good quality rhythmic handwriting is in question, and there is reason to believe that the only disguise has been the substitution of alternative letter formations, there is the possibility, no more, of applying a test for their presence. In a handwriting of good quality, the extent of the variation of any letter design about its master pattern is slight, accidental formations are few, and even these depart only slightly from the master pattern. In such a handwriting, the substitution of a letter design with which the writer is not very familiar will tend to disturb the general consistency of the writing. It is probable that the substituted letter design will exhibit considerably more variation about its master pattern than that which is found with the normal letter designs. It is also likely that accidentals will be more frequent, for these will have occurred whenever the writer inadvertently commenced to write the usual letter design, but, realising his mistake, changed it to the substituted form as best he could.

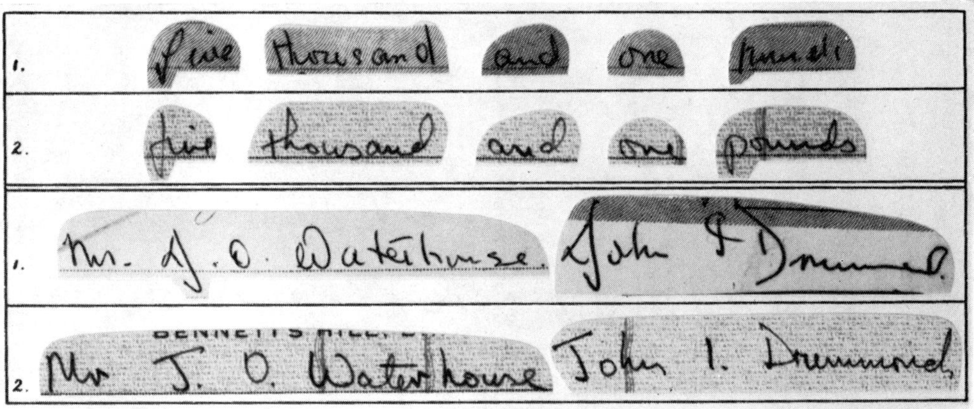

Fig. 10–4. The writing on line " 1 " is the natural handwriting, whereas that on line " 2 " has been disguised when filling in a forged cheque. Note the use of (a) block letters instead of cursive capitals; (b) alternative forms for " s," " p," " t " and " r."

(5) The Internal Consistency of Handwriting is Disturbed by the Introduction of Disguise

Including capital letters, the alphabet may be considered to be made up of about forty different letter formations in extensive use, for little heed need be taken of such letters as " Z," " X " and " Q " which are rarely encountered in English handwriting. Every individual letter of this fairly large number, although of unique design, is in reality constructed by combining a few of a relatively small number of structural elements. These structural elements are the loops, arches, troughs and short straight lines from which all systems of contemporary handwriting are constructed. Therefore, it is not surprising that many letter designs have much in common. In some instances the resemblance is very close indeed; in alphabets based on Roman script the cursive forms of " a " and " d " differ very slightly. Consequently, in practically every specimen of undisguised handwriting selected for examination it will be found that the " d " has been constructed by the slight, sometimes very slight, lengthening of one of the strokes of the " a." It might be

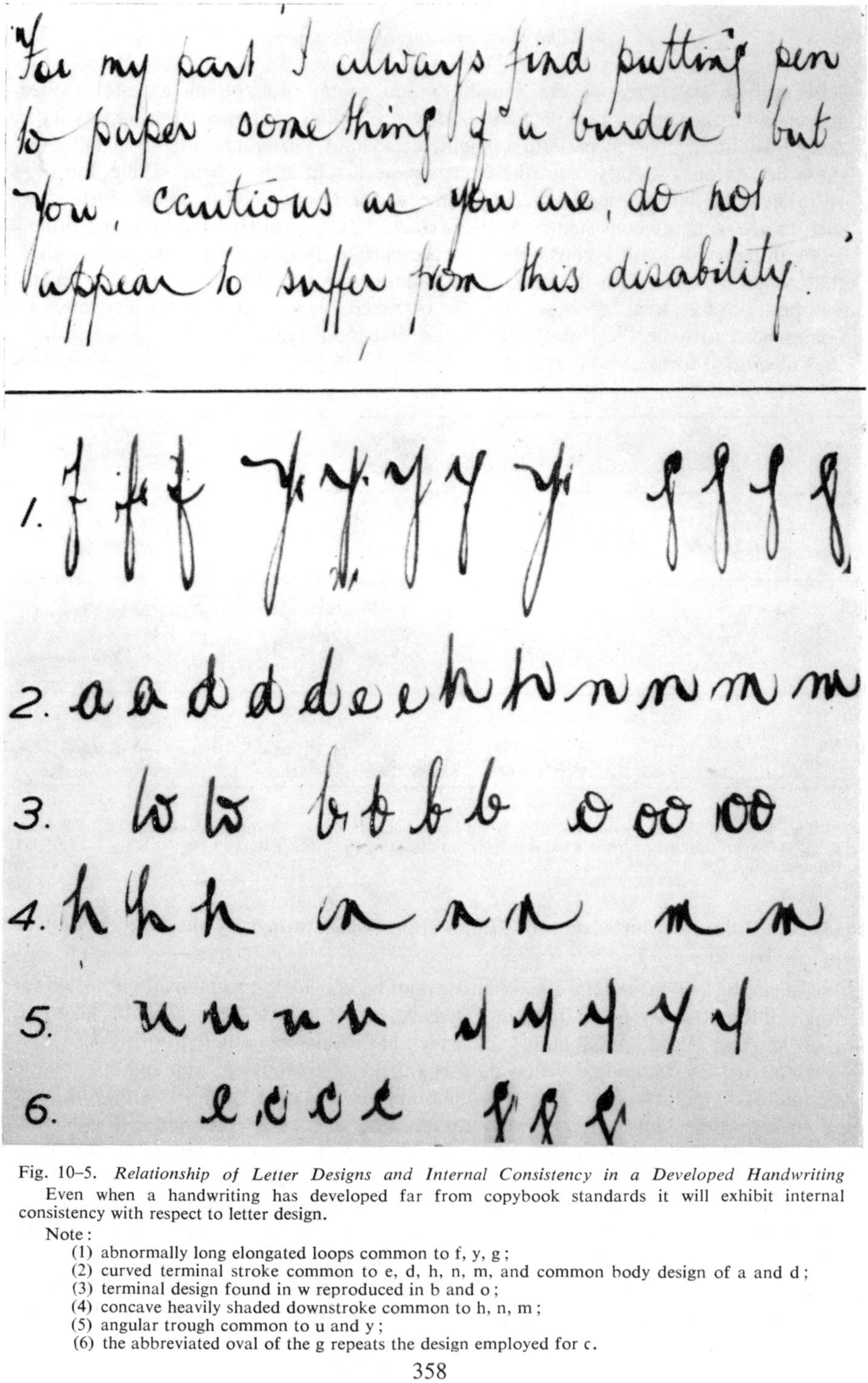

Fig. 10–5. *Relationship of Letter Designs and Internal Consistency in a Developed Handwriting*
Even when a handwriting has developed far from copybook standards it will exhibit internal consistency with respect to letter design.

Note:

(1) abnormally long elongated loops common to f, y, g;
(2) curved terminal stroke common to e, d, h, n, m, and common body design of a and d;
(3) terminal design found in w reproduced in b and o;
(4) concave heavily shaded downstroke common to h, n, m;
(5) angular trough common to u and y;
(6) the abbreviated oval of the g repeats the design employed for c.

mentioned in passing that the degree to which this stroke is lengthened is an important, though inconspicuous, feature of a handwriting.

In addition to the pairs of letters which are so alike that there is a risk of confusion when they are carelessly written, there are other groups of letters which have a number of less conspicuous features in common, in spite of their differing widely in design. For example, in many handwritings, a design favoured for the upper loop of " b " will be found to be followed closely for the upper loops of other letters, such as " h," " k," " l," and possibly " f." A similar state of affairs will be found to hold for the lower loops of letters such as " g," " j " and " y," no matter how far from copybook standards the handwritings may have departed. From this it appears that any developed handwriting in its normal state can be expected to exhibit a marked degree of internal consistency. This is of fundamental importance when considering the problem posed by disguised handwriting, for it implies that if the internal consistency of the handwriting is to be preserved, any appreciable alteration in the design of one letter must be accompanied by a corresponding change in the design of structurally related letters. This will impose a severe restriction on both the nature and the extent of any disguise which can be introduced into the letter designs without its presence becoming patent.

Unfortunately, certain forms of disguise are exempt from this restriction. Change of slope and the consequent change in letter design which stems from it is probably the best example; if the slope is changed for all the letters, the handwriting will retain its internal consistency unaltered. Neither can the test of internal consistency be applied to indicate every altered letter design which has been introduced. For example, if the disguise consisted in lengthening the stroke which converts " a " into " d," a comparison of the related letters " a " and " d " which could be counted on to expose any other type of alteration in either of these letters, cannot be relied on to expose this lengthening, for it is in the possession of an extended stroke that the " d " differs from " a," so that there is no basis for comparison of this particular feature.

This internal consistency in the design of the letters is by no means exclusive to connected cursive handwriting, for both block letters and the Tudor style of

Fig. 10–6. This shows the close structural relationship between the block lettering formations of two writers—an example of the internal consistency of block lettering.

disconnected " script " letter formations exhibit a similar relationship. Incidentally, block letters are rarely disguised, as those who use block letters to conceal the identity of their writing consider that this in itself constitutes an impenetrable disguise.

(6) Originality in Disguise is Rare

The large-scale examination carried out by the author on disguised handwriting has revealed that, as in so many other human activities, originality in disguise is rare. That disguise tends to follow a regular pattern is a finding of some importance, for it allows the document examiner to lean heavily on his experience when he has to decide which features of a handwriting under examination are disguised.

By far the most surprising fact which emerged from the survey of disguised handwriting is that less than about one person in nine is able to disguise his cursive handwriting to such an extent that it is unrecognisable at a glance by anyone familiar with it. This is yet another illustration of the fixity of handwriting habits, and it is hardly any exaggeration to state that, for many practised writers, writing has become a reflex action over which they find some difficulty in exercising any appreciable control. It may not be surprising that it was the writers of highly individual and often beautiful hands who proved unable to produce handwriting so devoid of their own personal touch that it was effectively disguised. The poorer the handwriting, the less difficulty seemed to be experienced in making it unrecognisable on cursory inspection.

This seeming inability of many skilled writers to make any effective alteration in the general appearance of their handwriting may provide an explanation for events which will often puzzle a court, and incidentally provide the defence with a red herring they are rarely loth to trail before the jury.

In the course of proceedings, particularly when there appears little option, the defence will concede that certain handwriting, such as that of an anonymous letter or damning entries in an account book, bears an uncanny resemblance to that of the accused, but, the jury will be asked, " can anyone credit that a man of intelligence such as that of the accused would have been so foolish as to employ his very distinctive natural handwriting in the course of wrong-doing, when it was sure to be recognised by anyone acquainted with such an individual hand?" Once this point has been made, the jury are invited to consider the possibility that the easily recognised handwriting of the accused was copied by someone who wished to shield himself by throwing the blame on to an innocent man. The truth in practically all these cases is that the accused persons are among those who are incapable of making any really effective alterations in their normal handwriting.

Block Letters as Disguise

Inability effectively to disguise the connected cursive style of handwriting is but one of the reasons why block letters are favoured by about twenty-five per cent. of those who wish to avoid recognition of their handwriting. The popularity of block letters, inconvenient as they are for writing at speed, is probably due to the general but quite erroneous impression which is abroad that no effective comparison can be made between different specimens of block lettering to determine whether or not they are of common authorship. This is undoubtedly why the great majority of those who use block letters as a disguise make little or no effort to depart from the letter designs they employ for legitimate purposes.

The idea that nothing can be done to identify the block lettering is quite erroneous, for handwriting in this style may exhibit as many identifying characteristics as the connected cursive hand customarily employed by the writer. Whilst it is true that block letters are comparatively simple in design when compared with cursive capitals, and that the absence of connecting strokes restricts the amount of evidence which is available, there are other compensating factors.

Fig. 10–7. A rare example of disguise being introduced into block letters when addressing an anonymous letter.

Because block lettering is rarely taught with the thoroughness devoted to the acquisition of a good cursive hand, comparatively few know how to write the correct or, what might better be termed, the " conventional " forms of all the letters. From this it follows that the block lettering of even the unpractised writer is unlikely to bear a very close resemblance to the standard copybook style, which cannot be said of connected cursive handwriting. The " block lettering " of the majority is a mélange of correct block letter formations, " script " designs and modified cursive capital letters. As this is so, it is not surprising that the " block lettering " of many illiterate persons is far more individual and easy to identify than their undeveloped cursive handwritings.

The only real advantage gained by the employment of block letters as a disguise is two-fold. In the first place, block lettering is unlikely to be recognised at a glance by those familiar only with the cursive handwriting of the writer, and secondly, it is impracticable to attempt to compare block lettering with cursive handwriting. Specimens of block lettering of the suspect must be available if the document examiner is to have any chance of proving authorship.

Whilst it is generally a simple matter to obtain specimens of cursive handwriting for purposes of comparison, this is rarely the case where block lettering is concerned. It is because of this fact alone that the use of block lettering as disguise is sometimes effective.

Copied Block Lettering

Compared with connective cursive handwriting, the copying of detached and simply formed letters is much simpler to effect and correspondingly more difficult to detect, so that there is always the remote possibility that a specimen of suspect block lettering is a careful copy of the block lettering of an innocent person. Whilst the physical process of copying block lettering would present less problems than the imitation of a connected cursive hand, it does not follow that successful forgery of even block letters is simple and straightforward. Apart from the fact that the writing skill of the forger would have to be of a higher order than that of the intended victim, close study of a very considerable amount of his block lettering would be an essential preliminary to any attempt at forgery. Following upon this, considerable practice would be required before sufficient facility would be acquired to render success at all probable.

Cases involving copied block lettering are rare. In one which stands out in the recollection of the author, he was asked to compare the block lettering on a postcard with that attributed to the secretary of a society. The committee had such little confidence in the ability of any document examiner to make an effective comparison of block lettering that they decided to prove their point by setting to work with similar postcards, so that each member made a careful copy of the block lettering on the offending postcard. These copies were enclosed with the other material with no hint of what had been done. The author was asked to examine the documents submitted, with a view to determining "whether any two or more were written by the same person." At first sight it appeared that all were the work of the same person, but a more thorough examination showed quite conclusively that this was not the case. The fluency of the block lettering of the genuine writings was in marked contrast with the laboured appearance of the copies. It was only when it was reported that one postcard had been written by the writer of the extended specimen, and that the others were crude copies written by a number of different persons, that there was any disclosure of the trick which had been played.

"Script" as Disguise

From the beginning of the century, school children in England and Wales have been taught to write a disconnected hand, based on that popular in Tudor times. This "script," like every other style of handwriting which dispenses with connecting strokes, has so little to recommend it for everyday use that in later life it is almost invariably dropped or modified into a more speedy connected cursive hand. As the "script" letter formations which closely resemble lower-case printed characters are unlikely to be forgotten, they may be used, often together with block letter formations, for disguised writing.

The problems presented in the examination and comparison of "script" letter formations used for disguise are on all fours with those encountered in the comparison of block letters, except that there are two sources of added difficulty. The first derives from the nature of the "script" letter designs, for they are even more simple, affording less scope for modification, than block letters. The second stems from the fact that as those who use "script" forms for disguise have abandoned them for general use comparatively early in life, they are unlikely to have developed letter designs which have departed appreciably from copybook standards. This means that highly developed and individual forms of "script" letters are unlikely to be characteristic of disguised handwriting.

Unlike block lettering, which is rarely taught in school, and has to be picked up haphazardly, great care is taken in the early stages of instruction to ensure that the copybook form of every "script" letter is acquired. As they are written separately, " script " letters, unlike their cursive equivalents, are unmodified in design by the letters which flank them in the word.

This means that the " script " hands of those whose connected cursive handwritings may have little in common, often prove fairly difficult to distinguish. Even more so than with block lettering, the document examiner has to exercise great caution before committing himself about the authorship of small amounts of " script," especially when it has been used as disguise. As " script " is characterised by extremely simple letter formations, and is devoid of connecting strokes, a good penman will experience little difficulty in copying the " script " of another person, providing he has sufficient material for study. The copy can be built up, a letter at a time, without betraying the fact that it has been a slow and laboured production, for the forgery is unlikely to exhibit the loss of rhythm and abnormal pen-lifts which would immediately arouse suspicion in a copied cursive connected handwriting. If, to make matters worse, a ball-point pen in poor condition has been used, it may even prove impossible to determine the exact structure of many of the letter formations.

Although the introduction of " script " coupled with the ever-increasing use of the ball-point pen has facilitated the task of the forger, it by no means follows that the document examiner can do nothing when confronted with a comparatively small amount of suspect " script," for, as previously emphasised, a handwriting is far more than a collection of letter designs strung together along a line. Whilst a skilful forger may copy the " script " letter formations of his victim to perfection, he may well fail to perceive and reproduce certain quirks of letter proportions and spacing which are inconspicuous but none the less important characteristics of the genuine writing. Every feature of a suspect handwriting has to be taken into account before it is regarded as genuine.

Alteration in Size as Disguise

It has been pointed out in Chapter 9, which deals with handwriting, that the absolute size of handwriting is subject to variation according to the circumstances in which the writing act takes place, although most writers have a preferred size for what might be termed every-day use. When the size of a disguised hand is compared with that which is normal to the writer, it will be found to have been modified—almost invariably increased in size—in about fifty per cent. of the cases.

Where a small amount of very large disguised handwriting is being dealt with, it is fairly safe to assume that the design of most of the letters has been modified in some respect; it is in the over-large hand that grotesque letter forms are found. In some cases there will be good reason for refusing to regard an abnormally large script as a true handwriting, for it may be more in the nature of a series of drawings of letters conjured up in the mind of the writer, as unlike his normal handwriting as he can devise. Any attempt to compare such grotesqueries with natural handwriting will be a waste of time.

On occasion, extreme alteration in size will be utilised as a disguise, by making the writing so small that the details of letter design are concealed in the thickness of the line. With the pen in good condition, a photographic enlargement may serve to render the details of letter design sufficiently clear to enable a comparison to be made, but where a thick pencil or a defective ball-point pen has been used, neither microscopic observation nor photographic enlargement is of much avail. The writing may be so devoid of detail, that few of the letters can be positively identified and decipherment is largely a question of guesswork.

A.

B.

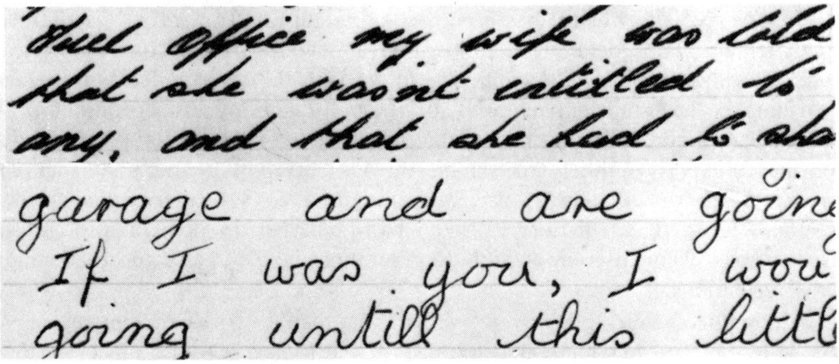

Fig. 10–8. " A " is a specimen of the normal handwriting of a suspect later convicted for attempted blackmail. " B " is a specimen of disguised writing presented to the police.
Note (a) the increase in size and (b) the reversion to copy-book style of the disguised writing " B."

The identification of handwriting of this description can be counted on to test the patience and the capability of the document examiner to the utmost, but no case should ever be considered as hopeless. On many occasions, the author has been able to discover sufficient evidence to implicate the writer of matter which was practically illegible. Even when care is taken to render the outlines of the majority of the letters indistinguishable, those who rely on this disguise often neglect to change those writing characteristics which are independent of letter design. These include letter spacing, marginal habits, the extent of indentation associated with paragraphs, and the other features of handwriting which have been considered in some detail in Chapter 9. Evidence drawn from such considerations can often be used to reinforce the little derived from letter structure to indicate the most probable author from a number of suspects.

Copied Handwriting

When a forger copies the handwriting of another, the motive generally extends beyond the desire to conceal authorship, but copied handwriting will be considered here because it affords an excellent example of what is a most effective disguise.

It is stated in Chapter 11, that a good copy of a genuine signature cannot effectively be compared with the normal handwriting of a suspect, so that a forgery may be considered to be an example of handwriting which has been perfectly disguised. This is because forged signatures, whether a free-hand simulated copy or a tracing, will be more in the nature of a drawing than a true handwriting.

In view of the foregoing, it might be concluded that the copying of the handwriting of another person should prove a perfect technique for disguising a handwriting. Whilst this is true in theory, serious difficulties are certain to be encountered if any attempt is made to put the idea into practice on any but the smallest scale. A signature may be copied with fair success, because the forger will take care to acquire and study a number of genuine specimens. The actual copying will take only a short time for little more than a single word is likely to be involved. On the other hand, if an extended passage has to be written in an imitation of the handwriting of another, the initial difficulty will be the acquisition of sufficient suitable material for study before the pen is put to paper. Even where this has been done and the details of the letter design have been mastered, the production of a copied handwriting with but a tithe of the fluency and rhythm of the original is extremely difficult to accomplish. In those cases which have been investigated by the author, it has been found that the copyist is usually content to introduce into his handiwork the most outstanding and individual features of the handwriting being imitated.

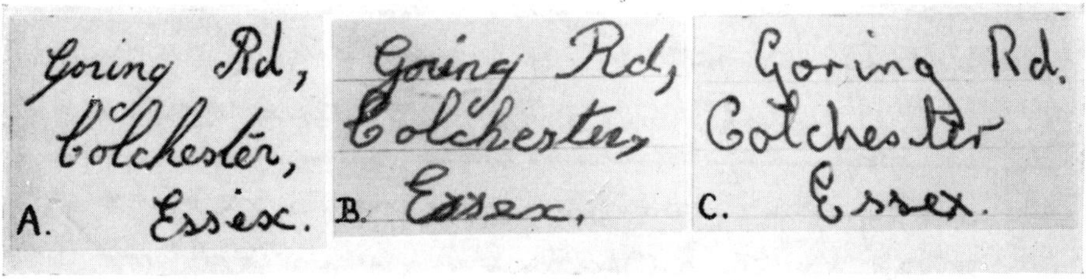

Fig. 10–9. " B " is a portion of an address on an anonymous letter in which the writer of specimen " C " attempted to copy the handwriting of the person who wrote specimen " A." The capital letters as well as certain of the others have been carefully copied so that " A " and " B " bear a superficial resemblance to each other. Note, however, in " B " the altered " r " of " Colchester " and the " ss " of " Essex " where additional strokes have been inserted. The ratio of " B " resembles that of " C " rather than " A." The variable slope of " B " is often characteristic of a copied handwriting.

Apart from these, in every case, the final copy has been found to consist entirely of an easily recognisable specimen of the handwriting of the copyist, complete with all the minutiae which give it individuality and enable it to be identified. It may safely be concluded that the danger that an innocent person may be implicated because the real criminal has copied his handwriting as a form of disguise is far more apparent than real.

Writing with the Unaccustomed Hand

The term " writing with the unaccustomed hand " is used in preference to the more common expression " writing with the left hand," for the case of the naturally left-handed person writing with his right hand is indistinguishable from that of the right-handed person using his left hand.

Anyone who has attempted to write with his unaccustomed hand will probably have noticed that the resultant script bears little general resemblance to that normally written with the other hand. This is why about one person in twenty who wishes to disguise his handwriting will employ this simple method for the production of what he thinks will prove to be an unrecognisable script. This figure would probably be much greater if it were not for the fact that many, without making any real attempt to do so, consider that they are quite unable to write with the unaccustomed hand.

This is made manifest when, in the course of a criminal investigation, suspects are asked to furnish specimens of writing done with each hand, a course which is invariably taken when there is any reason to believe that the questioned handwriting has been disguised in any way. It is curious how, once they have been persuaded to make the effort, many of those who have professed complete inability to write at all with the unaccustomed hand, are surprised to find that it is less difficult than they had expected. With a little practice, most people are capable

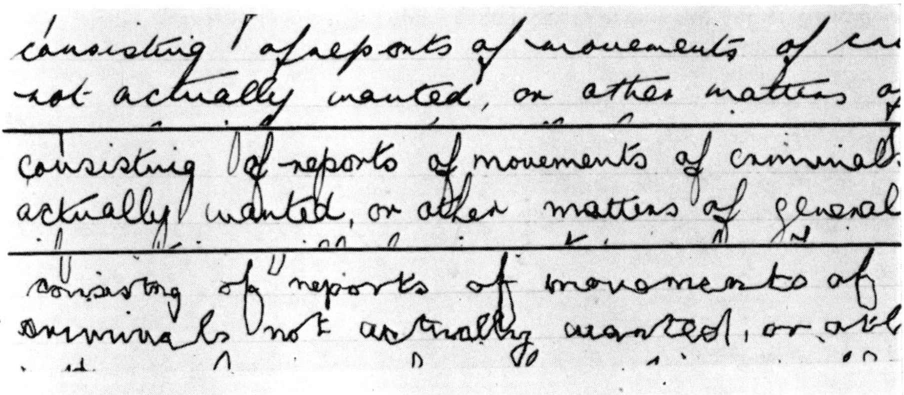

A.
B.
C.

Fig. 10–10. Three specimens of handwriting by the same person: (a) normal handwriting; (b) handwriting with a back slope; and (c) handwriting with the unaccustomed hand. Note the close resemblance between specimens " B " and " C."

of furnishing a legible if rather crude and inelegant script with either hand. Not unnaturally, speed and fluency will be lacking, as these things are the last qualities of a handwriting to be acquired, since their development demands a considerable period of practice.

Experience has shown that those who rely on the use of the unaccustomed hand for disguise rarely consider that there is any need to go further and introduce grotesque letter designs into the script as an extension of the disguise. They probably feel that the gross alteration in the appearance of the handwriting is sufficient disguise, and that there is no need for them to complicate the already considerable difficulty of the task they are undertaking.

It has already been stated that the adoption of a pronounced back slope will profoundly change the appearance of a handwriting, and the reasons for this have already been discussed in some detail. If a specimen of handwriting made with the unaccustomed hand is compared, not with the normal handwriting but with one made with an exaggerated back slope, it will be discovered that these two specimens bear a considerable resemblance to each other, practically the only difference being that the former exhibits even less fluency and grace of outline. This comparison justifies the conclusion that it is the change in slope which is largely responsible for the change in appearance of writing made with the unaccustomed hand. In addition, the lack of muscular control exhibited by the unaccustomed hand will be reflected in a lack of fluency, poorer rhythm and a crudity in the formation of loops, curves and eyelets which is absent from the normal handwriting.

The essential resemblance between the writing of the two hands is not surprising when it is realised that developed handwriting is substantially the unconscious product of the mind; it is only reasonable to conclude that if a man is blessed with artistic ability which is expressed in the adoption of a well-proportioned handwriting, it is unlikely that this quality will be suppressed merely by changing the hand which has acted as the servant of the brain. This statement may seem to argue that there may be substance in the claims of those graphologists who profess to delineate character from handwriting, but whilst it is manifestly unreasonable to assert that the nature of the handwriting is completely divorced from the mental and physical abilities of the writer, it is difficult to see how there can be sufficient evidence in a small specimen of handwriting to justify a tithe of the far-reaching and often contradictory speculations of the graphologists who examine it.

While the document examiner may be quite certain of the accuracy of his identification when he has compared left-handed with right-handed writing, it is sometimes difficult to convince a court and lay jury that two such apparently different handwritings are by the same person. In such cases it is well to have available for comparison specimens of writing done with each hand; if the disguised handwriting is then compared with that written by the suspect with the unaccustomed hand, the problem reduces itself into the proving that two specimens of handwriting of poor quality are of common authorship.

In the past, children who were naturally left-handed were forced to write with the right hand. Once schooldays were past, many of these unfortunates changed over to the left hand for writing, although as a result of long training, they were capable of writing fluently with the other hand; an ability often retained throughout life. As such persons are naturally ambidextrous as far as handwriting is concerned, it may well happen that specimens of the writing with the two hands will be both fluent and rhythmic, exhibiting slight but consistent differences which will enable the work of a particular hand to be identified. If the document examiner is presented with a suspect specimen of writing in the one hand, whereas all the comparison specimens are in the other, it is probable that whilst he will suspect that he is confronted with the work of a truly ambidextrous writer, he may not be able to prove that this is so on the material which is available to him. On one occasion, the author was placed in this difficult position. Whilst he strongly suspected that certain anonymous letters had been written with a hand different from that used for making the very fluently written standards, he was unable to express any definite opinion as to authorship. However, when extra standards written with the other hand were forthcoming, no further difficulty was experienced.

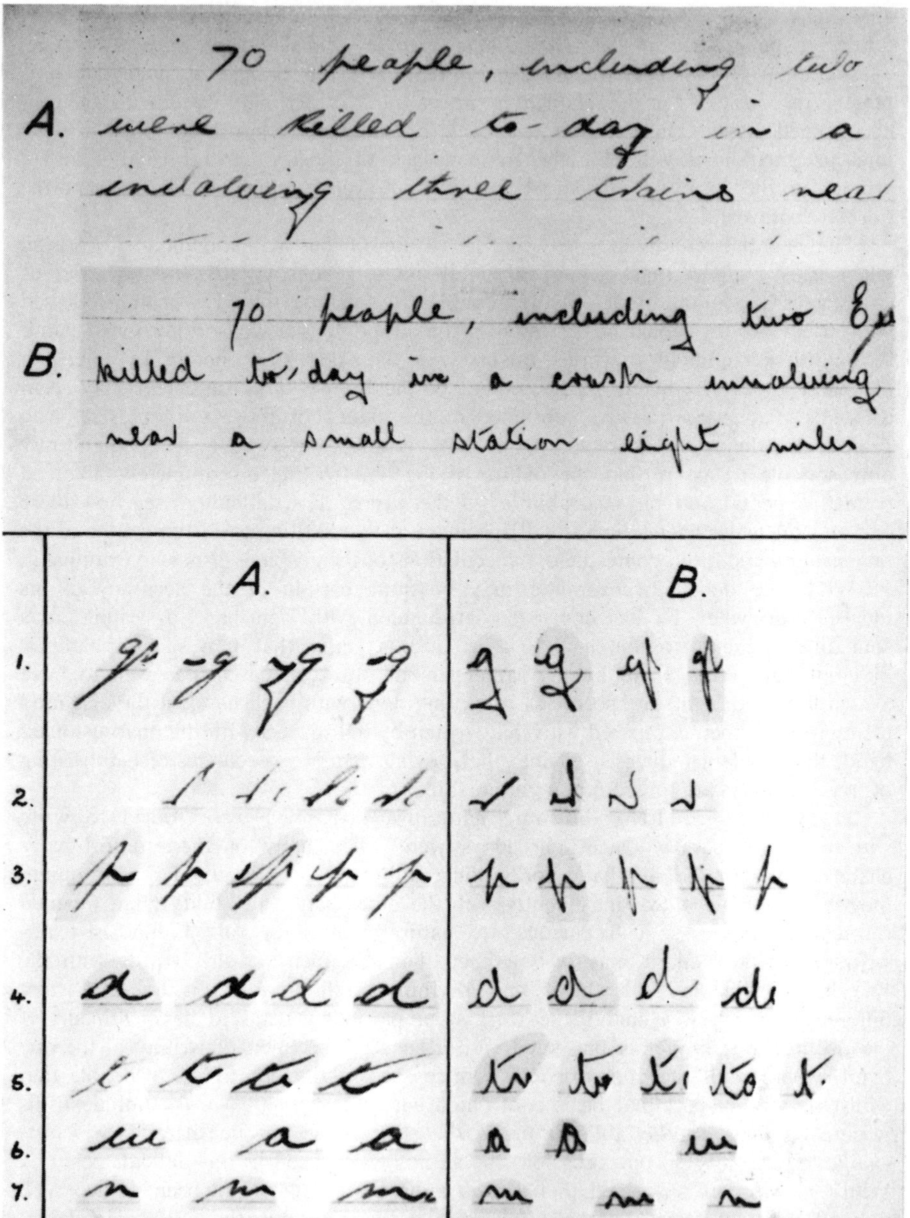

Fig. 10–11. " A " is the normal and " B " a disguised writing. The comparison table indicates how the master patterns for both writings are fundamentally the same although the writings differ greatly in appearance.

As it is now considered inadvisable to force left-handed children to write with the right hand, the number of fluent ambidextrous writers in the next generation will be considerably reduced, much to the relief of the document examiner.

Some graphologists, without giving details, claim that they are able to decide which hand was used from the appearance of the handwriting. Whilst it is true that many who habitually use the left hand adopt a most peculiar writing position which might have some effect upon the writing, the author has to confess that this feat is beyond his powers, for he has been unable to discover any consistent feature of a handwriting which would infallibly indicate which hand was used.

(7) Disguise is Rarely Consistent

With the obvious exception of the use of the unaccustomed hand, few forms of disguise are consistently retained throughout the whole of an extended passage of handwriting. Apart from the relaxation of the disguise, which is usually characteristic of the latter part of a passage and which is due to the writer becoming tired, with the consequent loss of concentration, certain portions of a disguised document can be counted on as having been much less thoroughly disguised than others.

For example, where disguised writings are enclosed in an envelope, either for transmission through the post or for delivery by hand, it is rare for the handwriting on the envelope to be disguised with anything like the same thoroughness as its contents. This is but one of the reasons why the envelopes of anonymous letters should invariably be preserved for investigation.

Apart from any relaxation of disguise in the handwriting, it will usually be found that the arrangement of the inscription on the envelope is that favoured for the writer in his normal correspondence; more than one anonymous letter writer has been traced by this unwitting retention of a highly individual style of arranging the inscription on an envelope. Figures which form part of the address on an envelope are rarely disguised, and, with the possible exception of the substitution of block letters for cursive capitals, the same may be said for titles such as "Mr.", "Mrs.", "Dr.", etc. Even in the anonymous letter itself, these titles are unlikely to be disguised, and the figures, especially those used for numbering the pages, will probably be those in normal use.

From this it must not be assumed that figures are invariably left undisguised; on the contrary, the figures found in fraudulent entries in account books and on printed forms are almost invariably disguised. This disguise will sometimes take an insidious form, for it is quite common for the criminal to copy the figures of someone who has also some legtimate access to the documents. When unsuspected, this form of disguise will serve not only to conceal the identity of the forger, but to direct the investigation into unprofitable channels. In a surprisingly large proportion of cases this wicked form of disguise may be penetrated with some ease, for the forger, whilst taking care to make an exact copy of his victim's figures, will often neglect to perfect his forgery in other equally important but less obvious respects. For example, in a number of cases investigated by the author, the forgers followed their own practices instead of those of their victims with respect to the arrangement of the figures in relation to the line and other printed matter on the page.

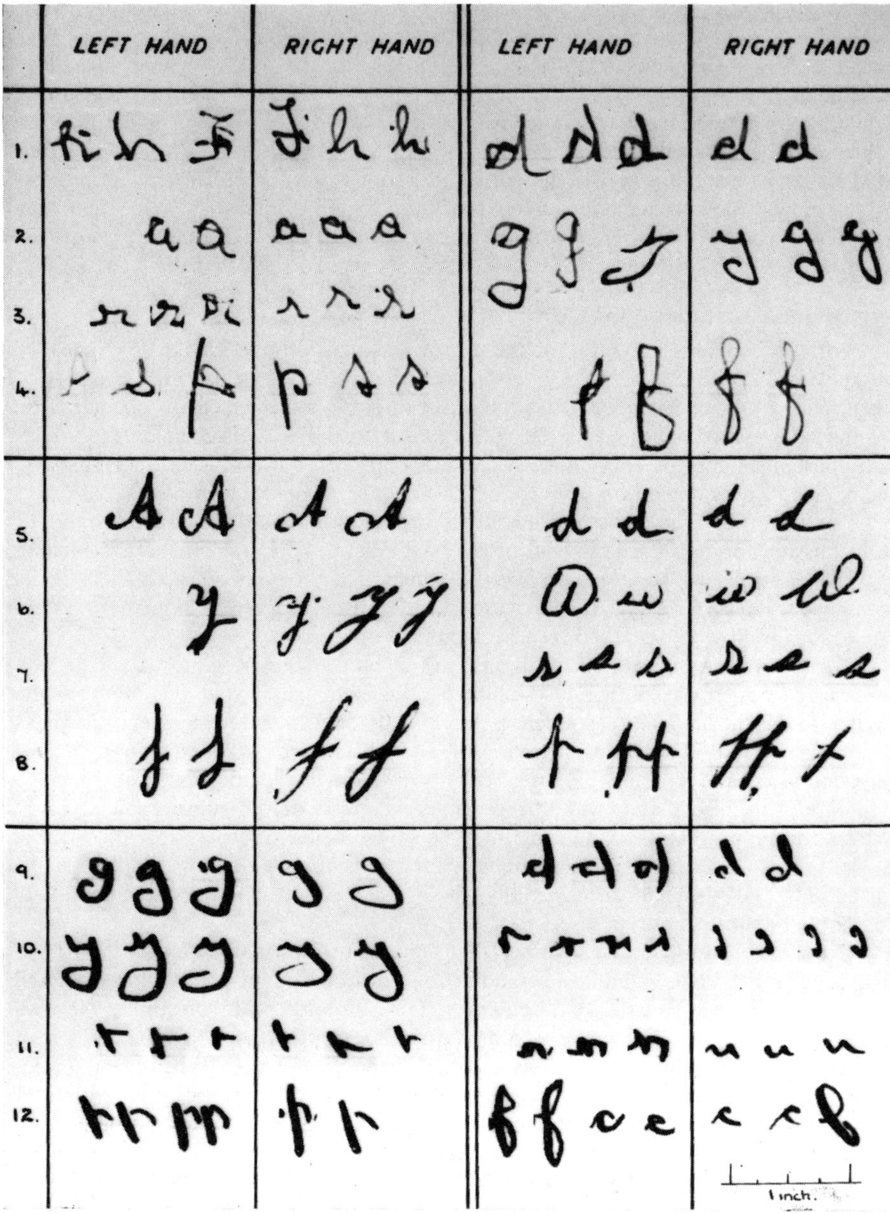

Fig. 10–12. Lines 1–4, 5–8, 9–12 contain extracts from the writing of three persons. Note (a) the close resemblance in structure of the various letter formations; (b) the increased back-slope of the left-hand writing; (c) the comparative crudity of the curves of the left-hand writing.

When such inconsistencies are observed, a decision has to be made as to which features are the consequence of disguise—the design of the figures or the way in which they are arranged. This is not difficult, for it is unreasonable to assume that anyone wishing to conceal his identity would retain his normal figure designs, and rest content with a subtle change such as an alteration of the way in which they are sited on the document.

As it is difficult to maintain a disguise consistently throughout a long passage, the final paragraphs of a disguised handwriting will bear a closer resemblance to the normal handwriting than any which have gone before; any feature which remains unchanged throughout is probably undisguised. Any feature which can be shown to be present unchanged throughout a number of specimens written over a fair period of time may safely be assumed to be undisguised. The only exception to this rule is where the feature is very obvious and is of comparatively rare occurrence. Consistent disguise is restricted to the more outstanding features of a handwriting, and the less conspicuous the characteristic, the less likely is it to be disguised in any way. This must not be taken to imply that subtle changes are never introduced into a handwriting as disguise, but the introduction of subtle changes is almost invariably unwitting, for they are generally the consequence of deliberate gross changes such as that of slope.

(8) Certain Features are Rarely Disguised

Experience has shown that certain features of a handwriting are rarely changed, however thorough the disguise may be in other respects; some of these have already been referred to in the chapter which deals with the structure of handwriting.

A general principle which admits of no exception is that no one is capable of writing a disguised handwriting which is of higher quality with respect to fluency, rhythm and letter design than that which is normal to the writer. Whilst this may seem a statement of the obvious, this principle is often overlooked when a comparison has to be made between a disguised handwriting and specimens drawn from a large number of suspects. On many occasions, a great deal of unnecessary work would have been saved if this had been borne in mind, for it is manifestly a waste of effort to seek specimens from poor writers when the suspect disguised script displays a high degree of pen control and artistic ability.

The general appearance of a handwriting may give a useful pointer to its probable author, no matter how carefully it has been disguised. Many handwritings are characterised by abnormal spacing of the words; in some the words are separated by less than a width of a letter, whilst in others the spacing may be as much as the width of four or five letters. Close spacing is so common that its occurrence is of little evidential value, but extremely wide spacing is comparatively rare. In the majority of disguised handwritings the word spacing is almost certain to be that of the normal script, a fact which may prove of some evidential value.

Excessive ornamentation in the form of flourishes, the underlining of words and the use of the rubric, is a feature of only a minority of hands, but it is worthy of note that the writers find considerable difficulty in pruning their scripts of these revealing features when attempting to disguise their handwriting.

In most disguised handwritings, what might be termed the arrangement of the writing—the marginal habits, line spacing, the extent to which the paragraphs are inset, etc.,—is rarely affected by the disguise. Of the thousands of specimens of disguised handwritings examined by the author, not a single one was found to depart from this rule. There also appeared to be complete conformity even in such details as the manner in which the writing is arranged with respect to the printed line when lined paper was used.

Bibliography

Conway, J. V. P., "The Identification of Handprinting," *Journal of Criminal Law, Criminology and Police Science,* Vol. 45, No. 5, January–February, 1955.

Downey, J. E., "Disguised Handwriting," *Journal of Applied Psychology,* Vol. 1, December, 1917.

Harris, J., "Disguised Handwriting," *Journal of Criminal Law and Criminology,* Vol. 43, No. 5, January–February, 1953.

Hilton, Ordway, "Influence of Serious Illness on Handwriting Identification," *Post-graduate Medicine,* 19 (2) A–36—A–48, February, 1956.

11

FORGED SIGNATURES

UNTIL public prejudice has been overcome and the fingerprint is willingly given and accepted as an identifying symbol on all important documents, the written signature must continue to exercise this function. That the signature is not entirely satisfactory as a means of positive identification is witnessed by the fact that convictions for forgery are not uncommon, and that an appreciable part of the work of the document examiner is concerned with the examination of questioned signatures.

For convenient treatment, suspect signatures may be divided into seven classes. These are:

(1) Forged signatures where no attempt has been made to make a copy of the genuine signature of the person purporting to sign the document.
(2) Forged "signatures" of fictitious persons.
(3) Forged signatures which closely resemble the genuine signature since they have been produced by a tracing process.
(4) Forged signatures which resemble the genuine signature, written free-hand to produce what is known as a "simulated" forgery.
(5) Genuine signatures which have been obtained by trickery.
(6) Genuine signatures which the writers are honestly unwilling to accept as genuine.
(7) Genuine signatures which have been deliberately written illegibly or in an unusual manner, so as to afford the signatories some plausible grounds for disclaiming them, should they deem it expedient.

DISTINCTION BETWEEN "GENUINE" AND "LEGALLY GENUINE" SIGNATURES

Some confusion may be avoided if it is made clear at the outset that the lawyer's criteria as to what does or does not constitute a legally genuine signature are not necessarily those of the document examiner when he has to decide whether, in his opinion, a signature is genuine or a forgery.

If, for example, a lawyer were confronted with a practically illegible signature on a will which, from other evidence in his possession, he is confident was made by the inert hand of the dying testator guided by that of one of the witnesses to form the signature, stroke by stroke, at the request of the writer who well knew what he was attempting to sign, he would have no hesitation in accepting this signature as legally genuine.

If, on the other hand, a document examiner were asked to compare this co-operative effort on the will with genuine signatures written by the testator when hale and hearty, it would probably be difficult for him to produce evidence that the signature on the will was a genuine signature of the testator. Again, a lawyer would undoubtedly regard as fraudulent a document bearing a signature obtained by trickery, whereas to the document examiner the signature would clearly be a genuine specimen.

In view of the foregoing, throughout this chapter, the terms "genuine" and "fraudulent" will be applied from the point of view of the document examiner, because he has to base his views entirely on what evidence he can adduce from the documents presented to him for examination. It is for the lawyer, who alone is able to view the case as a whole, to decide whether what the document examiner may characterise as a genuine signature from his point of view, may or may not legally be held to be a valid signature and vice versa.

Authorship of Forgeries

When a suspect signature is submitted for examination, the document examiner is first asked to determine whether, in his opinion, the signature is genuine or forged. If the signature is pronounced fraudulent, the question of the authorship of the forgery is very often raised. It will be shown that while it is often possible to express and justify a definite opinion as to whether a signature is genuine or forged, it is rarely that the identity of the forger can be established by comparing the handwriting of the forgery with specimens of the handwriting of suspects.

In some cases what matters is the authenticity of the signature, in others the identity of the forger. With certain types of forgery, such as those of the signatures on old wills and agreements, the proof that the questioned signatures are not genuine is often regarded by the parties as more important than the determination of the identity of the forger, who may well be dead by the time inquiries are made into the authenticity of the signatures.

On the other hand, especially where signatures of fictitious persons appear on bogus receipts for money or for the return of lost property, or on fraudulent hire-purchase forms, the fact of forgery is often patent once suspicion has been aroused, and the investigation is wholly directed to the discovery of the forger.

The Characteristics of Genuine Signatures

Before embarking on a discussion of the failings which enable forged signatures to be distinguished from those which are genuine, it is necessary to consider the features which characterise a genuine signature.

Whilst a person's signature may have a great deal in common with his handwriting in general, it is, fortunately for the document examiner, set apart in many respects from the usual run of handwriting. For many people, the signature is the word in the writing of which they have had most practice and are most fluent; indeed, it is the only word the illiterate can write with any degree of confidence. The signature is also the word with which a person identifies himself, and as such will have a greater personal significance than any other word he may write.

By anyone but the novice, the signature is written with little attention to spelling or to the details of letter design. It is probable that when a signature is being written, the attention is directed more to what is being signed than to how the letters of the signature are being put together. The signature, above all others, is the word which is written automatically and without conscious thought about the mechanics of its production.

Pen Movement

The novice will slowly lower his pen on to the paper and allow the point to rest momentarily before beginning to trace out the line. This is not the practice of the fluent writer whose pen point is in motion before touching down on the paper. This forward motion of the pen point is continued when the word has been completed and the pen is being lifted from the paper. A similar state of affairs applies to the writing of a fluent signature, possibly more so, for a signature is generally written with a dash and flourish absent from the normal handwriting.

Fig. 11–1. The left hand " B " from a forged signature is characterised by poor line quality and blunt ends to the strokes. The right hand " B " from the genuine signature has good line quality and more pointed line endings.

The microscopic examination of the ends of an ink line will usually indicate whether or not the pen point was in motion before touching down onto the paper. When the pen point is already in motion at the instant of making contact with the paper, the line will often exhibit a pointed end. A similar feature will be found when the motion of the pen point is maintained as it is being lifted off the paper at the end of the word. This pointed appearance is in marked contrast with the thickened and sometimes club-shaped ends which are found when the pen point has rested on the paper for any appreciable time before being put into motion or after the writing has ceased.

The thickening of the ends of the line is due to the continued flow of ink from the pen nib on to the paper whilst it is stationary, and the extent of this thickening depends upon a number of factors. If the pen nib is well charged with ink, especially if it be an ink which flows very freely, such as one of the recently introduced alkaline inks, the clubbed ends of the lines may be apparent to the naked eye, especially if the paper has a soft surface which readily absorbs ink. If, however, the pen nib is running short of ink, the amount of thickening as it rests momentarily on a highly glazed paper surface may be imperceptible. In all cases, the condition of the ends of the ink lines is relative. Where there is no apparent thickening where the pen point rested momentarily on the paper, it will probably be found that the ends of the lines which had been written with the pen point in motion before touching the paper are not so much pointed, as deprived of ink for some distance after the pen had touched the paper. These inkless traces of the pen point can best be seen by having the light at grazing incidence.

Whilst on the subject of barely perceptible scratches made with the dry pen, it may be of some interest to record that, like the golfers who waggle the club behind the ball before driving, some writers are in the habit of making a few nervous scratches with the pen before beginning to write. Whether this is a nervous " tic " or due to their being accustomed to write with reluctant fountain pens which need some preliminary manipulation before the ink can be expected to flow, the fact is that any genuine handwriting of these persons is invariably prefaced by these initial scratches.

Ball-point Pen Movement

The thickening of the ends of ink lines has been attributed to the increase in the flow of ink on to the paper as the pen nib remains stationary, but with a ball-point pen, there can be no direct flow of the ink from the reservoir to the paper. In these pens the ink is conducted by capillary action from the reservoir to the rotating ball, which picks up a thin layer of the thick viscous ink which is transferred to the paper as the ball revolves. The amount of ink transferred to the paper is proportional to the area of ink-covered ball surface which is brought into contact with

Fig. 11–2. The poor line quality of the writing is caused by the use of an early type of ball-point pen and is not indicative of forgery.

the paper and not to the duration of the time of contact. As this is so, no thickening of the line endings can be expected as the result of momentarily halting the pen point before writing.

When a swiftly moving ball-point is applied to or lifted from the paper, some tapering of the ends of the lines may be observed, but the nature and extent of this is dependent upon the state of the pen; unless the inkfeed is working at its highest efficiency, the line produced by a ball-point pen is rough and irregular. Some ball-point pens refuse to write until the ball has been rotated to a considerable extent. This is why many signatures written with one of these pens are accompanied by a number of preliminary scratches. These should not be confused with the nervous scratches to which reference has already been made, for they are more in the nature of abortive starts to the writing.

Pen-lifts, Halts and Hesitations

Many signatures, particularly those of few letters, are written with a continuous line, the pen being neither lifted nor even halted in its progress from start to finish. In a minority of signatures, well-defined breaks occur. Sometimes the break takes the form of a pen-lift where, after being lifted, the pen is replaced on a line so that no obvious break in the continuity of the line can be seen with the naked eye. When the pen is not replaced on a line, a hiatus will be formed in the signature. A hiatus between the initial capital letter and the remainder of the signature is fairly common, but a hiatus elsewhere in a signature is comparatively rare.

It is uncommon to find a signature with more than one hiatus, although on one occasion the author encountered the signature of a well-educated adult where every letter was made separately as though it were written in script, although the letter formations were substantially cursive rather than script forms.

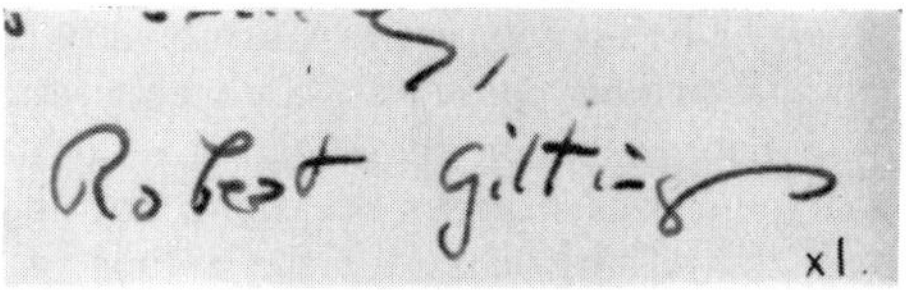

Fig. 11–3. A signature characterised by the presence of many hiatuses although the letter formations resemble those characteristics of connected cursive handwriting rather than disconnected " script."

With the great majority of people, whatever plan be followed, whether the use of an unbroken line or the formation of the signature in separate pieces, it will be found that the manner of writing is consistent in this respect when *contemporary* signatures are examined. The habits of some writers in this respect are subject to change, and if a series of signatures written over a period of years is studied, a regular gradation of writing practice will probably become apparent. This discovery may prove of importance, since many an excellent forgery has been exposed because certain characteristics of the suspect signature could not be regarded as consistent with the date attributed to it.

Increase in Pen-lifts due to Ill-health

When a writer is seriously ill or senile, it is scarcely to be expected that the normal practice of writing the signature with a single continuous line or with only few breaks will be adhered to, and common sense must be applied when suspect signatures are alleged to have been written under these conditions.

Sometimes these signatures also exhibit considerable departures from the normal letter design, and usually the attempt is made to explain these on the grounds of fatigue on the part of the writer. This plausible explanation can sometimes be negatived by demonstrating that the forged signature, presumably written by a fatigued person, is devoid of any pen-lift, whereas all genuine contemporary signatures exhibit this feature. It is most unreasonable to assume that anybody too fatigued to form the letters correctly would fail to take advantage of the breaks normal to the signature.

It will be explained later that a forged signature which bears a close resemblance to the genuine signature is generally laboriously constructed from a comparatively large number of separate portions. The natural consequence of this—the presence of a correspondingly large number of pen-lifts—when the signature is attributed to a sick person, is almost invariably explained as due to the signatory finding it necessary to rest after the effort of writing each portion. This argument can sometimes be exposed as fallacious by demonstrating that no pen-lift has occurred in places where they are invariably found in genuine contemporary signatures. It is manifestly unlikely that anyone seeking rest whilst signing will pass over any place where he usually lifts his pen and pauses when in good health.

Detection of Pen-lifts in Signatures

A hiatus in a signature is easily seen, but where, following a pen-lift, the pen point is restored to the paper on the ink line itself so that no gap appears in the writing, examination with a microscope will probably be needed to establish the presence of a pen-lift. Where ordinary writing ink has been used in a conventional pen, the detection of a pen-lift affords little difficulty, but with writing done with pencil or ball-point pen, it will probably prove impossible to determine where, if at all, the writing point was lifted and restored to the paper. If a ball-point pen is in poor condition the situation is even worse, for the signature will be graced with numerous hiatuses occasioned by the defective action of the ink feed rather than the writing habits of the author of the signature.

Other Characteristics of Genuine Signatures

General Similarity

The signatures of a good writer are certain to bear a strong resemblance to each other, but experience has shown that no matter how many are examined, no two will be found to be perfect replicas of each other, always provided that the signatures are of reasonable length and do not consist of but two or three letters. This should not be an unexpected finding because human beings cannot be expected to function with the precision of machines. The extent of the divergence is, however, much greater than might be expected. Even when a careful selection has been made from a large number of the signatures of a skilled penman, any two of which are chosen for their close resemblance will be found to differ in many respects when they are compared by being superimposed before a strong light. This plays an important part in the detection of traced forgeries.

Alignment with Respect to Guide Lines and Printed Matter

When a multitude of signatures on printed forms are examined, a number of important conclusions may be drawn concerning the alignment of signatures with respect to the guide lines and other printed matter thereon.

One group of writers will be found always to write their signatures accurately aligned along the dotted line whenever this is provided, whilst another slightly larger group will consistently write just above it. A third minority group will be found to write their signatures through the line. Out of a large number, a few will be found who seem to care little whether they write on, above or through the line, but with these the handwriting itself will also show a marked reluctance to conform to any standards.

Fixed habits will also be found with respect to the alignment of the signature in the space provided for it along the line. Many begin to write as close as possible to any printed matter such as (signed), whilst others shun the print and cram the signature into a small space at the extreme right of the line. The great majority will neatly frame their signatures in the centre of the space provided.

If no dotted line is provided, the majority of the signatures will be given a slight upward slope, many will be fairly horizontal whilst others will slope downward.

In this respect also, it will be found that the habit of any particular signatory will remain fairly fixed.

Other minor but nevertheless significant habits may be noticed. Some writers seem incapable of writing a signature without the immediate use of blotting-paper. Even in the use of periods after the initials, and sometimes after the surname itself, it will be found that there is a marked tendency for the majority of writers to develop habits from which they rarely depart. On occasion, commas rather than periods will be found to be favoured.

If a fair number of the genuine signatures of any particular person are examined in the light of what has already been stated, it will almost certainly be possible to list a number of personal idiosyncrasies in the writing and placing of the signature on a document which are additional to those mentioned above by way of example.

All these personal features connected with the writing of a signature help to characterise it and they show that any signature must be regarded as something far more complex than a collection of letter designs strung together in a particular order.

Letter Design and Range of Variation

As no two genuine signatures are identical, it follows that in signatures, as with handwriting in general, a certain amount of natural variation in letter design must be expected and consequently allowed for, whenever signatures are being compared to determine whether or not they are of common authorship. Occasionally, as with other handwriting, accidentals may occur in genuine signatures, but it is fortunate that this is a comparatively rare occurrence because their presence is often wrongly regarded as a definite indication that any signature so modified cannot be considered genuine.

The existence of natural variation means that, as with other handwriting, a reasonable amount of standard material in the form of genuine signatures must be available for comparison, because it is essential that the range of variation in letter design which might be expected in a genuine signature should be determined before any comparisons are attempted with signatures of unknown authorship.

Nothing is more calculated to bring the comparison of handwriting into contempt than the attitude of the witness who declares a genuine signature to be a forgery because it departs in some detail of letter design from either of *the two genuine specimens* he has used as the basis of his comparison. This kind of folly has happened within the experience of the author.

Methods for the Production of Forged Signatures

Many forgeries are so crudely executed and bear such a remote resemblance to the genuine signatures, that their spurious nature is evident on the most cursory examination. These crude forgeries find their way to the document examiner only when evidence leading to the discovery of the forger is required. Other forgeries are so skilfully written that proof that they are not genuine can be adduced only on microscopic examination of the structure of the ink line. To appreciate the significance of the evidence which may be gleaned from the microscopic examination of the ink line of a forgery it will be necessary to consider in some detail the principal methods whereby convincing forgeries are fabricated. As full details of these methods have been published far and wide, in novels as well as in technical works, there is small risk of forgery being facilitated by their being referred to once again.

There are two main methods whereby a forgery which bears a close resemblance to a genuine signature may be fabricated.

Simulated Forgeries

The first involves the careful study of a genuine specimen of the signature it is intended to copy, so that the forger may acquire a mental picture of the letter design, letter spacing, shading and any other prominent feature which endows the genuine signature with its general pictorial effect. This study is combined with many practice attempts at the reproduction from memory, first of portions of the signature and then, when these elements have been mastered, of the signature written as a whole.

After each attempt, the reproduction is compared with the genuine signature which is being copied and any shortcomings are noted for correction in future attempts. The study and practice are continued until the forger feels that he is capable of writing a convincing forgery on the required document.

A freehand forgery made in this way is known as a " simulated " forgery, and in the hands of an expert this method of writing forgeries is least liable to detection. Most of the notorious forgers of a past generation have relied on the simulated forgery when practising their craft. It is fortunate that the number of persons who have both the skill and application, to say nothing of the motive, to enable them to produce a convincing simulated forgery is extremely limited. One limiting factor is that no one can hope to make successful attempts at the production of a simulated forgery of the signature of a more skilful penman than himself.

Traced Forgeries

The alternative method, and for a poor penman, the only practicable way of forging a signature, is to make use of one of the tracing procedures employed by artists and draughtsmen when they have to make accurate copies of outlines in the course of their work. Tracing is resorted to by all who are not sufficiently confident of their ability to write a convincing simulated forgery, for this process can be counted on to furnish a forgery which can be made to bear an exceedingly close resemblance to the genuine signature used for the tracing.

Direct Tracing

The simplest tracing procedure, direct tracing, is accomplished by holding the paper bearing the genuine signature against a window and then adjusting the position of the document which is to bear the forgery so that the outline of the signature can be seen through the document in the required place. All that then remains to be done is to ink-in the outline of the genuine signature. As a window is rarely found in a convenient position and at a comfortable angle for writing, a photographer's retouching desk is far more satisfactory; if a retouching desk is not available, it is easy to improvise an effective substitute.

In essentials, a retouching desk is little more than a sloping sheet of glass illuminated from below with a powerful source of light. The paper bearing the genuine signature and the document to be forged are placed together on the sloping sheet of glass which is more convenient for the careful outlining of the genuine signature than the average window.

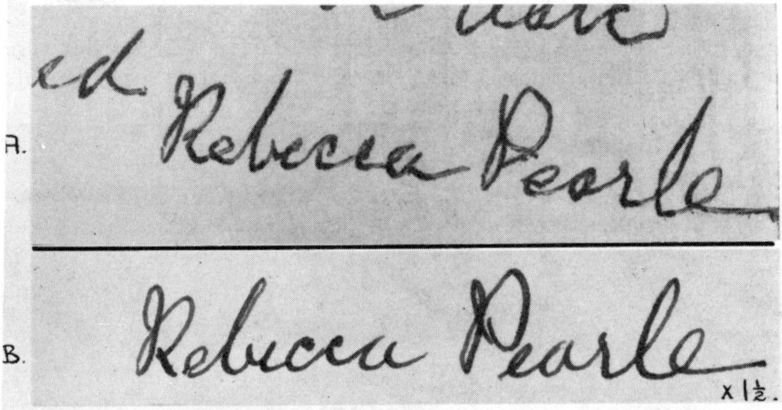

Fig. 11–4. The lower signature " B " is a tracing prepared from the upper genuine signature " A." This example of a traced forgery is interesting in that the line quality of the forgery is superior to that of the original genuine signature from which it was prepared. The line quality of the genuine signature " A " is extremely poor because of the age and infirmity of the signatory.

It is curious how the majority of traced forgeries seem to have been outlined with the signature held upside down. Experiments carried out by the author indicate that it is far simpler to trace the signature when it is correctly orientated, so that it is hard to account for this curious practice. One explanation may be that with the signature held upside down, the attention can better be directed to the accurate tracing of what then will be a meaningless outline, rather than to the writing of a recognisable name in which the forger's own handwriting tendencies may influence the final result.

Direct tracing may not always be practicable, as it necessitates the availability of a genuine signature written on a translucent sheet of paper with nothing printed or written on the back in the neighbourhood of the signature. Unless these conditions are complied with, there will be insufficient light transmitted to enable a clear outline of the signature to be distinguished. In spite of this limitation and the fact that the forger has to trace an outline which, at its best, is rather tenuous and lacking in detail unless both sheets of paper concerned are fairly translucent, the direct method has the great advantage that no separate "guide" line has to be made on the forged document.

If a guide line is allowed to remain associated with the forgery, the discovery of its presence will be sufficient to expose it as fraudulent. If attempts are made to erase a guide line, it will be found very difficult to effect a thorough erasure, and in any event, the surface of the paper in the neighbourhood of the forgery will be disturbed and so be likely to arouse suspicion.

Projection Tracing

When direct tracing is not practicable, recourse has to be made to methods for the projection of the outline of the genuine signature on to the document which is to be forged.

Some system of optical projection would probably be ideal for this purpose, and it would be a simple matter to make the size of the forgery somewhat different

Fig. 11–5. A traced forgery showing where the ink line has departed appreciably from the horizontal impression formed as a guide line. When an impression is being inked in it is difficult to adjust the illumination so that both horizontal and vertical impressions can be clearly distinguished at the same time. In this case the impressed signature was illuminated from the side. This enabled an accurate register of the vertical lines with the impressions to be made but as the horizontal impressions were difficult to distinguish considerable errors may be seen throughout the whole of the signature.

from that of the genuine signature, and in this way complicate the proof that the forgery was derived from the genuine signature which had been utilised. It may be fortunate that there is no commercial apparatus which can readily be adapted for this purpose and the majority of forgers are incapable of devising and putting into operation a workable scheme for themselves. For obvious reasons no further details of the method are given here.

By far the simplest way of projecting an outline of a genuine signature on to the document to be forged, is to place the genuine signature over the place where the forgery is to appear, and then to pencil along its outline so heavily that a groove appears on the undersheet. This groove can then be conveniently inked-in. Despite the crudity of the outline produced in this simple way, this method was successfully used by a bank manager over a period of years to forge the signatures of the bank's customers.

Use of Carbon Paper

The use of carbon paper will provide a more detailed outline with the application of less pressure to the genuine signature. Whilst on many grounds, it would be more satisfactory to utilise a smooth hard point, such as that on a coarse metal or plastic knitting-needle, for tracing out the outline of the genuine signature, it is curious how often a pencil is used for this purpose with no attempt made to erase the pencil line at the completion of the tracing.

It is hard to credit that sometimes, in an endeavour to secure acceptance of the forgery, a genuine signature bearing this obvious sign of having been used as the basis of a traced forgery is introduced as evidence to show how closely a questioned signature resembles the admittedly genuine signature from which it had actually been traced. Even if the stupid mistake of using a pencil on a genuine signature intended for production at a later stage is guarded against, traces of the faint groove which is inevitably formed along the outline of the genuine signature by the passage of the tracing point are almost sure to be found on close inspection.

Carbon paper is not entirely satisfactory, and apart from general smudges wherever it has made contact with the document, leaves a greasy line which cannot easily be erased when the inking-in has been completed.

As the presence of traces of carbon paper markings associated with a suspect signature are fatal to its chances of acceptance once they have been detected, other methods for the projection of a desired outline are preferred by the competent forger. Whilst these methods may vary in detail, the general procedure is the same for all, in that tracing paper is used for the preparation of an intermediate copy of the signature.

Use of Tracing Paper

A sheet of transparent paper, such as tracing paper, or even paper which is highly translucent such as grease-proof paper, is placed over the genuine signature and pressed into close contact so that it shows through quite clearly. The signature is then copied on to the tracing paper with soft pencil or ink. If gentle pressure is employed, there will be no indication that the genuine signature has been used as the basis of a tracing.

After removal from the genuine signature, the back of the tracing paper is given a coat of graphite by being rubbed over with a soft pencil. Considerable control of the nature and the depth of the coating and hence of the guide line can be exercised at this stage. The tracing paper is then lowered on to the required place on the document which is to bear the forgery, and the outline of the signature is once more traced out with a pencil or other pointed implement. This will transfer to the document an outline which can subsequently be inked-in. Unlike the greasy guide line and smears which are produced by the use of carbon paper, any graphite left on the forged document by contact with the coated tracing paper can be removed by gentle erasure with artist's gum or an india rubber.

The only disadvantage of a tracing made in this manner is that it is twice removed from the original, and considerable care has to be taken at all stages if all the details in the genuine signature are to be reproduced in the forgery.

Guide Lines

Except for those directly traced, every traced forgery will have a guide line which, usually, will be left without any attempt being made to erase it. This may seem a stupid omission on the part of the forger, but there are good reasons for this.

In the first place, the average forger has not available nor is experienced in the use of the microscope, and if the inking in of the guide line has been accomplished with care, little if any trace should be apparent on the closest inspection with the naked eye. Few forgers are aware that it is by no means easy to ink in a guide line, especially when care has to be taken not to venture beyond the limits of the trace, for almost invariably, parts of the guide line will be found uncovered at the ends of the strokes and at the centres of curves. Even when the guide line has been completely covered by the ink line, it is often possible to distinguish traces of it mingled with the ink when a high-power microscope is used for the examination of the line. Furthermore, if graphite has been used for the guide line, and a dyestuff ink for the inking-in, a photograph of the signature taken by infra-red will record the whole of the guide line, because of the opacity to infra-red of graphite or other forms of free carbon. The ink is unlikely to interfere because of the transparency to infra-red of most of the dyestuffs used for the preparation of writing ink.

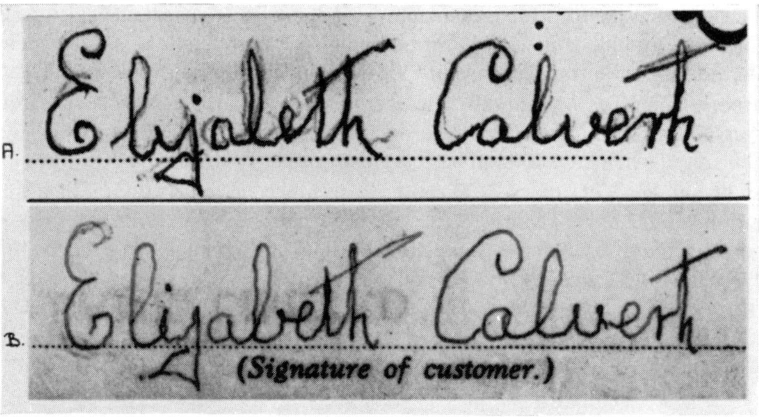

Fig. 11–6. " A " is a photograph of a traced forgery in which the pencil line may be seen in its entirety. " B " is a photograph of a traced forgery from the same case, in which the greater part of the pencil line has been erased. The forger failed to erase the faint pencil line associated with the extreme upper and lower portions of the initial " E." In each case the appearance of the pencil line has been enhanced by the appropriate photographic procedure. On the original document these pencil lines appeared very faint indeed.

In the second place, a forger may be reluctant to attempt to clean up a traced forgery because of the disturbance this would almost certainly cause to the surface of the paper in the neighbourhood of the signature. Nothing is so certain to excite suspicion as signs of abrasion in the neighbourhood of a signature.

When erasure is attempted there are often abundant indications of abortive attempts having been made to erase the guide line. As a rule the most thorough erasure is accomplished in the middle of the signature, for the ends are rarely so thoroughly cleaned up. This is probably due to the fact that when the eraser is swept to and fro, the rubbed area has not been extended appreciably beyond the ends, because of the risk of signs of abrasion becoming apparent on the blank areas of paper which flank the signature. This means that the speed of the eraser, and hence its cleansing power, is at a maximum at the centre of the signature, falling to very low values at the ends of its travel.

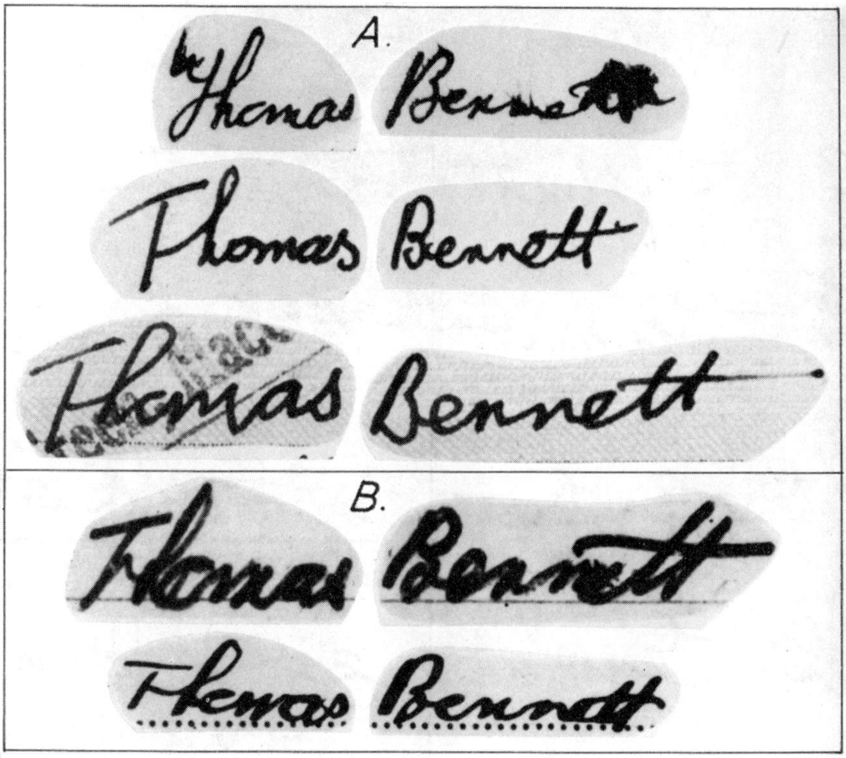

Fig. 11–7. *Identification of a forger.* " A " illustrates three forged signatures of a non-existent person. " B " illustrates two examples of the same name written by the suspect who was eventually convicted of the forgery. In " A " little attempt was made to disguise the handwriting of the forger except by the adoption of a slightly more upright slope.

Investigation of Forged Signatures

The investigation of a suspect signature is governed largely by the nature of the class of forgery to which it may be assigned. The principles which are invoked to prove that a group of signatures are all traced forgeries derived from one original genuine signature will have little in common with those applied to the examination of a single simulated forgery. As this is so, each class of forged or suspect signature will be considered independently.

The first class of forgeries to be considered will be that which includes those "signatures" where no attempt has been made to make a close imitation of the handwriting of some other person.

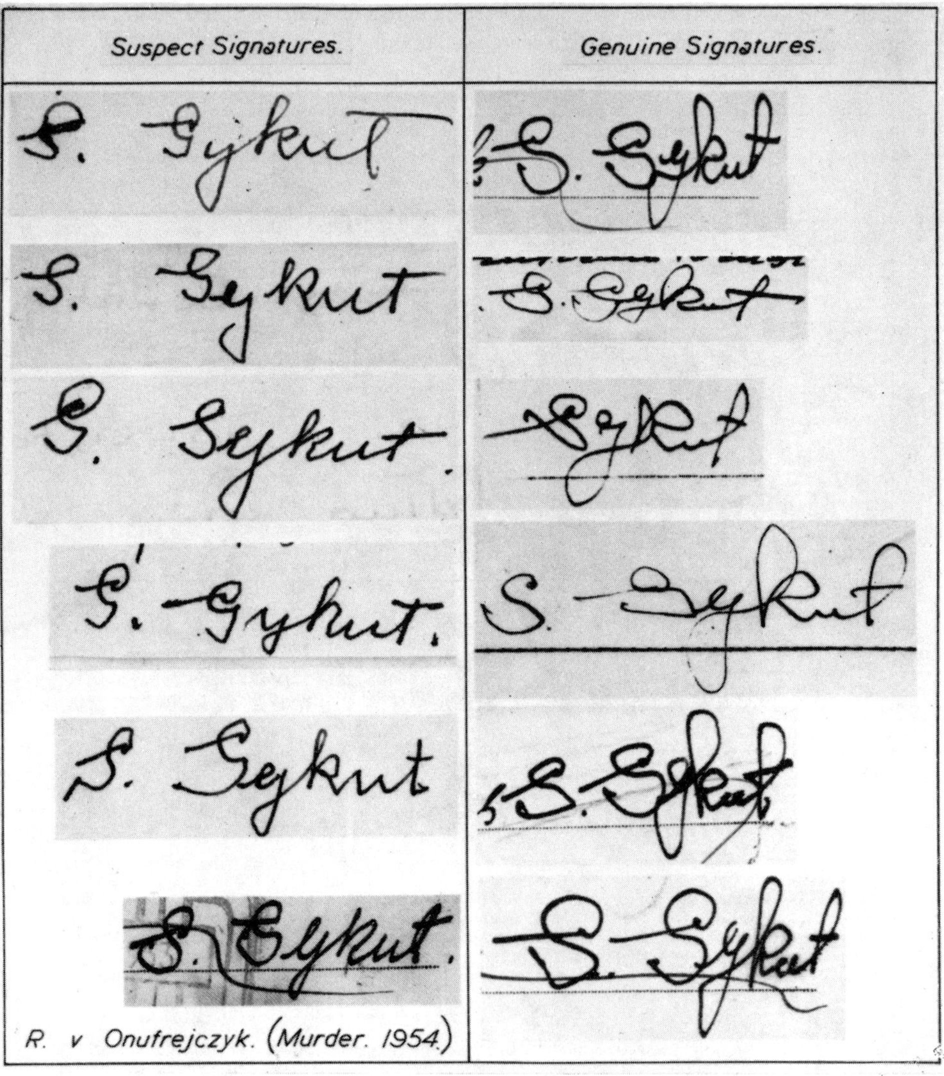

Fig. 11–8. The suspect signatures in the left hand column are characterised by (i) poor line quality, (ii) different letter alignment and (iii) greater degree of general resemblance to each other than the freely written and genuine signatures shown in the right hand column. This illustrates the tendency for a group of forged signatures to bear a close resemblance to each other and to show faults in the relative alignment of the letters even when care has been taken to make a fair copy of the letter design.

When these signatures have been dashed off by the forger without any attempt being made to copy any particular outline, there is rarely any difficulty in proving that they are fraudulent and as a rule the only question with which the document examiner has to deal is the determination of the authorship of the forgeries. This usually resolves itself into the proof of the authorship of a limited amount of handwriting, although the problem is often complicated by the forged signatures rarely being written in a natural handwriting completely free of disguise. It is fortunate that a fair proportion of people are unable to introduce any appreciable disguise into their handwriting, so that it is often possible to prove the authorship of these forgeries to the degree of certainty required in a criminal prosecution.

Even where there is insufficient evidence to prove authorship, it is often possible for the document examiner to indicate the probable author out of a considerable number of suspects and so direct the investigation into profitable channels.

This aspect of the work occupies a considerable proportion of the time of any document examiner working for law enforcement agencies, for since the establishment of the Welfare State, some millions of postal drafts for considerable sums of money are posted to the recipients every week. As might be expected, a proportion of these are misdelivered or are stolen to be cashed by people who have no right to the money. As personal identification of the person cashing the orders by busy Post Office employees is generally out of the question, the only means whereby the culprits may be brought to justice is by the comparison of the handwriting on the postal drafts which acknowledges receipt of the money, with specimens of the handwriting of any suspects.

It is where these small amounts of disguised handwriting are concerned that every advantage must be taken of the habits, other than mere letter design, associated with the writing of a signature, which have already been referred to.

Signatures of Fictitious Persons

The second class of forgery includes the signatures of fictitious persons, such as those which are found on bogus receipts for money or for the return of stolen or found property. Signatures of this class naturally cannot be shown to be fraudulent by producing genuine signatures to which it is obvious that they bear no significant resemblance.

Theoretically, this end might be attained by showing that the persons to whom the signatures refer are fictitious, but in practice it is exceedingly difficult to prove that any particular person has no existence outside the imagination of the forger. This difficulty is not reduced when it is suggested by the defence that a fictitious name might have been used by a real person who wishes for good reason to remain unknown.

In these circumstances, it is often best to concentrate on seeking evidence which might connect the handwriting of the forged signature with that of the person who is most likely to benefit from the forgery. If it can be shown that there is a substantial amount of evidence which is consistent with this suspect having written the questioned signature, this will reinforce other evidence which tends to show that the signatory has no real existence. The fact of forgery and its authorship are proved simultaneously.

When, to his own advantage, a forger puts forward a document which bears the signature of a fictitious person, it may confidently be expected that he will have taken considerable trouble to ensure that the forgery bears little obvious resemblance to his normal handwriting. If this fraudulent signature purports to have been " witnessed " it is well to remember that these extra signatures will also have to be forged. It is very noticeable how often the imagination of the forger as to the form of disguise will become impoverished when a second or third signature has to be disguised on the one document. Whilst, in many instances, it has proved impossible to prove that the principal signature is in the handwriting of the forger, it has been comparatively easy to show that he was responsible for those of the " witnesses."

General Line of Attack on Forgeries which Resemble the Genuine Signatures

If the suspect signature is an integral part of a document, the initial attack should be aimed at the document as a whole, because it is well known that it is far more hazardous to attempt to fabricate a signature which is an integral part of a document than one which is an isolated example. It is for this reason that forged autographs of the historically famous are generally found written on strips of paper or parchment hardly large enough to accommodate them, or on documents whereon their appearance seems to be completely fortuitous.

It has already been mentioned that the design of most people's signatures is slightly but steadily modified with the passage of the years, a fact which appears to be unknown to many otherwise quite skilful forgers. As this is so, there is always the chance that the document which may be said to " frame the signature in time " will bear a date or furnish evidence from which it can be dated, which is at variance with the style of the signature it bears. Considerable doubt can be cast upon the authenticity of a suspect signature when it can be shown to be of a pattern which had been discarded by the writer before the date attributed to the document on which it appears, and even less credence will be given to a signature which considerably antedates the style of genuine signature to which it conforms.

The importance of this preliminary investigation cannot be over-estimated, because even the most skilfully executed simulated forgery is not proof against attack on the grounds of style related to date. This line of attack is of the greatest utility when applied to documents which have conveniently come to light some years after they are supposed to have been drawn up. It is of less general application when contemporary signatures on contemporary documents are the subject of investigation.

Every document which bears a suspect signature should be given a close general examination on the lines laid down elsewhere. Special attention should be paid to the search for abraded areas in the neighbourhood of the signature and for smears of colouring matter caused by contact with carbon paper. In particular, a close examination with strong light at grazing incidence should be made of the whole of the document for, on more than one occasion, impressions of practice attempts at writing a forged signature have been discovered on the document. These were occasioned by the forger carelessly resting scrap-paper on the document while rehearsing the writing of the forgery.

Any peculiarity in the positioning of the signature or in its alignment with respect to the remainder of the written or typewritten matter should be noted, as from such observations it is sometimes possible to draw the conclusion that the signature must have antedated some at least of the other matter on the document.[1]

Detailed Examination of Suspect Signature

Those who wish to make a successful attack upon the authenticity of any forged signature which bears a distinct resemblance to the genuine signature must bear in mind three facts.

The first is that any forgery will, of necessity, exhibit a considerable degree of similarity to the general run of genuine signatures in the more obvious features of letter design. The reason for this is simple—what else could any forger be expected to ensure if he wishes his handiwork to be accepted as genuine?

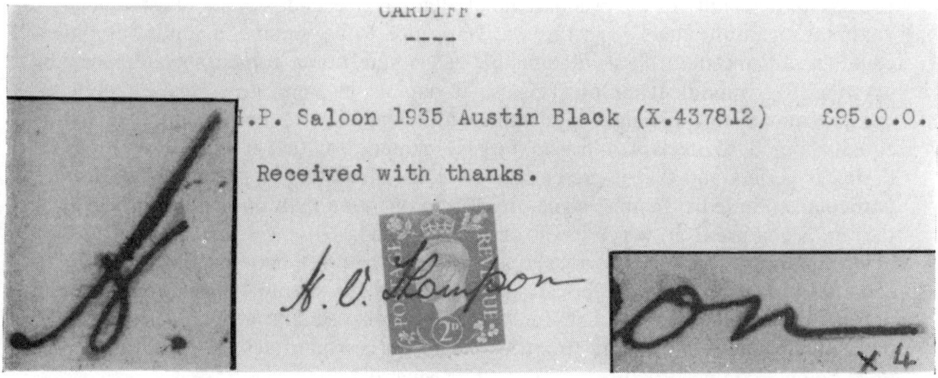

Fig. 11–9. The signature across the stamp has been traced over a faint pencil outline. The two enlarged inserts show where the ink line has departed from the pencilled guide line.

The second is that some forgeries will resemble at least one genuine signature to an uncanny extent. This is to be expected, for all that the forger has to do to accomplish this feat is to run his pen accurately along a traced outline. The close resemblance follows automatically from the nature of the process—tracing—used for fabricating the forgery.

The third is that no two genuine signatures of any length are replicas of each other. The existence of natural variation and the occasional occurrence of accidentals already referred to ensure that there will always be some variation in letter design and general structure among a group of genuine signatures.

In view of the foregoing facts, it is more than unscientific, it is puerile, to attack any signature as a forgery simply by stating that it exhibits some obvious feature of letter design which cannot be matched in any of the genuine signatures which have been made available for examination.

Those who are putting forward a forgery can be counted on to have a complete

[1] See " Signatures obtained by Trickery."

answer to this argument. They may well have available either the genuine signature from which the forgery was copied or one very like it, and it is quite probable that this particular genuine signature will exhibit the very feature to which exception had been taken; otherwise it is extremely unlikely that this feature would have been included in what would have been an admittedly good copy of the general features of the genuine signatures taken as a whole.

If by any chance a suitable genuine signature cannot be produced to counter this attack, the examiner may be asked whether, owing to the existence of natural variation and the occurrence of accidentals, every feature of a genuine signature can be expected to be matched in one or other of a comparatively small group of admittedly genuine signatures. If the answer is rashly given in the affirmative, a genuine signature will then be carefully selected and presented with the request to match every obvious feature of its letter design in one or other of a small group of genuine signatures. When it is patent that this cannot be accomplished, the stupidity of the original line of attack is revealed.

If the signature attacked in this way happened to be genuine, a similar argument could be advanced to show that neither a genuine nor a forged signature can be described as fraudulent simply because it departs in some gross feature of letter design from a few genuine specimens with which it has been compared. It is equally stupid to declare a traced forgery genuine on the grounds that its letter design is perfect and that it presents no obvious differences in pictorial effect from a particular admittedly genuine signature which, on more than one occasion, has been the very signature from which it was originally traced.

From the description previously given of the contrast between the writing of a genuine signature and the fabrication of a forgery, it should be apparent that the only fundamental difference between a genuine signature and a good forgery lies in the manner in which they are produced. Any successful attack on a skilful forgery must be made on its structure, and not on its general appearance.

Attack on Traced Forgeries

Where traced forgeries are concerned, the most devastating attack which can be made on their authenticity is to demonstrate the presence therein of a guide line or traces of a guide line which has been wholly or partially erased.

A stereoscopic microscope is best suited for the preliminary examination of the signature. The search should be concentrated on the ends of strokes, and at the centres of curves where the guide line is least likely to be completely covered by the superimposed ink line. If it is suspected that an attempt has been made to erase a guide line, the extremities of the signature should be examined with thoroughness before the search is abandoned, for it is here that the erasure is least likely to have been effective.

If an attempt at erasure is suspected, the area should on no account be dusted with graphite in an effort to find evidence of abrasion until the search with the microscope has been abandoned. Once the area has been dusted with graphite, no matter how thoroughly the loosely adherent particles are removed by rolling with a cylinder of plasticine, any subsequent discovery of graphite or of graphite-like material associated with the ink line would be of no significance, for there could be no certainty that the graphite discovered had not come on to the document as a consequence of the dusting treatment.

The shining particles shed from a pencil are readily seen, but the certain detection of traces of the dull, black, waxy material derived from carbon paper is by no means a simple matter, and the stereoscopic microscope may have to be supplemented by a high-power monocular instrument for the thorough examination of the ink lines.

In spite of what has so facilely been written, the proof by microscopic examination of the presence of traces of a guide line in a heavily inked traced forgery is not always a simple matter. If the ink has been derived from an open ink well, it is almost certain to contain dust particles, and the presence of these in the ink line of a suspect signature may well be misinterpreted as evidence of the presence of traces of a guide line. This is one reason why it is advised that the search for traces of a guide line should be concentrated on the ends of strokes, because any graphite-like material found *beyond* the ink line cannot be explained away as being due to dust in the ink.

The use of photographic methods for the detection of graphite in ink lines has been discussed elsewhere, so that any suspect signature which is thought to be a tracing should be photographed in an effort to discover any guide line or traces of a guide line which has eluded microscopic examination.

If all other methods have failed and it is thought, from the evidence of coloured smears in the neighbourhood of the signature, that a faint carbon paper line may lie concealed in the ink line, the ink line may be touched, after all the usual precautions outlined elsewhere have been taken, with a tiny drop of mixed solvent. The object of this is to liberate the dyestuff of the carbon paper from the waxy material in which it is bound, and cause it to bleed out of the ink line so that it can more easily be seen.

A suitable solvent is a mixture of methylene dichloride to dissolve the wax, and ethyl acetate to dissolve the dyestuff should it be insoluble in the first solvent. If bleeding of dyestuff can be demonstrated, this will indicate the presence of something foreign to the ink line. Care must be taken to ensure that the appropriate blank tests are carried out on other ink lines before the ink of the signature is tested.

If a ball-point pen has been used for inking in the outline, it is obvious that any tested with solvent would be more likely to disfigure the signature than to disclose the presence of a guide line containing dyestuffs, so that the procedure cannot be recommended for signatures written with these pens.

Detection of Impressions Associated with Traced Forgeries

A guide line will leave a shallow impression or indentation in the surface of the paper, even after all trace of it has been erased. Similarly, the indentation utilised in the simple method of transferring a required outline previously described will remain associated with the inked-in signature. It is inadvisable to jump to conclusions, for if impressions are found associated with signatures even in regions suffering from abrasive damage, this must not be taken as definite evidence that the signatures are tracings. The presence of impressions may be indicative that the signatures are genuine and, as such, have been used as the basis of a tracing, the impressions being caused by the passage of the tracing point.

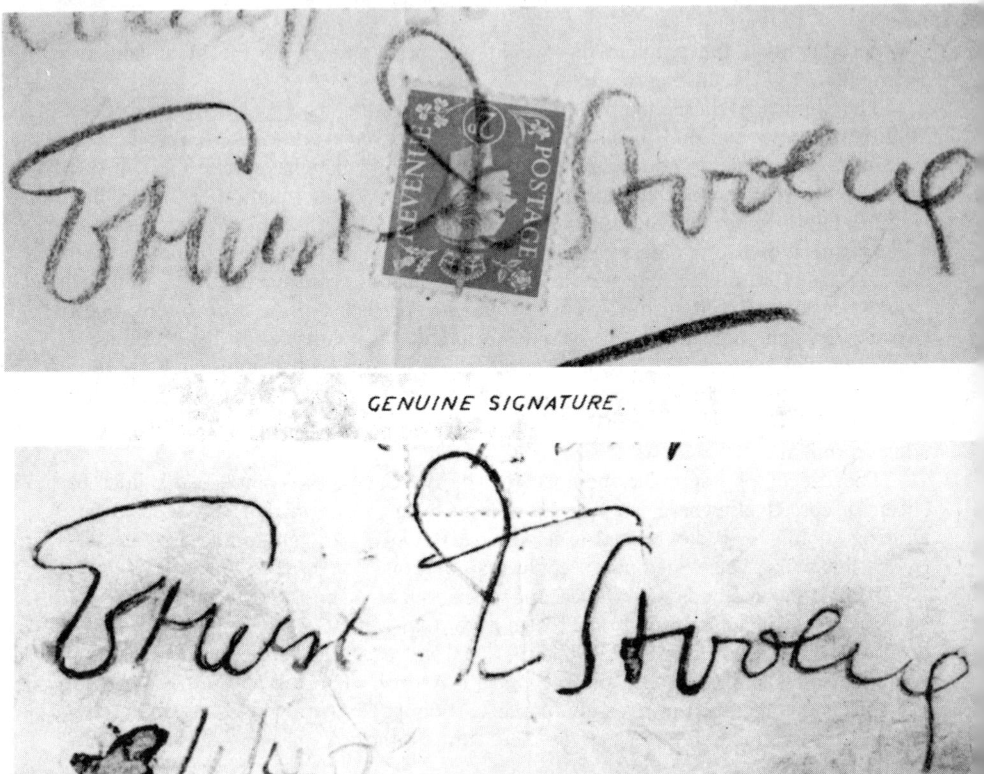

Fig. 11–10. *Traced Forgeries*

The two lower signatures were traced from the upper genuine signature of the financier Ernest Terah Hooley.

Even if the upper signature had not been available for comparison, the bad line quality and the thickened line endings would have betrayed these two signatures as fraudulent.

All that can be hoped for from the discovery of impressions is that they may strengthen other evidence that the signatures with which they are associated are tracings. Even then, to be significant, they should be shown to extend beyond the ends of the ink lines so that they cannot be explained away on the grounds that they were caused by the pressure of the pen, especially if it be a ball-point.

Impressions are best detected by examination with light at grazing incidence, so that their presence should be revealed during the general examination of the documents bearing the suspect signatures.

Guide Lines which are not Indicative of Forgery

It has already been mentioned that the presence of a pencil line closely associated with a suspect signature is by no means a positive indication that the signature is a traced forgery. This is because of the fairly prevalent practice, among those who should know better, of pencilling in a vague outline of a signature in the place where important documents have to be signed by not very intelligent clients.

If the signatory has sufficient common sense to take no heed of the pencil marks and to sign his normal signature at the place indicated, a close examination of the signature will reveal that the pencilled outline and the signature have little in common, and that what is present is a *mélange* of the same name written in two different hands. If the signatory stupidly follows the pencilled outline and makes no attempt to write his usual signature, he will be copying the tricks of a forger and will produce something which will present the conventional appearance of a traced forgery with but one important difference.

This difference is all-important. The final signature will bear little, if any, resemblance to the normal signature of the signatory, so that the most prominent feature of a traced forgery—its uncanny resemblance to the genuine signature—will be entirely lacking.

Many genuine signatures which appear in evidence are found to have either a pencil line or traces of pencil marks closely associated with their outlines. These are the genuine signatures which have been used for the preparation of traced forgeries by the use of carbon paper or by making an indentation where a pencil has been used as the tracing point.

A pencil line closely associated with a signature may be capable of an even more innocent explanation. On more than one occasion, the author has had submitted to him for examination, tracings of signatures on documents it was considered inadvisable or impracticable to submit in the original. After it had been explained that tracings were useless for the purpose, and the original documents were forthcoming, it has been discovered that the tracings first submitted had often been made by running a pencil over the suspect signatures with sufficient pressure to transfer an outline on to another sheet of paper with the aid of carbon paper. It might be thought that it is a simple matter in such cases to determine which was written first, the pencil line or the ink line. This is never so simple or so certain as might appear from what has been written on the subject, and is dealt with in detail elsewhere. (See p. 232.)

A double line in a signature might be due to the overwriting of a genuine signature from one of a number of motives. The most common motive for the

A
Chief Constable.
B
x1·5
Chief Constable.

overwriting of a genuine signature is to disguise the fact that alterations or additions have been made to the document in an ink which has dried a different colour from that of the original ink. By overwriting the whole of the entries with new ink, it is hoped that the additions will pass unnoticed. On other occasions, a genuine signature may be overwritten just because it appears to the writer to be too faint in its original state. This often happens when a defective ball-point pen is used.

Whilst the foregoing may prove acceptable explanations for the presence of pen, pencil, or faint ink markings in a signature, there can be no excusing any traces of carbon paper markings which might be present.

Abrasions in the neighbourhood of a suspect signature may also be reasonably explained. Where a pencilled outline of the name of a signatory has stupidly been placed in the required position, it is sometimes the practice to make matters worse by erasing it once the document has been signed. The reason which has been given for this most inadvisable practice is to " clean up " the document before photography for purpose of record.

Whilst the microscopic examination of a traced forgery will often yield sufficient evidence of the presence of a guide line to enable it to be branded as spurious, it will fail to do so, not only in those cases where the forgery has been directly traced without a guide line, but also where a complete erasure has been effected on rough-surfaced paper of good quality. On such a paper, an erasure of a faint pencil line may sometimes be effected without leaving any trace of the line or of any definite evidence of an erasure having been accomplished.

In certain circumstances, traced forgeries devoid of any guide line can successfully be attacked and revealed as fraudulent on other grounds. It may appear strange that the very perfection of form of a traced forgery may prove to be its undoing! Experience has shown that the reason for this is that, although well-written genuine signatures of a particular person may have a great deal in common, no two which are perfect replicas of each other are likely to be encountered. Even a skilled penman would find it impossible, deliberately, to write two signatures of medium length which are so similar that no differences between them can be demonstrated on careful comparison.

It sometimes happens that when a traced forgery is challenged, the very signature from which it was traced can be discovered; it may even happen that it is brought forward to demonstrate how closely the forgery resembles at least one genuine signature! This may prove dangerous for the forger. In the first place, unless the genuine signature has been handled with extreme care, it will yield some direct evidence that it has been used as the basis of a tracing. Whilst it may be too much to hope to find an obvious pencil line associated with the outline of the genuine signature (although in one case in the author's experience this was actually found), there may be indentations or possibly indentations plus signs of erasure thereon, if

---

Fig. 11–11 (opposite). The lower signature " B " bears a very close resemblance to the upper genuine signature " A." The line quality is poor, notably in connection with the upper loop of the " J " and the long curved down stroke of the " a " which follows this letter. In the lower portion of the figure the same pair of signatures is shown photographed under a transparent scale. From this it can be seen that " B " is a replica of " A." This indicates that not only is " B " a forgery but that it must have been produced by tracing from the genuine signature " A " in order to achieve such identity of form.

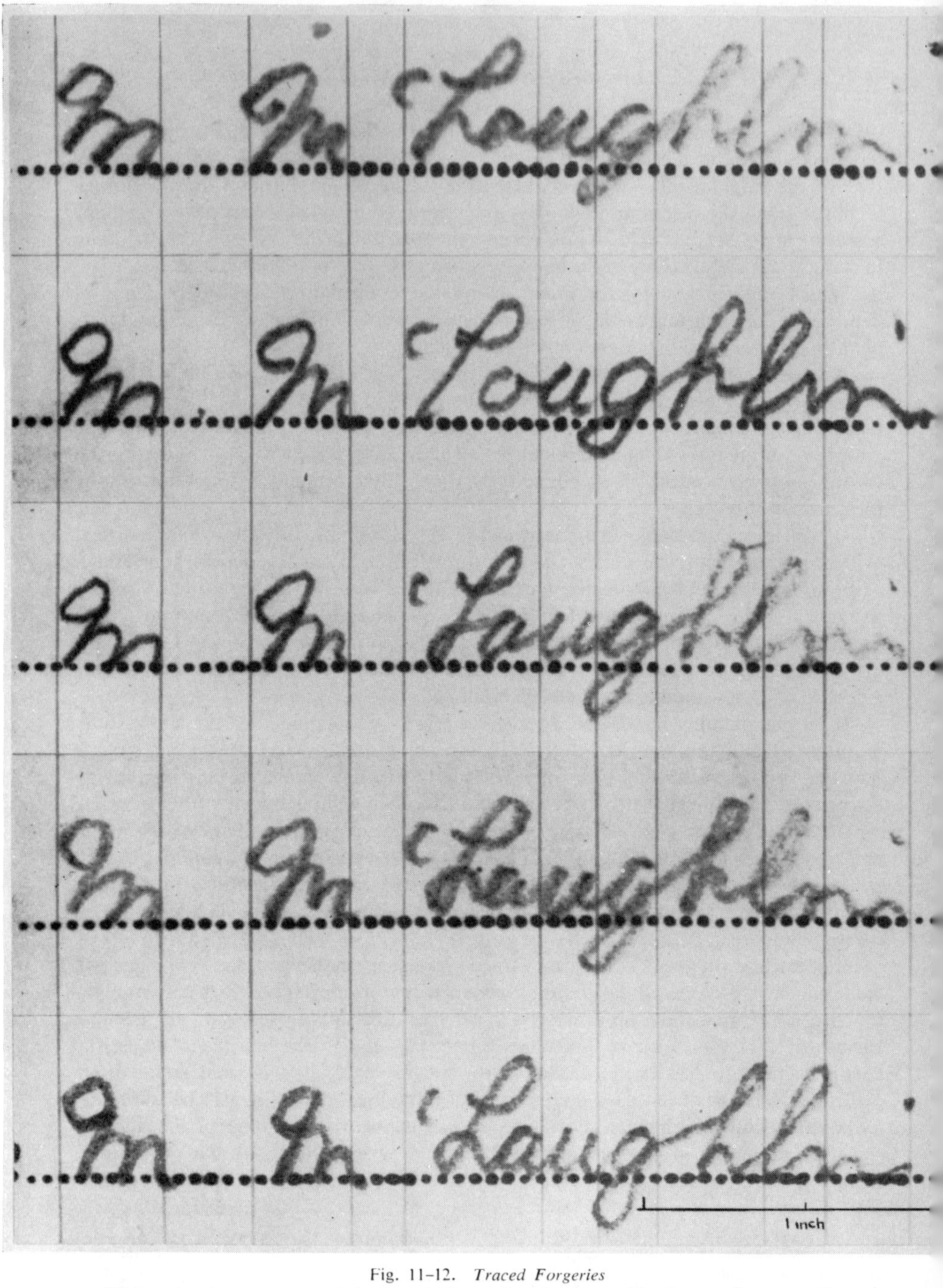

Fig. 11-12. *Traced Forgeries*

All five signatures were traced from a single genuine signature. The degree of correspondence is much closer than that found among five genuine signatures of the same man chosen at random but is insufficient to prove the fact of tracing.

The tracing was very crudely carried out by the forger, who had become careless. The guide line was not continuous so a fair amount of each signature was filled in freehand.

the forger was stupid enough to use a pencil rather than a smooth metal stylus for making the tracing.

Incidentally, any indentations which might be present will be more apparent as raised outlines on the back of the document bearing the genuine signature.

Secondly, although neither indentations nor other signs of the genuine signature having been used as a tracing may be apparent, it will be possible to demonstrate that the forgery is too similar to the genuine signature for the resemblance to be fortuitous, or to be explicable on any grounds other than its having been produced by tracing from that particular genuine signature. Occasionally, it has happened that one or two genuine signatures have been used to produce a fair number of tracings, the record number in the experience of the author being fifteen traced forgeries derived from a single genuine specimen.

Once it is realised that suspect signatures have been made by tracing, proof of forgery is generally simple, for whilst the odds against two genuine signatures being replicas are very great, the chance that a number of replicas are anything but tracings is infinitesimally small.

Traced Forgeries in Court

In the event of court proceedings, the most convincing demonstration that a suspect signature is a tracing of a genuine specimen is the production of an enlarged print of the one and a transparency of the other made on the same scale. All that remains to be done is to arrange for the transparency to be superimposed on the print, when the exact degree of correspondence will be made manifest.

This demonstration material is not as easily prepared as it might appear, and in most cases, it is advisable to be satisfied with a moderate degree of enlargement, of approximately three diameters, otherwise there may appear to be a considerable discrepancy between the signatures when the transparency is applied to the print. The reason for this has already been discussed when the dimensional stability of photographic materials was being considered. Wet paper stretches to a considerable degree when handled to any great extent, and even if a sheet of paper is merely wetted, it stretches and, what is worse, fails to return to its original dimensions when it dries. This means that, whilst the image of the signature projected in the enlarger can be made of the exact size required, the dimensions of the completed print on bromide paper may be appreciably different. The same distortion does not occur in the transparency, for in this the emulsion is sited on film which has a reasonable degree of dimensional stability.

The difficulty of matching the size of print and transparency can be sidestepped should a considerable degree of enlargement be necessary for the demonstration. All the positives should be prepared on film to form transparencies. One should then be dry-mounted on to a sheet of white card to take the place of the print.

It is true that the use of printing paper which has been interleaved with metal foil can be counted on to solve all problems of dimensional stability, but this material is very expensive and not easily procurable. Bromide paper which has been waterproofed with a nitrocellulose varnish before coating may be substituted for the interleaved paper with little loss of accuracy, but here again, this special paper may not always be available when required.

From the foregoing, it must not lightly be concluded that the exposure of every traced forgery as fraudulent is a simple straightforward matter, even when the original genuine signature is available for comparison. If no guide line, or any trace of a guide line can be detected, and if the signature is a short one and the tracing has been carelessly carried out, it may be inadvisable to make any attempt to demonstrate that the tracing is a replica of the genuine signature for the sufficient reason that it is not!

No attempt should be made to rely on the demonstration of an imperfect fit and then to endeavour to explain the differences which are apparent on the grounds of careless workmanship on the part of the forger. The signature, if forged, almost certainly can, and should, be attacked on other grounds; it should be treated as though it were a simulated forgery and its spurious nature demonstrated in accordance with the principles laid down below.

It goes without saying that if only one traced forgery devoid of any guide line has been submitted for examination, and the genuine signature from which it was traced is not available, the comparative method of attack is not applicable and this, too, must be treated as a simulated forgery.

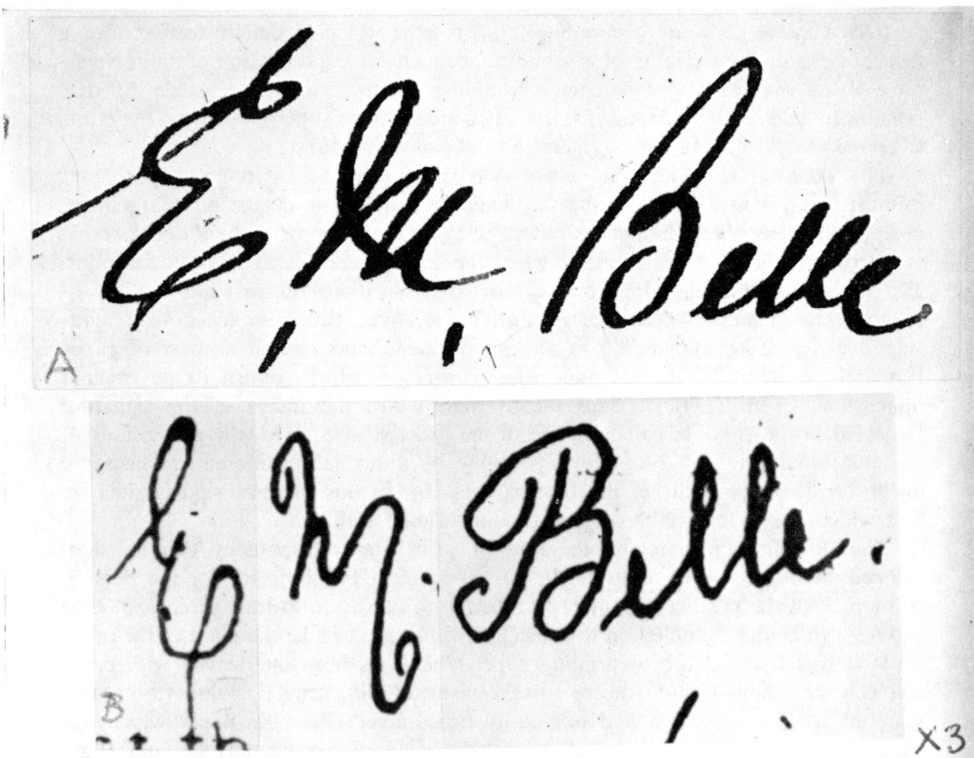

Fig. 11–13. " A " is a genuine signature of which " B " is a simulated forgery. The poor line quality made manifest by the considerable degree of enlargement is strongly indicative of forgery.

Authorship of Traced Forgeries

From what has already been said of the mode of production of a forgery, there is no doubt that the process of inking-in a tracing cannot be considered to have anything in common with normal handwriting. All that the forger has to do is to follow a line, an activity which has little in common with the normal writing action, which is the substantially reflex reproduction of letter designs that the writer has memorised from childhood and become accustomed to write for years.

It follows from this that there is little that can be done by comparing a traced forgery with normal handwriting, to link the person who has merely run his pen along an outline with the writer of a specimen of normal handwriting. A few general observations may be made. For example, if the traced forgery has been written in a neat and skilful manner, the opinion may be justified that somebody whose normal handwriting exhibits a persistent tremor or exceptionally poor control over the pen was not responsible for the forgery on the grounds of sheer incapacity.

In general, therefore, it may be said that whilst there may be evidence which tends to exclude a particular suspect from suspicion, it is very unlikely that any particular person could be implicated as the writer of the forgery by comparison with his normal handwriting.

Detection of Simulated Forgeries

Mention has already been made of the fact that a genuine signature, particularly that of a practised writer, is written fluently and without conscious thought being given to the exact form of the letters, simply because of the familiarity of the writer with the task he is accomplishing.

In marked contrast, when an outline is copied to complete a traced forgery or when a form is produced from memory, or perhaps copied from one which is before the writer, to form a simulated forgery, there can be no swift, carefree movement of the pen. Unlike the casual writer, the forger has to concentrate on the task in hand if he is to ensure that his pen point is reproducing the letter designs he has memorised or is observing with half his attention whilst giving the remainder to the writing.

Instead of a swift and sweeping movement of the pen, there has to be a slow and careful motion which is the product of care from the moment the pen is cautiously applied to the paper until it is finally lifted from its surface. The forger has a double care; not only has he to copy the handwriting of another, but he must continually be on the alert to suppress his own handwriting instincts. Therefore that which is finally committed to the paper, be it either traced or simulated forgery, cannot be termed "handwriting" in the normal sense of the word; it is more accurately described as a careful and painstaking "drawing" of the handwriting of another person. It may well be argued that many a simulated forgery, written by an expert, has passed muster as a genuine signature which appeared to have little, if anything, wrong with it. This is quite true, but forgeries are usually accepted as genuine simply because the eye is apt to judge any handwriting by its general appearance, by what has been termed its "pictorial effect."

The forger will continue to flourish because life is too short for every signature to be given the close scrutiny which alone is capable of revealing its structure, as opposed to the casual glance which merely gathers the general impression afforded by its outline.

When an enlarged photograph of a forgery, whether it be simulated or traced, is compared with a similarly enlarged photograph of the genuine signature, it becomes patent that there is a world of difference between the two signatures in spite of the general similarity in their appearance, for it is only when they are magnified several diameters that the details of the construction of any signature can be appreciated by the naked eye. When photographic enlargements of signatures are examined, the most striking observation will be that, however much a genuine signature is enlarged, the curves which constitute the greater part of the

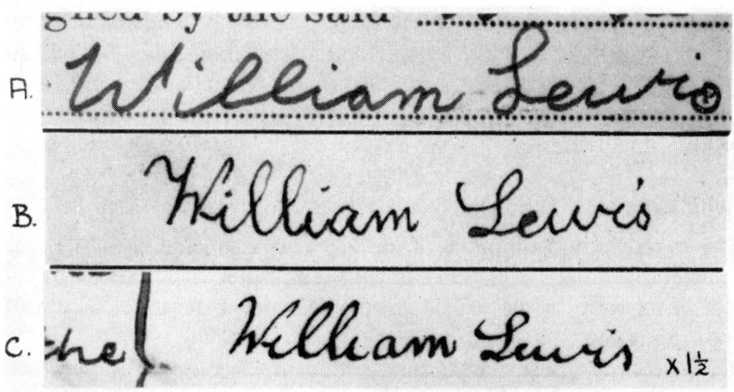

Fig. 11–14. " A " is a genuine signature, " B " a suspect signature on a will, " C " the signature of a witness on the same will as " B." The signature " B " bears a closer resemblance to " C " with respect to letter design, slope and writing habits than it does to " A."

handwriting lose none of their grace because, as they have been formed as the result of a smooth regular movement, their curvature will appear smooth and even throughout; and what is more, the signature will seem to be a coherent whole. However, with the enlarged photograph of a forgery, whether traced or simulated, once the eye is able to study each stroke and curve as an individual element of the signature, the ragged and hesitant curves and, what is even more significant, the patchwork appearance of the signature as a whole can be fully appreciated. Most people who view an enlarged photograph of a forgery are surprised that it was ever accepted as genuine.

Line Quality of a Forgery

With sufficient magnification, there will be no difficulty in recognising the frequent hesitations and changes of direction undergone by the pen point as it is forced along the path chosen by the forger. The frequent correction of the direction of motion reveals the attention which must have been paid to the path taken by the pen point. The resultant abrupt changes in pressure, direction and speed of the pen as the forger momentarily slows its motion whilst he takes stock of his handiwork and contemplates the next move, have their inevitable consequences in bad line quality of the writing.

It is this defective line quality, only appreciated to the full when visual comparison is made with that of a genuine signature, which is one of the most revealing characteristics of a forgery, whether it be traced or simulated, for no ink line can present a smooth and well-graduated appearance on high magnification unless it has been fluently and evenly written.

Line Endings of Forgeries

The appearance of the line endings of a suspect signature is often highly significant. It has already been pointed out that with a genuine, fluently-written signature, the pen, being in motion before it touches the paper, tends to produce tapered ends to the ink lines. With a carefully written forgery the pen usually has to be deliberately placed on the paper at the desired position before any appreciable motion is imparted to it. When each pen movement is complete, a forger will often allow his pen to rest momentarily on the paper while he takes stock of the position. Under these conditions, the ends of the ink lines in a forgery tend to be thickened rather than tapered.

Pen-lifts

Most genuine signatures are written with a continuous line which exhibits neither halts nor hesitations. Whilst a genuine signature may have one or two places where the pen is habitually halted or even raised, these generally occur at places where a pen-lift may be expected. These are governed largely by the letter which has to be written after the pen-lift and it will be found that most pen-lifts are made to avoid having to form a retrace. Few forgeries are written with one continuous stroke, or even with the pen-lifts which are characteristic of the genuine signature, for many forgers find it necessary to stop and take stock at regular intervals, indeed many forgeries will be discovered to have been written a letter at a time. Occasionally, a forger may be found to have had such little confidence in his ability that he works by linking up a succession of single strokes. These multiple hesitations, halts and pen-lifts rarely have anything in common with the pen-lifts characteristic of some genuine signatures; sometimes, a forgery exhibiting multiple pen-lifts will be seen to have omitted a pen-lift in the place where it invariably occurs in the genuine signature.

If the conventional form of pen nib is used with fluid ink, whether in an ordinary pen holder or in a fountain pen, there will usually be little difficulty in determining where the pen-lifts, halts and hesitations have occurred, for the effect of these on the ink line may easily be seen on microscopic examination.

If the suspect signature has been written in pencil or with a ball-point pen, which in many respects may be considered to be an ink pencil, it is often impossible to detect these stops and hesitations of the pen point because of the fundamental difference between the mode of action of a conventional nib and that of the pencil and ball-point. Both the pencil and ball-point may be lifted from the paper and replaced without leaving any indication that there has been any interruption in the writing.

Although the use of a pencil or ball-point pen deprives the document examiner of the valuable evidence of forgery afforded by the presence of a superabundance

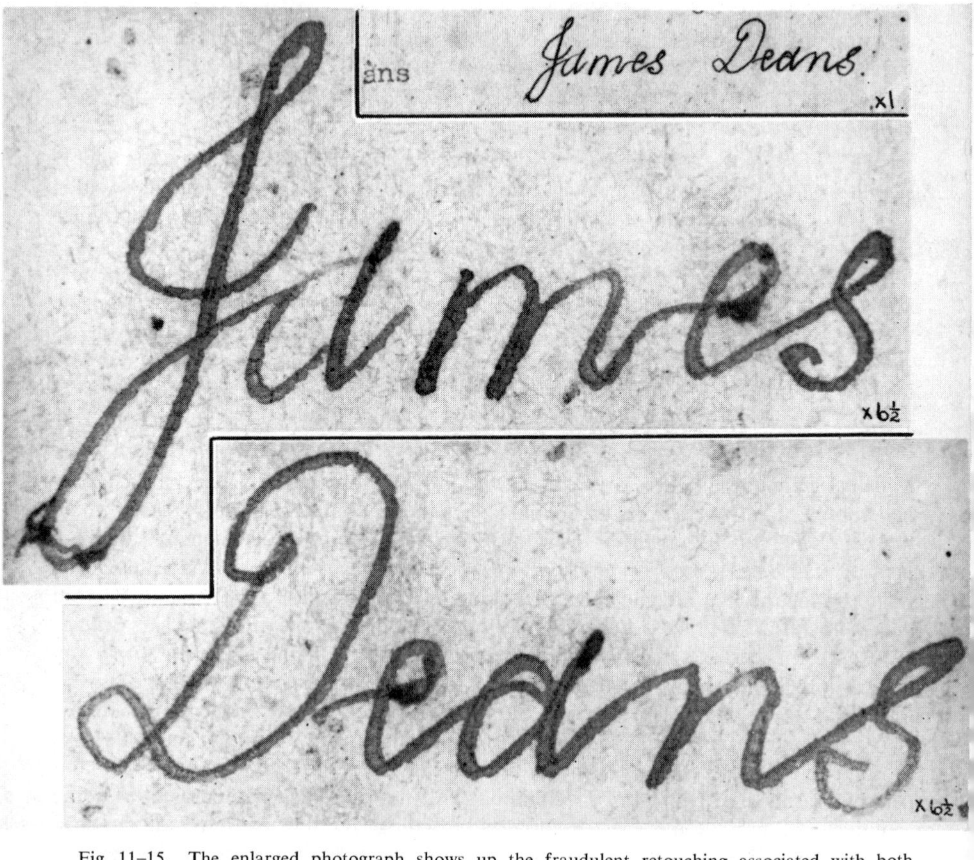

Fig. 11–15. The enlarged photograph shows up the fraudulent retouching associated with both "a" and "e" of the signature "James Deans" on the document illustrated in Figure 3–13. There has also been a certain amount of smoothing of the connection from the "m" to the "e."

of pen-lifts, halts and hesitations in a suspect signature, it does nothing to improve the poor line quality of a slow deliberately written forgery. However, some forgers are so skilful, and there are signatures which are so easy to forge, that the loss of any sources of evidence which has a bearing on the authenticity of a suspect signature is greatly to be regretted. No one would think of using a pencil for writing an important signature, and it would be as well if the same caution were displayed with respect to the use of a ball-point pen.

Retouching

Until a forgery is received for examination at a document laboratory its most exacting critic is undoubtedly the forger who wrote it, for he, more than anyone else, having studied the genuine signature most carefully, is fully aware of any short-comings it may show. As this is so, few forgers are able to resist the temptation to try to improve their handiwork. The only form this improvement can take is that of delicate retouching to introduce shading, improve the letter outlines and to round off curves, in an endeavour to remove the more obvious signs of strain commonly referred to as the " tremor of forgery."

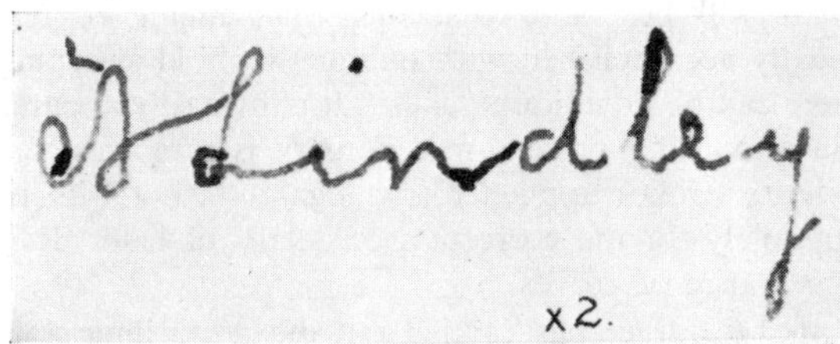

Fig. 11–16. This is an excellent example of non-fraudulent retouching made by a poor writer to correct imperfect letter designs.

It must be emphasised that the presence of retouching or of modified letter designs in a signature is by no means an infallible sign that the signature is fraudulent. Some careless writers habitually retouch their signatures—the author is numbered among them—but this retouching should never be confused with the type of retouching characteristic of a forgery.

Fig. 11–17. *Shading Habits*

The lower signature " B " was suspect because of the over-writing of the " J " and of the suspicious thickenings in the lower portion of the " l," " e " and " o." A similar thickening was observed in the admittedly genuine signature " A." This thickening in both signatures was caused by an abnormal pen-hold.

Retouching found in a genuine signature has been done with but one object in view, and that is to improve legibility. For example, when the arcade form is used and the letters are carelessly written, the " rr " in the middle of the author's surname may be, and indeed, often are, mistaken for the letter " m." A little retouching serves to obviate this possibility, and for this reason some retouching of the " rr " will often be found in his genuine, but carelessly written, signatures on some comparatively unimportant documents.

It will be found that this what might be termed " genuine retouching " is usually accomplished with one or two bold sweeping strokes, about whose presence there can be little doubt, as it is usually easily apparent to the naked eye. In contrast, the retouching present in a forgery is unobtrusive; it is made up of a number of delicate strokes applied to the signature, not with the object of improving legibility but solely for the correction of details of letter design and the improvement of the appearance of curves.

If the forger has carried out the retouching skilfully and with a delicate touch, it may be necessary to examine the signature with a microscope to detect its presence and to prepare any photographs with a considerable degree of enlargement —up to six diameters—to be able to demonstrate the nature and extent of the additions.

As there is no reason for anyone writing a genuine signature to indulge in this careful and painstaking retouching, no matter how carelessly it has been written, the discovery of fine retouching is perhaps the most convincing proof that a suspect signature is a forgery.

Detection of Retouching and Additions. Once the ink of a signature has begun to sink into the paper, it is difficult, if not impossible, to add a stroke in such a way that it merges completely into the original line. It is because of this that microscopic examination of a signature written with a conventional pen and ink can generally be relied upon to furnish evidence of retouching, no matter how carefully it has been carried out.

If either a pencil or a ball-point pen is used the forgery may be retouched with impunity, as microscopic examination of the rough tracks made by either cannot be counted on to reveal the added strokes, which is yet another reason why neither pencil nor ball-point pen should be used for writing important signatures.

Shading

Some signatures of today, like many of those of a previous generation, are written with due regard being paid to the capabilities of the pen as a medium of artistic expression. These signatures not only exhibit a graceful succession of letter designs, but also utilise to the full the ability of the pen to produce variations in the width of the ink line. This variation in width, produced by control of the pen position with respect to the direction of pen motion and of the pressure exerted, is known as shading. Not only do these shaded signatures grace any document on which they are found, but they provide a most difficult problem for the would-be forger, however skilful he may be.

If a forger is allowed to hold his pen in the manner with which he is most familiar, he may have little difficulty in making a fairly accurate copy of the outline of any signature he wishes to forge, providing it is the outline alone on which he has to concentrate his attention. If the outline being copied features well-shaded ink lines, he can make a convincing copy with identical shading only if he is able to copy the penhold and reproduce the pen action of the writer of the signature he is attempting to copy. If he cannot accomplish this by no means simple feat, he will be forced, first to reproduce the unshaded outline, and then to try to imitate the shading by the delicate retouching of every stroke which has insufficient width in the outline he has drawn.

This again is a most formidable task, comparable in difficulty with the imitation of the penhold and writing action of the original writer, for not only have the shaded strokes to be thickened, but any thickening must shade gradually into the finer strokes at the ends of each shaded stroke.

Fig. 11–18. Example of a genuine signature exhibiting tremor. This tremor was characteristic of the whole of the handwriting of this person throughout life.

If the forger doubts his ability to accomplish this piecemeal shading in a convincing manner, he has no alternative but to experiment with different penholds until he finds one which will give a close approximation to the required effect as he draws the outline of the forged signature. Any slight deficiencies can be retouched subsequent to the writing. This laboriously acquired penhold is almost certain to be one to which he is unaccustomed. The combined effects of unaccustomed penhold and efforts to copy both outline and shading are certain to be reflected in the line quality of the writing. The forgery will have few of the characteristics of a fluent and carefree writing, and the strain under which it was produced—the tremor of forgery—will become obvious when an enlarged photograph of his final accomplishment is compared with one of the genuine signatures.

Unfortunately, shading in most contemporary handwriting is most conspicuous by its absence. The advent of the ball-point pen, with its symmetrical writing point which makes a deeper rather than a wider line on the application of excess pressure, has done much to banish shading from contemporary handwriting and so to facilitate the task of the forger.

It matters little how a pencil or a ball-point pen is held; the line remains practically unaltered whatever the angle, and the amount of turning of the pen in the fingers as the writer proceeds. This is yet another reason why important

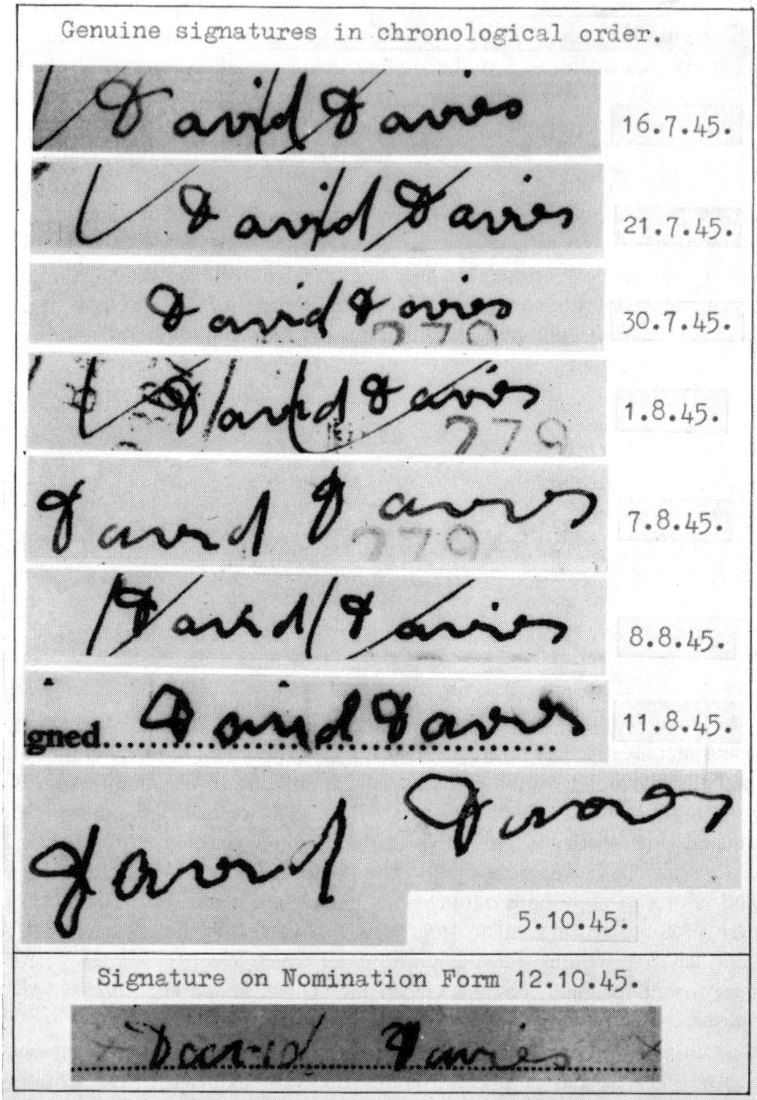

Fig. 11–19. This shows the rapid deterioration caused by illness during a period of less than three months before death. This deterioration is most marked when the signatory was in hospital in October, 1945. The suspect signature dated 12.10.45 exhibits a degree of pen control which had departed during August—note particularly the terminal "d" of "David" and the "ies" of "Davies."

signatures should never be written with other than the conventional type of pen. Many forgeries made with a ball-point pen remain undetected through lack of evidence to show how they were written.

Deficiencies in Signatures Caused by Ill-Health

Once adolescence is past and a handwriting has become formed, it is most exceptional for it to undergo any rapid development which results in any fundamental change, provided the health of the writer remains unimpaired. This does not exclude the slow development of the signature over a period of years which, with some people, enables an opinion to be given that a certain signature has been written within a specified period of time. This absence of any extensive change over sometimes quite considerable periods of time enables a suspect signature to be compared effectively with standard specimens which are not necessarily strictly contemporary.

This is not the case when ill-health or senility has to be taken into account. When anybody has become senile or is mortally ill, there is often such a rapid and complete loss of muscular control that the handwriting, and with it the signature, may be altered to such an extent as to become practically unrecognisable in a very short period. As this is so, when a signature is attributed to someone who is senile or gravely ill, it is imperative that any signature or other handwriting used for comparison be as contemporaneous as possible, for even the lapse of a few days may make all the difference, so rapid is the deterioration of the handwriting as death approaches.

It is not unusual for wills to bear signatures alleged to have been written when the signatory was at the point of death. When these are suspect, three possibilities have to be taken into account. The first is that the signature is genuine and that the manner in which it differs from the normal signature is due entirely to failing of the physical faculties of the writer; the second is that the signature is what is sometimes termed a " guided hand " signature; the third possibility is that the suspect signature is a forgery.

Genuine but Deteriorated Signatures

If the signature is genuine, but the handwriting has seriously deteriorated, it will certainly be difficult and may, in some cases, be impossible to prove that the signature is genuine. The first step in this direction is that taken with any signature—that is, to examine the document and the signature itself for evidence which is indicative of forgery. If nothing suspicious can be discovered, efforts must be made to obtain a number of genuine signatures written over a fair period of time.

The signatures should extend in time from those written in good health to others as nearly contemporary with the suspect signature as possible. If any genuine signatures written after the suspect signature are available, these will prove especially valuable.

In the case of elderly persons who have been ailing for some time, it is imperative to guard against the inclusion of forgeries among the supposedly genuine signatures, which is one reason why signatures written when in good health and in full possession of the faculties should always be included. This warning is not given lightly, for the author has had to deal with many cases where the majority of the supposedly genuine signatures have eventually proved to be forgeries. Very often these forgeries included among the supposedly genuine signatures have proved to be by the same hand as the forged signature sent for investigation, which makes this unwitting inclusion especially dangerous.

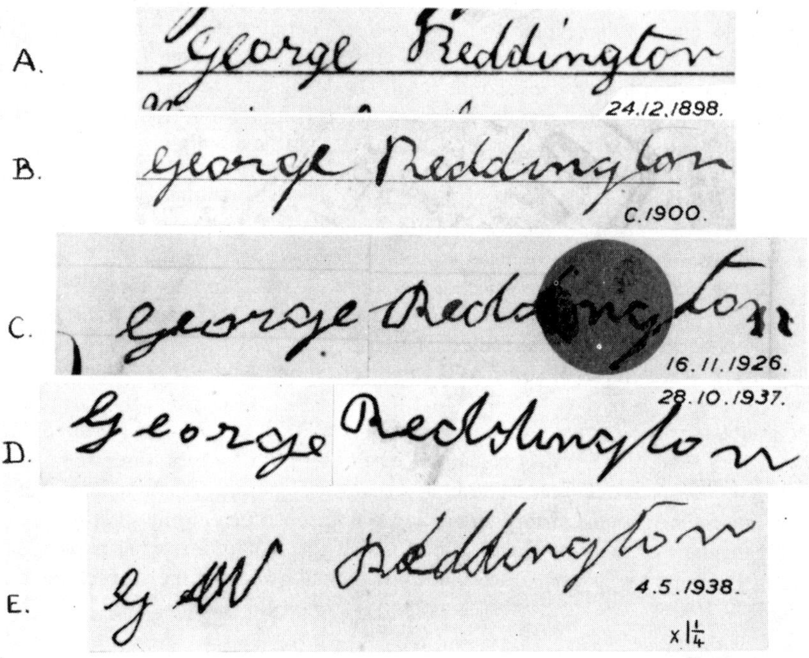

Fig. 11–20. This illustrates the change occurring in a signature over a period of 40 years.

If enlarged photographs of the genuine signatures are mounted in chronological order, it will often be possible to trace the continued deterioration of the handwriting as the illness progresses. If the standard signatures do not reach as far forward in time as the suspect signature, it may be possible, by a process of extrapolation, to determine whether the suspect signature falls neatly into the series as a natural development of tendencies already foreshadowed. If the suspect signature can be bracketed in time by the genuine signatures, the task can be simplified, for all that has to be done is to mount the suspect signature in its correct place in the chronological order and to see whether it fits in with those which come both before and after.

If no signs of forgery have been detected and the signature falls into line with the range of standards examined, it may safely be declared to be genuine, because the successful forgery of a signature in a deteriorated handwriting is not nearly as simple as might be thought.

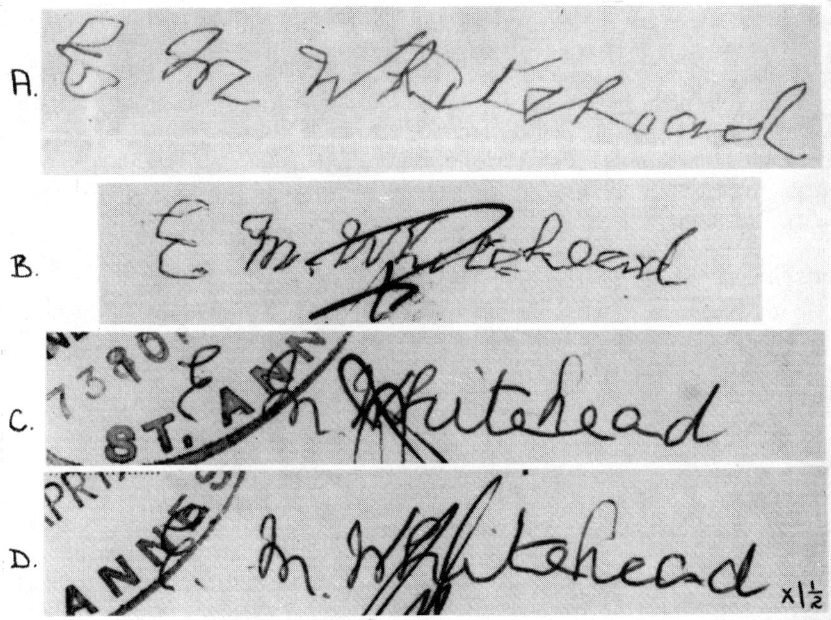

Fig. 11–21. " A " and " B " are suspect signatures, " C " and " D " are contemporary genuine signatures. The genuine signatures " C " and " D " are characterised by pen-lifts between the last five letters of the surname. This characteristic has not been reproduced in " A " and " B." The tremor in " A " and " B " is not the tremor of forgery but has been deliberately introduced to simulate the tremor of old age characteristic of " C " and " D."

" Guided Hand " Signatures

This is the description given to a " signature " supposedly written by the signatory with his hand " guided " by that of another person. Under certain conditions, the " guided hand " signature may be quite acceptable to the lawyer. However, every " guided hand " signature examined by the author has been declared by him to be a forgery, and the explanation concerning the " guided hand " has been forthcoming only after he explained how far from genuine the disputed signatures appeared.

This should underline the warning previously given that every detail concerning the signing of a disputed document should be elicited and written down at the very beginning of the inquiry. If this is done, stories about " guided hands " cannot conveniently be trumped up at the last moment to explain away features of the signatures which would otherwise prevent them from being accepted as genuine.

If a signature is said from the beginning to be by the " guided hand," it can be expected to resemble anything from a genuine signature of the signatory to something which might be written by anybody chosen at random, and merely asked to write the name of the signatory. The " guided hand " signature can be written with one continuous line or in a series of short strokes; it can have good line quality or bad. With one exception, whatever may be its faults as a signature, the document examiner is powerless to damn it as a forgery, however fraudulent it may appear on close examination.

The exception is important. A " guided hand " signature should be devoid of any fine retouching, but here again, if the forger decides to pass off a forgery as a " guided hand " signature, once inquiries are made there is nothing to stop him describing how he touched-up the signature at the request of the testator. It is possible that even in this case the signature would have to be accepted as valid from the legal point of view.

Forgeries Simulating Deteriorated Writing

Many forgers are under the impression that it is a simple matter to make a detection-proof forgery of the signature of a sick or senile person. They consider

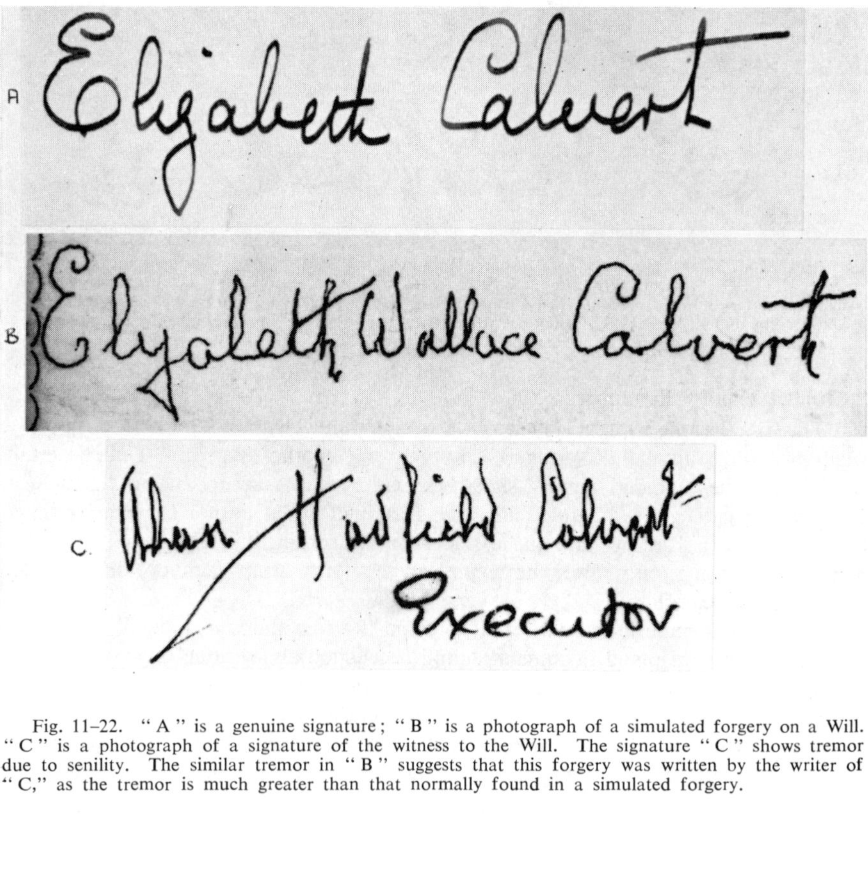

Fig. 11–22. " A " is a genuine signature; " B " is a photograph of a simulated forgery on a Will. " C " is a photograph of a signature of the witness to the Will. The signature " C " shows tremor due to senility. The similar tremor in " B " suggests that this forgery was written by the writer of " C," as the tremor is much greater than that normally found in a simulated forgery.

that any deficiencies will be ascribed to ill-health with its failing muscular control rather than to forgery. It is not denied that the investigation of a signature written in a deteriorated handwriting presents its own peculiar difficulties, but the forgery of the signature of anyone in a parlous state of health is not nearly so simple as might at first sight be supposed.

The first difficulty is one with which the forger of a normal signature is never faced, that is, he must decide the general appearance of the forgery. Many forgers have failed lamentably at this first hurdle by being satisfied with a rather tremulous copy of a signature written in good health. All that has to be done to expose these miserable efforts is to place in juxtaposition enlarged photographs of the forgeries and those of genuine signatures written before and, if possible, after the date borne by the forgery. If this is done it will be seen that the forgeries entirely fail to fit into the general picture presented by the genuine signatures.

If genuine contemporary signatures are available and the forger has the wit to use them this difficulty can be overcome, and all that he has to do is to make a copy by one of the methods already described.

It has been explained how the unnatural nature of the effort and the strain involved in writing a forgery result in poor line quality, uneven curves and similar imperfections which are sometimes summed up in the term the " tremor of forgery." Many forgers of the signatures of the sick and aged consider that any tremor of forgery, or indeed any other faults their work may exhibit, will be overlooked on the grounds that they are caused by the feeble signatory's lack of muscular control, rather than the excessive control of the pen point by a forger as he seeks to force his pen to follow an unfamiliar course.

Tremor of Sickness and Senility

To consider that the tremor and associated imperfections of a forgery can be passed over as due to ill-health is wishful thinking, for although a deteriorated handwriting may fall far below normal standards and exhibit a marked degree of tremor caused by lack of muscular control, it will still possess a certain amount of internal consistency that will be lacking in a forgery, which exhibits either natural tremor of forgery or an assumed tremor.

For example, a sick person may find it difficult to form smooth rounded troughs to the letters, in which case all the troughs in a genuine tremulous signature will be defective. On the other hand, the forgery will often contain some poorly rounded troughs, like those of the genuine signature, but may also include one or more troughs written to perfection, a feat beyond the power of anyone grievously ill. Again, when contemporary signatures of those in ill-health are characterised by the presence of gross tremor, the forger has to make an attempt to copy this feature of the handwriting. In these instances, many forgers begin with an extremely tremulous letter formation to suggest loss of muscular control, but later in the same signature spoil the effect by writing a similar letter formation in a smooth, fluent fashion—a fatal inconsistency. On other occasions, copies of signatures in deteriorated handwriting will inadvertently be adorned with one or more examples of perfect pen control, attributable only to those in possession of all their physical and mental faculties.

The tremor which is characteristic of forgery is generally most apparent in the long curved strokes which form part of the capital letters and of the lower and upper loops of certain of the letters, for it is extremely difficult to make a slowly written accurate copy of a long curved stroke. The pen in the shaking hand of the unfit will produce tremor throughout the whole of the writing. Often no attempt will be made to write a smooth sweeping curve to the extended loops, instead, they will be represented in a genuine deteriorated handwriting by three or four short strokes to form a rough triangle or quadrilateral, with little or no attempt being made to round off the corners.

Sometimes the forger will consider that the tremulous signature he has written is too fluent in places to be likely to pass muster, in which case the obvious remedy, retouching, is applied. The presence of delicate retouching in an apparently tremulous signature is of course inexplicable on any grounds other than forgery. In general, it may be said that internal lack of consistency will expose the majority of forgeries of signatures written in a deteriorated handwriting.

Illegible Signatures

Sometimes a genuine signature written by someone who has lost practically all control of the pen will be found to be almost illegible. It might well be thought that nothing can be done to establish whether such a signature is either genuine or forged, but when an enlarged photograph of a genuine illegible " signature " is compared with that of a normal signature, written when the writer was in good health, it will generally be found possible to relate each fragment of the illegible signature with a formation found in the genuine specimen. When attempting this, it must be borne in mind that it is not uncommon for a writer in ill-health to miss out a whole syllable of his name, but as a rule it will be possible to discover what the writer has endeavoured to represent in every stroke he has succeeded in making.

In marked contrast, where the illegible matter is a forgery which purports to be an illegible signature, it is often impossible to correlate many of the strokes in this way. Not only is the forgery illegible, but it is devoid of either rhyme or reason. Furthermore, in a totally illegible signature, it is often possible to determine in which direction the majority of the strokes are written, and in this respect, the strokes will conform to the related structures in the normal signature. With a forgery, although similar strokes may be present, they will not necessarily have the same direction of writing as those they pretend to represent.

Ornate Signatures

Some writers take pains to acquire a florid and ornate signature which displays a superabundance of unnecessary strokes and flourishes, in the hope that such a signature will be both distinctive and proof against forgery. Distinctive these signatures may be, but far from being difficult to forge, they are easy game for the forger with any pretension to a modicum of skill.

When these elaborate signatures are carelessly written, their essential letter formations are hidden under a mass of superfluous strokes, so that little is discernible save a vague " pictorial impression " of the signature as a whole. In many instances, all that the forger has to do to make a most convincing forgery, is to construct a hotch-potch of lines to form a whole which conveys to the mind a general impression similar to that of the genuine signature. Without a microscopic examination to determine the exact form and direction of writing of each stroke, no decision can be made concerning its authenticity. When this is done, these signatures have to be treated as illegible signatures.

A similar difficulty is experienced when the authorship of groups of initials is in dispute. Many people who write normally in other respects initial documents with a group of closely entwined, floridly written, capitals. Initials written in this way are easily forged, because all that the forger has to do is to reproduce the general outline of the group without being concerned with details, which would be the case if the initials were clearly and simply written. Suspect illegible groups of initials have to be treated as though they are illegible signatures, but here in the majority of cases the amount of evidence will be too limited to enable a decision to be made.

Forgery-proof Signatures

The type of signature which is the most difficult to forge is not that which approximates to a florid and practically illegible scrawl, but one which is carefully and accurately written with shaded strokes, and in which every letter can be distinguished. To copy such a signature, the forger has first to master and be able to copy every stroke, which in itself is no mean task, and also ensure that the writing is fluent and not laboured. At the same time, he has to manipulate his pen so as to produce the same shading as the original signature, another matter of extreme difficulty. If he fails to do this at the same time as he is reproducing the outline of the letters, he is faced with a long and delicate retouching operation in which a single slip will ruin the whole of this work.

Forgery of Poorly Written Signatures

In the foregoing treatment of the forged signature, it will be apparent throughout that the emphasis has been placed on the contrast between the laboured, tremulous and piecemeal written forgery, and the unconscious fluent handwriting of the genuine signature of the practised writer.

This might be termed the classical treatment of the subject of forged signatures. In the past, the document examiner was concerned mainly with signatures of this description, for it was rarely worth while attempting to forge the signatures of the poor and illiterate since there was little of which they could be robbed by means of a successful forgery. The position is different today. Forgery, instead of being a comparatively rare offence on the grand scale, where large estates could be plundered if only a few signatures could be forged with sufficient skill to escape detection, has become both widespread and squalid. Nowadays, the poor and sick are regularly being cheated out of the small sums sent through the post to them by the Ministry of Health or the Ministry of Pensions, etc. At the same time, Post Office Savings Bank accounts are daily being robbed, a few pounds at a time, by means of forged withdrawal forms used with stolen bank-books.

The vast majority of the genuine signatures which acknowledge the receipt of moneys from the public funds, or which appear on the Post Office Savings Bank withdrawal forms, are written by those who are unaccustomed to the regular use of the pen. Nearly all the signatures are written with a slow and laborious action, a letter at a time, in very much the same way as a forger writes when copying a signature. To make matters worse, when the genuine signatures of the illiterate, written over a period of time are examined, they are found to be extremely variable, so that in many cases there is insufficient evidence to enable the document examiner to decide whether a suspect signature is a forgery or an extreme variant of a genuine specimen.

Suspect signatures on these postal drafts fall into two classes. The first, which will be considered in more detail at a later stage, consists of genuine signatures which have been disclaimed by the writers. The second consists of forged signatures, and this again may be sub-divided into two further groups.

The first, and by far the larger group is made up of signatures on drafts stolen from the post; and since the genuine signatures of the recipients are known neither to the forger nor to the clerk who cashes the draft, no attempt is made to copy the genuine signature of the true payee. Any resemblance which might appear will be fortuitous. All that is required from the document examiner in these cases is the formal statement that the signature on the draft is a forgery, so that another payment may be made out of State funds to the loser. In these cases, the main interest is not centred on the fact of forgery, but on any evidence of authorship which might be gained by the comparison of the forged handwriting with that of any possible suspects.

The problem then resolves itself into the determination of the authorship of small amounts of handwriting, often fairly thoroughly disguised. This may seem an unrewarding task, but over the past twenty years the author has examined many hundreds, possibly thousands, of examples of this type of forgery, and has been able on many occasions to indicate to the investigating officers a fruitful line of inquiry, even where the ill-formed handwriting of some dozens of suspects has had to be compared with a forgery which consisted of a few ill-written letters made with a ball-point pen. This has been possible only by making full use of every feature on the handwriting on the forms, and not restricting the examination to the details of letter design.

The second group is made up of forgeries where some attempt has been made to copy the signature of the loser. This group includes the forged signatures which appear on withdrawal forms when stolen Post Office Savings bank books are being exploited.

If a stolen postal draft bears a signature which exhibits a strong general resemblance to that of the loser, this will constitute a valuable clue to the identity of the thief, for it has to be someone who is clearly acquainted with the genuine signature, and this means that either a relative or a close friend of the family is concerned. The forged signature on a Savings Bank withdrawal form must also bear something approximating to the genuine signature of the owner of the stolen book, but this fact in itself is of no evidential value, for the signature is usually forged by being copied from the signature of the depositor which has to appear in the bank book so that a comparison may be made by the counter clerk before paying out the money. The scrutiny which can be given by a clerk in a busy post office is necessarily cursory at the best, so that forged signatures which bear rather a remote resemblance to the genuine are readily accepted.

Many of those who steal Savings Bank books are unskilful forgers who inadvertently include many of their own less conspicuous features of handwriting in both the signature and the other particulars which have to be written on the withdrawal forms. In these cases, there is generally enough evidence to be derived from the comparison of the handwriting to indicate which of a number of suspects is responsible for the forgery and, on many occasions, convictions have been obtained merely on the evidence of opportunity for the theft and the resemblance of the handwriting of the accused with that on the forged withdrawal form.

Practically all these forgeries of the signatures of the illiterate are simulated, for tracing is rarely resorted to, so that even proof of forgery is sometimes very difficult to obtain. Comparison of the letter design of the suspect signature with that of the genuine signatures is often fruitless because of the variability of this feature throughout the genuine signatures.

Line quality is bad in many of the signatures of the illiterate, which in this respect are not greatly distinguished from the forgeries. To make matters worse, the favourite writing instrument is the ball-point pen, so evidence of patching, pen halts and hesitations is hard to come by.

It is extremely fortunate that amidst all this variability, one characteristic of the illiterate signature remains remarkably fixed. Practically all illiterate writers have fixed habits with respect to the way they append their signature to a document. In view of the deliberate way in which a signature is written by those unaccustomed to the task, it is perhaps not surprising that this deliberation extends with equal force to the positioning of the signature on the document.

It will generally be found that if one genuine signature is written carefully on the line, then all the other genuine signatures, no matter how they may vary with respect to the details of letter design, will also be written on the line; if one genuine signature is commenced right up against any printed matter which occurs on the same line as the signature, then all the others will be found written in the same way; if one genuine signature is finished off with a full-stop or period this feature is unlikely to be found wanting in other genuine signatures written by the same person.

Herein lies a trap into which many forgers of the signatures of the illiterate fall. Whilst they may make a convincing copy of the relatively undeveloped letter design of the genuine signature, and run no risk of betraying the forgery by the slow, careful nature of their handiwork, for this will also be a feature of the writing of genuine signatures, they almost invariably employ their own personal preferences with respect to the other features of the signing of a document, the placing of the signature on the line, etc.

These extraneous matters which have little to do with the mechanics of the construction of a signature are all important, not only in providing a reliable touchstone for judging the authenticity of the suspect signature but also for giving some indication as to which one of a small group of suspects is most likely to be responsible for writing the forgery.

Signatures of Principals Signed by Subordinates

In some businesses it is considered bad policy to allow certain classes of correspondence emanating from principals to be signed " *per pro,*" so that, in the absence of the principal, it becomes the custom for the letters to be signed by someone in a position of trust who is capable of writing a colourable imitation of the principal's signature. With practice, some of these " signing assistants " become so proficient that it is often impossible to find any obvious signs of forgery in their handiwork.

This stems from the fact that as the signatures are quite legitimately written in the course of business, there can be no feeling of guilt or any apprehension that a serious crime may be detected and brought home to the penman. At the same time, there is no need for any retouching of the signature or for taking such pains with the copying that the deception will be able to defy detection on the closest of examinations. In view of this, it is not surprising that in these circumstances the writing is almost invariably fluent and free from any of the tremor of forgery.

When the principal is a poor penman and writes variable and rather illegible signatures, it is sometimes impossible to be certain that any specific signature written in the course of business is genuine or not. In many cases, in the experience of the author, the principal has been unable to say with any certainty, unless he can recall the circumstances in which the document was drawn up and signed, whether or not he himself was responsible for the signature.

To allow anyone to copy and use in the course of business the signature of the principal of a firm is bad policy, because once the copyist knows that his imitation is accepted without question as genuine, he may be tempted, and often is, to use the skill he has acquired to his own advantage.

In these circumstances, the investigation of questioned signatures is fraught with pitfalls. As the questioned signatures rarely bear any of the classical signs of forgery, all that can be done is to gather together as many specimens of the signature of the principal as possible. This collection should contain examples of both genuine and copied signatures, when in the majority of instances it will be possible to divide the signatures into two groups by virtue of some detail of letter design or by the way the signature is positioned on the document. When this has been done, the principal should be able, by taking into account the nature of the documents and the dates on which they were signed, to indicate which group he considers to bear his genuine signatures. This should then afford a basis from which the investigation of the suspect signatures may proceed.

Criminal proceedings against the forger in these circumstances are almost invariably followed by disputes which may give rise to civil actions, for when a trusted servant has been convicted of forgery of signatures on cheques, there is almost certain to be some disagreement between the bank which has paid out on the forgeries and the employer who has been robbed. When many cheques have been forged, criminal charges are often restricted to comparatively few to avoid undue waste of time. With the cheques which have been the subject of successful proceedings against the forger, there is rarely any dispute; contention arises out of cheques which have not been proved to be fraudulent in court. It is not uncommon for a bank to have good reason to suspect that in some of these cases, genuine signatures are either carelessly or wilfully disclaimed by the signatories, and in these cases they rightly refuse reimbursement unless forced to do so. Investigations of doubtful signatures in these cases are often fraught with considerable difficulty.

Genuine Signatures which are Disavowed

Apart from the foregoing examples, there is a growing number of genuine signatures which are quite honestly but mistakenly disclaimed by their authors. One reason is the ageing population, with the consequent increased incidence of failing memory. Many elderly people who find themselves able to recall trivial matters which happened in their youth, regard this as a proof that their memories are still excellent rather than as a sign that old age is advancing on them. They do not realise that although ancient events are recalled as though they happened yesterday, actions which are much more recent are being completely forgotten. The author is constantly having documents submitted to him for examination by the legal advisers of elderly people who have no recollection of signing them and who cannot or will not recognise the signatures as their own. In many of these cases the first mistrust of the signature occurs when the elderly person, who cannot recall writing it, observes some obvious feature which he says, often quite correctly, cannot be matched in its entirety with any of the genuine signatures in his possession. As few people have available for comparison large numbers of what they know to be genuine signatures, this is not surprising when it is remembered that the signatures of the most skilled writers exhibit a certain amount of natural variation.

These investigations present little difficulty. As a rule, the indications of forgery —tremor, retouching and poor line quality—are absent and the obvious feature which has occasioned the first suspicion can usually be found, probably in a less developed form, in other genuine signatures. Provided the minutiae of the genuine signatures are correctly reproduced, there is little probability that a forger of sufficient experience to include the insignificant details of the handwriting would make such an obvious gross error. As a general rule, it is safe to conclude that any forgery which has been so well written that it bears a close and detailed resemblance to the genuine signature, is extremely unlikely to resemble the genuine signature in details whilst departing from it in an obvious fashion.

In the majority of cases, once this has been pointed out, and the opinion that the signature shows no sign of having been forged is reinforced by a simple demonstration of the facts which can be appreciated by any intelligent person, the signature is accepted without more ado. Occasionally, elderly people refuse to listen to reason and persist in disclaiming their genuine signatures, sometimes on a wholesale scale. Whether this course is taken through senility or whether it is an example of the cunning of old age is often hard to determine. Every large banking concern has had experience of some of its elderly customers disclaiming their signatures on cheques which have been paid out, although there is no prima facie case that they are the victims of fraud.

They are almost invariably people who have suffered financial reverses which they refuse to attribute to their own lack of acumen; instead they blame the bank for depleting their resources by paying out on forged cheques. There must always be the suspicion that they know that if this allegation can be established the bank will have to refund the money and that it is this which inspires this wholesale disclaiming of genuine signatures. In these cases, the investigation of the authenticity of the signatures should follow along conventional lines. Whilst the old adage about there always being fire wherever there is smoke may not be true, nothing is lost by making sure that where there is some smoke, no fire can be found. Even where there is proof of wholesale exaggeration, all signatures should be scrutinised with care, even when they occur on cheques paid to the credit of the complainant in settlement of genuine accounts. Wealthy elderly people are the natural prey of the modern forger and the signatures on these cheques may be practice efforts or designed to establish confidence in a forgery. This is dealt with in greater detail at a later stage.

Genuine Signatures Deliberately Modified

The fraudulent disavowal of signatures is not confined to the elderly, for when a deal has proved to be unsatisfactory, it is simple to avoid responsibility by disclaiming the signatures on the vital documents. Another comparatively common example of the disclaimed signature is that on a delivery note which has to be signed as the proof of receipt of goods.

The routine investigation is often complicated by the fact that at the time of signing, the signatory foresees circumstances in which it might be to his advantage to disclaim the signature. When this is so, the signature is written in a careless and illegible fashion or is deliberately modified in some particular. This deliberate alteration is introduced to supply a plausible pretext for eventual repudiation.

The illegible signature is employed on documents such as delivery notes, because the delivery-man is generally satisfied if any written matter appears on his copy of the note, the signing of which he regards as a formality because deliveries are so rarely challenged. It is on the more formal documents, where a scrawled and illegible signature would be the subject of comment, that the signature exhibiting a deliberate modification is found.

When illegible signatures or scrawled initials are being investigated, it is well to preface the examination by preparing considerably enlarged (up to five times linear) photographs of both questioned and comparison signatures. Whenever possible, the comparison signatures should be drawn from contemporary, similar, documents signed under identical circumstances. In the enlarged photographs, it will be possible to relate certain formations in the illegible signature with the letters they purport to represent. When this is done, it will be seen that even in the most illegible signature and scrawled initials, there is some justification for the outline which has been written, and this will go some way towards establishing its authenticity.

It is more difficult to forge an illegible signature than is realised, for the enlarged photograph of the forgery of a scrawl will often make clear that many of the strokes are meaningless and, unlike those in a genuine scrawl, cannot be related with any specific letter or group of letters in the genuine signature. If the enlarged photograph of a disclaimed, scrawled or illegible, signature shows no sign of forgery, and it has been orientated on the document in a way similar to that shown in documents bearing undisputed signatures, then providing that its outlines can be related even remotely to those of the genuine signature, it may be reported that available evidence is consistent with the scrawl being a genuine signature written by the person to whom it was attributed. If these conditions cannot be fulfilled, the matter will have to be left open.

When the signature on a formal document has been deliberately modified, two discoveries may confidently be expected on close examination. The first is that the modification is in some rather prominent feature of the letter design which is almost invariably pointed out by the person disclaiming the signature, and the second is that, apart from this one obvious feature, the rest of the signature appears to be normal. The tremor of forgery and any delicate retouching are absent, and all the minutiae of the handwriting of the genuine signature are present in the disclaimed specimen.

Before the discrepancy can be accepted as proof of forgery, one has to accept a forger who is sufficiently skilful to reproduce the minutiae to perfection and yet is sufficiently stupid to introduce, quite unexpectedly, a feature which, according to the person disclaiming the signature, has never appeared in a genuine signature. The extreme unlikelihood of this will negative the suggestion that the signature is forged.

A signature which reproduces all the grosser features of the genuine but none of the lesser, may safely be denounced as a forgery. The converse does not apply, for a signature which produces to perfection all the less conspicuous features is unlikely to have been written by anyone other than the presumed signatory, in spite of some obvious difference in letter design which could have been deliberately introduced.

It is curious how signatures on documents which are signed with some misgivings tend to fade away at the end of the word, sometimes to such an extent as to omit the final letter altogether. When these signatures are disclaimed and the incomplete nature of the signature cited in support, it can be pointed out that in a forgery the last letters can be expected to be as fully and completely represented as the first. There are few forgers who would content themselves with the writing of an incomplete signature; this would be sure to invite the most stringent scrutiny because of its obvious departure from the normal.

Signatures Obtained by Trickery

Occasionally the author receives for examination signatures which by any test are genuine, and yet which any lawyer would rightly regard as fraudulent because they appear on documents which the writers of the disputed signatures would never willingly have signed. These are signatures which have been obtained on the documents through trickery. Trickery should always be suspected when the person who puts forward a document from which he hopes to profit and which the presumed signatory disclaims, demands to have it submitted to any document examiner of standing the other side may choose and agrees to abide by his findings.

There are innumerable devices by which a genuine signature may be caused to appear on a document which the signatory has never willingly signed. Although some of these have already been referred to and others are mentioned below, it is impossible to draw up a comprehensive list of tricks which must be guarded against.

The simplest and perhaps the most popular is to trim off the unwanted material from a sheet of paper which bears a genuine signature that is somewhat isolated from the other matter on the document. The only disadvantage of this simple scheme is that the area of blank paper which appears over the signature is certain to be limited and the shape of the trimmed sheet is unlikely to be conventional. These two difficulties can be surmounted in a number of simple ways. If the document is supposed to be anything but very recent, another matching sheet of paper can be fixed with either stamp-edging or cellulose tape to the upper edge of that bearing the signature, to simulate a much larger initial sheet which has become torn and roughly repaired. To lend colour to this suggestion, some of the added material is placed so that the " tear " appears to have cut through a line of writing or of typescript. At first sight, this device will lend credence to the story that the original document was torn at a time which was subsequent to the writing or typing. On the other hand, once a microscope has been used on the raw edges, a different state of affairs may be disclosed. If the paper has either a watermark or well-defined wire marks, it may be possible to show that the extra sheet does not exactly fit that bearing the signature, because of the lack of continuity of the water or wire marks.

Another way of surmounting the difficulty is to use the sheet of paper bearing the genuine signature as the last of a number of sheets on which the remainder of the document has been drawn up. In this case, there will be no necessity for any water or wire marks to be matched, so this difficulty is avoided. There is the chance that suspicion may be aroused when the complete document is found to consist of a number of different types of paper with the edges possibly showing different signs of wear and tear. At all times the shape of the trimmed sheet is unlikely to be conventional, and this is a feature which should arouse suspicion once a disclaimed signature has been found to be devoid of any evidence of forgery. Another suspicious feature is the occurrence of cramped or unevenly spaced matter above the signature, which is often coupled with large blank areas below.

If an isolated genuine signature is not forthcoming, the victim is induced to sign a document, usually in the form of a receipt, made specially for the purpose. A considerable space is deliberately left between the written matter and the place where the signature has to be written, so that the document may subsequently be trimmed. Alternatively, the paper is chosen and the entries on the document are such that a thorough erasure can be effected of everything but the signature.

If this trick is suspected, a careful search should be made for signs of erasure. Treatment with powdered graphite can usually be relied on to indicate the site of erasures if examination with light at grazing incidence has failed. Whenever possible, once an erasure is discovered, the nature of the erased matter should be elicited in an effort to recall to the signatory the circumstances in which he signed the original document.

If a name is short, consisting of but few letters, an example of a genuine signature may be discovered written across and wholly on a stamp on a genuine document. Once the stamp has been removed by judicious peeling, a process aided by cautious steaming, it can serve as the basis of a most convincing forgery. The only evidence of the swindle may be that the stamp shows indications that it has been removed from one document and stuck on to another. Even this discovery may not be sufficient to expose the trick, because it may be argued that the stamp might have been placed on the wrong document before being removed and stuck down in the correct place in readiness to receive the signature. This argument is difficult to refute if the whole of the signature is on the stamp, but there is always the possibility that the style of the signature is significantly older than the document on which it appears—a finding which would reinforce the suggestion of forgery.

Fig. 11–23. This is an enlarged photograph of a genuine signature written across a stamp which was removed and re-fixed to a fraudulent document. The initial " J " and the final " es " were added and the whole overwritten to conceal the fact that additions had been made.

Sometimes it is necessary to add a stroke at each end of the signature which has proved too large to be accommodated on the stamp in its entirety. This addition is not easy to accomplish, and it is often possible to show that part of the signature has been written twice, once on the edge of the stamp and a second time just under the edge of the stamp. This is a discovery which admits of no plausible interpretation and is wholly indicative of forgery. It may happen that, in those instances where two portions of the signature cannot be shown to overlap, the ink used for making the additions to the signature does not match that in which the main portion has been written; another discovery which is fatal to the forgery.

On more than one occasion, the author has received for examination documents where disclaimed signatures were undoubtedly genuine, but where there was no evidence of either trimming or erasure. In all these cases the circumstances indicated that the signatures had been obtained by bare-faced effrontery.

Many busy executives, and chairmen of committees in particular, have many more or less formal documents to sign; when these documents are placed before them for signature at the end of a long session, they are often signed with little attention to the exact nature of the document to which the signature is being applied if their attention is distracted. In these circumstances, there is often little risk in including an extra document which will be signed along with many others of similar general appearance.

A safer device is to prepare a composite document for signature. The smaller upper portion may be a copy of a genuine document which has to be signed in the normal way of business. This is tacked with a few spots of gum on to the lower sheet on which the signature is required. If the sheets overlap at a fold or along a line, it is possible to prepare the composite so that anyone signing in a hurry will not notice that it differs in any way from a normal document. Once signed, the composite is hidden and another copy of the genuine document offered for signature. If there is any suggestion that this has already been signed, there will naturally be no trace of the earlier document. Unless traces of the spots of gum can be discovered, here again there will be no way of showing that the disclaimed signature is anything but genuine.

The device of obtaining a signature on a document, usually a receipt which is so arranged that a carbon copy is made at the same time on another sheet of paper, is an ancient device which requires a certain amount of stage management if it is to be successful. Even when the trick is successful the carbon copy obtained in this way is of little use, except in the case of documents such as delivery notes, where a carbon copy of a signature is to be expected. Any disclaimed signature which is a carbon copy should be immediately suspect.

The use of the recently introduced N.C.R. paper which has been described elsewhere will undoubtedly simplify matters for the trickster. The special properties of this paper which does not require the use of carbon paper to form copies, enable a signature to be obtained on an under-sheet which to the eye is indistinguishable from ordinary paper, and on which the document to be signed can be placed in full view of the signatory. The signatures obtained in this way are blue in colour at first, slowly changing in a matter of days to a bright green, not unlike the colour of Superchrome Jade Green ink. The writing appears to have been made with a stylo or a ball-point pen adapted for use with ordinary writing ink, and bears little resemblance to the conventional carbon copy. If rubbed with the thumb there is no smearing; it is to be hoped that this paper is not developed further to give a black rather than a green copy!

Forgery of Signatures of Elderly Persons

The forgery of the signatures of elderly and, in particular, senile persons has become increasingly prevalent in recent years, and the author has had many cases of this type of crime whereby those most in need of care and protection have been stripped of their savings. With the advance of medical science, many elderly people, more often women, live on for years after their mental powers have failed.

Sometimes, these elderly people live with companions, but in other instances their relatives seek relief from having to tend them personally, a situation complicated by the absence of domestic assistance, by placing them in privately managed homes for the elderly often situated in the south of England. Whilst they are well tended in some of these places and their last years made comfortable, in others, every opportunity is taken to rob them of their money, a fact which is only discovered by the relatives when they find on their decease, that their estates are considerably reduced in value or bequeathed to strangers in a new will drawn up just before death. Some companions are honest, but others cannot resist the temptation to make use of their unique opportunities to forge their employer's signature to any documents which do not have to be witnessed.

The simplest method of swindling an elderly person is by means of the " raised " cheque. The trusted companion, or nurse, kindly assumes the boring task of filling in the entries on cheques for the victim who has nothing to do but add her signature. If a cheque is cunningly drawn, using a ball-point pen, it can easily be " raised " after signature with no evidence to show that it is other than genuine. Additions to the original amount can be made in the spaces which have been left for the purpose and where a ball-point pen has been used, microscopic examination cannot be counted on to reveal the fact that any addition has been made. Of course if the mistake is made of using a conventional pen, then it is often possible to prove that the cheque has been raised in instances where six has been raised to sixty, or eight to eighty. Another mistake is to have a raised cheque made payable to a fictitious person or to the forger personally, a feature which is calculated to give rise to some suspicion when the matter is finally investigated. In one case in which the author was concerned, where a very wealthy senile woman was systematically robbed by her companion-housekeeper, suspicion was aroused by the fact that large numbers of cheques had been made payable—allegedly for nursing services—to some dozens of different nurses, all of whom had but a single initial and a three-letter surname. The woman, who was later sentenced for this and similar offences, had collected practically every three-letter surname it was possible to find, the object being to reduce the amount of handwriting needed when the cheques were endorsed, so as to minimise the chance of proving that all the endorsements had been, in fact, written by the same person.

More cunning forgers ensure that raised cheques are made payable to reputable tradesmen and collect the difference in goods ostensibly supplied to the victim.

When mere raising of the occasional cheque is regarded as too slow a procedure, downright forgery of the signature itself is resorted to. These forgeries may pass undetected in spite of investigation, unless it is realised how thoroughly the ground is often prepared. The first stage is for the forger to undertake the writing of everything on genuine cheques except the signature. When the officials at the bank have become accustomed to seeing the handwriting of the would-be forger appear on practically all the cheques drawn by the victim, the first attempts at forgery are made on cheques issued in payment of accounts due to such bodies as the Commissioners of Inland Revenue, the Electricity Board, the Gas Board, etc. For obvious reasons, signatures on cheques such as these are rarely the subject of close scrutiny, and if sufficient of these forged cheques flow through an account, any imperfect forgery will soon come to be regarded as a variant of the genuine signature with any differences from previous signatures attributed to the onset of old age.

If the first forged cheques fail to pass muster at the bank, the excuse can be made that the signature was made to save trouble for the elderly person and that no harm could have been done because the money paid out on the cheque would, in any case, have been credited to the account of the victim.

The next stage is to write to the bank in the name of the victim for an extra cheque-book and, when this is forthcoming, forged signatures may be written with impunity as long as the account is not overdrawn.

Once the forged cheques are accepted without question, a forged will may be prepared and held in readiness for the decease of the victim. A stupid forger will draw up the will so that he or she benefits directly, but a far more subtle variant which the author has observed on more than one occasion, is to have the money disposed of in the forged will bequeathed to another elderly person who has made no secret of the fact that all he or she possesses is to be left to the forger. When this person dies the forger can enjoy the ill-gotten gains with comparative impunity.

Whenever inquiries are made, the document examiner is asked to examine only those cheques which there is good reason to believe are forged. It is not very probable that any contemporary signatures other than those on cheques will be available for comparison, because these are practically the only documents signed by the elderly infirm. The signatures which are likely to be chosen as standards of comparison are those on cheques which are considered unlikely to be forgeries, since it is to no one's interest to forge them. These, of course, are the cheques made payable to the Commissioners of Inland Revenue, etc., referred to above. If this is the case, the investigation is hamstrung from the very beginning, as forged signatures are being compared with other forgeries, so that no significant difference will be seen.

The only safe course is to go sufficiently far back in time to ensure that any signatures used for comparison are without question genuine. It is only with these as a basis that it will be possible to establish which subsequently written signatures are forged and which are genuine. It is very unwise to assume that any signature or other writing made whilst the suspect was on the scene is genuine, because even " witnessed " signatures have on occasion been proved to be forged. The witnesses may have been in league with the forger, or the witnessed signatures may appear on documents which in reality bear two or three signatures, no two of which were written at the same time or with the signatories in the presence of each other.

Forgery of Complete Letters

Occasionally, not only signatures but whole letters are written in an imitation of the handwriting of another person. If this very difficult task is to have any hope of success the first essential is that ample specimens of the handwriting of the victim must be available to the forger. It is practically impossible to make a convincing forgery of a large amount of cursive handwriting of good quality, although there is no reason why a fairly successful attempt might not be made with disconnected script handwriting. The reason for this is dealt with in the chapter on " Disguise."

The most astounding examples of the attempted forgery of a whole letter in the handwriting of another person in the experience of the author was made by an eleven-year-old girl who was charged with theft. She produced to the police a letter which she said was sent to her by her mother who lived in a distant town. In this, she was instructed to steal and send the proceeds of her thefts to her mother with the threat that, if she failed to do so, she would be sent to an orphanage. The police were so impressed with this story that they obtained a specimen of the mother's handwriting with a view to charging her with writing the letter, the handwriting of which bore a very close resemblance to that she had written at their request.

It required a critical examination of the handwriting to show that the mother had had nothing to do with the writing of the letter; after the handwriting of the letter had been attributed to the child it required a complete confession on her part before the police force concerned was completely satisfied that she was guilty. The natural handwriting of both mother and daughter was, as is often the case with such near relatives, very similar to begin with, and the child cunningly copied the more outstanding characteristics of the mother's handwriting and suppressed her own to a considerable extent. Certain differences between the handwriting of the mother and that in the letter were considered by the police to be due to disguise, and it was only when the minutiae of the handwriting in the letter were shown to be those of the child rather than of the mother that the true state of affairs was revealed.

Another case in the author's experience is that of another young girl, fifteen years of age, who fabricated a whole series of letters which purported to come from a young man, in order to support a successful application for an affiliation order. The man strenuously denied authorship of the letters on oath, but when the magistrates had compared his handwriting with that of the letters they refused to believe him, granted the order and referred the matter to the local police so as to charge the man with perjury. The documents were referred to the author so that expert evidence could be called to refute the denial of authorship by the man. The final result was that the man was exonerated of perjury, and the girl found herself in the dock at the assizes charged and convicted of that crime.

These two cases illustrate that tender age is no bar to the committal of a serious crime, and that children can and do embark on projects which the majority of adults would hesitate to attempt. In both cases, without expert examination of the documents concerned, there was a definite risk of a serious miscarriage of justice taking place.

Bibliography

Bruning, A., "A Genuine Counterfeit," *International Criminal Police Review,* No. 58, May, 1952.

Frazer, P., "The Application of Composite Photography to Handwriting and Especially to Signatures," *Proc.Am.Phil.Soc.,* 1886.

Guven, E., "The Signature," *International Criminal Police Review,* No. 58, May, 1952.

Hardless, C. E., *The Identification of Handwriting and the Detection of Forgery,* The Hardless Press, Calcutta, India, 1912.

Hilton, O., and Stein, E. W., "Ballpoint Pens, Use for Signing Documents Considered," *American Bar Association Journal,* May, 1948.

Hilton, Ordway, "Can the Forger be Identified from his Handwriting?" *Journal of Criminal Law, Criminology and Police Science,* Vol. 43, No. 4, November–December, 1952.

Keeler, K., " A Study of Documentary Evidence in Election Frauds," *Journal of Criminal Law and Criminology,* Vol. 25, No. 2, July–August, 1934. " Documentary Evidence Involved in an Election Dispute," *Journal of Criminal Law and Criminology,* Vol. 27, No. 2, July–August, 1936.

Le Clerc, M., " The Protection of Banking Documents against Forgery," *International Criminal Police Review,* No. 58, May, 1952.

Locard, E., " The Inert Hand," *International Criminal Police Review,* No. 45, February, 1951.

Osborn, Albert S., " Difficulties in Proving Forgery." Reprinted from *Virginia Law Review,* Vol. XVI, No. 5.

12

THE PRELIMINARY PHASE OF A DOCUMENT EXAMINATION

DESPITE the many thousands of forged documents that are put into circulation every year and the innumerable scurrilous anonymous letters which call for investigation, genuine documents are so numerous that it is only on relatively rare occasions that a lawyer or even an investigating officer of a large law enforcement organisation comes into contact with a case which involves the examination of forged, anonymous or suspect documents.

Whilst the average lawyer or investigating officer is, at the beginning of such a case, apt to find himself at a loss as to how best to proceed, it is unfortunately only too true that the best opportunity to expose fraud and forgery or to prove the authorship of anonymous letters may be lost for ever if the preliminary stages of the investigation are not carried out, not only properly, but promptly. This is why it sometimes happens that when the case comes for trial the truth cannot be established, in spite of the assistance of an able and conscientious document examiner and the best efforts of the advocate. The loss of a case which should have been won can usually be attributed to one or both of two reasons.

In the first place, at the trial there proved to be a dearth of suitable comparison material in the form of specimens of handwriting, authentic signatures, or of work done on known typewriters and the like, in spite of the fact that a sufficiency of these might have been had for the asking at the outset of the inquiry. Secondly, the initial statements made by those who proved to be adverse witnesses were not sufficiently precise and detailed to prevent considerable modifications being fraudulently introduced with impunity at the trial, in an effort to explain away some of the more awkward facts which had been brought to light as the result of the scientific examination of the documents concerned.

To ensure the proper action on the part of those initially engaged in any matter involving forged, anonymous or suspect documents, there should be knowledge of what can be accomplished by the document examiner in connection with the examination of a forgery or a group of anonymous letters, and in particular a good idea as to what data he needs to carry out the examination. The first enables the investigator to know what help and information he can reasonably demand from the document examiner in the type of case concerned, and the second, in particular, will tell him what material in the way of comparison writings, etc., he will have to supply to the examiner, if full advantage is to be taken of his skill and experience.

INITIAL STATEMENTS

It is curious how forged wills and kindred documents, especially those which have made a belated appearance on the scene, are almost invariably brought forward by people who are only too eager to tell their stories, for forgery is rarely unsupported by perjury. This is a good thing, and anybody who is willing to make a statement in connection with the signing of a will, the discovery of hidden documents or the receipt of anonymous letters should be interviewed and allowed—nay, more—encouraged, to tell his story as completely and with as much detail as possible.

The story is best taken down word for word by an unobtrusively placed shorthand writer or, better still, recorded on an unobtrusive tape recorder. So many legal advisers now make a practice of recording all interviews on this useful machine that its presence should occasion no surprise at the interview.

In connection with the use of a tape recorder it must not be assumed that what is reproduced from a tape is necessarily a complete and accurate record of what was said. Recordings from tape machines can be edited by deletion, addition, or even alteration of sequence, by one who has some experience in these matters, and it may be a matter of extreme difficulty to discover, much less prove, that this has been done. Although it may sound incredible, it can be arranged that a considerably altered version of an interview can be played back from the actual tape which was used for the initial recording.[1] In spite of this possibility of abuse a tape recorder has a great deal to recommend it if its limitations are kept in mind.

During the interview, while the witness is talking of, for example, the discovery of a hidden will, etc., no prompting should be given and not the slightest doubt as to the truth of the story should be allowed to show itself in the manner or voice of the listener. It is only at the end of the story, which in the majority of cases has been carefully, sometimes too carefully, prepared, that there comes the time for questions. The questions should be designed not only to fill in any gaps in the record, but also to investigate the surroundings of the story which has been related. As many details as possible should be extracted, since the more detailed the story the more chance there is of discovering anachronisms and facts at variance with the account when a forged document is subsequently submitted to detailed physical examination. If, on the other hand, the document is genuine and the story is true, then the extended agreement between what can be gleaned from the document and the associated story will be such that no hesitation need be felt in finally accepting it as genuine.

When there are two or more witnesses they should be examined separately, and the fullest details should be required from each, especially those concerning the actual signing of documents such as agreements and wills, as well as the circumstances in which discoveries of hidden documents and the receipt of anonymous letters occurred. Far too often such details are neglected in the early stages of a case, so that at the trial witnesses sometimes appear with hitherto unrelated stories of "guided hand" signatures to wills, which may undo all the patient work of the document examiner who may have been at pains to show how extensively the questioned signature on the will differs from any genuine signature of the testator. In many such cases a comprehensive initial statement would have disposed quite effectively of such last-minute testimony which often is quite untrue, having been

[1] The possibility of this being done and the sequence of operations necessary have been pointed out by T. B. Radley in an article in the *Criminal Law Review* ([1954] Crim.L.R. 96). Subsequently a case where this was admitted to have been done was heard at Southwark County Court. This case was reported in *The Solicitor's Journal*, Volume 98, p. 794.

trumped up to explain inconsistencies which might otherwise seriously damage the chances of a forgery being declared genuine. False witnesses often carefully rehearse their stories which, when compared, show a remarkable similarity in far too many details which seem to be perfectly recalled with amazing facility, sometimes over a period of years; whilst other occurrences, which are often found to differ in the several accounts, seem to be recalled with the utmost difficulty, if at all.

Sometimes a great deal of forethought is taken by those who proffer forged wills. In a recent case involving forgery of a will [2] evidence was given at the trial as to how the two " witnesses " whose names appeared on the forged will were, some months after the death of the testator, instructed to make each other's acquaintance for the first time over a glass of beer, in case either was cross-examined as to the other's appearance when the court hearing took place. At the same time one of the " witnesses " was presented with a typewritten brief, which he was requested to study before appearing at a solicitor's office to make an affidavit concerning the supposed signing of the will. Fortunately in this case, a fairly full statement had been taken initially, and the first stage of the investigation, which eventually led to the conviction of both the principal beneficiary and one of the " witnesses " for forgery, was the proof that the will was actually typed on a machine belonging to this " witness," who had declared that the first time he saw the will was when he was asked to sign as a witness to the testator's signature.

If a witness has related a story concerning the signing and witnessing of a signature to a will or agreement, he should be taken back over the actual ceremony of signing and the following important points settled and put on record.

In the first place, questions should be put concerning the will or agreement itself. The witness should be asked whether he had ever seen the will before being asked to place his signature thereon. This may prove an important point to have established, because it may subsequently be shown that the " witness " was actually responsible for writing or typing the will himself, for a high proportion of forged documents are manufactured by one of the " witnesses." The witness should be asked how the will was produced, whether from an envelope or pocket in a folded state, or lying flat on a table when first seen. The point as to whether the will was folded before or after signing should be thoroughly probed. The significance which folds in any document may have is dealt with in another chapter, but where a will is concerned they may prove of paramount importance. On examination, some wills afford evidence that they were devoid of folds when signed by the testator, but that the signatures of the witnesses were added after the paper had been folded. Whilst this fact may be capable of reasonable explanation, it may sometimes prove fatal to the establishment of the will as a legal document.

The details concerning the actual signing of the will by the testator should next be ascertained. The preliminary questions to this end should concern the writing instrument employed, and whether blotting paper was used or not. The most vital questions deal with the position assumed by the testator. Frequently the presence of unusual features in a questioned signature is " explained " by last minute accounts that the testator signed in bed, without his spectacles or with his nerveless

2 *R.* v. *Kirven,* unreported.

hand guided by that of one of the witnesses. If the precaution had been taken of getting a full account of what was supposed to have happened, before the " witnesses " had been placed upon their guard by the discovery that the will was being submitted for expert examination, there would have been no opportunity for these after-thoughts.

If there is available more than one witness to the alleged signing of a will or agreement, it is unlikely that they will have agreed upon a similar story which will cover all the points raised by these questions, so that it will be possible to test the truth of the stories, for answers which show a good measure of agreement will tend to establish the veracity of the witnesses.

Sometimes traces of pencil writing are found associated with the testator's signature on a will or agreement. This discovery, whilst often very significant, does not necessarily indicate that the signature is a traced forgery, for it is a regrettable practice of some solicitors' clerks who have to deal with an undue proportion of stupid clients, to pencil in the client's signature in the appropriate place. Sometimes the client is sufficiently foolish as to trace over this pencilled signature with ink in the confident hope that by doing so he cannot have gone far wrong. This innocent association of pencil writing with genuine signatures is sometimes invoked to account for the presence of the pencil writing sometimes found in a traced forgery. If a definite statement is obtained from a witness that the will form was devoid of any pencil indications as to where the testator should sign, the presence of any pencil marks found on subsequent examination cannot be accounted for in this way and some other plausible excuse must be found for their presence.

The surface on which a document rests whilst being signed sometimes has an effect on the handwriting. If the paper rests on wood with a decided grain, writing done with a pencil or a ball-pointed pen will often show the influence of the grain in the unevenness of the writing. In the same way, any unnatural position assumed by a person writing will have an effect on the writing. The nature of the surface on which a document is supposed to have rested whilst being signed, as well as the position of the writer, whether standing up, sitting up or even lying down in bed, have been used at various times to explain awkward facts which the careful examination of questioned signatures has brought to light.

If the witness states that the will was signed in some peculiar way or in strange circumstances which may possibly affect the handwriting, then a full account should be recorded so that the document examiner can be informed in good time. He can then consider the matter at leisure and, if necessary, perform experiments to determine how much significance these peculiar circumstances would be likely to have.

By far the worst time for such considerations to be sprung on the document examiner is during his cross-examination in court, when he may be asked, " Do you not think it possible that the suspicious features you have mentioned in your evidence in connection with this signature might conceivably have been caused by. . . ? " And then counsel continues by outlining some peculiar and highly improbable conditions surrounding the signing about which he intends to call evidence. If the unfortunate witness agrees that the theory outlined to him might be true, his evidence is considerably weakened. If he takes his courage in both hands and rashly answers " No—such considerations will not, in my opinion, justify the presence of the suspicious features I have referred to," he will afterwards have to think very quickly as he faces a barrage of awkward questions designed to exploit his almost certain inability to consider this new evidence in all its implications whilst on his feet in the witness box.

Sometimes a curious story is told of the signing of a will, not in a testator's home or at the office of his legal adviser, which would make it difficult to account for its subsequent wanderings, but in some peculiar place which the normal person would consider the last anyone would visit to make his will. Improbable stories should be deeply probed. The locus of the signing should be identified beyond any doubt whatsoever, and also the reason for choosing such a place. In a recent case, a will disposing of large tracts of valuable ground in London was supposed to have been signed and witnessed in a certain public shelter, associated with a line of street cars, after which the will was lost to sight for some years and came to light subsequently only as the indirect result of damage done in an air raid. The initial questioning of an aged " witness " to the will established the position of the shelter beyond any doubt, and when the case was heard, evidence was given that this particular shelter was not even built at the time the will was supposed to have been made. Any vagueness about the exact site of the shelter would have reduced the crushing effect of this evidence which contributed largely to the refusal of the court to accept the document as genuine. If a lost will has been " discovered " in some peculiar place and the witnesses to the will are either deceased or cannot be traced, the full story of the events leading up to the discovery should be obtained.

It should always be borne in mind that whilst the majority of documents encountered are genuine, the odds against a perfectly genuine will coming to light as a " romantic " discovery are very great indeed. In the experience of the author, *every* will he has been asked to examine which was found in peculiar circumstances, has been fraudulent. This may be even more surprising when it is known that in nearly half the cases, the examination was made at the request of the parties who hoped to establish the authenticity of the documents they submitted for examination. Every will or document which is " discovered " at an opportune moment should be viewed with grave suspicion unless its authenticity can be established beyond reasonable doubt.

The first step in the investigation of the circumstances in which the will or other document was discovered is to find out whether the discovery was the result of deliberate search or was quite fortuitous. If a search was conducted, the reasons for choosing the correct place should be elucidated, for should a will have been " planted " by the discoverer or by someone who is making use of him, a great deal of light may be thrown upon the matter when questions are asked as to why the search was made in the unlikely places where these documents are invariably found.

Even if the will has been discovered accidentally, it may prove to be of some importance to find out who was present or was first informed of the discovery. Care should be taken to ascertain whether the finder told anyone of the testamentary dispositions, because it may happen that someone who should have been ignorant of the contents of the will has indicated that he knew more than he should have done.

If a forged will is produced which makes testamentary dispositions that should occasion some surprise, such as the replacement of a favoured relative by someone who might be considered most unlikely to benefit, the forger is often nervous of his handiwork and endeavours in the will itself to make some explanation for the change. Occasionally supporting documents in the form of letters written by the testator explaining his motives are subsequently "found," if the possibility of their existence is strongly hinted at during the preliminary inquiry. If such additional documents are already in existence or make their appearance later, it is as well to have them produced in time for a thorough investigation of these also. Sometimes the forger overreaches himself by including matter which the testator could not have known of, or would be unlikely to put in a will. It is too much always to expect to find such expressions as "who so kindly looked after me until my death," which have occasionally been found in such letters, but similar if not such blatant slips may be found if the possibility of their existence is kept in mind.

Occasionally the use of an unusual legal phrase in a suspect document may be worth investigating. A member of a firm of solicitors was astonished to have presented to him as genuine a will which had certainly not been drawn up by his firm, but which employed an abbreviated and rather curious attestation clause which as far as he knew was used only by his firm. His interest was further roused when he saw what purported to be the signature of a deceased client for whom he had actually drawn up a much different will some little time previously. The former will could not be found, so acting on the deduction that this new will had been drawn up illicitly by copying from the genuine will the legal phraseology but not the names of the original beneficiaries, he had this strange new will scientifically examined. A few months later, as a direct result of this examination, the beneficiary in the new will was convicted for forging it.

The way in which the interview of the recipient should be conducted in an inquiry into the receipt of anonymous letters is dealt with in detail elsewhere.[3] Before the interview is concluded, permission should be sought for the documents to be examined and photographed. The question of photography is considered elsewhere, but suffice it to say that a mere "photostat" or contact print of a questioned document is of little more use than a typewritten copy; a properly prepared photograph should invariably be insisted on.

Armed with the foregoing data, the legal adviser or investigating officer who has reason to believe that he has been presented with a forgery is in the position to make the preliminary physical examination of the suspect document as outlined elsewhere in this book.[4] He will naturally select only those tests which are applicable to the case, so that this examination need not take an inordinate time. While making his examination he will keep in mind the salient points of the story which has been related, so that he can detect any anachronisms or other evidence in the documents which does not agree with the story told of them.

Selection of Document Examiner

If, at the end of the examination, when due consideration has been given to what has become apparent to the investigating officer, it is decided that the documents

[3] See Chapter 14.
[4] See Chapter 3.

could with advantage be submitted to a professional document examiner, then a decision has to be made on the choice of a consultant. This, as explained in the introductory chapter is not an easy decision to make by anybody who has had no personal experience in these matters, for anyone who chooses may term himself a " document examiner " or " handwriting expert."

Owing to the increasing complication of the scientific apparatus which nowadays is essential for the thorough examination of documents, the practice of referring the matter to a local schoolmaster or bank official is not likely to be the best course today. It is true that some of these gentlemen not only have a flair for examining signatures, but have studied deeply what has been written on the question of forgery and so vicariously have shared in the experience of others, but in this, as in many other subjects, the day of the amateur or the semi-professional is past Many of these people may be quite capable of giving a correct opinion on the genuineness or otherwise of documents put before them and their help in the initial stages of an investigation should never be spurned. In these days, however, the courts are rarely interested in mere " opinions " about documents, however accurate they may be, for the modern tendency is to rely, where disputed documents are concerned, on a *demonstration of the facts* on which any opinions are advanced. This demands an experience of court work and the availability of laboratory facilities which few except professional examiners of documents are likely to have.

If inquiry of legal brethren for advice on the choice of a document examiner does not result in a name or names being given with confidence, then an inquiry at the headquarters of a large city or county police force will almost certainly meet with success. In Great Britain at any rate, the standing and ability of most of the experts who regularly give evidence in the criminal courts are well known to the police and the inquirer is not likely to go far wrong if he acts on the advice they give.

Comparison Material

Immediately it has been decided to consult an expert, efforts should be made to obtain the necessary comparison material he is sure to want. If an " expert " is chosen who is satisfied with the production of scanty comparison data, if he is willing to give an opinion on a signature straight away after merely glancing at a single standard, the inquirer may congratulate himself that he has been saved the possibly difficult task of obtaining dozens of genuine signatures for comparison. But his congratulations are likely to end here—he will probably receive few from his unfortunate client—for an " expert " who is so easily satisfied himself is unlikely to satisfy others.

The sooner a search is made for comparison material the better, for not only is there more time available if difficulty is experienced in finding it, but at the beginning of a case, not only are the people concerned more liable to talk freely, but they may go further and furnish specimens of their own as well as of other people's handwriting. This they may be loth to do at a later stage when doubts have crept in and they are not so confident that their forgery can withstand the scrutiny they discover it is receiving.

The golden rule when seeking comparison material is to give the document examiner the opportunity to compare like materials. For example, if a document bears a questioned signature, then signatures must be available for comparison. Furthermore, if the questioned signature is written in a confined space, then signatures written in similar confined spaces whenever possible should be made available as standards of comparison.

Sometimes a document examiner who has pointed out a whole series of differences between a signature on a will or other important document and those undoubtedly genuine is asked: " the signature on the will (or document) was a most important signature, so could not the importance and uniqueness of the situation have influenced the testator and occasioned the slight differences you have pointed out?" The only satisfactory answer to this or similar questions is, " I have examined signatures of the testator on other documents of equal importance, and consequently I am in the position to state in what way, if any, the importance of the occasion affects the signature of the testator." This answer could not be given if the investigating officer had not taken the trouble to obtain as comparison material, signatures on other important documents, instead of, for example, being satisfied with a few signatures on cancelled cheques for small amounts.

In cases involving forged signatures not only should comparison signatures be obtained from documents of similar importance, but if possible also from documents which are roughly contemporary with those in question.

The writing of an adult, once formed, rarely changes until disease or old age takes its toll, but often it happens that a signature will show an obvious steady change with the passage of time. In these circumstances the provision of a whole set of signatures written over a period of years will prove of inestimable value to the document examiner. On many an occasion, armed with such data, not only will it be possible to prove that a questioned signature is forged, but also that a signature of a certain period was used as a copy. (See Figure 11–19.) Furthermore, if there is exhibited an enlarged photograph of a number of signatures in chronological order set alongside the questioned signature which itself is placed level with a contemporary genuine specimen, the obviously " out-of-date " appearance of the forgery is often sufficient to condemn it, irrespective of any further evidence which points in the same direction.

When serious illness occurs, or death is near, a signature often undergoes a remarkable change in a very short period and if a suspect will is dated near the day of death, then signatures covering this period are essential if reliable evidence of the authenticity or otherwise of the signature is to be gleaned by any process of comparison.

On making inquiries it may be found that the most valuable comparison signatures are on documents in the custody of banks and other institutions unable to release documents for examination of signatures unless a number of time-consuming formalities have been complied with. These formalities should be set in motion as soon as possible, so that the required documents may be available for examination in time for full advantage to be taken of them.

In no case is the value of an immediate start by the legal adviser or investigating officer in the gathering of specimens more imperative than in cases involving the examination of typescript. The chapter on the examination of typescript explains how and why a machine leaves its imprint on every document which is typed thereon. It is emphasised also that all machinery is subject to the effects of wear and, in particular, of misuse. Every time a typewriter is used, and particularly when it is cleaned, slight alterations in the alignment and other characteristics are occasioned, so that work done on a much-used machine at a specified time may bear very little significant resemblance to that typed on the same machine a few months before. Consequently, with typewriting even more than with handwriting, there is an imperative need for contemporary standards of comparison. It may happen that even after a lapse of some years, it will be possible to find examples of typescript which are contemporary with the questioned document, but there is no guarantee that these specimens will prove to be altogether satisfactory for the document examiner's purpose. Contemporary copies made on the suspect machine specifically for the examination are far more preferable as standards of comparison.

In the investigation of anonymous letters, no time should be lost in setting inquiries in motion, because it often happens that others besides the complainant have received offensive letters from the same source and if the investigation is delayed, most of this valuable material may have been destroyed by the recipients. If this has happened it may prove a serious handicap, as there is a much greater chance of tracking down the author of a series of such letters than if a solitary example is all that is available.

It should always be borne in mind that in cases involving the examination of documents and the comparison of handwriting, the limiting factors are nearly always the nature and amount of standard material. All too often this comparison data has proved so scanty and of such an unsuitable nature that little positive can be accomplished.

More than twenty years of experience have proved to the author one important fact in connection with the supply of suitable standard comparison material. It is not usually circumstances which restrict the nature and quality of the comparison data which is supplied to the document examiner. Almost invariably two other factors play important parts. The first and the more important is that the legal adviser or investigating officer does not know what is actually required by the document examiner in the way of comparison material. This perhaps is understandable because document examination has become a highly technical matter. When consulted, the document examiner can of course indicate quite clearly what he needs for his examination, but all too often he is consulted at the last moment—sometimes after the court hearing has begun—and the other parties to the action no longer show the co-operative spirit which probably prevailed in the very early stages of the case. Secondly, the document examiner is often told that the material he has been supplied with is all that is available, and that he must do his best with what he has. Here again, experience has shown that if he takes a firm stand and refuses to attempt to solve a problem using material he knows will prove inadequate, but at the same time indicates where extra specimens are likely to be found, it is remarkable what is subsequently done to help him. It seems that some legal advisers and investigating officers are not aware of the many sources from which specimens of writing and signatures can be derived. This is the one advantage of the flood of paper which is characteristic of life today.

The provision of suitable standards is so often the very crux of successful document examination that great prominence is given to the matter by the author when he lectures at Detective Training Courses. The results of emphasising this aspect of the work have been most gratifying. Standard handwriting which is far superior in quantity and quality is much more readily forthcoming. Incidentally, this proves that in the majority of cases suitable comparison material exists and is forthcoming if a sufficiently thorough search is made in the correct places.

Where standard or comparison handwriting is concerned, whether in the form of signatures or letters, the first essential is that the comparison material be reliable. The risk of including among comparison writings only a single specimen of handwriting not written by the person to whom it is attributed should never be taken, for the inclusion of a false standard of comparison may very well invalidate any conclusion based on this faulty material. For example, if a single forged signature is included among those described as genuine, then it may very well be that those features which would otherwise suggest that the questioned signature on a will or other document is fraudulent would be present in the false comparison signature. Consequently, it would be difficult for any document examiner to reach a confident opinion concerning the authenticity of the questioned signature. To guard against the possibility of false standards of comparison being included in a group, the first care of the document examiner is the inter-comparison of any material described as the genuine writing of an individual, to detect any specimens which appear to be of doubtful authenticity. When such specimens are discovered and referred back to whoever supplied them, they almost invariably prove to have been mistakenly included with the genuine specimens.

The value of this preliminary work, which in the ideal state of affairs should never be necessary, has been proved time and time again. Unfortunately, when only a single comparison document is available—which often happens in criminal cases involving persons who write very little—this test by inter-comparison cannot be applied, and everything then rests on the care which has been taken by the investigating officer who has obtained and established the authenticity of the standard document.

In particular, signatures should never be taken at their face value. Cases are known where correspondence has been carried on for years, presumably by persons who subsequently have been proved to be incapable of writing a single word. Even officially witnessed " signatures " have been made by near relatives, who have persuaded minor officials to certify the " signatures " on the grounds that they undertake all the correspondence " for poor father (or mother or brother, as the case may be), who has never learned to write."

In addition, there are many who carry on correspondence and conduct business in the name of near relatives, although these relatives can write quite well and could if necessary conduct their own business. Many people sign the names of near relatives without giving any indication that the signature has been signed by someone else, and after some years of this it is often difficult to disentangle the correspondence, especially if, as is often the case with near relatives, the handwritings of the people concerned are very similar in appearance.

One solicitor's clerk was the unfortunate (for him) victim of this state of affairs. He investigated the correspondence his firm had had over a period of many years with a wealthy client and decided that her signature, of which he had numerous examples, was an easy one to forge on a fraudulent mortgage which he drew up on some property belonging to this client. He accomplished the forgery very skilfully, but when the case was investigated he was shocked to find that he had made a copy of the handwriting of his client's niece, who, unknown to him or to anyone else in the firm, had been looking after her aunt's financial affairs for years. This only came to light when the documents in the case were received for examination at the author's laboratory. As is the custom, the writings attributed to the old lady were compared with each other when it was found that the handwritings of two persons who wrote a very similar hand were concerned. Subsequent inquiries soon showed what had happened. At the trial, the defence made no effort to prove that the questioned signature on the mortgage was genuine, which in the circumstances was not surprising.

If proceedings are contemplated, it is of the utmost importance that two conditions should apply to any comparison signatures or specimen handwritings utilised by the document examiner. In the first place the specimens should all be available as evidence, and in the second they must be capable of being proved to be what they purport to be.

Very often when inquiries are made into the authorship of anonymous letters, comparison material in the form of personal letters written by the suspect to friends is readily supplied during the initial stages of the investigation. Whilst it is usually a simple matter for an investigator to obtain possession of such letters for purposes of comparison, it is different when there is the prospect of the lender of the letters having to give evidence in an assize trial; potential witnesses fear the serious inconvenience and loss of time occasioned, as well as the unwelcome publicity. If there is any threat of issuing a subpoena to an unwilling witness it is quite usual for him to suffer a sudden loss of memory concerning the authorship of the letter about which he was previously so certain.

The difficulties which are experienced by the document examiner when it is discovered at the last moment that certain documents are either not available or are inadmissible as evidence are dealt with more fully in the chapter which deals with the conduct of a disputed document case in court.

Admissibility of Standards

It is essential that all the standard comparison material needed by the document examiner is admissible as evidence. This is not always the case with a fair proportion of otherwise excellent comparison material. Many crimes are committed by criminals who have spent some time in prison, and specimens of their handwriting in the form of petitions and similar communications to the authorities are usually to be found among the prison records.

From the scientific point of view these documents concerning whose authorship there can be no shadow of doubt, furnish excellent comparison data in cases where notes are left at the scene of a crime. They are also very useful for comparing with the writing on envelopes used to return to the owners valueless stolen material. Unfortunately, these invaluable specimens of handwriting are invariably written on prison notepaper. Consequently they are not admissible in evidence, as it is considered that their contents might convey to a jury something derogatory about the character of the person they are trying.

Occasionally these incriminating documents are all that are available. In such cases they can be bound between two sheets of thick cardboard with holes cut in one sheet, through which some of the more innocuous words and phrases may be seen by the jury who are theoretically supposed to be in ignorance of the real nature of the document and of the reason why some of it is obscured. Whilst this idea will appeal to a keen detective officer, the defence can be expected to make every effort to have the obscured document excluded from the jury on the grounds of prejudice.

On the admissibility of documents in general the usual rules of evidence apply, but as they are based largely on common sense, an experienced lawyer or investigating officer should experience no difficulty in knowing whether a particular document is likely to be admissible or not.

Proving of Standards

It is important that somebody who can " prove " the comparison standards should be available in court. The proving of a standard writing or specimen of typescript is a legal matter, the details of which have no place here, but, broadly speaking, standard comparison handwriting or typescript is proved by the evidence of:

(a) someone who has seen the handwriting actually being written, or has seen the typescript typed on a particular machine;
(b) the admission of any person that a certain specimen of handwriting was written by him;
(c) someone who is in the position to recognise the handwriting as that of a particular person.

Obtaining Handwriting of Deceased Persons

It is the signature of a deceased person which is most likely to be questioned, so that the problem becomes one of discovering suitable comparison writing, as there is no possibility of obtaining " request " writings from someone who is no longer alive.

Whilst it is obvious that genuine signatures which are roughly contemporary with the questioned signatures form the best comparison material, the document examiner is sometimes asked whether he can utilise writings other than signatures as his comparison material. Alternatively, he may be offered these other writings as a supplement to a rather meagre supply of standard handwriting in the form of signatures.

A signature is in every respect a special word or phrase which is peculiarly representative of the writer. The majority of people do not use their ordinary handwriting when signing their names. A signature is often more floridly—and generally more illegibly—written than normal. As signatures fall into a class by themselves, other signatures constitute the only really satisfactory standards of comparison. Although other handwritings of the person concerned may assist the document examiner in a variety of ways when he is examining a questioned signature, they cannot be regarded as a satisfactory substitute for genuine signatures.

The possibility of variation in the fluency or carefree nature of a signature when applied to a solemn document such as a will, mortgage, or contract, has already been mentioned, as this is a favourite red herring trailed during cross-examination in an effort to explain away any divergences from normal exhibited by a forgery. This is yet another reason for obtaining signatures on other important documents as standards of comparison.

When cheques have to be signed with two or possibly three signatures, the final signature on the cheque will usually have to be written in a cramped space. This may affect the fluency of the writing, should the signatory be compelled to write a signature which is appreciably smaller than he is accustomed to make. Signatures written on similar cheques or in other cramped situations are obviously the optimum comparison material in these cases.

Many people have remarkably fixed ways of signing or endorsing cheques, especially with respect to the way the endorsement is positioned on the back of the cheque, and the way the signature is placed with respect to any printed matter such as " signed .... " and to any dotted line which may be present. Habits vary considerably. Some people begin their signatures close to the printed word, whilst others leave considerable gaps; some write above the dotted line, whilst others write on or even through it. All these points may be significant, so signatures signed on documents or under conditions as near as those applying to the questioned document should be sought for as comparison material.

The minimum number of signatures which should be made available for comparison depends on many factors. If the handwriting of the testator is good and the will or agreement was signed when in good health, then a dozen contemporary signatures should be sufficient in the majority of cases. If the handwriting of the testator is of poor quality and variable, then the more signatures made available for comparison the better. It is one thing to have to say in evidence, " I have examined six undoubted signatures of the testator, but although they all showed considerable variation I failed to find in any one the combination of handwriting characteristics found in the questioned signature, consequently I consider it unlikely to be a genuine signature "; but it is far better to be able to state that a considerable number of genuine signatures had been examined with the same result. The more signatures of a poor and variable writer available, the stronger is the opinion which can be expressed as to the authenticity of a questioned signature.

With respect to the writing instrument, more must be said nowadays than hitherto. No one would think of signing an important document with a pencil, but today an incredible number of these are signed with a writing instrument which from the forger's and the document examiner's point of view is really an ink pencil—though commonly known as the ball-point pen. It should be more widely known that a signature written with a ball-point pen can be forged as easily as though a pencil were used. It is most unfortunate that it is often a matter of extreme difficulty to decide whether a signature written with a ball-point pen is a forgery or not. The reasons for this are given in some detail in Chapter 11 on " Forged Signatures."

If the questioned signatures have been written with a ball-point pen they can be compared quite satisfactorily with genuine signatures written with a conventional form of pen, but not always vice versa.

If a will or other questioned document bearing signatures of witnesses is in question, it is advisable to obtain standard signatures of the witnesses if by any chance they can be identified as real persons. There is a good reason for taking this extra trouble. Many forgers take extreme care when forging the signature of a testator, for they know that this is the vital signature to which the greatest attention is likely to be paid. Once this signature has been painstakingly forged, attention often lapses, for many cases are known where the most careful forgeries of the most important signature on a document have been accompanied by the crudest forgeries of those of the witnesses. Sometimes the forger just dashes these off, employing his natural handwriting for the one and a back-sloped handwriting for the other. The identity of more than one forger has been established by the comparison of the handwriting of forged signatures of witnesses with specimens of the handwriting of the suspects.

Where " family forgeries " of wills are concerned, it is remarkable how often the forger of the testator's signature signs the name of the first " witness," whilst an accomplice—usually a brother or sister—signs the other. (See Fig. 11–14.)

A real difficulty sometimes arises in connection with the documents signed by very busy men. Some fall into the habit of having their unimportant correspondence signed, not with a rubber stamp, which is regarded as unsatisfactory, but by one or other of their subordinates, without the fact being clearly indicated in the conventional way. In many organisations there are juniors who through long practice have become capable of writing, quite legitimately of course, a more than passable imitation of the principal's signature. This saves a busy man much of the time which would otherwise be spent in signing routine correspondence, and incidentally facilitates the work of the clerks, who have not to wait to get unimportant correspondence signed when the principal is engaged or absent.

This signature-writing sometimes becomes almost second nature to the man who is entrusted with this work, and it frequently happens that the " signatures " he writes are quite as fluent as the genuine specimens. Sometimes they are even better and more legibly written. After a lapse of some years, a man who has allowed this very unwise practice to be carried on may be unable to decide, when dealing with long-previously written correspondence, which signatures are his and which the clerk's. This may throw doubt on the authenticity of some of the comparison standards obtained in these circumstances. The source of the difficulty experienced in picking out the signatures written by the clerk is that, unlike forgery, where mental tension results in the production of slow, laboured " drawings " of the genuine signatures, these non-fraudulent copies have been written light-heartedly with no fear of the consequences of failing to make a copy which must pass muster on critical examination. Should sufficient signatures be available, it is often possible to divide them into two groups, and then to determine which group represents the genuine signatures. The copies can usually be found to have some inconspicuous feature in common which serves to differentiate them from the genuine signatures.

The next question to be considered is where signatures of deceased persons can best be sought. At the outset, inquiries should be made at banks where the accounts of the deceased person were kept. When anyone opens a banking account several witnessed signatures are invariably obtained on a special card, and there is little fear of any substitution by relatives here. Associated with the banking accounts are the bank mandates, deeds of assignment, receipts for material removed from the safe-keeping of the bank, correspondence and cancelled cheques. Signatures on the latter should be regarded with some care as bank clerks are not infallible, and the possibility should be kept in mind that some of the cheques have also been forged by the person responsible for the forgery being investigated.

Closely following banks as repositories of specimen signatures are legal firms who have conducted business for or with the deceased. Here one can expect to find signatures on correspondence, deeds, mortgages, and the host of legal documents a person is called upon to sign from time to time. Among these documents there may be superseded wills. This will prove a valuable find should a forged will be the subject of investigation.

If the foregoing sources do not yield sufficient material, then recourse must be had to documents concerned with applications for permits, applications for services such as water, gas and electricity, and the host of forms involved with living in a house, finding employment and running a motor-car.

Most people are under the unpleasant necessity of making returns in connection with taxation in some form or other; the majority having to submit annual returns of income. If they run a car they have to make application for renewal of driving licences and for the taxation of the vehicle. If they have the telephone installed, and if they want gas, water, or electricity, almost invariably witnessed signatures have to be applied to agreements.

The difficulty in exploiting these sources is two-fold. In the first place it may not prove easy to obtain access to the required documents. For example, the Commissioners of Inland Revenue are extremely unlikely to satisfy a request for permission to examine the returns of income so that signatures thereon can be used as a basis of comparison, but when the issues at stake are vital, even this may be accomplished at the direction of the court. The second difficulty is the " proving " of the signature once the document has been obtained. This is often a major difficulty if the person concerned is deceased. If witnessed, the witnesses may be alive and available. Where this is not so, someone who " knows the handwriting " of the signature may be found to testify concerning the authorship of the signatures.

Even if the search at these sources has proved fruitless, a great deal can still be done. Very few people are able to go through life without transacting some business which needs a signature. Receipts for parcels and articles delivered by registered post are signed by those who rarely indulge in correspondence, and the widespread adoption of hire-purchase ensures that a very considerable number of witnessed signatures are made annually by persons in many walks of life. Again, insurance in one form or another is bought by a large proportion of the population today, and most proposal forms require witnessed signatures.

Finally, a man's vocational, religious and social activities may be reviewed. Many employers insist on a long and detailed questionnaire being completed and signed before an applicant is given work, and these forms are usually carefully filed and retained even when the employee has severed his connection with the firm. It is interesting to note how signatures and other handwriting on such forms are playing an increasingly large part as standard comparison material in document examinations. Also, many firms retain and file any correspondence they receive from employees. This includes excuses for absence and requests for wages to be paid to friends or members of their families when they are themselves unable to be present on pay-day.

Most young men now have to undertake a period of National Service, and during this period many official forms have to be filled in and signed. The Army Records constitute a mine of handwriting specimens, the difficulty here being that of access.

The sources described above are intended to be illustrative of what material exists for the uncovering; the list is by no means comprehensive and any legal adviser or investigating officer could probably double it with very little thought.

Request Writings

What has been said about the steps which can be taken to obtain specimen signatures and writings of deceased persons applies to living persons as well, only in this case the investigator may possibly be able to persuade the persons themselves to write something suitable for the investigation.

Anything written specifically for an investigation is commonly termed a " request writing," and falls into a special category of standard comparison material. There are a number of reasons why " request writings " cannot always be accepted at their face value as satisfactory standards of comparison. Even if a person is quite willing to give specimens of his handwriting on request, the question can be asked whether any reliance dare be placed on these being in every respect natural writings. Even if the person concerned has a clear conscience, there is the possibility that the unnatural circumstances, or perhaps the uniqueness of the occasion will cause him, albeit unwittingly, to modify his handwriting. Where signatures are concerned, it is very unlikely that he will dash off his signature as he usually does when signing documents in the ordinary way of business; he is far more likely to take care to write signatures which are as legible, or perhaps as impressive, as he can make them. Should the person concerned be guilty of some offence then, knowing that he is guilty, he may feel that he is betraying himself if he writes normally and consequently will be tempted to disguise what he is writing.

This is why no effort should be spared to find handwriting specimens not written specifically for the occasion, even where the person concerned is willing to write all that is requested of him.

Unwillingness to give specimens of handwriting is not necessarily a sign of guilt. There are many honest but cantankerous people who are unwilling to allow their fingerprints to be taken for the purpose of elimination when a serious crime is being investigated, and these are they who are also unwilling to give specimens of handwriting on request.

In spite of the sometimes unsatisfactory nature of request writings, if a person is willing to write, he should be encouraged to do so irrespective of whatever other handwriting of his may be available, for no document examination is ever prejudiced by there being too much standard material at the disposal of the examiner. Even if it is almost certain that the request writing will be disguised, which is quite common since many criminals think they are clever enough to disguise their handwriting so that the furnishing of specimens will actually divert suspicion from them, this should never deter the investigator from accepting everything which is offered in the way of handwriting specimens.

Whilst the obtaining of a set of request signatures or other writings is a simple task, it is very often bungled by the inexperienced and it is most exasperating to a document examiner to receive useless material from an occasion, which, if rightly exploited, should have yielded him sufficient data to satisfy all his needs.

For an investigator to push a piece of paper under the nose of the intending writer and a ball-point pen into his hand and say " sign here three times " is a stupid and senseless proceeding, and the evidential value of the handwriting obtained is usually about equal to the thought which had been given to the matter—practically nil in each case.

Procedure for Obtaining Request Writings

Certain preparations should be made well in advance.

If the questioned signature were made on a large sheet of unlined paper, then similar large sheets of unlined paper should be available, and conversely, if the questioned handwriting were done on lined paper, then similar lined paper should be provided for the request writings. If the questioned signature occurs in a cramped space on an official form, then a similar form or failing this a typewritten copy, approximately the same size, should be used. If the official form had a dotted line on which the signature was written, then the copy should have a similar dotted line. If the questioned signature occurs either on the face of a cheque or as an endorsement on the back, a similar blank cheque should be provided. If a conventional form of pen were used for the questioned signatures, then a similar pen and nib should be available. If there is evidence that the questioned signature was blotted, blotting-paper should be provided. Where a ball-point pen was used for the questioned signature, a ball-point pen, *tested and found to be in good condition,* should be used for the request writing also.

This list of suggestions could, of course, be extended almost indefinitely, but it should indicate the general lines on which one should proceed in setting the scene for the taking of specimen standard request writings.

Whenever possible, efforts should be made to reproduce as closely as the occasion admits, the conditions under which the questioned signature or other writings were made. Before any handwriting is taken, it is essential to ensure that the writer is quite comfortable in posture and has everything to his satisfaction. If the person writing appears very nervous he should be asked to write a few formal words stating that he is writing in a certain place and at his own free will, before embarking on the comparison signatures or other writings. In this way he will get the feel of the pen, and also have his muscles and emotions under control before coming to the all-important comparison material.

Unless it is unavoidable, the investigator should never rest content with a single specimen signature or sample of handwriting, especially if there is any suspicion that the writer is nervous or attempting to disguise his handwriting. Although a second and in some cases a third specimen should be obtained, they should not be asked for as soon as the first has been completed. If the sheet bearing the first writing is removed from sight, then an interval filled with casual conversation will tend to rid the nervous of apprehension, and what is far more important, allow the exact tricks of disguise used by the cunning to fade somewhat in the mind.

If some unwillingness on the part of the writer to write a second or third set of handwritings or signatures is anticipated, different types of pen should be available so that the request may appear more reasonable and likely to be complied with when put in the form of a question—" Will you please be good enough to use *this* pen now? " A blunt request for another set of specimens, which may suggest that the person writing is not playing fair in some way, may cause resentment and result in a refusal to write any more.

On many occasions a single sheet of paper bearing three signatures made at the one time is submitted as a standard. Such a sheet is often referred to as " a sheet bearing three signatures of X Y." A more accurate description for purposes of comparison would be " a sheet bearing three examples of one signature of X Y," which is a quite different description from the first, especially if X Y were writing disguised signatures for the occasion.

If the writer produced a disguised signature for his first example, he could easily copy the second and third signatures from it, and would consequently produce three consistently written disguised signatures. The document examiner might be misled and come to the erroneous conclusion that the standard consisted of the normal undisguised signatures of the writer.

It is to guard against this that, once a specimen handwriting has been written, the sheet is placed out of sight before any subsequent specimens are commenced on another sheet of paper.

The Form of Request Writings

When signatures are in question, the form a request writing should take has already been settled—the writings need consist of nothing but signatures. When, however, the document examiner has to deal with handwriting other than signatures, signatures by themselves are of little use as standards of comparison so that other considerations apply.

Two questions must be settled before the suspect is asked to write. One is concerned with what should be written, whilst the other has to do with the style of script to be employed.

The majority of people are able to write in two distinct styles of script, whilst many have three at their disposal. Everybody except the very young and the illiterate can write in what is termed cursive handwriting, which is alternatively known as ordinary or business handwriting. In this style of handwriting, the letters of a word are joined so that the pen runs fluently from one letter to the next without having to be lifted from the paper. The second style of handwriting which most people can write is referred to by many names, the most common being " block lettering," " block capitals " or " pen printing." In this style, the letters are written separately, and are very close in design to the Roman capitals devised some thousands of years ago to facilitate the cutting of inscriptions on stone with a hammer and chisel. Incidentally, it is from these Roman block capitals that cursive handwriting has been developed by a long process of evolution.

Illiterate persons favour block lettering because of the greater skill needed to produce legible cursive handwriting. Block letters are often used by those who fear discovery if they use their normal cursive handwriting. These two styles of handwriting are often mixed. Block letter formations are used as capitals in a high proportion of cursive hands, and many writers of block lettering utilise the cursive form where they are uncertain of the design of certain letters, notably the G, I and Q.

Various other styles of handwritings are in use. In the thirteenth century, the best handwriting in Italy reached a high standard of beauty as an art form, and efforts are being made to popularise the use of this " Italic " hand which is one which also employs detached letters. In Tudor times, handwriting in England consisted of detached letters which closely resemble the lower case characters used today as print. At the beginning of this century this style of handwriting was adopted for use in many of the elementary schools in England and Wales because of the theory that as the designs of its letters resembled print more closely than do the conventional cursive forms, it would be easier for the child to learn both reading and writing if taught to write in this style.

The majority taught in this style of handwriting soon discover that speed can only be gained if the pen is not raised after writing each letter. Consequently as they grow older they increasingly tend to join the letters after the manner of cursive handwriting, until finally they write a connected hand which, however, retains many of the " script " formations. A minority, usually women, retain the disconnected style all their lives, and if skilful with the pen are often able to write it with both speed and elegance. There are many critics of this style of handwriting who are sceptical of any advantage its adoption may have, and who do not hesitate to point out the difficulties encountered in later life should a speedy legible handwriting be desired.

Apart from the possibility of making a few generalisations, it is impracticable to attempt to compare any one of the above-mentioned styles of writing with one of the others, so that if the questioned material consists of block letters, then the comparison writing must also consist of block letters. Similar conditions apply for cursive, script, Italic or any other style of handwriting.

The style of handwriting required should be made quite clear to the person who is to give the specimen, but in spite of considerable explanation, some people will persist in using script forms when block capitals are required and vice versa. It is inadvisable to give instruction as to what exactly constitutes block capitals by writing an example, because this may result in the copying of the exact form of the letters shown. It is far preferable to have ready a specimen of printed block capitals—many public notices are printed in this form—and to show this, along with a specimen of newsprint which will resemble the script form of writing. The difference between block capitals and script may easily be demonstrated in this way to even the dullest subject. After this demonstration there should be no difficulty in obtaining a specimen of handwriting of the required style.

Preparation of Passage to be Written

To prepare the most suitable text it should be remembered that the best comparisons are made between things which resemble each other to the greatest extent, so the rule becomes " dictate something approximating to the handwriting, figures, signatures, etc., which appear on the questioned documents."

For example, if the questioned documents contain names and addresses, or figures, then the piece to be dictated should contain similar names and addresses and figures; if addresses on envelopes are included in the questioned documents, then envelopes should be addressed as part of the test. Abbreviations, titles, dates, etc., are often written in peculiar ways, and if these are present in the questioned documents, then similar formations must be included in the matter to be written.

Spelling Mistakes

A great deal of nonsense has been written about spelling mistakes, and they are often made to play far too great a part in court proceedings. They can only be assessed at their true worth as evidence if some thought is given to the matter.

There is no doubt that some words in the English language are so difficult to spell that most people are as likely as not to spell them incorrectly. Not only are these difficult words often misspelled, but many writers do not use a consistent misspelling even in the same passage. It may very well happen that a correct spelling has been achieved by accident in a passage which includes several different misspellings of the same word. It follows from this that if in a questioned handwriting a difficult word is correctly spelled on a solitary occasion, whilst in a specimen written at dictation it is found to be incorrect, this in itself can suggest nothing about the authorship of the questioned handwriting.

If in a questioned handwriting, a difficult word is invariably correctly spelled on a number of occasions, it may safely be assumed that the writer knew the correct spelling. If in a specimen writing the same word was written incorrectly on most occasions, then unless the writer was very cunning, it may safely be concluded that he was uncertain of the correct spelling.

In these circumstances, the presence of spelling mistakes on the one hand, and proof of ability to spell difficult words correctly on the other, may well be thought to have some significance when the problem of common authorship is being considered.

Spelling mistakes are sometimes found in simple words. These mistakes may be the result of habitual mispronunciation on the part of the writer, or of some personal misapprehension as to how these simple words should be spelled. The significance of such misspelling may be considerable because, unlike the misspelling of difficult words which is a failing common to the majority of persons, these misspellings of simple words are often personal idiosyncrasies and are likely to be restricted to a very small number of people. For example, if anonymous letters are found to contain consistent misspellings of simple words, this fact should be kept in mind in case other documents of known origin are discovered to contain the same errors. On one occasion the word " ashamed " was repeatedly spelled "ashaned" throughout a group of anonymous letters, and this curious misspelling was also found in the handwriting of a suspect. This spelling mistake was regarded as being highly significant and an investigation in this direction was suggested. This led to the exposure and conviction of the writer of the anonymous letters. The spelling of proper names affords a useful test. Proper names are often difficult to hear correctly and many a man is addressed and spoken of by a name which is incorrect though sounding very like the correct version.

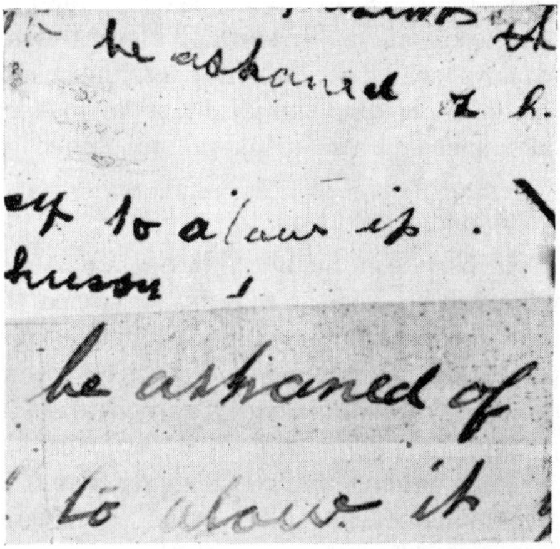

Fig. 12–1. *Spelling Mistakes.* The upper photograph is of a portion of an anonymous letter in which "allow" is spelt "alow" and "ashamed" written as "ashaned." The lower photograph is of extracts from the handwriting of a suspect which incorporates the same spelling mistakes. The misspelling of "alow" in both is of little significance because many illiterate persons might make this mistake. The writing of "ashamed" as "ashaned" is of far greater significance as this is a consequence of an uncommon mispronunciation of a fairly simple word. (Note the back-slope of the anonymous writing.)

Whilst misspelling of proper names often occurs through illiteracy, this misspelling is not so significant as misspelling due to faulty appreciation of the name. This faulty appreciation of a proper name will often assist the tracing of the writer of anonymous letters containing such misspelling. Inquiries will often lead to information being given of persons who are in the habit of making the same mistake in conversation.

If spelling mistakes occur in the questioned handwriting, these words should be included several times in the piece prepared for dictation, so that a thorough test may be made of the spelling ability of the suspect. Sometimes during a dictation, the writer will pause and ask how to spell a certain word. This request should never be complied with. The answer should be "have a shot at it and don't worry if you don't get it quite right." Much more can be learned from an unsuccessful attempt at spelling a word than by the correct spelling being written down from dictation, letter by letter.

When the text of the piece to be written has been prepared in the light of the foregoing hints, garnished with the application of common sense to the many points not specifically dealt with, preparations for the actual writing may go forward. The would-be writer is furnished with a comfortable seat and a table which suits him for height. He is handed a fountain pen and an appropriate sheet of paper, which is lined or unlined depending on the nature of the questioned document.

Margins

If the questioned document has no ruled margin the paper provided should be devoid of a margin also. If a sheet of paper is devoid of a ruled margin it is the habit of some persons to crease the paper lightly so as to provide a rough indication of where to begin each line of writing. If the person writing does this, no effort should be made to prevent his doing so, but a note should be made of the fact.

If the questioned document is in the nature of a questionnaire or an official form, the most strenuous efforts should be made to obtain similar blank forms for the dictation. If suitable blank forms cannot be obtained it may be possible to have something which approximates to them prepared on a typewriter. If this is done, care should be taken to keep the dimensions of the writing spaces the same, and also to put in any dotted lines on which writing has to be placed.

Dictation

It has been assumed throughout that any passage the suspect is asked to write will be dictated rather than copied from manuscript or typescript. Although the inexperienced often find difficulty in writing from dictation, this method of presenting the material the suspect is required to write should always be adhered to. A great deal may be learned about a writer who is allowed to arrange the passage himself, rather than copy the ideas of another.

Punctuation, spelling, marginal habits and the indentation given to paragraphs are all characteristic of a writer, and these cannot be ascertained if copying from a script is allowed.

The passage to be dictated should be typewritten with double spacing so that there will be ample room for any annotations the person giving the dictation may wish to make thereon. For the first dictation, a conventional pen should be provided and an effort made to match the nib used for the handwriting on the questioned document. Although an effective comparison can be made between handwritings written with widely differing nibs, the more closely the conditions of writing the questioned document can be produced, the better.

Before starting on the prepared dictation, the writer should be given an opportunity to get accustomed to his surroundings and to the feel of the pen. To this end he should be asked to write his name and address, the date and a short statement to the effect that he is giving a specimen of his handwriting at his own volition. This is far better than making an abrupt start on a piece of dictation. It is too much to expect natural handwriting from someone taking dictation to which he is probably unaccustomed before he has had the chance to settle down. This preliminary writing will also be of value to the investigator. As everybody should know how to write his own name and address, this writing should be done without undue hesitation. If this preliminary writing is fluent, and there is no indication that the suspect is attempting to disguise the handwriting, the dictation should be proceeded with.

The dictation should be given at a speed which is well within the capacity of the writer to maintain, so that his mind is not being strained by having to deal with too many words at a time. If the suspect continues to write smoothly and fluently, it may safely be assumed that a genuine undisguised handwriting is being produced.

The investigator should be on the alert for any attempt to disguise the writing. Here the important thing to bear in mind is that disguise requires effort and takes time. Experiments have proved that disguised handwriting can rarely be written quickly and fluently. If, during the preliminary writing of the name and address, etc., the writer appears to hesitate or to produce grotesque handwriting, certain precautions should be taken.

As the dictation is commenced, an unobtrusive note of the time should be made on the copy. Whenever the writer appears to hesitate at a word or even at a particular letter a coded pencil mark should be made at the appropriate place on the prepared piece of dictation. The code should be simple. A dot may indicate a slight pause, whereas two or more would indicate pauses of greater duration. If the document examiner is provided with this coded script accompanied by an explanation of the code, it will help him considerably if the writing has been disguised. Anyone who is seen to be taking thought as he writes should never be hurried, for if he is disguising his handwriting he should be given a good opportunity to do so thoroughly.

At the end of the dictation the time should again be noted and the sheet of manuscript removed. If there is reason to think that the handwriting has been disguised, a second specimen should be insisted on. No hint should be given that there is any suspicion of disguise but a different type of pen should be produced as a pretext for requiring the additional writing.

If possible, a fair interval, filled with conversation, should be allowed to elapse before the second dictation. During this interval the suspect is almost certain to forget some of the details of the disguise he has used in writing the first specimen. The second dictation should be given as quickly as possible so as to defeat attempts at disguise. If an air of urgency is introduced and the suspect is continually pressed to maintain a high speed of writing, he will find considerable difficulty in applying his mind to the consistent repetition of the earlier disguise.

The only way in which anyone can write at speed is by employing those letter formations he has practised over and over again—that is, the writer's usual form of handwriting. Whilst some disguise may be retained, it is not likely to be consistently applied throughout the handwriting and any lapses which occur will constitute valuable evidence that an attempt has been made to introduce disguise. If the person writing is doing so honestly, then the increased speed of dictation will not serve to embarrass him in any way; his second handwriting specimen will merely show the differences one would expect of more hurried handwriting.

It is better to obtain the second rather than the first specimen at speed because, by this time, the writer will have become acquainted with what he is writing and also more practised in taking dictation, a feat which many find extremely difficult to master at a first attempt.

Left-handed Writers

The question of left-hand writing may now be considered. The method taught in the schools for holding the pen and the positioning of the wrist is the most convenient for the right-handed person, because the handwriting is written from left to right. If the ordinary type of pen nib is used and the left hand holds the pen, considerable difficulty is met with in writing from left to right, unless the position of the left hand is altered from that normally maintained by the right hand. Consequently, many left-handed writers take up what appears to be a most awkward hand position and method of holding the pen.

Apart from this, there is no reason why handwriting should not be written equally fluently with either hand. Experience shows that with the vast majority of practised left-handed writers there is nothing in the writing to indicate which hand held the pen. With a pencil or ball-point pen no modification of hand position need be made.

The question of left-handed and right-handed writing is considered in some detail elsewhere, but when taking specimens it is advisable to ask the suspect to furnish some handwriting written with the unaccustomed hand.

Sometimes the writer disclaims the ability to write at all with the unaccustomed hand, but in fact very few people are incapable of writing with either hand. With a little persuasion many will make an attempt and do much better than they had thought possible. There are some persons who are truly ambidextrous where handwriting is concerned. They were probably born left-handed but trained to write with the right hand at school. The former insistence on the use of the right hand by all the pupils is now no longer observed, as medical opinion is inclined to the view that if this is done with children who are naturally left-handed, it may result in certain psychological disturbances in later life.

Whilst there is usually a great deal which is common to the right- and left-handed writing of an ambidextrous person, there are sometimes sufficient differences to cause real difficulty. These can only be resolved if specimens of handwriting from both hands are available for comparison.

Unwilling Writers

The foregoing has been based on the assumption that the person concerned is willing to write. It is when all attempts to obtain written matter have failed and the suspect refuses either to acknowledge any handwriting as his, or give a specimen of his handwriting at dictation, that the investigating officer can show his skill and cunning.

In a certain Investigation Bureau well known to the author for its efficiency, a subtle device is used. An unwilling suspect is first told that while he is under no obligation to write anything, he has nothing to fear if he is innocent, so that there is no point in his refusing to be co-operative. If this plea fails to move him, he is then informed that he is quite within his rights in refusing to write, but that his definite refusal to do so must be put in writing as it is such an important and significant stand he is taking. Without further ado, a pen is put into his hand and paper placed before him. He is told to write that he is standing on his constitutional rights and refusing to incriminate himself in any way by writing from dictation. Finally, he is asked to sign this statement.

According to the members of this organisation, when stage-managed slickly, quite a high percentage of " hard citizens " can be persuaded to write by this simple ruse, and before they have realised what they have done, the investigators have obtained a useful if not an ideal specimen of handwriting. If this is considered to verge on sharp practice, the answer is that the innocent person has nothing to fear from giving a specimen of his handwriting, even when it is obtained by a trick.

There are many other methods employed by investigators who wish to obtain a specimen of the handwriting of a suspect who is to be kept in ignorance of the investigation. There is no place here for the details of these methods, some of which are of such dubious propriety that a court would be unlikely to accept as admissible, evidence obtained in such ways. The least dubious method is to write to the person concerned a letter so phrased that no suspicion is aroused and that a reply will almost certainly be called for. No standard form is laid down for such letters, which must vary with the circumstances of the case. In seaside districts letters seeking accommodation almost invariably bring replies, whereas in country districts inquiries about the possibility of purchasing eggs, fruit and vegetables are most efficacious. In large towns these gambits are ignored and the most reliable letters of inquiry seem to be those requesting some details concerning previous occupants of the premises or information about neighbours.

The letter is then followed up by a personal visit, during which the letter received from the suspect in reply to the inquiries is produced and the question put as to who was the writer. An admission by the writer of the letter will serve to " prove " authorship at any subsequent proceedings. Incidentally, any correspondence received from suspects in the form of replies to inquiry letters should be carefully examined for evidence which may serve to link it with the questioned documents. This is referred to in some detail in the chapter on the preliminary examination of documents.

Typescript Specimens

Handwriting specimens are only part of the comparison material which may be required by the document examiner. A steadily increasing proportion is typewritten, and it may be necessary to obtain specimens of typescript from a suspect machine.

The preparation of a specimen of typescript on a suspect machine is dealt with in the chapter dealing with typewriting, but when the machine itself is not available the same methods may have to be employed to obtain specimens of typescript as those outlined for getting handwriting. The business inquiry letter often produces results, especially if this letter is itself typewritten.

It should be borne in mind that most people are fairly consistent in their behaviour. A person who writes a series of anonymous letters containing criticism and complaints about the behaviour of others is not usually content to write anonymous letters on this subject. He will often send similar letters of complaint to the police, the sanitary inspector, education authorities, to the editors of local newspapers—in fact to anybody he thinks is in a position to receive complaints. The majority of these letters are signed, and on many occasions the author has been provided with useful comparison standards of both handwriting and typewriting from these sources.

When investigating anonymous writings, especially those left behind at scenes of crime, or the names and addresses written on envelopes in which empty wallets or personal papers are returned to the losers, two things should be borne in mind when all other leads seem to have failed. The first is that criminals are often related to other criminals, and the second is that the handwriting of relatives is often very similar. If a specimen of questioned handwriting is available to the investigator it should be compared with the handwriting of criminals from the locality, and a list of possible writers drawn up, taking care to spread a very wide net. It often happens that the list contains the name of the writer, or may be of a near relative of the writer. This may seem a forlorn hope, but in the experience of the author this procedure, although time consuming, gives a useful lead more often than might be expected.

A good example of this was where a persistent thief, who had never been in police hands, stole little but money from the numerous dwelling-houses and office premises he entered. When his crimes had become very numerous and he was becoming careless, he stole a fountain pen bearing the name of the owner and also a postal order for a small amount. He signed the postal order with a fictitious name in order to cash it, and eventually it came into the hands of the police. As a last resort, the author was asked to examine this small amount of handwriting and to make what comparison he could with the enormous mass of handwriting from persons of bad character contained in the police records. It proved a long and difficult task and finally it was reported that the handwriting of the thief was probably not among the thousands examined. However, two handwritings were picked out as being somewhat similar to that of the fictitious signature on the postal order. The writer of one specimen was found to be in prison, and the other specimen was that of a female juvenile delinquent. A very experienced detective officer hearing this rather discouraging news remarked that the girl came of a very bad family and had a half-brother of pronounced criminal tendencies. He decided there and then to go and interview this man. As soon as he met him he saw he had a fountain pen in his breast pocket, and without any hesitation demanded it for examination. It proved to be the stolen pen with the name of the owner still on it. Eventually the man made a full confession. His room contained a large number of reference books on crime and its detection, but significantly none on the examination of handwriting! His handwriting proved to be very like that of his half-sister, and it was this that led to his eventual detection.

Once it has been decided to consult a document examiner, the investigating officer or legal adviser should get in touch with him as soon as possible, because he may require some special investigation to be carried out or some additional comparison material. It should be remembered that expert examinations take time, and that nothing is less conducive to a thorough examination than haste. No expert welcomes having to give evidence in a difficult case within a very brief period of having been consulted. When the expert has been supplied with all he wants in the way of information and standard comparison material, the preliminary phase of the case may be regarded as complete. It is now the province of the document examiner to apply his skill and experience to the matter. It may very well happen that only an interim report will be furnished at first, and that the investigating officer or legal adviser will have to make a further search for comparison material, but any subsequent work will be on similar lines to that already carried out.

When all this has been done it is inadvisable for the investigating officer or legal adviser to consider that their part in the matter is complete and that nothing further remains for them to do. On the contrary, they should endeavour to put themselves in a position to understand the significance of everything in the report made to them by the document examiner, so that they will be able to apply his findings to the case as a whole. To do this they should obtain as many books as they are able—there are in fact very few—dealing with the subject of document examination, and read those chapters dealing with the points at issue. To this end a bibliography is given at the end of the chapter dealing with the conduct of a questioned document case at court. If the case involves forgery, then the chapters on traced and simulated forgeries should be read, so that some idea can be gained of how much assistance can reasonably be expected from the expert examination of the signatures. No expert relishes being expected to perform the impossible.

If typewritten documents are in question, a perusal of the chapter on the examination of typescript will probably cause surprise, because of the wealth of information which may confidently be expected after the examination of typewritten documents.

Some persons have a touching faith in the power of science, and may ask a document examiner what they consider to be important but simple questions, such as whether some handwriting was written three weeks ago as alleged, or whether it is actually a month old. It comes as a shock when they are informed that no reputable expert will attempt to answer such questions by analysis of the ink or any other method. Reference to a book on the subject of document examination will make it quite clear why this is so. On the other hand it is occasionally possible to give answer to what, to the uninitiated, may appear to be impossibly difficult problems, and it is only by extensive reading that some knowledge of the wide scope of modern document examination may be gathered.

The report which is eventually received from the document examiner can best be appreciated if the work of document examination is understood in outline, and in particular that part dealing with the case concerned. Unless the report is understood in all its implications, the best use cannot be made of the findings expressed therein. It is only if both the report and the background to the expert examination are understood that the expert can be asked those further questions which would tend to clear up any points with which the report has not quite satisfactorily dealt.

It might be objected that the subject of document examination is nowadays so highly technical that reading a book on the subject would be likely to be a waste of time, as little would be understood by a layman. It is true that this may rightly be said of many books on scientific subjects, but there are one or two books on the scientific examination of documents which are so clearly written that they can profitably be read by anyone with a good general education; there is no need to master the details of a particular manipulation before one can understand its significance. The important thing to know is what results may be obtained and not the details of the best technique for obtaining them, for this is the task of the expert and the reason for employing him.

With all the preliminary work thoroughly carried out, the legal adviser may now consider which counsel he will advise his client to brief for the trial. Although occasionally a weak case involving a document examination is carried to a triumphant conclusion largely through the efforts of skilled and resourceful counsel, many strong cases have been lost because counsel has failed to play the powerful cards put into his hand as the result of the scientific examination of the documents concerned.

The co-operation of counsel, legal adviser and document examiner, and the conduct of the case, especially with regard to examination, re-examination and cross-examination of expert witnesses, is so important that this matter is dealt with in a separate chapter. (See Chapter 15.)

Bibliography

Hardless, C. E., Standards for Comparison, The Document Examiner and Scientific Detective (India) 1 (2) + 21–24.

Smith, S., " Obtaining Document Standards for Comparison," *Journal of Criminal Law and Criminology,* Vol. 40, No. 1, May–June, 1949.

" The Collection of Writing Standards," *Journal of Criminal Law and Criminology,* Vol. 32, No. 2, July–August, 1941.

13

THE CARE, PRESERVATION AND CLEANING OF DOCUMENTS

Deterioration of Paper in Storage

It is sometimes hard to realise that any document, written in ink or pencil on ordinary paper, not only has a limited life but suffers some damage every time it is handled.

The damage caused by careless handling may not be readily apparent, nor may it seriously diminish the legibility of the writing of typescript at the time, but nevertheless carelessness may seriously reduce either the value of any less obvious evidence it may possess as to its origin or authorship, or the possibility of proving that forgery has been committed when the document is subsequently examined minutely in the laboratory.

Paper is by no means a homogeneous material like metal foil or even cellophane, which it resembles very closely in the chemical sense; actually it consists of a web or mat of interlaced delicate cellulose fibres, with the spaces between partially filled with clay-like materials and the surface by a coating of sizing material.

For over a century fears have been expressed that many important documents which have been written with too acid an ink on poor quality paper will be likely to have a very limited life.[1] The more alarmist theories, which suggested that the majority of such documents would be likely to fall to powder before reaching a respectable age, have fortunately proved incorrect. But the fears proved so well founded that a sub-committee of the International Institute of Intellectual Co-operation of the League of Nations was set up in the thirties to make inquiries as to the state of preservation of publications and records in different countries, and to circulate information concerning the remedies for the rather serious state of affairs which was uncovered by the inquiries.[2] The result of the inquiry seemed to suggest that, in the majority of cases, the use of inferior paper and ink were more to blame for deterioration than the conditions of storage, although with the general rise in the level of atmospheric pollution, this would not necessarily apply today.

In Great Britain, the greatest concern was expressed about the condition of books and documents printed on paper made between 1890–1900 due to faulty methods of manufacture. In America, the importance of the nature of the fibrous constituents of the paper was brought out by a study made under the auspices of the National Bureau of Standards and the Carnegie Foundation; this showed

[1] *The Durability of Paper.* Report of Special Committee set up by the Library Association, London, 1930.

[2] Whalley, M. E., *Abstract of a Report on the Permanence of Paper Prepared by the League of Nations.* National Research Council, Ottawa, 1932.

that newspapers printed on paper containing 75 per cent. of ground wood fibres showed obvious signs of disintegration, although it was only in the late sixties that newspapers began to use this type of paper. On the Continent of Europe a much more serious state of affairs existed, especially in those countries which suffered financially during the First World War and were unable to do very much active work on the preservation of their records. Here again, the use of inferior materials was regarded as the primary reason for the trouble being experienced.

The influence of the acidity of the ink has gradually become recognised as an important factor in the life of a document. All papers, whatever their source, consist of fibres of cellulose, and all normal iron-inks contain acid; any acid causes a slow but sure degradation of the cellulose molecule.

Nevertheless we can now be confident that if documents are prepared on good paper carefully made with a foundation of rag or chemical wood pulp, using ink which contains the minimum amount of acid consistent with other desirable qualities, then they may be expected to reach an age of some hundreds of years, providing the acids present in the polluted atmospheres, which are becoming increasingly common, are not allowed access to the documents during storage.

The deterioration of a document usually consists of a fading of the ink, coupled with the discoloration of and even the partial disintegration of the paper. Discoloration in bulk is generally due to traces of chemicals left over from the manufacturing process—particularly that of bleaching the fibre. Discoloration confined to the edges of sheets is usually due to the action of light, or of those acids in the atmosphere derived from the sulphur in solid fuel and coal gas.

Loss of strength which determines the extent to which a document can be handled without permanent harm may be due to a number of causes.

In the first place, certain papers which incorporate a high proportion of clay-like materials for improving the surface and opacity are much less resistant to the stresses imposed by folding, since the loading material they contain has to be paid for by a corresponding deficiency of the much stronger fibre. Heavily loaded papers are invariably weak and cannot withstand much handling. Secondly, energetic bleaching to obtain a white fibre often results in the slow but certain deterioration of the cellulose fibres, especially if all traces of the bleach have not been washed out.

The wearing qualities of paper are also influenced by the treatment of the fibres during paper making. If they are cut very short as is the case with blotting-paper, the paper will wear rapidly even if the original stock was good quality rag. In the case of blotting-paper the looseness of the fibres, which is essential if the paper is to be really absorbent, also contributes to its lack of strength.

A good paper is produced by the correct treatment of suitable raw material; any deficiency in either respect will be reflected in the lowering of the quality of the paper.

Action of Moisture on Paper

Paper readily absorbs moisture from wet air to become limp and weak, but tends to dry out in a dry warm atmosphere to regain much of its original stiffness and strength. Each change in its water content alters its dimensions, and consequently to a slight degree, the dimensions of everything written or printed thereon. Printers go to a great deal of trouble to control the water-content of their paper, especially in colour work where a number of printings have to be done in accurate register on one sheet. The average paper is at its best when it contains about 7 per cent. of its weight of water. If it contains less than 7 per cent. the paper tends to become harsh and brittle, with more the paper stretches and tends to become limp.

All papers contain air spaces which vary from about 30 per cent. for heavy dense paper to 70 per cent. for light bulky paper. These air spaces accommodate to some extent the expansion undergone by the fibres when they absorb moisture. Owing to the way in which machine-made paper is fabricated the fibres tend to align themselves with the direction of the moving web of paper—known as "machine direction." This is important for the following reasons.

When a cellulose fibre absorbs water, it swells rather than lengthens, so that when a sheet of paper absorbs water its maximum expansion is across the machine direction. In the case of the majority of papers this expansion across the machine direction varies from 2–4·5 per cent., with a mere ·1–·8 per cent. in the direction at right-angles. With hand-made paper there is no "machine direction" and the expansion is slight and fairly uniform—hence the superiority of this material for drawing accurate plans and diagrams. The optimum condition for paper storage is at about 70°–75° F., with a relative humidity of about 50 per cent.

One unfortunate result of changes in humidity is the tendency for any impressions in the paper to become more and more shallow until they may disappear altogether, with the consequent loss of possibly valuable evidence. Again, if the surface of the paper has been wetted by the use of chemical ink-eradicators or written on with invisible ink, there are procedures which enable these wetted regions to be detected, but if the document has been allowed to become very damp these methods lose much of their efficiency.

Prevention of Attack by Insects, Bacteria and Fungi

Apart from the alteration of dimensions with change in humidity, documents should never be exposed to humid conditions for long. In extreme cases the documents are subject to microbiological attack, especially in the neighbourhood of any adhesives.[3]

If, owing to climatic conditions, documents have to be stored under very humid conditions, one or two precautions can be taken to minimise the possibility of damage. The first is to store the document in an air-tight container together with a proprietary silica-gel desiccant which is colour-coded to indicate when it has ceased to absorb moisture. A crude substitute for the silica-gel is a lump of quicklime, which will serve much the same purpose but which is neither so effective nor so convenient. If neither of these courses can be followed, some crystals of thymol may be packed along with the document. This substance will tend to discourage

[3] Minier, D. W., "Mildew and Books," *The Library Journal,* No. 20, November 15, 1932; Mitchell, C. A., and Wood, D. R., "Action of Molds on Ink in Writing," *Analyst,* 63, 111, 1938.

bacterial action as it is a volatile disinfectant, although it is of doubtful efficiency against moulds.

A new and most promising development in the protection of documents against the destructive effect of insect and microbiological attack is the use of either pentachlorphenol or its sodium salt. These compounds were first manufactured in 1936 and distributed by the Monsanto Chemical Company and were marketed under the names of Santophen 20 and Santobrite. Santophen 20 is nowadays sold under the trade name of Monsanto Penta.[4] These products are toxic to a wide range of micro-organisms. They are low in cost and their physical and chemical properties enable them to be used for the preservation of documents.

Work in this connection has been carried on by the experts at the British Museum in conjunction with the Record Office, House of Lords.[5] Their recommendations include the use of tissue paper impregnated with Pentachlorphenol as an interleaving for any documents which are susceptible to attack. There is no need to introduce the tissue between each page of a book—the normal usage is to have one sheet of tissue to approximately every eight pages. The protective agent is sufficiently volatile to impregnate the book sufficiently to check the growth of fungus and bacteria, and also to check insect attack at the same time. The impregnated tissue should be prepared by first soaking tissue paper in a 10 per cent. aqueous solution of Santobrite, and then draining and drying. John Dickinson, the well-known paper makers, supply double crown 9 lb. tissue paper impregnated with Santobrite to H.M. Stationery Office for this purpose. This material has proved of considerable assistance in preserving documents in hot humid climates.

There is no reason why envelopes made of stout paper which has been impregnated in this way should not be used for the storage of documents under difficult conditions of heat and humidity.

Glue or paste is protected by including about one part in two hundred of Santobrite, whilst glue-size or parchment-size is adequately protected by half this concentration. If there has been a serious attack these concentrations may be increased. Incidentally, experiments have shown that the paste and glue are better made up with distilled water. If used in the concentration stated, there should be no danger to health in the handling of these chemicals, which seem to confine their toxicity to vegetable and insect life. The odour associated with these substances is so slight as to be unnoticeable, even when they are used in the maximum concentrations advised.

Action of Light on Documents

Very few materials of either animal or vegetable origin are unaffected, either in colour or strength, by exposure to sunlight; paper and ink are no exceptions. The deep yellowing of the cheaper grades of paper and the rapid fading of coloured inks, especially those used in typewriter ribbons, when they are exposed to sunlight immediately spring to mind in this connection. Eventual deterioration is experienced by the best qualities of paper and the majority of inks, only the process takes longer.

[4] " Monsanto," Technical Service Bulletins, Nos. 12D/5, 2D2.
[5] The Record Office, House of Lords. Reports for 1951–52, –53.

It follows from this that the exposure to strong sunlight of important documents should be restricted to the absolute minimum, especially if the documents bear coloured ink or typescript.

In the course of laboratory examination, documents may have to be exposed to powerful sources of ultra-violet light or infra-red radiation. It should be borne in mind that a short exposure to a powerful source of ultra-violet radiation is likely to do far more harm than months of exposure to ordinary daylight. Infra-red sources will cause a serious rise in the temperature of a document unless suitable precautions are taken with respect to ventilation. It should be a matter of routine to mask as much of the document as possible and to use all possible means to decrease the time of exposure.

Exposure to strong light also tends to make paper brittle. If the temperature of paper is raised even to the boiling point of water it soon becomes very fragile, and may even crumble to dust on being handled after some hours of exposure to these conditions.

PHOTOGRAPHS

Photographic reproductions on a paper base are even more subject to deterioration than other documents because of the heavily loaded paper and the presence of a layer of gelatine which holds the image-forming material. This is why the conditions under which photographs should be stored are dealt with in some detail in Chapter 6.

PROTECTION OF DOCUMENTS FROM THE EFFECTS OF HANDLING

Being an excellent absorbent of both oil and water, paper is profoundly affected by perspiration; the deleterious effects of constant handling on paper may be seen by examining a reference book which is in fair demand. As important documents should be subjected to the minimum of contact with the hands, they should be kept in transparent envelopes of ample size. In this recommendation, the word " ample " is significant, because nothing is worse for a document than being thrust in and out of an envelope which is just about large enough to accommodate it.

The celluloid map-cases used by the Armed Forces make excellent temporary containers for documents which are subjected to the unavoidable handling involved in the course of court proceedings. Their disadvantages are bulk, expense and fire-risk, but these are outweighed by their unrivalled strength and transparency.

Where these rigid containers are not available, envelopes made of heavy-gauge polythene or cellophane make good substitutes.

Whilst plastic containers are excellent for the temporary protection of documents, they should never be used for permanent storage. Many plastics slowly evolve vapour, generally from the plasticiser almost invariably present, and this has been blamed for the deterioration of documents after long storage in such containers. With celluloid there is an added risk; not only is this plastic extremely inflammable, but it evolves dangerous fumes at temperatures considerably below those which cause paper to char.

For more permanent storage, box files should be used. The Record Office, House of Lords Library, uses box files of the following specifications. Two sizes are standardised: 17¼″ by 12¼″ by 6″, and 14½″ by 10¼″ by 6″, being inside measurements. The box has sides of three-eighths of an inch wood, the base and lid are strawboard and all joints are strengthened with holland. The box and lid are covered with red leatherette and a metal cup handle is riveted to the side of the tray. The interior is lined with plain paper, and three-quarter inch holes are drilled through each end of the box.

Documents should never be placed on a spike-file or pinned together; even the use of spring clips should be avoided as they produce shallow grooves in the paper, and these may be the subject of speculation at a later date when the spring clip is no longer remembered as the cause.

Documents which are seen to bear impressions which may be thought significant, should never be subjected to pressure by being piled up or kept in envelopes. They should be kept in a shallow box and, incidentally, examined scientifically as soon as possible because impressions tend to fade with the passage of time. They soon become shallow and tend to lose their sharp outline, which renders them much more difficult to decipher.

Torn Documents

If a document is torn, the pieces should be kept in a shallow box. If it is necessary to reconstruct the document, each piece should be fixed to a glass or plastic sheet with a tiny speck of adhesive. Then another sheet of glass or plastic should be bound in position so as to hold the paper fragments securely sandwiched in place between the two sheets.

An alternative method of assembling torn fragments is to coat a suitable surface with either rubber solution or with one of the proprietary coatings made by the photographic companies—such as "Film Flat," or something similar. Scraps of paper adhere tightly to such surfaces, especially when they are freshly prepared, but, when necessary, the paper may easily be peeled away from the treated surface without leaving even a trace of the adhesive on the paper or harming it in any way.

Folds

Documents should not be folded and unfolded unnecessarily, as some poor quality papers cannot often undergo the considerable stresses imposed by the folding process. Even if the paper does not tear along the fold, the surface in its neighbourhood is sufficiently broken up to render microscopic examination of any ink or pencil line in the region of the fold quite useless.

Folded documents should be protected from dust. The fretting action of dust in the folds is one of the main causes of the tearing of dusty documents along the folds if they are subjected to much handling.

New folds should never be introduced into a document. The reason for this will become apparent when the significance of the folds of a document is considered.[6] One thing that should be avoided is the reversal of the direction of a fold, as this not only seriously weakens the paper at the fold but may lead to serious difficulties

[6] See Chapter 3.

or even incorrect deductions in a later examination of the document to learn something of its history from its condition.

Copying of Documents

It may seem unnecessary to give a warning that tracings of signatures and other writings should never be made from a document, but in some quarters this ill-advised practice is still carried on. The maltreatment of a document which has been traced-over may result in considerable difficulty in a subsequent examination, should the examiner be unaware of what has happened. He may well, though quite erroneously, come to the conclusion that the document bears some of the hall-marks of being a tracing itself, especially if the handwriting traced is of poor quality or is stilted in appearance.[7]

If a record of what the document has to convey is all that is needed, a cheap " photostat " or similar form of reproduction may prove quite satisfactory, but if a complete record of the appearance of the document is required, then a properly prepared photograph is essential. The differences between a photograph and a " photostat," which are often confused, is explained in Chapter 6. " Photostat " is the proprietary name given to a method of copying photographs, which relies upon the production of paper negatives that can also be read as reversed positives. The term photostat is often, popularly but incorrectly, applied to any form of photographic reproduction of a document made by this or any similar process.

Marking Documents

It should not be necesary to state that documents should never be cut, torn, or trimmed, nor should large adhesive labels be carelessly applied, but unfortunately such stupid actions are still carried out by persons who should know better. A malign fate seems to ensure that the adhesive label is stuck onto what subsequently proves to be the most vital part of the document—from the point of view of the examiner—in the same way that the cashier's cancelling pencil or pen stroke invariably seems to cross the most interesting place in the signature on a forged cheque.

Similarly, identification marks and rubber stamps are often placed haphazardly upon many documents which are court exhibits, whereas a little thought will usually indicate where the stamp is least likely to be harmful.

Many investigating officers and some solicitors, all of whom should know better, are apt to underline or " ring around " those letter formations to which they consider the document examiner they consult should pay particular attention. Whilst advice is always welcome, the proper place for it is in the accompanying letter, never on the document which is being submitted for examination.

Charred Documents

Paper which has been subjected to a high temperature—even though the exposure is insufficient to discolour the paper much less char it—loses practically all its strength and readily breaks up when handled. If the heating has gone on until

[7] See Chapter 11.

the paper has turned brown or black then it may fall to a powder on the slightest handling.

It is sometimes of the greatest importance to decipher and maybe preserve a document in this state, and for this purpose the charred material must be transferred to a laboratory without suffering any further damage or disintegration. Charred documents should be treated as described in Chapter 5. No attempt should be made to stiffen the document by spraying with an alcoholic solution of shellac—a practice sometimes advocated—for the solution dries slowly to a tacky mass before hardening. Another disadvantage is that after exposure to light shellac becomes less soluble in alcohol and is difficult to remove by subsequent treatment with solvent. When toughened by spraying, a charred document needs no further preservative treatment, but if it has to be handled it should be bound between two sheets of glass or transparent plastic as advised for torn documents.

It is sometimes recommended that charred documents should be soaked in warm water or in water containing gum, so as to toughen them sufficiently for handling. This method may be of some value when a scorched document is concerned, but any treatment involving the use of water is extremely hazardous for any document be it charred or not. Water is ever the enemy of documents and its use or that of aqueous solutions should be avoided wherever possible, although many writers on the examination of documents advise the application of chemicals or even soaking the document in water to test water-marks.

Chemical Treatment to Preserve Documents

The main cause of the deterioration of paper is acidity. Papers are generally acid because of residual chemicals derived from the sizing process. Papers with a pH above 5 will probably deteriorate and should acidity rise above this, a life of about twenty-five years may be all that can be expected. As the paper deteriorates the acidity rises and brittleness increases in proportion.

To prevent this rise in acidity, documents may first be soaked in lime water and then in a solution of calcium bicarbonate or a mixture of calcium and magnesium bicarbonates. This neutralises the acid and deposits small concentrations of alkaline earth carbonates which will tend to keep the paper neutral in reaction. After treatment the paper is air dried. To protect the surface and increase tear-resistance the sheet may be laminated by heat-pressing with tissue paper between films of cellulose acetate.

The whole will then form a homogeneous unit which has much the appearance of the original document. The treatment is slow and expensive, special heated presses being required for the lamination.[8]

Cleaning of Documents

Occasionally a document is received for examination in such a state that cleaning, to some extent at any rate, is an essential preliminary to its examination especially where any writings thereon have to be deciphered.

[8] *Industrial and Engineering Chemist,* P.25A, Vol. 40, No. 11, November, 1957.

Sometimes these documents have been soiled through having been buried in the earth or, as in the case of one document whose discovery played a great part in the conviction of a murderer,[9] through lying on the oily dirty floor of a garage. On other occasions documents are received in a filthy state through having been treated with graphite powder, in a generally fruitless attempt to develop fingerprints or to render more legible any surface impressions of writing which might be present. The use of the ninhydrin spray to develop fingerprints also leaves a document in a very "sensitive" state, because unless steps are taken to remove the ninhydrin, every time the document is handled a fresh crop of red fingerprints will slowly develop.

There is no general method which can be guaranteed to clean a document and leave any writing thereon unharmed.

An essential preliminary is to attempt to determine both the chemical nature of the contaminant and also whether the writing or printing which has to remain unaffected consists of pencil, copying or indelible pencil, iron-ink, dyestuff ink, ball-pointed pen ink, wax crayon, carbon paper, or printing ink. Without this preliminary information any blind attempts at cleaning are as likely to remove the wanted material as the unwanted—probably the wanted is more liable to be removed as there is usually less of this than of the contamination. The safest procedure is to hasten slowly, bearing in mind that the effect of any treatment once embarked upon cannot always be judged and, if necessary, stopped in time to prevent harm.

Before any cleaning process is commenced it is as well to try all the resources of photography. This not only gives a record of the document as it was received and before any risk is taken with it, but sometimes the use of special methods, such as the preparation of a series of photographs of different exposures by infra-red, may enable the cleaning process to be dispensed with altogether. Photography by infra-red is of the greatest utility when pencil writing is concerned because pencil marks, unlike many inks, are opaque to infra-red radiation.

The commonest contaminant is water or aqueous solutions of chemicals used in industry. If a wet document is encountered it should not be dried before testing it for acidity or alkalinity with litmus paper. This is important because paper soaked in very dilute sulphuric acid will last for days without taking much harm; whereas if such paper is dried without treatment, this results in the concentration of the acid to such an extent that when dry the paper will immediately crumble into dust owing to the energetic action of the concentrated sulphuric acid on the constituents of ordinary paper.

If the paper is already wet with acid no further harm can be done by a further bathing in a very dilute solution of calcium bicarbonate which will neutralise the acid present. A rinse with water will remove most of the excess bicarbonate and any soluble salt of the acid which has been formed; following careful blotting, the document can quite safely be slowly dried in a current of warm air.

As most paper is normally slightly acid owing to the alum which is added during manufacture, the litmus paper should turn a definite red shade before any chemical treatment to effect neutralisation is carried out. If the litmus paper turns

9 *R.* v. *Podmore* (1930) 46 T.L.R. 365.

blue, this indicates the presence of an alkali, and once again treatment with a bath of dilute calcium bicarbonate solution is the safest preliminary treatment, as this chemical will neutralise caustic alkalis as well as acids. Paper treated with alkali becomes very tender, and so it should be subjected to the minimum of handling before treatment and subsequent washing and drying.

The easiest documents to clean by chemical means or the action of organic solvents are those written in pencil, because the graphite fragments which make up a pencil line are resistant to the action of all chemicals except those which would make short work of the paper itself. All that affects pencil writing is abrasion, and this should be borne in mind when there is any temptation to aid the cleaning process by swabbing with solvent-impregnated cotton wool.

Oily stains associated with dirt are commonly found, as paper readily absorbs oil of any kind, and if such stains are encountered on documents written in either pencil or iron ink, the cleansing effects of solvent should first be tried. The best solvent for initial use is petroleum ether with a boiling range of up to 100°C. This will remove most hydrocarbon oils and so loosen any dirt they hold. Pure solvent should be used as impure petroleum ethers (usually sold as benzine) often leave stains on paper since they contain coloured impurities which will not evaporate with the remainder of the solvent.

Before using any solvent, a little should be spotted on to a corner of the sheet and its effect noted after it has evaporated. In the majority of cases the paper will appear unchanged, so that it will be safe to proceed with the major operation. The document should be held in a shallow dish and flooded with the solvent. If this becomes discoloured it is poured off and the process repeated with clean solvent until it ceases to be discoloured. At this stage the document should be removed and dried in a current of warm air. Petroleum ether will affect papers which have been sized with wax but these are fairly rare.

The vapours of most solvents are toxic and some, for example, petroleum ether, white spirit, benzene, ether, are very inflammable and highly explosive when mixed with air, so that the greatest care must be taken when large shallow dishes are being flooded with fair quantities of these very dangerous liquids. Ample ventilation should be assured and all naked lights within a wide radius extinguished. A most powerful solvent for oils is "white spirit" which has a fair content of aromatic hydrocarbons. This should be used in a similar way to petroleum ether: it is just as inflammable and the vapour even more toxic.

If neither of these solvents serves to remove the oily stain then ethylene trichloride should be tried. Before pouring this or any other chlorinated solvent onto a document it is just as well to sniff at the bottle. If chlorinated hydrocarbons are kept for any length of time in the presence of air, light and moisture, decomposition occurs and hydrochloric acid is formed. This pungent-smelling substance is most harmful to paper, so that any chlorinated solvent such as ethylene trichloride, methylene dichloride, or chloroform, which has not a sweet non-acid smell should never be used on a document. Ethylene trichloride is easily obtained as it is extensively used for degreasing metal in engineering works. Methylene dichloride is an even more powerful solvent than any of the foregoing and can be used to remove most oils, fats and waxes as well as oil-paint from paper or cloth.

Some oily stains resist the foregoing solvents but are soluble in alcohol or acetone. The best form of alcohol to use is either rectified spirit or methylated spirit with synthetic denaturant. The commercial blue-tinted methylated spirit should never be used. Alcohol is used in the same way as the above-mentioned solvents but the vapours are neither so toxic nor so inflammable.

If cellulose lacquer or nail-varnish has been spilled on a document then other solvents should be tried. Amyl acetate mixed with an equal volume of acetone will dissolve nitrocellulose which is the basis of most lacquers. Failing this, recourse must be made to any of the other non-aqueous solvents available—and the number of these is legion.

Useful though the foregoing solvents are with documents written in either pencil or iron ink, their solvent power usually prevents their being used on documents written with ball-pointed pens, indelible or coloured wax pencils or carbon paper, as the oil or wax which carries the pigment in these instances may very well be dissolved away with the contaminant. The safest principle to act on in such cases is that of trial and error. To do this in the most convenient fashion, a tiny wooden splint is dipped in the selected solvent and, using a hand lens, the wet end is applied to a portion of the line of writing. If there appears any sign of spreading of the colour when the solvent is thus applied, then it is unsafe to use that particular solvent for cleaning.

Solvents usually act in groups. If benzene has proved useless it is generally a waste of time to try either toluene or xylene. Similarly, if carbon tetrachloride attacks the line of writing, one can be sure that chloroform, trichlorethylene and methylene chloride will act in a similar manner. Similar behaviour may be noticed in connection with the group—ethyl alcohol, methyl alcohol and acetone.

If the document has been disfigured by the use of graphite or other similar powder which has been brushed on in the hope of detecting finger-prints, or if it is very dusty, the only effective treatment involves the use of "Plasticine," a proprietary form of modelling clay. A thick cylinder of this material is first softened in the hand and then rolled back and forth across the document. This will pick up any loosely adhering powder but will leave any writing, whether it be with pen or pencil, completely unaffected. If there is a considerable amount of dust to be removed, the surface of the plasticine roller should be renewed either by scraping or by re-forming.

If the document is oily or greasy, it is likely that some of the dust will resist removal by the plasticine. In this event, the document should be treated with an oil or grease solvent such as benzene before attempting renewed rolling with the plasticine.

Although the use of the organic solvents mentioned above serves to clean a large proportion of the soiled documents encountered with no ill effect on the paper, or on the writing or printing if the solvent is chosen with care, there are many stains which resist all such solvents and in such cases more heroic measures must be adopted. These generally involve the use of aqueous solutions of various kinds, and this should only be embarked upon as a last resort.

In the first place, before any application of an aqueous solution is made, the document should be photographed, so that in the event of complete disaster some record remains. Before any new treatment is commenced, the document should be freed, by thorough washing, from all traces of the chemicals previously used.

The mildest treatment, which will often remove a great deal of non-oily surface contamination, is to swab the document very carefully and lightly with water containing a few drops of a wetting agent or detergent—not soap, which should never be used. Detergents have a powerful cleansing action, and if used with vigour may even remove printing ink from the paper. As this is so, anything else in the way of writing is likely to fare ill under such treatment.

To remove stains caused by iron-rust or clay, which chemically have much in common, bathing with a dilute solution of oxalic acid may prove very effective. A dilute solution of this acid, which is very poisonous, has little immediate effect on ink which is well dried and aged, but it rapidly dissolves fresh iron-ink, hence its use for removing fresh ink stains from old documents. The action of this solution on the document should be watched carefully and when no further improvement can be noticed, the solution should be poured off and the document well washed with distilled water to remove all traces of the acid.

Stains caused by mildew and those known as "foxing," which are also caused by micro-organisms, are difficult to remove, especially as the paper is often seriously weakened by the action of the fungus.

Some improvement may be obtained by the action of a suitable bleaching solution. Very dilute sodium hypochlorite solution, made just acid by the addition of hydrochloric acid, may effect some improvement but this solution rots paper very quickly. After use the document should be washed with water and then soaked in a solution of sodium thiosulphate—"photographer's hypo"—to remove the last traces of the bleach, before being once again washed in distilled water and dried. Instead of the hypochlorite solution, chlorine water may be used. These bleaching solutions will also serve to remove dyestuff stains as well as ink stains, whether the ink is a dyestuff or the more difficult resistant iron-ink.

If these bleaches fail to remove a stain caused by a dyestuff, a solution of sodium hydrosulphite—not to be confused with "photographer's hypo" which is sometimes known as sodium hyposulphite—may be used. If this powerful reagent does not work, there remains little hope of ever getting rid of the stain by chemical means.

Blood stains come into a category of their own. When fresh, the best treatment is gentle washing with physiological saline—a teaspoonful of salt to a pint of water. If this is ineffective, as it will be if the stain has been heated, then the bloodstain is probably there for good. The action of boiling acetic acid may remove some of it but this is hardly the treatment that a document can be expected to survive.

In the larger cities there are usually one or more dry-cleaning establishments. A great deal of research has been done on behalf of the dry-cleaning industry on methods for removing stains without harming the most delicate fabrics and their dyes. Each establishment handling very much such work usually has an expert at what is termed "spotting" on the premises. It is the duty of this person to work out methods for the removal of unusual stains which do not yield to the conventional treatment with a solvent which is similar to the petroleum ether mentioned above. The advice of such a person may be of great value where a soiled document is concerned. It should, however, be borne in mind that documents differ in many respects from clothes, and a trial on a very small scale should be made before any risks are taken with important documents.

Documents are sometimes treated with a solution of ninhydrin in order to develop latent finger-prints which, on heating the document for a short time at 80°C., appear as purple markings. After photography, the document should be washed in several changes of acetone to remove residual ninhydrin. The finger-prints are not affected by the acetone treatment, but certain ball-point pen inks are affected as is the dyestuff used in some makes of copying or indelible lead pencils.

A special example of a document which may have to be " cleaned " to enable useful evidence to be extracted therefrom is well-used blotting paper. Sometimes such sheets are so well-used that nothing of value can be distinguished. In such cases appropriate treatment may remove ink by stages and enable valuable information to be obtained. If a variety of inks has been used, the blotting paper should be photographed under different lighting conditions and with different negative material, until no more evidence can be obtained in this way.

Many inks sold for use in fountain pens are of the washable type, so that the first cleansing procedure is to soak the blotting paper in cold water in a shallow dish containing a glass sheet which can act as a support for the blotting paper when it has to be removed from the dish. If the water is discoloured through the removal of any of the ink, the water should be renewed until no further colouring matter diffuses out of the blotting paper. The water is drained off and the dish is flooded with methylated spirit with synthetic denaturant. This removes the water from the paper, which, supported on the sheet of glass, is lifted out of the dish and the alcohol dried off in a current of warm air before the sheet is photographed once more.

The same procedure should be repeated using a dilute aqueous solution of oxalic acid. This has a slow but continuous action on ink so the process should be interrupted occasionally, the document washed and dried as described above until sufficient of the ink has been removed. Oxalic acid solution acts quickly on freshly applied ink but very slowly on ink which has blackened by oxidation. Many inks contain but little iron and owe their tinctorial power mainly to the presence of dyestuff—like the modern fountain pen ink. These are often quickly bleached by the oxalic acid solution, so that by its use the blotting paper may be slowly cleared of the markings.

The effect of the foregoing treatment is gradually to clear the document of water-soluble (washable) inks, then dyestuff inks and finally the more recently applied ink until all that remains are the oldest and most oxidised inks which were on the blotting paper. The effect of this progressive treatment, if pursued with care and patience, is gradually to reveal much of what was overlaid by the multitude of markings.

Frequent photography is essential, as the action of the bleaching solutions is progressive, and useful evidence may only be apparent for a short time before it too disappears.

Bibliography

Grant, J., *Books and Documents. Dating, Permanence and Preservation* (Grafton and Co., London, 1937).

Johnson, C., *The Care of Documents and the Management of Archives* (London Society for Promoting Christian Knowledge, 1919).

Langwill, W. H., Permanency of Paper, Process and Technical Section of the British Paper and Board Makers Association, 36, 199, 1955. Technical Bulletin of the British Paper and Board Makers Association, 29, 21, 1952. Technical Bulletin of the British Paper and Board Makers Association, 30, 170, 1953. Tappi, 38 (g), 190A, 1955. " Action of Sulphur Dioxide in air on paper," *Nature,* September 18, 1956, p. 590.

Zimmerman, Weber and Kimberley, " Relation of Ink to the Preservation of Written Records," *Journal of Research of the National Bureau of Standards,* 14, 463–468, 1935.

Effect of Sulphur Dioxide in the Atmosphere on Books and Paper, National Bureau of Standards Miscellaneous Publications, M154.

14

ANONYMOUS LETTERS

It is not necessarily an offence to send letters which are unsigned or which contain no obvious clue to the identity of the writer. If, however, the letter is indecent, threatening, or in any way likely to cause a breach of the peace, then the writer puts himself in peril of legal proceedings. Whilst many cases are dealt with as civil offences, writers of blackmailing, threatening and criminally libellous letters come within the ambit of the criminal law and are liable to long sentences of imprisonment.

Few people realise the extent to which malicious anonymous letter writing is indulged in, and the misery and dislocation of social life caused thereby. Whilst a persistent writer of scandal in a large city may be little more than an objectionable nuisance, similar activities in small and closely knit communities undoubtedly cause considerable unhappiness and distress. It is for this reason that in the provinces police forces usually endeavour to identify anonymous letter writers who are not regarded as such a menace in large centres of population. If the anonymous letters are of a threatening or blackmailing character, strenuous efforts are made to detect the offender wherever the offence takes place.

Whilst the detection of the author of an anonymous letter is not necessarily as hopeless as it may at first sight appear to an investigator presented with a few sheets of almost illegible manuscript, or what is worse, a sheet of typescript apparently devoid of any clue to the sender, the investigation will call for the highest qualities of observation, deduction and patience if success is to be ensured.

Collection of Material for Investigation

The first step in the investigation is simple. As much anonymous material as it is possible to find should be gathered together, for whilst the chance of detecting the author of a single letter may be good, it is increased out of all proportion when two or more letters from the same source are available. Therefore, discreet inquiries should be made to ascertain whether similar letters had been received by relatives, friends and neighbours of the complainant. The net cannot be spread too far or too wide. The writer might very well have been active for years before the complaint was made to the authorities and other persons not known to the complainant might have been pestered in the same manner.

If inquiries fail to reveal any further specimens, an effort should be made to induce the writer to try again. The victim should be warned to be silent and to give no outward sign of having received the offending letter. This action will have a two-fold effect. In the first place, the writer will be deprived of the satisfaction of observing any sign of the success of his misdoing. Secondly, he will be forced to wonder whether his letter has actually reached its destination. This is often sufficient to provoke him into further and often more extravagant efforts, in which the attempts to hide his identity may not prove so successful.

When the various letters which have come to light are collected, a note as to how and when they were received should be made while the events are still fresh in the memory. This information may prove of paramount importance at a later date when a suspect is being challenged as to his whereabouts and movements at significant times.

From the beginning, the investigator should bear in mind that in a fair proportion of cases the letters are written by the complainant himself, so that caution should be adopted whenever the investigation is being discussed with him. Some suggestions as to the form the interview with the complainant should take are given later in this chapter.

Every communication should be thoroughly examined as laid down in the chapter on the preliminary examination of documents. As a result of this preliminary examination, evidence may be found which will make it worth while having the letters submitted for examination in a laboratory which specialises in document examination.

Unopened Letters

If a constant stream of letters is being received, so that they can be recognised before the envelope is opened, instructions should be given that they should be preserved and handed over for examination, unopened. One reason for this is the possibility of developing fingerprints by means of the ninhydrin process, but apart from this, the investigator can be sure that no one but the writer can be acquainted with the contents. This assurance is valuable when the recipient is also the writer, for it may happen that an incautious remark on his part will arouse suspicion at a later date if the investigator has taken the precaution of keeping to himself the contents of any letters he has gained possession of unopened.

The speedy receipt of an unopened letter will enable any odour associated with the paper to be detected with greater certainty than if the letter had been opened and well handled before being handed over for examination. Odour may be of some significance, because the majority of anonymous letters are written by women and are often carried along with cosmetics in their handbags before being posted.

Envelopes

The envelopes or other wrappings in which anonymous material is sent should be preserved for examination. Not only is the handwriting thereon less likely to be disguised, but it sometimes happens that "foreign bodies" found in the envelopes have furnished valuable evidence as to the source of the letters. On one occasion an anonymous letter submitted for examination was found by the author to contain a small filter paper of very high quality. The anonymous letter had been made by laboriously piecing together letters cut from newsprint, and the filter paper had been used for blotting the excess gum. Inquiries showed that there was only one place in the neighbourhood where such filter paper was easily available, and with this information to give a start to the investigation, the sender of the anonymous letter was eventually discovered.

False Clues

The investigator should always be on his guard against being deceived by the deliberate " planting " of clues designed to implicate an innocent person as the writer. The formation of easily seen impressions of addresses has already been mentioned, but this does not exhaust the list of false clues. Sometimes in an effort to implicate an innocent person, considerable trouble is taken to secure a sheet of headed notepaper, which is cunningly torn as though the intention were to remove the printed heading, but sufficient is left for it to be identified. The re-use of envelopes on which the original name and address can still be seen is another common trick. The test which should always be applied to " clues " such as these is that of consistency with other less obtrusive and, consequently, more reliable evidence.

Reading Aloud

Once all the material has been gathered, the letters should be arranged in chronological order and slowly read aloud. This is most important, for not only does it focus attention on points which would escape notice if the reading were swiftly done by eye, but certain tricks of expression and emphasis which may indicate the sex and character of the writer are better thrown into relief when they are heard as well as seen.

This reading aloud is essential when a mass of anonymous material written in heavily disguised handwriting is being dealt with. Whilst at first sight it may appear that more than one person must be concerned, because of the variation in the handwriting and arrangement of the written matter, during the reading, when attention is focused more on the style, choice of words and phraseology, it will often become apparent that there is only one mind behind the whole. The differences observed can then be put down to deliberate attempts to confuse the issue. Once it is clear that only a single person is involved, the investigation and comparison of the handwriting is greatly simplified.

Once the letters have been read aloud, it should be possible to proceed with the next step in the investigation. This is the classification of the letters into one of a number of groups, based on the motives which prompt the production of anonymous letters. As soon as it is possible to establish the motive, the field of likely suspects will be considerably narrowed, so that neither time nor effort need be wasted in pursuing inquiries in unlikely quarters.

Classification Based on Motive

With anonymous letters demanding blackmail, making indecent suggestions or indulging in spiteful abuse, the motive is plain. In other cases, the true motive may be hard to ascertain from a single letter, and may become apparent only when a series is read as a whole.

It may happen that the true motive is concealed and only appears late in the investigation. Cases are known where the character of someone practically unknown to the writer is bitterly assailed in terms calculated to cause the utmost resentment. In these cases, the letters are actually aimed at a third party, whose name is never mentioned, but who is intended to be harmed by being blamed for writing the libels because of cunning clues deliberately planted and intended to be discovered when the letters were investigated.

Blackmailing Letters

While many letters which demand money with menaces are exactly what they appear to be, it should not be assumed that every letter of this type is a blackmailing letter and that a conviction for this offence will automatically follow once the writer has had authorship proved against him. The senders of many letters which demand money with menaces do not expect to receive anything in the way of financial gain, their motive being merely to frighten and annoy the recipient.

If a blackmailing letter is to be taken seriously at its face value it should fulfil certain conditions:

1. The sum of money demanded may reasonably be thought by the blackmailer to be within the capacity of the victim to pay.

The author once had a case where a farm labourer received an anonymous letter in which he was threatened with violence if he did not hand over £20,000. In the circumstances, this was a sum of money so great that it is ridiculous to think that the half-witted youth who was proved to have written the letter ever expected to receive it. In spite of this, it required much argument before the aggrieved person dropped his intention of bringing a charge of demanding money with menaces.

This charge would have been laughed out of court by any competent defending counsel, and the letter writer who deserved and received punishment for a lesser offence would have gone free.

2. There should be practicable instructions whereby the money is to pass from the victim to the blackmailer.

Many letters contain demands and threats without a hint as to how the victim is to comply with the demands even if he were willing to do so. No instructions are given as to how the money is to be handed over, nor is there any obvious clue as to the identity of the person who is expected to benefit.

Sometimes the most fanciful instructions are given with respect to the handing over of the money. These letters generally come from juveniles who write from a spirit of mischief, anticipating amusement from watching the victim endeavouring to comply with the instructions.

3. A genuine blackmailing letter should contain a hint, if nothing more definite, of some reason why the victim should be called upon to pay.

This almost invariably takes the form of the writer assuming a nauseating hypocritically moral tone, rebuking the recipient either for some form of sexual delinquency or for an evasion of income tax, which the writer feels should be punished by the extortion of money, to be regarded by the victim as a well-merited fine for the offence.

The blackmailer may relate a story of misfortune which seeks to justify his action as one of taking from the rich for the benefit of the poor. He may also state that he intends to regard the payment he has demanded as a loan which will, in due course, be repaid perhaps with interest, when times are better. Sometimes the writer is at pains to impress on his victim that his demands must not be considered as blackmail, but are merely a request for assistance; however, the dark hint of the unpleasant consequences of a refusal to pay is quite sufficient to justify such demands being treated as demanding money with menaces.

4. There must be a threat to ensure both compliance and silence. The threat is generally that of exposure of wrongdoing on the part of the victim. Nowadays these threats take one of two forms to the practical exclusion of all others.

The most popular, often addressed to business men who handle large sums in cash, is the threat to inform the revenue authorities of alleged wholesale evasions of income tax. If there is any substance in the allegation, the blackmailer feels confident that not only has his victim good reason for avoiding investigation of his affairs but is also in possession of a large sum in ready cash from which he should be able to draw sufficient unidentifiable money to pay blackmail, without having to raise it specially for the purpose. This threat is often backed by reference to newspaper accounts of the conviction of offenders for offences similar to those alleged.

The second, and by far the more serious, is the threat of exposure of alleged sexual aberrations on the part of the victim. This is a most evil and potent threat and even if there is little substance in the allegations there is a natural reluctance to follow the only safe course of defying the blackmailer and reporting the matter to the authorities.

5. No genuine blackmailing letter is completely without the promise that the current demand is positively and definitely the last, and that if it is promptly complied with no more will ever be heard of the matter.

It is a matter of bitter experience that this promise, which is intended to reinforce the threat and incline the victim towards compliance instead of taking the only sensible course, is never kept. Any subsequent demand is much more difficult to resist, because the initial submission is regarded by the blackmailer as evidence that his allegations are well founded and that his threats are irresistible.

Sometimes a complaint is made of the receipt of communications which make demands far beyond the power of the victim to pay, coupled with accusations and threats of exposure of having committed some serious but unspecified crime. There may also be the declared intention of the infliction of bodily harm, or even of the burning down of the victim's home. The strong probability is that these letters have been written by the recipient himself, who is endeavouring to obtain a certain and possibly a sympathetic hearing of his troubles in this way. The threats are rarely spared, so that when he complains he feels he runs no risk of being advised merely to ignore the letters, which might well happen if they were not couched in such strong language.

Threatening Letters

These are fairly common, but if legal proceedings are contemplated when the author has been identified, it is important to distinguish between those threats which are real and intended to terrorise, and others which are so extravagant that the writer is never likely to implement them. It is almost impossible to obtain a conviction on a charge of uttering threats to kill in the face of a defence which points out that, not only must the jury be satisfied that the accused made the threats but that, at the time he made them, he fully intended to carry them out. In nearly all of these cases it is safer to bring a lesser charge which will have some chance of being brought home to the accused.

It is the threatening letter more than any other which sometimes contains the " planted " clue, which has deliberately been inserted to throw the blame for the threat on to the person the writer desires to harm. It is noteworthy that the threatening letter where the writer intends and is in the position to carry out his threats is comparatively rare, and in these cases the recipient usually has an excellent idea of the identity of the person responsible. If he can be persuaded to speak, the investigation is simplified from the outset.

Letters of Revenge

A desire for revenge is the motive behind a large proportion of anonymous letters. Included in this group are the " tip-off " letters sent to the police, tax officials, Customs and Excise, and to those in authority in business and other organisations. They contain allegations of some wrongful act on the part of the person it is desired to harm in the hope of bringing them into conflict with authority. It is the threat to write these letters that is most favoured by the blackmailer, and very often it is the only threat he dares to carry out.

The allegations may be wholly or partially correct, or thought to be correct by the informant when he seeks his revenge in the punitive action taken against his victim because of the information he has supplied. On the other hand, the informant may be well aware that there is no substance in his allegations, but hopes to have the affairs of his victim made the subject of inquiry with all the inconvenience, if not worse, that this will cause.

Once it is realised that jealousy is often the driving force behind the writing of such letters, the circle of possible offenders is considerably narrowed. The nature of any well-founded allegations may prove a valuable clue to the direction in which to make inquiries, for accurate information which is discreditable to anyone is likely to be in the possession of someone who belongs to a strictly limited group. Care should be taken not to narrow the circle of inquiry by too much, because the accuracy of the information may be more the result of shrewd guesswork than of definite knowledge. It should also be borne in mind that what is sometimes considered to be fairly exclusive information may have leaked out to be picked up by the most unexpected person.

An example of this occurred when a series of anonymous letters was found to contain references to many facts which it was thought certain could have been known only to the members of a certain organisation. Comparison of the handwriting proved quite conclusively that no one in this organisation had written the letters, nor was there any evidence that the letters had been written from a copy or by dictation. Matters remained in this unsatisfactory state until it was discovered, quite by chance, that the lift attendant employed in the building was the culprit. He was not a member of the staff of the organisation concerned, but his duties gave him the opportunity of picking up a multitude of chance remarks and fitting them together to obtain an intimate and fairly accurate, knowledge of the internal affairs of those firms whose staff and clients habitually used his lift.

The identity of the writers of a fair proportion of these letters of revenge may be ascertained merely by reading them carefully. In many cases, not only is the victim of the attack castigated in unmeasured terms, but to make his offence more rank, his behaviour is unfavourably contrasted with that of a third party who receives both sympathy and praise from the writer. The writer is often at great pains to emphasise that he knows this most estimable person but slightly, and is himself unknown to him. In practically every case, once the identity of this praiseworthy citizen has been established, nothing more remains to be done to discover the writer. Experience shows that not one anonymous letter in a thousand contains a kindly word for anybody but the author.

Letters of Recommendation

It may happen that allegations of wrongdoing or of general inefficiency are stated in such general terms and are applied to so many people that the true object is not revenge as at first sight may appear. On the contrary, the sole aim is merely the recommendation of someone whose good character and efficiency is highlighted by the disparagement of others. Whilst the source of these letters is not difficult to determine, the person recommended may not have written the letters, especially if his handwriting is likely to be known to the recipient. Wives, husbands or other near relatives may have been pressed into service to do the actual writing so as to prevent the identification of the source of the letters.

Sexual motives often lie behind the writing of a variant on this type of letter. It is not uncommon for a person who desires someone of the opposite sex to write numerous letters to a number of persons, often including himself, in which the person desired is accused of having sexual relations with the writer, who is named or otherwise identified in the letters. The motive behind this action is rarely to bring discredit upon the persons named in the letters, for they are often praised for their good taste, so that the writing of such letters can be attributed neither to spite nor to a spirit of revenge. Whether the act of writing such accusations gives some satisfaction to the author, or whether they are intended to bring the writer to the notice of the desired person, or perhaps to put ideas into his or her head, must be left to the psychiatrist. From the standpoint of the investigation, it is important that these writings be recognised for what they are, and not dismissed as spiteful libels. Recognition of their true nature will often serve to identify the author and save much fruitless investigation.

It is an adolescent version of this type of letter which plagues the senior forms of girls' schools from time to time. In these letters, reference is made to someone having what is termed " a crush " on one of the mistresses or senior girls. The investigation usually shows that the letters have been written by the person accused of " having the crush on " the elder person.

Spiteful Letters

The majority of anonymous letters are actuated by malice and spite. They range from the abusive and rude, which are best ignored, to the grossly libellous, which should be the subject of a criminal charge once the identity of the perpetrator has been established. The malicious anonymous letter is written so that the writer, almost invariably a middle-aged woman, can let her evil tongue run unchecked with little risk of having to answer for her actions.

The investigation of letters which are merely expressions of malice and spite is often very difficult, because little can be learned about the writer from a consideration of the subject-matter; the obvious conclusion that the author is a spiteful person often does little to direct the inquiry. Even the inclusion of the foulest and most indecent language cannot justify any narrowing of the range of inquiry, because many of these most offensive letters have been proved to have emanated from the most unlikely sources—educated and respected women of gentle upbringing, generally considered to have been unacquainted with the language they have used with such abandon.

Whilst the straightforward unsigned letter of abuse is unpleasant enough, those which cause most harm profess to report unpleasant things said about the recipients by third parties in the hearing of the writers. By this cunning device, not only are the recipients made the target of abuse, but they are often provoked to make trouble with the other parties, because their minds have been inflamed by what has been reported to have been said about them. Sometimes they are goaded to write anonymous letters to the persons accused of having abused them, without considering the tainted nature of the information on which they are acting. This snowballing of anonymous letters not only increases the mischief, but may cause confusion in the investigation, unless it is realised that more than one person has become involved in the writing of the letters.

When this has become the state of affairs, the earliest letters should be examined to determine whether they may reasonably be considered as provocation for the writing of others, and, if so, by whom and to whom. Then, if anonymous letters have been received by those suggested by this test, it may be possible to deduce who the writers are, and so eliminate them from consideration when investigating the author of the prime cause of the mischief.

Letters Written by the Person Maligned

If letters impugn the character of an individual, and particularly if threats are included, the possibility of this individual being the writer should never be lost sight of, even if it is hard to credit that the apparent victim could be guilty of the offences charged or acquainted with the foul language in which the threats are couched.

Whatever the reason which prompts these letters, whether desire to be the object of attention and sympathy, or the onset of mental illness, such complaints form a fair proportion of those brought to the notice of the authorities. As this is so, no investigation should proceed very far until the possibility of their being self-written has been considered and eliminated.

Special attention should be paid to the business man who receives letters which contain threats to burgle or set fire to his business premises. These are almost invariably self-written, to provide a plausible explanation for a faked burglary or a fire which he is thinking of staging to cover defalcations or bad business investments. The complainant is rarely able to account for the threats in any reasonable manner and can give no assistance to the investigation into their origin. Should it become necessary for the faked crime to be staged, then the letters are referred to as the obvious explanation for what has occurred.

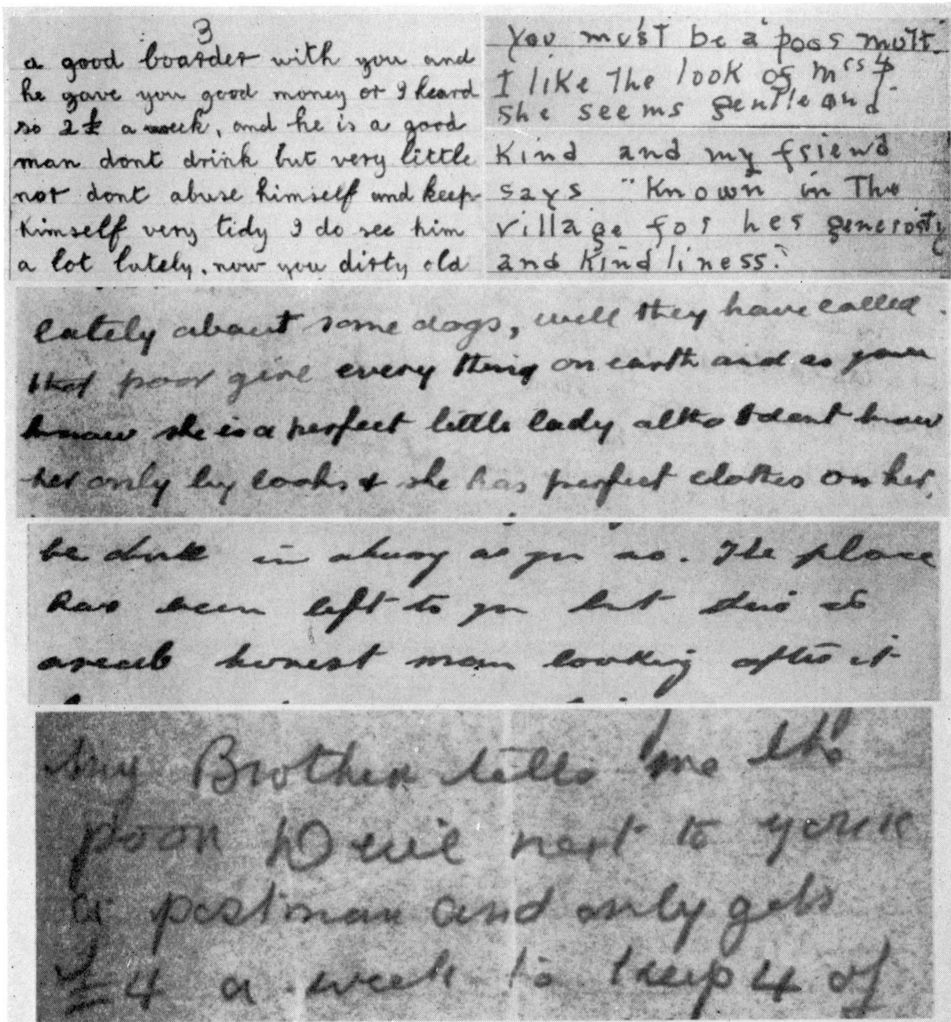
3
a good boarder with you and
he gave you good money or I heard
so 2£ a week, and he is a good
man dont drink but very little
nor dont abuse himself and keep
himself very tidy I do see him
a lot lately, now you dirty old

You must be a poor mutt.
I like the look of Mrs 4.
She seems gentle and
Kind and my friend
says "Known in the
village for hes generosity
and Kindliness."

lately about some dogs, well they have called
that poor girl every thing on earth and as you
know she is a perfect little lady altho I dont know
her only by looks & she has perfect clothes on her,

be drunk in always as you are. The place
has been left to you but there is
a real honest man looking after it

My Brother tells me the
poor Will next to your
postman and only gets
£4 a week to keep 4 of

Fig. 14–1. Five examples of the indication of authorship contained in the text of anonymous letters. In each case the person praised or sympathised with, eventually proved to be the author.

Miscellaneous Anonymous Letters

Many anonymous letters are either completely illegible or so incoherent that they can be dismissed as the productions of disordered minds, whilst others leave no doubt in the mind of the recipients that the writers are suffering from mild delusions. It is not easy to be sure of this when the degree of mental unbalance is small. In these cases of mild insanity on the part of the writer the best indications are the occurrence of incoherent phrases and the introduction of matters which have little or no apparent connection with the main theme of the letters. It is when these letters are read aloud that these characteristics are most forcibly brought to the notice of the investigator.

Into this class of letters written by the mildly insane fall those invariably received by those in the public eye, or who have gained some publicity in the national press. These communications, which range from the admonitory to the foully abusive, pour in from busybodies and other mentally unstable persons from far and wide.

As the writers and recipients are rarely acquainted with each other, the range of suspects is very wide. As most of these letters follow a curiously similar line of thought, little can be learned from their contents. If they are quite harmless—and as any successful investigation of their origin is unlikely—they are best consigned to the fire.

Practical Jokes

Some people with a perverted sense of humour cause annoyance by sending written instructions in the name of the victim for the insertion of advertisements in the local press. These letters are often followed by others giving fictitious news of engagements and marriages, in the hope that reference will be made in the gossip column of the paper concerned. Numerous tradesmen may also be written to and requested to deliver goods at the victim's house at the same time, with the object of creating confusion as well as annoyance.

These practical jokes may best be regarded as a form of revenge, so that the investigation should follow the lines laid down under that heading.

Letters Accompanying Stolen Property which is Returned

Anonymous letters are often sent with the empty handbags and personal papers returned, either to the victim or the police, by the thieves. These are rarely sent by professional thieves, but by amateurs who wish either to minimise the evil effect of their crimes by returning to the owner what is of no use to them, or to put false clues before the police, who, they suspect, may be getting close to them in their inquiries. In the latter case, they are wasting their time; the police never believe the lies in the letters and, in many cases, the handwriting has proved to be the vital clue which has led to the identification of the criminal.

Even when no letter has been enclosed, the handwriting or typescript on the envelope or wrapper has often proved sufficient to direct the investigation into profitable channels, so that all wrapping papers and envelopes used to return stolen property should be preserved and submitted for laboratory examination. It has often happened that the envelope or wrapper had been used before, and photography by infra-red has revealed the details of post office cancellation marks and, occasionally, whole names and addresses which had been overlooked by the thief, because they had been almost entirely erased. While not apparent to the naked eye, laboratory examination enabled them to be deciphered to the undoing of the thief.

Notes Left at Scenes of Crime

Some thieves feel impelled to leave behind them at the scene of crime a note addressed either to the occupant of the premises or to the police. This is not invariably a stupid proceeding on their part, because people who have been robbed of large sums of ready money found concealed on their premises are sometimes warned that to report the theft to the police will result in their receiving attention from the tax inspectors for suspected evasion of income tax. Sometimes this may be a very potent threat indeed.

In some cases of arson there will be found a note, which has apparently escaped destruction by a miracle, to the effect that someone other than the occupier of the premises has been responsible for the fire which was caused for revenge. On more than one occasion the discovery and the subsequent proof of the authorship of such a note has been the only evidence that the fire was deliberately caused by someone who hoped to profit by it.

Many of the notes which are left behind at a scene of crime, such as housebreaking, are but the expression of high spirits and defiance of authority by juveniles. When these notes are signed " lone rider " or " Robin Hood II " one can be fairly sure that a juvenile is responsible.

Indecent Writings

The last group of anonymous writings to be considered are those placed in public lavatories to enable vicious men to get into touch with others of like mind. These filthy things are often the subject of investigation, because they play a large part in the securing of convictions for attempted procuration and gross indecency.

Classification into Groups of Common Authorship

It is while a group of letters is being studied to decide to which class they belong that the decision can best be made as to whether they are all the work of the same person. In many cases this presents no difficulty, as the same style of handwriting or the one typewriter has been used throughout. It may happen, however, that some letters are written in cursive handwriting and others in block capitals, with the remainder typed on a number of different machines. Even if cursive handwriting is employed throughout, it may be presented in several elaborate disguises chosen, so as to convey the impression that more than one writer is involved.

In spite of the difficulties raised by the different forms the letters take, by the time all have been read aloud the problem can usually be regarded as solved. However many times the handwriting is varied or the typewriters changed, the ideas expressed in the letters and the quality of the phraseology, which reflect the personality behind the letters, must be the same for every letter written by this person, irrespective of the manner in which these ideas are committed to paper. If more than one person is responsible, there is usually little difficulty in arranging all the fair-sized letters into groups where each group is obviously the work of but a single person. In this work the investigator should be careful to err, if at all, in the direction of forming more groups than there are individuals involved. The inquiry is less likely to go astray if more persons are sought than are, in fact, responsible.

Some anonymous letters are very short, containing but a few words of abuse. With these short letters, if there is any doubt as to which group they should be assigned, it is as well to leave them out of reckoning for a while.

The investigation proceeds by the rereading of those letters which can unhesitatingly be considered to be the work of a single person. From this second reading it should prove possible to draw a number of conclusions which can be used to narrow the search for the culprit.

Conclusions Derived from Context

Sex of Writer

There is no infallible method whereby the sex of a writer can be determined by the examination of the handwriting. Even those graphologists who profess to be able to furnish every detail of anybody's character from a specimen of handwriting never claim to be able to determine the sex of the writer, which must be disclosed to them before they are able to perform their near-miracles. This hesitation on their part to deduce something which can so easily be checked for accuracy must be commended, because if they worked by guesswork, they would be wrong about as often as they would be right.

On the other hand, it is often possible to make a shrewd guess about the sex of the writer by considering *what* has been written rather than *how* it was written, although the problem is made more difficult by the existence of masculine women and effeminate men. When attempting a determination of the sex of a writer, the investigator must not neglect the warning already given, and assume that letters containing the foulest language and filthiest abuse could not have been written by a supposedly respectable woman. Experience has proved the opposite; women are quite the equal of men in this respect.

If the motive is spite and jealousy, the overwhelming probability is that a woman is responsible, especially if there is abuse of young and attractive girls. Accusations which almost invariably indicate female authorship are those in which the objects of their spite are either " exhibiting themselves," dressing and making-up so as to attract masculine attention, or keeping a dirty house and neglecting their children. There is often priggish advice concerning the future conduct of the victim, who is often advised to leave the district.

No reliance should be placed upon the truth of any statement the letters may contain about the sex of the writer; it is more likely to be false than true. If a series of letters written by the one person over a long period of time is available, then a list of the dates at which they were sent should be made. If it is found that the letters were sent in groups at regular intervals of about a month, this will be a fairly reliable indication that a woman is responsible, because the mental unbalance which is responsible for most anonymous letter writing tends to recur in monthly cycles.

Self-inflicted Letters

Men rarely write anonymous letters to themselves. The only exception to this rule is the "warning" letter already referred to, which is sent to render plausible and capable of explanation some crime such as arson which is contemplated by the writer.

The self-inflicted letters written by women can readily be picked out by studying their wording, as the abuse and accusations are curiously selective. There are never any of the accusations of uncleanliness, vanity or neglect of children almost invariably found when other women are attacked. On the other hand, it is not uncommon to find the most outrageous attacks on the morals of the recipient, expressed in such crude terms that there is often the greatest difficulty in convincing anyone that the letters are self-inflicted.

Indications of Male Authorship

Whilst many anonymous letters may be attributed to women with some degree of certainty by a consideration of their contents, the same confidence can rarely be felt that any particular letter is the work of a man. Reliable indications of masculine authorship are so rare that there are only two types of communication which can be reasonably assumed to have been written by men when judged solely on their contents.

The first is where the sexual act is described in detail and with evident relish from the point of view of a man, and where the person addressed, usually a young woman, is urged to indulge in some indecent behaviour for the benefit of the writer. The second includes indecent letters addressed to very young girls. These, contrary to the general opinion, are rarely the work of young men, for they are almost invariably written by elderly men, often the kind of person who would be the last to be suspected of such behaviour.

Age of Writer

This is most difficult to estimate, either from the handwriting or the context of the letters. Whilst the young and immature person is extremely unlikely to be the author of writings which exhibit mature arrangement and the logical development of a theme, the reverse is not necessarily the case. Some people who can normally command a flow of verbal expression become the equivalent of tongue-tied whenever a pen is placed in their hands. Words fail them and the expression is stilted, so that the result is a composition which would never be attributed to its author by anyone acquainted only with his feats of verbal expression. Added to this, the writings of persons who are passing through the initial stages of senility sometimes bear a distinct resemblance to those of adolescents.

The only safe conclusion which may be made about the age of the writer is that the adoption of a querulous and censorious tone may be regarded as a sign that the youth of the writer is long past.

The class of person who has received the anonymous letter will sometimes give some idea of the probable age of the writer. Grossly indecent letters received by very young girls are almost invariably the work of men in their fifties, whilst similar letters received by women in their twenties are more likely to be from much younger men.

Where the influence of the cinema and the horror comic is shown by the use of signatures, such as " lone rider " or " the Ghoul," it may be assumed that an adolescent is involved, although it is remarkable how long adolescence can last with some persons.

Handwriting affords little help in judging the age of the writer, for while a developed style is unlikely to be that of a young person, the reverse is not always the case.

Occupation and Social Circle of Writer

An assessment of the social circle in which the writer moves may be made by attention to names of people, places and events which are mentioned. Phraseology, the mode of setting out the communication and the occurrence of technical terms and words of special usage will often suggest the occupation of the writer. Accurate reference to matters concerned with the internal routine of an organisation unlikely to be known to outsiders will do more than hint at the occupational circle of the writer, especially when things are referred to by initials. A good example of this occurred in an anonymous letter wherein the Daily Orders, which were a feature of the organisation of a certain police force, were referred to as " D.O.'s," an abbreviation which would have quite a different significance for anyone not intimately acquainted with the internal organisation of that force.

The names of people which are mentioned may prove of great evidential value if it is possible to establish something they have in common, such as membership of a club or particular drinking place. If this can be done, the probability is that the writer is either a member of the group referred to or at least well known to them.

National, Political and Religious Groups

Letters may contain terms, expressions and phraseology which can be recognised as characteristic of a special group in the community. Membership of a group is most apparent where religion is concerned, for those who have the strongly emotional nature which is so often coupled with some degree of instability, frequently attach themselves to the more extreme religious bodies. These people often betray their strong convictions in the manner in which they treat the subjects about which they feel impelled to write. This goes beyond religion, for members of minority groups the world over seem sensitive to what they consider to be unfair discrimination against them; and any anonymous letters written by members of such groups are coloured by the phraseology associated with the complaints of their particular group.

The handwriting will often provide some indication of the nationality of the writer because of the variation in design found in the handwritings taught in different countries. This is dealt with in some detail elsewhere, but the possibility of the nationality, or at least the country where the writer was taught to write, being determined from handwriting should not be lost sight of, especially when the offence occurs in an area of mixed population. The occurrence of a few letter designs which are characteristic of the handwriting taught in a particular country, should never be seized upon as evidence of the nationality of the writer, because foreign forms of letter design are often included in a handwriting either as an affectation or as a disguise. The handwriting, as with all handwriting which might be disguised, must be considered as a whole before any conclusion as to the nationality of the writer can safely be drawn.

The smallest and the most fundamental group is the family, and it is a melancholy fact that a large proportion of anonymous letters are written by close relatives of the victim. The source of such letters is generally revealed by the authors betraying an intimate knowledge of family affairs, particularly in connection with those financial matters which are unlikely to be known to outsiders. The recipients of the letters are often aware of their probable authorship, but as faults exist on both sides, they are apt to conceal vital information from the investigator. Whilst they resent receiving abusive letters, the last thing they desire is to have the matter pushed to such a definite conclusion that family dirty linen would have to be washed in public. The complaint is often made to the authorities so that the sender will become scared at the prospect of a police inquiry and consequently desist from further misconduct of this nature.

Medical men in general practice are a favourite target for the anonymous letter, which is nearly always written by a female member of a small group—one of his own patients. Sometimes the letters are restricted to the man himself when they can do little harm to a member of a profession so well acquainted with human ill, both mental and physical, but there is always the risk that they may end in being circulated among the other patients. Unless this state of affairs is checked by vigorous action, the medical man may risk professional ruin. The complaints follow a familiar pattern. They range from neglect of duty toward certain patients or classes of patients, with inevitable complaint of undue attention being paid to others, to downright accusations of immorality with some if not all of his female patients.

Whilst these letters are almost invariably the work of a woman, it must not be assumed that she is either elderly or unattractive (which is almost invariably the case with female anonymous letter writers), especially if the medical man is young or has recently become engaged or married.

It is not uncommon for a medical man to be called upon to treat an elderly patient, nursed by a daughter or other young female relative who had devoted her life to this purpose. The doctor's natural admiration and approval of such devotion is often mistaken for something much more personal by the woman who may no longer be young enough to anticipate making a good marriage. When events convince her that the hopes she has nourished are likely to be baseless, this otherwise estimable person may be prompted to take revenge, for what she regards as her wasted and frustrated life, by writing the most damaging libels on both the medical man and any woman she imagines has supplanted her in his affections. When the culprit has been discovered, it is often a matter of the utmost difficulty to convince anyone inexperienced in this type of investigation of her guilt. Her blameless character and long years of service are invariably quoted in her favour, in ignorance of the fact that these are the very things for which an experienced investigator would look when surveying the field for the most likely suspect.

Even when proof of authorship or an admission of guilt has been secured, it is difficult to decide what should be done. Legal proceedings are certain to spread the libels even further afield and there are never lacking those who declare that there is no smoke without fire, and yet if no definite steps are taken to deal with the matter, the consequences may be serious.

A procedure which has much to recommend it is to confront the suspect with overwhelming proof that she is known to be the author of the libels, and then to demand a signed confession of guilt and an expression of regret, together with a statement that she knows the libels to be entirely without foundation. If she agrees to do this, little more remains to be done except to point out that the most serious consequences will be certain to follow any repetition of the offence.

If no confession and expression of regret is forthcoming, the matter should be allowed to rest in the hope that the fright administered during the confrontation will prove sufficient to prevent any repetition of the offence. It is comforting to remember that once an anonymous letter writer has been detected and challenged, it is but rarely that any further trouble is experienced.

Educational Qualifications of the Writer

Disguised handwriting is often accompanied by attempts to convey a misleading impression of the educational qualifications of the writer by the use of bad grammar, poor punctuation and spelling errors in simple words. An assumed illiteracy is the only possible form of disguise of this nature, because no one can assume a higher standard of phraseology, grammar and skill in the selection and use of words than is normal to him, any more than he can disguise his normal handwriting by a substantial improvement in its general quality.

Illiteracy is more difficult to assume than is generally realised because, like every other form of disguise, it must be applied uniformly if it is to have any chance of success. To take an extreme example, the popular use of a small or lower-case " i " for the personal pronoun, to convey an impression of a very low educational standard, will accord ill with the correct but pedantic use of the subjunctive in the same sentence.

Deliberate misspelling is a well-used device, but on closer examination it will be found that while the simplest words may be misspelled, other more difficult words are invariably correctly spelled. If the writing of a truly illiterate person is examined, it will be found that not only are many of the more difficult words incorrectly spelled, but that several versions of the same word may be encountered on the same page. Where a long word is concerned, it will often be found that an attempt has been made to write it as it is *pronounced by the writer*. This in itself may prove a useful clue to the writer, especially in the case of mispronounced and consequently misspelled proper names. This often happens with uncommon names which have been misheard at the outset and consequently mispronounced on all subsequent occasions. Many anonymous letters have been traced in this way. On being passed round in the society thought to be frequented by the writer, the misspelling has been noticed by an acquaintance of the writer who has passed a remark that a particular person he knew was in the habit of using this mispronunciation.

Associated with the misspelling of the simple word are the grammatical errors of the " I is " and " you was " type. These crudities are often exposed as deliberate errors by their association with correct punctuation and division of the written matter into sentences and paragraphs, as well as with the correct division of words at the ends of lines.

When the foregoing and similar inconsistencies betray the fact that the writer has deliberately introduced these errors, the assessment of his educational qualifications must be made on what remains when these features have been eliminated from consideration. The most reliable indication of the educational standard of the writer may be gained from the logical development, or otherwise, of the theme of the letters. The uneducated have a limited vocabulary and tend to repeat themselves. On the other hand, the educated betray themselves by the use of the appropriate word and the smooth development of what they wish to say, no matter how crude the spelling errors and grammatical constructions employed.

If a letter is found to be very crudely written, and it is hard to determine whether the illiteracy is assumed because of the limited amount of written matter, it is as well to examine the envelope. In a surprisingly large number of cases, it will be discovered that the writer has addressed the envelope in his usual style, with little or no attempt at disguise. Many have a fairly definite style of addressing envelopes from which they rarely depart, even when they have disguised their handwriting. Recognition of this fact may serve to narrow the search for the writer. Extreme disguise is rarely assumed when an envelope is being addressed, possibly through inadvertence, or because it may be thought that any peculiarity associated with the writing on the envelope would call attention to it and assist in the discovery of the writer.

The document examiner is sometimes asked in cross-examination whether he does not agree that the occurrence of an undisguised but nevertheless crude and unlovely handwriting does not exclude the possibility of an educated person being the writer. The answer is that neither high mental stature nor a good education are a guarantee of even passable handwriting, for it is well known that many able professional men write an extremely bad hand. All that can be learned from the handwriting about the educational standard of the writer is that the possessor of a smooth and flowing hand could have achieved such proficiency only by much practice.

Devices to Defy Detection

The investigator sometimes feels that he is faced with a contradiction between the matter and the way in which it has been set out. The thought and phraseology will be that of an adult, whilst the handwriting and the setting out will appear immature. The most likely explanation for inconsistencies such as these is that he is examining something which has been copied or written from dictation.

Some people are unable to disguise their handwriting or may fear that even disguised handwriting may be identified by someone who will have a shrewd idea from the text who is most likely to be responsible. They feel that under these circumstances the safest plan is to have what they have written copied by a near relative who can be trusted to hold his tongue.

When the persons thought to be responsible for the letters are challenged with authorship, they are loud in their denials and demand that specimens of their handwriting be sent to an expert for comparison with that of the anonymous letters. When a suspect takes this line, it may safely be assumed that he has little to fear from any comparison of his handwriting with that of the letters, so the net should be spread a little wider, and a request made for specimens of the handwriting of any near relatives who might have done the actual writing on his behalf.

It is often possible to determine whether a letter has been written from dictation. When writing from dictation, unless both the writer and the person who is dictating are experienced in this work, it is difficult to match the speed of dictation with that of the writing. This tends to destroy any rhythm the writing may normally have. Words are left out or sometimes repeated, as the writer, who is usually struggling to keep up with the dictation, loses all sense of what is being written down, because his attention is concentrated on the mechanical process of transferring to paper what is being dictated. Punctuation and arrangement suffer badly, and even the most experienced writer is apt to split a long sentence in the middle so that neither portion by itself makes sense. The presence of this last error is an almost certain indication that the matter has been dictated, for it could hardly occur if the writer were fully aware of the sense of what was being written down.

Instead of being dictated, the letter may have been copied from a script. In this case it is unlikely that sentences split into two parts will be found, but copying from a script has its own pitfalls. It is hard for the inexperienced to keep an eye both on what they are writing and reading. This results in the missing out of words and sometimes of whole phrases. The missing out of a word will sometimes happen with normal writing when a writer's mind runs away from his pen, so that this alone must not be taken as a proof that the writing has been done from a copy. The most revealing characteristic of writing copied from a script, is a pronounced tendency to make false starts to sentences. Sometimes the false start can be seen to be that of a paragraph which has already been written or which occurs a little further on. If both the correct paragraph and that which has incorrectly been begun commence with the same word, this will explain how a mistake came to be made; it will also be strong confirmation that the writing was done from a copy.

A trick which is sometimes attempted in the hope that it will confuse the issue and nullify any attempt to identify the handwriting as that of any particular individual, is to have the anonymous letter written a word at a time by more than one person. Unless this possibility is realised at the outset, it will be an impossible task to match the handwriting of the letter with that of any one suspect.

If the handwritings of the persons taking part in this deception are fairly well developed and individualistic, there should be no difficulty in seeing through the trick and separating out the different handwritings before attempting any identification. If, on the other hand, the handwriting of the persons involved are relatively undeveloped, or worse still, are those of near relatives (sometimes uncannily alike), it may prove very difficult to effect a separation which can be relied on. This will greatly complicate, if not completely defeat, any identification of the writers.

Block Capitals

The commonest device for shielding the writer from discovery is the use of block capitals instead of the more familiar cursive handwriting. This has one merit as a disguise. Whilst someone familiar with the normal writing of the author of an anonymous letter may recognise the handwriting even when it is disguised, this is not likely to happen when the less familiar block capitals are employed.

The experienced examiner of questioned documents is unlikely to be defeated by the use of block capitals, for the only difficulty he is likely to experience will be in connection with the standards of comparison on which he has to rely for his identification. Block capitals are essential for his purpose, as it is difficult, if not impossible, to make an effective comparison with cursive handwriting. Whilst it is usually a simple matter to obtain specimens of the cursive handwriting of a suspect, it is another matter where block capitals are concerned. Fortunately nearly everybody is now called upon to fill up numerous official forms which require the use of block capitals, and to an investigator armed with the necessary authority, this multitude of forms should prove a fruitful mine of comparison material.

Typewritten Letters

A generation ago, it was the exception rather than the rule to encounter a typewritten anonymous letter. Today, with typewriters in many homes and quite serviceable machines obtainable at fairly low prices on the second-hand market, the position has altered appreciably. Many still think that it is impossible to carry out any worthwhile investigation into the source of a typewritten document, and a typewriter is used for anonymous letters in the confident expectation that thereby the author will be immune from discovery. That this is by no means the case is shown in the chapter on the examination of typescript, which should be referred to for details of the principles on which the investigation is based.

The laboratory examination of a typewritten document may be relied upon to provide information about the make and age of the machine. At the same time, an investigation of the surface of the paper can be made in an effort to find impressions of other typescript made when the sheet of paper concerned was used as a backing sheet. Information about the make and age of the machine will furnish a clue as to where the machine is likely to be found. An ancient machine is unlikely to be in use in the general office of a large firm, nor is a recent model of an expensive full-sized machine usually found in a humble dwelling.

The way in which the document is set out will give some indication of the skill and experience of the typist. The work of an expert typist is unmistakable in the even impression of the typescript as well as in the care taken with spacing, especially that associated with the punctuation signs. A skilful typist may introduce deliberate errors to suggest the work of an amateur, but the test is one of consistency coupled with probability, as is the case with other errors deliberately introduced into anonymous letters.

The striking of incorrect letters is one of the most common errors deliberately introduced, but if the letters " a " or " e " appear instead of " i," the substitution must have been deliberate, because it is very unlikely that these letters could have been struck by mistake. If, on the other hand, the letters " u " and " o " appear instead of " i," this may have been caused by poor typing, because these letters flank the required " i " on the standard keyboard.

Letters Built up with Printed Characters

Anonymous letters are sometimes constructed by the laborious device of selecting letters and wherever possible, whole words, from printed matter and then sticking these on to a sheet of paper to make words and sentences. If the envelope has been addressed in the same manner, there is little hope of tracking down the perpetrator by identifying the source of the lettering. This is generally derived from newsprint, and the mutilated papers are burned so as to reduce the risk of discovery. When a book has been used, there is always the possibility of finding the mutilated copy, as books are not always easy to destroy.

The investigation of an anonymous letter of this type is not quite the hopeless task it might seem at first sight. In the first place, much may be gathered of the character of the sender from the method he has chosen as well as from the sentiments expressed in the letter. On one occasion an investigator solved the problem by looking up a local man who had previously been convicted of the same offence by means of evidence obtained from the handwriting, and so had every reason to fear detection if he relied on conventional methods for producing his missives.

Even the most careful criminal may make a mistake. Reference has already been made to the man who used this method but who made the mistake of leaving in the envelope a piece of filter paper he had used for blotting up the excess gum, and was eventually identified through an investigation which began with the filter paper.

Further Investigation

Once the investigator has completed his reading of the letters, he should be in possession of a good idea of the motive which inspired them, as well as an impression of the probable age, educational standard and sex of the writer. He should then draw up a list of names and of places of resort mentioned in the letters. He should also make a note of any complaints which have been voiced, for these may serve to cut short his investigation when properly followed up.

Throughout the examination of the material, the investigator should be on the lookout for any special feature which might be used to give a lead to the investigation. On one occasion, the author was asked to examine some hundreds of indecent anonymous postcards which had been sent to many people in the district. It was observed that all four postcards which had been addressed to one of the recipients had been sent inside envelopes. When the handwriting of this person was compared with that on the postcards, their authorship was immediately established.

The sending of false orders to tradesmen to cause embarrassment to the victim has already been mentioned. The successful investigation of these cases is not always possible, so that anything which can be used to narrow the investigation should be assiduously sought.

A retail tradesman was overwhelmed when he received from a number of wholesalers floods of goods fraudulently ordered in his name. The investigating officer inquired why the tradesman was so annoyed when he could have made the best of a bad job by explaining what had happened to the firms concerned and asking for credit while he sold the goods. The reply was that the goods were *all* slow-selling lines. This gave the clue which solved the case. The officer reasoned that it was almost certain to be a local man in the same line of retail trade who would have this specialised knowledge. He consequently obtained specimens of the handwriting of local retailers of the same lines of goods. These were sent to the author's laboratory with the fraudulent order forms which had been filled up in a disguised hand. Comparison of the handwriting led to the discovery and confession of the culprit.

Interview with Recipient

All is now set for the all-important interview with the recipient.

If, from his study of the letters the investigator has any reason to suspect that they are self-inflicted, he should clear up this point at the very outset. The investigator will choose his own line of attack based on his experience and the kind of person he has to deal with. In the event of a denial of self-infliction, he will insist on the provision of suitable standards of handwriting by the complainant, or of typescript from any typewriters available, so that a thorough comparison may be carried out.

The recipient should be required to give a full account of the receipt of the letters, especially if they did not come through the post. This account should be written down, so that it cannot be altered to suit any modified story the recipient may wish to tell if it is later proved that the letters are self-inflicted. Even if this is not regarded as very likely, the information should be recorded while it is fresh in the memory, so that the whereabouts of any suspects at the material times can be checked at a later stage in the investigation.

It should be made clear to the investigator who, if anybody, has been told of the receipt of the letters and whether anything has been disclosed about their contents. It may happen that someone will subsequently be interviewed who betrays an unexpected knowledge of things legitimately known only to a very limited number of people, a fact which might direct the investigation into a profitable channel. At the same time, the recipient should be warned to disclose nothing concerning any letters he may receive in the future.

Every name of a person and place that appears on the list which has already been prepared should be put to the recipient for his comments and any information he can give concerning them. If any of the persons mentioned seem to fit the mental idea the investigator has formed of the sender of the letters, the fullest details of the relationship of this person with the recipient should be extracted for consideration as possible suspects. It is rarely worthwhile asking the recipient about the allegations as they are invariably denied.

Finally the recipient should be asked whether he suspects anybody in particular. To assist his thoughts in this direction, questions should be put about those with whom he has quarrelled, or who may be jealous of any good fortune or success he has recently had. It must be remembered that the tendency is always for the recipient to accuse those *he* dislikes rather than the people who have reason to dislike *him*. These may of course be the same people, for dislike is usually mutual, but this is not always the case. People who are sufficiently unbalanced to send anonymous letters are sometimes aggrieved by the most trivial actions of which the offender may be quite unconscious.

The author has given evidence in many serious cases of criminal libel where the aggrieved parties have gone into the witness box, one after the other, and have declared on oath that they have always been on excellent terms with the accused and cannot credit the possibility of their being responsible for the dreadful things which had been written about them. Even when the proceedings are terminated by admissions of guilt which leave no room for any doubt, they have seemed unable to believe their ears.

At the end of the interview, the recipient should be instructed in the most definite terms not to repeat his suspicions to anyone. This should be followed by the warning that an action for slander is likely to prove more distressing to him than the receipt of anonymous letters, however abusive they may be. A similar warning should be given to all who are interviewed in the course of the investigation, because one of the most distressing features of these cases is the snowballing of accusation and counter-accusation among those originally but remotely concerned.

Comparison with other Complaints

If the letters seem to have been written by people of more than average intelligence, any complaints therein should be listed. With this in hand, a search should be made among the great mass of letters of expostulation and complaint which are regularly received and preserved for a period by the various organisations to which such letters are addressed. Mention can here be made of the police, the local authorities, especially the sanitary inspector, and the local press. Other sources may occur to the experienced investigator. In a fair number of cases, signed letters having much in common with those being investigated will be found, and when these are followed up, they may very well lead to a successful conclusion of the investigation.

When the letters are not only abusive but show signs that they are the work of an illiterate person, inquiries should be made at the various drinking places in the locality for anyone heard uttering similar abuse, or expressing similar sentiments.

Vital assistance may be forthcoming from the most unexpected direction. The author has a vivid recollection of a case of abusive anonymous letters which plagued a populous industrial area for years. A new detective officer was given the hoary assignment with little hope that he could do any better than the able men who had preceded him. He soon realised that he would have to clutch at any straw if he wished to make headway where others had failed, so he carried a selection of the letters around with him, producing the envelopes to anyone he thought might be willing to look at them. One day the man he was casually showing them to replied that he could not recognise the handwriting, which was not surprising because it was very thoroughly disguised. There was something about the letters which did, however, remind him of something. When pressed to try to remember what it was, he replied that he knew an old man who was in the habit of collecting stamp edging which he used to secure the flaps of any envelopes he sent through the post. He was reminded of this because one of the envelopes had a strip of stamp edging sticking to it. The detective officer followed up this tenuous hint and obtained specimens of the handwriting of the old man when he had succeeded in identifying him. When these were submitted for examination, it was realised that the long quest was at an end.

Although the letters had been pored over for clues by many able officers, nobody had paid any attention to the presence of the strip of stamp edging. The attention of the old man, who was a recluse and thought to be of good character, had been relaxed on this one occasion, when he persisted in a habit which led to his eventual identification.

When everything the investigator can think of has been tried without avail, he must set about his task in the hard way. He must endeavour to discover the culprit by having the handwriting of the anonymous letters compared with that of all possible suspects. He will begin with that of the recipient, passing on to relatives, neighbours and friends, in the hope of eventually coming up with the perpetrator. This method is quite satisfactory if, like every detective officer in England and Wales, he has behind him the resources of a laboratory equipped and staffed for carrying out the multitude of handwriting comparisons which may be called for, but is certain to prove very expensive for anyone who is not so fortunately placed.

It is by no means a simple task to obtain suitable comparison specimens of the handwriting of a large number of persons, especially if block capitals are required, so that this blunderbuss method should only be resorted to when all else has failed.

The nature and amount of the specimens required by the document examiner have already been dealt with in the chapter on the preliminary phases of a document examination, which also includes suggestions about the way in which a specimen of handwriting should be obtained from anyone willing to write. The same chapter mentions many of the sources of comparison handwriting which are available for exploitation by an investigating officer armed with the necessary authority.

Interview with Suspect

The success of an interview with someone suspected of writing anonymous letters depends more on the investigator's experience of the world and his knowledge of human nature than on the depth of his acquaintance with the details of the scientific examination of documents. For this reason, there is little point in attempting to give more than a hint or so about the conduct of the interview. Some officers prefer to open the interview by stating briefly the nature of the complaint they have been called upon to investigate. They make no suggestion that they consider that the suspect has any guilty knowledge, but ask him whether he has been pestered in the same way. Many guilty persons are taken off their guard by this approach and are more willing to co-operate than if they are bluntly told that they are suspect.

If the suspect admits receiving anonymous letters, the officer should ask to see them. He should not be surprised to find that they are not forthcoming, but should ask the suspect to have them ready for him when next he calls. If it should be necessary to pay another visit, and the letters are produced, it will probably be found that no envelopes are included. The reason for this is that the letters will probably have been written after the previous visit.

If the suspect admits that he has heard of the receipt of anonymous letters, he should be questioned about his knowledge of them, in particular their distribution and the nature of the allegations. While he is complying with these requests, the source of his information should be probed to test his veracity and to suggest other persons who may be questioned.

The suspect should be asked whether he has any idea of the identity of the writers and the reasons for his choice. The answers to these questions are often very revealing. An inquiry about the whereabouts of the suspect when the letters were posted or delivered should invariably be made and the answers written down, so that there can be no dispute if the statement is later found to be inaccurate.

Even if the investigating officer has in his possession ample specimens of the handwriting of the suspect, before the interview ends he should be asked to give a specimen of his handwriting. If he has declared his innocence but refuses to write, he should be asked what he, as an innocent man, has to fear from giving a specimen of his handwriting, which if he were truthful would merely reinforce his denial of authorship.

If he agrees, but writes in a disguised hand, the officer should accept the disguised writing and then produce some undisguised handwriting of the suspect. He can then demonstrate the obvious differences and ask for an explanation. This will often lead to the suspect breaking down and confessing. If the suspect agrees to write and does so in his normal hand, this will mean that there is an extra specimen of authentic handwriting available for comparison.

Fingerprints on Anonymous Letters

It is only on the rarest occasion that fingerprints of any value are found on anonymous letters. There is little point in trying to develop prints with powders, because not only do the powders disfigure the document, but the moisture to which the powder adheres, slowly dries and diffuses into the paper, so that the fingerprints lose definition.

The ninhydrin process, to which reference is made in another chapter, affords the best hope of developing fingerprints on paper, but even this process is subject to severe limitations as it cannot be applied to all classes of paper.

Writing on Walls

When indecent writing on walls is being investigated, it is much simpler to provide a photograph than to remove that part of the wall bearing the writing, although even this has been done on more than one occasion. If a photograph is all that the document examiner is to see, it is essential that two things about the writing should clearly be indicated. The first is the size of the writing. This is best accomplished by including a rule or tape measure in the photograph. The second is some indication of the height of the writing above the floor. This latter does not necessarily allow the height of the writer to be estimated, because it might have happened that the space available for writing was very restricted. This is a point which should be cleared up in the report of the investigator, as well as the nature of the surface and the medium in which the writing was done.

It is not essential that the handwriting supplied for comparison should also have been written standing against a wall, although if the suspect can be persuaded to write in letters of the same size on a sheet of paper held at the same height against a wall, it will certainly facilitate the work of the document examiner.

15

A DOCUMENT CASE AT COURT

WHILST the author lays no claim to any special knowledge either of law or advocacy, he feels nevertheless that having attended numerous courts over a period of more than twenty years as an expert on documents his experience may assist in indicating what he regards as the most desirable technique for dealing with such evidence both before and during the court hearing.

A contested case which involves expert testimony on the scientific examination of documents is comparatively rare in the experience of most counsel, so that the difficulties invariably associated with the presentation of expert evidence are intensified through counsel's unfamiliarity with this work. What is more, the day is long past when all that was expected of counsel was to put his man into the witness-box, ask him to recite his qualifications, and then to be satisfied with the mere expression of his opinion on the documents he had examined.

The importance once attached to opinions unsupported by reasons has declined. Any documents examined by the witness can be placed before the court, and the resources of photography enable everyone concerned to see for themselves practically everything the witness is to refer to, even that which can only be seen directly by the aid of the most powerful microscope. Therefore, more reliance is now placed upon an exposition of the facts which are relevant to the issue, rather than on the unsupported opinion of any expert, however experienced he may be.

Some counsel, who would never consider shirking the infinitely more difficult task of putting before a jury the most abstruse legal technicalities, regard the adequate presentation of expert evidence on documents as beyond their powers, and take a very simple way out of their difficulty. Just prior to the hearing, they briefly discuss the case with their expert witness and wind up the discussion with the words: " This seems to be rather technical, so I propose to call you and then leave you to it. I'm quite sure you know more about these things than I do, and as you've had plenty of experience giving evidence you can probably put it over better than I can myself."

Whilst, at first sight, this course may appear very flattering to the witness, it cannot be recommended, however experienced the witness and reluctant the advocate. Trouble may be experienced at the outset. It often falls to counsel to open his case with a preliminary statement in which, among other things, he may consider it advisable to state exactly what he hopes to prove by means of expert evidence on documents. Unless he has made an effort to grasp both the extent and the significance of the evidence his expert witness is prepared to give, he will either understate his case, or more likely and much worse, will give the court the impression that the expert evidence will carry matters much further than the witness dare go on the facts available to him.

If this unfortunate impression is created, not only does the expert evidence fail to reach the heights predicted, but is almost certain to end on a note of anticlimax. Incidentally, the other side is unlikely to miss the opportunity of stressing how far the expert testimony has fallen short of what was promised. In doing this, they will probably cause much of what was of value in the evidence to be under-estimated if not completely overlooked.

When, deprived of the assistance of his counsel, a witness embarks upon what can only be described as a statement to the court, he will find great difficulty in the logical presentation of both the facts and the conclusions he has formed. He will become increasingly aware that a long and necessarily involved statement made by a single voice tends to become monotonous and even boring to the jury, whose attention is consequently apt to wander. On the other hand, if the same evidence is presented by means of question and answer, interest is maintained. Not only are there two alternating voices to break any monotony, but any remark in the form of a question is likely to arouse the interest, because the audience experiences a feeling of expectancy as they await the answer.

Counsel is not restricted in his remarks to the mere asking of questions, because he can at intervals inform the witness, and incidentally his audience, what he hopes to establish by the answers to the questions which he is about to ask. This device may prove especially valuable when the witness is about to explain the principles which govern any particular investigation he has made; the court is able to appreciate the point of counsel's questions, so that all can follow the logical development of the theme which otherwise might not have appeared to have very much relation to the matters in issue.

Another advantage of the unfolding of evidence by means of question and answer is made manifest should the witness fail to make a point clear. Most experts are so familiar with their subject that they fail to realise the difficulties it presents to most other people. What may seem to an expert to be a perfectly satisfactory answer to a question may strike very few of his audience in the same way. Counsel is in a much better position to judge of the adequacy of any explanation offered by an expert witness, and, where necessary, will repeat or rephrase his question so that the answer it brings forth makes everything clear to all.

Even if a witness, unaided by counsel, is able to give his evidence clearly, it may happen that he will be interrupted by questions from the judge, to whom something of purely legal significance may have occurred arising out of what the witness has been saying. The witness may not understand what the judge has in mind, and may unwittingly give misleading answers to his questions. If he is being examined by an experienced counsel, who will undoubtedly appreciate the point the judge is making, the examination-in-chief can be so directed that the witness will be able to remove any misunderstanding.

The great disadvantage of following the course of leaving everything to the witness is revealed when his cross-examination has been completed, for it is now that counsel has the valuable right of re-examination.

Even where the most experienced witness is presenting an extremely strong case, an able cross-examination can be counted on to diminish the effect of his evidence, for an experienced counsel will give the witness the very minimum of opportunity of replying fully to his criticisms of the evidence he has given. It is here that re-examination can be so valuable. Whilst a witness cannot very well make another statement at the end of his cross-examination, an experienced counsel who has so mastered the subject that he knows what answers he may confidently expect from the witness, can ask just those questions which will give him the opportunity to deal thoroughly and effectively with the issues which were raised in cross-examination.

It is when the time comes for counsel to cross-examine any expert witness called for the other side that any inadequacy in his preparation of the case is fully exposed. If he adheres to the wise rule of never asking any question in cross-examination to which he does not know the answer, there is little he can safely ask. If, as is sometimes the case, he rashly asks the witness why he does not agree with the opinions expressed by counsel's own expert, this will give the witness the opportunity of once more placing before the court arguments unfavourable to counsel's case.

It may be that no cross-examination is called for, but it is a bold counsel who takes the bull by the horns and informs the judge that, from what he has heard, it is patent that the witness knows so little about his subject that any cross-examination would merely waste the time of the court. This course is sometimes taken with telling effect, but only by counsel who are confident of their grasp of the matter.

It is fortunate that the majority of counsel take a different line from those who are content to leave all technical matters to the expert witness. The following suggestions are designed to assist them as they co-operate with their expert witnesses in an endeavour to present the strongest case before the court.

Reports on the Examination of Documents

The parties who submit documents for expert examination are concerned with the conclusions which are reached by the document examiner rather than the evidence on which his conclusions are based.

For example, they may wish to know whether a signature is a forgery or not, or whether a specimen of handwriting has been written by the person they suspect. It is for this reason that the first report submitted by the document examiner is often very bare of detail. Whilst the conclusions at which he has arrived are given fully, the grounds on which the conclusions are based and the arguments which lead up to them are rarely given at any length, because of the considerable and probably wasted photographic and clerical work which would necessarily be involved. If, for example, several specimens of handwriting had to be compared to determine their authorship, the document examiner would find it necessary to have enlarged photographs of all the documents, and from these he would have to prepare a number of detailed comparison charts, were he required to explain in any detail the grounds on which his opinions were based. In the majority of cases, this time-consuming and expensive task would be pointless, because those commissioning the work should have sufficient faith in the ability of the man they consult to accept his opinion, without putting him to the trouble and expense of proving his words to the standard required in a criminal prosecution.

Again, it may very well happen that, for a preliminary examination where the only desire is to ascertain the facts, the document examiner will have been supplied with comparison material in the shape of genuine signatures and specimens of handwriting of known authorship, of which a considerable proportion may be material which is either unavailable or inadmissible at any contemplated court proceedings.

Once it has been decided that the case is to go for trial, counsel has to make a decision as to what documents he intends to produce. He must also ascertain what comparison material is both available and admissible in evidence; he may decide not to use all the documents on which the document examiner has reported. This is often so in criminal prosecutions, where a multitude of possible charges is reduced to a manageable number so as to facilitate the work of the court. Alternatively, he may call for an examination to be made on documents which had not been included among those submitted to the expert in the first instance.

If there has been any serious reduction in the amount of standard comparison material, it will almost certainly be essential for those remaining documents which are to be used at court, both standard as well as questioned, to be submitted to the document examiner for reconsideration. It might very well have happened that some of the standard comparison material which the document examiner considers vital to the satisfactory demonstration of the grounds on which his opinion is based is no longer available. In these circumstances, he may be forced to reduce the strength of the opinion originally expressed, for the strength of any opinion is governed by the nature and the amount of the material which is available for examination and comparison. Whilst a witness may be fortified in his own mind as a result of his examination of documents which cannot be placed before the court, he is not in a position to utilise this knowledge to supplement his evidence.

An early decision as to what documents are to be produced is essential, for there is little which is more disconcerting to a witness than to be told as he is about to step into the witness-box that certain of the documents he is relying on as standard comparison material are not going to be made available to him, or that his opinion will be sought on a document which will be shown to him for the first time during his examination-in-chief. This may seem improbable but both these very unpleasant experiences have occurred to the author on more than one occasion. Another reason for an early decision as to which documents are to be produced is because on that decision depends the choice of photographs and comparison charts to be prepared.

It is a simple matter to withdraw any photographs of documents which it may be decided at the last moment to leave out, but if extracts from the withdrawn documents figure in any of the comparison charts prepared to illustrate the grounds on which the expert's opinions are based, one of three courses, all most undesirable, must then be embarked upon.

The first is to scrap all those charts which include any extracts from the documents which have been withdrawn. This is certain to weaken the effect of the

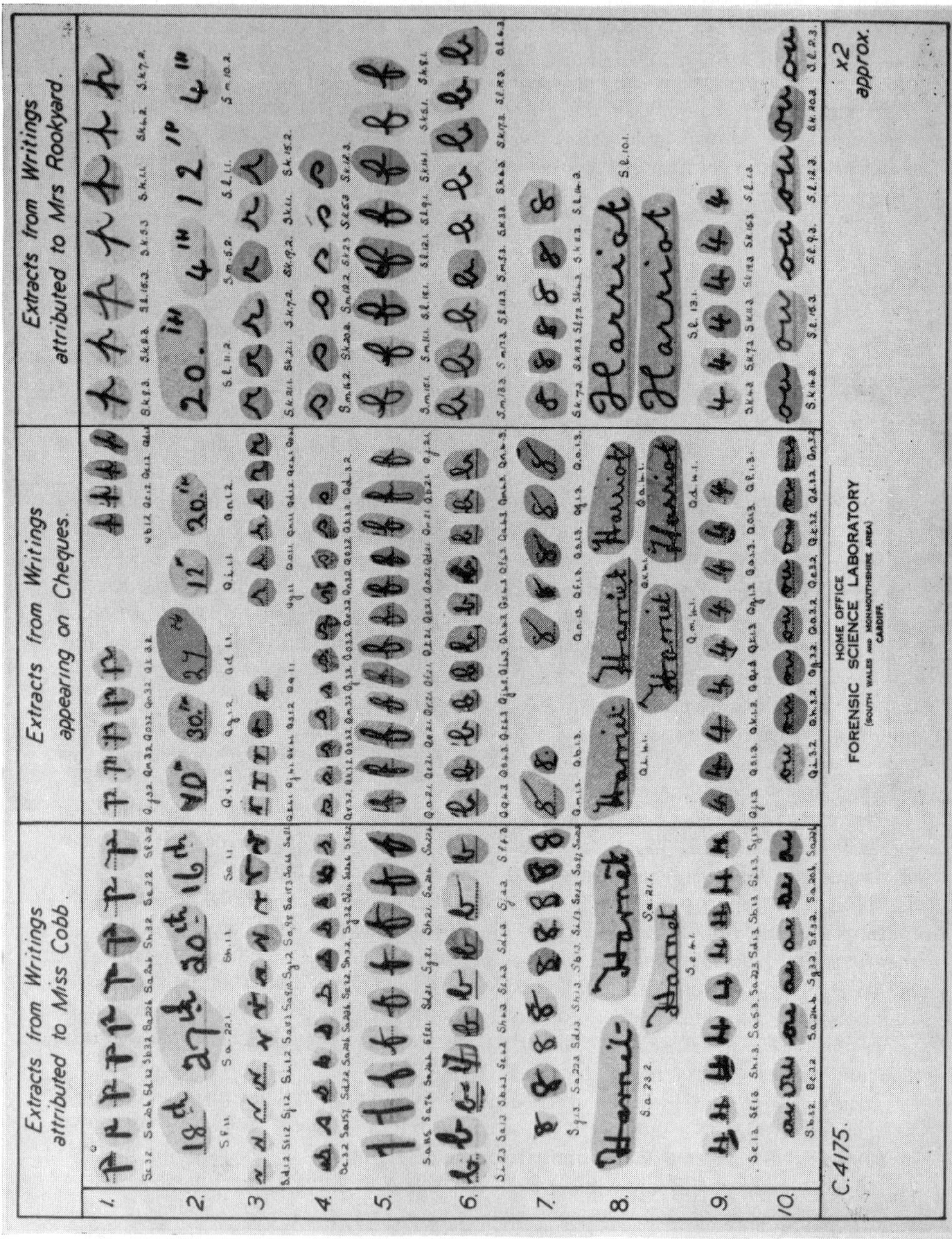
Extracts from Writings attributed to Miss Cobb.
Extracts from Writings appearing on Cheques.
Extracts from Writings attributed to Mrs Rookyard.
1.
2.
3.
4.
5.
6.
7.
8.
9.
10.
C.4175.
HOME OFFICE
FORENSIC SCIENCE LABORATORY
(SOUTH WALES AND MONMOUTHSHIRE AREA)
CARDIFF.
x2 approx.

expert evidence; it may even prevent its being presented in anything approaching a satisfactory manner.

The second is to cut out with a knife or scissors all the inadmissible extracts. This operation can usually be counted on to reduce the charts to the semblance of embroidery and should be avoided at all costs.

The third is to block out the unwanted extracts with either adhesive tape or black paint. Neither of these two commodities is easily come by at the last moment and the use of either will disfigure the comparison charts so treated. Incidentally, the blacking out of the unwanted extracts is almost certain to unbalance the charts, which will consequently lose much of their effect on the jury.

Detailed Reports and Statements of Evidence

When the document examiner knows for certain with which documents he will be required to deal at the hearing, he should prepare such a detailed report on those particular documents that in effect it is practically a statement of evidence. From this detailed report, counsel should be able to ascertain not only the conclusions which have been arrived at, but also everything but the most trivial details of the evidence on which the conclusions are based.

This detailed report should be supplemented by suitable photographs, a fair proportion of which will consist of enlargements of selected portions of the documents examined. If the comparison of handwriting or of typescript is involved, there will probably be, in addition, one or more comparison charts made up of enlarged extracts from the handwriting or typescript placed in juxtaposition so as to facilitate comparison. Comparison charts of this nature are indispensable when the witness wishes to illustrate the grounds upon which his opinion is based. (See Figures 15–1, 15–2.)

It is the responsibility of the document examiner to prepare for the approval of counsel those photographs and charts which he considers he will need for the adequate presentation of his evidence. Close co-operation with counsel is essential, for there may be some documents which are not in dispute but which nevertheless have to be proved formally. In these circumstances any elaborate preparation will be unnecessary, as all that will be required of the witness will be a formal opinion which is unlikely to be challenged.

Although enough enlarged photographs and comparison charts should always be available for a proper presentation of the evidence of the document examiner, nothing is gained if meaningless photographs are produced in an effort to bolster up weak and inconclusive testimony.

Whilst this photographic work is being put in hand, counsel who has no intention

---

Fig. 15–1 (opposite). This is a reduced (approximately half size) photograph of a typical comparison chart produced to illustrate document evidence in court. For the comparison of handwriting a magnification of approximately twice linear is found most appropriate. The sub-script letters and figures associated with each extract on the chart enable its source to be traced in the original documents. In this case a number of cheques purporting to have been written and signed by Miss Cobb were examined and found to be forgeries written by Mrs. Rookyard. The chart illustrates how the writing on the cheques resembles that of Miss Cobb in certain obvious features but is more like that of Mrs. Rookyard in less conspicuous, but none the less important, characteristics. Note, for example (line 10), the close spacing of " ou " in the handwriting of Miss Cobb, but the relatively wide spacing of these letters in the writing on the cheques and that of Mrs. Rookyard.

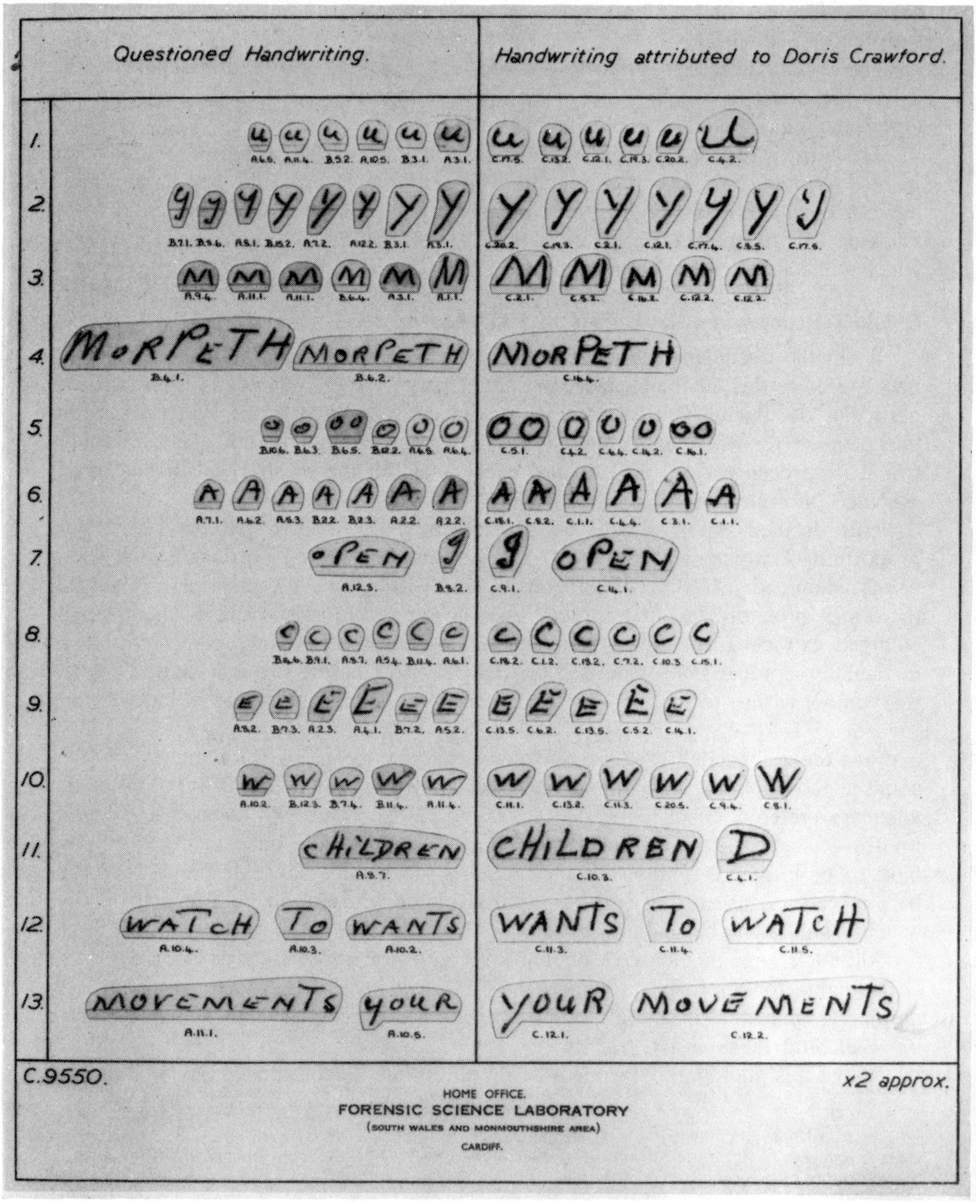

Fig. 15–2. This is a reduced (approximately half size) photograph of a comparison chart produced to illustrate document evidence in court. The case involved the comparison of block lettering taken from a series of anonymous letters. By means of the chart it was possible to show not only the similarity in the design of the letters, but also the relative heights of the letters in the words. The chart also illustrates the occurrence of cursive formations in block letters (see lines 1 and 7).

of leaving everything to his expert witness will have been far from idle. When he realises that technical evidence on documents is likely to play an important part in the case, he will be well advised to undertake some general reading on the subject of document examination, so as to provide himself with a background of knowledge which may serve him in good stead as the case proceeds. He may find some difficulty in securing suitable reading matter, for little of value in the form of textbooks has been written in recent years.

There are, however, some books which will repay study, and a list of some of these is given at the end of this chapter. Another source of up-to-date information are certain law reviews, and those journals which deal with " Police Science " as it is termed in the U.S.A.[1] Whilst textbooks deal more generally with the subject of document examination, the review articles often treat of recent developments which may be of interest to their readers. There is no doubt that the document examiner who is concerned with the case will be in an excellent position to advise and possibly supply counsel with all the reading matter he might require. It goes without saying that any counsel who has acquired some background in this fashion is more likely to appreciate the points made by the document examiner in his detailed report on the documents in the case.[2]

No matter how carefully and comprehensively this report has been drawn up, there will remain some points on which counsel will require further enlightenment. To this end he should draw up a detailed questionnaire to be sent for consideration to the document examiner, who should give his answers in writing. Should these answers fail to afford sufficient clarification, counsel should continue with his questions until he is confident that he possesses an intimate and thorough understanding of the expert evidence which will be at his disposal. During this process of question and answer he will probably have gained a good idea of how this evidence is likely to fare under cross-examination.

One thing that counsel will make sure of from the beginning is that both he and the document examiner are speaking the same language, and he will have taken pains to ensure that he is fully familiar with the exact shade of meaning that the document examiner attaches to all the technical terms he makes use of in his report. Whilst this is highly advisable for the adequate examination of his own witness, a perfect acquaintance with technical terms is essential when any expert called for the other side is being cross-examined, so that counsel cannot be misled by being unaware of the exact meaning attached to any term used by the witness.

1 Articles on various aspects of document examination may be found scattered in a number of journals. In England the *Criminal Law Review* (Sweet & Maxwell, London) publishes a regular series of short articles on aspects of forensic science which includes document examination. In America, articles dealing with document examination appear fairly regularly in the Police Science section of the *Journal of Criminal Law and Criminology* of the North Western University. The *International Criminal Police Review* publishes articles on all aspects of document examination drawn from authors all over the world. This monthly journal is published in several languages but unfortunately is available only to those who are connected with some law-enforcement organisation. Articles written in German appear in the *Archiv Fur Kriminal-Anthropologie-Und Kriminalistik*. The *Gazette of the Royal Canadian Mounted Police* is published monthly and is for the use of accredited police forces only. It occasionally publishes articles on document examination. It is impossible to list all the journals which occasionally publish material which has a bearing on some aspect of document examination. All that can be done by those interested is to follow up any references given in an article.

2 Mitchell, C. A., " Scientific Documentary Evidence in Criminal Trials," *Analyst*, 57, 1932.

When a criminal prosecution in connection with a serious charge is being conducted in England or Wales, it is necessary for the prosecution to establish a prima facie case against the accused at a preliminary hearing before the justices who, if they consider that a case has been made out, will commit the accused to trial before a higher court. As a rule, the evidence given by a document examiner before the justices in the committal stage of a case which is going for trial is rarely more than an expression of his opinion on the documents which are before the court. He does, of course, produce all the enlarged photographs and comparison charts which he intends to use to illustrate the evidence he will be called upon to give in detail at the trial, but will not deal with them in any detail. It is usually considered sufficient if he refers to them as "photographs I have prepared to illustrate some of the more obvious grounds on which I have based my evidence."

It is only occasionally that he will be asked to do more than to indicate, quite briefly, what part the photographs are to play, and to tell the court some of the grounds on which he has formed his opinion, but this evidence is rarely written down to form part of his deposition.

In nearly every instance, the defence will reserve cross-examination. The only exception to this rule is when it is considered that the accused's best interests will be served by an effort to have the case thrown out by the justices. In these circumstances a severe attack may be made on the evidence about the documents. The defending lawyer is invariably in a most difficult position, for he has to cross-examine the expert witness immediately his evidence-in-chief has been concluded. He often has little or no opportunity to consider at any length the evidence he is called upon to challenge, much less to obtain expert assistance in his attack upon it.

It is not surprising that, in these circumstances, the cross-examination is usually restricted to an attack on expert evidence in general and on evidence on documents in particular. It is rarely that the defence succeeds in these tactics and the accused is usually committed for trial.

Counsel is rarely briefed to conduct a prosecution in a higher court until the accused has been committed for trial. He is then supplied with copies of the depositions and of any photographs which have been put in as evidence. It is on this not very satisfactory basis that he has to build his case, for when he reads the deposition of the document examiner he is unlikely to receive a great deal of enlightenment about the case because of its extreme brevity. Even the close study of the photographs and the comparison chart is unlikely to afford any further help, for without some explanation of their nature they will appear little more than a confusing jumble of fragments of handwriting or typescript. Counsel is in approximately the same position as if he were being briefed in a civil action, and had at his disposal little more than the original report of the document examiner. As this is so, his obvious course is to seek further information from the document examiner as described above.

Before the hearing of the case, counsel will probably have a conference with the document examiner, during which any matters which are still doubtful can be cleared up. It sometimes happens that, being human, counsel is dissatisfied with any expression of opinion which is in any way qualified or guarded, because he thinks that qualified opinions tend to weaken his case. It is during this conference that counsel may, and sometimes does, sound the witness as to whether he is willing to use a modified form of words when he is giving his evidence. This new form may be quite acceptable to the witness, and at the same time will assist counsel in the presentation of his case.

Photographs

The preparation of the photographs, which play such an important part in any trial involving expert evidence of documents, has been dealt with in some detail elsewhere in this book, but when considering the presentation of a document case at court, it may be of assistance to recall that the photographs may be divided into four main groups.

Photographs in the first class may be regarded as devices for duplicating the information contained in the documents. There is no reason why every document should not be copied in this way so as to facilitate reference. A cheaply prepared "photostat" is quite adequate for this purpose, and the copying of documents by this or some similar process is best carried out by specialist concerns. It is a waste of money for the document examiner to be required to produce "by hand" numerous copies of a multitude of documents purely for record purposes.

In the second class are those photographs which reproduce the surface of the document so accurately that the reproduction of all the details of any handwriting or typescript thereon is ensured. These photographs should be prepared by the document examiner himself, as it is with the aid of these photographs that his audience will be able to follow and appreciate his verbal evidence. As photographs of this quality are neither cheap nor easy to prepare, their numbers should be strictly limited to what is essential.

The third class of photographs includes all those which might be termed "specialist" productions, *i.e.,* those taken by ultra-violet, infra-red, transmitted or oblique lighting. It is likely that only selected portions of some of the documents will be treated in this way.

The fourth group consists of composite photographs prepared for demonstration. The majority of these will consist of comparison charts, whereon enlarged extracts from different documents are mounted in juxtaposition to facilitate comparison. This class will also include those composite photographs in which a transparency prepared from one document is mounted so that it coincides with a photograph of an extract, usually a traced signature, from another document to demonstrate beyond any question the exact correspondence which exists. These composite photographs are indispensable for proving traced forgeries, as there is no other way in which the facts can be made so manifest.

These two latter groups of photographs must be the work of the document examiner himself, for they form an essential part of his evidence.

As the evidence on the documents is being unfolded, certain features of the handwriting or typescript illustrated in the photographs have to be brought to the attention of the court whilst their significance is being explained. In order to accomplish this, some experienced witnesses advise the preparation of a single very large specimen of each photograph. These photographs, which may be as much as several feet across, are erected on an easel in the court so that they can easily be seen by judge, counsel and jury. While testifying, the witness stands by the easel and uses a pointer to indicate those features to which he wishes to call the attention of the court.

At first sight, this idea may seem to have a great deal to recommend it as preferable to the preparation of sets of much smaller photographs which are supplied to each individual concerned in the case. It is much quicker and easier to indicate with a pointer on a large picture of the document the exact feature being considered than it is to describe its position on a sheet held in the hand; for when these individual photographs are used, there is invariably some delay while everybody finds the place, no matter how careful and detailed the description. Another advantage which is possessed by the single large photograph is that everybody can concentrate his attention on the person who is addressing him, and at the same time follow what is being pointed out. The attention is not divided as it is when the eyes have to be switched backwards and forwards from the speaker to photographs held in the hand.

Attractive though this idea of using large photographs on an easel may appear at first sight, it would prove quite impracticable in the great majority of British courts. It would be difficult to carry out such a demonstration from any witness-box however well it might be situated, and in many courts it would be impossible to find any position from which all concerned could watch the demonstration and hear the witness at the same time. In many of the older courts, the lighting is poor, and because of defective acoustics it has been found necessary for judge, counsel, jury and witness to be placed very close together if all concerned are to hear all that goes on during the trial.

Even if the conditions in the courts are ideal, one serious objection could still be taken to this scheme. Many jurors have defective eyesight, and whilst everybody will take sufficient trouble to be fitted with spectacles which will enable him to read a newspaper, most people are not so particular in making sure that their distant vision is equally effective. On an average jury it is probable that there would be at least two persons who would be quite unable to distinguish any but the crudest features on an enlarged photograph viewed at a distance, no matter what degree of magnification were employed.

As already mentioned, the alternative to the single large chart is the preparation of a number of small charts which can be held in the hand.[3] Witness, counsel and judge are supplied with their own copies, but the jury are given only one between every two. This is not merely for economy. Experience has shown that the most serious objection to the use of individual charts is the complete inability of some people to take in and act on oral instructions, no matter how carefully worded and detailed they may be. If each member of the jury is provided with his own chart, there is invariably considerable delay before the witness can be sure that all have identified any new character he refers to at any time. If two jurymen share a chart, then one of each pair can be relied on to find the place fairly quickly and so delay is minimised.

[3] Hilton, O., Doud, D., and Hall, G. E., " Elements of Effective Expert Testimony and Compensation for Expert Witness " (*Journal of Forensic Sciences,* 2 (1), 73, January, 1957).

This difficulty in finding a place on a chart is why great care should be taken when comparison charts are being drawn up. They should never be overloaded with material, for too much on a chart is more likely to cause confusion than result in enlightenment. It is far preferable to produce three simple charts, each of which deals with one aspect of the evidence, than to make an effort to include everything on a single chart.

The witness should always bear in mind that a shorthand note may be taken while he is giving evidence and that it is on this note alone that a higher court will have to work when considering his evidence in the event of an appeal. The judges sitting in the appellate court will not have had the opportunity of watching the witness while he was pointing out features shown in the enlarged photographs, so that unless great care is taken while the evidence is being given, much of what is taken down by the shorthand writer will be quite incomprehensible to the appellate court.

Every comparison chart of photographs produced in evidence should be clearly titled, and the lines and columns thereon lettered and numbered. When any feature shown in a photograph is mentioned in evidence, the title of the photograph, as well as the line and column where that feature appears should be referred to, so that it can be written into the record.

It may be thought advisable to indicate certain places on the photographs by marks applied by the document examiner. This is a dangerous practice, because a successful objection may be made to the marked photographs on the grounds that they are no longer true records of what appears on the document. If the marks are obviously an addition and cannot be confused with the photograph proper, then it may be submitted that any such objection is unreasonable and raised solely in the hope of excluding unwelcome evidence. If the marking of photographs cannot be avoided, it is best to use red ink for this purpose. As red ink is simply an aqueous solution of one or more red dyes, it merely tints the photograph and cannot be said to obscure any features of the photograph, the whole of which can clearly be seen through the red ink line. Even when red ink is used as a marking medium, marks on the photograph itself should be kept to a minimum; the mount which surrounds the photograph is the obvious place on which to write titles, and any other marks of identification.

Every photograph produced should bear an indication of the degree of enlargement. An approximate value is quite satisfactory because, owing to the change in the dimensions of paper when treated with aqueous solutions and subsequently dried, a definite figure is not justified. It is, however, a good idea to have included in the photograph a scale which may be used should it be thought desirable to make a more exact determination of the degree of enlargement employed. The figure which is quoted for the enlargement will refer to the degree of linear enlargement, so that an enlargement of three times or 3X, as it is usually written, will mean that every line of the photograph is three times as long as it is in the original document. It is not generally realised that this means that every area on the photograph is no less than nine times as great as on the original. Sometimes a request is made for photographs to be enlarged " five times." If this is carried out literally, the recipient of the final print is very surprised when he receives something twenty-five times as big as the original, when what he really wanted was an enlargement of just over twice.

For the appreciation of the details of the structure of handwriting, an enlargement of about twice is ample, but a little more may be given when typescript is concerned.

One of the mistakes made by the inexperienced is the use of too great a magnification for the purpose in hand. Unless greatly enlarged photographs are severely restricted in the amount of handwriting or typescript they display, they tend to become very unwieldy in use, and too much magnification of handwriting will cause the attention to stray from the significant details of letter design to the fortuitous variations in the structure of ink lines which are present in all handwriting, and which may have very little to do with the investigation.

Where forged signatures are concerned, the position is very different. Here, within reason, it is difficult to effect too great an enlargement because the greater the magnification, the more does the appearance of a carefully written forgery depart from that of a genuine signature. Forged signatures should be enlarged at least five times, even if a special mount has to be made to accommodate the finished print. A device which does away with the necessity of using a very large rigid mount is to photograph the signature on a single negative, but to print it in two portions with a generous overlap at the join. Still separate, the two prints are mounted together so that when they are opened out one overlaps the other and shows the signature as a whole.

It is advisable for all the special photographs submitted by the document examiner to be mounted on a folder or bound into an album. The author has found it most convenient to have all the individual photographs he produces mounted on to a green cardboard folder, which when closed measures twelve and a half inches by eighteen. When opened out, this folder gives an area of twenty-five by eighteen inches, which is large enough to enable a fair number of photographs to be accommodated. This relatively large area obviates some of the confusion which results when comparisons have to be made between photographs mounted on a multitude of smaller sheets bound into an album.

Should this area be insufficient to accommodate all the photographs required, extra cards each twelve by seventeen inches are inserted in the folder, and secured in place by string tags which run through small holes punched in the cards and the folder. Instead of these tags, the extra card can be fixed in position with adhesive tape.

It is inadvisable to have the folder any larger than the size recommended, because it becomes awkward to handle within the confines of the average jury-box. When photographs are mounted in this way, not only are they kept together, but it is possible to give each photograph an identifying mark on the card mount alongside it.

Comparison charts should be limited to a size of twelve by eighteen inches, when one will fill one side of the folder. If the magnification of the extracts is about one and a half to twice as previously recommended, each chart will hold sufficient material to be convincing, and yet not appear to be overcrowded and difficult to follow when the evidence is being given.

Presentation of Specialised Photographs to Jury

When counsel is making his opening statement to the court he will often hand to the jury photographs of the documents with which he is dealing so that they can more conveniently follow what he is saying. These photographs are proved at a later stage by one of the witnesses.

Whilst there is no harm in putting in these ordinary photographs at this stage, experience has shown that it is inadvisable for him to give the jury copies of any specialised photographs, such as enlargements of portions of the documents or comparison charts, while he is opening his case. If counsel puts these in and endeavours to explain their significance in any detail, he will be giving evidence which by right should come from the document examiner who will probably be in a better position than counsel to deal with these matters. If, on the other hand, they are put in with but a modicum of explanation, some members of the jury will almost certainly give their attention to the photographs rather than to what they are being told about the case.

It is good practice to hold back any specialised photographs until both counsel and expert witness are in a position to deal thoroughly with them. If it proves necessary to put in a whole album or folder of photographs in order to refer to one or two of them, before it is convenient to deal with the remainder, counsel should suggest to the jury that they pay no attention to any but those being referred to.

Evidence Obtained through Examination by Oblique Lighting

Much of the obloquy which in the past attached to evidence on documents stemmed from its being almost entirely intuitive and subjective. Today the pendulum has swung so far the other way that many consider that what cannot be demonstrated about a document is not reliable evidence. This healthy doctrine cannot be applied in its entirety, for there is one exception to this rule. This has to do with the examination of documents for impressions made by writing or typing which has either been erased, or embossed from writing or typescript from another sheet which was in close contact with that bearing the impressions.

As described elsewhere, these impressions are best seen to advantage when the light is thrown across the surface of the document at grazing incidence—sometimes termed oblique lighting—at right angles to the line of the impressions. This means that it is often impossible to make a really satisfactory photograph of impressions on paper, for all that will properly be reproduced will be those impressions which were favourably situated with respect to the direction of the light when the exposure was made. Impressions are best observed by lighting the document a little at a time with a lamp held in the hand and moved about so as to bring into successive prominence all the impressions on the area being examined. The eye can register and the brain integrate to form recognisable letters and figures from the succession of changing shadow patterns made by the moving light. For these reasons, a witness who is testifying on the interpretation of impressions can often only state what he has observed, and may be unable to produce any really satisfactory demonstration material to support his recollection and interpretation.

It is unfortunate that matters are aggravated by the relative impermanence of impressions. No matter how carefully a document is preserved, the impressions tend to smooth out and eventually disappear with the passage of time. Should the document be subjected to handling, this process is accelerated until very little may remain of the original impressions when the case comes for trial. Impressions are far more difficult to interpret than is generally considered, so that any attempt to demonstrate their existence to a court is almost certain to fail, as even under the optimum conditions of controlled lighting even a practised observer may find difficulty in seeing them.

A magnifying glass is worse than useless for revealing the presence of shallow impressions, and should either the judge or any member of the jury produce a glass with the obvious intention of making a search, counsel should be quick to dissuade him. If this cannot be done by his pointing out that special conditions of lighting rather than magnification are called for, failure to observe anything with the magnifying glass will leave the observer with the conviction that there never were any impressions on the document. This is no exaggeration, because the author has seen more than one fruitless search for impressions conducted in the course of a trial with the aid of a magnifying glass. In every case, the searcher was convinced that there were no impressions on the document.

The Use of Instruments in Court

Some document examiners, invariably the least experienced, arrive in court armed with an array of instruments, including high-power microscopes, which they invite the judge and jury to use for themselves and so obtain confirmation of their findings. The use of a microscope requires special lighting which is rarely available, but much more to the point, it demands some experience in the art of managing this by no means simple piece of apparatus. The average juror is quite incapable of observing anything with a microscope, for even if the instrument were perfectly focused for him to use, he would be very unlikely to be able to interpret what he saw. It is impossible for the inexperienced to realise that the whole of the field covered with a high-power objective is a tiny area no larger than one of the full stops on this page of print.

High-power microscopes are sometimes necessary for the examination of documents, but their place is in the laboratory rather than the court. If anything observable only with a microscope has to be shown to the court, the proper course is to prepare a photomicrograph, which all can examine with the naked eye and which needs no training for its comprehension.

The only instruments which should be taken into court are a graduated metal scale and a hand magnifier. The metal scale is useful for making rough measurements and for checking alignments on documents which might be handed up for inspection. As the lighting in courts is poor, the best type of magnifier is one which incorporates an electric torch which is arranged so that its light falls on the place on which the lens system is focused.

Whilst it is inadvisable for scientific instruments to be brought into court for the use of those unaccustomed to them, certain instruments should be available for the use of the document examiner. This is because it may become necessary to make an examination of documents produced for the first time during the hearing.

Although a high-power microscope is rarely required, and in any case is cumbersome to transport, a good stereoscopic microscope which can be safely and easily carried in its case will enable practically any " on-the-spot " examination to be carried out. The question of illumination is easily solved by the use of an electric torch. Unlike high-power microscopes, stereoscopic microscopes have a long working distance, which enables a torch to be used. All that is required in addition to the torch and the microscope is a chair and a table. Even the simplest stereoscopic microscope is preferable to the best pocket magnifier which has a restricted field of view and does not give a stereoscopic image.

Should there be any prospect of typescript having to be examined, one or two of the special scales made on glass by a photographic process as described elsewhere should be available.

It is a mistake to attempt to set up in court apparatus such as the ultra-violet or the infra-red viewer described elsewhere. Whilst it may be possible to get the apparatus to work after a fashion, courtrooms are not laboratories, so that the apparatus has to be manipulated under unfavourable conditions. Most apparatus is designed for the use of but one or two persons at a time, so that any attempt to put on a mass demonstration is doomed to failure. Any failure is invariably attributed to the apparatus, the operator, or the method, rather than to the conditions under which the apparatus has to be used, so that an unconvincing demonstration is liable seriously to reduce the value of the other evidence associated with it. Any phenomenon which can be observed with the aid of the apparatus mentioned above is best demonstrated by means of photographs. Portable ultra-violet lamps for use outside the court can be plugged into the electric light mains, but difficulty may be experienced in finding a suitable dark room. This problem can sometimes be solved by the use of a few rugs allied with some ingenuity on the part of the experimenter.

Nothing else in the way of apparatus need be taken to a court hearing, because no matter how simple and portable any individual item may be, the total weight of reference books, microscope, torch and portable ultra-violet lamp is bound to be formidable.

The witness, and counsel as well, should provide themselves with pads of unlined paper about a foot square on which can be roughed-out any drawings to be shown to the court in the course of evidence, should there arise any point which needs the assistance of a sketch to make it clear. Ordinary pens and pencils are useless for making these sketches, as the thin lines they make cannot easily be seen across a court in poor light. Thick leaded pencils, or better still, wax crayons, are ideal for they can be used to make a line of any desired thickness. Two contrasting colours should be chosen so that, where necessary, different strokes can be rendered in easily distinguishable colours.

Reference Books

Copies of standard works on the subject of document examination should be available in court. It is important that these should be the most recent editions because sometimes authors modify their views in the light of greater experience. It may well happen that the other side may make use of a statement in one of these earlier editions to support their theories.

Where this is done, it is useful to have that book available, because a quick reference may show that what is being quoted is substantially modified in some other paragraph or a later edition. This material for cross-examination might not have been available had the book not been in court. It is the responsibility of the document examiner to see that all suitable reference books are in court, and from his experience he should know whether any quotation from them is fair and reasonable. If it is not, then it is to him that counsel will look for information as to how best he can deal with it in cross-examination.

Examination-in-chief

There is some difference of opinion among experienced counsel as to how the examination-in-chief of a document examiner should be conducted, but whichever course is taken, there are certain preliminaries which cannot be dispensed with.

The document examiner must establish his status as an expert by giving the court information as to his qualifications and experience. How much it is thought desirable to do in this connection will depend largely on the witness. Should he occupy an official position as a document examiner he will naturally be treated somewhat more summarily than if he were comparatively unknown and in private practice.

Where official experts are concerned, most counsel just ask for university degrees, the nature of the official position and the number of years' experience in the examination of documents. In the author's experience, even this is sometimes abbreviated to a single question about the official position he holds, and hitherto there has never been any question raised as to whether this is sufficient to establish his status as an expert witness on documents. Other counsel take a different view, and expand this phase of the examination-in-chief. They bring out in evidence the scope of the work he undertakes; the names of the various official bodies such as the police, Government Departments, the armed forces, etc., for whom he undertakes this work; the official training courses at which he lectures on document examination to detective officers; and the journals for which he writes articles. Whilst the matter is one for counsel, it is probable that time spent in acquainting the jury with the status, experience and other qualifications of the expert witness they are to hear is never wasted, especially when both sides happen to call experts whose views are not in complete agreement.

Once the status of the expert witness has been established, the documents on which he has reported are put to him for identification. It is at this point that there is a serious difference of opinion among counsel as to the best procedure. Some counsel at once ask the witness whether he has reached any opinion on the documents and, if so, to tell the court what it is. They leave any discussion or demonstration of the grounds on which the opinion is based until afterwards.

Others embark on a different course. Instead of asking the witness for any opinion, they take him through the documents in great detail so that he has ample opportunity to explain to the court all the factors he considers significant. It is only when the court has been fully informed as to the nature of the documents and the examination which has been carried out that the witness is asked to express any opinion whatsoever. Counsel who advocate this procedure consider that by the time the witness has described the documents and the examinations and comparisons he has carried out, the minds of the jury will have been prepared to receive the final opinion as reasonable, if they have not already arrived at the same conclusions of their own volition.

There is no doubt that once a jury has been successfully indoctrinated in this way, so that they hear the final opinion as merely a confirmation of their own conclusions, it is unlikely that any contrary opinion from another expert witness or any appeal from counsel on the other side is likely to shake their belief. Whilst extremely effective, this course demands much of counsel, who must not only acquire a complete understanding of the expert evidence he is to present, but be an adept at the unfolding of evidence in a manner and at a rate which keeps pace with the collective understanding of the jury.

Some counsel combine these two lines of approach. They ask for an opinion at the outset, work steadily through the evidence which supports it, and then ask the witness to summarise his findings at the end of the evidence.

For what it is worth, it is the opinion of the author that where the witness is to express an opinion which, to the average layman, may at first sight seem to contradict his own observation and common sense, it is better to reserve the opinion until the minds of the jurymen have been conditioned by careful preparation.

Consider, for example, two specimens of handwriting by the same person, one written in a normal manner but the other disguised by the adoption of a much different slope. At first sight, to a layman, these two specimens of handwriting will appear to have nothing in common, as their general appearance will be so different. It will come as a shock to the average juryman to be presented with photographs of these two specimens of writing and straightway to be told by a witness that both were written by the same person. The tendency will be for his mind to recoil from the idea, and once this has happened it will be difficult to persuade him to consider any evidence which might force him to change his mind. Once a juryman has made up his mind, it is very difficult to eradicate his first impressions and substitute something quite different.

If, however, the two writings are shown to him without any indication as to the conclusions reached by the witness, he will probably examine them with some interest while he is being shown a number of what are to him unsuspected resemblances in their structure. If this process is continued and he is persuaded to look further into the writing than its superficial appearance, it will gradually dawn on him that, in spite of their unlike appearance, the two writings have a great deal in common. Eventually he will not be surprised to hear and may readily accept the opinion of the witness that the two writings are very probably the work of a single person, and that the differences which they exhibit are superficial only, being due to disguise having been introduced into one of them.

Traced forgeries offer an even better illustration. A tracing, by its very nature, must appear very similar to a genuine signature, and few jurymen are willing to accept any opinion that such apparently flawless signatures are fraudulent, unless it has first been explained to them that this perfection in letter design is just what must be expected in a forgery made by tracing. If, instead of offering a jury an opinion which is bound to surprise them, counsel opens with a discussion of the methods whereby traced forgeries are made, the jury will be on the alert for and will be suspicious of that very deceptive appearance of perfection which otherwise would have closed their minds to the truth.

It does not always rest with counsel as to which course should be adopted. On occasion, once the documents have been put to the witness some judges interpose to ask whether he has formed any definite opinion on them. Once this opinion has been given, they tell the witness that, if necessary, he can give his reasons when he is being cross-examined. When this course is taken by the judge, there is little counsel can do, except possibly in re-examination, to show the jury the grounds on which the witness has reached his opinion. It may be that these judges think that once a properly qualified and experienced expert witness has reached a definite opinion, the jury should give that opinion full weight, and that they are unlikely to be any wiser and more able to give a just verdict, even if the whole matter were to be placed before them in detail. Other judges take a different view, and in cases where counsel has done little more than ask for an opinion, invite the witness to explain to the court the grounds and the reasoning by which the opinion was arrived at.

Whatever may be the private views of a witness, it is a matter for counsel as to how the expert evidence is to be presented, for he alone is in a position to fit the evidence into the case as a whole. He will know which of the expert's findings should be stressed and what can be left with the most cursory treatment.

Disclosure of Inconvenient Facts

Whenever a fair-sized group of genuine signatures is examined, a few will be found to exhibit features which at first sight might be regarded as evidence that they are not genuine, should there arise any question as to their authenticity. In a similar way, if two specimens of handwriting by the same person are critically examined, certain differences, all of which are capable of reasonable explanation, will be sure to be found.

A document investigation where all the evidence points unmistakably the same way is comparatively rare. It is most important that witness and counsel discuss any difficulties that may require explanation and come to a definite understanding as to how these should be dealt with when evidence-in-chief is being given. Some counsel take the view that as any apparently divergent features are capable of reasonable explanation and consequently do not affect the truth of their contentions, they should not be referred to in evidence-in-chief. They consider that any disclosure of features which need to be explained away may provide the other side with ammunition for cross-examination, of whose existence they might otherwise have remained in ignorance. When this view is taken, the expert witness has no option but to follow the lead given by counsel whatever his own views may be.

Other counsel take the opposite view that the sooner any objections which might be raised by the other side are brought to light and adequately dealt with the better. They consider that any apparent contradictions to their thesis can most satisfactorily be explained away by their own expert witness when he is being examined by his own counsel, so that he can take his time and deal with the matter fully. If this course is followed, the impact of the discovery of what might at first sight appear to be contradictory facts can be toned down and they can be disposed of without undue prominence being given to them. Should they be again referred to when the witness is cross-examined, he can truthfully reply that he has neither overlooked them in his examination of the documents or tried to conceal their existence in his evidence-in-chief.

In many ways this is far better for the witness than having apparent contradictions revealed for the first time in cross-examination, when any explanation given in the face of a hostile counsel is made to take on the appearance of an excuse either for his failure to observe them during his examination of the documents, or for his attempt to conceal them until questioned on the point by his opponents.

Matters may be even worse if the apparent contradictions are glossed over during cross-examination and then produced with an air of triumph by the expert called by the other side, who will be given every encouragement to develop his theme before an interested court before he can be cross-examined. Even the most vigorous cross-examination is unlikely to dispose of the matter in as satisfactory a fashion as a full disclosure at the earliest opportunity.

Determination of Line of Attack on Conclusions

It is during cross-examination that an expert witness gains his first idea as to the evidence which is likely to be given on the other side, so that he should be alert for any indication which might be given. It is probable that if photographs have been prepared by an expert witness who is to be called at a later stage, these will be shown to him during his cross-examination when he is being questioned on some feature they are alleged to illustrate. He should neglect no opportunity of making as complete an examination as possible in the time available, especially if the photographs take the form of comparison charts, for it is unlikely that anything thereon will have been included without good reason. In this way he may be able to glean sufficient information to ensure that his counsel is not taken completely by surprise when he hears the testimony given by the opposing expert witness.

In criminal prosecutions, the prosecution are bound to disclose the conclusions of their expert witnesses, and also supply the defence with copies of any photographs they intend to put in. All this has to be done in good time, so that the defence have ample opportunity to study the case they have to meet. They can consult their own expert advisers, who need not disclose their views until they are called to give their evidence. There is rarely any time for the views expressed by the expert witnesses called by the defence to be considered in any detail, or for any photographs they produce to be subjected to critical examination. As soon as the defence experts have completed their evidence, prosecuting counsel has to rise and cross-examine without having any opportunity for consultation with his own expert advisers, unless he has been very fortunate with the timing of the case. If the court should adjourn at the completion of the examination-in-chief, counsel may be considered fortunate as he will have some time for consideration of the evidence.

It is where counsel has to cross-examine at once that the value of careful preparation on his part becomes apparent. If he has discussed the technical details of the case very fully with his own expert and has also provided himself with a background by reading, a few words with his expert will be all that is necessary to start him off on an effective cross-examination.

Under certain circumstances, counsel may be able to recall his own expert witness to give evidence in rebuttal. This seems to be a very rare practice, as the author has been called upon to give evidence in rebuttal only once in a period of over twenty years' experience in the courts. The possibility of calling evidence in rebuttal does nothing to relieve counsel of his burden, for should he, by means of a vigorous cross-examination, succeed in confounding the witness and show him to be both incompetent and mistaken in his views, this will have a much greater effect than any expression of a conflicting opinion by his own witness.

Cross-Examination

Many books have been written on the difficult art of cross-examination, but when they come to deal with the cross-examination of expert witnesses, the authors generally content themselves with the remark that counsel should be wary of pursuing an expert witness on to his own ground. This is accompanied by the warning that most expert witnesses have had considerable experience of cross-examination, so that any question put to them at random may elicit an answer which counsel is unlikely to relish.

It is true that if counsel is himself calling expert evidence he can expect to receive a certain amount of technical assistance and possibly some helpful suggestions for cross-examination from his own expert, but this does little to relieve him of his onerous duty.

Incidentally, when seeking advice from his own expert, an experienced counsel will probably insist that everything shall be put in writing, whether answers to his own queries or suggested questions to be put to the expert on the other side. It goes without saying that all these suggested questions should be accompanied by the answers they should bring forth.

When dealing with expert witnesses who are testifying on scientific subjects such as chemistry, physics and medicine, counsel is usually at a double disadvantage. In the first place, it is very unlikely that anybody but the expert witness has had any opportunity of examining the material on which the evidence is being given, so that counsel has had to rely upon the witness, not only for the opinion which he is giving in evidence, but also for the facts upon which this opinion has been based. Indeed, in the majority of cases, even if the material were before the court, counsel would probably be little wiser. Secondly, most branches of science have their own highly specialised vocabularies, which are made more difficult by the fact that many of the terms used do not necessarily bear their everyday meaning when used in a specialised context. The use of a specialised vocabulary cannot very well be avoided, for it would be unreasonable to ask these experts to confine themselves to the use of everyday language which is rarely sufficiently precise for their purpose.

Where expert evidence on documents is concerned, the case is entirely different, and no counsel, even if unprovided with expert assistance, need feel diffident about his ability to submit any witness tendering expert evidence on documents to a searching cross-examination. In the first place, counsel will have the inestimable advantage of having the actual material the witness is dealing with displayed before his eyes, so that there need be no dispute about the *facts* which everybody present can observe for himself at first hand. Added to this, documents are so common a feature of everyday life that, with the possible exception of a few technical terms all of which are capable of simple explanation, the whole of the expert evidence can be given in language which everybody can understand. It is because of this that a fair proportion of the testimony in a contested document case can be removed from the sphere of opinion to become a demonstration of facts which are made patent to all.

As cross-examination should invariably be directed towards the detection and exposure of error, it may be helpful to list those sources of error most frequently encountered.

The first type of error is encountered when incorrect positive identifications have been made. The commonest examples are forged signatures which are declared to be genuine, or handwriting attributed to the wrong person.

The reasons for falling into this type of error may be summarised as follows:

(a) basing conclusions on those general features which are to be found in the majority of handwritings but which have incorrectly been assumed to be individual characteristics of the handwriting in question;
(b) failing to observe inconspicuous features of the handwriting in question which would point away from its having been written by the person to whom it was incorrectly attributed;
(c) interpreting consistently different characteristics as being due either to variation or disguise, whereas they really point to different authorship.

The second type of error is the reverse of the first in that genuine signatures are declared to be forgeries, or that handwriting is not that of the actual writer.

The reasons for falling into this type of error may be summarised as follows:

(a) failing to take into account the effects on handwriting of differences in age, mental and physical condition and the conditions under which it was written;
(b) misinterpreting differences which are due to natural variation or accidental formation and treating them as evidence of different authorship.

Errors in general may be due either to incompetence or to deliberate testifying against the facts caused by enthusiasm for a cause or for profit. Over confidence may also cause error, in that definite conclusions are reached on material which is too scanty to justify any definite opinion being given.

Competence of Witnesses

Incompetence

There is no doubt that incompetence lies at the root of the greater part of any incorrect testimony which may be given on documents, so that time and effort spent on probing the qualifications of any witness whose standing has not been established, is rarely wasted.

For most branches of science there are well recognised standards of attainment, such as university degrees or the membership of learned societies, which may confer on a man a prima facie right to speak as an expert, but unfortunately this is not yet the case where document examination is concerned. No recognised university college conducts courses or grants degrees in document examination, nor is there yet in this country any learned society, membership of which may safely be assumed to confer a recognised status as a document examiner. The unfortunate result is that the courts are open to anyone who chooses to style himself a document examiner or handwriting expert, whether he knows anything about the subject or not. It is due to the mistakes of these incompetents, whose pretensions have not been exposed by ruthless cross-examination, that serious miscarriages of justice have occurred and the impression is abroad that in any case involving the examination of documents there may be as many different opinions as there are expert witnesses.

The truth is that, owing to the fact that all the material is before the court, there is probably less conflict of opinion between *honest and competent* document examiners than exists between experts in any other field. In many of the highly publicised cases where there has been a serious conflict of opinion, it will generally be found that at least one of the so-called experts is qualified neither by experience nor training to express a worthwhile opinion. In some countries it is the practice to call such men in apparently hopeless cases in order to establish a "conflict of opinion," which can be used as the basis of an appeal to the jury to enable guilty persons to escape conviction. Otherwise it is difficult to account for the appearance time and time again of the same men who invariably stoutly maintain that the experts called for the prosecution are wrong in their conclusions. Some of these are by no means incompetent, so that they undoubtedly fall into the category of those who are prepared to testify against what they must recognise as the facts, and it is they who justify the sneer that an expert can always be found who will find similarities or dissimilarities in any two handwritings according to order. Many of these so-called experts have an assured manner and give evidence garnished with a profusion of high-sounding technical terms designed to hide their ignorance and impress a jury. It sometimes happens that once their entire lack of any qualifications has been exposed to the jury, there is no longer any need to waste any time on cross-examination of their findings. The cross-examination to this end may be considered under the following headings.

Membership of Societies and Diplomas

Practically anyone may obtain membership of certain scientific societies, some of which are of high repute, by application in the right quarter or even merely by the payment of a fee. For example, the Fellowship of the Chemical Society, a most reputable society, may be obtained by nomination and the payment of a fee which helps to finance the famous Journal of the Society, but fellowship of this Society is no guarantee of any standing in the world of science. Much the same state of affairs holds for the membership of certain other societies, less well known than the Chemical Society.

Certain foreign police forces have forensic science laboratories where persons of little or no scientific experience may work in some capacity or other and eventually qualify for a diploma. It is not suggested that all such diplomas are valueless, but they should never be taken at their face value until a searching inquiry has been made as to what course of study has to be undertaken to qualify for them, and how it relates, if at all, to the study of documents. This latter point is important. If a witness states that he is a Fellow of the Royal Photographic Society, this should be enough to establish his status as a photographer if he is merely producing photographs of documents. It will not serve to qualify him as an examiner of handwriting. All too often men who are experienced photographers come into the witness-box and produce photographs. If there appears little chance of their conclusions being challenged they go on from there to offer opinions on handwriting or typewriting. If they should be cross-examined, they speedily retreat into the position that they are only pointing out something shown on the photographs which they consider to be of some interest to the court.

Experience

Time is rarely better spent than in probing the meaning which is given by the self-styled expert to the term "experience," which is invariably claimed to cover the lack of any other qualification. These claims are generally greatly exaggerated, so inquiry should first be made as to whether the term of years mentioned in evidence-in-chief refers to the time during which the witness has considered himself to have been an expert or whether it includes a period devoted to training. If this is the case, the training period can be subtracted from the original claim. If, on the other hand, the period mentioned is that over which the witness claims to have worked as an expert, the number of years spent in training should be ascertained, and the total subtracted from the witness's age if he appears to be fairly young. The result of this calculation will usually show that the study was begun at a very tender age!

Owing to the limited amount of work available, very few persons can make a whole-time living as document examiners, so that questions as to what other occupations have been followed will often reveal that document examination has occupied only a small proportion of their attention over the years they have claimed were devoted to it.

Experience may prove to be only an opportunity for repeating one's mistakes unless the correctness of any opinions expressed can be checked in some measure against the facts. As this is so, the witness should be asked how many opinions on document examinations he expresses in an average year and what percentage of these he has been able to check for accuracy. It is obvious that few experts in private practice in this country have any opportunity of checking the accuracy of their opinions, which is perhaps unfortunate as some of them might thereby learn whether they were becoming more proficient with increasing experience or not.

Those who are in the fortunate position of working in one of the British Home Office Forensic Science Laboratories are at least able to make a partial check on the accuracy of their findings. This is because they are usually consulted very early in the inquiries into the very numerous cases of fraud, forgery and anonymous letter writing which arise. At this stage their work often takes the form of sifting the handwritings of very many possible suspects in an effort to narrow the subsequent investigations by the police. A fair proportion of these cases, where the most likely forger or writer of anonymous letters is picked out, end in confessions by the guilty parties, so that the document examiner concerned can be sure that his opinions as to the authorship of handwriting or the authenticity of a signature were correct in these cases at least. In some of the remaining cases, where no confession of guilt has been forthcoming, other evidence is discovered which confirms the original findings of the document examiners.

Experimental Material

If the witness can be induced to agree that document examination is a study which can only be firmly established on a basis of experiment, he should be asked the source of the large number of handwriting specimens he must have had available to enable him to familiarise himself with the raw material of handwriting comparison. Whilst it may be a simple matter to obtain large amounts of ordinary handwriting, it is by no means easy to get hold of specimens written by large numbers of people under different conditions such as fast, slow, and medium speed, with the left hand and the right, in both normal and disguised hands. The study of books is no satisfactory substitute for this practical experience with the actual materials.

Graphologists

There can be no doubt that every handwriting does, to some extent at least, reflect the personality of the writer. A neat and elegant handwriting is more likely to be the work of someone who has at least a modicum of artistic ability, muscular control and careful habits than that of a person who is entirely lacking in these respects. It is when efforts are made to extend general conclusions and a detailed character analysis is attempted from the consideration of small amounts of handwriting—sometimes a single signature seems to be all that is needed—that the graphologist lays himself open to criticism.

There are different schools of graphology, each with its adherents, who stoutly maintain that theirs and theirs alone are the true principles on which correct conclusions can be reached. Many of the books which have been written, either on graphology or on the psychology of handwriting, seem to have only one feature in common—whilst the preliminary chapters appear reasonable enough, the arguments employed become increasingly vague as they are developed in greater detail, until finally it becomes obvious that the majority of the conclusions of any graphologist must be reached by intuitive methods, since they appear to have little or no experimental foundation.

In most of these books, the illustrations are almost wholly confined to the signatures of well-known people. Certain features which are to be found in these rather limited handwriting specimens are then correlated with the characters and known abilities of the writers. It is not denied that this correlation may have some basis in fact, but the argument would have much greater force if it were also shown that similar features were common in the signatures of practically all the people of similar abilities and traits of character, but were never present in the signatures of those who were not similarly endowed.

It is unlikely that graphology will ever be raised to the status of an experimental science because of the formidable difficulties certain to be encountered in assembling and analysing numerous specimens of the handwriting of a great many people whose character and capabilities, both realised and latent, are known. This would be an essential preliminary if the principles on which character assessment is to be accomplished are to be sufficiently reliable to allow the conclusions of graphologists to be seriously considered in the courts.

If a witness proclaims himself a follower of any school of graphology, he should be asked if he can guarantee to determine the sex of a writer from handwriting. This, one would think, should be an easy task for any graphologist who professes to be able to deduce so much from so little in the way of handwriting, but this test is never likely to be accepted. It is perhaps uncharitable to conclude that this simple request is invariably refused because the conclusion reached by the graphologist in this case can so easily be checked.

Authorship as a Qualification

The claim to expert status as a document examiner is sometimes bolstered up by the witness claiming to have published articles or even books which refer to the scientific examination of documents. This impressive claim should be scrutinised with care, because it is quite a simple matter to get articles or even books published without the author possessing more than a superficial knowledge of the subject he is treating.

Details of the publications in which the articles have appeared should be sought, as well as the titles. The answers may show merely that the witness was able to write in a sufficiently facile manner to ensure the publication of articles of merely popular interest in periodicals whose mission is to entertain rather than instruct. At the same time, he might be asked if he had written on other subjects, and if he has done so, whether he poses as an expert on these as well.

Any scientific book published by a reputable firm is almost certain to have been reviewed in *The Analyst* or in the *Journal of the Medico-Legal Society,* if it has any substantial forensic interest. In the U.S.A. it will probably have been reviewed in the Police Science section of the *Journal of Criminal Law, Criminology and Police Science,* North Western University.

If the book is unsatisfactory in any respect, the reviewers in these journals may be counted upon to say so. If unfavourable reviews in these journals are discovered, it may be as well to have them at hand so that the witness may be challenged with them; certain authors have proved to have had very poor memories for any unfavourable reviews of their works when being cross-examined.

If possible, the books published by the witness should be inspected, for much may be learned about the author from the preface. This may contain gross exaggerations of his prowess and experience, which should prove embarrassing to a boastful witness when he is asked to justify his claims. Added to this, there is always the possibility that something stated in the book may flatly contradict some of the theories included in the evidence.

Testimony Against the Facts

Whilst it may be a comparatively simple matter to negative the erroneous opinions of witnesses who can be shown to be incompetent and unqualified to give expert evidence, the difficulties are considerable with witnesses who are technically proficient, yet testify against the facts either deliberately or through failure to see where they clearly point.

Even when everwhelming evidence is tendered that two handwritings are by the same person, they will stoutly maintain the contrary on one of three standpoints. They may declare that the resemblances which have been demonstrated are the result of careful copying by a forger whose aim is to implicate the writer of the handwriting which has been copied. They point out differences which are obviously disguised features, but which they refuse to accept as disguise and which they state are significant indications that the handwriting of a different person is concerned. They refuse to recognise the fact that in two handwritings of the same person there can be found slight variations which are a feature of all handwriting. These variations they insist are indicative of different authorship.

A more subtle approach is where the whole of the facts brought forward are grudgingly admitted as accurate, but considerable doubt is expressed as to whether there is sufficient evidence to justify any definite opinion of common authorship being given. Sometimes this attitude is reinforced by reference to one or other of the arguments referred to above.

In each case, there is a preferred line of cross-examination.

Resemblances Alleged to Result from Copying

When evidence which is indicative of the common authorship of two handwritings is wrongly interpreted as being the product of deliberate copying by someone who desires to implicate the writer of the one handwriting as the writer of the other, the cross-examination may take the following form.

The witness should be asked whether he agrees with the universally accepted dictum that, on close examination, any handwriting can be shown to be something more than a combination of obvious features such as letter design and slope. He should then be invited to describe these other features which go so far to give any handwriting individuality; in particular he should mention the oft-repeated, tiny and often quite inconspicuous characteristics of which a writer is rarely aware, and which can only be appreciated by someone who examines the handwriting with a magnifier.

The next step is to establish that it would prove impossible for even the most skilled forger to reproduce every characteristic, whether obvious or concealed, of the handwriting he is attempting to copy *and yet write fluently*; also the fact that when a handwriting is copied, it is generally sufficient for the forger to concentrate on reproducing the pictorial effect which is largely governed by slope and the more obvious features of letter design. This aspect of the cross-examination is rounded off by an inquiry as to whether a forger, unless he were a professional document examiner, would even suspect the existence of the finer structure of the handwriting which is only fully revealed upon magnification.

If there is any hesitation on the part of the witness in agreeing that a forger would be unlikely to include the finer details if he had anything more than a few words to copy, he should be challenged to point out any definite indications that what he is declaring to be copied handwriting has been written more slowly and carefully or with less fluency than the comparison material. The difficulty encountered by anyone who wishes to make a perfect copy of a handwriting could be emphasised by extracting from the witness the admission that whilst writing, the copyist would also have to suppress all hint of his own handwriting style, an extra burden which would make the production of the copy even more laborious.

The cross-examination could be completed by eliciting the fact that were the handwriting a copy, the successful copyist must have had at his disposal many specimens of every letter, groups of letters and possibly whole words represented in the alleged copy, written by his victim, so that the exact form of these letters and groups of letters, together with the nature and extent of the natural variation could be ascertained and copied.

Disguised Features Alleged to be Dissimilarities

In cases where disguised features are incorrectly interpreted as dissimilarities which point away from the same person having written both the comparison handwriting and another which he has attempted to disguise, the cross-examination may be conducted on the following lines.

The foundation that disguise must be expected and taken into consideration in cases involving anonymous letters is laid by establishing the fact that the letters are anonymous because the writers do not wish to be known; and that, fearing their handwriting might be recognised by anyone familiar with it, or who compares it with handwriting they are known to have written, the writers can be relied upon to attempt as thorough a disguise as they know how.

The witness should then be asked whether he has ever examined a disguised handwriting, and if so, how he found it to differ from the undisguised writing of the same person. The answer would probably be to the effect that the general appearance of the handwriting had been altered by change in its slope and in the design of some of the letters, particularly the capitals. There might have been, in addition, the use of alternative forms of letters such as " r " and " e." The ability of the witness to test for disguised formations in handwriting should now be examined. He should answer that disguise in slope is recognised by the variability the slope of the disguised handwriting portrays, especially towards the end of the writing; that disguised formations are rarely written with the same consistency in design, speed and fluency as the forms they replace; that with alternate forms of letter, it may happen that a few examples of the more usual form may have slipped in, or that some of these usual forms have been commenced and then altered or overwritten so as to conceal their presence.[4] The witness is then pressed to admit that if

[4] See Chapter 10

disguised formations can be identified and allowed for, their presence does not necessarily debar handwriting from being identified and attributed to the person responsible for it. Finally, admissions are extracted that handwriting contains a large number of repeated inconspicuous features which, being unknown to the writer, are extremely unlikely to be deliberately disguised, and that where these characteristics are shown to be present as fluently written formations, they are *certain* to be undisguised and consequently may be used as a basis for the comparison of disguised with natural handwriting.

The cross-examination of a witness who wrongly identifies the handwriting of different persons as that of a single writer, because he has mistaken for disguise those differences in the writings which point to different authors being involved, is dealt with later.

Natural Variations Alleged to Indicate Different Authorship

Where the witness maintains that admitted differences between two handwritings, actually due to natural variation or accidental formation, indicate that they were written by different people, the cross-examination should be designed to show that no two passages written at different times by the same writer can be expected to be absolutely alike.

The preliminary questions should bring agreement that human beings cannot be expected to perform with the precision of machines, so that it is unreasonable to expect two passages which are replicas to be produced by anyone at a sitting, much less at different times and under different conditions. The further admission is then invited that even with single words, such as signatures of reasonable length, the appearance of perfect replicas is invariably regarded with the gravest suspicion, the generally accepted inference being that the replicas are forgeries, as it is only by tracing that such a marked degree of consistency of letter design can be achieved.

The influence on the handwriting of different conditions including ill-health, fatigue or carelessness, on the part of the writer, the nature of the writing and the circumstances under which it was written should be inquired into so that it can further be agreed that all these factors might be expected to cause some modification of the handwriting.

The next step is to take one of the handwritings being compared and to obtain agreement that *in itself* it exhibits certain variations in letter design from line to line. The witness should be invited to find examples and to point them out to the court with promptings from counsel if he appears insufficiently observant. The variations pointed out by the witness in the design of any letter should be considered. It will be found that these variations group themselves about a norm or " master-pattern," to which they all with but few exceptions will approximate. The witness should be asked whether he can find this same master-pattern or norm for this letter in the other writings. If they are indeed by the same person, there is no doubt that they will be present. The investigation should then be extended to other letters, with the same result.

The witness should then be invited to consider what reasonable explanation for the existence of practically identical norms or master-patterns for all the letter formations in all the handwritings can be offered, except that of common authorship or of extreme coincidence. He may still refuse to admit common authorship, but he has been forced to modify his original view that the differences were not due to natural variation, but were only explicable on the ground of different writers being responsible.

If the presence of accidental letter formations has been made a part of the argument that different writers are involved, the witness should be asked whether whilst writing he has ever changed his mind as to the exact letter he should write, due to doubts about the spelling of a word or for any other reason, and then converted it into another letter. He will have to admit that any letter written in this way may look appreciably different from the other specimens of the same letter in this or any other writing he may have written. From this, it is simple to gain assent to the fact that any specimen of handwriting may include accidental features which cannot be matched in other writing by the same person.

If at this stage the witness persists in his opinion that the presence in two specimens of handwritings of differences, really due to natural variation and accidental formations, show that different persons must have written them, his attention should be called once more to one of the specimens. He should then be asked to compare two lines which contain variations and accidentals, and challenged to say that this proves that more than one person was concerned in the writing of the one specimen.

Witness Relying on Practical Experience Rather than Skill

It may happen that a forged signature is declared to be genuine by a bank clerk, schoolmaster or someone who claims a practical experience of handwriting rather than any skill in its microscopic examination.[5]

The cross-examination should commence by asking questions which emphasise that the witness claims neither possession of, nor experience with, microscopes or similar apparatus, the use of which is sometimes essential for revealing that a signature is a forgery. Once the admission has been obtained that reliance has been placed upon the naked eye, with or without the aid of a simple hand magnifier, it should be followed up by establishing that many forgeries have escaped the scrutiny of experienced bank clerks and that money is being paid out daily on forgeries; also that banks are chary about cashing cheques for large sums of money over the counter for unknown persons, unless inquiries have been made to verify the signatures.

The question is then asked as to what the forger has to achieve so as to deceive people into thinking that a forgery is genuine. This is to imitate the general appearance of a genuine signature selected as a model by concentrating on reproducing its slope and letter design.

Agreement is then sought to the proposition that a careful tracing of a genuine signature must result in the production of a forgery which resembles a genuine signature very closely indeed, as it only differs from a genuine signature in those

5 Inbau, F. E., " Lay Witness Identification of Handwriting " (*Illinois Law Review*, Vol. 34, No. 4, December, 1939); Swett, G. G., " The Use of Individual Photographic Charts in Presenting Questioned Testimony " (*Journal of Criminal Law, Criminology and Police Science*, Vol. 42, No. 6, March–April, 1952).

aspects which are governed by the way in which it was written—a little at a time instead of with a free, fluent motion of the pen. At this stage the witness is asked whether he would guarantee to pick out a skilfully traced forgery on the basis of its appearance from a large number of genuine signatures. If a number of traced forgeries, all made from the same model are considered to be genuine, the witness should be asked for any reason he can suggest for all of the group being so alike, whereas the admittedly genuine signatures exhibit a noticeable amount of variation. This point may also be made in many cases where a number of simulated forgeries are involved, for since a forger has difficulty enough to learn and perfect himself in the copying of the genuine signature he has chosen for his model, it will be this one signature that he will endeavour to reproduce whenever he writes a forgery. Very often a group of simulated forgeries written by the same man may be shown to have what might be termed " errors of forgery " in common.

It may happen that the forger has chosen for his model an outdated signature. This affords an opportunity for asking the witness for an explanation of the curious behaviour of the presumed signatory in returning to a former fashion of writing his signature, behaviour all the less explicable in that it has been confined to the signatures under question.

Where an incompetent witness is unable to point out any reason for his declaring a signature to be a forgery, other than that it diverges in some respects from the letter design of the signatures with which it has been compared, it should be firmly established that divergences in some detail of the letter design is all that is complained of, and that there are present none of the delicate retouchings, unusual pen-lifts and hesitations or the bad line quality indicative of forgery. Once this has been done, he should be asked whether he expects to find every signature which is genuine conforming strictly to the same pattern.

Whatever the answer to this question, the inquiry should then be directed to the influence of conditions on handwriting as a whole. Instead of counsel putting to the witness the various conditions which would be expected to modify handwriting, he—the witness—should be asked whether such conditions exist and then to enumerate them. If the list does not include such factors as the physical and mental conditions of the writer, as exemplified by ill-health, fatigue, preoccupation with other matters than writing, fear and anger, together with the influence of the physical conditions in which the writing is done, such as writing done standing, in a poor light or with defective writing materials, then prompting should be given.

Once it has been agreed that conditions can be expected to have some effect on writing, the witness should be asked how many genuine signatures, written under the most diverse conditions, he has had the opportunity of examining. Frequently it will be confessed that very few signatures had been made available to him, so that he has not had any opportunity of determining what range of variation is likely to be present. It may even be disclosed that the signatures which were used for the comparison are by no means contemporary with the questioned signature. This is an important admission because some people introduce considerable modifications into their signatures at certain periods in their lives. In this connection it is interesting to study the far-reaching changes which take place when a man suddenly changes his status, so that he has many more documents to sign than formerly. Some of the books on graphology illustrate this point very well with the signatures of politicians who have suddenly achieved fame and responsibility, and with it the task of writing hundreds of signatures daily.

As a general rule, nothing is gained by asking expert witnesses to give opinions on writings they see for the first time when they are handed to them in the witness-box. This is because any document needs careful study before any worthwhile opinion can be expressed about any feature of it, but there is no harm if the witness in the case now being considered is handed a group of genuine signatures with the warning that he is not going to be asked to express any opinion on their authenticity. He is merely asked to pick out any two from the group which resemble each other so closely that he can find no obvious differences between them. This task is unlikely to be achieved by any honest witness, as it is rarely that two genuine signatures are found where there is not some difference to be found on careful search. The conclusion is driven home that there is obvious variation to be found in the way in which genuine signatures of the person concerned are written. Therefore the witness is asked whether or not he now considers that the differences in letter design he found in the questioned signature he pronounced as a forgery might not be explicable on the grounds of natural variation.

Instances are regularly occurring where incompetent document examiners denounce as forgeries signatures which exhibit some feature of letter design not present in the one or two admittedly genuine signatures they had available for comparison. Very often a search amongst a fair number of genuine signatures will reveal some containing this very feature. These genuine signatures should be reserved for production at the very end of the cross-examination, when the witness has fully committed himself and the court has been fully informed of the fact of and reasons for the presence of natural variation in the signatures of even the most consistent writers.

It may not always prove possible to have available a suitable genuine signature with the exact feature desired so as to confute completely the incompetent witness, but where a single obvious discrepancy has been relied upon to show that a signature is a forgery, he can be asked whether or not the remainder is satisfactory. If so, the comment can be made that apart from this one rather obvious feature the forgery is practically perfect. The conclusion then drawn is that a skilled and observant forger must have been at work with a genuine signature at his disposal for copying. If this is granted, then the witness should be asked how he thinks that the feature on which he relies came into the signature, if it is never present in a genuine signature and a skilled forger was responsible for writing what he considers to be a forgery.

Assumptions by Witnesses

Unless the truth of any principle or assumption made by an expert witness on documents is self-evident, he should be asked for his authority for the statement. On one occasion in the author's experience, a witness in an important trial stated that the presence of an upward concavity in the horizontal stroke which formed part of a block capital " T " indicated that the writer must have been left-handed.

This ridiculous statement, for which no justification whatever exists, was left unchallenged. The witness should have been asked in cross-examination for any reasons he might have had for making such a sweeping statement. The only acceptable answer would be for him to refer to extensive experiments he had carried out himself, or he had seen reported in some publication of standing and which he had confirmed from his own experience. Dubious assumptions are almost invariably found in the evidence of those who are, either knowingly or unknowingly, testifying against the facts, and these, unless they are vigorously attacked at the source, may confer an air of plausibility on the opinions of the witness.

There are other witnesses who claim to be able to determine the extent and sequence of every stroke in a writing by microscopic examination, a feat which no reputable document examiner who did not suffer from self-deception would claim to be able to accomplish. Where two obviously similar signatures are in question, these witnesses can be counted on to find that, although the letter formations may appear to everybody else to be very alike, one set, invariably that found in the questioned signature, has been constructed out of a surprisingly large number of separate strokes which seem to run in all conceivable directions. From this it is concluded that this signature is fraudulent, a conclusion which would be inescapable if, and only if, the preliminary assumptions were correct and the forger crazy enough to have written the signature in such a manner. Similar arguments are sometimes used to show that obviously similar handwritings are made by different persons.

Frequently these witnesses produce grotesquely enlarged photographs of selected letters to support their conclusions, knowing full well that extreme enlargement will bring into prominence all the jagged edges which are a feature of any ink line. These rough edges are produced by the irregular flow of ink into the relatively rough mat of fibres which make up the surface of even the smoothest papers. Taking these enormous enlargements in hand they explain to the jury that the crude letter formations which are shown thereon could only have been made by this and that stroke and movement of the pen. What they neglect to point out is that their evidence might have some basis in fact only if letters of the actual size of the photographs they are demonstrating had to be written with a pen of conventional size. When cross-examined on this point they claim a magnification of only ten times, but they neglect to add that this makes every area with which they are dealing no less than a hundred times as great. In point of fact, the majority of the operations they claim have been carried out could hardly have been effected by a skilled engraver working on a copper plate with a fine steel point, much less by the use of a pen on paper.

It is difficult effectively to deal with these witnesses, who are often most evasive. The only policy which is likely to be successful is to put it to them bluntly that the majority of their findings are purely imaginative without the slightest basis in fact. There should be a refusal to accept any conclusions based on the "eye of the expert." It should be maintained that what cannot unequivocally be seen either by the naked eye or in a properly prepared photograph is not evidence. It is useless to offer to these gentlemen, for examination and the determination of stroke number and sequence, signatures which have been written under controlled conditions, because these witnesses are too wary to attempt to accomplish what they know to be impossible, under conditions which would lead to their exposure.

Technical Terms

Most of the technical terms used in connection with document examination are simple and, unlike many of those in use in other sciences, have the obvious meanings which might reasonably be attached to them. As stated earlier, some witnesses who wish to invest their evidence with a weight and meaning which is undeserved, are apt to make use of high-sounding terms behind which they take refuge when being cross-examined. If a witness uses a term whose meaning is not immediately apparent, he should be asked to explain its significance in ordinary language. Whilst, for the sake of clarity, this is important when the witness is giving his evidence-in-chief, it is essential when he is being cross-examined.

Disguise

The failure of an incompetent witness to recognise disguised features in a handwriting has already been touched upon, but it may happen that " disguise " is the explanation which is incorrectly tendered to explain away facts which do not square with his theories. It is fatally easy to " prove " that any two specimens of handwriting are of common authorship by pointing out the similarities which are present, and then dismissing as disguise any consistent significant dissimilarities which cannot reasonably be explained as being due to natural variation or accidental formation.

The cross-examination of a witness who has fallen into such an error should be conducted in stages.

He should first be asked how handwritings are disguised. It should be put to him that the aim of any disguise is to effect the maximum change in the appearance of a handwriting in the simplest manner, and that this is almost invariably accomplished by a profound alteration in slope, the use of alternative forms of letters, etc.[6]

He should then be asked to agree that inconspicuous features of the structure of a handwriting are not often disguised because the writer is rarely aware of either their existence or their importance as identifying features of a handwriting.

If two handwritings are indeed by different authors, it is certain that a number of dissimilarities in these inconspicuous features can be pointed out to the witness and the extreme improbability of these being disguised to the exclusion of the more usual methods should be emphasised. In this way, whilst the witness may not be induced to change his opinion, its lack of any reasonable basis in fact can be demonstrated.

Presenting a Case in Cross-Examination

Where expert witnesses are being called by both sides, counsel may have to put his own case before the court during his cross-examination of the expert called by the other side, instead of being able to leave it until his own expert gives evidence.

[6] See Chapter 10 for details.

Technical evidence is never easy to put before a court, and in some cases it can be presented in a manner which is likely to carry conviction only by the united work of counsel and witness, who will supplement each other's efforts to ensure that the exposition proceeds at such a rate and in such a manner that its full impact is being felt. The greater part of the talking and demonstration will be done by the witness with occasional prompting from counsel, who will be keeping his eye on the jury to see that they are not being outpaced by the witness who, being fully conversant with his case, may be inclined to hurry over important matters if not checked. Only if the case is unfolded systematically and thoroughly will the court be left in no doubt as to the tenor of the evidence.

In contrast to this, when a new point of view has to be advanced in the course of a cross-examination, there will be little opportunity for any careful introduction and systematic leading up to conclusions, which will probably be adverse to those which have been advanced by the witness who is under cross-examination. As a rule the witness may be counted upon to extend to counsel the very minimum of co-operation, and it is only natural to expect that he will lose no opportunity of throwing as much cold water as he conscientiously can on conclusions and opinions with which he does not agree.

The greatest difficulty will be found in laying the necessary foundation, as the opponent's witness will be chary of agreeing too readily to any propositions put to him, and his answers will be so guarded and qualified that the thread of the argument is likely to be lost in a maze of " ifs " and " buts." Counsel will find himself in real trouble if he is relying on assumptions and statements of general principle made by his own expert, of which the witness challenges either the validity or the applicability to the problem under consideration. From this point onward, counsel may be forced to rely on hypothetical questions, and matters will become further complicated if yet more propositions are challenged and not accepted by the witness.

The confusion may be increased by the bad habit some experts have of using technical terms whose meaning, if any, is known to themselves alone. Should these terms be used in examination-in-chief, the witness is able to explain what he means by them, but if they are introduced into the case by counsel in the course of cross-examination, the witness will protest his inability to answer the question because he cannot understand some of the terms in it. It is most embarrassing for counsel to have to break off his cross-examination to consult his expert for the meaning of a term which should never have been used in this way.

As far as he is able, counsel should confine to its essentials any case he is putting before the court for the first time as part of his cross-examination of the expert called for the other side; details should be left until he can call his own expert.

Photographs

A witness who seeks to destroy in the minds of the jury the effect of testimony that two specimens of handwriting were written by the same person may produce distorted photographs to support his contention.

Experience has shown that the resources of the photographic process are fully exploited in the production of these illustrations. An apparent difference can always be created between two specimens of handwriting by photographing them under different conditions. The one may have its contrasts greatly increased in the preparation of the negative by the selection of a process plate and the appropriate developer. This negative is then printed on to a hard paper which is slightly under-exposed. In this way a print is produced which shows handwriting of a sketchy and scratchy appearance wherein many of the more delicate strokes to which the handwriting owes its character are not reproduced. The other handwriting is photographed on to a soft gradation plate which is not very critically focused, and the resulting negative is printed on to soft paper which is slightly over-exposed. By this treatment a print is produced which exhibits handwriting with a smoothed-out and thickened line with a certain amount of filling up of the smaller eyelets.

Extracts from these photographs are finally placed in juxtaposition to form comparison tables, without any hint being given that the two handwritings being compared have been photographed under totally different conditions, so as to create and emphasise differences which do not exist in the original material.

The selection of letters or other features of the handwriting for inclusion in the table may be as unfair as the photography, if, as is often the case, it is restricted to accidentals and examples of extreme variants carefully chosen to exhibit the maximum amount of divergence. It is not unknown for the differences to be emphasised, in the case of not very legible handwriting, by the comparison of different letters of the alphabet!

The production of photographs of this type should be welcomed, as they may be used to stigmatise the whole of the evidence of the witness. Little technical knowledge is needed to conduct that portion of the cross-examination which deals with the photographs. If one of the handwritings appears in the photograph as unduly scrappy, search should be made in the original writings for a couple of letters which exhibit fine, delicate strokes. It will then be discovered that in a " scrappy " photograph in which the contrasts have been greatly over-emphasised there will have been a failure to reproduce the whole of these strokes. In cases where the writing has had its contrast reduced so as to give it an unduly smooth appearance it will probably be discovered that some of the finer loops and eyelets in the original handwriting are shown as solid formations in the prints.

These faults are put to the witness, who is then asked whether he still maintains that his photographs are true and accurate reproductions of the original handwriting. If he has claimed to be a skilled and experienced photographer, it may be thought proper to go further and suggest that there has been deliberate faking, as different treatment must have been applied to the handwritings to make them appear different in appearance when judged from the photographs. Too much should not be hoped for from this line of questioning because these witnesses are very cunning, and may try to explain away the differences by saying that circumstances over which they had no control forced them to use different qualities of printing paper for making the final photographs.

The suggestion that the photographs have been faked may be reinforced when the basis of the selection of the letter formations in the comparison tables is investigated.

Frequently it will be found that the chart is very narrow when compared with its length. This is rarely accidental; a narrow chart admits of but few specimens of each letter being included, so that the space can appear to be adequately filled by the accidentals and extreme variants which are present in each specimen of the handwritings being compared.

In cross-examination, one of the letters included in the chart should be chosen and the witness asked how many specimens he has illustrated, and how many they have been chosen out of. He might not know the answer to this question, so a count may have to be made. The next question is whether the specimens on the chart are supposed to be representative of that letter as it appears in the mass of the handwriting. If this is stated to be so, the witness is asked to observe certain forms of the letter which are present in fair numbers in the handwriting, and asked to point out on the chart which specimen he has chosen to represent them. If the chart follows the usual pattern, it will be found that the selection has been made in an unfair manner and is not truly representative of the handwriting, so that the witness is unable to comply with this request.

Evidence on Typescript

Evidence relating to the comparison of typescript is rarely challenged, as the production of suitably enlarged photographs to show the resemblance between the questioned typescript and that from the suspect machine is often all that is necessary to carry conviction. Very occasionally difficulties and possibly errors in identification may arise from a variety of causes.

In the first place, very old machines may have worn bearings which may cause considerable variation in the alignment of the typescript. This variation may be regarded as the mechanical equivalent of the natural variation which is found in handwriting. If reasonable amounts of typescript are available for examination, then the nature and extent of these variations may be estimated and allowed for. If, however, but limited amounts of typescript are concerned, then there may be room for a difference of opinion concerning the significance of any slight differences in the alignment of the typescript. Should a witness attribute any differences in alignment to worn and loose bearings, he should be questioned on his reasons for so doing. He should, of course, be able to point to other signs of extreme age and bad mechanical conditions in the typescript, otherwise he will have no justification for his attitude.

Secondly, every time a typewriter is used, and particularly after it has been cleaned, a certain amount of wear and tear takes place with consequent slight alterations in the characteristics of the work done on the machine. If specimens taken at different periods in the working life of a busy machine are compared, a steady deterioration of the typescript with use will be seen.

If a witness wishes to ascribe differences in typescript to wear and tear, he should be in a position to prove that the typewriter concerned had had considerable use in the interval between the typing of the specimens he is dealing with. This should be followed up by a demonstration that what is presumed to be the later specimen includes the majority of the errors found in the earlier together with others which occurred at a later date. This is a reasonable request, for whilst a typewriter might become less perfect in alignment with usage, increased wear and tear cannot be relied upon to correct more than a small percentage of any of the earlier imperfections.

General Considerations

During cross-examination care should be taken with the form of the question when a reluctant witness is being pressed to admit that certain features of the handwriting under consideration are not in complete agreement with his conclusions. It is inadvisable to put to the witness—for example—that two letter formations which appear to counsel to be somewhat different, are *completely* different. Few witnesses are likely to accept such a sweeping statement literally, so that the answer might very well be an uncompromising "No." When, with some surprise, counsel asks the witness whether he expects the jury to accept his view that the two letter formations are similar, the witness explains that he was asked whether or not the two letter formations in question were *completely* different, to which he still replies that so far from being *completely* different, they actually have certain things in common, and some witnesses, if not checked, will proceed to point out these similarities to the jury, and so spoil the effect of the point counsel had intended to make. In any event, time is wasted and the cross-examination loses something of its effect.

In these circumstances, it is better for counsel to ask the witness whether he considers that the two formations are *exactly* similar. On receiving the only possible answer, counsel should then ask the witness to explain in what respects they differ. It may very well happen that the witness has noticed even more points of dissimilarity than were apparent to counsel, who is always in a position to prompt the witness if he appears to be overlooking any. In this way counsel will establish his point in the words of the witness. The majority of witnesses will not split hairs, and will always try to answer the question they know counsel is attempting to put.

Frequently, a witness is asked at the end of his examination-in-chief to summarise his conclusions. This summary should be listened to with great care, because many a witness testifying against the facts grows in confidence as he unfolds his views, and is tempted to summarise on a much stronger note than is justified by the evidence he has given in detail. On more than one occasion, an indiscreet witness has stated that in his opinion there is no evidence to support the case for the other side, or more rashly still, that two handwritings which he has declared to have been written by different persons have not a single characteristic in common. A cross-examiner who seizes on a foolish statement like this and invites its withdrawal or a denial of facts which are patent to all will have made a good beginning.

On the other hand, counsel may have the task of cross-examining a witness who has reached well-argued conclusions, firmly based on facts which are patent to all. Experienced counsel often content themselves with getting the witness to repeat any doubts he has expressed about his ability to decide certain questions in a positive manner, so as to emphasise any weakness in the evidence. Some counsel merely attempt to discredit the witness by criticising all expert evidence in general, and by suggesting that evidence on documents is conflicting in the extreme, and receive with incredulity the answer that competent document examiners are rarely in conflict.

If counsel has been unable to present expert testimony of his own, he sometimes suggests that if he were to call another expert, the court might hear a different opinion expressed. Sometimes this question is put in a manner calculated to enlist the sympathies of the jury, and it requires some care in answering if the witness is not to make any damaging admissions on the one hand or appear cocksure on the other. If the evidence on which the witness has based his opinion is overwhelming, he should answer that he can see only one reasonable explanation for the facts he has brought forward. If the case is not so strong, he should admit the possibility of there being someone who might reach not so definite or even a contrary conclusion.

Sometimes a cross-examination is completed by counsel putting to the witness that all his evidence is a matter of opinion. The answer to this is usually to point out that a large proportion of the evidence has consisted in pointing out to the court facts upon which anybody present may easily form his own opinion.

The strange question " Are you always correct in your opinions? " is still heard, and counsel who ask it are sometimes slightly hurt to receive the answer that no man can claim to be infallible. This is especially so when the witness adds that in this particular case he feels sure that he is expressing a correct opinion.

Sometimes the comment is made that witnesses from the Home Office Forensic Science Laboratory at Cardiff, who are responsible for carrying out practically all document examinations for the police where opinions have to be expressed, invariably appear for the prosecution. The answer to this is that, in cases where questioned documents are involved, unless the experts at this Laboratory are satisfied that there is an overwhelming case, they are unlikely to be called as witnesses for the prosecution. On those occasions where the evidence from the documents is inconclusive or appears to contradict other evidence for the prosecution, it is offered to the defence who may call the witnesses themselves or may ask to have them called by the prosecution.

Seminar on Testimony

Ashton, H. M., " Illustrating Testimony," *Journal of Forensic Sciences.*
Brooks, C. D., " Cross Examination," *Journal of Forensic Sciences.*
Doud, D., " Special Problems," *Journal of Forensic Sciences,* 2 (2), 177, April, 1957.
Elliott, D. W., " Mechanical Aids to Evidence," *Criminal Law Review,* January, 1958.
Hilton, O., " Organisation and Presentation of Testimony," *Journal of Forensic Sciences.*
Purtell, D. J., " Qualifications," *Journal of Forensic Sciences.*

Suggestions for Further Reading

Books on the subject of document examination which include matter which is of interest to those engaged in litigation concerned with forged, anonymous or suspect documents are few. Below are listed about a dozen or so which are likely to be still in print or available at a good library. Saudek's book is one of the best which has appeared on the subject of graphology and is included as a matter of interest in spite of the fact that in the view of the author many of his conclusions are not borne out by experience.

At the end of *Questioned Documents* will be found a full bibliography of the older works on document examination and related subjects. The majority of these books are out of date and have but an historical interest. Many will probably be unobtainable by the ordinary reader. It is for these reasons that Osborn's list is not duplicated here.

Brewester, F., *Contested Documents and Forgeries* (The Book Company, Limited, Calcutta, 1932).

Carter and Pollard, *An Enquiry into the Nature of Certain Nineteenth Century Pamphlets,* 1934 (Constable, London).

Farrer, J. A., *Literary Forgeries* (Longmans, Green & Co., London, 1907).

Grant, Julius, *Books and Documents,* 1937 (Grafton & Company, London) ; *Science for the Prosecution,* 1941 (Chapman and Hall, London).

Haselden, R. B., *Scientific Aids to the Study of Manuscripts* (The Bibliographical Society, London, 1935).

Hilton, O., *The Scientific Examination of Documents* (Callaghan & Co., Chicago, 1956).

Locard, E., *Manuel de Technique Policiere,* 1923 ; *L'Enquete Criminelle et les Methods Scientifiques,* 1920.

Mitchell, Ainsworth, *Documents and their Scientific Examination,* 1935 (Chas. Griffin & Company, London) ; *The Expert Witness and the Applications of Science and of Art to Human Identification, Criminal Investigation, Civil Actions and History,* 1923 (W. Heffer & Sons, Ltd., Cambridge).

Osborn, Albert S., *Questioned Documents,* 2nd ed., 1929 (Boyd Printing Company, Toronto, Sweet & Maxwell, Ltd., London) ; *The Mind of the Juror* (Osborn, Broadway, New York) ; *Questioned Document Problems,* 2nd ed., 1946 (Boyd Printing Company, Albany, N.Y.) ; *The Problem of Proof,* 2nd ed., 1926 (The Essex Press, Newark, N.J.).

Quirke, A. J., *Forged Anonymous and Suspect Documents,* 1930 (George Routledge & Sons, Ltd., London).

Saudek, Robert, *Experiments with Handwriting,* 1928 (George Allen & Unwin, Ltd., London).

Scott, Charles C., *Photographic Evidence,* 1942 (Vernon Law Book Company, Kansas City, Mo.).

GLOSSARY

EVERY science has its own specialised vocabulary and that of document examination is no exception. Many of the terms used have been derived from the trades concerned with the manufacture of the materials which make up a document and others from the branches of physical science employed in their examination. Only a small number of terms are peculiar to the field of document examination itself.

Owing to the richness of the English language, the grafting of trade terms on to those in common usage and the lack of standardisation of the terms used in document examination, it is not uncommon to find the same thing referred to in a number of different ways, all equally appropriate but confusing to those with little acquaintance with the subject.

Throughout this book an effort has been made to explain the meaning of any specialised term used in connection with document examination, but for those who are not familiar with the terminology of the physical sciences a glossary of terms is appended. No attempt has been made to give a strict definition of any term; the intention is to provide a few words of explanation which may render the text more comprehensible.

Å	Ångström Unit—one hundred-millionth of a centimetre.
ABERRATIONS	See Lens Aberrations.
ABRASION	Rubbing or scraping.
ABSORPTION SPECTRA	A record of the way in which a substance absorbs or transmits light of different colours.
ACTINIC LIGHT	Light, generally blue or ultra-violet light, which has the power to initiate or speed up chemical reactions.
ALCOHOL	A colourless liquid; also referred to as "rectified spirit" or "methylated spirit." Used as a solvent.
AMINO-ACIDS	Organic acids which contain nitrogen combined in a particular way. They may be regarded as the structural units from which proteins are built.
APERTURE	That area of a lens through which light is allowed to pass. It is controlled by the "stop."
ASTIGMATISM	A type of defect found in lenses of poor quality.
AZO-DYE	A synthetic dye containing two atoms of nitrogen, linked together in the molecule.
BENTONITE	A type of clay.
BLEEDING	The seepage of colour from an ink line.
BLOCK LETTERS	Also known as "block capitals," "Roman capitals," "pen-printing."
BLOOMING	When applied to a varnish or a binder for charred documents, this term refers to the milky opaque appearance of the film. When applied to lenses it means a special treatment whereby a very thin layer of material has been applied to the surface of the lens to improve its performance.
BROMIDE PAPER	The name often applied to the printing paper used in conjunction with an enlarger to make the final photographic print.
BULL'S EYE	The term applied to a large lens such as that found in a reading glass.

Caesium-silver cathode — Prepared by evaporating atoms of caesium on to a very thin layer of silver oxide. When light strikes such a surface electrons are liberated—the number of electrons being proportional to the brightness of the light.

Catalysis — The speeding up of a chemical reaction.

Chlorinated solvents — These may be regarded as solvents similar to petrol or benzene in which some of the hydrogen has been replaced by chlorine. This makes them less inflammable and even better solvents. Chloroform, methylene dichloride and carbon tetrachloride are examples of chlorinated solvents.

Chromatographic analysis — In this the substance to be analysed is carried along a strip of paper by a fluid generally referred to as the "running fluid." The different constituents in the mixture are carried different distances along the filter paper. This both separates and allows them to be identified.

Civil Service handwriting — A 19th century derivative of "Copper Plate" and the old-fashioned "Round Hand."

Clogged type — Also referred to as "filled ovals" or "blocked type." Unless cleaned, type faces become filled with dirt and debris, particularly the depressions in letters such as o, e, d and g. This results in the hollows of the typescript being printed as either shaded or solid black.

Coma — A fault found in lenses.

Composite negative — This is made up of an ordinary negative combined with a transparency whose function it is to eliminate certain matter from the negative. Composite negatives are used in photographic masking.

Condenser — A lens or lens system used in microscopes and enlargers for obtaining parallel or convergent light from a point source.

"Copper Plate" handwriting — A style of handwriting formerly popular in England. The writing was based on a compressed oval sloping forward at an angle of 15–40° from the perpendicular. The pronounced shading was produced by variable pen pressure on a flexible nib.

Development — The process of converting the latent image which is formed by the lens on the photographic plate, into a heavy deposit of silver which can be seen and which can be used for producing the final print. The process of development can roughly be divided into two classes. In the first, which is "chemical development," the latent image controls the reduction by chemicals of the silver halide present in the emulsion; in the other, known as "physical development," silver is deposited upon the latent image to such an extent that it eventually becomes visible.

Discharge lamp — In the conventional filament lamp, light is produced by heating a metal filament to incandescence. The discharge lamp contains no filament intended for the emission of light; instead light is produced by passing an electric discharge through gases or mixtures of gases inside the tube. If the tube contains mercury vapour, ultra-violet light is produced. If instead of mercury vapour the rare gas neon is present, then light of a reddish hue is produced. If sodium vapour is present, then yellow light is the principal product of the discharge.

D-LINE — The name given by physicists to the yellow monochromatic light produced when an electric discharge is passed through a lamp containing sodium vapour.

DYESTUFFS—SYNTHETIC — Until about a hundred years ago dyes were derived from natural products such as plants but with the rise of chemical industry greatly improved products were made from simple products found in coal tar or petroleum. This is why synthetic dyestuffs are often referred to as " coal tar colours."

ELECTRON LENS — In the electron microscope, the image converter and the television tube, the final image is produced by electrons rather than light waves. Whereas light waves can be focused by means of glass lenses, electrons have to be focused by means of magnets or coils through which currents are passed. This coil or magnet system is known by analogy as an electron lens because it performs the same function for the electrons as the glass does for the rays of light.

ELECTROPHORESIS — The movement of charged particles in solution under the influence of an electric field. The different particles travel at different speeds so a separation can be effected under the appropriate conditions. This is the basis of the electrophoretic method of analysis.

ESCAPEMENT — The control mechanism on the typewriter which allows the carriage to go forward an equal distance, generally a tenth of an inch, each time a key is pressed. Mechanically it has a certain amount in common with the escapement on a watch or clock.

ETHYLENE GLYCOL — A liquid which resembles glycerine. By appropriate chemical treatment the molecules can be made to combine with each other to produce a wax-like solid—usually referred to as polyethyleneglycol. This can be used as the basis of a viscous ink for ball-point pens.

EXPOSURE — The time-interval in which light is allowed to act on the photographic plate while a photograph is being taken. To produce a satisfactory photograph the exposure must be very carefully controlled.

FERROUS AND FERRIC COMPOUNDS — Chemical terms applied to iron compounds.

FIELD CURVATURE — A fault found in photographic lenses.

FILAMENT — A fine thread.

FLARE SPOT — A fault in a photograph produced by internal reflections inside a lens. It has been largely eliminated in modern high-class lenses by " blooming."

FLUORESCENCE — The visible light which is emitted when ultra-violet light is absorbed by fluorescent material. Fluorescence can vary in colour from blue, through the spectrum, to dark red.

FLUORESCENT TUBES — Discharge lamps in which the tube which contains the electric discharge is coated with powders which fluoresce to produce visible light under the action of the invisible ultra-violet light produced by the discharge.

“ FOREIGN ” TYPE FACES — If broken or defective type on a Royal typewriter were replaced with type designed for use on an Imperial typewriter then these replacement letters would be referred to as “ foreign ” type faces.

GRAIN — The unpleasant mottled effect sometimes found on photographs where the degree of enlargement has been excessive is known as “ grain.” It is not due to the size of the grains of silver in the original negative from which the enlargement was made because these are very small indeed. The graininess is produced by a clumping of the very small grains to form masses sufficiently large to affect the definition and detail in the final photograph. Grain can be reduced or eliminated by appropriate development conditions.

GRAPHOLOGY — The attempt to interpret the character of an individual from his handwriting.

GRATICULE — A very small scale generally used in conjunction with a microscope.

GRAZING INCIDENCE — The term used when light is allowed to pass over the surface of a document so that its direction is almost parallel with that surface so that any irregularity is thrown into prominence. Other terms for the same thing, used almost indiscriminately, are “ oblique lighting ” and “ side-lighting.”

ILLUMINATOR — The term applied to the apparatus used at the Cardiff Laboratory for the photography of documents.

IMAGE CONVERTER — In this apparatus, light rays strike a caesium-silver photocathode from which electrons are emitted. The electrons are accelerated electrically and then allowed to strike another surface where their energy is converted into light waves. The light waves going into the apparatus can be infra-red whereas those coming out can be arranged to be visible. With such an apparatus it is possible to “ see ” by infra-red.

IMPRESSIONS — Sometimes referred to as “ indentations ” and occasionally as “ embossing.”

INFRA-RED — The term given to radiation of too long a wave-length to be perceived by the human eye. Infra-red rays may be detected either by photography or by the image-converter.

INK, BLUE-BLACK — The term which is applied to ink which is also known as “ iron ink,” “ iron gallotannate ink,” or “ nutgalls ink.”

INVISIBLE INK — Sometimes termed “ secret ” or “ sympathetic ” ink.

ITALIC HAND — Also known as Italian Hand, Chancery or Cancellaresca. A style of handwriting dating from the 14–15th century in Italy and the 16th century in England. An attempt is being made to revive this style for contemporary use. The shading is produced by adjusting the angle of presentation of a stiff stub pen.

LENS ABERRATIONS — Aberrations are faults in the lens which prevent it from forming a perfect image of the object on which it is focused. A simple lens suffers from many aberrations. In an achromatic lens an effort is made to correct for the worst faults in the focusing of colours. An anastigmatic lens corrects not only faults in the focusing of different colours but also removes some of the other aberrations at the same time. An apochromatic lens has even better colour correction than the anastigmatic lens and as it contains a larger number of components the lens designer is also able to reduce the residual aberrations which are present in the anastigmatic lenses.

LITMUS PAPER — Paper which has been soaked in coloured dyestuff which turns red with acid and blue with alkali.

METHYLENE DICHLORIDE — A very powerful solvent for oils, paints, fats and waxes. It is one of the chlorinated solvents.

MICROAMMETER — An electrical instrument for measuring exceptionally small currents.

MICRO-PHOTOGRAPH — Strictly speaking, an extremely small photograph of an object. If a whole newspaper were reduced to the size of a postage stamp this would be a micro-photograph of the newspaper. This term is loosely and incorrectly applied to what is more correctly spoken of as a photo-micrograph, which is an enlarged photograph of a very small object.

MICROSPECTROPHOTOMETER — A spectrophotometer enables the absorption spectrum of a substance such as a dyestuff to be recorded. A microspectrophotometer would enable this operation to be carried out on an extremely small specimen of dyestuff.

MYCELLIUM — The portion of a fungus which grows beneath the surface. The mould which can be seen on the surface consists largely of the fruiting bodies.

NERNST FILAMENT — A fine wire which has been coated with a layer of oxides of rare metals. When heated by an electric current it becomes red-hot and acts as a source of infra-red radiation.

NITROCELLULOSE — This is made by the action of nitric acid on cellulose. It is a major constituent of certain explosives and of the plastic " celluloid."

NUTGALLS — These are growths which are found on oak trees. When extracted with water they yield a solution of tannin, used largely in the manufacture of ink.

OLEIN — Olein is another name for oleic acid, an oily liquid which is extracted from fats such as olive oil.

OPTICAL BLEACHES — Colourless substances which absorb ultra-violet light and emit either blue or green light.

OPTICAL FLATS — Sheets of glass, the surfaces of which have been rendered perfectly flat and parallel by very careful grinding and polishing.

OPTICAL GLASS — A soft glass with very special qualities often made out of expensive ingredients. It is used in the manufacture of camera lenses.

OSMIUM — A metal similar to platinum. When finely divided it is a deep black.

OSMIUM TETROXIDE — A compound of osmium and oxygen. When heated it becomes vaporised. It will react with fats to form metallic osmium.

OXALIC ACID — A poisonous acid which has the power of dissolving old hardened ink which will not dissolve in water.

Oxidation	The change which takes place when the oxygen of the air combines with a substance, *e.g.*, a dyestuff can take up oxygen from the air to become a colourless material. This is the main cause of fading of dyestuffs in inks and typewriter ribbons. Another oxidation change is the change from soluble colourless ferrous salts in ink to the black insoluble ferric salts.
Ozone	This gas may be regarded as an extremely active form of oxygen. It has an acrid smell and an irritating effect on the air passages.
Panchromatic emulsion	This is a photographic emulsion which by treatment with dyestuffs has become sensitive to light of all colours.
Paper negative	A photographic emulsion may be coated on glass to form a plate, on transparent plastic to form a film or on translucent paper to form a paper negative.
Parallax focusing	It is possible to find which of two objects is the further from the eye by moving the head. The object which appears to move in the same direction as the head is the further. In parallax focusing the head is moved. If the photographic image appears to move the same way as the eye, this means that it is further from the eye than the cross on the screen. If the cross on the ground glass screen appears to move with the eye then the image is between the eye of the observer and the ground glass screen.
Pen-printing	Also called " block lettering " or " Roman capitals."
Pentachlorphenol	A powerful fungicide made by acting upon phenol (commonly known as carbolic acid) with the poisonous gas chlorine.
Perspex	The trade name for a very clear plastic known scientifically as polymethylmethacrylate.
Petroleum ether	A very volatile solvent made by the distillation of crude oil. It is sometimes referred to as benzine. It is very similar to a highly refined petrol.
pH	This is a symbol introduced in 1909 to denote the acidity (or conversely, the alkalinity) of a solution. A neutral solution of water itself has a pH of about 7, a lower figure denotes an acid solution whereas a higher value for the pH indicates that the solution is alkaline.
Phenol	The scientific name applied to carbolic acid.
Photoelectric cell	The device which is able to convert light into a feeble electric current.
Photoflood lamps	These are tungsten filament lamps which are over-run to a considerable extent. This makes a very bright light which is achieved at the expense of lamp life. Whereas an ordinary tungsten lamp will burn for some thousands of hours a photoflood lamp when used at the recommended voltage has a life of a few hours only.
Phthalocyanines	A group of comparatively recently discovered dyestuffs of high quality.
Physical development	See Development.
Pigment	Colouring matter.
Platen	A name given to the roller on the typewriter around which the paper is wound.

Pliofilm	A transparent plastic in sheet form used for packing.
Polarisation	Light consists of vibrations. By the use of an appropriate device it is possible to ensure that light issuing from the apparatus is vibrating in one particular plane. Such light is known as "plane-polarised light."
Polar screen	The name applied to a special type of filter which has the power of polarising light.
Polyethyleneglycol	See Ethylene Glycol.
Polymethylmethacrilate	See Perspex.
Polystyrene	A hard transparent plastic.
Polythene	A soft flexible translucent plastic.
Polyvinylacetate	A plastic which is very flexible. When dissolved in solvents it can be used as an adhesive.
Polyvinylchloride	A tough plastic. It is usually supplied in the translucent rather than transparent state.
Prism	This usually consists of a piece of glass so shaped as to bend light, reverse an image or separate light into its component colours to form a spectrum.
Process lens	A lens which is highly corrected for use in industries where accurate photographs are essential.
Process plates	Plates with a photographic emulsion which is extremely fine-grained to achieve high resolution. Process plates are very slow compared with ordinary plates.
Protein	Nitrogen-containing compounds which make up a fair proportion of the animal body. Gelatine is an example of a protein.
Prussian blue	A blue colouring matter which contains a high proportion of iron. It is sometimes referred to as an Iron Blue.
Rectified spirit	See Alcohol.
Red lead	A red powder consisting of a combination of lead and oxygen, used in paint.
Refractive index	A measure of the manner in which a light-wave is bent when it passes into transparent substance.
Relative humidity	A measure of the amount of moisture in the air.
Resin, photo sensitive	A resin which becomes insoluble in certain solvents after exposure to light.
Rheostat	Another name for a variable resistance used to control an electric current.
Rolling	The name given to the process of manufacture of type faces by squeezing the metal into contact with the hard die.
Running fluid	In chromatographic analysis it is the running fluid which is used to carry the constituents of the ink along the blotting paper, so as to effect a separation.
Scalpel	A small sharp knife used by surgeons.
Scotch tape	A strip of plastic coated with an adhesive.
Selenium cell	A type of photoelectric cell based on the use of a very thin layer of selenium.
Shellac	A brown, naturally occurring plastic.
Shredding	The cutting of teeth in the surface of typefaces to drive the ink into the body of the paper.

SIDE LIGHTING	An alternative term for "oblique lighting" or "light at grazing incidence."
SILICA-GEL	A substance which resembles brown sugar in appearance and which has the power of absorbing moisture from the air without becoming wet. As it is impossible to see when the silica-gel has become saturated with moisture, it is the practice to add a colouring matter to the silica-gel which changes when it will no longer absorb moisture. Such silica-gel is referred to as colour coded. When the silica-gel has become saturated with water it can be reactivated by heating to drive off the water.
SILICONE, WATER REPELLENT	A thin oily liquid which, when baked on to the surface of glass, renders the glass water-repellent.
SOXHLET THIMBLE	A piece of filter paper shaped like a thimble used in the Soxhlet apparatus which is a device for facilitating the extraction of fat.
SPECTROGRAPH	An apparatus for recording photographically the colour of light which is emitted when a substance is burned in an electric arc. This light is analysed by a prism and recorded on a photographic plate as a series of lines. Each element present is represented by its own particular lines.
SPECTROPHOTOMETER	A piece of complicated apparatus which enables the absorption spectrum of a substance such as a dyestuff to be recorded.
"SPOTTING" OF PHOTOGRAPHS	The term applied to the removal of defects caused by pin holes and other imperfections.
STABILISATION	Once a photographic print has been prepared it is necessary to remove the unchanged silver salts, otherwise the print would quickly become black all over. In the conventional process this is done by treatment with a hypo bath, which involves soaking and long continued washing. A simpler process is to sponge the document with a stabilising solution which does not remove the excess silver salts but converts them into a form which is no longer acted upon by light.
STANDARDS	These are specimens of handwriting or of typescript which are of known origin. They are also referred to as "comparison data."
STANDARD WHITE	This is a compressed block of magnesium carbonate viewed through various coloured glasses when colours are being recorded on the Lovibond system.
STARCH IODIDE	This is the name given to the blue colour produced when iodine is mixed with starch.
STEAM-SETTING PRINTING INKS	These are printing inks which are fixed on the surface of paper by treatment with steam after printing.
STOPPING-DOWN	A term applied to decreasing the size of the aperture through which the light passes when an image is being formed by a lens.
STRIATIONS	Another term for streaks.
THIOCYANIC ACID	A poisonous gas containing sulphur, carbon, hydrogen and nitrogen. It gives an intense red colour with traces of ferric salts.
THIOSULPHATES	Sodium thiosulphate is the correct name for what is commonly called "photographers' hypo."

THYMOL — This is a white solid with a powerful smell reminiscent of thyme.

TITANIUM DIOXIDE — This is the chemical name for titanium white, a white powder which is used as a loading for paper and also as the colouring ingredient for certain white paints.

TOLUENE — This is an odorous liquid found in petrol. It is a powerful solvent.

TRACING PAPER — Paper which is translucent so that when placed on a signature the outline of the signature may clearly be seen through it.

TRANSFORMER — A device for increasing the voltage of the mains.

TRICHLORETHYLENE — An example of a chlorinated solvent containing a high proportion of chlorine. It is an excellent solvent for fats and waxes.

TUNGSTEN — A heavy metal with a high melting point. If a tungsten filament is heated by passage of an electric current, it acts as an efficient generator of light.

ULTRA-VIOLET LIGHT — Invisible light of short wave-length generated by passing an electric discharge through mercury vapour contained in a quartz tube. Ultra-violet light is highly actinic and can excite fluorescence in many substances.

VANADIUM — A comparatively rare metal used for alloying with steel. Its salts, such as ammonium metavanadate, are found in certain classes of ink.

VEILING — This is the obscuring of an image by a layer of fog, which reduces both contrast and crispness in the final photograph.

WAVE-LENGTH — Electromagnetic radiation is in the form of waves which differ according to their wave-lengths. Those of very long wave-length form the wireless waves used for telephony, shorter wave-lengths are used for television, even shorter as registered by the body as heat. A small group of very short wave-lengths are appreciated as light. Different wave-lengths in this group are registered as light of different colour ranging from red through yellow and green to blue as the wave-length decreases. Radiation of wave-length slightly too long to be seen by the human eye is known as infra-red whilst wave-lengths just too small to be seen are known as ultra-violet. When the wave-lengths are further decreased the radiation is known as X-rays whilst radiation of the shortest wave-length is known as the gamma-rays from radium and the atomic bomb.

WETTING AGENT — A substance which when dissolved in water enables a surface to be wetted more easily. Soap and detergents are wetting agents in common use.

XENON — A rare gas used in discharge lamps to give brilliant white light.

X-RAY DIFFRACTION — When X-rays are passed through a powder, the beam is scattered by the individual crystals of which the powder is composed. The direction and intensity of the scattered rays can be recorded photographically in an X-ray powder diffraction camera. This enables the powder to be identified.

XYLENE — A solvent similar to benzene.

ZINC-WHITE — A compound of zinc and oxygen used in white paint.

INDEX